MANHATTAN LSAT

Logic Games

LSAT Strategy Guide

This comprehensive guide breaks down the logic games section and arms you with the tools to tackle any game. Written to be a teacher-in-a-book, this guide also includes numerous drills and solutions to push you to your top form.

Logic Games LSAT Strategy Guide, 3rd Edition

10-digit International Standard Book Number: 1-935707-84-1
13-digit International Standard Book Number: 978-1-935707-84-4
eISBN: 978-1-937707-26-2

Layout Design: Dan McNaney and Cathy Huang
Cover Design: Evyn Williams and Dan McNaney
Cover Photography: Alli Ugosoli

INSTRUCTIONAL GUIDE SERIES

Logic Games
(ISBN: 978-1-935707-84-4)

Logical Reasoning
(ISBN: 978-1-935707-85-1)

Reading Comprehension
(ISBN: 978-1-935707-86-8)

PRACTICE BOOKS

10 Real LSATs Grouped by Question Type
Practice Book I

(ISBN: 978-1-937707-36-1)

15 Real, Recent LSATs
Practice Book II

(ISBN: 978-1-937707-12-5)

MANHATTAN
LSAT

October 23, 2012

Dear Students,

In your hands is the end result of years of hard work. At the core of this book is the brainpower of the most talented teachers and curriculum developers that I know. Many moons ago, Mike Kim and Dan Gonzalez pored through years of LSATs to figure out what makes the test tick and together they wrote our original Logic Games Strategy Guide. One found mastering the LSAT to be nearly effortless while the other had to work hard to unlock the LSAT's inner logic and tendencies; it is the combination of the two that underlies our curriculum.

We pride ourselves on teaching that goes far beyond lecture-style classes. This means not only that our students are actively engaged in the material, but also that our teachers are always rethinking how to unlock complex ideas in ways that make students truly understand. Each new edition of this book incorporates what we've learned from helping our students learn. So, along with thanking our teachers and book team for their invaluable input—especially Brian Birdwell, Dmitry Farber, Cathy Huang, Elizabeth Krisher, Dan McNaney, Charmayne Palomba, Matt Sherman and Patrick Tyrrell—I must thank our students for raising their hands to ask and answer interesting questions.

At Manhattan LSAT, we're always looking to improve and to provide you with the best prep available. While we hope that you'll find the book you're holding to be exactly what you need, we appreciate any feedback you may have, whether it's positive or not. Please e-mail me at noah@manhattanlsat.com with any comments, and we'll be sure to consider them for future editions.

Good luck as you prepare for the LSAT!

Sincerely,

Noah Teitelbaum
Executive Director of Academics
Manhattan Prep

HOW TO ACCESS YOUR ONLINE STUDY CENTER

If you...

> ## are a registered Manhattan LSAT student

and have received this book as part of your course materials, you have AUTOMATIC access to ALL of our online resources. To access these resources, follow the instructions in the Welcome Guide provided to you at the start of your program.

Do NOT follow the instructions below.

> ## purchased this book from the Manhattan LSAT online store or at one of our centers

1. Go to: http://www.manhattanlsat.com/studentcenter.cfm.

2. Log in using the username and password used when your account was set up. Your one year of online access begins on the day that you purchase the book from the Manhattan LSAT online store or at one of our centers.

> ## purchased this book at a retail location

1. Create an account with Manhattan LSAT at the website https://www.manhattanlsat.com/createaccount.cfm.

2. Go to: http://www.manhattanlsat.com/access.cfm.

3. Follow the instructions on the screen. Your one year of online access begins on the day that you register your book at the above URL.

You only need to register your product ONCE at the above URL. To use your online resources any time AFTER you have completed the registration process, log in to the following URL: http://www.manhattanlsat.com/studentcenter.cfm.

Please note that online access is nontransferable. This means that only NEW and UNREGISTERED copies of the book will grant you online access. Previously used books will not provide any online resources.

> ## purchased an eBook version of this book

1. Create an account with Manhattan LSAT at the website https://www.manhattanlsat.com/createaccount.cfm.

2. Email a copy of your purchase receipt to books@manhattanlsat.com to activate your resources. Please be sure to use the same email address to create an account that you used to purchase the eBook.

For any technical issues, email books@manhattanlsat.com or call 800-576-4628.

TABLE *of* CONTENTS

TABLE *of* CONTENTS

Chapter 1

of

Logic Games

Introduction

In This Chapter...

Logic Games

The Logic Games section of the LSAT is designed to test your ability to make inferences—to figure out what must be true based on given facts—and to organize lots of pieces of information. When you get past the fact that you're asked to put clowns in cars, patients in waiting rooms, and dogs into an order for grooming, it's not too hard to see how this section is useful in showing that you will be a successful law student. In law school, you'll be asked to organize lots of information, and you'll be asked to draw many inferences. And, if you are working during law school, you might even be putting dogs in order.

In order to do well on the Logic Games section, you need to be organized and consistent. You also need to be creative and flexible. These characteristics might seem like polar opposites, but in fact, being organized is what will allow you to be creative, just as being consistent will allow you to be flexible.

The Logic Games section of the LSAT is often more intimidating to students than Reading Comprehension or Logical Reasoning. Few of us have played more than the occasional Sudoku puzzle, but all of us have read passages and answered questions about them. And it's safe to say that all of us have had to reason logically! This intimidation factor actually works in your favor. With the proper preparation, you will be confident during a section that leaves many people cowering on test day. Dramatic improvements on this section are definitely possible, but it's hard to do this alone! So, commit to mastering this crazy section; we're right beside you.

By the way, it's not smart to start our relationship with a lie, so we must confess that the Logic Games section of the LSAT is really called "Analytical Reasoning." But that's the last time we'll ever refer to Logic Games by the official name.

Where Logic Games Fit in the Big Picture

The Logic Games section is comprised of four games, each of which has between 5–7 associated questions. Overall, the section usually has 22–23 questions. The games tend to be arranged in ascending order of difficulty. However, it's unusual that you will experience the four games of a section in exactly that way. Don't be surprised, for example, if the second game is tougher for you than the third.

1

The entire LSAT exam is comprised of the following sections:

Section	Questions	Scored?	Time
Logic Games	22–23	yes	35 minutes
Reading Comprehension	26–28	yes	35 minutes
Logical Reasoning (1)	24–26	yes	35 minutes
Logical Reasoning (2)	24–26	yes	35 minutes
EXPERIMENTAL	22–28	no	35 minutes
Essay	1 essay	no	35 minutes

The first five sections can come in any order. The essay will be your final section, and it will not factor into your overall score.

Talking about not counting, the experimental section is used by the LSAT wizards (test writers) to test-drive questions and sections and calibrate their difficulty. You won't know which section is experimental, and it will be an additional Logical Reasoning, Reading Comprehension, or Logic Games section. Thus, you might receive two Logic Games sections on your LSAT.

Every question outside of those in the experimental section is worth exactly one point. Guessing is not penalized, so it's to your advantage to bubble in an answer for every question! It's also to your advantage to move on quickly from questions that seem impossibly difficult and invest your time in questions that seem within reach.

In total, you'll see 100 or 101 scored questions. The number of questions you answer correctly is your raw score, which is then converted into a scaled score from 120–180, and a percentile. That scaled score and percentile ranking tells law school admissions officers how you rank compared to other test-takers. The calculations done by LSAC (the organization that writes and administers the LSAT) are perhaps fascinating, but generally irrelevant to your preparation. One thing to know is that because each test is slightly different in difficulty, the conversion scale (used to convert raw scores to scaled scores) varies slightly from test to test. However, the variation is not large.

Here's a sample conversion scale that is representative of the most recent LSATs:

Raw Score (minimum correct out of 100 total questions)	Scaled Score	Percentile Rank (the percentage of test-takers you outperformed)
98	180	99.9
94	175	99.5
88	170	97.5
81	165	92
75	160	80
66	155	64
56	150	44

Since your score depends on how many questions you get correct, it's actually helpful to think about how many you can get wrong and still reach your goal score. Is your goal score a 180? Probably not! If you don't have a goal score in mind, go ahead and do some research on the schools that interest you and what GPA and LSAT score will give you a good chance of getting in. If you poke around on the LSAC website, you'll find a calculator that can help you do that. Set an initial goal for yourself based on the "easiest" school you'd be happy to attend, and once you reach that score, raise the bar.

One more note about the scores: some people spend a lot of energy worrying about whether a particular LSAT is going to be hard or difficult. But since the scores are scaled, the difficulty of a particular test is generally of no importance to your performance. If you get an "easy" LSAT, so will everyone else, and thus the "curve" will be a bit less generous. Instead of focusing on issues that you can't control and that don't really affect your score, let's start learning about logic games!

A Quick Vocabulary Lesson

So that you know what we're talking about, let's define the terms we'll use to discuss logic games.

1. The **scenario** introduces the **elements**, usually people's names or letters representing objects, and provides the context in which those elements are to be organized:

> On Monday, seven trains—F, G, H, J, K, M, and N—leave Rivertown Station consecutively and one at a time. No other trains leave the station on Monday.

We sometimes refer to the set of elements as the **"roster."**

2. The **rules**, or **constraints**, impose limitations on the relationships between the elements and the **positions** in which they are to be placed (in this case, the positions are ordered):

> Train J is the first or seventh train to leave the station.

Train H leaves the station before M, and exactly two trains leave the station between H and M.

Train N leaves the station either immediately before or immediately after train M.

Train K leaves the station third.

3. The **questions** ask you to make inferences based on the scenario, the rules, and perhaps an additional limitation introduced by the question. We sometimes refer to the question itself as the "**question stem**." Here's an example of a question stem and the answer choices:

If Train H leaves the station first, then which one of the following must be true?

(A) Train F leaves the station second.

(B) Train F leaves the station fifth.

(C) Train M leaves the station fifth.

(D) Train N leaves the station fifth.

(E) Train G leaves the station second.

Did you go ahead and solve that? The answer is (D). We'll talk about games like this soon enough!

Logic Games Today

Logic Games were first introduced on the LSAT in 1982. The section has not officially changed since then, but there is a noticeable difference between Logic Games sections administered before 2000 and those administered after. In general, we're seeing:

1. Fewer total questions. Exams pre-2000 commonly had 24 questions per Logic Games section. We're now at 22 or 23.

2. Slightly lower difficulty. On average, post-2000 games have less involved setups and require less advanced inference skills. We're NOT saying that these more recent games are easy! Instead, we're mentioning this in case you do some pre-2000 practice LSATs (PrepTests) and find yourself feeling queasy.

3. Less variation. Recent games tend to follow more predictable patterns than those from earlier exams.

4. Some new question types. We've seen some types of questions sent into retirement, while a few new types have been brought in. We'll discuss these in the next few chapters.

This strategy guide is designed to prepare you for the sorts of Logic Game sections we're now seeing, so we have focused our research on recent LSATs. This doesn't mean that we have reduced the rigor of our approach, or that when you see us throw you an old game, you should discount it. We invite you to use some of the old LSATs to push your ability to be flexible (and there are some of them in this book), but for the most part, we are going to teach you what we have found effective for the sort of LSAT you're going to face.

5. More space. The most recent LSAT, as of this writing, provided more space for scratch work. We assume that this trend will continue. The impact of this change is neglible for all but the messiest of us.

Game Types

While at this point it may seem to you that every game is unique, soon you'll see that there are only a few basic structures that are used to build all recent LSAT logic games.

All recent games ask you to assign elements to positions. This means your first thoughts should be "what are the elements?," "what are the positions?," and "what is the relationship between the two?" That might seem confusing, but it's not that complex since there are only two basic relationships:

1. Elements can be ordered. This is what you saw in the train game above. This is the most common task LSAT Logic Games ask of you.

2. Elements can be placed into groups. This might look like this:

> Eight students—Mary, Noel, Orpheus, Perla, Quinn, Rheanna, Simone, and Tyrrell—
> are to be seated in two rows.

We have eight elements, and each of these has to be placed in two different rows.

Along with games that simply do one or the other, some games ask you to order positions **and** put them in groups. We can tweak the example above to have it include both:

> Eight students—Mary, Noel, Orpheus, Perla, Quinn, Rheanna, Simone, and Tyrrell—
> are to be seated in two rows. In each row there are four chairs, numbered from 1–4,
> from left to right.

Simple, you say? Bring on the three twists! (Actually, they're pretty simple, too.)

1. Mismatches. There can be a mismatch between the number of elements and positions. For example, imagine there were only six students but eight seats (or nine students and seven seats).

2. Element subsets. There can be different categories of elements. For example, the sample game we're using could have told us whether each student is a boy or girl. In that case, some of the rules could have hinged on that (for example, "A boy cannot sit in a seat numbered 3").

3. **Position subsets.** Similarly, the positions can be categorized. Perhaps the first seat in each row is reserved for a class leader (or troublemaker).

Those are the families and twists you are going to face. It may seem like a lot of work to keep track of all of this, but the good news is that a single game won't have all or even most of the above variations going on—we rarely see more than two or three element–position relationships and twists in total. Also, we're going to arm you with the tools to deal with each of the above. Finally, while the crew of geeks that wrote this book think deeply about how to categorize every nook and cranny of every game, and occasionally end up in fisticuffs over whether it's best to say that a certain game has element subsets or position subsets, your job is simpler. You just need to figure out how to incorporate a twist into your diagram and get the questions right! Various approaches and diagrams to a given game can each work just fine.

Here is the general breakdown of games in recent years:

Ordering	
Basic Ordering	18%
Relative Ordering	13%
3D Ordering	10%
Mismatch Ordering	9%
Grouping	
Open Conditional Grouping	8%
Closed Conditional Grouping	4%
Closed Grouping	9%
Open Grouping	11%
3D Grouping	2%
Hybrid	14%
Misc.	2%

No doubt those categories don't mean much to you yet, but even when they do, the goal is not to become a master categorizer or a strict executor. Instead, your goal is to be able to adapt to twists, and to be able to make even a poorly constructed diagram work.

Every quest must have a hero, and on the Logic Games road to 170+ it's MacGyver, the man who could use a lightbulb, a pipe, and a chunk of ice to break out of a meat locker (look up the show if you don't know it). MacGyver was able to evaulate his situation and creatively adapt whatever he had at hand to solve the problem (and, usually, save someone). So how do we mortals develop our inner 170+ MacGyver?

From Here to 170+

Flexibility is just one of the characteristics that separate high-scorers from the average test-taker. Let's consider some of the others.

MOST LSAT TEST-TAKERS	170+ TEST-TAKERS
Fail to recognize the different game types.	Quickly recognize the game types; use this recognition to inform approach.
Lack consistent and effective diagramming methods.	Develop and maintain consistent diagramming methods.
Spend too little or too much time on the setup.	Use instincts and experience to help them allocate time wisely.
Use trial and error as a primary approach.	Use key inferences to save time and work.
Get confused when a game or constraint strays from the norm.	Are able to adapt their methods to work on the "curveball" game or constraint.
Struggle to apply the methods and aspproaches in a real test environment.	Practice enough to achieve flexibility and proficiency.
Are scared of logic games.	Enjoy doing Logic Games!

Bridging the Gap

So how do you move from the left column to the right? There are three keys:

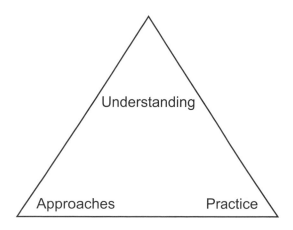

1. Understanding. You must learn about the tendencies and nature of LSAT Logic Games.

2. Approaches. You must develop an approach that aligns with the exam and that you feel comfortable employing.

3. Practice. In order to make your approaches smoother, and in order to gain a thorough understanding of this test, you must practice a lot. This doesn't mean that you must do every Logic Game ever—though you should do many of them—but it does mean that you should replay tough games multiple times in order to deepen your understanding and hone your approach.

How to Read This Book If You're Already Really Good at Logic Games

Most people who buy a book on logic games are not already good at them, but we tend to see a lot of high-caliber students (it's one of our specialties), so if you happen to be already scoring in the high 160s on Timed Practice LSATs, you might want to adjust how you use this book.

So that we can have high-level discussions about game playing with every student, we devote some time to exploring basic issues about games. It's tempting to skip parts that seem too basic for you, and we invite you to do so. However, be careful that you don't skip where we teach you how to solve logic games better than you already do! Skip too much and you will finish this book simply relying on the same skills and knowledge that you entered this book with. One way to check your understanding on a section that you're skipping is to try out the drills for that section. If you can solve them the way we do, then bravo.

To get the most out of this book, make sure you're aligning your approach with ours. If you have experienced success with a different approach on a specific game type, be sure to check out how we do it and make an informed decision on whether to jump over to ours.

Enough talk about what we will do; let's do it!

Chapter 2

of

Logic Games

Basic Ordering

In This Chapter...

> As of PrepTest 66, the June 2012 LSAT, Logic Games have been printed on two pages. This leaves you with lots of space for drawing your diagram. To save space, we've printed all games on one page, so feel free to grab a blank sheet of paper for each game to enjoy the extra space you'll see on test day.

Getting Familiar

You're probably wondering why we're throwing a game at you when we haven't taught you much of anything. No matter how much you prepare for the LSAT, there are going to be some unexpected curves on your test. One way we'll train you is by throwing curveballs at you from time to time—like a timed trial you're not ready for! Do your best to complete the following game in **8 minutes or less**. Use whatever approaches you see fit.

Exactly seven swimmers—Hewitt, James, Kopov, Luis, Markson, Nu, and Price—will race in the 50-meter freestyle event. Each swimmer will swim in exactly one of seven lanes, numbered 1 through 7. No two swimmers share the same lane. Lane assignments comply with the following conditions:

James swims in a lower-numbered lane than Kopov.
Nu swims in either the first lane or the seventh lane.
Markson swims in a lane numbered two lower than Price's.
Hewitt swims in lane 4.

1. Which of the following could be an accurate list of swimmers, listed in order from lane 1 through lane 7?

    (A) Nu, Luis, James, Kopov, Markson, Hewitt, Price
    (B) James, Luis, Markson, Hewitt, Price, Kopov, Nu
    (C) Nu, Kopov, Markson, Hewitt, Price, James, Luis
    (D) Luis, Markson, James, Hewitt, Price, Kopov, Nu
    (E) Markson, Nu, Price, Hewitt, James, Luis, Kopov

2. Which one of the following must be false?

    (A) Price swims in lane 5.
    (B) Price swims in lane 7.
    (C) Markson swims in lane 2.
    (D) Kopov swims in lane 3.
    (E) James swims in lane 6.

3. If James swims in lane 1, then each of the following could be true EXCEPT:

    (A) Kopov swims in a lower-numbered lane than Hewitt.
    (B) Luis swims in a lower-numbered lane than Hewitt.
    (C) Markson swims in a higher-numbered lane than Hewitt.
    (D) Kopov swims in a lower-numbered lane than Price.
    (E) Luis swims in a lower-numbered lane than Markson.

4. If Price swims in lane 3, which one of the following could be true?

    (A) Kopov swims in lane 2.
    (B) James swims in lane 6.
    (C) Luis swims in lane 2.
    (D) Nu swims in lane 1.
    (E) Kopov swims in lane 7.

5. Which of the following could be a partial and accurate list of swimmers matched with the lanes in which they swim?

    (A) lane 1: Nu; lane 2: Markson; lane 6: Luis
    (B) lane 5: James; lane 6: Kopov; lane 7: Luis
    (C) lane 3: Luis; lane 4: Hewitt; lane 5: James
    (D) lane 4: Hewitt; lane 5: Luis; lane 7: Kopov
    (E) lane 2: James; lane 5: Markson; lane 6: Kopov

We will revisit this game later in the chapter. We promise.

2

Ordering

Order is the most common means by which the LSAT writers assign elements to positions. Nearly two-thirds of LSAT games require you to order elements. This is a big topic!

Ordering games come in several flavors. In the following chapters, we will go into great detail about each of these variations, and suggest specific strategies for each of them. In this chapter, we will lay the groundwork for the entire **Ordering Family** of games by discussing Basic Ordering games. We're also going to discuss the two most common question types you're going to face.

Basic Ordering

It's usually smart to define things by their characteristics, but Basic Ordering games are best defined by what they *don't* have: Basic Ordering games do not involve subsets of the elements or positions, and they do not involve a mismatch between the number of elements and the number of positions. They're the vanilla of ordering games.

While you can think of Basic Ordering games as "simple" games that do not have adornments, by no means do we mean to suggest that all Basic Ordering games are *easy*. Admittedly, Basic Ordering games do tend to fall on the lower end of the difficulty scale, but there have been a few Basic Ordering games that have been quite difficult. If you run into a Basic Ordering game as your fourth game, it's much more likely that you'll find it to be on the higher end of the difficulty scale.

Basic Ordering games are extremely common. They show up about once in every five games. Let's get friendly with these games!

Picturing Basic Ordering Games

Basic Ordering games are simple to picture. For the purposes of discussion, let's use the following hypothetical game scenario:

> Seven runners—K, L, M, N, O, P, and S—finish a race in order. There are no other runners, and there are no ties. The following conditions apply:
>
>> S finishes before O.
>> N finishes fourth.
>> L finishes two spots ahead of P.
>> K is either first or seventh.
>> If L finishes third, M finishes before K.

Start all games by reading the scenario and quickly scanning the rules. Don't start diagramming until you've taken a peek at the rules, as they will often tell you what sort of diagram to use. Once you recognize that you're dealing with a Basic Ordering game, write down the elements to be placed and draw slots for positions.

$$\underset{1}{\rule{1cm}{0.4pt}} \quad \underset{2}{\rule{1cm}{0.4pt}} \quad \underset{3}{\rule{1cm}{0.4pt}} \quad \underset{4}{\rule{1cm}{0.4pt}} \quad \underset{5}{\rule{1cm}{0.4pt}} \quad \underset{6}{\rule{1cm}{0.4pt}} \quad \underset{7}{\rule{1cm}{0.4pt}} \qquad \textsf{K L M N O P S}$$

This is probably what you would do naturally, but maybe it seems more natural to you to put the first position to the far right, and to go from right to left. That can work, but we recommend that you stick with left to right, since that's how the elements in a game will be ordered in answer choices and that's how we tend to read in English! But we admire rebels; just be a consistent rebel. Develop a system and stick with it.

Keep an eye out for situations where slot 1 could be the lowest or highest value (e.g., "most popular to least popular" or "tallest to shortest"). Check which side of the spectrum gets assigned to 1. And, while we're talking about twists, there also have been some ordering games that are naturally easier to imagine in a vertical organization. Imagine you were assigning businesses to different floors of a building—floors 1 through 7—and all of the rules were about above and below; in that case, it would likely be to your benefit to visualize the game this way:

$$\begin{array}{l} \underline{} \\ 7 \\ \underline{} \\ 6 \\ \underline{} \\ 5 \\ \underline{} \\ 4 \\ \underline{} \\ 3 \\ \underline{} \\ 2 \\ \underline{} \\ 1 \end{array}$$

Or, perhaps you'll soon be so used to ordering games that you will feel perfectly comfortable thinking about the order of floors as going from left to right. With these types of minor decisions, go with whatever feels most comfortable for you. (By the way, that's not some "let's all get along" sort of broad advice. It is *critical* that you are comfortable with your diagram, because you need to be able to manipulate it in order to answer questions.)

Now we can move on to thinking about the rules in greater detail.

Basic Ordering Rules

The rules that accompany Basic Ordering games will give you information that falls into two general categories. They will give you details about either **assignment** or **order**.

Rules of Assignment

As we discussed in the introductory chapter, all LSAT games are about assigning elements to positions. Therefore, all games are likely to have some **rules of assignment**, and rules of assignment are the simplest rules that we will encounter.

Assignment rules give us one of two types of details:

1. An element will be assigned to a position. In our hypothetical game, we had the assignment rule "N finishes fourth."

We can notate this by placing N in the fourth position, like so:

$$\underset{1}{\underline{}} \quad \underset{2}{\underline{}} \quad \underset{3}{\underline{}} \quad \underset{4}{\underline{N}} \quad \underset{5}{\underline{}} \quad \underset{6}{\underline{}} \quad \underset{7}{\underline{}}$$

(We know, this is pretty straightforward so far!)

2. An element will not be assigned to a position. Imagine that instead we were told, "N does not finish fourth." We could notate this information like so:

$$\underset{1}{\underline{}} \quad \underset{2}{\underline{}} \quad \underset{3}{\underline{}} \quad \underset{4}{\underline{}} \quad \underset{5}{\underline{}} \quad \underset{6}{\underline{}} \quad \underset{7}{\underline{}}$$
$$\cancel{N}$$

Rules about Order

Naturally, ordering games will also have rules about order. Let's consider the range of ordering rules that are possible.

Ordering rules can relate elements to elements (for example, "S finishes before O") or elements to positions (for example, "M finishes no later than third"). Most ordering rules that appear on the LSAT relate elements to elements. They can do so in a few different ways:

1. Ordering rules can relate elements without giving us any specific information about how many spaces are between them.

These rules are very common, and we call these **Relative Ordering** rules.

The rule "S finishes before O" is an example of a relative ordering rule, and we can represent it this way:

$$S - O$$

We can draw this on the side of our number line or below it.

From this rule, we know S must be before O, but we don't know much else. They can finish right next to one another, or fthey can be further spread apart.

Note that we could be given the same rule with slightly trickier wording: "O does not finish before S."

If this rule were part of a game in which elements could tie, it would mean something different (it would mean that O could tie with S or finish after it). However, since elements can't tie in this game, "O does not finish before S" means S finishes before O.

Relative Ordering rules can sometimes involve three and (rarely) even four elements.

For example:

"L finishes before M but after P."

or

"S finishes after both L and N."

We can diagram these rules, respectively, as follows:

$$P - L - M \qquad \begin{matrix} L \\ \searrow \\ N \nearrow \end{matrix} S$$

The dash (—) will be a significant symbol in our notation system, and it will always mean the same thing: we know of a *relative* relationship between elements, but nothing more specific than that.

2. Ordering rules can tell us the exact number of positions between elements.

In our Getting Familiar game, we had the rule "L finishes two spots ahead of P."

We can diagram this as follows:

L	_	P

This rule seems simple enough, but it's very easy to misinterpret as

L	_	_	P

2

You must be vigilant about, and practiced at, interpreting and diagramming these common rules accurately.

You probably already figured out that we're using an underscore (_) to indicate a known space between elements. Just to clarify the difference, "J–S" means that J comes sometime before S, while "J_S" means that J comes exactly two spots before S.

When elements have a known number of slots in between them, they form what we'll call a **chunk**. While the name is sort of gross, as you start to solve ordering games, you'll quickly see that chunks are crucial.

3. Ordering rules can give us a somewhat specific, but not exact, relationship between elements.

Imagine that in our initial example we had the rule "L finishes at least two spots ahead of P."

In this case, we'd know something specific—L can't finish right before P—but the information is also somewhat diffuse; we don't know more beyond that. By the way, terms like "at least" might be small, but they can have a huge impact on how a game works.

This type of rule is less common than the previous two types, but it is challenging and thus important to be prepared for. We can represent this rule as follows:

$$\boxed{\text{L \_ + P}}$$

"_ +" indicates that there is at least one space, and possibly more, between L and P. (Some people prefer "L _ ... P".) While the exact number of spaces isn't known, we'll still often refer to this as a chunk.

4. Ordering rules can specify the distance between elements, without indicating order.

Imagine we had the following rule: "Exactly two people finish between K and P."

In this case, we would know that there are two spots between K and P, but we wouldn't know whether K went before P, or vice versa. We could represent this situation in the following manner:

$$\boxed{\text{K \_ \_ P}}$$
↑_____↑

The double-sided arrow might be a bit awkward at first, but if you are consistent in your notation, it should be intuitive soon enough. Some students have found it helpful to use this alternative notation:

$$\boxed{\text{K \_ \_ P}} \quad \text{or} \quad \boxed{\text{P \_ \_ K}}$$

Similarly, the rule "G and R finish consecutively," could be represented in one of these two ways:

We think it's faster to use the one on the left, but follow your heart on decisions like this, and then stick with your decision.

Keep in mind that many of these ordering rules could be given to us in terms of "nots." For example, we could have a rule that states, "L does not finish exactly two spots ahead of P." These types of "not" rules are rare, but if they appear, we can just adjust our common notation with a cross out, like this:

As mentioned above, almost all ordering rules relate elements to one another, but if we do happen to get an ordering rule that relates an element to a position, we can handle it easily enough.

If we take the example "M finishes no later than third," we can represent this in one of two ways:

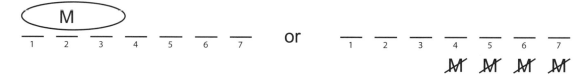

Either method would be fine, although, depending on the particular game, one might be a smidge more useful than the other.

The oval notation on the left, which we call a **cloud**, is frequently used for situations in which we know elements must fit in a certain range, but we don't know the exact positions of these elements. For example, we might know that K, L, and M have to go in the first three positions, but not know their relative order. In this case, we can put them in a cloud.

Here's a table that includes all of our diagramming suggestions thus far:

Rules of . . .

Assignment	
N finishes fourth.	$\underset{1}{\_}\ \underset{2}{\_}\ \underset{3}{\_}\ \underset{4}{N}\ \underset{5}{\_}\ \underset{6}{\_}\ \underset{7}{\_}$
N does not finish fourth.	$\underset{1}{\_}\ \underset{2}{\_}\ \underset{3}{\_}\ \underset{4}{N\!\!\!/}\ \underset{5}{\_}\ \underset{6}{\_}\ \underset{7}{\_}$
Order	
S finishes before O.	S – O
L finishes two spots ahead of P.	⎡ L _ P ⎤
L finishes at least two spots ahead of P.	⎡ L _ + P ⎤
Exactly two people finish between K and P.	⎡ K _ _ P ⎤ ↑＿＿↑
M finishes no later than third.	⟨ M ⟩ $\underset{1}{\_}\ \underset{2}{\_}\ \underset{3}{\_}\ \underset{4}{\_}\ \underset{5}{\_}\ \underset{6}{\_}\ \underset{7}{\_}$

In addition to the type of information that they can give, rules are further defined by the manner in which they give that information.

Most commonly, rules give us information in a simple way:

> S finishes before O.
> N finishes fourth.
> Q finishes immediately before T.
> L finishes two spots ahead of P.

However, rules can also give us information in two other ways:

1. Rules can present *either/or (but not both)* scenarios. We've actually already dealt with a "hidden" either/or (but not both) scenario above: "Exactly two people finish between K and P" means either

⎡ K _ _ P ⎤   or   ⎡ P _ _ K ⎤

Additionally, the test writers are apt to take many of the other types of rules given above and convert them into either/or (but not both) scenarios. Here are some examples of common rules, as they would apply to the runner game above, along with suggestions for how to diagram these rules:

MANHATTAN
LSAT

K is either first or seventh.

$$\underset{1}{K/} \quad \underset{2}{\quad} \quad \underset{3}{\quad} \quad \underset{4}{\quad} \quad \underset{5}{\quad} \quad \underset{6}{\quad} \quad \underset{7}{/K}$$

Either L or P finishes third.

$$\underset{1}{\quad} \quad \underset{2}{\quad} \quad \underset{3}{L/P} \quad \underset{4}{\quad} \quad \underset{5}{\quad} \quad \underset{6}{\quad} \quad \underset{7}{\quad}$$

L finishes before S or N, but not both.

The last rule is certainly the most challenging of the set above to diagram. Before you read on, take a moment to sketch how you might diagram that one.

Many test-takers would stop at this:

L – S

or

L – N

However, keep in mind that if L finishes before S, it can't finish before N, and, since they can't tie, that must mean that N finishes before L. If L finishes before N, it must finish after S. Basically, L is in the middle. We could actually write this:

$$N - L - S$$

Also, keep in mind that unless the design of a game prevents it, or unless it is explicitly stated, the phrase "either/or" does not exclude the possibility of both. The reason we know that the rule "K is in either 1 or 7" means K is in 1 or 7, but not both, is that we know, based on the parameters of the game, that K won't finish twice. For the rule "L finishes before S or N, but not both," if instead we had simply been told, "L finishes before S or N," without the "but not both," then three options would be valid:

$$S - L - N \qquad\qquad N - L - S \qquad\qquad N \overset{L}{\underset{S}{<}}$$

Again, unless explicitly stated or prohibited by the nature of the game, the either/or phrase does not exclude both. This is a tricky concept, but fortunately one that is not particularly significant for the vast majority of ordering games. We'll cover this concept in greater detail in the chapters for which it's more relevant.

2. Rules can be _conditional_. Conditional logic is central to the construction of the LSAT, and we'll discuss it at length in other parts of this book (and also in even greater depth in our Logical Reasoning Strategy Guide), but one easy way to think about conditional rules is that they are triggers that set off a certain outcome or guarantee.

The most common marker of a conditional rule is the word "if." We had one conditional rule in our original hypothetical game:

> If L finishes third, M finishes before K.

We recommend that you diagram this type of rule below or off to the side of the diagram, and we recommend that you diagram it like this:

$$L_3 \rightarrow M - K$$

Note that we do not want to put L into the third slot in our main diagram, because L may or may not be in that slot. We can use subscript for this situation. We could just as easily represent it in either of the following ways:

$$L_3 \quad \text{or} \quad \frac{L}{3}$$

Use whatever feels best for you.

Let's think for a moment about the specific significance of a conditional statement. So that we can stay focused on the reasoning involved, let's use a simple conditional:

> If K finishes fifth, N will finish third.

We can represent this rule as follows:

$$K_5 \rightarrow N_3$$

Let's look at various scenarios to see what this rule does and does not mean: *What do we know if K finishes fifth?*

We know for sure that N **must** finish third. Pretty straightforward, right?

Take a moment to consider what we could infer—know for sure—in each of these situations:

    a.   K doesn't finish fifth.   b.   N finishes third.   c.   N doesn't finish third.

Figured those out? Let's take a look:

a. What if K doesn't finish fifth?	*b. What if N finishes third?*	*c. What if N does not finish third?*
Does that mean N won't finish third? Not necessarily. If K doesn't finish fifth, this rule doesn't apply, and **we can't infer anything.**	Do we know for sure that K finished fifth? No. It could have, but we don't know that for sure. **We can't infer anything.**	Do we know anything about K? Yes! We know that K did not finish fifth (otherwise, N would have finished third). We know K **must not** have finished fifth.

MANHATTAN
LSAT

We know that if N does not finish third, K does not finish fifth. If we wanted to, we could notate this as follows:

$$-N_3 \rightarrow -K_5$$

Notice the relationship between the original conditional statement and this valid inference—the elements have been *reversed* and *negated*. We can **always** derive inferences from conditional statements by reversing and negating both sides of the statement, and these inferences have a special name: contrapositives.

Generally, students choose to deal with contrapositives in one of two ways:

1. By diagramming them along with the original conditional statements.

This is simple enough, and it's a habit you will quickly become comfortable with.

2. By being mindful of them.

For certain game types that we will explore in depth later in the book, conditional statements are the heart and soul of the game, and for those games, we'll strongly recommend writing out all contrapositives. However, for other types of game, such as Basic Ordering, we're also fine with you not writing out contrapositives, and instead being mindful of their significance. If you feel more comfortable writing out the contrapositives, especially while you're still new to games, go for it. Figure out what works for you.

For logic games, the concept of trigger and consequence can be useful in wrapping your head around the contrapositive. Put simply, the contrapositive simply means that **if the consequence didn't happen, the trigger didn't happen.**

Here are a few examples of conditional rules, along with suggestions for how to notate them:

Statement	Notation	Contrapositive
If S finishes second, O will finish sixth.	$S_2 \rightarrow O_6$	If O doesn't finish sixth, S doesn't finish second.
If L finishes before S, P will finish before O.	$L - S \rightarrow P - O$	If P doesn't finish before O, L doesn't finish before S.
If L and O finish next to one another, though not necessarily in that order, M will finish second.	$\boxed{LO} \rightarrow M_2$	If M doesn't finish second, L and O don't finish next to one another.

Smart Tip: Combine Rules as You Go

It is fairly common that you will find the same element mentioned in more than one rule, and oftentimes when that happens you can combine the two rules. Combining rules will pay off nicely by helping you fill in the number line and reducing the amount of uncertainty in the game.

For example, imagine we had the following two rules for a game:

K finishes before S.
S finishes immediately before T.

We can combine these two rules in the following notation:

K — ⎡ST⎤

Keep in mind that the test writers will not always conveniently place rules sharing like elements next to one another. Some test-takers aggressively look to combine rules as they first notate them. For example, when they've dealt with a rule about G and P, instead of simply moving to notate the next rule, these folks will scan the other rules looking for a reference to G or P. For some games, "reordering" rules is essential, so it's not a bad habit to employ all the time. At a minimum, try to combine related rules as you notate them.

Here are five other pairings of rules that can be notated together. See if you can figure out a way to bring the two rules together and sketch out the combined notation before looking at the solutions. Keep in mind that we're still working with the same basic race scenario:

1. S finishes immediately before or immediately after L.
    K finishes before L.

2. S finishes before O.
    K finishes after O.

3. P finishes after N but before L.
    M finishes immediately before or immediately after P.

4. N finishes fourth.
    K finishes before N.

5. O finishes at least two spots ahead of or behind M.
    Exactly one runner finishes between L and O.

MANHATTAN
LSAT

Solutions

1. S finishes immediately before or immediately after L.
    K finishes before L.

    $$K - \boxed{SL}$$

2. S finishes before O.
    K finishes after O.

    $$S - O - K$$

3. P finishes after N but before L.
    M finishes immediately before or immediately after P.

    $$N - \boxed{PM} - L$$

4. N finishes fourth.
    K finishes before N.

    $$\boxed{K} \quad N$$
    — — — — — — — —

    or

    $$K - N_4$$

5. O finishes at least two spots ahead or behind of M.
    Exactly one runner finishes between L and O.

    Did you struggle with this one? Curveball! While you could write out a pretty complex notation for this combination of rules, since there are so many options, it's fine to not combine their notations but simply know that you'll have to keep an eye on how they interact. If you were brave, perhaps you came up with something like this:

    $$\begin{array}{c} L\_or\_L \\ \boxed{M\_\_ + O} \end{array}$$

    or

    $$\begin{array}{c} L\_or\_L \\ \boxed{O\_\_ + M} \end{array}$$

DRILL IT: Basic Ordering Diagrams

Now that we've discussed the full spectrum of rules that you are likely to see for a Basic Ordering game, let's practice setting up our diagrams.

In this drill, we've got four stripped-down mini versions of Basic Ordering games. For each one, practice creating your diagram and notating rules. As you are doing so, you may notice and uncover additional truths about the game—inferences—by bringing the rules together. Notate these inferences as you'd like.

Two last tips before you start:

1. When you're done notating all the rules, **circle any elements that are not obviously affected by any rules**. (One of our teachers calls them "free radicals.) This will tighten your grasp on how a game works, and once in a while the move pays off handsomely in the questions.

2. As much as possible, put the rules *into* the number line instead of off to the side. The more that your rules are in the number line (or whatever diagram a game requires), the more they'll be front and center in your mind. That said, some rules are too complex to be immediately included, and others, like conditional rules in Basic Ordering, don't really fit into the diagram at all.

Timing is less important at this stage in your prep, but if you can complete each setup accurately in one and a half minutes or less, you are in great shape at this point.

1. Seven circus clowns—Roy, Stew, Tony, Urma, Xi, Yang, and Zip—are to emerge one at a time from a suitcase. No other clowns are to emerge from the suitcase. The following conditions apply:

   Urma emerges either first or last.
   Stew emerges immediately after Xi.
   Yang emerges at least two spots before Roy.
   Tony emerges at some point after Xi.

2. A scientist is testing each of seven experimental medicines—N, P, Q, R, S, T, U. No medicine can
   be tested at the same time as another, and the scientist will test only those medicines. The testing of
   the medicines must be conducted according to these rules:

   > If R is tested third, N cannot be tested first.
   > If S is tested first, T is tested immediately after P.
   > P is tested either fifth or seventh.
   > If U is tested before S, Q is tested after N.

3. Six race cars—F, G, H, I, J, K—will be lined up in starting positions 1–6, going from left to right.
   The following conditions apply:

   > J is not in position five.
   > H is positioned to the left of K.
   > Either G or K is in position four.
   > F is after G or J, but not both.

4. Six office departments—legal, management, operations, personnel, shipping, and tech—are to be
   assigned to floors 1–6 in a new office building. Each department will occupy its own entire floor and
   no other departments will be in the building. The assignment of departments to floors must follow
   the following rules:

   > Tech cannot occupy the top or bottom floor.
   > Management must occupy either the fifth or sixth floor.
   > Shipping must be placed directly above or below operations.
   > Personnel must be placed either on a floor higher than tech or on one higher than
   >   shipping, but not both.

SOLUTIONS: Basic Ordering Diagrams

Here are solutions to the diagramming drill. Note that in some places you may have put in additional inferences that we did not, and perhaps in other places we notated inferences that you did not. This is fine. We'll discuss inferences in greater detail in just a bit. For now, the most critical thing to review is that you notated each rule correctly.

1.

$$\frac{U/}{1} \quad \frac{}{2} \quad \frac{}{3} \quad \frac{}{4} \quad \frac{}{5} \quad \frac{}{6} \quad \frac{/U}{7} \qquad R S T U X Y \cancel{Z}$$

$$\boxed{XS} - T$$

$$\boxed{Y\_ + R}$$

2.

$$\frac{}{1} \quad \frac{}{2} \quad \frac{}{3} \quad \frac{}{4} \quad \frac{P/}{5} \quad \frac{}{6} \quad \frac{/P}{7} \qquad N P Q R S T U$$

$$R_3 \rightarrow \cancel{N}_1$$

$$S_1 \rightarrow \boxed{PT}$$

$$U-S \rightarrow N-Q$$

3.

$$\frac{}{1} \quad \frac{}{2} \quad \frac{}{3} \quad \frac{G/K}{4} \quad \frac{}{5} \quad \frac{}{6} \qquad F G H \textcircled{I} J K$$

$$\cancel{J}$$

$$H-K$$

$$G-F-J$$

4.

6 <u>M</u>/ ̶T̶

5 <u>M</u>   Ⓛ M O P S T

4 __

3 __

2 __

1 __ ̶T̶

Inferences

If an LSAT question asks, "Which of the following must be true?" the right answer will *not* be something that must be true directly according to the rules that we are given.

Huh?

Here's what we mean. If we're given a rule that specifically tells us that T must go in the fourth position, we'll never be asked "Which of the following must be true?" and have "T is fourth" as an answer choice.

The correct answer to that problem will be one that we can **infer**, or deduce, by bringing together the various things we know about the game. When it comes to logic games, inferences are our best friends. We love inferences because they frequently allow us to answer a question in ten seconds rather than a hundred, or to solve a complete game in six minutes rather than twelve. We're going to be making inferences at every point in our game-solving process: as we initially picture games, as we absorb the rules, and as we answer the questions.

Inferences are the key to solving logic games quickly, but before we talk about what to do, let's lay out some common misunderstandings on either side of the inference spectrum.

At one end are test-takers who do not understand the significance of inferences. These students often fail to make up-front inferences, and, even more commonly, fail to make inferences when questions include a new rule (such as "If G is fourth, which of the following..."). Failing to make inferences forces these students to use more deliberate, error-prone, and time-consuming methods, such as trial-and-error.

At the other end of the spectrum are test-takers who are overly eager to make all inferences—to "solve" games—during the initial setup of a game. This mentality can lead to false inferences, and it can also lead to a lot of extra work that ultimately proves to be of little worth. Finally, this mentality can lead to panic when games are invariably *not* solved during the setup.

The reality is, certain games are "front-end" games, designed to yield key up-front inferences, while others are "back-end," designed with few inferences up front and more work in the questions. You want to able to recognize and be comfortable with both of these tendencies. As we discuss individual game types, we'll talk about the front-end/back-end tendencies of each type of game. More importantly, you'll develop your own ability to see which category a game falls into.

Let's discuss inferences in more specific detail. It can be helpful to organize our thinking in terms of inferences made during the setup and inferences made during the questions themselves.

MANHATTAN
LSAT

Inferences in Our Setup

As we just mentioned, *front-end* games yield significant inferences during the setup stage of a game, and *back-end* games do not. In general, Basic Ordering games are back-end games. We may be able to uncover a few truths up front, but it's likely we will do most of our inferring in the questions themselves.

Still, there are usually a few front-end inferences we can make that we definitely want to put down on our papers, and often there are even more that we can make that we simply want to keep in mind. (Since you're just starting out with Basic Ordering games, err on the side of over-diagramming inferences until you figure out for yourself which inferences you don't need to write out.)

Remember that inferences are based on bringing information together, and, when it comes to Basic Ordering games, we are simply bringing together information about order and assignment. Let's use the hypothetical ordering rule "K is two positions ahead of N" to illustrate all the ways one ordering rule might come together in holy inference matrimony with another piece of information in the game.

We can diagram the rule like this:

$$\boxed{\text{K \_ N}}$$

Using that, here are three types of combinations you'll encounter:

1. Ordering Rules + Other Ordering Rules.

We already worked on this a bit—when two ordering rules share a common element, they can often be combined.

For example, what do we know if "L is immediately before K" and "K is two positions ahead of N?" We can infer that L is three positions before N, and we can diagram the combination like this:

$$\boxed{\text{L K \_ N}}$$

While some rules easily fuse together like that, sometimes we can make inferences by thinking about how ordering rules link up, even if they don't share a common element.

For example, imagine that we have a game involving six slots, and along with the rule "K is two positions ahead of N" is the rule "There are three people who finish after L but before P."

This second rule we could diagram like this:

$$\boxed{\text{L \_ \_ \_ P}}$$

Now, before you read on, think for a minute about how these two rules interact with one another.

Is it possible for the two chunks not to overlap? No. We'd need a minimum of eight spaces for them not to overlap. In how many different ways could they overlap? Not too many. Here they are:

```
KL N _ _P
_ L K _ N P
L K _ N P_
L _ _ K P N
```

2. Ordering Rules + Rules of Assignment

Very commonly, Basic Ordering games are defined by the interaction between an ordering chunk and the assignment of an element to some position in the middle of our order.

Imagine that, in addition to our "K is two positions ahead of N" rule, we had one that stated, "F is fourth." What could we infer in our six-slot game? Take a moment to think about it before reading on.

If K is exactly two positions ahead of N, and if F is fourth, K cannot be second. Furthermore, N cannot be sixth. Did you figure out where the K _ N chunk can go? It can go only in slots 1 _ 3 or 3 _ 5. Notice a commonality between those options? Wherever that chunk goes, part of it is going in slot 3, so we can write "K/N" there.

This sort of inference is not too easy to spot, and will surely be useful during the questions, so we definitely want to note it on our diagram:

Far less commonly, we may also make inferences based on "not" assignment rules. If, in addition to knowing "K is two positions ahead of N," we knew "N is not fifth," we would know that K could not be third.

3. Ordering Rules + The Construction of the Game

Almost all ordering rules will allow us to make at least some inferences about where elements can't go, based on the construction of the game—more specifically, based on the fact that there is a beginning and an end to the number lines we're using!

Again, imagine that our rule "K is two positions ahead of N" came in a game involving six positions. What would we know about where K and N could and, perhaps more importantly, could not go?

MANHATTAN
LSAT

N cannot be in positions one or two, because then there would be no place for K. Similarly, K cannot be in positions five or six, because then there would be no place for N.

We *could* notate these inferences as follows:

To Note or Not to Note, That Is the Question

Did you notice we just said that you *could* notate those inferences? For some folks, perhaps you, those inferences are so obvious, it wouldn't be worth writing them out, especially if there were multiple restrictions for various slots. In terms of what you do actually diagram on your paper and what you don't, there is no perfect diagram, and the "right" amount of inference-notating is based in large part on your personal preferences, strengths, and style. In general, we suggest that you start off by overdoing it; diagram more rather than less, especially whenever you are not confident that you will remember a particular inference.

However, inferences that involve ordering rules coming into conflict with the beginning or end of the order are so common that after serious prep, most people end up not needing to notate them on their diagrams. There are also certain games for which there are so many such inferences that, if one were to carefully diagram each one, it would be a waste of time and energy. It's tempting to write these out since it *feels* like productive work, but start noticing whether noting that particular level of inference is actually productive.

Speaking of temptations to resist, you may be tempted to look for inferences based on conditional rules. After all, if they give you a rule that begins "If P is second…," it makes sense to think about the consequences of P being second. However, this generally will not be to your advantage. Usually, we want the inferences we make up front to be always true. Conditional rules, by definition, are rules that are triggered *only in certain situations.* That means that when you make inferences from conditional rules, these inferences represent what *could* be true of the game. That's why it's usually best to put these types of inferences to the side, to be reached for when necessary.

Again, you want to be on the lookout for inferences in all parts of your setup. We also strongly recommend pausing at the end of the rules to take one last look for inferences. We call this step in the problem-solving process *The Big Pause.*

The Big Pause

Imagine that you are a participant on a game show that somehow has managed to combine the quiet challenge of solving crossword puzzles with the frenetic ordeal of grocery shopping. Here's how the show works: first, you have to use a series of crossword puzzle-like clues to uncover eight items that exist on a grocery store shopping list. Second, you have to run through a supermarket finding the elements on that list. The contestant who finds all items first wins.

The game is on! You've just had a hell of a time figuring out the word clues. Finally, you figure out the list of elements: ice cream, toothpaste, milk, cheese, sugar cookies, frozen peas, orange juice, and earwax remover.

It took you longer than you'd like, and your competition finished figuring out the same list about ten seconds before you did.

So, as soon as you are done with figuring out the last item, you rush into the aisles, looking for the first element on your list: ice cream.

If Manhattan LSAT were coaching you for this competition, we would *not* suggest that you rush in looking for that ice cream.

Why not?

Because we recognize that a few seconds spent organizing what you know can prevent you from wasting a ton of time and energy going about your task in an inefficient manner.

It would take hardly any time at all to consider the fact that ice cream and frozen peas are likely very close to one another. The milk, cheese, and orange juice are similarly likely to be adjacent, and both the toothpaste and earwax remover are likely to be found in the "non-foods" sections. Perhaps in this pause you consider which elements are easiest to find, and you start with those. Or, you see that earwax remover may be the toughest element to find (you've never had to look for it before!), and you come up with a plan of attack that focuses on that.

Whatever the strategy, a few seconds of organization and reflection can save a lot of time on the back end.

This is consistently true of LSAT games as well.

The LSAT is a time-pressured test, and it's easy to get in a mind-set where we think we have to rush, or go as fast as possible, through each part of the process. However, this reaction to the time pressure can be detrimental.

2

It can be helpful to think about the time pressure not as something that forces you to go faster in your general thinking, but rather as something that forces you to make decisions about where and how to invest your time. Solving a game well is somewhat like dancing well—you need *rhythm*. You have to understand when you should be swift and clean, and when you should be slow and deliberate.

One of the critical points at which it's super-helpful to remember to give yourself a beat, or a **pause**, is between setting up your diagram and jumping into the questions. At this critical moment, you are often going to feel like the person in our game show example—like you are already behind and you've got to get going. However, the way you spend the few seconds during the transition is likely going to have a key impact on how easy or how difficult the questions feel to you.

We want you to use this pause to get comfortable with your diagram and to get ready for the questions. Specifically, we want you to get in the habit of using this pause to think about three critical aspects of game solving:

1. Get comfortable with your notations.

Go one notation at a time, and make sure you've correctly understood and represented each rule. For each rule you diagrammed off the board (i.e., not on the slots), think quickly about how that rule would play out on the board.

Note which elements have no rules attached to them, and circle them.

2. Take one last look for significant inferences or possible frames.

While they're usually back-end games, Basic Ordering games do often have one or two significant inferences. You will generally be able to catch them as you diagram, but it's good to be in the habit of double-checking. Some up-front inferences for Basic Ordering games are so key that missing them will cause you significant delays when you get to the questions.

We'll talk about frames later, but in short they are diagrams to represent two (maybe three) general directions in which the game could go. Frames are rarely necessary or even useful for Basic Ordering games, but they will be more important for other types of games.

3. Pick your key rules.

As we go through the process of solving questions, over and over again we are going to have to think about how the various rules come together with one another, and with the layout of the slots. The order in which you think about these rules can have a significant impact on your pace and overall success.

Put simply, there are certain rules that are more important than others. It can be very helpful to identify and prioritize these key rules.

2

On a general level, we can think of the most useful rules as those that help us understand the most about a game.

For Basic Ordering games, the most significant rules are generally those that give us a chunk. A two-element chunk is great. A three- (or four-) element chunk—a "super chunk"—is even better. And of course, the more specific the relationship between the elements, the better. Often, games will have two chunks, and the key to success will involve thinking about the limited ways in which these chunks fit together. Other times, games will involve a limiting relationship between a chunk and an assignment somewhere in the middle of the board, and the key to success will be to think of the limited ways in which the chunk interacts with that assignment.

For Basic Ordering games, the least significant rules are typically conditional rules. In general, you will want to make it a habit to think about these rules last. As you go through hypotheticals in the process of solving problems, you will generally want to use other rules to fill in as much information about the board as possible, and then move on to the conditional rules if and when they're needed for a few final decisions.

MANHATTAN
LSAT

DRILL IT: Basic Ordering Inferences

Let's take some time to practice diagramming games and taking the Big Pause.

In this drill, we've got another four stripped-down mini versions of Basic Ordering games (and there are some more online). For each one, practice creating your diagram and notating rules. As much as possible, get those rules *into* the diagram, not on the side. As you are doing so, you should be able to make more inferences about the game by bringing the rules together. When you're done diagramming the rules, take a moment to consider the game in general—the Big Pause! There isn't always some large inference to figure out, but you want to be in the habit of leaving some space for that discovery to occur, and it's also useful to notice which elements are "rule-less" and which rules you want to prioritize.

Again, timing is less important at this stage in your prep, but if you can complete each setup accurately in two minutes or less, you are in great shape at this point.

1. Six high school marching bands—Kearny, Linden, Manchester, Newark, Orange, and Patterson—will parade in front of a grandstand consecutively, one at a time. No other bands will be in the parade. The following conditions will apply:

    Kearny will parade either first or fifth.

    Newark will parade third.

    Manchester will parade immediately after Kearny.

    Patterson will parade two spots after Linden.

2. Six different surgeries—N, O, P, Q, R, and S—are to take place in one operating room and one at a time over the course of 24 hours. No other surgeries will be performed in that operating room. The scheduling of the surgeries must adhere to the following conditions:

    R is scheduled at some point after both N and O.

    Q cannot be scheduled third.

    If N is scheduled first, P is scheduled last.

    O is scheduled immediately after S.

3. A rock band will make exactly seven consecutive stops during its next tour. The stops are Pasadena, Rialto, Sonoma, Tustin, Vallejo, Woodside, and Yucaipa. The following rules apply to the tour schedule:

    Woodside is the stop immediately after Sonoma or Vallejo.

    The Rialto stop is scheduled for some time after Pasadena or Yucaipa, but not both.

    Sonoma is exactly two stops before the Vallejo stop.

    Tustin and Vallejo are consecutive stops.

4. A secret society is planning to meet annually from the year 2020 to the year 2025 using six different locations—K, L, M, N, O, and P. Each location will be used exactly once. The meetings will take place only at those locations, and no more than one meeting can take place in any given year. The schedule of meetings must adhere to the following requirements:

    P must be used for a meeting in 2022.

    K and M must be used two years apart.

    N and O must be used in consecutive years.

    M cannot be used until L has been used.

🖰 Log in to your online Student Center for more questions for this drill (look at page 7 for instructions on how to do that). Throughout the book, 🖰 means a drill has more questions online.

SOLUTIONS: Basic Ordering Inferences

1.

$$\frac{K/}{1} \quad \frac{\_}{2} \quad \frac{N}{3} \quad \frac{L/P}{4} \quad \frac{/K}{5} \quad \frac{\_}{6} \qquad K L M N \textcircled{O} P$$

K　P　　　　P　K
P　　　　　　K
M　　　　　　M

KM

L_P

The L/P in slot 4 inference was tough to figure out! It's clear that this game will hinge on the placement of the two chunks.

2.

$$\frac{\_}{1} \quad \frac{\_}{2} \quad \frac{\_}{3} \quad \frac{\_}{4} \quad \frac{\_}{5} \quad \frac{\_}{6} \qquad N O P Q R S$$

R　R　Q　　　S　N
　　　R　　　　　O
　　　　　　　　　S

N ⟍ R
　　⟍
SO ⟋

$$N_1 \rightarrow P_6$$

The most important issue in this game will be the N, R, SO group.

We could have noted that R is "floating" above slots 4–6 since it cannot go in slots 1–3.

3.

$$\frac{\_}{1} \quad \frac{\_}{2} \quad \frac{\_}{3} \quad \frac{\_}{4} \quad \frac{\_}{5} \quad \frac{\_}{6} \quad \frac{\_}{7} \qquad P R S T V W Y$$

W　Y　　　　　　S　R
R　　　　　　　　　S
Y

SW or VW

P - R - Y　　　S_V

SWVT or STVW

VT

Bravo if you figured out how to combine the SW or VW chunk rule with the S_V and VT rules! These super chunks will determine four of the assignments in the number line, with the P – R – Y rule taking up the other three.

4.

Did you figure out the K/M inference? We saw the same sort of thing in the game 1 (L/P in slot 4).

This game, like most Basic Ordering games, will be ruled by the placement of its chunks! In this case, the placement of one chunk will determine the placement of the other. In fact, we could sketch out each of these "frames" (we'll discuss framing in much detail in a future chapter).

Here's the frame for when the NO chunk is in the first two slots:

And here is the frame for when the NO chunk is in the last two slots:

2

Inferences in the Questions

Because Basic Ordering games are generally back-end games, we will typically be making most of our inferences as we solve the questions themselves.

We will make these inferences at two different points—mostly, we'll make them at the point of the question stem, but sometimes we will make them in the answer choices themselves. In some ways, where you should be spending your thinking time is built into the design of each question. While certain questions require you to spend considerable thought-time in the answer choices, we want you to develop a habit of doing as much work in the question stem as you can *before* considering the answers—this is another pause that ultimately saves time.

Some question stems provide no new information; we call these **unconditional questions**. These will ask you to consider something specific about the game as a whole—say, which elements can go in the final three spots, or, quite broadly, what must be true. Other unconditional questions will ask something specific about a position or an element—who can go third, where F can go. If the question limits itself to a certain element or part of the number line, make sure to run through these considerations before evaluating the answers. If the question asks something broad such as "What could be true?," you'll have to spend more time considering the answer choices, although a well-developed diagram and approach will help you quickly tackle these questions.

Conditional questions contain new information that we need to incorporate into what we know about a game. The new piece of information is applicable only to that question. That's why you should leave your original diagram alone and create a new one for most every conditional question. Often, especially for back-end games, it should feel like the new piece of information in the condition is that central jigsaw piece that allows you to assemble a bunch of different rules that weren't coming together before. The new question-specific diagram that you create should provide one or more satisfying inferences. Knowing that, you want to be in the habit of fleshing out these inferences—"doing your homework"—before moving on to the answer choices. Simply reading the new condition and then testing out the answer choices will slow you down. The LSAT is designed to test your ability to make inferences; your ability to figure things out through trial and error is not particularly important to law schools! If you're going to score your best, you need to use the mental muscles the LSAT is evaluating, your inference-making muscles.

While the new condition in a conditional question might trigger a breathtaking cascade of inferences, some are just not so impressive. It's rare that the condition will totally determine each element's position; at least a couple of elements are usually left "floating." Don't force the inferences and make false ones. Instead, be comfortable noting which elements are left to take the remaining positions (noting whatever rules are left attached to them). Asking yourself "who's left?" is crucial to quickly solving many questions. With "could be true" questions, the answer will generally involve one of the strays.

If you're tempted to get an LSAT tattoo (don't), consider having it read, "Know what you know; know what you don't."

DRILL IT: Inferences in the Questions

Inferences are better learned through experience than through reading, so let's do a drill that exercises the inference-making muscles that you will rely on to solve questions. You will be given three Basic Ordering examples. After diagramming these examples and making any front-end inferences you can, you will be provided with a series of statements to evaluate. Some of them will be *unconditional*, in that the statements will not provide you with further information. Some of them will be *conditional*, in that they will ask you to evaluate the situation in light of additional information. For conditional statements, make sure to infer from the new condition the best you can before evaluating the statement. In all cases, your task is to figure out whether the statement must be true, must be false, or neither (i.e., could be true or false).

The two key skills we want you to work on are:

1.   Being able to distinguish between what you know and what you don't
2.   Inferring fully, but not over-inferring, when given conditional information in the statement

We suggest that you do your work and note your answers on a piece of scratch paper so that you can redo this exercise later if needed. Also, check your answers after each game to make sure you're on the right track.

1. Six movies—*Justice, Karina, Liberation, Martians, Naples,* and *Originals*—are to be played during a film festival, one at a time and consecutively. No other movies are to be shown and each movie is shown only once. The schedule of movies must adhere to the following conditions:

> *Naples* is shown third.
> *Liberation* and *Originals* must be shown consecutively.
> Exactly one movie is shown between *Martians* and *Justice*.
> *Karina* is not shown second.

Statement	Must be true	Could be true or false	Must be false
1. *Martians* is shown first.			
2. *Liberation* is shown second.			
3. *Originals* is shown fourth.			
4. *Justice* is shown last.			
5. If *Karina* is shown first, *Justice* is shown last.			
6. If *Justice* is shown last, *Karina* is shown fifth.			
7. If *Liberation* is shown first, *Martians* is shown fourth.			
8. If *Naples* is shown after *Justice*, *Originals* is shown next to *Martian*.			

Remember to check your answers after each game.

2. Seven singers—S, T, V, W, X, Y, and Z—will perform on a variety show, one at a time and in order. The following conditions apply:

> Both T and W perform before Z.
>
> Exactly two singers perform after S but before V.
>
> Either V or X performs last.
>
> W does not perform immediately before or immediately after T.

Statement	Must be true	Could be true or false	Must be false
1. S performs first.			
2. W performs sixth.			
3. Z performs fourth.			
4. V does not perform third.			
5. If S is third, Z is fourth.			
6. If V is fifth, Z is sixth.			
7. If Z is fourth, Y is sixth.			
8. If W is fifth, Y is first.			

2

3. Seven different appetizers—P, Q, R, S, T, V, and W—are to be brought out during a cocktail party one at a time and in order. No other appetizers are to be served. The order in which the appetizers are served must adhere to the following conditions:

> Exactly two appetizers are served both before T and after R.
>
> V is served before W, with exactly one appetizer served in between them.
>
> Q is served fourth.
>
> If V is served before R, P must be served immediately before or after T.

Statement	Must be true	Could be true or false	Must be false
1. R is served third.			
2. V is served fifth.			
3. V is served first and P is served last.			
4. T is served immediately before V.			
5. If P is served second, W is served last.			
6. V is served third.			
7. P is served last.			
8. S is served immediately before R.			

> 🖱 For more practice, log in to your Student Center!

SOLUTIONS: Inferences in the Questions

Note that your diagram might have more inferences than ours. We limited our inferences to the first and second levels of inferences that one would probably make in real time. Also note that you might later find writing out all the inferences for Basic Ordering games to be overkill. As we've mentioned before, for now, err on the side of overdoing it.

1.

Statement	Must be true	Could be true or false	Must be false
1. *Martians* is shown first.			X
2. *Liberation* is shown second.		X	
3. *Originals* is shown fourth.			X
4. *Justice* is shown last.		X	
5. If *Karina* is shown first, *Justice* is shown last.			X
6. If *Justice* is shown last, *Karina* is shown fifth.	X		
7. If *Liberation* is shown first, *Martians* is shown fourth.		X	
8. If *Naples* is shown after *Justice*, *Originals* is shown next to *Martians*.		X	

1. **Must be false.** If M were first, J would have to be third. Since N must be third, this is impossible.

2. **Could be true.** If L is second, then O must be first. Then the M/J ___ J/M chunk must go in 4–6, leaving K to go in 5:

      <u> O </u>   <u> L </u>   <u> N </u>   <u> M/J </u>   <u> K </u>   <u> J/M </u>

3. **Must be false.** This would leave nowhere for the M/J ___ J/M chunk:

      <s><u>   </u>   <u>   </u>   <u> N </u>   <u> O </u>   <u> L </u>   <u>   </u></s>

(It's a good idea to strike through any invalid hypothetical you write as you work through a game—that way you don't mistake it later for a valid one and base, for example, a could be true answer on it.)

2

4. **Could be true.** If J is last, M must be in 4. This leaves room for the O/L chunk in 1 and 2:

  __   __   N   M   __   J

5. **Must be false.** With K in 1, the only way to properly arrange our chunks is to place the L/O chunk in 5 and 6, leaving space for the MJ chunk to straddle N:

  K   M/J   N   J/M   O/L   L/O

6. **Must be true.** J in 6 puts M in 4, and the OL chunk in 1 and 2. The only space left for K is 5:

  O/L   L/O   N   M   K   J

7. **Could be true.** L first puts O second, and the M/J __ J/M chunk in 4 and 6. It's acceptable for M to be in either slot:

  L   O   N   M/J   K   J/M

8. **Could be true.** The only way for J to go before N is for J to be in 2. If J were in 1, M would have to be in 3:

  __   J   N   M   __   __

This leaves only the last two slots for O and L, and while O could go in 5, it could also go in 6.

2.

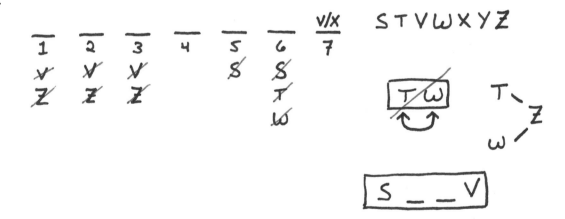

By the way, you could have combined the rules about T, W, and Z into something like this:

Statement	Must be true	Could be true or false	Must be false
1. S performs first.		X	
2. W performs sixth.			X
3. Z performs fourth.		X	
4. V does not perform third.	X		
5. If S is third, Z is fourth.			X
6. If V is fifth, Z is sixth.		X	
7. If Z is fourth, Y is sixth.	X		
8. If W is fifth, Y is first.		X	

1. **Could be true.** If S performs first, we have this framework:

<u>S</u>   __   __   <u>V</u>   __   __   <u>X</u>

And here's one possibility:

<u>S</u>   <u>T</u>   <u>Y</u>   <u>V</u>   <u>W</u>   <u>Z</u>   <u>X</u>

However, S certainly doesn't have to go first, as we will see below.

Note that in the hypothetical we created above, T and W could switch places. This will always be true in this game—we will stop noting it—unless we see a condition that states the placement of one or the other.

2. **Must be false.** Z must follow W, and this breaks the rule that V or X must be last.

3. **Could be true.**

<u>T</u>   __   <u>W</u>   <u>Z</u>   __   __   __

This leaves only one place for our <u>S</u> __ __ <u>V</u> chunk:

<u>T</u>   <u>S</u>   <u>W</u>   <u>Z</u>   <u>V</u>   __   __

We can place X last and Y right before it.

But we also have seen examples in which Z is not fourth.

4. **Must be true.** If we were to place V third, where would S go?

5. **Must be false.**

__   __   <u>S</u>   __   __   <u>V</u>   __

2

To fill in Z, we need the T and W chunk to come before it. Since we only have 2 spaces available before slot 4 and they are consecutive, we can't place Z fourth.

6. **Could be true.**

   ___   S   ___   ___   V   ___   X

At this point, do we have to put Z sixth? We know we need T and W before Z, perhaps like this:

   W   S   T   ___   V   ___   X

Z and Y are the only elements left, and there's a space for each of them. Z might go sixth, but it could also go fourth.

7. **Must be true.** If Z is fourth, there is only one spot for our S _ _ V chunk:

   T   S   W   Z   V   ___   ___

We'll have to place X last, and Y must go sixth.

Note that placing Z fourth determines the placement of every element except T and W.

8. **Could be true.**

   ____   ____   ____   ____   W   Z   V/X

If we place X in 7, we will need the S _ V chunk in 1–4:

   S   ___   ___   V   W   Z   X

However, if we place V in 7, we *can* place Y first:

   Y   ___   ___   S   W   Z   V

3.

P Q R Ⓢ T V W

R _ _ _ T

V _ W

V - R → [P T]

Statement	Must be true	Could be true or false	Must be false
1. R is served third.		X	
2. V is served fifth.		X	
3. V is served first and P is served last.			X
4. T is served immediately before V.			X
5. If P is served second, W is served last.	X		
6. V is served third.			X
7. P is served last.			X
8. S is served immediately before R.		X	

1. **Could be true.** We have no written inferences indicating that this is prohibited. We could do a quick mental hypothetical:

   __ __ R Q __ T __

There's still space for the V __ W chunk, and the V–R rule is not triggered. It's totally fine for R to go third.

2. **Could be true.** The last question set us up for this. This definitely can work:

   P/S   P/S   R   Q   V   T   W

But, we also could place V somewhere else:

   V   R   W   Q   T   P   S

3. **Must be false.** From the last question, we see that P doesn't have to be last in this situation. But could it be? If V is first, it must come before R, meaning T and P must be consecutive. That gives us:

   V __ W Q S T P

But we can't correctly place the R three spots before T.

4. **Must be false.** This would create an R _ _ TV _ W super chunk. Wow—that spans all seven slots and pushes Q out of slot 4! This is a common issue with two chunks: they often have trouble coexisting without causing trouble.

5. **Must be true.** With P in 2, where can we fit R _ _ T? Only in 3–6:

<u> Q </u> <u> P </u> <u> R </u> <u> Q </u> <u>   </u> <u> T </u> <u> Q </u>

The VW chunk must go in slots 5–7.

6. **Must be false.** If V is in 3, W is in slot 5:

<u>   </u> <u>   </u> <u> V </u> <u> Q </u> <u> W </u> <u>   </u> <u>   </u>

The RT chunk can't fit anywhere. We should add to the original diagram that V can't go third.

7. **Must be false.** If P is last, it seems we have plenty of room to place everyone. We can place the RT chunk in 3–6:

<u>   </u> <u>   </u> <u> R </u> <u> Q </u> <u>   </u> <u> T </u> <u> P </u>

But we can't fit our VW chunk anywhere. If we place the RT chunk in 2–5, we bypass that problem:

<u>   </u> <u> R </u> <u>   </u> <u> Q </u> <u> T </u> <u>   </u> <u> P </u>

We can put V in 1–3, but now V is before R, which requires TP.

Regardless of where we put the RT chunk, P last doesn't work.

8. **Could be true.** We saw in #2 that S could go right before R—and we saw that it could not!

Did you notice how restricted this game is? We could actually break up the diagram (frame it) according to where we place the RT chunk:

<u> V </u> <u> R </u> <u> W </u> <u> Q </u> <u> T </u> <u> P </u> <u> S </u>

<u> (S </u> <u> P) </u> <u> R </u> <u> Q </u> <u> V </u> <u> T </u> <u> W </u>

With S and P perhaps switching places in the second frame, there are only three different arrangements in total. Consider how much easier it would have been to answer all the questions with those frames. Let's talk about that later!

For more practice, log in to your Student Center!

Question Type Spotlight: Orientation and Standard Questions

2

Mastery over logic games isn't just about being able to set up clever diagrams. It's necessary to be strong at each part of the process. One critical component of this mastery is the ability to attack questions in an effective, efficient manner.

Throughout these first few chapters, we will break down the various types of questions that will appear in logic games. For some of them, hopefully for many of them, the processes we recommend will be completely intuitive—processes you would have used anyway—and they will require no work for you to implement effectively.

However, for other types of questions, it is very likely that the most efficient approach might seem at first a bit counterintuitive or twisted to you. It's understandable why—some of the most challenging Logic Games questions are just like tongue twisters for your mind. It's going to take work and commitment to improve in these areas, because improvement not only requires learning concepts, it requires turning this understanding into habits.

Let's start by taking a close look at the two most common types of questions you will see in Logic Games: what we call *Orientation questions* and *Standard questions*. These question types together make up more than 80% of all questions that you will see in the games section.

Orientation Questions

Nearly every game that appears on the LSAT will begin with what we call an **Orientation question**. Orientation questions ask us to identify one arrangement of elements that is possible based on the game's rules. Every Orientation question we've seen asks us to identify one possible arrangement that *could* be valid, given the rules; the four wrong answer choices are arrangements that, per the rules, *cannot* work.

We've talked a lot about how important it is to make inferences, but for Orientation questions, you almost never need inferences to get the right answer. Each of the wrong choices will directly violate a given rule. This is different from all other question types.

Furthermore, for most games, Orientation questions are generally designed so that individual rules allow you to eliminate exactly one of the answer choices. If you have four rules in a game, it's highly likely that each of them will allow you to get rid of one of the four wrong answer choices. If you have fewer than four rules relating to the arrangement of elements, you should expect rules to eliminate more than one answer each. However, sometimes there's a rule embedded in the scenario. For example, a scenario might tell you that "every student performs exactly once," and one of the incorrect answers to the Orientation question might leave out a student and illegally list another twice.

2

Based on all of these characteristics, the general process that we recommend for Orientation questions is for you to use the rules, one at a time, to eliminate answer choices. You want to develop a good sense of when it might be possible for rules to eliminate more than one answer (such as when you have fewer than four rules about the arrangement of elements), but in general expect that if a rule eliminates an answer choice, it won't eliminate others, and you can save a little time by moving on to the next rule after eliminating one answer.

Let's return to the Orientation question from our Getting Familiar game to discuss this further.

James swims in a lower-numbered lane than Kopov.
Nu swims in either the first lane or the seventh lane.
Markson swims in a lane numbered two lower than Price's.
Hewitt swims in lane 4.

1. Which of the following could be an accurate list of swimmers, listed in order from lane 1 through lane 7?

   (A) Nu, Luis, James, Kopov, Markson, Hewitt, Price
   (B) James, Luis, Markson, Hewitt, Price, Kopov, Nu
   (C) Nu, Kopov, Markson, Hewitt, Price, James, Luis
   (D) Luis, Markson, James, Hewitt, Price, Kopov, Nu
   (E) Markson, Nu, Price, Hewitt, James, Luis, Kopov

All we need to do is read one rule at a time and scan the answer choices for one that violates the rule.

The first rule tells us that J comes before K.

We scan the answers quickly for the one answer we can eliminate based on this rule. We see that in (C) J comes after K. We can cross that out. It's unlikely that the LSAT will have two answers that violate this rule, so we can save time by "re-starting" with a new rule instead of seeing if J comes before K in (D) and (E)—most likely it does.

Now we're looking for N to be in 1 or 7.

Which of the remaining choices doesn't have N in either spot?

We can cross off (E) and move on.

Now we're looking for M to be two lower than P (M _ P). (D) violates this. (By the way, if you misunderstood this rule to mean M _ _ P, it should have been a red flag that *so many* of the answer choices violate that interpretation).

Easy so far?

Now we're down to one rule and two answers. H is in 4. We can eliminate (A). **(B) is correct.**

Do we need to verify it? It'd be nice to do so, but we don't have the time.

The correct answer for an Orientation question could turn out to be a valuable tool to be used for other questions—it is one order that you know for sure *works*. Especially when you are stuck on other problems, having one possible order can turn out to be very useful.

You may intuitively feel that it would be easier to evaluate the answer choices one at a time, comparing them against your diagram or against the rules. That's completely understandable. But for a variety of reasons, it's simply faster to work from rules to answers, rather than from answers to rules. We could go into a wordy explanation of why, but if you are interested, we suggest that you simply try both methods on various games and see which is faster.

Smart Tip: Rule Reordering and Using Your Diagram

One approach that you might want to try with Orientation questions is using the "simpler" rules first to evaluate answer choices. For example, imagine that a game includes these two rules:

H is either two floors below J or two floors above K.
K is fifth.

Which one of those do you want to use first to scan five answer choices? Clearly, it will be a lot faster to start with the second rule!

Try reordering the rules and see if it makes things easier. If it adds unnecessary complexity to your life, forget about it!

Another alternate strategy you might want to test out is to use your diagram to eliminate answers to an Orientation question. Each of the rules should be represented in your diagram! This can serve as a good check of your diagram and help you "own" the game more thoroughly. It's generally best to simply look at the rules, not the inferences you drew from those rules, although very occasionally you'll face an Orientation question for which working from the inferences you've made will speed up your work. In these cases, your comfort with working from the diagram will help you adjust to looking at the inferences when you realize that the original rules aren't doing the trick.

By the way, certain types of games will at times allow for alternative methods for solving Orientation questions. We'll discuss these methods in the respective chapters.

Standard Questions

We use the term **Standard questions** for a set of questions that are all very closely related to one another.

Standard questions ask us to evaluate five answer choices based on the information we've been given, and to determine what must be true, could be true or false, or must be false.

Certain Standard questions begin by giving us new, additional information that applies to that question only; for example, "If X is third … " or "If Y is before S …." We discussed these in the inferences section, and we think of these as **conditional questions**.

Here are some examples of unconditional and conditional question stems for Standard questions:

> *Unconditional*
> *Which of the following must be true?*
> *Which of the following cannot be false?*
> *Which of the following could be true?*
> *Each of the following must be false EXCEPT:*

> *Conditional*
> *If X is third, which of the following could be false?*
> *If K is before N, each of the following must be true EXCEPT:*
> *If G is on the same team as H, which of the following must be false?*
> *If M is not selected, which of the following cannot be true?*

Perhaps you noticed that some of these question stems represent different ways of asking the same question. When you encounter question stems that involve EXCEPT or CANNOT, and you find yourself a bit turned around, it can be helpful to think about the more basic equivalent question stem. Here's a chart of different ways of asking the same thing:

This...	Is equivalent to...	And...
Which of the following must be true?	Each of the following could be false EXCEPT:	Which of the following cannot be false? (rare)
Which of the following could be true?	Each of the following must be false EXCEPT:	
Which of the following could be false? (rare)	Each of the following must be true EXCEPT:	
Which of the following must be false?	Each of the following could be true EXCEPT:	Which of the following cannot be true? (rare)

Keep in mind that question stems in the second and third columns are generally far less common than those in the first. However, you certainly want to be prepared for anything that can come up, and if you understand the equivalents, it's easy enough.

MANHATTAN
LSAT

The manner in which a particular Standard question is asked should intuitively impact how you are going to approach and think about the five answer choices. Let's lay out a few key principles:

Evaluating answers is less about right and wrong, and more about what you know and what you don't.

Let's think about the most basic question stem possible:

"Which of the following must be true?"

On a different type of exam, if we were given five answer choices and told that exactly one of them must be true, we might expect that the other four answers must be false.

However, on the LSAT, except for a few rogue situations, the wrong answers to a "must be true" question will **not** be answers that must be false. The wrong answers will be ones that could be true, or could be false. In other words, **wrong answers to a must be true question will be answers about which we do not have enough information to make a determination**.

Here's a chart of the four different ways Standard questions can be asked, along with what you should typically expect from the correct and incorrect answer choices:

If the question stem is...	The right answer...	The wrong answers...
Which of the following must be true?	must be true	almost always could be true or false (though a few rare ones must be false)
Which of the following could be true?	could be true	must be false
Which of the following could be false? (rare)	could be false	must be true
Which of the following must be false?	must be false	are almost always ones that could be true or false (though a few rare ones must be true)

Focus on what you know, and worry less about what you don't.

As we mentioned earlier, the ability to differentiate between what "could be" and what "must be" is absolutely critical to a game's success—you simply will not be successful with these games unless you are able to organize information in this way.

Faced with this reality, many of us are inclined to try to keep track of both sides of the fence—all of those things that must be true or false, and all of those variations that could be true. And we can make things even more complex by trying to keep them separate in our minds. Trying to accomplish all of

2

this can make the games harder than they need to be, and we don't suggest this, particularly when you're early in your LSAT prep.

Instead, focus on correctly understanding that which *must* be—either must be true, or must be false, depending on the situation—and pay less attention (and time) to ways that rules or games *could* play out. That's not to say that you won't ever need to figure out what could be, but it's common for students to spend too much time on that side of the fence. You *always* need to understand what must be true, while you only *sometimes* need to know what could be true. Finally, what's particularly dangerous is figuring out something that could be true and mistaking it for something that must be. Keep yourself focused on the "must be" side of the fence, and when you need to peek over to the other side, do it.

Conveniently, it is far easier to keep track of what must be, and to recognize when inferences and answers don't fit into that bucket. It is much more difficult to keep track of what must be *and* what could be as you make your inferences and evaluate answer choices.

EITHER eliminate wrong answers OR search for a right answer (but not both).

For Reading Comprehension and Logical Reasoning, we recommend that you answer most every question by using a process of elimination. This is not what we recommend for Logic Games.

Rather, for Logic Games, we recommend that your process be driven by whether it will be easier to identify the correct answer or to knock out the wrong ones. You generally want to stick with one strategy on each pass through the answer choices. For instance, you might first do an elimination pass and then consider which of the remaining answers is correct.

Let's break down a couple of different question stems to see exactly what this might look like:

Stem 1: *"Which of the following must be true?"* For a question like this, we know that one answer, the correct answer, will be something that must be true. Keep in mind that in most instances, the right answer for this type of question should include information we *already* know to be true, based on an inference we made in the setup or a new condition in the question stem. The four wrong answers will be answer choices for which we can't make a determination, because we don't have enough information to say whether the answer is definitely true or false.

Knowing this, how should we attack such a question? By searching for the right answer!

This is the fastest way to get this question correct, because the correct answer is the one we know the most about.

In these situations, it'd be a waste of time to try to eliminate incorrect answers, because we don't know much about the wrong answers. We would likely have to go through some tedious work—creating hypotheticals—to confirm that they all could be false. It's much easier to look for the right answer, eliminating obvious wrong answers, and deferring judgment on answer choices that "smell" wrong.

One caveat—sometimes, you won't know what must be true. Perhaps you missed an inference. Or perhaps the way the question is designed, the right answer is one that you just can't anticipate before looking at the answers. That's fine; you can most definitely still get these questions correct, and we'll discuss secondary strategies for these situations in just a bit. However, do keep in mind that for the majority of "must be true" questions, the answer will be one that you should have uncovered to be true either in your setup, or from a condition in the question stem.

Let's take a look at another question stem:

Stem 2: *"Which of the following could be true?"* For this type of question, we know that the right answer could be true, and the four wrong answers must be false.

Will it be easy to spot what could be true?

Sometimes you'll know for certain that an answer could be true, but more often you won't. Most of the time, knowing for sure that an answer could be true will require you to invest some time and energy.

For a question that asks what could be true, it makes more sense to use a process of elimination. You know that four of the answer choices **must be false**, and it's easier to make quick decisions about what must be. So, in general, for a "could be true" question, you want to arrive at the correct answer by eliminating incorrect answers.

Stem 3: *"Which of the following could be false?"* Here, the four wrong answers will be things that must be true and should be the easier ones to spot.

Stem 4: *"Which of the following must be false?"* For these, the correct answer will generally be easier to find than the four incorrect, could be true, answers.

To summarize, we want you to develop the habit of either looking for the right answer or eliminating wrong answers, depending on the specific task the question requires from you.

What does it mean exactly to look for one right answer? It means that we're going to defer judgment on answer choices that don't necessarily seem right or wrong (we'll talk more about deferring judgment in a moment).

What does it mean exactly to eliminate wrong answers? It means we're actively going to seek out reasons why particular answers are incorrect.

If you have conceptualized the game correctly, these primary strategies will allow you to arrive at the correct answer as efficiently as possible.

Here's a chart listing the approaches:

Question Stem	Primary Strategy
Which of the following must be true?	**Find** the "must be true" right answer.
Which of the following could be true?	**Eliminate** the "must be false" wrong answers.
Which of the following could be false?	**Eliminate** the "must be true" wrong answers.
Which of the following must be false?	**Find** the "must be false" right answer.

When testing answers, break the must be trues and prove the could be trues.

Imagine you're looking to find the answer that must be true and it isn't jumping out. This doesn't mean you skip the question! It's time to go to plan B, **testing answers**.

You're down to (D) and (E):

(D) J finishes no later than fourth.
(E) F finishes no earlier than third.

Both look good on first glance, so it's time to dig deeper and test them. What do you do?

How does the following strategy sound? You test out (D) by placing J third and seeing if it works. It does! You pull the trigger on (D).

Sound good? No! You have not tested out whether J *must* finish earlier than fourth, you've simply confirmed that it *can*. When you want to test an answer choice for a must be question, you should try to "break it." You should see if J can be placed later than fourth. If (D) is the answer, you'll be unable to place J anywhere but in slots 1–4.

Confused? Imagine a mischievous farmer tells you that all carrots, tangerines, and melons must be orange, and your job is to figure out which one of those three "rules" is true. What would you do? Would you go looking for orange carrots? No! You would search for carrots (and tangerines and melons) that were not orange. You'd try to "break" these alleged rules. Finding an orange melon would not prove that melons must be orange (since some could be orange and others not), but finding a yellow melon would definitely prove something. **To test a "must be," see if you can "break it"!**

The rule of breaking must be's applies to both must be true and must be false questions. With must be true questions, you try to prove that answers can be false. With must be false questions, you aim to show that answers could be true.

Quick quiz: How would you check (E)? (F finishes no earlier than third.)

You would see if you can have F finish earlier than third.

Quick quiz #2: If you eliminated (D) in the scenario above, what should you do?

If you're short on time, pull the trigger on (E), put a star next to the question, and come back and confirm it if you have time. If you have some time in the bank, confirm it right then and there.

Now we have our rule about how to test must be questions, but what about *could be* questions? Consider it for a moment; how would you confirm that, for example, G could come before L? The way to test could be answers is probably more straightforward to you: simply see if it works! For could be false questions, you are working to prove that an answer could be false, which, a bit confusingly, means you are testing the opposite of the answer choice (e.g., if you're testing whether "K finishes fourth" could be false, you see if K could finish in another spot).

At this point we have our testing strategies—break must be's, prove could be's—but we shouldn't forget that testing answers is not necessarily the most efficient strategy. In fact, trial and error is a slow strategy and one that we should only use when the other tools in our arsenal are not working. That said, a MacGyver game player knows that there will be times when we need to test out answers. Sometimes we will need to test the final two choices after more efficient tools have eliminated the other three, and sometimes we will have to test four answers in a row, either because the question is designed to require that level of work or because we've missed an inference in our diagram.

Here's our chart again, this time with our backup strategies:

Question Stem	Primary Strategy	Backup
Which of the following must be true?	Find the "must be true" right answer.	Test answers by trying to prove they could be false.
Which of the following could be true?	Eliminate the "must be false" wrong answers.	Test answers by trying to prove they could be true.
Which of the following could be false?	Eliminate the "must be true" wrong answers.	Test answers by trying to prove they could be false.
Which of the following must be false?	Find the "must be false" right answer.	Test answers by trying to prove if they could be true.

2

If you're the type of student that is trying to memorize that chart, stop! You can't memorize your way to a great LSAT score; instead, make sure you *understand* the ideas, and then *practice* them on your way to a great LSAT score! Soon you'll find yourself naturally using the primary strategy and switching midstream to the backup strategy when needed. Great. This isn't an algebra exam we're preparing for—the LSAT rewards flexibility.

All of the question-specific advice can seem overly regimented if we get too lost in the details, but hopefully these processes will soon (or already) feel intuitive for you. In summary, when thinking about the answer choices, our first option is to use what we know to either quickly identify the right answer, or to eliminate wrong answers (and we want to avoid trying to do both of these things at once). If that isn't viable, then we want to evaluate answer choices efficiently, running through hypothetical scenarios in a way that allows us to know with certainty that each answer is correct or incorrect. You should soon find yourself switching strategies to match the specifics of each question.

When in doubt, defer.

One of the easiest ways to run out of time on the games section is to spend too much time investigating answers—particularly those that we end up eliminating. To avoid this, we want to work from what must be true whenever possible. We also want to be savvy, or what ordinary people refer to as "lazy."

Anyone who has played a few games has experienced what we'll call the "d'oh!" moment. It can look like this: it's the second question of a game, and you're asked to find what must be true. You are facing four could be true answers and one must be true. You look at (A) and can't quickly decide, so you start to test it. 10 seconds later, you've proven it's not a must be true. (B) also looks good, and it's only after 15 seconds of testing that it turns out to be a dud. (C) takes another 15 seconds to eliminate, and when you get to (D), it takes you only 5 seconds to realize that it's the correct answer—d'oh!

Wouldn't it have been lovely if you had looked at (A), **deferred judgment**, thinking, "Geez, I don't know, let me see if there's an easy answer," again deferred judgment on (B) and (C), and then quickly seen that (D) was correct? That sequence could take about 20 seconds as compared to the 45 the original sequence took. The key was to defer judgment, and that is one of the hallmark moves of high-level game players/MacGyvers.

Many Logic Game questions are designed so that the right answer will be easy to spot by anyone who has done his or her homework during the diagramming phase or after considering the new condition that an "If" question provides. The wrong answers, as we discussed above, can take a lot of time to confirm as incorrect, and thus deferring judgment can save you significant time.

But what if you end up deferring judgment on all five answer choices? That definitely happens, even to strong game players, but let's do the math and see how bad the damage is. Imagine there are five questions on which you whip out the deferring judgment tactic. For one of those questions, you end up not finding a "d'oh!" answer on the first pass. How much time have you wasted? It might be only 30 seconds. How much time do you save on the four other questions? Easily more than 30 seconds.

The key to deferring judgment is keeping your cool. It will happen at times that you cannot defer your way to an obvious answer, and in those situations you'll have to restart and use your other strategies. Probably, you'll need to dig deeper into answer choices.

Use your gut.

At times, you'll have no choice but to start testing out answer choices, and then the issue becomes which choices to test first. It definitely doesn't matter if you start with (A) or (E), but if you happen to have seen an answer that somehow strikes you as more tempting, start with that one! If it turns out to be the answer and this is a practice test, put a star next to the question and when you go back to review the question, figure out what about that answer might have made it more tempting. Perhaps it involved an element in a chunk, or perhaps it involved an element that had no rules attached to it.

It's impossible to say what would make an answer choice more tempting in general, but there are small issues that your deep LSAT brain might understand before the rest of you does! It might seem like we're suggesting you "use the Force," and if you do have some Jedi mind trick abilities, definitely use them, but what we're actually saying is to let all the patterns and understandings you gain through your study and practice inform your choices.

Smart Tip: The LSAT Likes Math

If you're not sure where to start looking at answer choices, and if two or three answers involve math (e.g., "G is assigned to no more than three groups") and the other two are more straightforward (e.g., "G is assigned to the Bluegrass group"), there's a slightly higher chance that the answer will be one of the "math" choices. Why? Because those answers are often harder to figure out, and the LSAT needs to put some tough questions in each LSAT to help make it easier to tell the difference between a 174 and a 178 game player.

We'll talk in later chapters about how to stay on top of the mathematical issues that arise in games, but for now, when in doubt, head towards the math answers. Are we saying that you can count on this and simply choose based on how the answers look? No.

Use hypotheticals.

At times, you might find that you'll need to draw out a scenario to test an answer choice. We call these **hypotheticals** (and we'll use this term to refer to valid hypotheticals only). While using hypotheticals is sometimes a sign that you're missing an inference in your diagram, or not approaching a question correctly, there may be times when there's not much else you can do. Even if it's not ideal, we want to make this approach efficient and effective.

2

Be very careful not to get turned around when using hypotheticals with must be true questions. It's not really possible for one hypothetical to prove that a situation must be true. That would be like looking at the sky, seeing a cloud directly above, and stating that clouds are always directly above you!

When you are facing a must be question, you more often use a hypothetical scenario to *disprove* answers. If you do need to confirm that something must be true with a hypothetical, you'll need to use multiple hypotheticals. If something must be true, it will be true in every hypothetical you can create. Clearly this is not a very efficient strategy. That doesn't mean we shouldn't understand how to use it, but we'll also want to note any question on which we find ourselves scrambling so dramatically, and later review that game and question to see how we could have avoided such a situation.

When you are facing a could be question, hypotheticals are more obviously useful. If you want to determine whether it could be true that Z comes before X, and you can make a hypothetical in which it is true, then that's the answer! However, what if you write out a hypothetical and X comes before Z? Should you eliminate the answer that states that Z can come before X? No! Just because your one hypothetical didn't work, that doesn't mean another one wouldn't. So again, you're forced to use multiple hypotheticals to work through the answer choices, and again, this is inefficient.

Make your previous work count.

Smart game players know that once they've answered a few questions, they're already armed with some hypotheticals. Let's imagine that the answer to an Orientation question for a Basic Ordering game was the following:

> (D)   R, M, O, F, T

And let's also imagine that we were subsequently asked the following:

3. Each of the following could be true EXCEPT:

   (A) M comes exactly two spaces before F.
   (B) M comes exactly one space before F.
   (C) R comes at some time before T.
   (D) O comes exactly two spaces before R.
   (E) O comes exactly two spaces after R.

Which answers can we immediately eliminate? Because we know that the correct answer to that earlier orientation question is a possible scenario, we can eliminate (A), (C) and (E), each of which describes that scenario, and therefore could be true.

Similarly, in the question below, which answers can we eliminate based on the answer to the Orientation question?

4. Which of the following must be true?

(A) R comes at some point after O.

(B) M and F are separated by at least two other elements.

(C) Either F or O comes last.

(D) F and R come consecutively.

(E) M comes third.

2

We're messing with you—they can *all* be eliminated, which only occurs in LSAT nightmares. They can all be eliminated because we see that none of the answer choices describe what is true in the scenario we compared them against. While you hopefully won't use this strategy to eliminate all five answer choices, you should look for opportunities to use previous work to eliminate and choose answers. If during your work on a question you draw out a scenario that is invalid, **be sure to cross it out** so that you don't later misguidedly use it as an example of a valid scenario.

The strategy behind using previous work is no different from what we discussed above. For must be questions, look for past examples that disprove answers, and for could be questions, look for examples that show them to be possible.

Move along or heed the warning!

If you are able to answer each and every question in every games section with enough finesse and speed to finish the section with a few minutes to spare, bravo! You can put this book down and pour yourself a drink. But if you're a normal person, you're going to find that some questions are stumping you. When should you move on and when should you not?

In general, if you're struggling with the first two questions of a game, it's an indication that either you're making a careless error on the question—perhaps misreading the word "before" as "after"?—or you've missed a big inference in your diagram. The questions in a game are very roughly organized in order of difficulty, so you should be able to nail the first two questions quickly. If you do find yourself spinning your wheels on question 2, for example, take one more look at the question stem and choices, and if you don't see that you've made a slipup, take a slow turn through your rules and then each choice. Most likely you've missed an inference, and this question is kindly telling you so. If after, say, 90 seconds, you're still stumped, it's time to move on. Hopefully you've actually just made a silly mistake on the question, and when you return to that question later, you will see the errors of your ways.

If you're struggling on a question later on in a game, it's more likely that it's simply a tougher question and you're missing the inference that is needed. Luckily, these questions are worth the same amount as the easier questions. If possible, move on from this question after just 40 seconds.

Get the right ones wrong.

Huh?

Yes, you will be more successful on the LSAT if you allow yourself to get a certain number incorrect. The key is to get the harder, time-consuming questions wrong, and the easier ones right. Ideally, by working speedily through the easy questions, and moving on when you encounter impossible questions, you will save time for the tough-but-not-impossible questions.

If you go into a test with this mind-set, you will be much more likely to finish a section on time, and get a score that accurately reflects your ability to reason the way the LSAT demands. If you lose three minutes on each of three impossible questions—probably still getting them wrong—and end up having to guess on five questions that would have been simple for you if you had simply had a bit more time, your score will reflect your inability to manage your time on the test, not your impressive brain power vis-à-vis logic and reasoning.

If you end up with extra time, go back and work on those impossible questions.

Become familiar with how many questions you generally can get wrong and still get your goal score, and go ahead and get that number incorrect.

Each time you get a higher score on a practice test, simply set your goal score two points higher than the last time, and reduce the number of questions you can get wrong by two. You may be surprised at the results….

Getting Familiar (Take 2!)

Now that we've laid out the primary strategies for setting up Basic Ordering games, let's return to the game we tried at the beginning of the chapter. We'll use it as an opportunity to practice what you've just learned, and we'll reinforce those ideas in the solution write-up. Try solving it again on your own before reading through our solution. (By the way, we suggest that you replay games regularly—it's a great way to master them.)

One last tip: keep an eye on how often the chunk is crucial!

Exactly seven swimmers—Hewitt, James, Kopov, Luis, Markson, Nu, and Price—will race in the 50-meter freestyle event. Each swimmer will swim in exactly one of seven lanes, numbered 1 through 7. No two swimmers share the same lane. Lane assignments comply with the following conditions:

James swims in a lower-numbered lane than Kopov.
Nu swims in either the first lane or the seventh lane.
Markson swims in a lane numbered two lower than Price's.
Hewitt swims in lane 4.

1. Which of the following could be an accurate list of swimmers, listed in order from lane 1 through lane 7?

    (A) Nu, Luis, James, Kopov, Markson, Hewitt, Price
    (B) James, Luis, Markson, Hewitt, Price, Kopov, Nu
    (C) Nu, Kopov, Markson, Hewitt, Price, James, Luis
    (D) Luis, Markson, James, Hewitt, Price, Kopov, Nu
    (E) Markson, Nu, Price, Hewitt, James, Luis, Kopov

2. Which one of the following must be false?

    (A) Price swims in lane 5.
    (B) Price swims in lane 7.
    (C) Markson swims in lane 2.
    (D) Kopov swims in lane 3.
    (E) James swims in lane 6.

3. If James swims in lane 1, then each of the following could be true EXCEPT:

    (A) Kopov swims in a lower-numbered lane than Hewitt.
    (B) Luis swims in a lower-numbered lane than Hewitt.
    (C) Markson swims in a higher-numbered lane than Hewitt.
    (D) Kopov swims in a lower-numbered lane than Price.
    (E) Luis swims in a lower-numbered lane than Markson.

4. If Price swims in lane 3, which one of the following could be true?

    (A) Kopov swims in lane 2.
    (B) James swims in lane 6.
    (C) Luis swims in lane 2.
    (D) Nu swims in lane 1.
    (E) Kopov swims in lane 7.

5. Which of the following could be a partial and accurate list of swimmers matched with the lanes in which they swim?

    (A) lane 1: Nu; lane 2: Markson; lane 6: Luis
    (B) lane 5: James; lane 6: Kopov; lane 7: Luis
    (C) lane 3: Luis; lane 4: Hewitt; lane 5: James
    (D) lane 4: Hewitt; lane 5: Luis; lane 7: Kopov
    (E) lane 2: James; lane 5: Markson; lane 6: Kopov

Step 1: Picture the Game

We recommend that you start every game by reading the scenario *and* skimming the rules before you set pencil to paper, in order to gain a big-picture, general understanding of the parameters. This game began with the following scenario and rules:

> Exactly seven swimmers—Hewitt, James, Kopov, Luis, Markson, Nu, and Price—will race in the 50-meter freestyle event. Each swimmer will swim in exactly one of seven lanes, numbered 1 through 7. No two swimmers share the same lane. Lane assignments comply with the following conditions:
>
> > James swims in a lower-numbered lane than Kopov.
> > Nu swims in either the first lane or the seventh lane.
> > Markson swims in a lane numbered two lower than Price's.
> > Hewitt swims in lane 4.

The first thing we recognize when we read this is that we are placing elements in order. We have seven elements for seven positions, we don't have anything else other than their names—such as whether the swimmers wear red or purple Speedos—and we don't see any strange issues, such as a mismatch between the number of elements and positions. The rules are all about order, with one about assignment. This has all the characteristics of a Basic Ordering game. We can start by setting up a board like this:

H J K L M N P

—— —— —— —— —— —— ——
1　　2　　3　　4　　5　　6　　7

Now that we've got the lay of the land, let's take a careful look at each of the rules.

Step 2: Notate the Rules and Make Inferences

We'll go one rule at a time and discuss our real-time processes:

> James swims in a lower-numbered lane than Kopov.

We can notate this next to the diagram like so:

We can infer at this point that J cannot go in lane 7, and K cannot go in lane 1. We'll add this to our diagram, but since this a pretty basic inference, advanced students might choose not to do so.

Next, we get the following rule:

> Nu swims in either the first lane or the seventh lane.

This we can notate much more directly. We suggest that you elevate it just a bit from the slot, so that you don't mistakenly assume that the slot is filled.

N/ ___ ___ ___ ___ ___ ___ /N   H J K L M N P
   1   2   3   4   5   6   7
K̶   J̶   J – K

Markson swims in a lane numbered two lower than Price's.

This is a rule that is very easy to misunderstand. It is often helpful to play out different hypothetical situations in order to correctly understand the meaning of rules. If P is in 4, M must be in … 2? Well, if the cost of M was $2 lower than the cost of P, and P was $4, then M would be $2. Yes, if P is in 4, M must be in 2. This rule means that we have M, one other swimmer, then P.

We can represent the rule this way:

N/ ___ ___ ___ ___ ___ ___ /N   H J K L M N P
   1   2   3   4   5   6   7
K̶ P̶   M̶ J̶   J – K
P̶   M̶   ⎡ M _ P ⎤

And we know this is an important rule—a chunk!

Finally:

Hewitt swims in lane 4.

At this point, perhaps we notice the significance of how the final rule relates to our chunk—M can't go in lane 2, and P can't go in lane 6. Because that might be difficult to see during the process of solving problems, it makes sense for everyone to notate that inference.

N/ ___ ___ ___ H ___ ___ /N   H J K L M N P
   1   2   3   4   5   6   7
K̶ P̶   M̶ J̶   J – K
P̶ M̶   P̶ M̶   ⎡ M _ P ⎤

It seems there are no other major inferences to extract.

2

Step 3: The Big Pause

Let's start by circling L, since it has no rules attached to it. Next, we'll check that we've understood and notated the rules correctly. We did, so now we'll prioritize the rules.

In this case, our instinct should be to prioritize the M _ P chunk. There are a limited number of places it could go—three to be exact—and placing it dictates and limits the possibilities for other elements. With that in mind, we know we're in great shape, and we can move on to the questions.

Step 4: Attack the Questions

Let's discuss the real-time processes we could use to solve these questions effectively and *efficiently*. We've split this process up into the thoughts we might have at the point of the question stem, and the thoughts we'd have as we walk through the answer choices.

1. Which of the following could be an accurate list of swimmers, listed in order from lane 1 through lane 7?

As we discussed earlier, the first question of the game is almost always an Orientation question. The approach: go through the rules one at a time, eliminating answers that violate that rule.

Remember, what we are suggesting is very different from going through each answer choice one at a time and comparing it against the rules. The method we suggest will generally prove to be far more time-efficient.

In this case, we are given four rules:

Rule 1: James swims in a lower-numbered lane than Kopov, eliminates (C).
Rule 2: Nu swims in either the first lane or the seventh lane, eliminates (E).
Rule 3: Markson swims in a lane numbered two lower than Price's, eliminates (D).
Rule 4: Hewitt swims in lane 4, eliminates (A).

    (A) ~~Nu, Luis, James, Kopov, Markson, Hewitt, Price~~
    (B) James, Luis, Markson, Hewitt, Price, Kopov, Nu
    (C) ~~Nu, Kopov, Markson, Hewitt, Price, James, Luis~~
    (D) ~~Luis, Markson, James, Hewitt, Price, Kopov, Nu~~
    (E) ~~Markson, Nu, Price, Hewitt, James, Luis, Kopov~~

We're left with (B), the correct answer. Unless we have plenty of time, let's skip confirming and move on.

2. Which one of the following must be false?

Aha! We know this sort of question. Four answers will be "could be false" answers, and the right one will be always false. Do you remember what to do? Let's find what must be false, and if we need to, confirm that some answers could be true. Since it's the second question of the game, we can expect that the answer will probably be based on a simple inference. It might be something we figured out while diagramming. Let's look:

(A) Price swims in lane 5.
(B) Price swims in lane 7.
(C) Markson swims in lane 2.
(D) Kopov swims in lane 3.
(E) James swims in lane 6.

(C) is correct—we know Markson can't swim in lane 2.

Second questions are often on the easier side, so feel free to be particularly "lazy," deferring judgment to see if an easy answer "jumps out."

3. If James swims in lane 1, then each of the following could be true EXCEPT:

This is a **conditional question,** and when they give us new information in the question stem, as they have done here, it's expected that we do our homework, making additional inferences from the new condition. Let's try doing that by placing J in the first position in a new diagram we draw for this question (and, by the way, we don't need to copy over every original front-end inference we made—we can always refer to our original diagram for those):

J ___ ___ H ___ N ___   H J K (L) M N P
‾1‾ ‾2‾ ‾3‾ ‾4‾ ‾5‾ ‾6‾ ‾7‾
K̶ P̶   M̶ J̶   J – K
P̶ M̶   P̶ M̶   ┌─────────┐
                    │ M _ P │
                    └─────────┘

If J is in 1, one thing we know directly is that N must be in 7. As usual, it's now helpful to think of our beloved chunk. M _ P can now go only in 3 _ 5. That leaves us with two open spaces—2 and 6—and we have two elements, L and K, that can fill either of those spaces.

With our inferences laid out, we can attack the answer choices. Since we are asked for the one answer that can't be true, we are looking for an answer that MUST BE FALSE.

(A) Kopov swims in a lower-numbered lane than Hewitt.

(B) Luis swims in a lower-numbered lane than Hewitt.

(C) Markson swims in a higher-numbered lane than Hewitt.

(D) Kopov swims in a lower-numbered lane than Price.

(E) Luis swims in a lower-numbered lane than Markson.

(C) is correct. Markson must swim in lane 3, and therefore cannot swim in a higher-numbered lane than Hewitt. Because of the uncertainty we have about Luis and Kopov, all other answers could be true or false. Notice that the wrong answers all include L and K, achieving "could be" status by relying on the uncertainty around the position of those two elements.

4. If Price swims in lane 3, which one of the following could be true?

This is another conditional question, but in this case we're asked to identify an answer that *could* be true. In general, the easiest way to separate out a could be true answer is to recognize the four answers that must be false.

But first things first—let's start by seeing what we can infer if we place P in position 3.

If P is in the third slot, M must be in the first slot, and N must be in the seventh slot. That leaves us with three elements for the three remaining slots. Though we know a bit about where these elements can go, there's a lot of uncertainty, so we'll just write them above to remind us of who's left:

Here are the answer choices:

(A) Kopov swims in lane 2.

(B) James swims in lane 6.

(C) Luis swims in lane 2.

(D) Nu swims in lane 1.

(E) Kopov swims in lane 7.

If we remember the J–K rule, then we know (A) can't be true.

By the same rule, (B) can't be true.

MANHATTAN
LSAT

(C) looks likely, so now either we defer judgment and see if (D) and (E) are indeed false, or we spend a moment to confirm that (C) is correct. Let's play out the first strategy—our diagram quickly tells us that (D) and (E) are impossible.

That leaves (C), the correct answer. It's easy to see that L could go in lane 2. We could put J in 5 and K in 6.

5. Which of the following could be a partial and accurate list of swimmers matched with the lanes in which they swim?

This is very similar to the Orientation question we began with—we're looking for a set of assignments that could satisfy the conditions. The big difference here is that the answer choices give us partial information.

The design of this question requires us to do some work to evaluate each answer choice—it's not easy to see why an answer is wrong with just a glance. However, we do know that four of the answer choices will violate our rules in one way or another. Let's go through each answer choice:

   (A) lane 1: Nu; lane 2: Markson; lane 6: Luis

We know M can't be in lane 2, and so we can eliminate this answer.

   (B) lane 5: James; lane 6: Kopov; lane 7: Luis

This is a tougher answer to eliminate, and perhaps one you wisely deferred judgment on, but if all these assignments were true, that would force N into position 1, and there would be no place for the M _ P chunk. Therefore, we can eliminate (B).

   (C) lane 3: Luis; lane 4: Hewitt; lane 5: James

If positions 3, 4, and 5 are all occupied, there is no place for the M _ P chunk. We can eliminate (C).

   (D) lane 4: Hewitt; lane 5: Luis; lane 7: Kopov

If positions 4, 5, and 7 are all occupied, N must go in 1, and there is no place for the M _ P chunk. We can eliminate (D).

   (E) lane 2: James; lane 5: Markson; lane 6: Kopov

At this point, depending on how confident you are in your eliminations, you can move on to the next question, quickly check this answer against the rules or, if you have any doubt, quickly prove that this answer can work with the rules:

$$\underline{N} \quad \underline{J} \quad \underline{L} \quad \underline{H} \quad \underline{M} \quad \underline{K} \quad \underline{P}$$

(E) is correct.

Smart Tip: Reviewing Practice Games

Now that you've had a chance to take another look at the game, and to read how another person might approach solving the questions, how do you feel?

As you review games you've completed, it can be helpful to compartmentalize the challenges you've faced, and it's always easier to address concrete concerns than it is to address vague ones, so you want to get to know yourself as a test-taker the best you can.

Here are some questions you can ask yourself in order to evaluate your understanding of a Logic Game:

1. Could I picture the game easily? Did I understand the general situation?

In this game, this step may not have been particularly challenging, but in other games, this will be a very important consideration.

2. Did I understand the rules correctly? Did I notate them in a way that allowed me to think about them easily?

For many students, this is the primary issue that prevents consistent success. However, this is an issue that is easily fixed. Almost all rules fall into very understandable and intuitive categories, and with the right practice you can get very comfortable at understanding and notating just about anything.

3. Did I make the key inferences at the right times? Did I understand which rules to prioritize?

We discussed this just before we re-solved this game. For this game, the key was to prioritize the M __ P chunk. "Chunk" rules are always rules that help us assign elements more easily.

4. Did I attack each question wisely?

In large part, this is about knowing when to look for the right answer, and when to eliminate wrong answers. It's also about knowing when to defer work, which is a critical component of high-level success.

Conclusion

You've learned your first game type, and along the way you've gotten some practice using the four-step process to tackle some common question types. That's a lot! What you've learned here is the bedrock of everything else you're going to do.

Here's a quick review:

1. General Process

- Read the scenario and scan the rules before you start diagramming—that will help you determine what sort of game you're facing and how to set up the basic framework of your diagram.

- When you work with the rules, notate them in a way that makes sense to you, and as much as possible, put the rules *into* the diagram, not on the side. Make inferences as you go along, look for connections between the rules, and…

- Pause before you start into the questions so that you can consider what the game's major issues are.

2. Orientation Questions

- For most Orientation questions, work from the rules, eliminating answer choices.

- Each rule is almost always used only once, so once you've found a "culprit," there's no need to evaluate the other choices.

3. Standard Questions

- If you're given a new condition, make inferences before you evaluate the answer choices.

- Your focus is generally on what you know must be true.

- When you use hypothetical scenarios, build them so that they can allow you to make eliminations, either proving or breaking answers as needed.

4. Basic Ordering Games

- Basic Ordering are ordering games with no bells and whistles. The rules will be about either the assignment of elements to positions, or the relative order of the elements.

- These games tend to be back-end. Pausing and identifying the game's big issues before you move into the answers is crucial.

- Chunks are important! Super chunks are super important!

P

Practice Game 1: PT32, S3, G3

Let's go ahead and try another full game. This one is on the high end of the difficulty scale, and was the third game of the section when it initially appeared. We recommend that you use this game to polish your complete four-step process for Basic Ordering games (and don't forget the Big Pause). Be extra conscious of making the correct moves, even if that means going a little slower at first. When you make the right moves, you often find that you can go slower and still finish games much faster! We recommend that you do your work on a separate piece of paper (perhaps write out seven (A) through (E) columns), so that you can replay this game later on.

At a concert, exactly eight compositions—F, H, L, O, P, R, S, and T—are to be performed exactly once each, consecutively and one at a time. The order of their performance must satisfy the following conditions:

> T is performed either immediately before F or immediately after R.
> At least two compositions are performed either after F and before R, or after R and before F.
> O is performed either first or fifth.
> The eighth composition performed is either L or H.
> P is performed at some time before S.
> At least one composition is performed either after O and before S, or after S and before O.

12. Which one of the following lists the compositions in an order in which they could be performed during the concert, from first through eighth?

    (A) L, P, S, R, O, T, F, H
    (B) O, T, P, F, S, H, R, L
    (C) P, T, F, S, L, R, O, H
    (D) P, T, F, S, O, R, L, H
    (E) T, F, P, R, O, L, S, H

13. P CANNOT be performed

    (A) second
    (B) third
    (C) fourth
    (D) sixth
    (E) seventh

14. If T is performed fifth and F is performed sixth, then S must be performed either

    (A) fourth or seventh
    (B) third or sixth
    (C) third or fourth
    (D) second or seventh
    (E) first or fourth

15. If O is performed immediately after T, then F must be performed either

    (A) first or second
    (B) second or third
    (C) fourth or sixth
    (D) fourth or seventh
    (E) sixth or seventh

16. Is S is performed fourth, which one of the following could be an accurate list of the compositions performed first, second, and third, respectively?

    (A) F, H, P
    (B) H, P, L
    (C) O, P, R
    (D) O, P, T
    (E) P, R, T

17. If P is performed third and S is performed sixth, the composition performed fifth must be either

    (A) F or H
    (B) F or O
    (C) F or T
    (D) H or L
    (E) O or R

18. If exactly two compositions are performed after F but before O, then R must be performed

    (A) first
    (B) third
    (C) fourth
    (D) sixth
    (E) seventh

Practice Game 1 Solution: PT32, S3, G3

Step 1: Picture the Game

At a concert, exactly eight compositions—F, H, L, O, P, R, S, and T—are to be performed exactly once each, consecutively and one at a time. The order of their performance must satisfy the following conditions:

> T is performed either immediately before F or immediately after R.
> At least two compositions are performed either after F and before R, or after R and before F.
> O is performed either first or fifth.
> The eighth composition performed is either L or H.
> P is performed at some time before S.
> At least one composition is performed either after O and before S, or after S and before O.

We can recognize that this is an ordering game, and we don't have any subsets or mismatches between the number of positions and the number of elements. Therefore, we can think of this as a Basic Ordering game, and start by setting up the following base for our diagram:

Step 2: Notate the Rules and Make Inferences

Here is our diagram with the rules notated. Check your work against it.

Keep in mind that the first rule, an "or" rule, does not exclude the possibility of both events happening at the same time—as far as we know at this point, T can be both immediately before F and immediately after R.

P

The other "or" rules do exclude the possibility of both, simply because it's not possible for both possibilities to occur at once—for example, O cannot be performed both first *and* fifth.

Overall, this is a complicated Basic Ordering game with a lot of rules and a lot of positions to be filled. However, as we notate the rules and think about how the game comes together, perhaps the most defining characteristic of this particular game is that there are very few up-front inferences. We can infer that S can't go first, and P can't go last. Other than that, there is very little else that we can figure out.

As mentioned before, Basic Ordering games tend to be more back-end than they are front-end. We can think of this example as an extreme back-end game, because there are hardly any inferences up front, and we can tell that we are going to have to do a lot of work within the individual questions.

With back-end games, it is critical that we clearly and correctly understand the exact meaning of each of our notations, and that we are able to prioritize the rules in terms of which will be most useful. This is exactly what we should do during…

Step 3: The Big Pause

For this game, the two rules to prioritize are the second rule—*At least two compositions are performed either after F and before R, or after R and before F*—and the last—*At least one composition is performed either after O and before S, or after S and before O*. These rules give us two chunks that both need to fit into the diagram, and that will, together, fill up four of the eight spots. They would be more useful to us if they were more exact (for example, if we knew that there were exactly two compositions between F and R) but they are still the most useful rules we've got. One could also think of those rules as defining what can't be true. For the second rule, for example, we can write that S and O cannot be consecutive, giving us a prohibited chunk.

The most challenging rule to deal with while answering questions is probably the first one—*T is performed either immediately before F or immediately after R*. Imagine that at some point we place T, F, or R on the diagram—it's not easy to see the exact ramifications of this rule.

Scanning the rules and the roster, we can see that every element is mentioned in a rule.

So here's what we know—this is an extreme back-end game with a lot of rules to keep track of, and we have two chunks that are going to help fill in our board. With that in mind, we take one quick look through each of our notations, and we get to work on the questions.

Basic Ordering **Chapter 2**

Step 4: Attack the Questions

12. Which one of the following lists the compositions in an order in which they could be performed during the concert, from first through eighth?

    (A) L, P, S, R, O, T, F, H
    (B) O, T, P, F, S, H, R, L
    (C) P, T, F, S, L, R, O, H
    (D) P, T, F, S, O, R, L, H
    (E) T, F, P, R, O, L, S, H

P

(A) is correct.

This is an Orientation question, and as we mentioned before, it is generally fastest to answer Orientation questions by going one rule at a time, eliminating answer choices that violate that rule.

"T is performed either immediately before F or immediately after R" eliminates (B).

"At least two compositions are performed either after F and before R, or after R and before F" eliminates (E).

"O is performed either first or fifth" eliminates (C).

"At least one composition is performed either after O and before S, or after S and before O" eliminates (D).

(A), the lone answer remaining, is our correct answer.

If you like to reorder which rules you use first based on how "easy" they are, you might start with the third rule, then perhaps the first, and finish off the remaining answer choices with the second and sixth rules.

13. P CANNOT be performed

    (A) second
    (B) third
    (C) fourth
    (D) sixth
    (E) seventh

(E) is correct.

We want to figure out where P can't perform before evaluating the answer choices.

MANHATTAN
LSAT

If we look at our diagram, there is only one rule involving P: P must be before S. We also know that either L or H has to go in the eighth spot. Putting these two things together, we can see that P cannot go second to last (because we'd have no space for S). There doesn't seem to be a reason why P cannot go in any of the other positions.

P

14. If T is performed fifth and F is performed sixth, then S must be performed either

    (A) fourth or seventh

    (B) third or sixth

    (C) third or fourth

    (D) second or seventh

    (E) first or fourth

(A) is correct.

This is a conditional question, and so we want to play out the information given in the question stem before evaluating the answer choices. We can draw a separate diagram next to this question.

We can make a couple of basic inferences once we place T and F. O must go first, since it's not going fifth.

Also, placing F in the sixth position limits where the R can go; in fact, R can go only in the second or third slot. There is little else that we can infer quickly.

The question asks specifically about the slots in which S can go, and makes it clear that S can only go in one of two slots. Let's go through the remaining open slots carefully.

Can S go in slot 1? Of course not, O is there.

Can S go in slot 2? No, because we know P must be before S.

Can S go in slot 3? No. This is a bit trickier, but we know R must occupy 2 or 3, and we know P must go before S. Therefore, there is no way S can go in 3.

We've effectively eliminated answer choices (B) through (E) since we've proven that S can't go in at least one slot mentioned in each choice, and if we're short on time, we'll choose (A) and move on, perhaps placing an asterisk next to this question to remind ourselves to come back and confirm if we have some extra time at the end of the section.

Can S go in slot 4? There doesn't seem to be a reason why not.

Can S go in slot 7? There doesn't seem to be a reason why not.

Therefore, **(A) is correct**.

15. If O is performed immediately after T, then F must be performed either

   (A) first or second
   (B) second or third
   (C) fourth or sixth
   (D) fourth or seventh
   (E) sixth or seventh

(E) is correct.

Again, since this is a conditional question, we want to do our inferring homework before evaluating the answers carefully. As in the last problem, it can be helpful to scan the answer choices to know, going in, that F will end up having just two possible positions.

Here's the diagram with the new condition and the inferences it brings about:

$$\underset{1}{\underline{\quad}} \quad \underset{2}{\underline{\quad}} \quad \underset{3}{\underline{R}} \quad \underset{4}{\underline{T}} \quad \underset{5}{\underline{O}} \quad \underset{6}{\underline{\boxed{F}}} \quad \underset{7}{\underline{\quad}} \quad \underset{8}{\underline{L/_{H}}}$$

If O is after T, we know that O must be fifth. Similarly, since this prevents a TF chunk, we are required to put R into the third position.

Once R is in the third position, we can see that F must go in either 6 or 7.

16. Is S is performed fourth, which one of the following could be an accurate list of the compositions performed first, second, and third, respectively?

   (A) F, H, P
   (B) H, P, L
   (C) O, P, R
   (D) O, P, T
   (E) P, R, T

(C) is correct.

This is another conditional question, and it's one that really tests our ability to recognize the significance of the new condition as it relates to several different rules.

For one, if S is fourth, O must be first, because it can't be directly next to S.

Next, we know that P must be before S, so it must occupy slot 2 or 3.

Finally, we know we have to fit the F/R chunk in somewhere. Since we can't fit the entire chunk after S, either F or R has to occupy one of the first three positions.

Here's our diagram with the inferences laid out:

$$\underset{1}{\underset{\rule{0pt}{0pt}}{O}} \quad \overset{}{\boxed{\underset{2}{P}\;\underset{3}{F/R}}} \quad \underset{4}{S} \quad \underset{5}{\_} \quad \underset{6}{\_} \quad \underset{7}{\_} \quad \underset{8}{L/H}$$

With these inferences made, (C) stands out as the correct answer.

17. If P is performed third and S is performed sixth, the composition performed fifth must be either

   (A) F or H
   (B) F or O
   (C) F or T
   (D) H or L
   (E) O or R

(C) is correct.

If S is sixth, O must be first. Notice at this point that we are now extremely limited in terms of where we can place either the TF or the RT—these pairings can only go in the 4/5 slots. Since TF or RT must go in 4 and 5, either F or T must go in slot 5.

Your diagram might look like this:

$$\boxed{\begin{matrix} RT \\ \hline TF \end{matrix}}$$

$$\underset{1}{O} \quad \underset{2}{\_} \quad \underset{3}{P} \quad \underset{4}{\_} \quad \underset{5}{\_} \quad \underset{6}{S} \quad \underset{7}{\_} \quad \underset{8}{L/H}$$

18. If exactly two compositions are performed after F but before O, then R must be performed

   (A) first
   (B) third
   (C) fourth
   (D) sixth
   (E) seventh

(D) is correct.

If O is not first, then O must go in the fifth position, and F in the second position. Once we make this inference, we know that R must go in the sixth or seventh position.

At this point, it would be efficient to simply try out one of these—if it works, then that's the answer! If it doesn't, the other one is correct. Can R go in the sixth position? Seems very possible, and here's one way it could work: P F S L O R T H.

Did you start by asking whether R can go in the seventh position? Let's play that out. Since there is now no room for R/T, we need T in the first position.

$$\frac{T}{1} \quad \frac{F}{2} \quad \frac{}{3} \quad \frac{}{4} \quad \frac{O}{5} \quad \frac{}{6} \quad \frac{R}{7} \quad \frac{T/H}{8} \qquad \boxed{F \_ \_ O}$$

We have a problem at this point—there is no way to put S at least two spaces away from O, while also allowing for P to finish before S. We can't have R in the seventh position.

P

Practice Game 2: PT19, S1, G1

Here is one final game for the chapter. This was a first game when it originally appeared on the LSAT, but it was fairly challenging nonetheless. Keep your focus on implementing the four-step process and see if you can finish the game within 9 minutes.

During a period of six consecutive days—day 1 through day 6—each of exactly six factories—F, G, H, J, Q, and R—will be inspected. During this period, each of the factories will be inspected exactly once, one factory per day. The schedule for the inspections must conform to the following conditions:

F is inspected on either day 1 or day 6.
J is inspected on an earlier day than Q is inspected.
Q is inspected on the day immediately before R is inspected.
If G is inspected on day 3, Q is inspected on day 5.

1. Which one of the following could be a list of the factories in the order of their scheduled inspections, from day 1 through day 6?

   (A) F, Q, R, H, J, G
   (B) G, H, J, Q, R, F
   (C) G, J, Q, H, R, F
   (D) G, J, Q, R, F, H
   (E) J, H, G, Q, R, F

2. Which one of the following must be false?

   (A) The inspection of G is scheduled for day 4.
   (B) The inspection of H is scheduled for day 6.
   (C) The inspection of J is scheduled for day 4.
   (D) The inspection of Q is scheduled for day 3.
   (E) The inspection of R is scheduled for day 2.

3. The inspection of which one of the following CANNOT be scheduled for day 5?

   (A) G
   (B) H
   (C) J
   (D) Q
   (E) R

4. The inspections scheduled for day 3 and day 5, respectively, could be those of

   (A) G and H
   (B) G and R
   (C) H and G
   (D) R and J
   (E) R and H

5. If the inspection of R is scheduled for the day immediately before the inspection of F, which one of the following must be true about the schedule?

   (A) The inspection of either G or H is scheduled for day 1.
   (B) The inspection of either G or J is scheduled for day 1.
   (C) The inspection of either G or J is scheduled for day 2.
   (D) The inspection of either H or J is scheduled for day 3.
   (E) The inspection of either H or J is scheduled for day 4.

6. If the inspections of G and of H are scheduled, not necessarily in that order, for days as far apart as possible, which one of the following is a complete and accurate list of the factories any one of which could be scheduled for inspection for day 1?

   (A) F, J
   (B) G, H
   (C) G, H, J
   (D) F, G, H
   (E) F, G, H, J

7. If the inspection of G is scheduled for the day immediately before the inspection of Q, which one of the following could be true?

   (A) The inspection of G is scheduled for day 5.
   (B) The inspection of H is scheduled for day 6.
   (C) The inspection of J is scheduled for day 2.
   (D) The inspection of Q is scheduled for day 4.
   (E) The inspection of R is scheduled for day 3.

Practice Game 2 Solution: PT19, S1, G1

Step 1: Picture the Game

P

During a period of six consecutive days—day 1 through day 6—each of exactly six factories—F, G, H, J, Q, and R—will be inspected. During this period, each of the factories will be inspected exactly once, one factory per day. The schedule for the inspections must conform to the following conditions:

> F is inspected on either day 1 or day 6.
> J is inspected on an earlier day than Q is inspected.
> Q is inspected on the day immediately before R is inspected.
> If G is inspected on day 3, Q is inspected on day 5.

Simple enough—we've got six elements for six slots. We can start off like this:

$$\underline{} \quad \underline{} \quad \underline{} \quad \underline{} \quad \underline{} \quad \underline{} \qquad F G H J Q R$$
$$\;\;1 \qquad 2 \qquad 3 \qquad 4 \qquad 5 \qquad 6$$

Step 2: Notate the Rules and Make Inferences

All of these rules should feel fairly comfortable to you by this point. One key is recognizing that the second and third rules can be brought together.

Here is the diagram with the rules notated. There are some things we know to be true about the order—for example, we know that neither Q nor R can be first—but there are no significant and difficult-to-recognize inferences that we *need* to mark.

Here is a completed diagram for this game:

$$F G H J Q R$$
$$J - \boxed{QR}$$
$$G_3 \rightarrow Q_5$$

Step 3: The Big Pause

There isn't too much to think about in this game. The J–QR chunk (chunk on a leash?) is going to be a key for us—it's going to fill in half of the available positions.

The F options will be important, too. We can expect to rely on the conditional rule from time to time, but only when it's triggered.

We should also note that H has no rules attached to it by circling it.

Step 4: Attack the Questions

1. Which one of the following could be a list of the factories in the order of their scheduled inspections, from day 1 through day 6?

    (A) F, Q, R, H, J, G
    (B) G, H, J, Q, R, F
    (C) G, J, Q, H, R, F
    (D) G, J, Q, R, F, H
    (E) J, H, G, Q, R, F

(B) is correct.

This is an Orientation question, and we can use the rules one at a time to eliminate the answer choices. The first rule eliminates (D). The second rule eliminates (A). The third rule eliminates (C). The fourth rule eliminates (E).

2. Which one of the following must be false?

    (A) The inspection of G is scheduled for day 4.
    (B) The inspection of H is scheduled for day 6.
    (C) The inspection of J is scheduled for day 4.
    (D) The inspection of Q is scheduled for day 3.
    (E) The inspection of R is scheduled for day 2.

(E) is correct.

We know that four of these answers could be true, and one must be false. We want to delay doing work on answers that feel uncertain—that could be true—and focus on identifying the answer that must be false.

With (A) through (D), there's no obvious reason why these placements can't be made.

With (E), we know of two elements that must go before R. Therefore, R cannot go second.

MANHATTAN
LSAT

3. The inspection of which one of the following CANNOT be scheduled for day 5?

   (A) G

   (B) H

   (C) J

   (D) Q

   (E) R

P

(C) is correct.

If we look at the fifth position and think about the rules we've been given, the only element we know for sure can't go in position 5 is J, which has at least two elements that go behind it. Therefore, we can look for J in the answer choices.

4. The inspections scheduled for day 3 and day 5, respectively, could be those of

   (A) G and H

   (B) G and R

   (C) H and G

   (D) R and J

   (E) R and H

(E) is correct.

This is a question that requires a little bit of work with each of the answer choices. We know four of them must be false, and we can identify those four by comparing the answers against the four rules we have diagrammed.

If G is third, then we know Q must be fifth. That allows us to eliminate (A) and (B).

If H is third and G is fifth, there is no place for the J–QR chunk. We can eliminate (C).

If R is third and J is fifth, there is no place for the QR block. We can eliminate (D). Plus, J could never be fifth!

We're left with (E). Depending on your confidence in your eliminations and the amount of time you have left, at this point you might choose to move on, or, if you were less certain, play it out. (E) can work out with the following order: J Q R G H F.

P

5. If the inspection of R is scheduled for the day immediately before the inspection of F, which one of the following must be true about the schedule?

(A) The inspection of either G or H is scheduled for day 1.
(B) The inspection of either G or J is scheduled for day 1.
(C) The inspection of either G or J is scheduled for day 2.
(D) The inspection of either H or J is scheduled for day 3.
(E) The inspection of either H or J is scheduled for day 4.

(D) is correct.

The condition in this question allows us to add F to our chunk, and since in this situation we know that F must finish sixth, we could draw the following next to this question:

We are unsure where J, G, and H will go, so we'll put them in a cloud above slots 1–3.

(Perhaps you notice something about G—more on this in just a bit.)

Let's go through the answer choices:

(A) doesn't seem like it must be true, because there doesn't seem to be a reason why J can't be in 1.

(B) doesn't seem like it must be true, because there doesn't seem to be a reason why H can't go in 1.

(C) doesn't seem like it must be true, because there doesn't seem to be a reason why H can't go in 2.

(D) is easy to lump in with the previous three answers, but when we try to put G into 3, we notice there is a consequence. If G is in the third position, Q must be in the fifth position, and we don't have that. Therefore, G can't go in the third position, and **(D) is correct**.

Perhaps you made the inference about G and the third spot up front. If so, terrific; that of course makes the problem much easier to solve.

You may also have noticed that these answer choices have a lot in common—they are all about the three elements we have remaining for the three slots, and they seem to be hinting at the fact that one of those slots is restricted to just two of the three elements. If, at that point, you had gone back to see if J, G, or H had some reason they couldn't go in 1, 2, or 3, that would have been a great strategy as well.

6. If the inspections of G and of H are scheduled, not necessarily in that order, for days as far apart as possible, which one of the following is a complete and accurate list of the factories any one of which could be scheduled for inspection for day 1?

(A) F, J

(B) G, H

(C) G, H, J

(D) F, G, H

(E) F, G, H, J

(D) is correct.

Here we've got a conditional question in which the condition given requires quite a bit of work from us. Still, it would be a mistake to move on to the answers before we go through our inference chain.

We want to think about how G and H can be as far apart on our line as possible—they can't go in 1 and 6, because F has to go in one of those two spaces. Therefore, it makes sense to think of G and H going in either 1 and 5 or 2 and 6.

Can G go in 1 and H in 5? Sure, and you can run through a quick hypothetical in your head to confirm: G J Q R H F.

Can H go in 1 and G in 5? Sure—we can use the same hypothetical and just switch G and H around to confirm: H J Q R G F.

Can F go in 1 and G and H in 2 and 6? Sure. We can think of a hypothetical if we want, but you can also just imagine taking some of the work we've just done, and flipping the F over from the back of the line to the front. Shifting everyone over one space to the right wouldn't violate any of the rules; one version that would work would be F G J Q R H.

Note that if we put another element into slot 1, then we'd have to put F in 6, and we would not have the maximum space between G and H.

Therefore, F, G, and H are the three elements that can go in slot 1.

7. If the inspection of G is scheduled for the day immediately before the inspection of Q, which one of the following could be true?

    (A) The inspection of G is scheduled for day 5.
    (B) The inspection of H is scheduled for day 6.
    (C) The inspection of J is scheduled for day 2.
    (D) The inspection of Q is scheduled for day 4.
    (E) The inspection of R is scheduled for day 3.

(C) is correct.

Like question #5, this question requires us to add on to our chunk. We can do so as follows:

We know that F is going to go at the beginning or the end, and that H is a stray. We also have to avoid triggering our conditional rule. We can't have G in 3, or Q would have to go in 5 instead of following right after G.

Using our diagram and our one conditional, we can get rid of (A), (D), and (E) immediately because they must be false.

(B) requires a bit more work—if H is on day 6, then the order would be set as: F J G Q R H. This would violate the conditional rule that if G is third, Q must be fifth.

Chapter 3 *of* Logic Games

Relative Ordering

In This Chapter...

Getting Familiar

Do your best to complete the following game in **8:30 or less**. Use whatever approaches you see fit.

Exactly eight rock bands—M, N, O, P, R, S, T, and V—perform consecutively at a showcase on Friday night. No band performs more than once, and no two bands perform simultaneously. The following conditions apply:

> T and P both perform at some time before O.
> S performs at some time before R.
> T performs at some time before N.
> V performs at some time after S.
> M performs at some time before V and at some time after O.

1. Which of the following could be the order of the performances from first to last?

    (A) P, T, O, M, R, S, V, N
    (B) T, N, M, P, S, O, V, R
    (C) P, T, N, O, M, V, S, R
    (D) T, P, N, O, S, M, V, R
    (E) T, N, O, S, P, R, M, V

2. Which of the following must be true?

    (A) At least four bands perform at some time after P.
    (B) At least four bands perform at some time after T.
    (C) At least two bands perform at some time after M.
    (D) At least two bands perform at some time before N.
    (E) At least two bands perform at some time before R.

3. If P performs fifth, then each of the following could be true EXCEPT:

    (A) R is the sixth band to perform.
    (B) N is the fourth band to perform.
    (C) S is the second band to perform.
    (D) T is the third band to perform.
    (E) R performs at some time before N but at some time after T.

4. If S performs at some time after N, and P performs at some time before T, which of the following could be true?

    (A) N performs earlier than P but later than O.
    (B) R performs earlier than M but later than N.
    (C) O performs earlier than N but later than S.
    (D) R performs later than S but earlier than T.
    (E) P performs earlier than O but later than R.

5. Each of the following could be true EXCEPT:

    (A) V performs earlier than N.
    (B) R performs earlier than T.
    (C) N performs earlier than P.
    (D) S performs later than O.
    (E) M performs earlier than P.

6. If T performs third and V performs sixth, then exactly how many different orders are there in which the bands can perform?

    (A) 1
    (B) 2
    (C) 3
    (D) 4
    (E) 5

7. There can be at most how many bands that perform after N but before S?

    (A) 1
    (B) 2
    (C) 3
    (D) 4
    (E) 5

Relative Ordering

About one in every eight games that appear on the LSAT is what we call a **Relative Ordering** game.

Hopefully, even if you found the Getting Familiar game to be a challenge, you didn't find it to be too unusual or unexpected. Hopefully, you saw it as related to the games we played in the previous chapter. Indeed, Relative Ordering games are a subset of Ordering games; however, because they are so common, and because they present a particular set of recognizable characteristics, it's useful for us to separate them out and discuss them specifically. Relative Ordering games are to general Ordering games as jeans are to pants—jeans are a type of pant, but so common that we also define them as a unique clothing category.

What Defines a Relative Ordering Game?

It's not the scenario given before the rules. To illustrate, let's take a look at the scenario for the Getting Familiar game you just played:

> *Exactly eight rock bands—M, N, O, P, R, S, T, and V—perform consecutively at a showcase on Friday night. No band performs more than once, and no two bands perform simultaneously. The following conditions apply:*

This introduction is not very different from the ones we saw for Basic Ordering games, and in fact, it could very well be the introduction to a Basic Ordering game.

What defines a Relative Ordering game are the rules themselves.

Let's take a look at the rules from the same game to illustrate:

> *T and P both perform* **at some time before** *O.*
> *S performs* **at some time before** *R.*
> *T performs* **at some time before** *N.*
> *V performs* **at some time after** *S.*
> *M performs* **at some time before** *V and* **at some time after** *O.*

Notice the similarity among all of the rules. They are all what we define as relative ordering rules—rules that inform us of a general ordering relationship between elements. None of these rules tell us exactly how many positions are between elements, and none of these rules tell us about specific assignments of elements to positions.

A Relative Ordering game is an ordering game for which all, or almost all, of the rules are about relative ordering. Relative Ordering games are one of the two types of games in which you'll always see all or almost all the rules conform to just one type. (The other type is Conditional Grouping, which we'll cover in a later chapter).

Picturing Relative Ordering Games and Notating Rules

When you first tried the Getting Familiar game, it's very possible that you drew a number line to get started. That's perfectly fine—there is no negative to drawing it, and it may serve as a useful reference later on.

However, notice that none of the rules are such that any elements can be placed on the number line. Other than some "not" inferences that you may or may not choose to notate, for this type of game, the number line is not particularly helpful in organizing the information given to us in the rules.

For Relative Ordering games, we recommend that you use another type of diagram that better represents the type of information these rules contain—we call this diagram the **Tree.**

To create a Tree diagram, we don't need to start with a "base" of slots. Once you've recognized that a game is a Relative Ordering game, you can start creating your diagram with the first rule that you read.

Creating a Tree diagram is actually quite simple, and it plays off skills that you already worked on in the previous chapter. Let's use the Getting Familiar game to illustrate how to set up the Tree diagram, step by step.

Here are the scenario and rules again:

> *Exactly eight rock bands—M, N, O, P, R, S, T, and V—perform consecutively at a showcase on Friday night. No band performs more than once, and no two bands perform simultaneously. The following conditions apply:*
>
> *T and P both perform at some time before O.*
> *S performs at some time before R.*
> *T performs at some time before N.*
> *V performs at some time after S.*
> *M performs at some time before V and at some time after O.*

Step 1: Start with the first rule, and draw lines between any two letters for which the relative position is known.

This form of notation should be familiar to you from the previous chapter. The line in between elements will always mean the same thing in our diagrams—we know of a relative relationship between elements, but not a specific one. Note that since we don't know, at least from this rule, the relationship between T and P, we don't connect these elements to one another.

3

Also notice that though we chose to draw T above P, we could just have well drawn it below P. When we construct a Tree diagram, the vertical organization of elements is irrelevant—all we care about is the horizontal relationship between elements. This notation allows us to see that both T and P are before O, but also that we do not know, specifically, the relationship between T and P.

Step 2: Move on to the next rule that can be connected to any part of the existing diagram.

You want to develop a habit, from early on and for any game, of handling the rules in an order that is most convenient for you.

For Relative Ordering games, that means looking out for rules that share a common element. In this case, once we've diagrammed the first rule, we want to skip the second rule, because it shares no elements in common with the first.

The third rule has a T, which also appeared in our first rule. So we want to add that third rule, like this:

Let's pause for a minute and think about what we know at this point, having brought these two rules together.

We know that T is before N, and that T is before O, but what about the relationship between N and O? Note that the way we drew in the second rule was somewhat arbitrary. We could have placed N a bit to the left of O, or a bit to the right, and either would have been fine. We don't know about the relationship between N and O. We know both come after T, but that's it.

What about the relationship between N and P? We never knew the relationship between T and P to begin with, so we certainly don't know the relationship between N and P.

Let's keep going.

Step 3: Repeat until all rules have been used.

It's a good idea to keep track of the rules we've already notated, and one way we can do so is to put check marks next to these rules. It might look something like this:

> ✓ *T and P both perform at some time before O.*
> *S performs at some time before R.*
> ✓ *T performs at some time before N.*
> *V performs at some time after S.*
> *M performs at some time before V and at some time after O.*

We want to look for the next rule that shares a common element with what we've got in our diagram so far, and in this case it is the fifth one, which tells us that we can place an M after the O we already have, and a V after our M, like so:

```
T — N
 >     O — M — V
P
```

If you were confused by that last rule, consider that it contains two pieces of information about M: M comes before V, and M comes after O. Once you've understood those pieces separately, it's easy to join them together.

Now let's pause again for a moment and think a bit about what we know of the relationship between P and V. It appears that P must be before V, but do we know that for certain?

Yes, we do, because we have a link of inferences that we can follow: P is before O, which we know is before M, which we know is before V. Therefore, P must be before V.

What about the relationship between N and V? N is positioned to the left of V, but do we know that N comes before V?

No, we don't. All we know about N, actually, is that it is after T. So it could be right after T, and well before V, or it could be well after T, and even after V.

Why can we infer something about the relationship between P and V, but not about N and V? At this point, it may be that you get why this is so, but perhaps not in a clear, definable way. Knowing when a relationship can be inferred is an important concept to understand, and one we'll revisit in just a bit. For now, let us plant this seed in your mind: we can "stretch" or "shrink" the T–N connection so that N appears to come before or after V. But no matter how you shrink or stretch the P–O–M–V connections, P will always be before V. Hmmm.

For now, let's get back to creating our diagram. We can move on to the fourth rule, which involves S, and add that rule to what we already have:

```
T — N
 >     O — M — V
P           S
```

Finally, we have a place to attach the second rule. We can finish up our diagram like so:

```
T — N
 >     O — M — V
P           S — R
```

Note that our final diagram could have ended up looking quite different, while giving us exactly the same information. Remember that vertical orientation, as well as the length of the lines used to connect elements, is not relevant to the inferences that this diagram is meant to yield. All we care about are the horizontal (left to right, or right to left) relationships between elements. Note that these three somewhat different looking diagrams all give us exactly the same horizontal relationships:

The Tree diagram consolidates the information from all the rules and gives us a clear picture of the relationship between the elements. The Tree does not give us the order of elements, nor is it meant to; we do not have enough information to make such a determination. The Tree does give us every single inference regarding relative relationships, and as you'll see shortly, these inferences are the key to success on Relative Ordering games. We will unlock the full power of the Tree momentarily when we discuss how to draw inferences from the diagram in order to answer questions. First, let's get more comfortable with the setup process by drilling the mechanics.

DRILL IT: Relative Ordering Setups

Each problem will contain one or more rules. Your task is to construct a Tree diagram for each one. Be sure to check your diagram against the solution on the next page AFTER EACH AND EVERY PROBLEM. Make sure you understand each exercise before moving on to the next one.

Example:

S departs at some point after R.

O departs at some time before P but at some point after Q.

P departs at some point after R.

```
    Q — O — P
           /
       R — S
```

1. X plays earlier than W but later than T.
    Y plays later than Z.
    Z plays earlier than X.

2. Both M and H are written later than N.
    O is written at some time before H but after J.
    J is written earlier than K.
    K is written earlier than N.

3. Both T and V call at some time before M.
    N calls at some time after R.
    O calls at some time before N but after M.
    P calls at some time before M.
    T calls at some time before S.

4. M arrives at some time after O.
    L arrives earlier than N
    J arrives at some time after L but before P.
    S arrives at some time after J.
    N arrives later than O.

5. Both S and Y finish at some time before R.
    T finishes at some time after X.
    S finishes at some time after W but before V.
    X finishes earlier than Z.

6. K is produced at some time after N but before O.
    Both L and J are produced at some time before N.
    M is produced at some time after P.
    R is produced at some time before O.
    J is produced at some time before M.

SOLUTIONS: Relative Ordering Setups

3

1. X plays earlier than W but later than T.
   Y plays later than Z.
   Z plays earlier than X.

   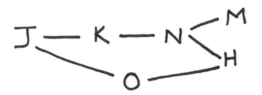

2. Both M and H are written later than N.
   O is written at some time before H but after J.
   J is written earlier than K.
   K is written earlier than N.

   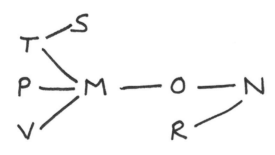

3. Both T and V call at some time before M.
   N calls at some time after R.
   O calls at some time before N but after M.
   P calls at some time before M.
   T calls at some time before S.

4. M arrives at some time after O.
   L arrives earlier than N
   J arrives at some time after L but before P.
   S arrives at some time after J.
   N arrives later than O.

   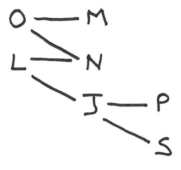

5. Both S and Y finish at some time before R.
   T finishes at some time after X.
   S finishes at some time after W but before V.
   X finishes earlier than Z.

   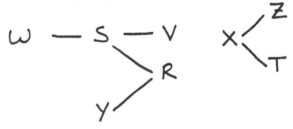

   (Yes, you might end up with two Trees! Don't try
   to force them together …)

6. K is produced at some time after N but before O.
   Both L and J are produced at some time before N.
   M is produced at some time after P.
   R is produced at some time before O.
   J is produced at some time before M.

   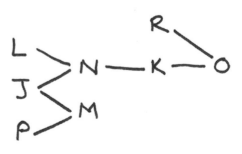

Using the Tree to Make Inferences

Now you know how to draw these fancy Trees, but how can you use them to answer the questions? Let's figure out how to use this powerful diagramming system.

If you have properly set up your Tree diagram, you have essentially uncovered **all** of the key relative ordering inferences required to answer the questions. Your ability to utilize these inferences, however, depends on your ability to correctly read the Tree. There are just two important rules that you must keep in mind. We'll discuss these rules one at a time using our completed Tree diagram from our rock band example:

```
T — N
  >   O — M — V
P       S — R
```

Rule #1: The relative position between two elements, or letters, *can* be determined if we can trace a continuous path between these two elements without changing the horizontal direction of our path.

It should make sense why this is so. If T is before O, and O is before M, and M is before V, we can say for certain that T must be before V. As long as we are linking our understanding in "one direction," we can make such valid inferences.

Example: P to V

Starting at P, we can follow a solid line to the right towards O, continue to the right towards M, and again trace to the right to arrive at V. Note that we have traced a *continuous* path from P to V, and we did not have to change horizontal directions to do so. We moved to the right the entire time. Thus, the position of P relative to V is known. Even though the rules never referenced a direct relationship between the two, we can infer that P sits somewhere before V (with at least O and M between them).

Example: M to T

From M, we can follow a solid line to the left towards O, then continue on a solid line to the left arriving at T. Thus, we can conclude that T sits somewhere before M.

Rule #2: The relative position between two elements *cannot* be determined if the path between them includes one or more changes in horizontal direction. In other words, if there's a zigzag connection between two elements, we don't know which one comes before the other.

Example: N to O

From N, we can follow a solid line to the left towards T, but then we must change horizontal directions, moving back to the right to arrive at O. Thus, the position of N relative to O *cannot* be determined. N could come somewhere before O, but it could also come somewhere after O.

Example: P to R

This is a tough one. It *looks* like P comes before R, but the relationship between them is actually unknown. Remember, the Tree is a map of relative position, NOT a physical picture of order. From P, we can follow continuous, solid lines to the right towards V, but then we must change horizontal directions back to the left towards S, and then change again to move right towards R. Thus, the position of P relative to R *cannot* be determined. P could come somewhere before R, but it could also come somewhere after R. This is tough for some folks at first since R is so far to the right of S in the diagram. But remember that since the connections between elements simply show that one precedes the other, we can make our lines as short or as long as we like. All you would need to do is stretch the S–V connection and your diagram could look like this (and still be correct):

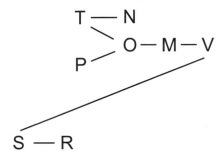

That's it! The Tree diagram presents a simple-to-understand visual representation of all that we know about the relative relationships between elements, and as long as you understand how to utilize the above two rules, the Tree can be a powerful tool for helping you get through a Relative Ordering game quickly and effectively.

Here are some additional tips for utilizing the Tree effectively:

1. Be mindful of "strays." We define a "stray" as an element that has a known relationship with just one other element.

If we take a look at our sample diagram:

The two "strays" for this game are N and R. We know that N comes after T, but we know nothing else about N. We know R comes after S, but we know nothing else about R.

Before you read on, identify all the various positions in the number line, one through seven, that N can occupy, and all the positions that R can occupy.

MANHATTAN
LSAT

N can occupy any position from two to seven, as can R. Because these elements have a lot of flexibility in terms of where they can be placed, they can often be the key "wrinkle" in a particular problem. Furthermore, because of the way we tend to represent these strays, it can be easy to forget them or misunderstand them. For our image above, for example, it can be very easy to forget that N could be the last element.

2. Become practiced at placing elements into positions during questions. Note that in setting up our diagram, we focused on the relationships between elements, rather than on where those elements can and cannot go. With most Relative Ordering games, we don't recommend spending time making additional inferences onto a number line diagram during your setup. However, when we get to the point of answering questions, we'll often need to transfer what we know about relative relationships to a set of concrete positions.

Let's think for a moment about the diagram we have set up. What positions in the order could M occupy? Think about it on your own before reading on.

Here's what we know about M: there are three elements—T, O, and P—that all MUST go before M, and there is one element—V—that MUST go after M. Therefore, M can't go in one of the first three positions, and M can't go in the last position. M could go in positions 4, 5, 6, or 7.

Let's think about the diagram from another perspective. Which elements could go first? Again, think about it on your own before reading on.

To answer this, it's helpful to know what prevents an element from going first. An element can't go first if there are other elements that have to go before (or to the left) of it. If we look at our diagram, there are three elements that have no other elements to the left of them—that is, no elements that must go before them. These three elements—T, P, and S—could all go first.

3. Know when to draw a new Tree. For conditional questions that provide an *assignment* (e.g., R is third), drawing out a number line makes a lot of sense. But for those times when we're provided with a new *relationship*—F comes before Q—drawing a new tree for that question generally is more appropriate.

Just like with conditional questions that tell us an assignment, with these relationship conditionals you might find that you can do the inference work in your head. Great. As you start your prep, default to writing out your work, and later, as you develop a strong grasp on your approach and an understanding of what your brain can actually handle under pressure, you can start to pull away from the paper for easier questions.

3

Using the Cloud to Represent Limited Uncertainty

Now, let's imagine that in a different question, we were told that T occupies the fourth position. We would start thinking about the situation by drawing a number line beside the question, and placing T fourth, like so:

$$\underline{\quad}\ \underline{\quad}\ \underline{\quad}\ \overset{T}{\underline{\quad}}\ \underline{\quad}\ \underline{\quad}\ \underline{\quad}\ \underline{\quad}$$

What do we know about T? We know that N, O, M, and V must all come after T. If T is fourth, there are four spaces after it—5, 6, 7, and 8—in which to place these four elements. However, we can't be sure exactly which position each element goes in. We do know something that severely limits our options—O must be before M which must be before V—but we don't want to waste time thinking about and representing every possibility for every position. Instead, we can do something like this:

$$\underline{\quad}\ \underline{\quad}\ \underline{\quad}\ \overset{T}{\underline{\quad}}\ \overset{\boxed{N,O - M - V}}{\underline{\quad}}\ \underline{\quad}\ \underline{\quad}\ \underline{\quad}$$

The cloud tells us generally where elements go, while also noting that there are still various options. It makes it easy to see that we have four elements to occupy four spots, and because the cloud preserves the known relationships between the elements, it's easy to do more specific deductive work about the specific positions elements can go in if the answer choices require that from us.

Note that we do not know anything about T's relationship with P, S, or R, and one way we know that we don't know anything is that we can't connect T to any of these elements without "crisscrossing" our horizontal direction. But since N, O, M, and V are taking up all the slots after T, we can infer that the rest of the elements fall before T.

We can finish off our diagram by placing the remaining three elements in a cloud in front of the T:

$$\overset{\boxed{P,S-R}}{\underline{\quad}}\ \underline{\quad}\ \underline{\quad}\ \overset{T}{\underline{\quad}}\ \overset{\boxed{N,O-M-V}}{\underline{\quad}}\ \underline{\quad}\ \underline{\quad}\ \underline{\quad}$$

DRILL IT: Tree Inferences

Each exercise will contain a completed Tree diagram. Your task is to answer the associated questions based on your understanding of the diagram. Be sure to check your answers against the solutions AFTER EACH SET OF QUESTIONS. Make sure you understand before moving on to the next exercise.

Exercise #1:

```
    T — S
P ──┤  M ── O ── N
    V   R
```

1. Does V come somewhere before O? Yes, no, or maybe?

2. Does T come somewhere before R? Yes, no, or maybe?

3. How many letters must come after P?

4. Of the eight letters, which ones could occupy the eighth position?

5. Of the eight letters, which ones could occupy the first position?

6. What is the earliest position that O could occupy?

Exercise #2:

```
        R
L           O
 ╲ N ── K ╱
J╱   ╲M
P
```

1. Does M come somewhere before R? Yes, no, or maybe?

2. Does K come somewhere before J? Yes, no, or maybe?

3. How many letters must come before O?

4. Of the eight letters, which ones could occupy the eighth position?

5. Of the eight letters, which ones could occupy the first position?

6. If N occupies the third position, what is the earliest position that M could occupy?

Exercise #3:

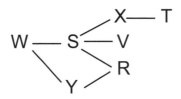

3

1. Of the seven letters, which ones could occupy the first position?

2. Of the seven letters, which ones could occupy the last position?

3. How many letters must come before J?

4. How many letters must come after L?

5. What is the latest position that O could occupy?

6. If J occupies the third position, list all of the possible positions that N could occupy.

Exercise #4:

1. What is the earliest position that R could occupy?

2. What is the earliest position that T could occupy?

3. If V occupies the third position, what is the earliest position that R could occupy?

4. What is the latest position that S could occupy?

5. If Y occupies the second position and V occupies the fourth position, how many different possibilities are there for the ordering of the seven letters? Write them out.

6. If T occupies the fourth position, which letters could occupy the seventh position?

🖰 For more practice, log in to your Student Center!

SOLUTIONS: Tree Inferences

Exercise #1:

1. Does V come somewhere before O? Yes, no, or maybe? **YES**

We can trace a solid line from V to M to O without changing horizontal directions.

2. Does T come somewhere before R? Yes, no, or maybe? **MAYBE**

From T, we can trace a solid line all the way to N without changing directions, but then we must move back to the left in order to arrive at R. Thus, we *cannot* determine the position of T relative to R. T could come before R or after R.

3. How many letters must come after P? **THREE**

Moving to the right, we can trace a continuous connection between P and M, P and O, and P and N. Thus, M, N, and O must all come after P. Remember, R is a stray! It could potentially come before P.

4. Of the eight letters, which ones could occupy the eighth position? **N, S**

Remember that S is a stray! The only thing we know about S is that it must come after T. Other than that, S is free to occupy any position, including the eighth position.

5. Of the eight letters, which ones could occupy the first position? **T, P, V, R**

Remember that R is a stray! The only thing we know about R is that it must precede N. Other than that, R is free to occupy any position, including the first position.

6. What is the earliest position that O could occupy? **5TH**

Notice that T, P, V, and M must all come before O. If these four letters must precede O, then the fifth position is the earliest position that O could occupy.

Exercise #2:

3

1. Does M come somewhere before R? Yes, no, or maybe? **MAYBE**

Tracing the path from M to R involves changing directions twice. Thus, the position of M relative to R *cannot* be determined. M could come before or after R.

2. Does K come somewhere before J? Yes, no, or maybe? **NO**

From J, we can trace a continuous path to the right to arrive at K. Thus, K comes *after* J, not before.

3. How many letters must come before O? **FIVE**

R, K, N, L, and J can all be traced back to O on a continuous, one-directional path.

4. Of the eight letters, which ones could occupy the eighth position? **O, M**

In this case, M functions somewhat like a stray. We know that M must be preceded by both J and P. Other than that, however, M is free to occupy any position, including the last position.

5. Of the eight letters, which ones could occupy the first position? **L, J, P, R**

Don't forget about the stray R! We know that R must come before O. Other than that, however, R is free to occupy any position, including the first.

6. If N occupies the third position, what is the earliest position that M could occupy? **5TH**

If N occupies the third position, L and J must occupy the first and second positions (not necessarily in that order). We know that P must come before M. With the first three positions filled, the earliest that P could come is fourth. Thus, the fifth position is the earliest position that M could occupy.

Exercise #3:

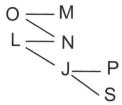

1. Of the seven letters, which ones could occupy the first position? **O, L**

Every other letter has at least one letter that must precede it.

2. Of the seven letters, which ones could occupy the last position? **P, S, M, N**

Watch out for the stray M! Also note that N functions somewhat like a stray in this case. We know that O and L must precede N. Other than that, however, N is free to occupy any position, including the last.

3. How many letters must come before J? **ONE**

L must come before J, and P and S must come after J. J's relationship with O, N, and M is uncertain because we cannot trace a one-directional line between J and O, J and N, or J and M.

4. How many letters must come after L? **FOUR**

N, J, P, and S must all come after L. L's relationship with O and M is uncertain because we cannot trace a one-directional line between L and O or L and M.

5. What is the latest possible position that O could occupy? **5TH**

All we know about O is that both M and N must come after it. Thus, O cannot occupy the sixth or seventh positions, but it could occupy the fifth position.

6. If J occupies the third position, list all of the possible positions that N could occupy. **4TH, 5TH 6TH, 7TH**

If J occupies the third position, L and O must occupy the first and second positions (not necessarily in that order). This leaves the fourth, fifth, sixth, and seventh positions for M, N, P, and S. Since there is no one-directional connection between any of these four letters, their relative positioning is uncertain. Thus, N could occupy any one of the last four positions.

Exercise #4:

```
              X — T
   W — S  <  V
        \    >  R
         Y
```

1. What is the earliest position that R could occupy? **4TH**

S, Y, and W must all come before R.

2. What is the earliest position that T could occupy? **4TH**

X, S, and W must all come before T.

3. If V occupies the third position, what is the earliest position that R could occupy? **5TH**

If V occupies the third position, W and S must occupy the first and second positions, respectively. Y must come before R. With the first three positions filled, the fourth position is the earliest that Y could occupy. R could occupy the fifth position immediately after Y.

4. What is the latest possible position that S could occupy? **3RD**

X, T, V, and R must all come after S. Thus, the latest position that S could occupy is the third.

5. If Y occupies the second position and V occupies the fourth position, how many different possibilities are there for the ordering of the seven letters? Write them out.

W Y S V R X T
W Y S V X R T
W Y S V X T R

If Y occupies the second position and V occupies the fourth position, W must occupy the first position and S must occupy the third position.

6. If T occupies the fourth position, which letters could occupy the seventh position? **V, R**

If T occupies the fourth position, W, S, and X must occupy the first, second and third positions, respectively. This leaves V, R, and Y for the last three positions. Y must come before R, so Y can't occupy the last position.

🖱 For more practice, log in to your Student Center!

Try It Again

Now that you've learned how to draw inferences from the Tree diagram, it's time to put your skills to good use. Let's revisit the rock band game introduced at the start of the chapter. Try developing your Tree from scratch, and then use it to tackle the questions. Again, limit yourself to **8 minutes and 30 seconds**. We'll work through the solutions together on the pages to come.

Exactly eight rock bands—M, N, O, P, R, S, T, and V—perform consecutively at a showcase on Friday night. No band performs more than once, and no two bands perform simultaneously. The following conditions apply:

> T and P both perform at some time before O.
> S performs at some time before R.
> T performs at some time before N.
> V performs at some time after S.
> M performs at some time before V and at some time after O.

1. Which of the following could be the order of the performances from first to last?

    (A) P, T, O, M, R, S, V, N
    (B) T, N, M, P, S, O, V, R
    (C) P, T, N, O, M, V, S, R
    (D) T, P, N, O, S, M, V, R
    (E) T, N, O, S, P, R, M, V

2. Which of the following must be true?

    (A) At least four bands perform at some time after P.
    (B) At least four bands perform at some time after T.
    (C) At least two bands perform at some time after M.
    (D) At least two bands perform at some time before N.
    (E) At least two bands perform at some time before R.

3. If P performs fifth, then each of the following could be true EXCEPT:

    (A) R is the sixth band to perform.
    (B) N is the fourth band to perform.
    (C) S is the second band to perform.
    (D) T is the third band to perform.
    (E) R performs at some time before N but at some time after T.

4. If S performs at some time after N, and P performs at some time before T, which of the following could be true?

    (A) N performs earlier than P but later than O.
    (B) R performs earlier than M but later than N.
    (C) O performs earlier than N but later than S.
    (D) R performs later than S but earlier than T.
    (E) P performs earlier than O but later than R.

5. Each of the following could be true EXCEPT:

    (A) V performs earlier than N.
    (B) R performs earlier than T.
    (C) N performs earlier than P.
    (D) S performs later than O.
    (E) M performs earlier than P.

6. If T performs third and V performs sixth, then exactly how many different orders are there in which the bands can perform?

    (A) 1
    (B) 2
    (C) 3
    (D) 4
    (E) 5

7. There can be at most how many bands that perform after N but before S?

    (A) 1
    (B) 2
    (C) 3
    (D) 4
    (E) 5

How Did You Do?

Since we discussed the setup of this game earlier, we're going to just transfer our diagram, and focus on the questions themselves. Please refer back a few pages if you need help with any part of the setup.

```
    T — N
      >  O — M — V
    P        S ⤸ R
```

3

The Big Pause

In Relative Ordering games, the Tree diagram serves as a thorough representation of all the inferences, so there's no need for any deep consideration of the game or prioritization of the rules. However, it's definitely worth checking that you've notated each rule correctly. At some point you'll see how time-consuming it is when you jump into the questions with a diagram based on "F is after G" when the rule actually says "F is before G"!

Attack the Questions

1. Which of the following could be the order of the performances from first to last?

    (A) P, T, O, M, R, S, V, N
    (B) T, N, M, P, S, O, V, R
    (C) P, T, N, O, M, V, S, R
    (D) T, P, N, O, S, M, V, R
    (E) T, N, O, S, P, R, M, V

(D) is correct.

This is an Orientation question, and we can use the rules to eliminate answers:

The first rule allows us to eliminate (E).
The second rule allows us to eliminate (A).
The fourth rule allows us to eliminate (C).
The fifth rule allows us to eliminate (B).

Alternately, if you are comfortable with your Tree diagram, you can use an approach that we call the "String Technique." Here's how it works:

Looking at our Tree, we see a P–O–M–V string. These four letters must come in that order (not necessarily consecutively, but certainly in that order). So let's start by eliminating any answer choices that do NOT contain the P–O–M–V string. (B) has M–P–O–V. Eliminate it. (E) has O–P–M–V. Eliminate it. Now let's take another string: S–V. Let's eliminate any choice that does NOT contain the S–V string. Eliminate (C). Lastly, we'll evaluate the S–R string. Eliminate (A). We're left with (D).

Note that the String Technique is just a different way of using rules to eliminate wrong answers.

2. Which of the following must be true?

   (A) At least four bands perform at some time after P.
   (B) At least four bands perform at some time after T.
   (C) At least two bands perform at some time after M.
   (D) At least two bands perform at some time before N.
   (E) At least two bands perform at some time before R.

(B) is correct.

N, O, M, and V must all perform after T.

Remember that a big key to questions such as this one is to not spend too much time on incorrect answers. If you are asked to identify an answer that must be true, or must be false, you want to focus on just finding the right answer, rather than on eliminating incorrect answers.

3. If P performs fifth, then each of the following could be true EXCEPT:

   (A) R is the sixth band to perform.
   (B) N is the fourth band to perform.
   (C) S is the second band to perform.
   (D) T is the third band to perform.
   (E) R performs at some time before N but at some time after T.

(A) is correct.

If P performs fifth, we know O, M, and V must follow it (in that order), and so O must be sixth, M seventh, and V eighth. That leaves T, N, S, and R for the first four slots. We can represent the information we know as follows:

$$\boxed{T-N,\ S-R} \qquad \underline{}\ \underline{}\ \underline{}\ \underline{}\ \underset{P}{\underline{}}\ \underset{O}{\underline{}}\ \underset{M}{\underline{}}\ \underset{V}{\underline{}}$$

We are looking for an answer that MUST BE FALSE. (A) must be false.

4. If S performs at some time after N, and P performs at some time before T, which of the following could be true?

   (A) N performs earlier than P but later than O.

   (B) R performs earlier than M but later than N.

   (C) O performs earlier than N but later than S.

   (D) R performs later than S but earlier than T.

   (E) P performs earlier than O but later than R.

3

(B) is correct.

Here's our second conditional question. Unlike the previous one, this question provides a *relationship* instead of a *position*. Therefore, instead of drawing a number line to make inferences, we'll want to draw a new tree.

We can start by simply notating the two relationships, roughly placing them in a position that might work in terms of where all the elements will eventually be placed:

Now we want to build the rest of the diagram around these relationships. No need to be fancy; simply take a rule and add it in. See if you can finish that off before reading on.

You could start by adding in that T must come before N, and then add that O must follow T:

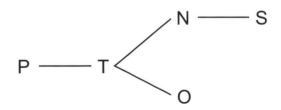

The final diagram for this question should look something like this:

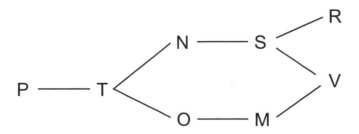

It may seem odd to build a new diagram for a question, but it shouldn't take long, and it will set us up nicely to move through the answer choices quickly.

We want something that could be true, so the four wrong answers must all be false.

(A) is clearly wrong—N can't perform earlier than P.

(B) is correct. R and M are connected by a zig zag, so R could definitely come before M, and R must come after N.

You wouldn't keep moving through the choices, but go ahead now and confirm for yourself why (C) through (E) must be false.

5. Each of the following could be true EXCEPT:

    (A) V performs earlier than N.

    (B) R performs earlier than T

    (C) N performs earlier than P.

    (D) S performs later than O.

    (E) M performs earlier than P.

(E) is correct.

This is another question that requires us to identify one answer that MUST BE FALSE. M cannot perform before P, because we know P performs before O, and O performs before M.

The other four answers represent relations about which we are not certain. For practice, you may want to think about how connecting each of the elements in the respective answer choices—V and N for (A), R and T for (B), etc.,—requires you to "crisscross" your horizontal path. Remember that a zigzag is the physical sign that allows us to see that we do **not** know the relationship between two particular elements.

6. If T performs third and V performs sixth, then exactly how many different orders are there in which the bands can perform?

    (A) 1

    (B) 2

    (C) 3

    (D) 4

    (E) 5

(D) is correct.

We will discuss this type of question in fuller detail shortly.

7. There can be at most how many bands that perform after N but before S?

    (A) 1

    (B) 2

    (C) 3

    (D) 4

    (E) 5

(C) is correct.

We will discuss this type of question in fuller detail shortly as well!

Review Questions

Now that you've had a chance to take another look at the game, and to read how another person might approach solving the questions, how do you feel?

Here are some of the review questions we discussed in the previous chapter. Let's apply them to this game, and use them to think about other Relative Ordering games.

1. Could I picture the game easily? Did I understand the general situation?

Do you understand what characteristics make this a Relative Ordering game? Will you able to recognize Relative Ordering games when you see them on the exam?

2. Did I understand the rules correctly? Did I notate them in a way that allowed me to think about them easily?

Were you able to correctly put together your Tree, or did you make an error somewhere? Do you feel confident that you can construct similar diagrams without error, or do you feel you need practice to get more comfortable?

3. Did I make the key inferences at the right times? Did I understand which rules to prioritize?

For Relative Ordering games, the Tree diagram gives us every up-front inference we need going into the questions. It will show us every "link" between relative relationships, and it will make it easy to see which positions elements can and cannot go into (and we need not and should not notate all of these possibilities up front). The Big Pause is simply a diagram check. The questions themselves will require us to make additional inferences, often by applying what we know to specific positions on a number line. Make sure you have a good understanding of how to think about inferences for Relative Ordering games.

4. Did I attack each question wisely?

In reading the solutions for this game, hopefully you were able to notice similarities and differences between your own thought process and the one we've outlined. If any questions took you more time than they should have, think carefully about the "unnecessary" steps you may have taken, or the moment at which your thought process may have gotten stuck. Perhaps just as importantly, think carefully about the questions that you answered very quickly and effectively. Walk through your thought process, and consider what the keys that led to such success were.

Spotlight on Question Types: Options Questions

In the previous chapter, we discussed the two most common types of questions, Orientation questions and Standard questions. On a typical exam, all but 2 to 4 of the questions that you will see in the games section will fit into one of those two categories (with Standard questions being, by far, the most significant category). In this chapter and the next, we will discuss the two "families" of minor question types—we'll discuss "Options" questions in this chapter, and "Rules" questions in the next.

Options questions require you to use what you know about a game to consider various possibilities for how to arrange the elements. Options questions come in five main types:

1. **Possible arrangements of all elements**
2. **Maximum or minimum**
3. **Possible elements for a particular position**
4. **Possible positions for a particular element**
5. **What would determine the complete assignment of elements to positions?**

The first two question types on the list are typically a bit more challenging, so we will focus our discussion on those two, but we'll also give suggestions for the remaining types of Options questions.

1. Possible Arrangement of All Elements

We had an example of this type of question in our Getting Familiar game:

> *If T performs third and V performs sixth, then exactly how many different orders are there in which the bands can perform?*

Almost all such questions that ask us to calculate total possibilities are conditional in nature; that is, they give us new information that will help us to further limit options before we have to count them. It makes sense why this is so; without new rules, there would generally be so many possibilities that it would be unreasonable to expect us to count them all in the course of a minute or so.

Therefore, you can expect conditions for these questions, and you should expect to be able to whittle down the uncertainty to just a few unset positions and a few unassigned elements.

Let's return to the question mentioned above to discuss these concepts further:

6. If T performs third and V performs sixth, then exactly how many
    different orders are there in which the bands can perform?

    T — N
    >
    P   O — M — V
        S ⟨ R

    (A) 1
    (B) 2
    (C) 3
    (D) 4
    (E) 5

We want to start by placing T third and V sixth. Initially, it might appear that those are the only as-signments we know for certain, but it would be a mistake, at this point, to move into thinking about the number of possibilities for each remaining position. With six positions open, the math is simply too much. We *know* we can uncover other assignments that are certain.

And if we think about it, there is more to uncover. Since there are two positions between third and sixth, and two elements—O and M—that must go between T and V, in that particular order, O must go in the fourth position and M must go in the fifth position.

That leaves P, S, N, and R for the remaining open positions—1, 2, 7, and 8.

We know we're going to get further limitations—if we just have four elements for four positions, with no other restrictions, that would yield 24 possible orders (we won't list them here), which is too many for the test writers to realistically expect us to calculate in the limited time frame (and is also not an answer choice).

We can figure out that P must go in one of the first two positions, and N in one of the final two posi-tions. Since S must perform before R, that means S must also go in one of the first two positions, and R in one of the final two positions. As we mentioned in the solution before, we end up with the following understanding:

$$\text{(P, S)} \quad \underline{} \; \underline{} \; \underline{T} \; \underline{O} \; \underline{M} \; \underline{V} \; \underline{} \; \underline{} \quad \text{(N, R)}$$

There are certain mathematical formulas that we can use to think about our possibilities. However, in general, we don't recommend that you use such formulas. Games often present unique limitations on where elements can go, and it's very easy to misrepresent these limitations when applying formulas under pressure. The situations presented are always simple enough that it makes more sense to manually count out the possibilities.

One tip we have is to focus on the positions that are uncertain. Once we've filled 3–6, we don't have to think about them anymore, and, mentally at least, the issue looks something like this:

Now it's a bit easier, perhaps, to walk through all possible permutations:

P, S   N, R
P, S   R, N
S, P   N, R
S, P   R, N

DRILL IT: **Possible Arrangements**

Here is a mini-drill to practice Possible Arrangement questions. Use the provided diagrams to solve each question.

1.

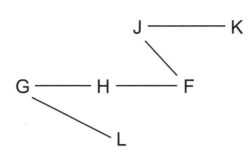

If H is third and L is fifth, how many possible sequences of letters are there?

(A) 2

(B) 3

(C) 4

(D) 5

(E) 6

2.

$$\underset{1}{\underline{H/}} \quad \underset{2}{\underline{}} \quad \underset{3}{\underline{J/F}} \quad \underset{4}{\underline{}} \quad \underset{5}{\underline{}} \quad \underset{6}{\underline{}} \quad \underset{7}{\underline{/H}}$$

H J F T (N) O P

P — O — T

If N comes immediately before H, how many orderings of letters are possible?

(A) 5

(B) 6

(C) 7

(D) 8

(E) 9

3.

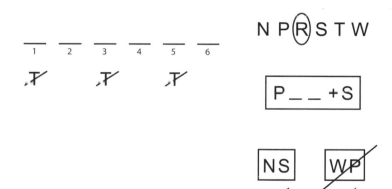

```
_  _  _  _  _  _        G F R S T W
1  2  3  4  5  6
```

If T is third and F is fourth, how many different arrangements are possible?

(A) 1
(B) 2
(C) 3
(D) 4
(E) 5

4.

```
_  _  _  _  _  _        N P Ⓡ S T W
1  2  3  4  5  6
```

If R comes fourth, how many different assignments are possible?

(A) 2
(B) 3
(C) 4
(D) 5
(E) 6

🖱 For more practice, log in to your Student Center!

SOLUTIONS: Possible Arrangements

1. **(C) is correct.** H must come after G and before F. So we know G is in either 1 or 2, and F is in either 4 or 6. J must come before F and K, so we know J is in either 1 or 2, and K is in either 4 or 6:

$$\overset{\boxed{G\ \ J}}{\underset{1\quad 2}{\rule{2cm}{0.4pt}}} \quad \overset{H}{\underset{3}{\rule{0.8cm}{0.4pt}}} \quad \overset{F/K}{\underset{4}{\rule{0.8cm}{0.4pt}}} \quad \overset{L}{\underset{5}{\rule{0.8cm}{0.4pt}}} \quad \overset{F/K}{\underset{6}{\rule{0.8cm}{0.4pt}}}$$

Thus, four scenarios are possible:

$$
\begin{array}{cccccc}
G & J & H & F & L & K \\
G & J & H & K & L & F \\
J & G & H & F & L & K \\
J & G & H & K & L & F \\
\end{array}
$$

2. **(D) is correct.** N must be in 6 to come immediately before H. We still have to determine the positions for P, O, T, and J/F:

$$\boxed{P - O - T,\ \ J/F}$$

$$\underset{1}{\rule{0.8cm}{0.4pt}} \quad \underset{2}{\rule{0.8cm}{0.4pt}} \quad \overset{J/F}{\underset{3}{\rule{0.8cm}{0.4pt}}} \quad \underset{4}{\rule{0.8cm}{0.4pt}} \quad \underset{5}{\rule{0.8cm}{0.4pt}} \quad \overset{N}{\underset{6}{\rule{0.8cm}{0.4pt}}} \quad \overset{H}{\underset{7}{\rule{0.8cm}{0.4pt}}}$$

Assuming that J goes third, there would be four places F could go: 1, 2, 4, or 5. Since it also could be F going third instead of J (and J going in 1, 2, 4, or 5), that gives us a total of eight arrangements.

3. **(D) is correct.** We have to place W in either slot 1 or 2. Because of the S, T, R rule, we'll have to place either R or S before T as well. That leaves the other (R or S) to slot 5 or 6, along with G. We have this so far:

$$\overset{\boxed{W\ \ S/R}}{\underset{1\quad 2}{\rule{2cm}{0.4pt}}} \quad \overset{T}{\underset{3}{\rule{0.8cm}{0.4pt}}} \quad \overset{F}{\underset{4}{\rule{0.8cm}{0.4pt}}} \quad \overset{\boxed{G\ \ S/R}}{\underset{5\quad 6}{\rule{2cm}{0.4pt}}}$$

However, we've ignored the W – G → S – R rule! Since W will definitely come before G in this case, S must come before R. Thus, we actually have this situation:

$$\overset{\boxed{W\ \ S}}{\underset{1\quad 2}{\rule{2cm}{0.4pt}}} \quad \overset{T}{\underset{3}{\rule{0.8cm}{0.4pt}}} \quad \overset{F}{\underset{4}{\rule{0.8cm}{0.4pt}}} \quad \overset{\boxed{G\ \ R}}{\underset{5\quad 6}{\rule{2cm}{0.4pt}}}$$

And from here it's easy to see that there are four possible arrangements:

MANHATTAN
LSAT

```
W S T F G R
W S T F R G
S W T F G R
S W T F R G
```

4. **(B) is correct.** Since R is in 4, T can only be in 2 or 6. However, T in 6 would leave only slots 1–3 for the NS chunk, and since P must come at least three spaces before S, that will not work. Thus, T must go in 2. There's now only one place to put the NS chunk—slots 5 and 6. If S is in 6, P can go in either 1 or 3, with W in the other. That's two arrangements so far. If S is in 5, P cannot go in 3, so P must go in 1, and W in 3. Thus, there are three possible arrangements:

```
W T P R N S
P T W R N S
P T W R S N
```

If T were in 6, the NS chunk would have to go in one of the first three spaces. However, that would not leave enough room to place P. Thus, T cannot go in 6.

🖱 For more practice, log in to your Student Center!

MANHATTAN
LSAT

3

The Possible Arrangement Flip Side

Like many questions on the LSAT, possible arrangement questions have a "flip-side" equivalent. While this *doppelgänger* is far less common, it is still worth discussing.

Here is the question we were looking at:

> *If T performs third and V performs sixth, then exactly how many different orders are there in which the bands can perform?*

Imagine if the same question were written in the following manner:

> *If T performs third and V performs sixth, then for exactly how many of the bands is their position in the order known?*

Note that both of these questions require the same type of work from us— we must take the given information and make inferences from it. The difference in the questions is that the answer choices are meant to test different aspects of our thought process.

For either type of question, the work we do gives us the following information:

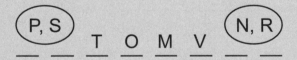

If we get the question in the first form, we find our answer in the positions still left uncertain. If we get the second, less common form of the question, we look at the positions that are now certain (the correct answer would be four—T, O, M, and V).

2. Max/Min

Another common form of the Options question involves consideration of minimums and maximums. These minimums and maximums can be about a few different types of issues. We can be asked about the maximum number of positions between two elements in an ordering question, or, in some other game that doesn't have anything to do with ordering, we can be asked the about the maximum number of elements in a particular group.

The final question from the previous game was an example of a Max/Min question. Let's break it down and evaluate it further:

7. There can be at most how many bands that perform after N but
before S?

(A) 1
(B) 2
(C) 3
(D) 4
(E) 5

```
T — N
  ⟩ O — M — V
P ⟋    ⟍
      S — R
```

When confronted with a Max/Min question during an ordering game, we want to think about three
possible issues:

1. What is the *earliest* that (in this case) N can perform?
2. What is the *latest* that (in this case) S can perform?
3. How many bands *must* (in this case) perform *between* the two?

Go ahead and think about these issues one at a time before reading on.

1. The earliest N can perform is second, because it must perform after T.
2. The latest S can perform is sixth, because it must perform before R and V.
3. Since there is zigzag between N and S, there are no requirements for how many bands
   must perform between them.

Therefore, there can be at most three (in positions 3, 4, 5) elements after N and before S.

3. Possible Elements for a Particular Position

Example: Which of the following is a complete list of bands, any one of which could perform third?

This is a more limited type of Options question—one that requires you to consider the options for just
one particular space.

When you're asked this question about a particular space, take a second or two to consider what other
elements *can't* go in the space. Armed with what you've figured out, you typically can eliminate several
answer choices.

Now you want to test the remaining elements strategically, and the elements that are most attractive to
test are the ones that differentiate the answers.

For example, let's imagine we have been given the question below, along with five answers. Let's also
imagine that our well-honed powers of deduction have allowed us to eliminate two of the answer
choices:

Which of the following is a complete list of bands, any one of which could perform third?

(A) M, N, O

(B) ~~M, N, O, P, Q~~

(C) M, N, P

(D) ~~M, N, Q~~

(E) M, N, O, P

3

If we are uncertain about which of the remaining answers is correct, it would make sense to try out O and P in the third slot, since the differences between the remaining answers involve O and P. As a counterpoint, trying out M or N in the third position would do us no good.

4. Possible Positions for a Particular Element

Example: Which of the following is a complete list of positions, any one of which can be occupied by O?

For most games, we probably won't already have thought out where O *can* go, but rather, we'll have considered where it *cannot* go. So, we'll start by thinking about where O can't go, and eliminate wrong answers. This will typically allow us to eliminate several answers.

When we're down to a few answer choices, we'll want to try out positions, and like on the previous type of question, we want to be strategic about the positions we try out—look for those that differentiate the answer choices from one another.

Note that this is the flip side of the question "O can go in each of the following positions EXCEPT:."

5. What would determine the complete assignment of elements to positions?

Example: Which of the following, if true, would determine the complete order of performances?

These questions, while not terribly difficult, are often time-consuming. Get ready to spend a bit of extra time if you run into this type of question.

Why is this question time-consuming? By its nature, this is a question that requires us to consider the answer choices. This is not a question where we can easily find an answer, or even eliminate wrong answers, based on our initial understanding of the game or the question stem.

We'll look at one of these questions in just a bit, but in general the most important thing to keep in mind is that four answers will *not* lead to a complete assignment of elements to positions. That is, four answers will eventually result in uncertainty about where elements can go. Uncertainty can lead to doubt and panic in the typical test-taker. A key to your success is that you understand the uncertainty for what it is and manage it.

For these types of questions, do not waste time on wrong choices. If you can't make complete inferences from an answer, the answer is probably wrong and you should move on. Try to find the one right answer that is "sticky"—that has multiple ramifications for the other elements—and that leads you on a chain of inferences. Even if you are a little uncertain of your path, if you find an answer that allows you to make three or four deductions, most likely that is going to be the right answer. Each of the wrong choices might lead to a deduction or two about where other elements will go, but those trails will quickly peter out.

A more high-level addition to your approach to this question type is to take a moment to consider the issues at play before you dive into the answer choices. Your understanding of the game's mechanics—an understanding you gained through the Big Pause and through your work on earlier questions—can help you speed up your work on this question type. For example, if you know that the answer must deal with the choice between F and G for the first position, as well as the ambiguous ordering of H, I, and J, keep that in the back of your mind as you evaluate answer choices. If an answer clearly leaves the relevant issues unresolved, then move on to the next one.

Practice Game 1: PT38, S2, G1

Note that on the next page we've added seven bonus questions for this game scenario. These are questions you can use to practice the minor question type processes we've just discussed. Note that these additional questions are NOT official LSAT problems, so don't go yelling at the nice folks over there if the questions are particularly hard.

Give yourself 8 minutes for the original game and questions (though if you feel very comfortable with Relative Ordering games, try to push the pace and go even faster!), and add 7 additional minutes for the seven bonus questions.

A car drives into the center ring of a circus and exactly eight clowns—Q, R, S, T, V, W, Y, and Z—get out of the car, one clown at a time. The order in which the clowns get out of the car is consistent with the following conditions:

V gets out at some time before both Y and Q.
Q gets out at some time after Z.
T gets out at some time before V but at some time after R.
S gets out at some time after V.
R gets out at some time before W.

1. Which one of the following could be the order, from first to last, in which the clowns get out of the car?

    (A) T, Z, V, R, W, Y, S, Q
    (B) Z, R, W, Q, T, V, Y, S
    (C) R, W, T, V, Q, Z, S, Y
    (D) Z, W, R, T, V, Y, Q, S
    (E) R, W, T, V, Z, S, Y, Q

2. Which one of the following could be true?

    (A) Y is the second clown to get out of the car.
    (B) R is the third clown to get out of the car.
    (C) Q is the fourth clown to get out of the car.
    (D) S is the fifth clown to get out of the car.
    (E) V is the sixth clown to get out of the car.

3. If Z is the seventh clown to get out of the car, then which one of the following could be true?

    (A) R is the second clown to get out of the car.
    (B) T is the fourth clown to get out of the car.
    (C) W is the fifth clown to get out of the car.
    (D) V is the sixth clown to get out of the car.
    (E) Y is the eighth clown to get out of the car.

4. If T is the fourth clown to get out of the car, then which one of the following must be true?

    (A) R is the first clown to get out of the car.
    (B) Z is the second clown to get out of the car.
    (C) W is the third clown to get out of the car.
    (D) V is the fifth clown to get out of the car.
    (E) Y is the seventh clown to get out of the car.

5. If Q is the fifth clown to get out of the car, then each of the following could be true EXCEPT:

    (A) Z is the first clown to get out of the car.
    (B) T is the second clown to get out of the car.
    (C) V is the third clown to get out of the car.
    (D) W is the fourth clown to get out of the car.
    (E) Y is the sixth clown to get out of the car.

6. If R is the second clown to get out of the car, which one of the following must be true?

    (A) S gets out of the car at some time before T does.
    (B) T gets out of the car at some time before W does.
    (C) W gets out of the car at some time before V does.
    (D) Y gets out of the car at some time before Q does.
    (E) Z gets out of the car at some time before W does.

7. If V gets out of the car at some time before Z does, then which one of the following could be true?

    (A) R is the second clown to get out of the car.
    (B) T is the fourth clown to get out of the car.
    (C) Q is the fourth clown to get out of the car.
    (D) V is the fifth clown to get out of the car.
    (E) Z is the sixth clown to get out of the car.

Bonus Questions

B1. How many different positions in the order are there at which T could get out?

(A) 2

(B) 3

(C) 4

(D) 5

(E) 6

B2. Which of the following is a complete and accurate list of clowns, any one of which could exit the car third?

(A) R, T, V

(B) W, T, V

(C) W, T, Z

(D) W, T, V, Z

(E) W, T, V, Y, Z

B3. If Y exits fourth and Q exits sixth, for how many clowns do we know the position in which they exited?

(A) 4

(B) 5

(C) 6

(D) 7

(E) 8

B4. What is the maximum number of clowns that can exit after Z but before V?

(A) 1

(B) 2

(C) 3

(D) 4

(E) 5

B5. Which of the following trio of clowns, exiting fourth, fifth, and sixth, respectively, would determine the complete order of exits for all clowns?

(A) W, Y, Z

(B) V, Z, Q

(C) W, Y, S

(D) W, S, Z

(E) V, Y, S

B6. If V exits fifth, which of the following is a complete and accurate list of all clowns who could exit fourth?

(A) T, Z

(B) W, T

(C) W, T, Z

(D) R, W, T

(E) R, W, T, Z

B7. If S exits fifth, which of the following could be a complete and accurate list of the clowns that exit before S but after R, though not necessarily in the order listed?

(A) T, V

(B) T, W, Z

(C) T, V, Q

(D) T, W, Z

(E) T, V, W, Y, Z

P

Practice Game 1 Solution: PT38, S2, G1

A car drives into the center ring of a circus and exactly eight clowns—Q, R, S, T, V, W, Y, and Z—get out of the car, one clown at a time. The order in which the clowns get out of the car is consistent with the following conditions:

> V gets out at some time before both Y and Q.
> Q gets out at some time after Z.
> T gets out at some time before V but at some time after R.
> S gets out at some time after V.
> R gets out at some time before W.

Setup

We want to think about the order in which the clowns get out of the car, and since it's our default, we'll use left for earlier, and right for later.

Apart from irrelevant issues like whether you placed W above or below the main R–T–V–Q branch, your diagram should look like this:

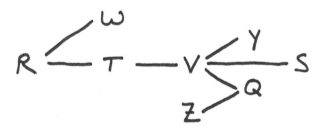

Keep in mind that in this instance we were able to handle the rules in the order in which they were given, but this won't always be the case. Make sure you are in the habit of taking the rules in an order that is best for *you*.

At this point, perhaps we double-check our rules against our diagram to make sure we've got a strong handle on the rules. With a Tree diagram, the inferences are baked in, so let's move on to the questions.

1. Which one of the following could be the order, from first to last, in which the clowns get out of the car?

    (A) T, Z, V, R, W, Y, S, Q
    (B) Z, R, W, Q, T, V, Y, S
    (C) R, W, T, V, Q, Z, S, Y
    (D) Z, W, R, T, V, Y, Q, S
    (E) R, W, T, V, Z, S, Y, Q

(E) is correct.

This is an orientation question, and we have a few options for how we can answer this. Let's go ahead and answer it by using the rules to eliminate answers:

> The first rule eliminates (B).
> The second rule eliminates (C).
> The third rule eliminates (A).
> The fifth rule eliminates (D).

That leaves us with (E).

2. Which one of the following could be true?

   (A) Y is the second clown to get out of the car.
   (B) R is the third clown to get out of the car.
   (C) Q is the fourth clown to get out of the car.
   (D) S is the fifth clown to get out of the car
   (E) V is the sixth clown to get out of the car.

(D) is correct.

Remember that for this type of question you are typically not going to see that one answer must be a possibility. Instead, you will see more easily that four answers are not possibilities:

> (A) must be false because at least three clowns must get out before Y.
> (B) must be false because only one clown can get out before R.
> (C) must be false because at least four clowns get out before Q.
> (E) must be false because at least three clowns get out after V.

3. If Z is the seventh clown to get out of the car, then which one of the following could be true?

   (A) R is the second clown to get out of the car.
   (B) T is the fourth clown to get out of the car.
   (C) W is the fifth clown to get out of the car.
   (D) V is the sixth clown to get out of the car.
   (E) Y is the eighth clown to get out of the car.

(C) is correct.

If Z is seventh, Q must be eighth, and we can see that the other clowns are mostly put in order. You can choose to keep these inferences in your head, or write them out like so:

We can see that (A), (B), (D), and (E) are all not possible, leaving us with only (C). Looking at our diagram for this question, we can see that W is free as a bird (within the cloud), making it a likely candidate for a correct answer.

4. If T is the fourth clown to get out of the car, then which one of the following must be true?

(A) R is the first clown to get out of the car.
(B) Z is the second clown to get out of the car.
(C) W is the third clown to get out of the car.
(D) V is the fifth clown to get out of the car.
(E) Y is the seventh clown to get out of the car.

(D) is correct.

Start by drawing a number line and placing T fourth. There are four clowns that must get out after T: V, Y, S, and Q. Since V must come before Y, S, and Q, it must be fifth. The remaining three clowns, R, W, and Z, must all get out before T. You can note these inferences like so:

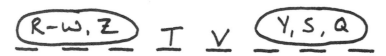

(D) must be true, and the other answers are all "could be true" possibilities.

5. If Q is the fifth clown to get out of the car, then each of the following could be true EXCEPT:

(A) Z is the first clown to get out of the car.
(B) T is the second clown to get out of the car.
(C) V is the third clown to get out of the car.
(D) W is the fourth clown to get out of the car.
(E) Y is the sixth clown to get out of the car.

(D) is correct.

If Q is fifth, we know the four clowns that must precede it: R, T, V, and Z. The remaining clowns must then get out after Q. We can note these inferences like so:

Since we are looking for an answer that must be false, (D) is correct. W, because it must get out after Q, cannot get out of the car fourth.

6. If R is the second clown to get out of the car, which one of the following must be true?

(A) S gets out of the car at some time before T does.

(B) T gets out of the car at some time before W does.

(C) W gets out of the car at some time before V does.

(D) Y gets out of the car at some time before Q does.

(E) Z gets out of the car at some time before W does.

(E) is correct.

If R gets out of the car second, Z must get out first, since no one other than R and Z can ever exit first. We can use our original diagram to consider how the other elements can go in spots 3–8, but it's clear that there's a lot of uncertainty. Since it must be true that Z is first, and this is a "must be true" question, it's very likely that Z will be a part of the correct answer. Why? Because Z exiting first is the only certain inference we were able to make. If we scan the answer choices for Z, we can save time and choose (E)—since Z is first, it must be before W.

7. If V gets out of the car at some time before Z does, then which one of the following could be true?

(A) R is the second clown to get out of the car.

(B) T is the fourth clown to get out of the car.

(C) Q is the fourth clown to get out of the car.

(D) V is the fifth clown to get out of the car.

(E) Z is the sixth clown to get out of the car.

(E) is correct.

It's fairly easy to picture this new rule using your original diagram, but for other variations of this type of problem it won't always be, so you want to develop the ability to quickly draw an adjusted diagram. In this case, if V is before Z, and we already know Z is before Q, we can adjust our diagram like this:

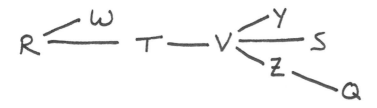

If Z is after V, (E) is the only one of the answer choices that could be true. (A), (B), (C), and (D) all must be false.

Bonus Questions

B1. How many different positions in the order are there at which T could get out?

    (A) 2
    (B) 3
    (C) 4
    (D) 5
    (E) 6

P

(B) is correct.

There is one element that must exit before T, so T can't go first. There are four elements that must follow T, so T can't be in one of the final four spots. That means T can exit second, third, or fourth.

B2. Which of the following is a complete and accurate list of clowns, any one of which could exit the car third?

    (A) R, T, V
    (B) W, T, V
    (C) W, T, Z
    (D) W, T, V, Z
    (E) W, T, V, Y, Z

(D) is correct.

We know that Y, S, and Q can't finish third because they all must have at least three clowns exit before them. This leaves us with R, W, T, V, and Z. No answer choice has all of these, so we know that there are more deductions to be made. R can't be third because at least six elements must go after it (R must be first or second). That leaves us with W, T, V, and Z.

At this point (B), (C), and (D) are all viable choices. Since V and Z are the only differences between the remaining answer choices, let's consider them. Since there is no reason why V or Z can't finish third (try placing them third in hypothetical orders to confirm if you'd like), (D) is correct.

B3. If Y exits fourth and Q exits sixth, for how many clowns do we know the position in which they exited?

    (A) 4
    (B) 5
    (C) 6
    (D) 7
    (E) 8

(C) is correct.

If Y exits fourth, we know R, T, and V must exit before it in positions 1, 2, and 3. If Q is sixth, Z must go before it in position 5. That leaves S and W for the final two positions.

Pop quiz! How many possible arrangements are there in this scenario?

That's easy—there are just two.

B4. What is the maximum number of clowns that can exit after Z but before V?

   (A) 1

   (B) 2

   (C) 3

   (D) 4

   (E) 5

(C) is correct.

The earliest Z can go is first, and if Z is first the latest V can go is fifth. Three elements (R, T, and W) can go in positions 2, 3, and 4 between them.

B5. Which of the following trio of clowns, exiting fourth, fifth, and sixth, respectively, would determine the complete order of exits for all clowns?

   (A) W, Y, Z

   (B) V, Z, Q

   (C) W, Y, S

   (D) W, S, Z

   (E) V, Y, S

(C) is correct.

This type of question requires us to evaluate each answer choice. With so many moving parts, how could we answer the question otherwise?

(A) W, Y, Z in 4, 5, 6 gives us the order of the first three elements (R–T–V) but leaves uncertainty about S and Q in 7 and 8.

(B) V, Z, Q in 4, 5, 6 tells us Y and S must follow, but doesn't give us an order for them.

(C) W, Y, S in 4, 5, 6 tells us that Z and Q must go in the final two positions, with Z before Q. R, T, V have to go in the first three positions, in that order. (C) gives us an exact order and is therefore correct.

In real time, you wouldn't continue to evaluate answers, but in case you're wondering today:

(D) W, S, Z in 4, 5, 6 leaves R, T, and V in 1, 2, and 3, respectively, but we are left uncertain about the order of Y and Q in positions 7 and 8.

(E) V, Y, S in 4, 5, 6 leaves us with many possibilities for order, in large part because both W and Z can be either in the first three positions, or in the final two.

B6. If V goes fifth, which of the following is a list of all clowns who could exit fourth?

   (A) T, Z

   (B) W, T

   (C) W, T, Z

   (D) R, W, T

   (E) R, W, T, Z

(C) is correct.

If V exits the car fifth, we know that Y, S and Q must all exit after V. The four clowns that exit before V would be R, W, T and Z. All of these can be fourth except for R, which must precede T.

B7. If S exits fifth, which of the following could be a complete and accurate list of the clowns that exit before S but after R, though not necessarily in the order listed?

   (A) T, V

   (B) T, W, Z

   (C) T, V, Q

   (D) T, W, Z

   (E) T, V, W, Y, Z

(A) is correct.

Notice the difference between the wording of this question and the previous one? Here, we're asked for *a list that could work*, while in the previous question we were asked for *a list of those that could work*. It's the same difference between a shopping list—a list of items you might buy—and a catalog—a list of all the items you could possibly buy!

If S exits the car fifth, we know that R–T–V must come before it, along with one other clown. The only possibilities for that one are W, Z, and Y. T and V must always come between R and S, so we can eliminate any answers without those two, leaving us with (A), (C), and (E). We can eliminate (C) since Q exiting before S would require Z to exit before S as well, and there isn't enough room before S for that.

(A) is a list that could work (i.e., a viable scenario), while (E) is the list of *all those* that could work. There isn't room for all of them at once! Since we're asked for what could be a list (not the list of those that could), (A) is correct.

In case you're wondering, one scenario in which (A) would work is Z R T V S W Y Q.

How Did You Do?

Again, you want to ask yourself the four basic questions:

1. Could I picture the game easily? Did I understand the general situation?
2. Did I understand the rules correctly? Did I notate them in a way that allowed me to think about them easily? Did I make the key inferences at the right times?
3. Did I understand which rules to prioritize? Did I have a solid sense of how the game works before starting the questions?
4. Did I attack each question wisely?

P

In particular, if some of the Options questions caused you more trouble than you'd like, it's worth your while to take note of them now. We're just getting started and we've got plenty of games in front of us. If you are aware of habits you need to develop, or question types you need to improve on, there will be plenty of time to practice and get those things taken care of.

Either/Or

The majority of Relative Ordering games that have appeared on modern LSATs have functioned very similarly to the two examples we've already discussed. However, the LSAT tends to throw in some curveballs, and so we should expect for games to stray from their basic templates. A common way in which test writers complicate otherwise standard Relative Ordering games is to introduce a relative rule that works in an "either/or" fashion.

To illustrate, let's use a simple game scenario. Let's imagine we have six appointments—M, N, O, P, Q, and R—to schedule, in order. No two appointments can happen at once, and in addition we get the following rules:

> M is at some point before O.
> Q and S are at some point after P.
> N is after P but before M.

Hopefully by this point you feel fairly comfortable diagramming the above situation.

We can start with M before O…

M — O

Connect the third rule…

P — N — M — O

And finally add the second rule…

```
         Q
       ⁄
P — N — M — O
       ∖
         S
```

Not too bad, right? Now let's complicate this by making the final rule into an either/or situation. Imagine the same scenario, but with the following three rules instead:

P

> M is at some point before O.
> Q and S are at some point after P.
> N is either after P but before M, or after M but before P.

Perhaps we think of starting our diagram the same way we did before, by notating the first rule, but when we go to connect the third rule, things become complicated. This third rule essentially means that N must go between P and M, but either P or M could go earliest among the three. In general, we recommend that you represent this type of situation as follows:

P — N — M

or

M — N — P

It's a bit of a challenge to figure out how to connect this to our first rule, and perhaps a bigger challenge still to consider how we would add on the second rule.

What we suggest is that during the Picture the Game phase, you take note of any either/or rules, and when it comes time to diagram, start with the either/or statement, and use it to create two separate diagrams.

We can start with something like this:

P — N — M   M — N — P

Now what we are going to do is build two separate diagrams that represent the two ways the game can play out, splitting at the either/or.

At this point, we can add the first and second rule to both diagrams, and end up with something like this:

```
       S                              Q
      /                              /
  P — N — M — O      M — N — P
      \                              \
       Q                    O         S
```

For this game, we would go into the questions with these two diagrams, which collectively represent the ways in which this game can play out.

When we use multiple diagrams, rather than just one, to represent a game situation, we call this **framing**. Framing is not a tool you will have to use on every game, but it can be a very effective way to take control of certain types of unwieldy games. By creating frames around the either/or, we can clearly lay out the various links and inferences that follow from the separate scenarios. If we kept it as one diagram, it would be tougher to consider various possibilities, especially when it comes to answering the questions.

We'll talk about framing in general more in just a bit, but for now let's get practiced at framing Relative Ordering games that have an either/or rule.

DRILL IT: Relative Ordering Frames

Here is a mini-drill involving stripped down Relative Ordering situations similar to the one we just discussed. For each one, practice working from the either/or statement to create frames for the game (if necessary). Assume there are no other letters to include in the diagram, that every letter mentioned is included, and that there are no "ties."

As usual, check your work after each one.

3

1.

S arrives at some point before W.

V arrives at some point after T.

R arrives at some point before Q.

Either T arrives before both R and S, or else T arrives before neither of them.

4.

N is placed immediately to the left of O.

S is placed to the right of N.

If O is placed to the left of P, L is placed to the right of R.

If P is placed to the left of O, R is placed to the right of L.

R is placed to the left of S.

2.

Both L and J are examined after G.

L is examined after F or after M, but not both.

K is examined after F.

5.

K performs before G and I.

H performs after F.

I performs after H.

M performs after G, or else before K, but not both.

M performs before J, or else before L, but not both.

3.

Y is interviewed prior to S.

Z is interviewed prior to T.

X is interviewed after both T and Y.

W is interviewed after Y, or else before S, but not both.

6.

R must sit immediately behind or immediately ahead of V.

T must sit immediately behind or immediately ahead of W.

V sits ahead of T, or else V sits behind S, but not both.

SOLUTIONS: Relative Ordering Frames

1.

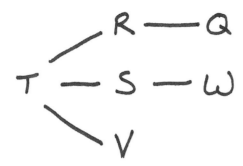 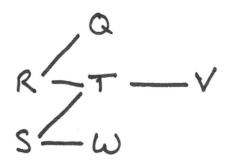

2.

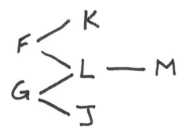 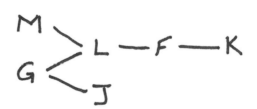

3.

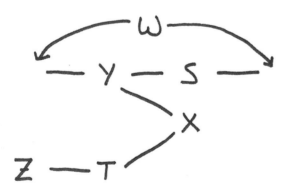

You could have written out a frame for each position of W, but isn't the above enough to keep the two options front and center in your mind? Don't use frames for tracking simple choices that have no consequences.

3

4.

5.

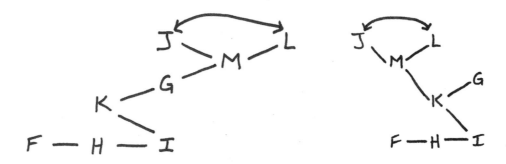

Tough one! You could have framed the issue of whether the order is J–M–L or L–M–J, but in this case, it's easy enough to notate those options without drawing out the frames.

6. This was a very difficult one! Furthermore, it's rare to have two chunks in a Relative Ordering game.

It was important to take a moment to think about the way the rules relate. Here are three ways to represent the game:

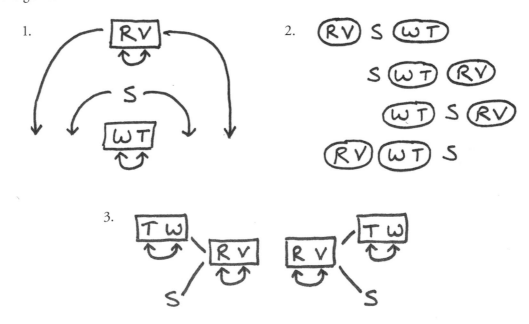

Basic Framing Concepts

As we just discussed, framing is a strategy of utilizing more than one diagram to represent the situation given to you in a Logic Game. For a few rare games, such as the ones we've just been discussing, frames are *essential* for representing the game situation in an easy-to-understand fashion. For some other games, frames are an optional tool that can help you to achieve greater accuracy and efficiency. We'll discuss general framing strategies in some detail here, and we'll also revisit the topic at various points throughout the rest of this book after you've gotten some more games under your belt.

We'll always design frames around some characteristic of a game that funnels the possibilities of that game into limited channels—what we will call a "division with consequences." "Either/or" statements are by their nature "divisions," and are thus some of the most likely restrictions we'll use to design our frames.

Earlier, we were given the statement "N is either after P but before M, or after M but before P." For many test-takers, this type of rule can inspire anxiety. However, for the veteran test-taker, these rules are often the key to handling a game quickly and easily.

We know that this rule limits us to two possible orders for M, N, and P:

P–N–M or M–N–P

Just as importantly, this rule prevents us from arranging the elements in any other fashion. (For example, the three elements will never go P–M–N, or M–P–N.) Thus, these two options represent an exhaustive set of possibilities. This is very important for framing. These frames wouldn't actually be frames if they were just two of many possible arrangements of P, N, and M. In fact, it's dangerous to mistake a nonexhaustive selection of possibilities for frames.

Looking at how different the two frames are, it's clear that this choice between P–N–M and M–N–P has **consequences**. The two diagrams are significantly different because there is a lot to infer based on which way the order of M, N, and P goes. For example, Q and S are forced toward the back of the tree in one frame, but have almost complete freedom of position in the other:

Other divisions we will encounter do not have consequences and are not worth framing. For example, on the next page is the diagram for the first game we played, back in Chapter 2.

$$\frac{\text{N/}}{1} \quad \frac{\ }{2} \quad \frac{\ }{3} \quad \frac{\text{H}}{4} \quad \frac{\ }{5} \quad \frac{\ }{6} \quad \frac{\text{/N}}{7}$$

H J K L M N P

~~K~~ ~~P~~   ~~M~~ ~~J~~   J – K

~~P~~ ~~M~~   ~~P~~ ~~M~~

$$\boxed{\text{M \_ P}}$$

N's placement does provide a division, but there are no significant consequences to that division.

Hopefully, it's clear by this point what we mean by a "division with consequences." Now we can discuss how to decide when to frame games.

1. DEFINITELY USE frames when a division prevents you from creating a normal diagram.

Relative to the LSAT definition of the word, we are using the term "definitely" somewhat loosely—it is certainly possible to nail these games without framing, and countless test-takers have done so. However, in our experience, there are certain situations in which not using frames will prevent you from being able to picture your game and will put you at a significant disadvantage.

The P–N–M scenario we started with is an example of this type of game. The last rule was such that we could not create a "Tree" diagram in the way we normally do, and any attempt at modifying the Tree to represent both possible worlds at once would have severely impacted our ability to read the Tree and make inferences.

In recent years, the vast majority of games that have "required" framing are Relative Ordering games that split on an either/or type of rule (hence the discussion of framing in this chapter). As mentioned before, situations that "require" framing are very rare, and in general, they are not too difficult to spot. If you find yourself unable to create any sort of base for your diagram because certain divisions seem impossible to represent in one diagram, most likely framing is required to make the game more manageable.

2. CONSIDER frames when a division stands in the way of making inferences.

In an ideal world, we want be able to think about a game and organize rules and inferences in a linear mental order; that is, we want one certainty to lead to another certainty to lead to another certainty and so on. For example, for a game in which six elements must be ordered, maybe we learn that R must go in position two, then, because of another rule, S must go in position three, and that forces T into position six, then V into position one, then W into position four, and finally the remaining element, Z, is left to go into the one open position, good ol' number five.

Oh, if only the LSAT were designed to be so! Alas, LSAT games are not Sudoku puzzles (which, by the way, aren't the worst extracurricular activities you could do as part of LSAT prep). On the LSAT, the inferences are likely to be far less definite, and the games are designed to tempt you into jumbling (and not seeing) the order of those inferences. And it makes sense that the LSAT would choose to do this. After all, LSAT games are designed to challenge your ability to organize information.

Frames can be a very useful tool for making concrete much of the uncertainty that games can present. A test-taker who needs to remain mindful of the various possibilities of a game is like a performer who's forced to juggle an unwieldy inverted pyramid of spinning plates.

The creation of frames is analogous to being able to "put down" the first couple of layers of plates that are being juggled. We can see how taking this one action can significantly lower the amount of uncertainty we're forced to manage during a game.

"Enough with the circus analogies!" you say. "Real LSAT examples!" Okay, okay, here's what we mean more specifically.

Let's imagine we had the following simple game scenario. Go ahead and try diagramming it, if you'd like, before reading further.

Seven people—G, H, I, J, K, L, and M—will be interviewed, one at a time. No other candidates will be interviewed. The following conditions apply:

> M will be interviewed second.
> H will be interviewed after I but before J.
> Exactly one person will be interviewed after G but before L.
> Either I or J will be interviewed fourth.

If we simply draw a number line, and notate the elements as we've done in the past, we should end up with something like this (your diagram may have more inferences written in):

3

$$\underline{\quad} \; \underset{2}{\overset{M}{\underline{\quad}}} \; \underset{3}{\underline{\quad}} \; \underset{4}{\overset{I/J}{\underline{\quad}}} \; \underset{5}{\underline{\quad}} \; \underset{6}{\underline{\quad}} \; \underset{7}{\underline{\quad}}$$

$$\boxed{\text{G \_ L}} \quad \text{I} - \text{H} - \text{J}$$

If this were a real LSAT game, at this point you might feel pretty darn good about the game. The information given to us poses some clear and significant restrictions on where we can place elements, and as we juggle information in the process of solving questions, we can imagine that this information wouldn't be terribly difficult to manage.

Still, let's consider what our diagram might look like if we set up frames. Of the four rules given, the final rule provides the clearest "division" for our frames.

If you didn't think to frame based on the fourth rule initially, try it now before reading on. Create two different diagrams, one with I fourth and one with J fourth, and try to apply the other rules to these frames.

Take a look at all you can infer in each frame.

$$\boxed{\text{G \_ L}}$$

$$\overset{\text{H}-\text{J}}{\bigcirc}$$

$$\underset{1}{\underline{\quad}} \; \underset{2}{\overset{M}{\underline{\quad}}} \; \underset{3}{\underline{\quad}} \; \underset{4}{\overset{I}{\underline{\quad}}} \; \underset{5}{\underline{\quad}} \; \underset{6}{\underline{\quad}} \; \underset{7}{\underline{\quad}} \qquad \underset{1}{\overset{I}{\underline{\quad}}} \; \underset{2}{\overset{M}{\underline{\quad}}} \; \underset{3}{\overset{H}{\underline{\quad}}} \; \underset{4}{\overset{J}{\underline{\quad}}} \; \underset{5}{\overset{G}{\underline{\quad}}} \; \underset{6}{\overset{K}{\underline{\quad}}} \; \underset{7}{\overset{L}{\underline{\quad}}}$$

Wow, is that satisfying!

With these two possible frames in hand, the questions will be markedly less difficult to solve.

As is often the case, one frame is more complete than the other. At this point, we could frame the two options of G _ L, or, more likely, just recognize that there are not many options left for that frame and trust that we can figure those out when and if needed.

3. There is usually no "right" answer to the framing question.

Hopefully, we've convinced you of the value and occasional need for frames. But it is easy for students to freak out about the framing decision. Trust us, there are only a few games that *need* to be framed.

One of our curriculum developers (a 99th percentile-scoring LSAT guy) was asked to make a video of himself solving a logic game. It was used to show students how a real LSAT geek solves logic games. He had not seen the game before, and when he solved it, he didn't use frames. It turns out that the game had been chosen as part of a lesson about when it can be useful to frame games. Clearly, it didn't matter *that* much. And we still showed the video because it reinforced an important message about how a flexible game player can make various approaches work.

Here are just a couple questions we'd like you to consider at this point.

1. Do all games present "divisions"?

Yes! Every game presents numerous either/or scenarios. Let's take a look at this super-simple scenario to illustrate:

> Four students—M, N, O, and P—compete in a race. They finish one at a time.
>
> > M finishes before P.
> > O does not finish third.

Here are some options sets this game presents:

> O could be first, or O could not be first.
> M can be either first, second, or third.
> O can finish first, second, or fourth.
> Either M must finish after N, or M must finish before N.
> Either N must finish second, or N must not finish second.

And so on. You get the picture. The much more important question is…

2. How will I know whether to frame a division, particularly for those games that don't "require" framing?

There is no easy answer for this, and to frame or not to frame is definitely a subjective decision; different students draw the line in the sand at different positions.

We've already discussed the rare situations in which we feel you "need" to use frames. For other games, if you need to decide whether to frame as a time-saving strategy, there are two primary considerations:

> 1. Do you feel uncomfortable with the number of plates that you are juggling? All games have uncertainty, but sometimes we feel that we can easily manage this uncertainty, and other times we feel less in control. Framing can be a helpful tool for the games that we find more difficult to conceptualize and control.

2. Do you see the division as having a direct consequence on the other rules? This is really the key sign that helps show us that framing around a particular division will end up being useful. Sometimes it's a bit more obvious that this is the case because you see the same elements in multiple rules (though this is almost always the case for Relative Ordering games, so here we're talking about other game types). This repetition might indicate that there are cascades of inferences waiting to be triggered.

Here are some final points before we return to our normal program!

- While it's rare, occasionally you'll encounter a game that is worth breaking off into more than two frames.
- Some *Conditional questions* will warrant framing! Usually the framing is pretty straightforward for these questions. We'll see examples of this later in the book.

Conclusion

Another power-packed chapter! (Don't worry, they get a bit shorter pretty quickly.) Let's quickly look back at what we've learned:

1. Relative Ordering Games

- With such front-end games, one of the largest dangers is incorrectly diagramming a rule. Slow down and get it right, and double-check your diagram against the rules.
- Remember the zigzag rule!
- For Conditional questions, draw a number line if you're given a specific position; re-draw a tree if you're given relationships that are hard to hold in your head.

2. Options Questions

- Avoid the math; just draw it out.
- Focus on the positions that are uncertain.
- For Max/Min questions, start with the extremes.
- For complete assignment questions, work wrong-to-right.

3. Framing

- Frame if there is a divide with consequences.
- In Relative Ordering games, be prepared to frame either/or situations.
- Look for opportunities to frame, but don't assume they are in every game. It's rare that a game MUST be framed.

Practice Game 2: PT51, S4, G2

Here is one final Relative Ordering game to finish the chapter. This is one of the more unusual Relative Ordering games that have appeared on the LSAT, so feel free to give yourself some extra time, especially during the setup phase. Do your best to complete this game in **9:30 or less**.

Six hotel suites—F, G, H, J, K, and L—are ranked from most expensive (first) to least expensive (sixth). There are no ties. The ranking must be consistent with the following conditions:

H is more expensive than L.

If G is more expensive than H, then neither K nor L is more expensive than J.

If H is more expensive than G, then neither J nor L is more expensive than K.

F is more expensive than G, or else F is more expensive than H, but not both.

6. Which one of the following could be the ranking of the suites, from most expensive to least expensive?

(A) G, F, H, L, J, K
(B) H, K, F, J, G, L
(C) J, H, F, K, G, L
(D) J, K, G, H, L, F
(E) K, J, L, H, F, G

7. If G is the second most expensive suite, then which one of the following could be true?

(A) H is more expensive than F.
(B) H is more expensive than G.
(C) K is more expensive than F.
(D) K is more expensive than J.
(E) L is more expensive than F.

8. Which one of the following CANNOT be the most expensive suite?

(A) F
(B) G
(C) H
(D) J
(E) K

9. If L is more expensive than F, then which one of the following could be true?

(A) F is more expensive than H.
(B) F is more expensive than K.
(C) G is more expensive than H.
(D) G is more expensive than J.
(E) G is more expensive than L.

10. If H is more expensive than J and less expensive than K, then which one of the following could be true?

(A) F is more expensive than H.
(B) G is more expensive than F.
(C) G is more expensive than H.
(D) J is more expensive than L.
(E) L is more expensive than K.

Practice Game 2 Solution: PT51, S4, G2

Picture the Game, Notate the Rules, and Make Inferences (sometimes it's all smooshed together like that)

P

Six hotel suites—F, G, H, J, K, and L—are ranked from most expensive (first) to least expensive (sixth). There are no ties. The ranking must be consistent with the following conditions:

> H is more expensive than L.
> If G is more expensive than H, then neither K nor L is more expensive than J.
> If H is more expensive than G, then neither J nor L is more expensive than K.
> F is more expensive than G, or else F is more expensive than H, but not both.

This is a Relative Ordering game in which it pays to take a moment to establish what first and last place represent. While we can imagine a game in which the last slot is the most expensive, in this game the first slot is. A quick first read through tells us that we are dealing with a "twisted" Relative Ordering game. We are placing elements in order, and all of the rules are relative ordering rules. The twist is in the fact that we have one either/or rule, and two conditional rules (conditional rules are extremely rare in Relative Ordering games).

How we choose to deal with the twists in this game is important. They can be handled cleanly up front in which case answering the questions becomes much more straightforward. If we push them under the rug, or if we go into the questions with significant doubt about the twists, or with an inability to picture them, we will undoubtedly run into trouble answering the questions correctly and efficiently.

The second and third rules are certainly the most difficult to understand completely, so let's take a moment to discuss them now before we delve fully into our diagramming process.

Each rule is designed to tell us that a certain relative relationship is true when another relationship is true.

If you struggled with decoding the second and third rules, practice untangling "neither...nor." For example, the second rule translates to "If G is more expensive than H, then both K and L *are less expensive* than J."

In most cases, conditional statements give us only part of the picture—rules that only apply sometimes. However, do you notice something unusual about the combination of rules two and three? Because there are no ties, the combination of "G is more expensive than H" and "H is more expensive than G" represents the complete range of possibilities for the relationship between G and H. We also learn a great deal about J. Since we know that in one situation the consequence is that J will come before K and L, and in the other it's that J will come after both K and L, we know that there will never be a situation in this game in which J will come between K and L.

The final rule is no walk in the park either if you're unaccustomed to that sort of language. If you struggled with it, take a moment to figure out which of these are the valid arrangements of F, G, and H according to that rule:

    i. F – G – H
    ii. G – F – H
    iii. H – F – G
    iv. H – G – F

Only two of those arrangements are valid—the second and third. So, what the fourth rule basically tells us is that F must be between G and H.

Of course, we've done a lot more thinking about, and categorization of, this game than you would during a real test. Let's move on to the task of diagramming the game as a whole.

Did you consider framing here? The clue that this is a game that should be framed is that the world of possibilities is split by the coupling of the second and third rules, not to mention by the last rule on its own. Furthermore, each of those sub-worlds (frames) carries its own set of inferences. The fact that we see G and H in the last three rules (and H in every rule) is a signal that there will probably be some inference chains to follow in the setup.

In terms of what division to frame, there are two options (which, in this game, take us to the same two frames). Since the two conditional rules divide the world of possibilities, we can frame using those options. In essence, these two rules represent an "either/or" situation. But it also makes sense—and is probably more intuitive for most of us—to start with the obvious "either/or" in the fourth rule. If F is more expensive than G, it will be less expensive than H, and vice-versa. So, we can start with these two frames:

$$H — F — G \qquad\qquad G — F — H$$

We can add the first rule easily enough to both frames. (Here's another example of why it's smart not to simply start diagramming rules the minute you get to them—a moment to picture the game and consider your plan of attack pays off handsomely.) Sure enough, these frames make it much easier for us to think about the second and third rules—the second rule applies to the second of our frames, and the third rule applies to the first of our frames. We can add this information into our frames as follows…

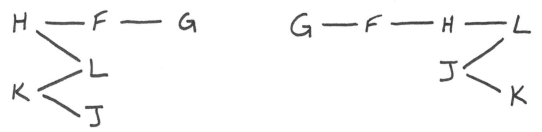

… and we are ready to go into the questions! Though the rules presented information in a challenging fashion, this information ended up coming together to create a fairly simple understanding of the game. As is often the case with Relative Ordering games, the Big Pause is superfluous here.

6. Which one of the following could be the ranking of the suites, from most expensive to least expensive?

   (A) G, F, H, L, J, K
   (B) H, K, F, J, G, L
   (C) J, H, F, K, G, L
   (D) J, K, G, H, L, F
   (E) K, J, L, H, F, G

(B) is correct.

This is an Orientation question, and we can use the rules to eliminate answers. These rules are a bit more challenging than normal, so if the process took you a bit longer that's understandable (and expected). If you tried the String Technique, you were in for a painful surprise. Because of the unavoidable frames, you need to use the old-fashioned approach for this Orientation question.

The first rule is a simple one to start with; it allows us to eliminate (E).

The final rule might be the easiest of the remaining three to use next. In short, we're looking for an instance when F is *not* in the middle, so we can eliminate (D).

The second rule, which applies when G is more expensive than H, allows us to eliminate (A).

The third rule, which applies when H is more expensive than G, allows us to eliminate (C).

(Note that the second and third rules could also have eliminated answers per their contrapositives.)

That leaves us with (B) as the correct answer.

MANHATTAN
LSAT

7. If G is the second most expensive suite, then which one of the following could be true?

(A) H is more expensive than F.

(B) H is more expensive than G.

(C) K is more expensive than F.

(D) K is more expensive than J.

(E) L is more expensive than F.

(C) is correct.

If G is the second most expensive suite, then we know we are dealing with the possibilities represented by the second of our frames, the one on the right. We know this to be true because G cannot go second in the first frame.

For the second frame, if G goes second, the only element that can go first is J.

That leaves the F—H—L chain, along with K, for the remaining four positions.

Now let's take a look at the answer choices. Keep in mind that we want to identify the could be true answer by eliminating the four must be false answers.

Alternately, seeing that K is a "stray," basically uninhibited from slots 3–6, it's likely that the answer will involve K.

(A) must be false—in the second frame, F is always more expensive than H.

(B) must be false—in the second frame, G is always more expensive than H.

(C) could be true, and is thus the correct answer. We do not know the relationship between K and F.

(D) must be false—in the second frame, K cannot be more expensive than J.

(E) must be false—in the second frame, F is always more expensive than L.

8. Which one of the following CANNOT be the most expensive suite?

(A) F

(B) G

(C) H

(D) J

(E) K

(A) is correct.

This is an unconditional question, and so we should consider the possibilities presented in both frames. We're looking for one element that can't be first in either frame.

F can't be first in either of the frames, and is therefore the correct answer.

During the test, we would suggest that you select (A) and move on. However, for the sake of discussion, let's quickly consider the other answer choices:

- (B) G can be first in frame 2.
- (C) H can be first in frame 1.
- (D) J can be first in frame 2.
- (E) K can be first in frame 1.

9. If L is more expensive than F, then which one of the following could be true?

- (A) F is more expensive than H.
- (B) F is more expensive than K.
- (C) G is more expensive than H.
- (D) G is more expensive than J.
- (E) G is more expensive than L.

(B) is correct.

We know that L can only be more expensive than F in frame 1, so we know that for this question we only need to consider that frame. While you might have felt comfortable enough to hold the new arrangement in your head, if not, the diagram for this question would be as follows:

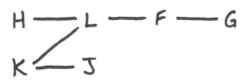

Since we're asked what could be true, it's likely that the answer will involve J's placement, since it is the most "stray" element, able to go in any slot from the second onward.

Let's evaluate the answer choices and knock off those that must be false:

(A) must be false in frame one—H is more expensive than F.

(B) must be false when we consider that L is more expensive than F (the new condition), and K is more expensive than L.

(C) must be false in frame one—H is more expensive than G.

(D) could be true, and is therefore correct. We know nothing about the relationship between G and J, and the new condition has no impact on that uncertainty.

(E) must be false per the new condition—If L is more expensive than F, and we already know F is more expensive than G, then it must be true that L is more expensive than G.

10. If H is more expensive than J and less expensive than K, then which one of the following could be true?

   (A) F is more expensive than H.
   (B) G is more expensive than F.
   (C) G is more expensive than H.
   (D) J is more expensive than L.
   (E) L is more expensive than K.

(D) is correct.

This question is a bit tougher to conceptualize than the last, so it might not be a bad idea to draw out the new condition and rebuild the diagram around it. We'll start by notating that H is more expensive than J and less expensive than K. It means K–H–J. This can't work in the second frame, where J is more expensive than K. Thus, we know that this question is giving us additional information about our first frame—H must come after K and before J. We can reimagine the Tree like this:

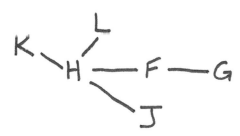

There are too many strays to consider what the answer will probably involve, so with our new diagram in hand, let's evaluate the answer choices:

(A) must be false.
(B) must be false.
(C) must be false.
(D) could be true and is therefore correct.
(E) must be false.

Note that in this case we were able to eliminate all four wrong choices simply by understanding which frame the condition put us in. We never actually needed to use the information about K–H–J! Solving this question boiled down to knowing which frame we were supposed to look at.

Chapter 4 *of* Logic Games

3D Ordering

In This Chapter...

Getting Familiar

Do your best to complete the following game. Use whatever approach you see fit. Give yourself **8:30 or less**.

A publishing company published exactly six novels—*Forgiven, Grain, Highwire, June, Lampoon,* and *Melted*—in the years from 1991 to 1996. Exactly one novel was published in each of the six years. Three authors—Robinson, Stewart, and Tamiko—each wrote exactly two of the novels. The following conditions apply:

> Exactly one of Robinson's novels was published before the first of Stewart's novels was published.
> Neither of Robinson's novels was published in 1991 or 1994.
> None of the authors had novels published in consecutive years.
> *June* was published in 1994.
> *Highwire* was published exactly two years after *Melted*.

1. Which of the following could be an accurate representation of the authors and the novels they wrote, listed in order of publication?

   (A) Tamiko: *Lampoon*; Robinson: *Grain*; Tamiko: *Forgiven*; Stewart: *Melted*; Robinson: *June*; Stewart: *Highwire*

   (B) Tamiko: *Lampoon*; Robinson: *Forgiven*; Stewart: *Melted*; Tamiko: *June*; Robinson: *Highwire*; Stewart: *Grain*

   (C) Stewart: *Melted*; Robinson: *Lampoon*; Stewart: *Highwire*; Tamiko: *June*; Robinson: *Forgiven*; Tamiko: *Grain*

   (D) Tamiko: *Melted*; Robinson: *Grain*; Stewart: *Highwire*; Stewart: *June*; Tamiko: *Forgiven*; Robinson: *Lampoon*

   (E) Robinson: *Forgiven*; Tamiko: *Grain*; Stewart: *Melted*; Robinson: *June*; Tamiko: *Highwire*; Stewart: *Lampoon*

2. Which one of the following must be true?

   (A) One of Stewart's novels was published in 1993.
   (B) One of Tamiko's novels was published in 1994.
   (C) One of Robinson's novels was published in 1992.
   (D) One of Robinson's novels was published in 1995.
   (E) One of Stewart's novels was published in 1996.

3. If *Forgiven* was published in 1995, each of the following could be true EXCEPT:

   (A) Stewart wrote *Grain*.
   (B) Tamiko wrote *June*.
   (C) Tamiko wrote *Highwire*.
   (D) Robinson wrote *Lampoon*.
   (E) Robinson wrote *Highwire*.

4. If Tamiko wrote *June*, then which one of the following must be false?

   (A) Tamiko wrote *Melted*.
   (B) Tamiko wrote *Highwire*.
   (C) Stewart wrote *Melted*.
   (D) Stewart wrote *Highwire*.
   (E) Stewart wrote *Forgiven*.

5. If *Lampoon* was published in the year immediately preceding the publication of *Melted*, which one of the following must be true?

   (A) Tamiko wrote *Forgiven*.
   (B) Tamiko wrote *Grain*.
   (C) Robinson wrote *Lampoon*.
   (D) Robinson wrote *Highwire*.
   (E) Stewart wrote *Melted*.

6. Each of the following could be true EXCEPT:

   (A) Tamiko wrote a novel that was published in 1995.
   (B) *Melted* was published exactly three years before *Grain*.
   (C) Stewart wrote *June*.
   (D) *Lampoon* was published before *Highwire* but after *Melted*.
   (E) Both of Tamiko's novels were published before either of Stewart's novels were published.

Try one more question on the next page…

7. Which of the following, if substituted for the condition that exactly one of Robinson's novels was published before the first of Stewart's novels was published, would have the same effect in determining the years in which the novels were published and the authors who wrote the novels?

(A) Neither of Robinson's novels was published in 1996.

(B) Neither of Stewart's novels was published in 1992.

(C) The earliest that either one of Stewart's novels could have been published is 1993.

(D) The earliest that either one of Robinson's novels could have been published is 1992.

(E) The earliest that either one of Robinson's novels could have been published is 1993.

4

3D Ordering

About 10% of all games that appear on the LSAT are what we call **3D Ordering** games.

You probably found that you were already familiar with most of the elements in the Getting Familiar game. Indeed, 3D Ordering games are firmly planted in the Ordering Family of games. But, as you surely noticed, there's a twist.

What Defines a 3D Ordering Game?

In short, a 3D Ordering game is a Basic Ordering game with an extra dimension. (While it sounds fun, in this case, we're not talking about quantum physics or anything deep like that.)

Imagine you were one of the devilishly brilliant folks who write the LSAT, and you were told to write a 3D Ordering game. If you were lazy, you could commit borderline plagiarism by simply taking a Basic Ordering game and adding on another dimension. Let's do it! Below is the game you saw in the Basic Ordering chapter. Take a quick moment to read it over:

> Exactly seven swimmers—Hewitt, James, Kopov, Luis, Markson, Nu, and Price—will race in the 50-meter freestyle event. Each swimmer will swim in exactly one of seven lanes, numbered 1 through 7. No two swimmers share the same lane. Lane assignments comply with the following conditions:
>
> > James swims in a lower-numbered lane than Kopov.
> > Nu swims in either the first lane or the seventh lane.
> > Markson swims in a lane numbered two lower than Price's.
> > Hewitt swims in lane 4.

Now, let's 3D it!

> Exactly seven swimmers—Hewitt, James, Kopov, Luis, Markson, Nu, and Price—will race in the 50-meter freestyle event. **Three swimmers will wear red caps, three will wear white caps, and one will wear a yellow cap.** Each swimmer will swim in exactly one of seven lanes, numbered 1 through 7. No two swimmers share the same lane and **no swimmer wears more than one cap.** Lane assignments comply with the following conditions:
>
> > James swims in a lower-numbered lane than Kopov.
> > **The swimmer in the sixth lane must wear a red cap.**
> > Nu swims in either the first lane or the seventh lane.
> > Markson swims in a lane numbered two lower than Price's.
> > **Hewitt wears a red cap** and swims in lane 4.
> > **Luis wears a white cap.**
> > **No two swimmers wearing red caps can swim in consecutively numbered lanes.**

4

It's clear (from the bold lettering, perhaps?) that we added the cap dimension to both the scenario and rules. Welcome to the third dimension!

Remember that in creating logic games, the test writers have many ways to pull their levers, but only have a few levers to pull! At the most basic level, the games can ask you either to order elements or to place them in groups (or, as we'll see later, both). 3D Ordering games clearly are based on ordering elements.

The next set of levers is about further defining elements or positions—creating subsets. And here's where we meet the 3D twist: the scenario introduces subsets of position. For example, a certain position will be held by either a French, Russian, or Polish speaker, or perhaps by a live or recorded performance, or, as we saw in the above game, by either a red, white, or yellow capped swimmer. Regardless of the actual categories, what is happening is that along with ordering elements into positions, we now must track categories of position.

Looking at the game above, we have several relationships to consider:

1. Swimmer and lane (element and position)
Which swimmer goes in which lane?

2. Swimmer and color (element and subset)
Which color cap is each swimmer wearing?

3. Color and lane (subset and position)
Which cap color does each lane correspond to?

That probably seems like a lot to keep tabs on, but this is where your diagram will come in handy. We'll get to that in a moment. In terms of recognizing when you're facing a 3D Ordering game, keep in mind two ideas:

1. Keep the order. If there's no ordering, it's not 3D Ordering!

2. Add another dimension. If it feels like Basic Ordering, but you're struggling to manage another dimension of the game, it's likely 3D Ordering.

Picturing 3D Ordering Games and Notating Rules

When you played the Getting Familiar game, you probably started with a number line. Perfect! As we just stated, a game is not 3D Ordering if there isn't ordering! But while we'll always start with a number line to anchor the ordering aspect of the game, that line is clearly not enough to represent the entirety of the game's structure. (Ideally, you would have realized that *before* you drew it, in the Picture the Game phase.) We need a second line for our additional dimension. This forms what we call a **3D Number Line**.

We suggest that the elements go on the bottom row, and the subsets, for which there are usually only two or three options, go on the top row. However you do it, definitely keep the ordering on the bottom of the whole diagram. (If you'd like to further distinguish between the elements and subsets, you can use lowercase for the subsets.)

Let's build one for the "3Ded" swimmers game from above. Write your rosters of elements next to the corresponding rows:

$$\underline{\quad}\ \underline{\quad}\ \underline{\quad}\ \underline{\quad}\ \underline{\quad}\ \underline{\quad}\ \underline{\quad} \qquad \text{R W Y}$$

$$\underset{1\quad 2\quad 3\quad 4\quad 5\quad 6\quad 7}{\underline{\quad}\ \underline{\quad}\ \underline{\quad}\ \underline{\quad}\ \underline{\quad}\ \underline{\quad}\ \underline{\quad}} \qquad \text{H J K L M N P}$$

If you might get confused, label the rows; in this case it would be "colors" and "swimmers," of course.

Before we go on, we should make one tweak to the team roster. Do you remember what the game says about the caps? Go back and reread the scenario if not.

It says that three caps are red, three are white and one is yellow. Don't forget that some rules are embedded in the scenario!

When you know how many of each subset are in a game, represent that in your diagram like so:

$$\underline{\quad}\ \underline{\quad}\ \underline{\quad}\ \underline{\quad}\ \underline{\quad}\ \underline{\quad}\ \underline{\quad} \qquad \text{R R R W W W Y}$$

$$\underset{1\quad\ 2\quad\ 3\quad\ 4\quad\ 5\quad\ 6\quad\ 7}{\underline{\quad}\ \underline{\quad}\ \underline{\quad}\ \underline{\quad}\ \underline{\quad}\ \underline{\quad}\ \underline{\quad}} \qquad \text{H J K L M N P}$$

Let's move to the rules. As we mentioned above, there are three different relationships in play in 3D Ordering games, and all three can show up in the rules. Sometimes two relationships will show up in one rule, as we see in the fifth rule of this game. Let's categorize the rules:

1. Swimmer and lane (element and position)

James swims in a lower-numbered lane than Kopov.

Nu swims in either the first lane or the seventh lane.

Markson swims in a lane numbered two lower than Price's.

4

You already know how to notate these rules.

2. Swimmer and color (element and subset)

Luis wears a white cap.

With these sorts of rules, you want to notate them in a way that is consistent with how your diagram is laid out. Since the caps are on the top row and the swimmers are on the bottom one, notate accordingly:

3. Color and lane (subset and position)

The swimmer in the sixth lane must wear a red cap.

No two swimmers wearing red caps can swim in consecutively numbered lanes.

As with the rules connecting the swimmers and the caps, represent these rules in a way that is easy to transfer into the diagram. The first rule above should go straight into the diagram, while the second one should go to the side:

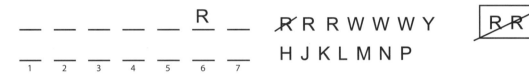

Notice we crossed out the items that were "used"—it's an easy way to keep track of who is left.

The fifth rule of the game references two types of relationships:

Hewitt wears a red cap and swims in lane 4.

But this is an easy rule to notate, and there's actually no reason to write it to the side. Let's throw it right into our 3D Number Line.

Go ahead and create a completed diagram (with inferences) before reading on. As you infer various restrictions, put them either above or below the 3D Number Line, depending on whether the restriction involves the teams or the swimmers. Here are the rules once again, and a template to fill in:

James swims in a lower-numbered lane than Kopov.

The swimmer in the sixth lane must wear a red cap.

Nu swims in either the first lane or the seventh lane.

Markson swims in a lane numbered two lower than Price's.

Hewitt wears a red cap and swims in lane 4.

Luis wears a white cap.

No two swimmers wearing red caps can swim in consecutively numbered lanes.

```
— — — — — — —    R R R W W W Y

— — — — — — —    H J K L M N P
1  2  3  4  5  6  7
```

Below is what we came up with—notice how we arranged things:

```
     R̸      R̸      R̸

— — — R — R —    R̸ R̸ R W W W Y    [R̸ R̸] ⟋  W
N/  — — H — — /N  H J K L M N P              L
1  2  3  4  5  6  7

K̸  P̸        M̸  J̸                  J — K   [M _ P]
P̸  M̸        L̸  M̸
          P̸
```

With so many relationships to keep track of, notating this way can help keep things clear.

As usual, your diagram might look a little different. Perhaps you wrote in "W/Y" in the top row of slots 3, 5, and 7. That's fine. A smart move you might not have done is crossing out the two R's that were placed. This helps you see who's left.

Talking about smart, if you started thinking about the remaining colors and where they can go, bravo! That last R can go only in either position 1 or 2. You can add that to your diagram using a cloud:

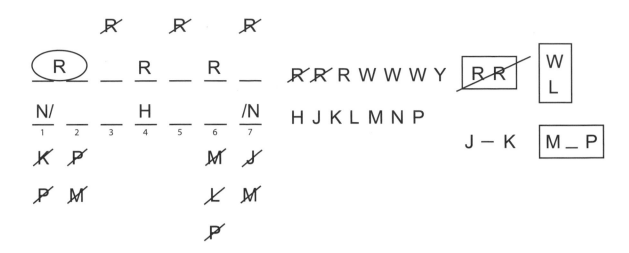

We'll do some more work on diagramming 3D Ordering games in a bit, but let's take a quick detour and look at some of the subtler issues of this game type.

Insider Overview of 3D Ordering

Historically, 3D Ordering games have been front-end games. They've called for a lot of up-front inference work. Lately though, the LSAT has been delivering more back-end versions.

As you practice, you'll come across more examples of front-end 3D Ordering games (and this makes sense, since with 20+ years of LSATs behind us, there are a lot more historical LSATs than recent ones). What does this mean for you? In short, be ready for either. Just because many of your practice 3D Ordering games can unfold with a dazzling sequence of inferences before you even look at the first question, don't force it. Some games simply are not designed to work that way.

If you sense that a 3D Ordering game is front-end, dive in! You know how to do this: work from the rules, look for restrictions, identify any divisions with consequences, etc.

If you quickly hit a brick wall, don't force it by writing out lots of hypotheticals, or by making frames where you shouldn't. Instead, know that you'll probably have more work to do in the questions and therefore be sure you have a firm grip on the rules. One way to see if you have a firm grip is to look at each of your notations, say to yourself what it means, and then check your interpretation against the written rule.

If you're unsure whether the game is front- or back-end, cover both bases: make sure you are in control of the rules AND consider how the game works during your Big Pause. The LSAT generously provides an early warning system: if the second (or first) question of the game stumps you—meaning you're not even sure how to approach it—you probably should go back and work on understanding the game.

DRILL IT: 3D Ordering Setups

Let's go back to working on diagramming 3D Ordering games. Work through the 3D Number Line setup for each of the games below. Be sure to check your work against the solutions after each game.

1. Exactly six items—F, G, H, J, K, and L—are sold at a yard sale. The items are sold one at a time and consecutively, and each item is sold for either $10 or $20. The following rules govern the sale of the items:

   > J is sold either first or sixth.
   > No two $10 items are sold consecutively.
   > The item sold third is sold for $10.
   > L is sold for $20.

2. Exactly seven students—Moore, Nelson, Polanski, Oh, Sullivan, Tang, and Webb—sit in the seats numbered sequentially 1 through 7 in the first row of a classroom. Exactly one student sits in each of the seven seats. Each student is either right-handed or left-handed, but not both. The seating arrangement adheres to the following conditions:

   > No right-handed student can sit in a seat numbered one lower than the seat of a left-handed student.
   > Moore sits in a seat numbered two lower than the seat in which Polanski sits.
   > A left-handed student sits in seat 3.
   > Tang is a right-handed student.
   > Oh sits in seat 6.

3. On Monday, exactly five flights—P, Q, R, S, and T—depart from the same airport. The flights depart one at a time, and each flight departs exactly once. Two of the flights are bound for Japan, two are bound for Germany, and the remaining flight is bound for France. The following conditions apply:

   > No flight bound for Germany can depart until at least one flight bound for Japan has departed.
   > Flight Q departs at some time before flight S and at some time after flight R.
   > The flight that departs first is not bound for Japan.
   > Flight P is bound for Germany.

4. One evening, a television station broadcasts exactly six programs: M, N, O, P, R, and S. No two programs are broadcast simultaneously, and no other programs are broadcast. Each program is either 30 minutes in length or 60 minutes in length. The following must be true:

   > N is 60 minutes in length.
   > The broadcast of S immediately precedes the broadcast of O.
   > Each 30-minute program is immediately followed by a 60-minute program.
   > P is broadcast at some time before O.
   > A 30-minute program is broadcast fourth.

4

SOLUTIONS: 3D Ordering Setups

1.

~~10 10~~

20
L

$$\text{item: } \frac{\cancel{J}}{1} \quad \frac{}{2} \quad \frac{}{3} \quad \frac{}{4} \quad \frac{}{5} \quad \frac{\cancel{J}}{6} \quad \text{F} \,\text{G}\, \text{H}\, \text{J}\, \text{K}\, \text{L}$$

$$\text{\$\$: } \underline{\quad} \quad \underline{20} \quad \underline{10} \quad \underline{20} \quad \underline{\quad} \quad \underline{\quad} \qquad 10 \quad 20$$

(F, G, H, K circled)

Under slot 3: ~~K~~

Note that an R must go in slot 7. If an L went in slot 7, the whole top row would be L's (since on R cannot immediately precede any L), and we know that we must have at least one R (Tang is right-handed).

2.

~~R~~L   R / T

M _ P

(arrow pointing down from note above into slot 7)

hand:	L	L	L	___	___	___	R	R L
student:	___	___	___	___	___	O	___	M N P O S T W
	1	2	3	4	5	6	7	
	~~P~~	~~P~~	~~T~~	~~M~~			~~M~~	
	~~T~~	~~T~~						

3.

J ⌐ J
J – G – G

R – Q – S

G / P

Japan can't go first (as the third constraint tells us), and since G can't go until after at least one J, G can't go in slot 1 or 2! This means P can't go in 1 or 2 either (since P is bound for Germany).

where:	~~G~~ ~~J~~ F	~~G~~ J	___	___	___	~~J~~ J G G ~~F~~
flight:	___	___	___	___	___	P Q R S T
	1	2	3	4	5	(T circled)
	~~Q~~	~~S~~		~~R~~	~~Q~~	
	~~S~~	~~P~~			~~R~~	
	~~P~~					

4.

If 30, then 30 60   60 N

P – 50

length:	___	___	60	30	60	60	30 60
show:	___	___	___	___	___	___	M N O P R S
	1	2	3	4	5	6	(M and R circled)
	~~P~~	~~P~~		~~N~~	~~P~~	~~S~~	
	~~S~~					~~P~~	

Try It Again

Now that you've learned how to identify and diagram 3D Ordering games, let's return to the initial game you played. Again, limit yourself to **8:30**. We'll work through the solutions together on the pages to come.

A publishing company published exactly six novels—*Forgiven, Grain, Highwire, June, Lampoon,* and *Melted*—in the years from 1991 to 1996. Exactly one novel was published in each of the six years. Three authors—Robinson, Stewart, and Tamiko—each wrote exactly two of the novels. The following conditions apply:

> Exactly one of Robinson's novels was published before the first of Stewart's novels was published.
> Neither of Robinson's novels was published in 1991 or 1994.
> None of the authors had novels published in consecutive years.
> *June* was published in 1994.
> *Highwire* was published exactly two years after *Melted*.

1. Which of the following could be an accurate representation of the authors and the novels they wrote, listed in order of publication?

   (A) Tamiko: *Lampoon*; Robinson: *Grain*; Tamiko: *Forgiven*; Stewart: *Melted*; Robinson: *June*; Stewart: *Highwire*
   (B) Tamiko: *Lampoon*; Robinson: *Forgiven*; Stewart: *Melted*; Tamiko: *June*; Robinson: *Highwire*; Stewart: *Grain*
   (C) Stewart: *Melted*; Robinson: *Lampoon*; Stewart: *Highwire*; Tamiko: *June*; Robinson: *Forgiven*; Tamiko: *Grain*
   (D) Tamiko: *Melted*; Robinson: *Grain*; Stewart: *Highwire*; Stewart: *June*; Tamiko: *Forgiven*; Robinson: *Lampoon*
   (E) Robinson: *Forgiven*; Tamiko: *Grain*; Stewart: *Melted*; Robinson: *June*; Tamiko: *Highwire*; Stewart: *Lampoon*

2. Which one of the following must be true?

   (A) One of Stewart's novels was published in 1993.
   (B) One of Tamiko's novels was published in 1994.
   (C) One of Robinson's novels was published in 1992.
   (D) One of Robinson's novels was published in 1995.
   (E) One of Stewart's novels was published in 1996.

3. If *Forgiven* was published in 1995, each of the following could be true EXCEPT:

   (A) Stewart wrote *Grain*.
   (B) Tamiko wrote *June*.
   (C) Tamiko wrote *Highwire*.
   (D) Robinson wrote *Lampoon*.
   (E) Robinson wrote *Highwire*.

4. If Tamiko wrote *June*, then which one of the following must be false?

   (A) Tamiko wrote *Melted*.
   (B) Tamiko wrote *Highwire*.
   (C) Stewart wrote *Melted*.
   (D) Stewart wrote *Highwire*.
   (E) Stewart wrote *Forgiven*.

5. If *Lampoon* was published in the year immediately preceding the publication of *Melted*, which one of the following must be true?

   (A) Tamiko wrote *Forgiven*.
   (B) Tamiko wrote *Grain*.
   (C) Robinson wrote *Lampoon*.
   (D) Robinson wrote *Highwire*.
   (E) Stewart wrote *Melted*.

6. Each of the following could be true EXCEPT:

   (A) Tamiko wrote a novel that was published in 1995.
   (B) *Melted* was published exactly three years before *Grain*.
   (C) Stewart wrote *June*.
   (D) *Lampoon* was published before *Highwire* but after *Melted*.
   (E) Both of Tamiko's novels were published before either of Stewart's novels were published.

Try one more question on the next page…

7. Which of the following, if substituted for the condition that exactly one of Robinson's novels was published before the first of Stewart's novels was published, would have the same effect in determining the years in which the novels were published and the authors who wrote the novels?

(A) Neither of Robinson's novels was published in 1996.

(B) Neither of Stewart's novels was published in 1992.

(C) The earliest that either one of Stewart's novels could have been published is 1993.

(D) The earliest that either one of Robinson's novels could have been published is 1992.

(E) The earliest that either one of Robinson's novels could have been published is 1993.

4

How Did You Do?

Picture the Game

We can be pretty sure we're facing an Ordering game from these clues in the scenario: "1991 to 1996" and "exactly one novel was published in each of the six years." We know this is a 3D Ordering game because we're dealing with three distinct variables: novels, authors, and years of publication.

We'll start with our 3D Ordering Number Line, and notate the two rosters:

author: __ __ __ __ __ __   R R S S T T

novel: __ __ __ __ __ __   F G H J L M
        1 2 3 4 5 6

Notate the Rules and Make Inferences

If you're pretty confident that you nailed this diagram, and would like to skip over the discussion of the setup, take a peek a few pages ahead and see if your diagram matches ours. If not, or if you'd like to get a guided tour regardless, let's go through the setup together.

> *Exactly one of Robinson's novels was published before the first of Stewart's novels was published.*

Since this rule references relative positions, we can express this relationship using Tree symbols. One R, and one R only, must come before the first S. The second R and the second S, therefore, must come after the first S (though we don't know in which order). Also note that this rule allows us to infer that R cannot be in 1991. If exactly one R must precede the first S, then an S cannot possibly occupy the first slot (otherwise, the R would fall off the left end of the diagram). We'll note this by using a cross out:

R — S <   R   author: S̶ __ __ __ __ __   R R S S T T
           S

                  novel: __ __ __ __ __ __   F G H J L M
                     1 2 3 4 5 6

> *Neither of Robinson's novels was published in 1991 or 1994.*

Once we've notated that R can't be in author slots 1 or 4, we should notice that neither R nor S can occupy slot 1. Thus, T must go in slot 1. Finally, if R cannot go in slot 1, then S cannot go in slot 2 (since exactly one R must come before any S):

```
                          R̶
              R           S̶   S̶       R̶
R —— S <               author:  T  __  __  __  __  __      R R S S T̶ T
              S           novel:                            F G H J L M
                                 __  __  __  __  __  __
                                 1   2   3   4   5   6
```

None of the authors had novels published in consecutive years.

This rule tells us that we cannot place like letters adjacent to each other in the author row. Also, this means that T cannot go in slot 2 (since T occupies slot 1). Thus, R must go in 2! Lastly, if R is in slot 2, R cannot go in slot 3 (we can't have two R's next to each other):

```
 ╔══╗                      R̶  T̶
 ║X̶X̶║                      S̶  S̶  R̶  R̶
 ╚══╝          R           author:  T   R  __  __  __  __   R̶ R S S T̶ T
R —— S <               
              S           novel:                            F G H J L M
                                    __  __  __  __  __  __
                                    1   2   3   4   5   6
```

June was published in 1994.

This is an easy one! That said, be sure to keep your elements straight. *June* is a novel; we must be sure to place the J in the correct row.

Highwire was published exactly two years after Melted.

A chunk! You should immediately recognize this as a crucial relationship. We can notate it to the side of the diagram, but we can (and should) also recognize some inferences that this chunk creates. If *Highwire* was published two years after *Melted, Highwire* cannot occupy the first or second slots, and *Melted* cannot occupy the fifth or sixth slots. Furthermore, the J in slot 4 means that H cannot occupy slot 6 (because that would put M in slot 4) and M cannot occupy slot 2 (because that would put H in slot 4):

```
 ╔══╗                      R̶  T̶
 ║X̶X̶║                      S̶  S̶  R̶  R̶
 ╚══╝          R           author:  T   R  __  __  __  __   R̶ R S S T̶ T
R —— S <               
              S           novel:             __  __  J  __  __  __   F G H J̶ L M
                                             1   2   3   4   5   6
       M _ H                         H̶  H̶          M̶  H̶
                                         M̶              M̶
```

The Big Pause

We should swing through our rules again, make sure we've understood them correctly, and see if there are any inferences we should add to our diagram. Since nothing jumps out at this point, our diagram is as complete as we can reasonably make it. Time for the Big Pause! What do you notice about this game?

One issue that should jump out is that the mini-tree of R's and S's is pretty limited in terms of where those authors could go. Also, for the novels row, the M _ H chunk is similarly limited. Indeed, there are only two places M could go.

Is this game worth framing? It's doable—you'd want to create a list of possible orders of authors and novels—but rather complex and unwieldy. The important takeaway from the Big Pause is to identify the two important limitations on the game.

Attack the Questions

1. Which of the following could be an accurate representation of the authors and the novels they wrote, listed in order of publication?

   (A) Tamiko: *Lampoon*; Robinson: *Grain*;
       Tamiko: *Forgiven*; Stewart: *Melted*
       Robinson: *June*; Stewart: *Highwire*

   (B) Tamiko: *Lampoon*; Robinson: *Forgiven*;
       Stewart: *Melted*; Tamiko: *June*;
       Robinson: *Highwire*; Stewart: *Grain*

   (C) Stewart: *Melted*; Robinson: *Lampoon*;
       Stewart: *Highwire*; Tamiko: *June*;
       Robinson: *Forgiven*; Tamiko: *Grain*

   (D) Tamiko: *Melted*; Robinson: *Grain*;
       Stewart: *Highwire*; Stewart: *June*;
       Tamiko: *Forgiven*; Robinson: *Lampoon*

   (E) Robinson: *Forgiven*; Tamiko: *Grain*;
       Stewart: *Melted*; Robinson: *June*;
       Tamiko: *Highwire*; Stewart: *Lampoon*

(B) is correct.

If a game has subsets, often the first question is not a standard Orientation question, in that we can't simply work from the rules. Rather, we have to work from the diagram and the inferences we made there. (Imagine that the answers to this question listed only the novels and not the authors.) We'll see plenty of these situations soon enough. Here, however, we're facing a standard Orientation question, so we know the drill!

The first rule allows us to eliminate (C).
The second rule allows us to eliminate (E).
The third rule allows us to eliminate (D).
The fourth rule allows us to eliminate (A).

Pull the trigger on (B), and let's move!

2. Which one of the following must be true?

   (A) One of Stewart's novels was published in 1993.
   (B) One of Tamiko's novels was published in 1994.
   (C) One of Robinson's novels was published in 1992.
   (D) One of Robinson's novels was published in 1995.
   (E) One of Stewart's novels was published in 1996.

(C) is correct.

Our hard work diagramming pays off—we can immediately see that (C) is the answer. There must be an R in author slot 2.

Consider how tough this question would have been if we had not made our inferences earlier. If we had skipped that step, this question would have been a wake-up call to go and do some more work on the diagram.

Again, during the exam, there would be no need to check the other answer choices. For the sake of practice, however, it would be a good idea to take a moment now to convince yourself that the four remaining choices need not be true.

3. If *Forgiven* was published in 1995, each of the following could be true EXCEPT:

   (A) Stewart wrote *Grain*.
   (B) Tamiko wrote *June*.
   (C) Tamiko wrote *Highwire*.
   (D) Robinson wrote *Lampoon*.
   (E) Robinson wrote *Highwire*.

(E) is correct.

Note that this is an EXCEPT question. We can translate "Each of the following could be true EX-CEPT" to "Which one must be false?" Also note that this is a Conditional question. We'll draw an abbreviated, temporary diagram that puts F in novel slot 5.

As we learned in previous chapters, chunks are the key to ordering. Once we put F in novel slot 5, we can see that the chunk M _ H must be placed in slots 1, 2, 3.

Now, as we look at the answer choices, we should NOT try to verify the answers that could be true. Rather, we should look for the answer that is obviously false. If an answer is not obviously false, defer judgment. It might be tempting, for example, to start with (A) and try to prove its validity, but we don't want to spend time on trial and error unless we need to. It's likely that the correct answer, once we get to it, will be obviously false. Nothing jumps out in answers (A) through (D). However, answer (E) clearly cannot be true. H is in slot 3, and R can never be there since we cannot have two consecutive R's.

4. If Tamiko wrote *June*, then which one of the following must be false?

    (A) Tamiko wrote *Melted*.
    (B) Tamiko wrote *Highwire*.
    (C) Stewart wrote *Melted*.
    (D) Stewart wrote *Highwire*.
    (E) Stewart wrote *Forgiven*.

(B) is correct.

This is also a conditional question, so we'll start by drawing an abbreviated, temporary diagram that puts a T with J:

$$\underline{\text{T}} \quad \underline{\text{R}} \quad \underline{} \quad \underline{\text{T}} \quad \underline{} \quad \underline{}$$
$$\underline{} \quad \underline{} \quad \underline{} \quad \underline{\text{J}} \quad \underline{} \quad \underline{}$$

There must be some inferences that we can draw based on this new information. With R in slot 2 and T in slot 4, neither R nor T can go in slot 3. (Remember, authors cannot publish books in consecutive years.) Thus, S must go in author slot 3.

Again, we'll work our way through the choices, deferring judgment on any answer that is not obviously false. Answer (A) would put an M in slot 1, under the T. There's no obvious rule against this, so we'll defer judgment on (A).

Answer (B) would put an H in slot 1, underneath the T. There IS a problem with this. Our original diagram tells us that H cannot go in slot 1. Thus, (B) must be false.

Notice that our inference (S must go in slot 3) didn't really help us here. That's okay. It's important to note these inferences whenever you see them. Most of the time they will come into play. In fact, this question is unusual in that the answer does not depend on the new condition.

5. If *Lampoon* was published in the year immediately preceding the publication of *Melted*, which one of the following must be true?

    (A) Tamiko wrote *Forgiven.*
    (B) Tamiko wrote *Grain.*
    (C) Robinson wrote *Lampoon.*
    (D) Robinson wrote *Highwire.*
    (E) Stewart wrote *Melted.*

(C) is correct.

Another Conditional question. This additional information adds to our M _ H chunk. If *Lampoon* is published immediately before *Melted,* we have: L M _ H. There is only one place this chunk can go. We'll draw an abbreviated, temporary diagram:

T   R   __ __ __ __
__ L   M   J   H   __

There doesn't seem to be anything else to easily infer, so let's move to the answer choices.

Again, we'll defer judgment on the answer choices until we find an answer that is obviously true.

Answer (A) isn't very obvious. It would probably take some trial and error to prove or disprove it. So we'll defer judgment for now.

Same story with answer (B). We could probably prove it or disprove it one way or the other, but this would require some time and energy. Let's bet that there will be a more obvious answer down the line. Defer judgment on (B).

Aha! We see that answer (C) is the obvious answer (assuming we were able to draw our temporary diagram correctly). R and L appear in slot 2.

6. Each of the following could be true EXCEPT:

    (A) Tamiko wrote a novel that was published in 1995.
    (B) *Melted* was published exactly three years before Grain.
    (C) Stewart wrote *June.*
    (D) *Lampoon* was published before *Highwire* but after *Melted.*
    (E) Both of Tamiko's novels were published before either of Stewart's novels were published.

(A) is correct.

This EXCEPT question can be rephrased to "Which one must be false?" We should try deferring judgment on answers that are not obviously false, but a quick scan of the answer choices gets us nowhere. None of the answers are obviously false given our diagram. This is not so uncommon on one of the last questions of a game. We must be prepared to spend some time on this question. Using previous work might be useful, but in this case, all that is clear is that the answer to question #1 eliminates (B); trial and error may be the best way to go.

Let's look at (A). We'll have to use a trial and error approach to see if Tamiko could have a novel in 1995. Let's try diagramming it. If T is in author slot 5, then S must go in author slot 3 (the two T's are used up and we can't put an R in slot 3 next to the R in slot 2). Thus, the second S must go in slot 6 (we can't put an S in slot 4 next to the S in slot 3). Therefore, the second R must go in slot 4.

Wait! Our original diagram tells us that R can't go in author slot 4. Thus, (A) must be false. While on the exam we wouldn't do this, take the time now to verify the possibility of the remaining four answer choices.

4

7. Which of the following, if substituted for the condition that exactly one of Robinson's novels was published before the first of Stewart's novels was published, would have the same effect in determining the years in which the novels were published and the authors who wrote the novels?

    (A) Neither of Robinson's novels was published in 1996.
    (B) Neither of Stewart's novels was published in 1992.
    (C) The earliest that either one of Stewart's novels could have been published is 1993.
    (D) The earliest that either one of Robinson's novels could have been published is 1992.
    (E) The earliest that either one of Robinson's novels could have been published is 1993.

(C) is correct.

This is an Equivalent Rule question. We will look more closely at this question type in the next section of this chapter, but let's take a quick look at this one.

Our task for this type of question is to choose an answer choice that has the same effect on the diagram as the rule being replaced. In other words, after the substitution, our diagram should provide the same exact information as the original—no more, no less.

The rule being substituted in this case (exactly one of Robinson's novels was published before the first of Stewart's novels was published) gave us a bunch of information in the top row of our diagram. Most importantly, we inferred from the rule that S can't go first. Later, based on the fact that R couldn't go in slot 1, we were able to infer that S couldn't go in slot 2. As seems to happen a lot on the LSAT, there was more to infer! With both S and R restricted from slot 1, T had to go there, forcing R into slot 2. Without that first rule, we are left with this:

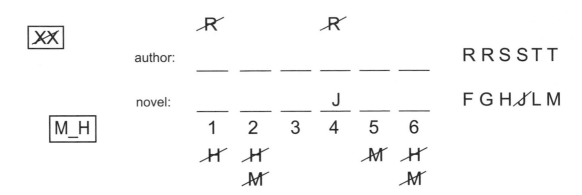

4

So which of the answer choices will give us back our T in 1 and R in 2 without adding any new information?

Answer (A) would prohibit an R from being placed in slot 6. This is information that does NOT exist in the original diagram. Eliminate (A).

Answer (B) would prohibit an S from being placed in slot 2, but this leaves open the possibility of an S or a T in slot 1 and an R or a T in slot 2. Thus, (B) does not have the same effect as the original rule. Eliminate (B).

Answer (C) would prohibit an S from being placed in slot 1 or 2. If S can't go in 1, and we already know that R can't go in 1, slot 1 must be filled with a T. Since no author can have books published in consecutive years, slot 2 could not get a T. Well, now we know that 2 can't get a T or an S, so slot 2 must get an R. This means R can't go in 3. This is starting to look like the original!

In fact, (C) gives us exactly what the original rule got us. You may be wondering, "What about the mini-tree notation involving the R's and S's? Does this new rule provide the same ordering rules?" Note that the new rule forces an R before either one of the S's (just like the original rule did) and, since R can't go in slot 3 or 4, we know that at least one S must come before the second R (just what we knew from the original rule). This is an equivalent rule, so (C) is the correct answer.

Go ahead and try (D) and (E) just for practice. You will find that neither leads to the same diagram as the original.

Spotlight on Question Types: Rule Questions

The last question of the game we just discussed was an example of one of the two types of **Rule questions** you will face on the LSAT:

1.   Equivalent Rule questions

2.   Rule Substitution questions

The first one has become increasingly common while the second one has become increasingly rare. While we'll focus more on the first one, let's take a look at both.

Equivalent Rule Questions

As we just saw, Equivalent Rule questions ask us to identify a replacement for a given rule that would result in the same possibilities and restrictions as the original. The four wrong answers affect the game in some other way; either they don't do what the original rule does, or they do too much, or both.

If you understand the original rule, the wrong answers to these questions are usually pretty easy to spot. In fact, don't be surprised if the correct answer is simply a rewording of the rule. Some answers are tougher to decode, but these will hinge on inferences that one could draw from that original rule. Thus, your best weapons for an Equivalent Rule question will be understanding the original rule and eliminating wrong answers.

To get a bit deeper into this question type, go ahead and diagram this game (and the major inferences):

> Five people—Q, R, S, T, and U—finish a race in order.
>   S finishes third.
>   T finishes immediately before or immediately after S.
>   Q finishes at some point before R.

Pretty straightforward, right? Here's the diagram with the basic inferences you should have drawn:

Now, let's give you a temporary job writing LSAT questions. Go ahead and write two (or more) possible correct answers to this question:

Which of the following, if substituted for the rule that T finishes immediately before or immediately after S, would have the same consequence on determining the order in which the five people finish the race?

Done? If so, *how* do you come up with the right answer?

For many, the first idea would be to reword the same exact information in a different way. We'll consider this as our first option:

Option 1: Reword It

Here are three equivalent rules for the original rule—T finishes immediately before or immediately after S—that are all simply rewordings of the rule:

"No one finishes between T and S."

"Either S finishes immediately before T, or T finishes immediately before S."

"Neither Q, nor R, nor U can finish between S and T."

Be ready for such simple answers. They are not uncommon.

Option 2: Match the Direct Consequences

What do we know about the spots that T can occupy? Because S must be in the third spot, and T must be next to S, T must be in the second or fourth spot. Imagine we were told one of the following:

"T must finish in the second or fourth spot."

"T does not finish first or last."

A direct consequence of either would be that T would have to be immediately before or after S. Thus these are valid matches for the given rule. They give us different information from that presented in the original rule, but when applied to the game, they produce the same results.

This is generally as tricky as the LSAT gets. But let's look at the fanciest type of answer choice we might face.

Option 3: Match the Indirect Consequences

In this option, the test writer creates an answer that doesn't relate directly to the original rule, but, in some incredibly clever way, ends up yielding the same consequences.

Instead of directly confining T to slots 2 and 4, as we did in Options 1 and 2, we could add complexity to our answer by limiting those who could finish first and last. It turns out there are only a few orders for this game:

QTSRU	UTSQR	QUSTR
QTSUR	QRSTU	UQSTR

So, we could write an answer like these:

"Either Q or U is first, and either U or R is last."

"If U is not first or last, then only Q or R can be first or last."

These rules look very little like the original rule that we were given, and they center on very different information, yet they ultimately have exactly the same impact on the game. Either of these rules would force T into two or four, and would thus force T to be next to S. These rules would also not have any other unintended, or mismatching, consequences.

It's rare that the LSAT will create such involved answers.

So now we know how the test writers can approach this question. What does this mean for *our* approach? Here are the keys:

1. Understand the original rule. Since most correct answers to Equivalent Rule questions have a relatively straightforward construction (they're based on Options 1 or 2), simply understanding the rule goes a long way. Especially if the rule is multifaceted, understanding the rule and its consequences will likely be all you need to eliminate several wrong choices, if not all the wrong choices. Don't rush this step.

2. Know when and where to spend your time. A big key here is to limit yourself. Do spend some time considering what the original rule means, but don't waste time looking for *all* possible secondary inferences when considering the meaning of the original rule. Per our understanding of how these problems work, that work will be unnecessary at best, and a distraction at worst.

3. Work from wrong to right. Eliminate choices that seem to have very different ramifications from those of the original rule. This may seem obvious, but if you are focused on advanced inferences, these answers can be some of the most tempting. It's useful to know that if an answer sounds way off, chances are it is.

However, as always, be cautious. Be mindful of the fact that you could have missed some initial inferences. Don't be afraid to slow down and confirm that certain answers are wrong. Depending on the difficulty level of the question, deferring judgment may leave you with most or all of the answer choices un-eliminated and glaring at you!

Assuming you have some time to spare, confirm that the right answer has the same consequences as the original rule—no more and no less.

Rule Substitution Questions

As we mentioned earlier, Rule Substitution questions are becoming passé. We're seeing them infrequently these days, while we're seeing a lot more Equivalent Rule questions. While we believe in focusing on recent trends, it's worth spending a bit of time looking at Rule Substitution questions. It's not unlikely that we'll see them make a guest appearance on some future LSATs, and they're a great way to work on developing a flexible approach to questions.

Rule Substitution questions can take three forms:

1. A rule is suspended, but all other rules remain in effect.

2. A rule is replaced with a different rule, and all other rules remain in effect.

3. A rule is added to the game, and all other rules remain in effect.

To be honest, the first and third versions aren't technically "substitutions," but the approaches are similar, so we'll discuss them here. In fact, the third version is basically a fancy Conditional question! Instead of a question introducing a simple condition such as "T is third," we are told something like "If T is third, it is not given a deluxe treatment." The difference is that we cannot apply this new rule until we get to the answer choices since we don't actually know if T is third! With a typical Conditional question, we should follow the inference chain *before* looking at the answer choices.

What all three options have in common is that, regardless of the change or addition, all the other rules remain in effect.

What might seem daunting to some test-takers is that they spend a significant amount of time mastering a game and then suddenly are forced to adjust the game. Success on LSAT Logic Games requires knowing what you know and what you don't, and Rule Substitution questions force us to change both! Fortunately, when these questions show up, they're usually the last question of a game, so we're not expected to learn a game, change our understanding for a Rule Substitution question, and then change back to our original understanding for another question. Even for the LSAT, that would be too cruel! Also, since this sort of question is usually the last one of a set, if we want to adjust our main diagram, we don't have to worry about having to "undo" our adjustments for the next question.

However, even though we're free to do so, we don't always want to adjust our original diagram. Sometimes a Rule Substitution question is better approached by *redrawing the entire diagram*. Indeed, there are two approaches to considering the new rule in Rule Substitution questions, each with their pros and cons:

1. Adjust your diagram to incorporate the change. This *tends* to be faster, but may lead you to miss important inferences. More specifically, you might miss that you should *undo* some of the original inferences. When you create a diagram, you don't simply notate each rule; you also notate the inferences that come from the interactions of the rules. With one rule removed or changed, we can expect some rule interactions to change as well.

2. Draw a new diagram from scratch. This *tends* to be slower and more accurate, but can be overkill; if you can avoid redrawing, do so. But sometimes the situation calls for it: perhaps you have time in the bank, and perhaps the change is connected to a chain of inferences.

Note that when we compare the relative strengths of each approach, we are speaking about *tendencies*. Exceptions abound, in part because of the particulars of this or that question, in part because of your timing on a particular game section, and in part because of your style and strengths. Each approach is useful, and each one can be used successfully in any situation. However, since one is sometimes more efficient than the other, you should be armed with both.

It would be unwise to have a hard and fast rule for when to redraw and when to amend, since the choice depends on several factors. Here are the main considerations:

1.   The complexity of the diagram.
     This issue cuts both ways. If the diagram is very complex, it may be too time-consuming to redraw, but the complexity might also make it hard for you to figure out the consequences of the new rule without redrawing.

2.   The complexity of the substitution's impact.
     The more consequences the rule substitution has, the more likely it is that you'll want to redraw.

3.   Your ability to reverse engineer the diagram.
     How easily can you undo the inferences you made originally? This depends on the issues above, as well as on your comfort with the game you're facing.

4.   How much time you have in the "bank."
     This is pretty straightforward. For example, if you're on the last question of the last game of the entire section, and you have four minutes to spare, the decision to do a possibly time-intensive redrawing is an easier one to make. On the other hand, if you've got one minute left on the section, you can't afford to do an involved redrawing.

Once you've done your "homework" and either redrawn the diagram or amended the one you have, it's time to attack the answer choices. Your approach at this point depends in part on whether you're facing a could be true or a must be true/false question.

If you're asked to identify what *could be true* (or, less frequently, false), then it's likely that you'll have to spend more time considering each answer choice. Along with figuring out how the diagram has changed from the rule substitution, you're also faced with putting that diagram to work.

If you're looking for an answer that *must be true* (or false), it's possible that your new or amended diagram already notes the answer. Deferring judgment in search of an obvious answer is a smart approach here, though at times you will be forced to do a second pass and dig a bit deeper into each choice.

Since you did all that work of changing your diagram to incorporate the new rule regime, the answer will more than likely require you to apply the new rule. Thus, be wary of answers that clearly don't involve the elements or positions that you had to adjust because of the rule substitution.

4

> If you'd like to get some targeted practice with Rule Substitution questions,
> log in to your Student Center!

DRILL IT: Rule Questions

Here's a devilish game designed to work your Rule question muscles. We suggest that you play it once under timed conditions, and then go back and slowly check your work, making sure to test any answers you deferred judgment on.

A tour company offers six tours each day, and each tour is led by one of six guides—Jack, Kaley, Lyle, Moquetta, Naru, and Olley. Each guide is assigned to lead one tour. In addition, each guide is either experienced or inexperienced. When scheduling the day's tours, the following rules apply:

> No two consecutive tours can be led by inexperienced guides.
> There are exactly two tours between the tour that Lyle leads and the tour that Moquetta leads.
> The tour that Kaley leads is either immediately before or immediately after the tour that Olley leads.
> Jack leads the fourth tour.
> The third tour is led by an inexperienced guide.
> Both Kaley and Olley are experienced.

1. Which of the following, if substituted for the rule that no two consecutive tours can be led by inexperienced guides, would have the same effect?

   (A) No two consecutive tours can be led by experienced guides.

   (B) An inexperienced tour guide can led neither the second nor the fourth tour.

   (C) Each tour led by an inexperienced guide must follow and be followed by a tour led by an experienced guide.

   (D) Naru and exactly one other guide are inexperienced.

   (E) Jack is an experienced guide, as are two of the guides who precede him and at least one of the guides who follow him.

2. Which of the following would have the same consequence on the order of the tours if substituted for the rule that there are exactly two tours between the tour that Lyle leads and the tour that Moquetta leads?

   (A) Either Moquetta or Lyle leads the third tour.

   (B) Either Moquetta or Lyle leads the last tour.

   (C) Either Kaley or Olley leads the first tour and Naru leads the fifth tour.

   (D) Either Kaley or Olley leads the first tour and either Lyle or Moquetta leads the third tour.

   (E) The tour led by Naru precedes the tour led by Moquetta or the tour led by Lyle, but not both

3. If substituted for the rule that Kaley and Olley must lead consecutive tours, which one of the following would have the same effect in determining the order of the tours?

   (A) Moquetta is inexperienced.

   (B) Lyle is inexperienced.

   (C) Either Kaley or Olley must lead the first tour.

   (D) Naru leads the fifth tour.

   (E) Neither Kaley nor Olley leads the sixth tour.

Continued on the next page...

4. If the rule that the tour that Kaley leads is either immediately before or immediately after the tour that Olley leads is replaced with a rule that says there must be exactly two tours between the tours that Kaley and Olley lead, which of the following must be true?

   (A) Olley must lead the second tour.

   (B) Naru must lead the fifth tour.

   (C) Moquetta must lead the sixth tour.

   (D) Naru's tour can neither directly precede nor directly follow any tour led by Moquetta

   (E) Jack's tour can neither directly precede nor directly follow any tour led by Lyle.

5. If the rule that there are exactly two tours between the tour that Lyle leads and the tour that Moquetta leads is replaced with the rule that there is exactly one tour between the tours that Lyle and Moquetta lead, how many different tours could Naru lead as an experienced guide?

   (A) 1

   (B) 2

   (C) 3

   (D) 4

   (E) 5

SOLUTIONS: Rule Questions

We will do only a brief discussion of the diagram for this game so that we can focus on the questions, the real emphasis in this devilish practice game.

The diagram for this 3D Ordering game is as follows:

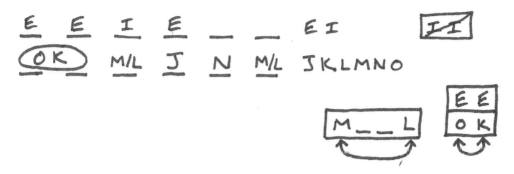

If your diagram was different—and we mean something other than cosmetically—take some time to work through the game again until you can understand all the inferences we drew, and then try your hand at the questions one more time. An incomplete diagram would make the questions almost impossible.

1. Which of the following, if substituted for the rule that no two consecutive tours can be led by inexperienced guides, would have the same effect?

   (A) No two consecutive tours can be led by experienced guides

   (B) An inexperienced tour guide can lead neither the second nor the fourth tour.

   (C) Each tour led by an inexperienced guide must follow and be followed by a tour led by an experienced guide.

   (D) Naru and exactly one other guide are inexperienced.

   (E) Jack is an experienced guide, as are two of the guides who precede him and at least one of the guides who follow him.

(E) is correct.

There are few inferences that we drew from the original rule prohibiting consecutive I's other than that slots 2 and 4 must have E's.

(A) This rule allows for consecutive I's!

(B) Both of those restrictions are in our diagram, but we need to prevent I I in 5 and 6, which this rule allows.

(C) This answer seems like a wordy way of saying the original rule! If you have an I, it must be sandwiched between two E's. If you fell for this answer, consider what inferences you would draw from this notation: I $\longrightarrow$ E – I – E. You would surely infer that I cannot go in the first or last slots. But in the original diagram, we can have I in slot 6.

(D) While it's true that the original rule requires that at most two guides are inexperienced, there's no reason that Naru must be inexperienced.

(E) If two of thes guides that precede J are experienced, these must be 1 and 2, as we already have an I in 3. After J, we can have E I, I E, or E E. This matches the restrictions in our original diagram.

2. Which of the following would have the same consequence on the order of the tours if substituted for the rule that there are exactly two tours between the tour that Lyle leads and the tour that Moquetta leads?

   (A) Either Moquetta or Lyle leads the third tour.
   (B) Either Moquetta or Lyle leads the last tour.
   (C) Either Kaley or Olley leads the first tour and Naru leads the fifth tour.
   (D) Either Kaley or Olley leads the first tour and either Lyle or Moquetta leads the third tour.
   (E) The tour led by Naru precedes the tour led by Moquetta or the tour led by Lyle, but not both.

(C) is correct.

The L M chunk, in connection with the other rules, required that M and L occupy slots 3 and 6.

(A) This provides only half of what we want!

(B) This provides only the other half of what we want.

(C) This rule forces K and O to occupy the first two slots—since they're a chunk—and with N occupying the fifth slot, the only places left for the remaining elements, M and L, are the third and sixth slots. Thus, this rule has the same effect as the original rule.

(D) This tempting answer allows either M or L to go in slot 5, followed by N.

(E) If we already know that K and O are in 1 and 2, this rule forces part of what we want—M and L on opposites sides of N. However, with only N between L and M, we could reach the following arrangement: L N M J K O.

3. If substituted for the rule that Kaley and Olley must lead consecutive tours, which one of the following would have the same effect in determining the order of the tours?

   (A) Moquetta is inexperienced.

   (B) Lyle is inexperienced.

   (C) Either Kaley or Olley must lead the first tour.

   (D) Naru leads the fifth tour.

   (E) Neither Kaley nor Olley leads the sixth tour.

(D) is correct.

This rule, in combination with the other rules, restricted the K O chunk to the first two slots.

(A) This rule means that M cannot go in slot 2, but L still could! This would allow O L N J M K. Also note that in our diagram, one of L or M must be inexperienced (because slot 3 has an I), but we don't know which one, so this rule adds an extra restriction.

(B) This answer is logically equivalent to the rule in answer (A), except that it switches L and M! We can eliminate for the same reasons.

(C) This rule doesn't restrict the elements enough. There's nothing keeping K and O together! For instance, we might arrange the elements like this: K L N J M O.

(D) If N is in slot 5, there's only one way to place the L M chunk—in slots 3 and 6—leaving K and O to the first two slots. That's what we want!

(E) This rule restricts K and O quite a bit. They can't go in 3, because they are both experienced, and now they can't go in 6. However, this rule would allow one of them to go in 5, as in the following: K N L J O M.

4. If the rule that the tour that Kaley leads is either immediately before or immediately after the tour that Olley leads is replaced with a rule that says there must be exactly two tours between the tours that Kaley and Olley lead, which of the following must be true?

(A) Olley must lead the second tour.

(B) Naru must lead the fifth tour.

(C) Moquetta must lead the sixth tour.

(D) Naru's tour can neither directly precede nor directly follow any tour led by Moquetta

(E) Jack's tour can neither directly precede nor directly follow any tour led by Lyle.

(D) is correct.

In this Rule Substitution question, we now have a K _ _ O or O _ _ K chunk. Since that chunk and the L _ _ M / M _ _ L chunk will have to overlap, it's wise to consider where they could go. With J in slot 4, there are only two slots—5 and 6—for the second element of each chunk. It seems that we have two options:

N L/M K/O J L/M K/O   N K/O L/M J K/O L/M

But be careful! One of those frames is not valid. Can you see which one and why?

It's important to remember that this is a 3D Ordering game! The guide in slot 3 must be inexperienced, and since both K and O must be experienced, neither can go in slot 3. Thus, only the second frame is valid. With that in hand, let's look at the answer choices:

(A) This answer is incorrect, because either K or O could be second.

(B) This answer would be correct if it said "first" instead of "fifth"!

(C) M might come last, but so might L.

(D) This answer translates to an anti-chunk: N and M cannot be consecutive. Since N is forced into slot 1, and M is in either slot 3 or slot 6, this is definitely true.

(E) L and J could be in slots 3 and 4, respectively.

5. If the rule that there are exactly two tours between the tour that Lyle leads and the tour that
    Moquetta leads is replaced with the rule that there is exactly one tour between the tours that Lyle and
    Moquetta lead, how many different tours could Naru lead as an experienced guide?

    (A) 1
    (B) 2
    (C) 3
    (D) 4
    (E) 5

(B) is correct.

Finally, a problem in which one of the first two answer choices is correct! (It's almost as if whomever
wrote this drill wanted you to have to wrestle with a lot of wrong answers....)

If the L _ _ M/M _ _ L chunk is replaced with L _ M/M _ L, what can we infer? There are now two
places that chunk could go: slots 1–3 or slots 3–5. These both work out fine (K and O stay clear of slot
3):

N can go in slot 2 or slot 6, and could be experienced in either case.

Conclusion

Even to the well-prepared test-taker, 3D Ordering games can be intimidating at first glance. And while some of these games are much more bark than bite, some provide a good serving of both. This is exactly the sort of game that separates the average test-taker from the more prepared one, and is thus *exactly the sort of game on which you can distinguish yourself.* Let's look at the three hurdles:

1. Identifying the game type.

- It's easy to confuse these games with others that we'll learn about later *if you ignore the ordering.* The ordering aspect of these games is their anchor.

2. Front-end or back-end?

- While we're seeing more back-end 3D Ordering games lately, you have to stay vigilant. The true danger is that you might not notice when a game is front-end. But thankfully, your experience on the first two questions will generally give you a not-so-gentle warning if you've done that.

3. Rule questions

- While not specific to 3D Ordering games, Rule questions can certainly be intimidating! They're often designed to take more time, so your best bet is to develop an efficient approach to the Standard questions. Since the majority of the questions you face will be Standard questions, gaining time on these will leave you the extra room you need to think through the occasional Rule question.

- That said, there are definitely some moves to speed up the process. For Equivalent Rule questions, spend a moment considering what the original rule means, and be ready for a surprisingly simple answer. For Rule Substitution, consciously decide whether the question warrants a new diagram, and look for answers that relate to the new rule's impact.

Practice Game 1: PT53, S2, G3

Let's put your new skills to work with TWO games. Try playing both of these back-to-back to work on your endurance. Give yourself a total of 20 minutes for both games (we added some tough extra questions).

Detectives investigating a citywide increase in burglaries questioned exactly seven suspects—S, T, V, W, X, Y, and Z—each on a different one of seven consecutive days. Each suspect was questioned exactly once. Any suspect who confessed did so while being questioned. The investigation conformed to the following:

> T was questioned on day three.
> The suspect questioned on day four did not confess.
> S was questioned after W was questioned.
> Both X and V were questioned after Z was questioned.
> No suspects confessed after W was questioned.
> Exactly two suspects confessed after T was questioned.

12. Which one of the following could be true?

    (A) X was questioned on day one.
    (B) V was questioned on day two.
    (C) Z was questioned on day four.
    (D) W was questioned on day five.
    (E) S was questioned on day six.

13. If Z was the second suspect to confess, then each of the following statements could be true EXCEPT:

    (A) T confessed.
    (B) T did not confess.
    (C) V did not confess.
    (D) X confessed.
    (E) Y did not confess.

14. If Y was questioned after V but before X, then which one of the following could be true?

    (A) V did not confess.
    (B) Y confessed.
    (C) X did not confess.
    (D) X was questioned on day four.
    (E) Z was questioned on day two.

15. Which one of the following suspects must have been questioned before T was questioned?

    (A) V
    (B) W
    (C) X
    (D) Y
    (E) Z

16. If X and Y both confessed, then each of the following could be true EXCEPT:

    (A) V confessed.
    (B) X was questioned on day five.
    (C) Y was questioned on day one.
    (D) Z was questioned on day one.
    (E) Z did not confess.

17. If neither X nor V confessed, then which one of the following must be true?

    (A) T confessed.
    (B) V was questioned on day two.
    (C) X was questioned on day four.
    (D) Y confessed.
    (E) Z did not confess.

Try a question that we wrote for this game:

18. Which of the following, if substituted for the rule that exactly two suspects confessed after T was questioned, would have the same effect both in determining the order in which suspects were questioned and in identifying which suspects confessed during questioning?

(A) The final suspect to confess was the sixth suspect questioned.

(B) W and the suspect questioned immediately before W were the last two suspects to confess.

(C) W was the last suspect to confess.

(D) The suspects questioned fifth and sixth both confessed.

(E) S was questioned last and immediately after W.

P

Practice Game Solutions: PT53, S2, G3

Picture the Game

Wow! What a tough game! We can get this, though, if we diagram effectively and use the diagram to make wise inferences. This is clearly an ordering game. The suspects will be interviewed in some order, 1 through 7. But there's an extra dimension here. Each suspect will either confess or not confess during the interview. So we have to put suspects in positions (day interviewed), and the positions have two subset options: confession or no confession. The 3D Number Line is the most appropriate diagram for this job. We'll use a "C" for confession and an "N" for no confession:

Confession: ___ ___ ___ ___ ___ ___ ___   CN

Suspect: ___ ___ ___ ___ ___ ___ ___   STVWXYZ
        1 2 3 4 5 6 7

Notate the Rules and Make Inferences

Here's where the tough work really begins. Making and tracking inferences during the setup is crucial. If we passively notate the rules without thinking about what the implications are, we won't have a chance to uncover the key inferences. Think as you diagram. Actively search for inferences. Let's walk through the rules slowly. The first two are fairly easy to deal with:

> T was questioned on day three.
> The suspect questioned on day four did not confess.

The next two rules are Relative Ordering rules. As always, we'll use connecting lines to indicate the relative ordering of the letters. We can make some standard inferences from them:

> S was questioned after W was questioned.
> Both X and V were questioned after Z was questioned.

Confession: ___ ___ ___ N ___ ___ ___   CN

Suspect: ___ ___ T ___ ___ ___ ___   STVWXYZ
        1 2 3 4 5 6 7
        S̶
        X̶   Z̶ W̶
        V̶   Z̶

W — S

Z < X , V

And now for the last two rules. Here's where we really need to do some thinking:

> No suspects confessed after W was questioned.
> Exactly two suspects confessed after T was questioned.

We already know that S comes after W, so S must NOT confess if no one after W confesses. Note that this says nothing about whether W himself confesses. We know that no one *after* W confesses, but we're unsure of W himself.

If exactly two suspects confess after T, well then W must come after T, right? Remember, no one can confess after W. So if T is in the third slot, we must have exactly two confessions after the third slot. Slot 4 is already a no confession slot (from a previous rule), so we must have exactly two confessions in 5, 6, or 7. But remember that we must leave room for S, a no confession suspect, after W. Thus, we must get confessions in 5 and 6, with W in 6 and S in 7:

Confession: _ _ _ N C C N   CN   W —S

Suspect: _ _ T _ _ W S   STVWXYZ   Z ⟨ X
          1 2 3 4 5 6 7   V
          8   Z W̶
          X̶   Z
          V̶

Now that we've got W and S in 6 and 7, we can see that Z can't go in 4 or 5. Remember, X and V must come after Z. We could put cross outs under 4 and 5 to represent this, or, as we've done here, we can put Z in a cloud over slots 1 and 2:

Confession: _ _ _ N C C N   CN   W —S

Suspect: (Z) T _ _ W S   STVWXYZ   Z ⟨ X
          1 2 3 4 5 6 7   V
          8   W̶
          X̶
          V̶

Phew! Take a minute to be sure you follow the logic above. Go through it again if you need to. If you can get to this point, you're 75% of the way to mastering this game.

The Big Pause

Looking back over the game, it's clear that about half of the elements and subsets are left undetermined. However, there are a lot of limitations on the remaining suspects. Because Z must come before both X and V, the order of the suspects is fairly limited. In fact, we're looking at two possible frames, which aren't necessary to write out, but are important to understand:

Z in slot 1	**Z in slot 2**
Z _ T _ _ W S	Y Z T _ _ W S

Notice that when Z is in slot 2, Y must be in slot 1, because it's the only remaining element that can precede Z. A quick scan tells us that every element is part of some rule. At this point, we're ready for the questions.

P

Attack the Questions

12. Which one of the following could be true?

    (A) X was questioned on day one.
    (B) V was questioned on day two.
    (C) Z was questioned on day four.
    (D) W was questioned on day five.
    (E) S was questioned on day six.

(B) is correct.

(A) No! We've got an X cross-out under slot 1. Z has to come before X, so X can't be first.

(B) Nothing seems to prohibit this, but let's defer judgment for now instead of trying to prove that it would work. Plus, since this is the first question, it's reassuring to confirm that our diagram allows us to eliminate all the other answer choices.

(C) No! Z can't be in slot 4.

(D) No! W must be in slot 6.

(E) No! S must be in slot 7.

This question is a breeze if we've done the hard, careful work of setting up the diagram and making inferences. Did you notice that this first question of the set is not an Orientation question? Even so, it was nearly as simple.

13. If Z was the second suspect to confess, then each of the following statements could be true EXCEPT:

    (A) T confessed.
    (B) T did not confess.
    (C) V did not confess.
    (D) X confessed.
    (E) Y did not confess.

(E) is correct.

We'll draw a temporary diagram next to the question (and, since slots 6 and 7 are determined, it would be acceptable to leave them out of it). We know that there are only two possibilities for Z: slot 1 or slot 2. If Z is the second to confess, then Z must be in the second slot, so we're dealing with frame #2: Y Z T _ _ W S. If Z is the second to confess, then both Y and Z must confess. The letters X and V will go into the remaining two spots, but we're not quite sure in what order.

$$\frac{C}{Y}\ \frac{C}{Z}\ \frac{\_}{T}\ \frac{N}{X}\ \frac{C}{V}\ \frac{C}{W}\ \frac{N}{S}$$
$$1\quad 2\quad 3\quad 4\quad 5\quad 6\quad 7$$

This "could be true EXCEPT" question can be translated to "Which one must be false?" We can expect the four wrong answers to be statements that could or could not be false, so we should immediately defer judgement on any answer involving X, V, or T, since each of those is undetermined in some manner.

(A) The correct answer is probably not about T. Indeed, we have no information about T's confession slot. Since it could go either way, this could certainly be true.

(B) Again, we have no information about T's confession slot.

(C) The correct answer is probably not about V. We know that V will go in slot 4 or 5. Slot 4 is a no confession slot, and slot 5 is a confession slot. So this could be true or false.

(D) The same is true for X. It could go in slot 4 or 5, so this could be true or false.

(E) In this scenario, Y must confess. Answer (E) must be false. Since the new condition forced Y and Z into certain slots and forced them both to confess, we could have expected that the correct answer would reference (incorrectly) one of those two elements.

14. If Y was questioned after V but before X, then which one of the following could be true?

   (A) V did not confess.

   (B) Y confessed.

   (C) X did not confess.

   (D) X was questioned on day four.

   (E) Z was questioned on day two.

(A) is correct.

If Y was questioned after V but before X, we must be dealing with frame #1: Z _ T _ _ W S. We'll sketch out the situation next to the question. If Y is after V but before X, Y must go in slot 4, V must go in slot 2, and X must go in slot 5. Since this is a "could be true" question, we can expect the answer to refer to Z, V, or T, the only three suspects for whom there is still something undetermined.

(A) This choice involves V, and nothing seems to prohibit V from confessing. Since it's the first answer, we'd probably spend an extra moment to confirm that it could be true instead of eliminating all the other answers. But we could also defer judgment for now.

(B) No! Y is in slot 4, which is a no confession slot

(C) No! X is in slot 5, which is a confession slot.

(D) No! X must be questioned on day five in this scenario.

(E) No! Even though this refers to Z, and we don't know if Z confessed, we do know that Z must be questioned on day 1.

15. Which one of the following suspects must have been questioned before T was questioned?

   (A) V

   (B) W

   (C) X

   (D) Y

   (E) Z

(E) is correct.

This is a free point if we've got the correct diagram, and even easier with the frames! Notice that Z is before T in either frame.

16. If X and Y both confessed, then each of the following could be true EXCEPT:

    (A) V confessed.

    (B) X was questioned on day five.

    (C) Y was questioned on day one.

    (D) Z was questioned on day one.

    (E) Z did not confess.

(A) is correct.

This "could be true EXCEPT" question can be translated to "Which of the following must be false?"

If X and Y both confessed, then neither X nor Y can go in slot 4 (since slot 4 is a no confession slot). We already know that Z can't go in 4, so this leaves V in slot 4. So V does not confess. (A) must be false.

17. If neither X nor V confessed, then which one of the following must be true?

    (A) T confessed.

    (B) V was questioned on day two.

    (C) X was questioned on day four.

    (D) Y confessed.

    (E) Z did not confess.

(D) is correct.

If neither X nor V confessed, then we can't have either in slot 5, since it is a confession slot. Thus, we are in frame 1, with Y in slot 5, Z in slot 1, and X and V in slots 2 and 4, not necessarily in that order:

$$\underline{\quad}\ \underline{N}\ \underline{\quad}\ \underline{N}\ \underline{C}\ \underline{C}\ \underline{N}$$

$$\underset{1}{\underline{Z}}\ \underset{2}{\underline{V/X}}\ \underset{3}{\underline{T}}\ \underset{4}{\underline{X/V}}\ \underset{5}{\underline{Y}}\ \underset{6}{\underline{W}}\ \underset{7}{\underline{S}}$$

We're looking for something that must be true, so we should be quick to defer on any answer that refers to the confession slots for Z, V, T, or X. We might want to go hunting for an answer that refers to Y, since its position and confession status are set.

(A) We don't have any information on T's confession slot, so this certainly could be true, but it doesn't have to be.

(B) Again, could be true, but doesn't have to be true. X could also go in slot 2.

(C) Could be true but doesn't have to be true. V could also go in slot 4.

(D) Yes! Y is in slot 5, which is a confession slot.

(E) We know nothing about Z's confession slot in this case. Could be true but doesn't have to be true.

18. Which of the following, if substituted for the rule that exactly two suspects confessed after T was questioned, would have the same effect both in determining the order in which suspects were questioned and in identifying which suspects confessed during questioning?

   (A) The final suspect to confess was the sixth suspect questioned.
   (B) W and the suspect questioned immediately before W were the last two suspects to confess.
   (C) W was the last suspect to confess.
   (D) The suspects questioned fifth and sixth both confessed.
   (E) S was questioned last and immediately after W.

(D) is correct.

We added this Equivalent Rule question to keep you on your toes (the LSAT didn't yet dish out this question type when this game came out).

The first step is to understand the original rule. What is the effect of exactly two suspects confessing after T is questioned? Since T is questioned third, this gives us two N's and two C's in slots 4–7. Another rule tells us that the suspect in slot 4 does not confess, so we're left with two Cs and an N to place in slots 5–7. From the fact that all suspects questioned after W must not confess, we can then infer that the order of these must be C C N.

The chain of inferences from the original rule looks like this:

2 C's after T ➞ 5–7 have 2 C's and 1 N ➞ C, C, N in 5, 6, and 7, respectively ➞ W and S in 6 and 7, respectively.

The three links correspond roughly to the three options that we discussed in creating Equivalent Rule answers. And the correct answer could provide us an equivalent for any part of that chain.

Let's dive into the answer choices, looking to eliminate but ready to defer judgement:

(A) This answer puts a C in slot 6, but what about slot 5? Eliminate.

(B) It would be very reasonable to defer judgment on this very tempting answer. It seems that if W confesses along with the suspect questioned before him, we can infer that W must go in slot 6. However, there's no reason that W couldn't go in slot 2, putting an N in each of slots 3–7. That's not allowed in the original diagram. Eliminate.

(C) As with (B), according to this rule we could have W in slot 2 (or, in this case, even slot 1), and have every subsequent suspect not confess. And, as with (A), we definitely have not determined from this rule that a C must go in the fifth slot. Adios.

(D) This might have been a tough answer to spot, but armed with a solid grip on the meaning of the original rule, we can see that this rule is an equivalent to the given rule. If the sixth suspect confesses, we know that W and S are in 6 or 7, because after W, no one else can confess. So now we have C C N in 5–7, with W and S in 6 and 7. This rule gives us the exact same consequences as the original rule.

(E) This answer doesn't establish that slot 5 has an N, or that W confessed.

P

MANHATTAN
LSAT

Practice Game 2: PT30, S1, G3

Exactly five cars—Frank's, Marquitta's, Orlando's Taishah's, and Vinquetta's—are washed, each exactly once. The cars are washed one at a time, with each receiving exactly one kind of wash: regular, super, or premium. The following conditions must apply:

The first car washed does not receive a super wash, though at least one car does.
Exactly one car receives a premium wash.
The second and third cars washed receive the same kind of wash as each other.
Neither Orlando's nor Taishah's is washed before Vinquetta's.
Marquitta's is washed before Frank's, but after Orlando's.
Marquitta's and the car washed immediately before Marquitta's receive regular washes.

11. Which one of the following could be an accurate list of the cars in the order in which they are washed, matched with type of wash received?

   (A) Orlando's: premium; Vinquetta's: regular; Taishah's: regular; Marquitta's: regular; Frank's: super

   (B) Vinquetta's: premium; Orlando's: regular; Taishah's: regular; Marquitta's: regular; Frank's: super

   (C) Vinquetta's: regular; Marquitta's: regular; Taishah's: regular; Orlando's: super; Frank's: premium

   (D) Vinquetta's: super; Orlando's: regular; Marquitta's: regular; Frank's: regular; Taishah's: super

   (E) Vinquetta's: premium; Orlando's: regular; Marquitta's: regular; Frank's: regular; Taishah's: regular

12. If Vinquetta's car does not receive a premium wash, which one of the following must be true?

   (A) Orlando's and Vinquetta's cars receive the same kind of wash as each other.

   (B) Marquitta's and Taishah's cars receive the same kind of wash as each other.

   (C) The fourth car washed receives a premium wash.

   (D) Orlando's car is washed third.

   (E) Marquitta's car is washed fourth.

13. If the last two cars washed receive the same kind of wash as each other, then which one of the following could be true?

   (A) Orlando's car is washed third.

   (B) Taishah's car is washed fifth.

   (C) Taishah's car is washed before Marquitta's car.

   (D) Vinquetta's car receives a regular wash.

   (E) Exactly one car receives a super wash.

14. Which one of the following must be true?

   (A) Vinquetta's car receives a premium wash

   (B) Exactly two cars receive a super wash.

   (C) The fifth car washed receives a super wash.

   (D) The fourth car washed receives a super wash.

   (E) The second car washed receives a regular wash.

15. Which one of the following is a complete and accurate list of the cars that must receive a regular wash?

   (A) Frank's, Marquitta's

   (B) Marquitta's, Orlando's

   (C) Marquitta's, Orlando's, Taishah's

   (D) Marquitta's, Taishah's

   (E) Marquitta's, Vinquetta's

16. Suppose that in addition to the original five cars Jabrohn's car is also washed. If all the other conditions hold as given, which one of the following CANNOT be true?

   (A) Orlando's car receives a premium wash.

   (B) Vinquetta's car receives a super wash.

   (C) Four cars receive a regular wash.

   (D) Only the second and third cars washed receive a regular wash.

   (E) Jabrohn's car is washed after Frank's car.

Try a question that we wrote for this game (assume that the rule change in #16 is not applicable):

17. Which of the following, if substituted for the rule that the first car washed does not receive a super wash, though at least one car does, would have the same effect in determining the order of car washes and the type of each?

(A) Vinquetta's car can receive only a regular or premium wash.

(B) No more than three cars receive a regular wash.

(C) Frank's car receives a super wash if, and only if, Taishah's car receives a regular or premium wash.

(D) All cars except Frank's and Taishah's must receive either a regular or premium wash.

(E) Either Frank's or Taishah's car receives a super wash, and no other car can receive that type of wash.

P

Practice Game Solutions: PT30, S1, G3

Picture the Game

Another tough game, with lots of rules and lots of inferences to make! The cars will be washed in some order, 1 through 5, and each car will receive one of three types of wash. So the cars are put in positions, and the positions have three subset possibilities. Clearly, the 3D Number Line is what we need for this job:

$$
\begin{array}{ccccc} \_ & \_ & \_ & \_ & \_ \end{array} \quad RSP
$$

$$
\begin{array}{ccccc} \_ & \_ & \_ & \_ & \_ \\ 1 & 2 & 3 & 4 & 5 \end{array} \quad FMOTV
$$

Notate the Rules and Make Inferences

With a lot of rules, and some rules having two parts, it's important to take our time. Take a look at how we notated each rule, and the basic inferences we drew (there's a bit more to infer—we'll get to that in a moment). If you have something radically different, take some time to figure out where your process went wrong. If you have a cosmetic difference—for example, perhaps you didn't note "R/P" in slot 1, or perhaps you didn't note the numerical limitations the same way—don't worry, those are basically issues of style. (Though feel free to "steal" our style!)

Exactly five cars—Frank's, Marquitta's, Orlando's, Taishah's, and Vinquetta's—are washed, each exactly once. The cars are washed one at a time, with each receiving exactly one kind of wash: regular, super, or premium. The following conditions must apply:

The first car washed does not receive a super wash, though at least one car does.
Exactly one car receives a premium wash.
The second and third cars washed receive the same kind of wash as each other.
Neither Orlando's nor Taishah's is washed before Vinquetta's.
Marquitta's is washed before Frank's, but after Orlando's.
Marquitta's and the car washed immediately before Marquitta's receive regular washes.

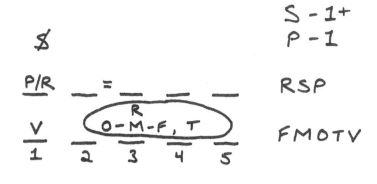

P

Did you catch the odd-looking way we combined the relative ordering rule and the rule about the type of wash R's car receives? If that doesn't work for you, discard it.

The Big Pause

We intentionally left out one major inference from the diagram above. It's likely that you didn't find it at all, or at least not until you took a moment to consider the game one last time. If you have no idea what we're talking about, take one more moment to look over the diagram again, considering the rules that have a strong connection with each other.

There are still inferences to mine from the intersection of the rule defining M's wash type (and that of the preceding car) and the rule that requires that the second and third cars receive the same wash type. From this intersection, we can determine the wash types for slots 2 and 3.

Because M is between O and F, it can go only in slots 3 or 4. If M goes in slot 3, both slots 2 and 3 receive an R, since we know that M and the car before it must receive an R. If M goes in slot 4, again because of the rule about M's wash type, we know that slot 3 must also receive an R. And, since slots 2 and 3 receive the same type of wash, slot 2 receives an R as well. Thus, regardless of whether M is in slot 3 or 4, slots 2 and 3 receive R's.

Another inference we can make is about S. Since it can't go in slots 1–3, and we must have at least one S, we know we have to place an S in slot 4, slot 5, or both.

Did you miss all of those inferences the first time you played the game? If so, it's probably a sign that you didn't take enough time to complete your diagram and consider the game as a whole.

Our final diagram looks like this:

Did you frame this game? It's definitely possible. There are some frameable divisions in this game, though probably the most promising is the two positions for M:

As is often the case, it's impossible to say if framing this game was the "right" thing to do. If you'd like, go ahead and replay the game with these frames. You'll see that it helps with several questions. Can you efficiently solve the game without these frames? Definitely.

Attack the Questions

11. Which one of the following could be an accurate list of the cars in the order in which they are washed, matched with type of wash received?

(A) Orlando's: premium; Vinquetta's: regular; Taishah's: regular; Marquitta's: regular; Frank's: super

(B) Vinquetta's: premium; Orlando's: regular; Taishah's: regular; Marquitta's: regular; Frank's: super

(C) Vinquetta's: regular; Marquitta's: regular; Taishah's: regular; Orlando's: super; Frank's: premium

(D) Vinquetta's: super; Orlando's: regular; Marquitta's: regular; Frank's: regular; Taishah's: super

(E) Vinquetta's: premium; Orlando's: regular; Marquitta's: regular; Frank's: regular; Taishah's: regular

(B) is correct.

With so many rules, expect that some will not yield any eliminations.

> The first rule eliminates (D).
>
> The second rule doesn't eliminate anything remaining (but would have eliminated (D) also).
>
> The third rule eliminates nothing.
>
> The fourth rule eliminates (A).
>
> The fifth rule eliminates (C). Down to (B) and (E).
>
> The sixth rule eliminates nothing!

P

Keep your calm, and swing through the rules one more time with (B) and (E). It turns out that the first rule eliminates (E) as well. If we had broken the first rule into its two components—no S in the first slot, and there must be at least one S—we could have avoided doing a second pass.

12. If Vinquetta's car does not receive a premium wash, which one of the following must be true?

   (A) Orlando's and Vinquetta's cars receive the same kind of wash as each other.

   (B) Marquitta's and Taishah's cars receive the same kind of wash as each other.

   (C) The fourth car washed receives a premium wash.

   (D) Orlando's car is washed third.

   (E) Marquitta's car is washed fourth.

(A) is correct.

We know that V must receive a regular wash. So what can we infer? Since we must have one premium wash, we know that slots 4 and 5 have an S and P, though not necessarily in that order. Since this is the second question, which is usually on the simpler side of the spectrum, we probably can get away without drawing out a new diagram. (If we use the frames we discussed, we can infer that we are dealing with the first one; therefore, we have O and M in slots 2 and 3.)

(A) Must be true. Since O must be in slot 2 or 3, it receives a regular wash. Pull the trigger and move on.

We wouldn't check, but of course, all the other answers could be false, or are false:

(B) Could be false. T is in slot 4 or 5, and so might receive a P or S wash.

(C) Could be false. Slot 4 might have an S wash.

(D) False! O is second.

(E) False! M is third.

13. If the last two cars washed receive the same kind of wash as each other, then which one of the following could be true?

    (A) Orlando's car is washed third.

    (B) Taishah's car is washed fifth.

    (C) Taishah's car is washed before Marquitta's car.

    (D) Vinquetta's car receives a regular wash.

    (E) Exactly one car receives a super wash.

(B) is correct.

What could those last two washes be? They must be both S's, since we need at least one S, and slots 1–3 can't have an S. Since we need one P, we put that in the first slot. But don't forget that this is a 3D game. What can we infer about the bottom row? Since M and the preceding car must receive an R wash, M must go in slot 3. Thus, we have the following:

We're looking for something that could be true, so let's scan our answers for something involving F or T, the two elements that are not completely determined. (B) is something that could be true   T is in slot 4 or 5. Of course, the other answers all must be false.

14. Which one of the following must be true?

    (A) Vinquetta's car receives a premium wash

    (B) Exactly two cars receive a super wash.

    (C) The fifth car washed receives a super wash.

    (D) The fourth car washed receives a super wash.

    (E) The second car washed receives a regular wash.

(E) is correct.

Our hard work in diagramming this game pays off. We know that the second car must have an R. Every other answer could be false.

15. Which one of the following is a complete and accurate list of the cars that must receive a regular wash?

(A) Frank's, Marquitta's
(B) Marquitta's, Orlando's
(C) Marquitta's, Orlando's, Taishah's
(D) Marquitta's, Taishah's
(E) Marquitta's, Vinquetta's

(B) is correct.

Let's look at our diagram before we look at the answer choices. We know that M has to receive a regular wash, along with whichever cars are in slots 2 and 3. Who must go in one of those two slots? O! We might quickly consider T, but we know that it could go in slot 4 or 5 and not receive a regular wash.

Alternately, you might have looked at the answer choices after a shorter consideration of the question stem. Since M is in every answer choice, no need to think about it. O is in two choices, so it's worth considering. Once we realize that it must receive a regular wash, we're down to (B) and (C). Confirm that T doesn't need a regular wash, and we're done.

Of course, if you framed this game, you probably took a quick look at your frames and saw that M and O are the only cars that must always receive an R.

16. Suppose that in addition to the original five cars Jabrohn's car is also washed. If all the other conditions hold as given, which one of the following CANNOT be true?

(A) Orlando's car receives a premium wash.
(B) Vinquetta's car receives a super wash.
(C) Four cars receive a regular wash.
(D) Only the second and third cars washed receive a regular wash.
(E) Jabrohn's car is washed after Frank's car.

(A) is correct.

A Rule Substitution question! Here we're adding a sixth car to the game. Though it's likely you redrew the diagram, a fine decision, let's take a look at how one might have done this by simply amending the diagram.

We'll start by adding another position:

S-1+
P-1

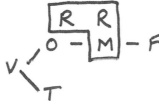

P/R   R = R   (S)   _   RSP

V   (O—M—F , T)   _   FMOTV J
         R
1   2   3   4   5   6

P

Now, what do we have to change? Perhaps the most obvious change is that there is now an element other than V that could take the first position.

Another important change is that we can no longer infer that slots 2 and 3 definitely receive R's. Perhaps M is in slot 5 now, requiring R's only in slots 4 and 5.

Also notice that S is no longer restricted to the last two slots. It's possible to place S's in both slots 2 and 3.

On this question, it's probably easier to work from scratch than to amend the diagram, but either way, you should have arrived at a diagram like this:

P/R   _ = _ _ _ _ _   RSP
                R R
         (V — O — M — F, T, J)   FMOTV J
1   2   3   4   5   6

There are a lot of restrictions we could write in—all the places where M cannot go, for example—but we don't have the time to do that just for this one question. We'll figure out those restrictions as we need them.

We've done enough homework—let's look at the answer choices. We're looking for something that must be false. Ideally, it would be notated in our diagram already, but considering how few restrictions we drew in, that's unlikely. Since four of the answers will be could be true scenarios, that might be time-consuming to confirm. Let's look for something that must be false.

(A) This calls for a bit of thought. Where could O go? With one element forced before it, and two forced after it, O can only go in slots 2–4. Could it receive a P in any of those positions? No. In slots 2 and 3, P is forbidden since those two slots must share a wash type, and there is only one P. If O is placed in slot 4, that means M and F are in slots 5 and 6, respectively, meaning that O must receive an R, since it would be the element directly before M.

All the other answers could be true.

(B) V could go in slot 2 and receive an S, along with whatever car is in slot 3.

(C) Slots 2–5 could receive R's, leaving a P for slot 1 and an S for slot 6.

(D) M could go in slot 3, slot 1 could be a P, and slots 4–6 could be S's.

(E) There are no restrictions on where J can go.

17. Which of the following, if substituted for the rule that the first car washed does not receive a super wash, though at least one car does, would have the same effect in determining the order of car washes and the type of each?

    (A) Vinquetta's car can receive only a regular or premium wash.

    (B) No more than three cars receive a regular wash.

    (C) Frank's car receives a super wash if, and only if, Taishah's car receives a regular or premium wash.

    (D) All cars except Frank's and Taishah's must receive either a regular or premium wash.

    (E) Either Frank's or Taishah's car receives a super wash, and no other car can receive that type of wash.

(E) is correct.

We wrote this Equivalent Rule question to give you more practice with this question type. Note that the LSAT would not ask such a question right after a Rule Substitution question! We'll ignore question #16 in solving this one.

We'll start by understanding the consequences of the original rule. If slot 1 (car V) cannot be an S, we know that it must be a P or an R. No other consequences may spring to mind, but remember that this is a two-part rule. The last part tells us that at least one car does receive an S. Since slots 1–3 can't receive an S (due to various rules and their interactions), we can infer that there must be an S in slot 4 or 5. It's important to note that S's could be placed in *both* slots 4 and 5.

Let's dive into the answer choices:

(A) We can eliminate this answer since it only deals with the first half of the rule.

(B) This answer provides an equivalent only for the second part! With (B) in place, we know that there must be at least one S, but there's nothing stopping us from placing an S in slot 1.

(C) This answer should be easy to eliminate, even though it's complex. We don't see any restriction placed on S going in slot 1. Eliminate! Furthermore, there's no reason that F and T can't both have S's.

(D) This answer restricts S to F and T. But we also need to require an S. With this answer, it's possible to avoid having any S's.

(E) Here we get both parts of the original rule. The second part of this answer restricts V from receiving a super wash. It isn't a problem that it also restricts O in the same way; we learned in question #15 that O must receive a regular wash. The first part of this answer requires either F or T to receive an S, and this can only happen in slots 4–5. Note that the answer does not state "but not both," so it's possible that both receive an S.

P

Chapter 5

of

Logic Games

Conditional Logic 101

In This Chapter...

> WARNING: If you have also been reading our *Logical Reasoning Strategy Guide,* there's a good chance you are already quite familiar with conditional statements. If you feel quite confident, we suggest you test your skills using the chapter drills to confirm that you don't need to read the bulk of this chapter.

(Re)Introduction to Conditional Statements

What is a Conditional Statement?

The most basic type of conditional statement is triggered by "If … then" phrasing:

> **IF** Jeremy eats a big lunch, **THEN** he won't be hungry for dinner.
>
> **IF** John lives in San Francisco, **THEN** John lives in California.
>
> **IF** Sue attends the concert, **THEN** her husband is at home babysitting the children.
>
> **IF** Hiromi wins the election, **THEN** she had the most organized campaign.

Sufficient vs. Necessary Conditions

The "If" part of the conditional statement is called the *sufficient* condition, because it is *sufficient* to guarantee the truth of the "Then" part of the statement. The "Then" part of the statement is called the *necessary* condition because, when the sufficient condition is true, it is required, or *necessary,* that the "Then" portion be true as well. To summarize:

> **Sufficient condition:** The "If" part of the statement. When satisfied, it guarantees the truth of the necessary condition.

> **Necessary condition:** The "Then" part of the statement. It is required if the sufficient condition is true.

Note that while the sufficient condition is *sufficient* to guarantee the truth of the necessary condition, it is not required to arrive at the truth of the necessary condition. Let's take a very simple example to illustrate:

> **IF** you give me a gift, **THEN** I will be happy.

In this case the condition, "you give me a gift," is *sufficient* to guarantee the truth of the necessary condition, "I will be happy." However, there could be other conditions that are sufficient to lead to the truth of the necessary condition:

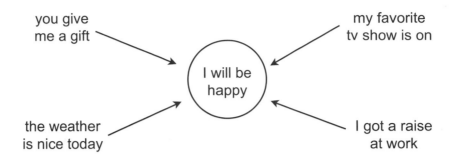

So, what can we conclude? Two things for now:

1.   Your giving me a gift is *sufficient* to guarantee that I will be happy.
2.   If I am happy, this does NOT guarantee that you have given me a gift (maybe I'm happy for a different reason). In other words, the relationship doesn't necessarily work the other way around.

This will be very important to keep in mind later on when we consider the types of inferences that can be made from conditional statements.

Conditional Statements in Logic Games

Conditional statements appear most often in Conditional Grouping games. We'll be covering Conditional Grouping in an upcoming chapter, but conditional statements can pop up in every single game type, including some Ordering games. Thus, it's worthwhile to introduce them here to provide some context for the conditional statements that we will discuss in the next chapter.

Conditional Inferences

Valid vs. Invalid

Before we get back to our "happiness" example, let's consider a simpler conditional statement:

IF Sally lives in Boston, **THEN** Sally lives in Massachusetts.

Now consider the following related inferences that might be made given the statement above:

1.   **Is the negative true?** If Sally does not live in Boston, then Sally does not live in Massachusetts.
2.   **Is the reverse true?** If Sally lives in Massachusetts, then Sally lives in Boston.
3.   **Is the negative AND reverse true?** If Sally does not live in Massachusetts, then Sally does not live in Boston.

Which of these inferences, if any, are valid? This is a simpler case because you already know that Boston is not the only city or town in Massachusetts. You can probably see already that the first and second inferences are NOT valid. Even so, let's use our picture to illustrate:

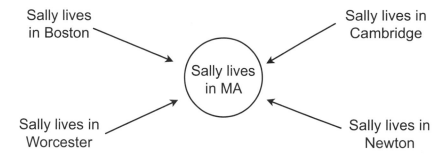

1. If Sally does not live in Boston, then Sally does not live in Massachusetts.

This, of course, is not necessarily true. After all, Sally could live in Newton, which would still put her in Massachusetts.

2. If Sally lives in Massachusetts, then Sally lives in Boston.

This isn't necessarily true either. There are many places Sally could live, including Cambridge, Worcester, and Newton, that are in Massachusetts but outside of Boston.

3. If Sally does not live in Massachusetts, then Sally does not live in Boston.

This, of course, MUST be true. This is the only inference of the bunch that is valid.

Let's now apply the same logic to the "happiness" example, which is a bit tougher:

> **IF** you give me a gift, **THEN** I will be happy.

Now consider the following related inferences that might be made given the statement above:

1. **Is the negative true?** If you do not give me a gift, then I will not be happy.
2. **Is the reverse true?** If I am happy, then you have given me a gift.
3. **Is the negative AND reverse true?** If I am not happy, then you have not given me a gift.

Which of these inferences, if any, are valid? To evaluate our potential inferences, let's consider our picture again, remembering that there may be other sufficient conditions that would guarantee my happiness.

1. If you do not give me a gift, then I will not be happy.

This, of course, is not necessarily true. Remember, while giving me a gift is *sufficient* to make me happy, it is not required. Maybe you haven't given me a gift, but perhaps I am happy because I got a raise at work today. Thus, this is an invalid inference.

2. If I am happy, then you have given me a gift.

Remember, there could be other reasons why I am happy. This is an invalid inference.

3. If I am not happy, then you have not given me a gift.

This MUST be true. If you give me a gift, it is guaranteed that I will be happy. So, if I am not happy, you could not possibly have given me a gift. This is the only valid inference of the bunch.

By now you may be noticing that the only correct inference, regardless of the original conditional statement, is the one that reverses and negates the original.

We can reduce this complex train of thought down to a reliable rule. To do so, let's start by organizing our thinking through the use of symbols. Let's use a G to symbolize "You give me a gift" and an H to symbolize "I will be happy." The arrow indicates the "If … then" relationship:

Statement	Symbols	Valid/Invalid	Description
If you give me a gift, then I will be happy.	$G \rightarrow H$	**GIVEN**	**GIVEN**
1. If you do not give me a gift, then I will not be happy.	$-G \rightarrow -H$	Invalid	Negate
2. If I am happy, then you have given me a gift.	$H \rightarrow G$	Invalid	Reverse
3. If I am not happy, then you have not given me a gift.	$-H \rightarrow -G$	VALID	REVERSE & NEGATE

You can see by looking at the symbols that the first inference simply negates the components of the original given statement. The second inference simply reverses the original components. The third inference both reverses and negates the components of the original statement. Thus, the only valid inference is one that reverses and negates the form of the original given statement. This is called the contrapositive.

Contrapositive: The valid inference derived by reversing and negating the components of a given conditional statement.

Let's generalize:

Statement	Symbols	Valid/Invalid	Description
If X, then Y.	$X \rightarrow Y$	**GIVEN**	**GIVEN**
1. If not X, then not Y.	$-X \rightarrow -Y$	Invalid	Negate
2. If Y, then X.	$Y \rightarrow X$	Invalid	Reverse
3. If not Y, then not X.	$-Y \rightarrow -X$	VALID	REVERSE & NEGATE

Take some time now to practice making inferences from conditional statements.

DRILL IT: Drawing Inferences from Conditional Statements

Diagram each of the conditional statements below, then diagram the contrapositive relationship by reversing and negating the components of the original. Finally, use the contrapositive diagram to write a statement that expresses the valid inference made. Be sure to check your responses against the solutions after each mini-exercise.

Example: GIVEN: If X is selected, then Y is selected.

GIVEN DIAGRAM: $X \rightarrow Y$

CONTRAPOSITIVE DIAGRAM: $-Y \rightarrow -X$

VALID INFERENCE: If Y is not selected, then X is not selected.

1. GIVEN: If Sid is on the committee, then Jana is on the committee.

GIVEN DIAGRAM:

CONTRAPOSITIVE DIAGRAM:

VALID INFERENCE:

2. GIVEN: If Raul is invited to the party, then Shaina is not invited to the party.

GIVEN DIAGRAM:

CONTRAPOSITIVE DIAGRAM:

VALID INFERENCE:

3. GIVEN: If Brooks is not on the bus, then Traiger is not on the bus.

GIVEN DIAGRAM:

CONTRAPOSITIVE DIAGRAM:

VALID INFERENCE:

4. GIVEN: If the tiger is not in the cage, then the lion is in the cage.

GIVEN DIAGRAM:

CONTRAPOSITIVE DIAGRAM:

VALID INFERENCE:

5. GIVEN: I will not go jogging if it is raining outside.

GIVEN DIAGRAM:

CONTRAPOSITIVE DIAGRAM:

VALID INFERENCE:

6. GIVEN: If Tamika gives the speech, then she won the speech competition.

GIVEN DIAGRAM:

CONTRAPOSITIVE DIAGRAM:

VALID INFERENCE:

7. GIVEN: Yohei plays guitar if Juan plays drums.

GIVEN DIAGRAM:

CONTRAPOSITIVE DIAGRAM:

VALID INFERENCE:

8. GIVEN: If T is not chosen for the team, then N is not chosen for the team.

GIVEN DIAGRAM:

CONTRAPOSITIVE DIAGRAM:

VALID INFERENCE:

9. GIVEN: G is not selected for the club if F is selected for the club.

GIVEN DIAGRAM:

CONTRAPOSITIVE DIAGRAM:

VALID INFERENCE:

10. GIVEN: If Beethoven is played, then Mozart is also played.

GIVEN DIAGRAM:

CONTRAPOSITIVE DIAGRAM:

VALID INFERENCE:

5

SOLUTIONS: Drawing Inferences from Conditional Statements

1. GIVEN: If Sid is on the committee, then Jana is on the committee.

GIVEN DIAGRAM: $S \longrightarrow J$

CONTRAPOSITIVE DIAGRAM: $-J \longrightarrow -S$

VALID INFERENCE: If Jana is not on the committee, then Sid is not on the committee.

2. GIVEN: If Raul is invited to the party, then Shaina is not invited to the party.

GIVEN DIAGRAM: $R \longrightarrow -S$

CONTRAPOSITIVE DIAGRAM: $S \longrightarrow -R$

VALID INFERENCE: If Shaina is invited to the party, then Raul is not invited to the party.

3. GIVEN: If Brooks is not on the bus, then Traiger is not on the bus.

GIVEN DIAGRAM: $-B \longrightarrow -T$

CONTRAPOSITIVE DIAGRAM: $T \longrightarrow B$

VALID INFERENCE: If Traiger is on the bus, then Brooks is on the bus.

4. GIVEN: If the tiger is not in the cage, then the lion is in the cage.

GIVEN DIAGRAM: $-T \longrightarrow L$

CONTRAPOSITIVE DIAGRAM: $-L \longrightarrow T$

VALID INFERENCE: If the lion is not in the cage, then the tiger is in the cage.

5. GIVEN: I will not go jogging if it is raining outside. = **If it is raining outside, then I will not go jogging.**

Be careful with this one! Notice that the original statement puts the "If" part second. This doesn't change the conditional relationship.

GIVEN DIAGRAM: $R \longrightarrow -J$

CONTRAPOSITIVE DIAGRAM: $J \longrightarrow -R$

VALID INFERENCE: If I go jogging, then it is not raining outside.

6. GIVEN: If Tamika gives the speech, then she won the speech competition.

GIVEN DIAGRAM: $T \longrightarrow W$

CONTRAPOSITIVE DIAGRAM: $-W \longrightarrow -T$

VALID INFERENCE: If Tamika did not win the speech competition, then she will not give the speech.

7. GIVEN: Yohei plays guitar if Juan plays drums. = **If Juan plays drums, then Yohei plays guitar.**

GIVEN DIAGRAM: $J \longrightarrow Y$

CONTRAPOSITIVE DIAGRAM: $-Y \longrightarrow -J$

VALID INFERENCE: If Yohei does not play guitar, then Juan does not play drums.

8. GIVEN: If T is not chosen for the team, then N is not chosen for the team.

GIVEN DIAGRAM: $-T \longrightarrow -N$

CONTRAPOSITIVE DIAGRAM: $N \longrightarrow T$

VALID INFERENCE: If N is chosen for the team, then T is chosen for the team.

9. GIVEN: G is not selected for the club if F is selected for the club. = **If F is selected for the club, then G is not selected for the club.**

GIVEN DIAGRAM: $F \longrightarrow -G$

CONTRAPOSITIVE DIAGRAM: $G \longrightarrow -F$

VALID INFERENCE: If G is selected for the club, then F is not selected for the club.

10. GIVEN: If Beethoven is played, then Mozart is also played.

GIVEN DIAGRAM: $B \longrightarrow M$

CONTRAPOSITIVE DIAGRAM: $-M \longrightarrow -B$

VALID INFERENCE: If Mozart is not played, then Beethoven is not played.

5

MANHATTAN
LSAT

Only If

Translate this statement into formal notation: **Carlos eats fish only on Fridays.**

Based on that statement, which of the following is true?

    (A)   If it's Friday, Carlos is eating fish.

    (B)   If Carlos is not eating fish, it is not Friday.

    (C)   If Carlos is eating fish, it is Friday.

    (D)   If it is not Friday, Carlos is not eating fish.

The first two cannot be inferred from the given statement. Even though Carlos only eats fish on Fridays, he doesn't *have* to eat fish on Fridays. He might eat nothing! If he does indeed eat nothing on Friday, we have not violated the given rule, and thus we have disproven (B).

(C) is inferable since Friday is the only day he eats fish! Similarly, (D) must be true. Thus, the translation of the given statement is CF ➞ Fri. or –Fri ➞ –CF.

"Only" or "only if" usually indicates the necessary part of a conditional statement. However, be careful not to apply this rule robotically. Translate this statement: **The only time Lucy was funny to me was in the chocolate-eating scene.**

If you placed "Lucy funny" in the necessary position, you missed the point of the statement. What is guaranteed in that statement is that if she was funny to me, it must have been the chocolate-eating scene. Thus, the translation is "funny ➞ chocolate." This is a rare twist on an only statement; the vast majority of the time, "only" does come right before the necessary condition. However, do not translate into formal logic with a rigid mind-set or you will get fooled from time to time. Instead, focus on what is guaranteed and place that in the necessary position.

MANHATTAN
LSAT

Biconditionals

Consider these two statements and take a moment to translate them into formal notation before reading on:

1. Ramona will eat if you bring her macaroni and cheese.

2. Ramona will eat only if you bring her macaroni and cheese.

They translate to the following:

1. M & C → RE

2. RE → M & C

And how would you combine the two statements into one sentence?

One way is to simply write a long sentence: Ramona will eat if you bring her macaroni and cheese, and Ramona will eat only if you bring her macaroni and cheese.

That's correct, but not very elegant! How can we shorten it? One way is this: Ramona will eat if, and only if, you bring her macaroni and cheese. Take a moment to confirm that the statement includes both rules established by the original two statements.

Now, how would we write that if and only if statement in formal notation? Since it communicates the same rules as the original pair, we could cheat and simply copy what we wrote before:

    M & C → RE   RE → M & C

But there's a fancier way. Probably you noticed that each statement is the reverse of the other. When that's true, we have a **biconditional**. We can—but don't have to—represent it like this: M & C ←→ RE.

Of course, we also have the contrapositives of the two original statements:

    –RE → –M & C   –M & C → –RE

And those, too, can be combined into one statement: –RE ←→ –M & C. Both sides of the statement are triggers!

For a tiny bit of practice, go ahead and write out in formal notation all the conditional statements you can draw from this rule:

    K will be fourth if and only if J is third.

You could have written out four statements, but you also could have combined them into two:

    $K_4 \longleftrightarrow J_3$ $-K_4 \longleftrightarrow -J_3$

Connecting Conditional Statements

In Chapter 9 you'll learn a couple of fancy moves you can use when working with conditional statements. You already know the most important move—creating contrapositives. Another that you want to know right now—and probably could figure out on your own—is how to connect statements. Consider these rules:

1. Trains only come to town on Wednesdays.

2. If Leo is not working, it is not Wednesday.

Go ahead and write those in formal notation, along with the contrapositives before reading on.

1. TT ➔ Wed

    –Wed ➔ –TT

2. –LW ➔ –Wed

    Wed ➔ LW

So, what can you infer if a train comes to town?

From the first rule you know that it's Wednesday. But you also know, per the second rule's contrapositive, that if it is Wednesday, Leo is working. The end of one rule links to the beginning of another: TT ➔ Wed ➔ LW. Furthermore, we can apply the contrapositive rule to that entire chain, reversing and negating the whole thing, starting with –LW: –LW ➔ –Wed ➔ –TT.

Linking conditional statements is an important move, and one you'll use often. For Conditional Grouping games, we will teach you a way to incorporate those links into a diagram, but when you see linkable conditional statements in other games, go ahead and link them as we've done here.

You've finished Conditional Logic 101! Let's apply what you've learned to the next game type….

Chapter 6

Mismatch Ordering

In This Chapter...

Getting Familiar

Do your best to complete the following game. Use whatever approach you see fit. Give yourself **8:30 or less**.

Doctor X will see exactly five of seven patients—K, L, M, N, O, P, and Q—that are all waiting in the lobby. She will see these patients one at a time and in order. The following conditions apply:

    She will see both K and M, and she will see K before M.

    If she does not see O, she will see P.

    She will see Q or P, but not both.

    If she sees either L or O, she will see them after M.

    If she sees N, she must see N first.

1. Which of the following could be the order of patients that Doctor X sees, from first to last?

    (A) N, Q, K, M, P

    (B) N, Q, K, O, M

    (C) N, Q, K, M, L

    (D) N, Q, K, M, O

    (E) N, Q, M, K, O

2. Each of the following could be true EXCEPT:

    (A) The doctor sees Q first.

    (B) The doctor sees M second.

    (C) The doctor sees K fourth.

    (D) The doctor sees P last.

    (E) The doctor sees Q last.

3. If the doctor sees K third, which of the following must be true?

    (A) She sees N first.

    (B) She sees Q second.

    (C) She sees L last.

    (D) She sees P.

    (E) She sees O.

4. Which of the following must be true?

    (A) If the doctor does not see L, she will also not see Q.

    (B) If the doctor does not see N, she will also not see P.

    (C) If the doctor does not see Q, she will also not see P.

    (D) If the doctor does not see Q, she will also not see O.

    (E) If the doctor does not see O, she will also not see Q.

5. If the doctor sees M fourth, which of the following could be true?

    (A) The doctor sees K first.

    (B) The doctor sees K second.

    (C) The doctor sees P first.

    (D) The doctor sees Q last.

    (E) The doctor sees P last.

6. Which of the following, if true, would determine which patients the doctor will see and the order in which she will see them?

    (A) The doctor sees N first and P third.

    (B) The doctor sees N first and Q third.

    (C) The doctor sees K first and M second.

    (D) The doctor sees K first and O fourth.

    (E) The doctor sees K second and M fourth.

Mismatch Ordering

As you just experienced, Mismatch Ordering games include a small but important departure from Basic Ordering games. Our elements and positions can no longer be matched up one to one!

What Defines a Mismatch Ordering Game?

There are two basic flavors of Mismatch Ordering games. There are either extra elements or extra positions.

Imagine you are a personal trainer with five consecutive training session slots at the gym tomorrow and seven people that need to be scheduled into those slots. You have *extra elements*. How could this be resolved in real life? Perhaps you'd tell two people that they have to skip their sessions, or maybe you'd turn a session into a group class and double up on elements.

The other mismatch flavor might involve a film festival with eight consecutive times for showings, but only five films to show. Here, we have *extra positions*. There are basically two solutions. Either some of those films need to be shown more than once, or some showtimes need to remain empty.

That's it! There are either extra elements, extra positions, or some combination of the two flavors. (If you're wondering how there can be extra elements *and* extra positions, just you wait and see!)

Extra Elements

The most common type of Mismatch Ordering game is one in which there are extra elements. The key to picturing these games is to draw slots where we can track excluded positions. For example, imagine there were six potential elements—P, Q, R, S, T, and U—but only four positions. Your diagram should look like this:

PQRSTU

$$\underline{}\ \ \underline{}\ \ \underline{}\ \ \underline{}\ \Big|\ \underline{}\ \ \underline{}$$
$$\quad _1 \quad\ _2 \quad\ _3 \quad\ _4$$

In the game above, we probably wouldn't come across a rule that tells us that R comes before S, since we're not even sure whether R and S are in! Instead, it's more common to see a conditional rule, something like "If R and S are both performing in the show, then R performs at some time before S." The conditional nature of that rule preserves the possibility of excluding either element.

Less commonly, you'll face a game in which the extra elements are included by having some of the positions hold more than one element—we'll call this "doubling up." At times, the rules will define which position or positions hold more than one element; at other times, it's left unclear. If you know which slots are to double up (or triple up…), then notate that accordingly:

$$\frac{\underline{\quad} \qquad\qquad \underline{\quad}}{\underset{1}{\underline{\quad}} \; \underset{2}{\underline{\quad}} \; \underset{3}{\underline{\quad}} \; \underset{4}{\underline{\quad}}} \qquad \textsf{P Q R S T U}$$

However, if you are not sure which position or positions will double up, you can place an extra line above every position, like so:

$$\frac{\underline{\quad} \; \underline{\quad} \; \underline{\quad} \; \underline{\quad}}{\underset{1}{\underline{\quad}} \; \underset{2}{\underline{\quad}} \; \underset{3}{\underline{\quad}} \; \underset{4}{\underline{\quad}}} \qquad \textsf{P Q R S T U}$$

Alternately, you can use a standard number line and remember that doubling up must occur. Often, the rules will help define where the doubling up can or does occur.

It's easy to incorrectly assume that every slot in an ordering game must be filled. Be sure to ask yourself whether that's true for each game. While it's probably unnecessary for most folks, if you like to be very thorough in your diagramming and want to make it clear that in a certain game each position receives at least one element, a way to notate that (and in a way that is consistent with how we'll handle some future game types) is to place a box over each slot on the bottom row:

Dealing with mismatches in your diagram isn't particularly difficult, but it's crucial that you clarify the mismatch issues before you reach the questions in a game.

Before we look at how to picture the other flavor of Mismatch Ordering games, let's return to the Getting Familiar game to look at an extra element diagram in action. If you struggled with the game and think that having the excluded slots in your diagram would have dramatically helped you tackle the game, feel free to replay it, but otherwise, let's dive into the solutions.

As you read through the solutions, keep an eye out for situations in which tracking the excluded slots is crucial.

Try It Again

Doctor X will see exactly five of seven patients—K, L, M, N, O, P, and Q—that are all waiting in the lobby. She will see these patients one at a time and in order. The following conditions apply:

She will see both K and M, and she will see K before M.

If she does not see O, she will see P.

She will see Q or P, but not both.

If she sees either L or O, she will see them after M.

If she sees N, she must see N first.

1. Which of the following could be the order of patients that Doctor X sees, from first to last?

   (A) N, Q, K, M, P
   (B) N, Q, K, O, M
   (C) N, Q, K, M, L
   (D) N, Q, K, M, O
   (E) N, Q, M, K, O

2. Each of the following could be true EXCEPT:

   (A) The doctor sees Q first.
   (B) The doctor sees M second.
   (C) The doctor sees K fourth.
   (D) The doctor sees P last.
   (E) The doctor sees Q last.

3. If the doctor sees K third, which of the following must be true?

   (A) She sees N first.
   (B) She sees Q second.
   (C) She sees L last.
   (D) She sees P.
   (E) She sees O.

4. Which of the following must be true?

   (A) If the doctor does not see L, she will also not see Q.
   (B) If the doctor does not see N, she will also not see P.
   (C) If the doctor does not see Q, she will also not see P.
   (D) If the doctor does not see Q, she will also not see O.
   (E) If the doctor does not see O, she will also not see Q.

5. If the doctor sees M fourth, which of the following could be true?

   (A) The doctor sees K first.
   (B) The doctor sees K second.
   (C) The doctor sees P first.
   (D) The doctor sees Q last.
   (E) The doctor sees P last.

6. Which of the following, if true, would determine which patients the doctor will see and the order in which she will see them?

   (A) The doctor sees N first and P third.
   (B) The doctor sees N first and Q third.
   (C) The doctor sees K first and M second.
   (D) The doctor sees K first and O fourth.
   (E) The doctor sees K second and M fourth.

How Did You Do?

Picture the Game

This is a somewhat straightforward version of a Mismatch Ordering game. The scenario makes it clear that only five of the seven elements will be ordered, and we see a lot of conditional rules, a common feature of Mismatch Ordering games. We'll set up our number line, with two slots to the side for the irate patients who don't get seen:

$$\underset{1}{\_\_}\quad\underset{2}{\_\_}\quad\underset{3}{\_\_}\quad\underset{4}{\_\_}\quad\underset{5}{\_\_}\ \Big|\ \_\_\quad\_\_ \qquad \textsf{K L M N O P Q}$$

Notate the Rules and Make Inferences

She will see both K and M, and she will see K before M.

The first rule gives us two of our five patients, as well as a relative ordering clue about them. That's easy to notate to the side, or right on top of the number line.

If she does not see O, she will see P.

The second rule takes a bit more thought. We'll start by writing this as a conditional statement: $-O \rightarrow P$ and $-P \rightarrow O$. So can we write something into our diagram? One option is to write "O/P" above the number line, since we know one of those will be there. More importantly, we should consider what is and isn't possible under this rule. Specifically, can we have both O and P? Yes! So, we're definitely not writing anything over the excluded slots.

So far, we have this:

$$\overset{\textsf{K}-\textsf{M}\quad\textsf{P/O}}{\underset{1}{\_\_}\quad\underset{2}{\_\_}\quad\underset{3}{\_\_}\quad\underset{4}{\_\_}\quad\underset{5}{\_\_}}\ \Big|\ \_\_\quad\_\_ \qquad \textsf{K L M N O P Q}$$

$$-O \rightarrow P$$
$$-P \rightarrow O$$

She will see Q or P, but not both.

This rule is similar to the second one in that it requires one of two specific elements to be included. However, unlike the second rule, with this one we cannot have both elements in. This helps us define who is out as much as who is in. What will this rule look like written out? Since we know we have Q or P in and the other one out, this is a biconditional: Q ←→ –P and P ←→ –Q.

We could (or could not) write "Q/P" over our number line, but we should definitely fill one of the out slots with "Q/P." Why the difference? For the included side, we don't know two things: whether it's Q or P, and where that Q or P will go. For the excluded side, since order is irrelevant we can simply write "Q/P" in either slot. It's also super helpful that we'll have filled one of the excluded slots. If we can fill that other one during the game, then we'll know who's in (everyone else), with the exception of the Q/P choice.

Notice that the two rules we have just notated share an element in common. For each rule, P being an included element would satisfy the rule.

> If she sees either L or O, she will see them after M.

The next rule is triggered only if the doctor sees either L or O. Let's not forget to note that; we don't want to fool ourselves into thinking that this rule tells us that L, O, or M are always in. Since either L or O would trigger this rule, we can split the rule in two: L → M – L and O → M – O.

On to our last rule, a pretty straightforward conditional. If N is in, N is first. It's easy enough to write the rule to the side, but let's see if we can put the rule into the diagram. We can't put an N in slot 1 since we don't know if there will actually be an N. But we know for sure where N *won't* go, namely slots 2–5!

At this point our diagram looks as follows:

$$\begin{array}{ccccc} \text{K} - \text{M} & \text{P/O} & \text{Q/P} \\ \hline 1 & 2 & 3 & 4 & 5 \end{array}$$

K – M   P/O   Q/P   K L M N O P Q

```
___  ___  ___  ___  ___  |  Q/P  ___
 1    2    3    4    5    |
      N̸    N̸    N̸    N̸    |
                         |
              N → N/1    |   -O → P
                         |   -P → O
                         |
                         |   Q ↔ -P
                         |   P ↔ -Q
                         |
                         |   L → M – L
                         |   O → M – O
```

Before we consider the game in general, we should see if our rules connect, since we've only looked at each one as if it were the only rule in the game.

It's pretty clear that there are a lot of connections between the three conditional rules written to the side. If you feel confident that you can remember to track the connections, there is no need to write them out, but for most of us, it's a good move to take the extra step and link the rules in writing. Take a look at how the link-ups can look:

Be careful with the double arrows! For example, the –Q at the end of the first rule leads back to P, but that P doesn't lead to –O.

The Big Pause

As usual, let's take a breath before diving into the questions. What seem to be the crucial issues in this game? With such long conditional chains, it's obvious that we're going to have to keep a close eye on all of those rules. But with two elements already definitively in, and two element pairs for which one must be included, there's not much wiggle room in terms of who else can be in. Similarly, we have one excluded slot filled with the Q/P option, so only one other element can be excluded. If N isn't first, we know it'll be N.

Is this a game worth framing? Probably not. We *could* frame the Q/P option, the O/P option, or even the N/–N option. (We don't usually recommend framing a conditional situation like the N rule, but since N's placement is so restricted, and excluding N forces the inclusion of several others, framing this conditional makes more sense than is usually true.) Feel free to play around with those frames to decide on their value for yourself.

Attack the Questions

1. Which of the following could be the order of patients that Doctor X sees, from first to last?

   (A) N, Q, K, M, P
   (B) N, Q, K, O, M
   (C) N, Q, K, M, L
   (D) N, Q, K, M, O
   (E) N, Q, M, K, O

(D) is correct.

The first rule eliminates (E).

The second eliminates (C).

The third eliminates (A).

The fourth eliminates (B).

2. Each of the following could be true EXCEPT:

   (A) The doctor sees Q first.
   (B) The doctor sees M second.
   (C) The doctor sees K fourth.
   (D) The doctor sees P last.
   (E) The doctor sees Q last.

(C) is correct.

If you see an Unconditional question second in a game, it generally should be easy to spot the right answer. Let's defer on any answers that don't catch our eye as we look for something that can't be true:

(A) forces P out and thus O in. Since N is not in the first slot, N is out as well. There doesn't seem to be a reason we couldn't organize the remainder—Q, O, L, K, M—with Q coming first. Eliminate (or, if we're feeling timid, defer).

(B) seems uncontroversial. Defer judgment.

(C) triggers M being last. That seems fine, but let's look for other consequences. M shows up in the rules about L and O. If M is last, we can't have either L or O. That doesn't work, since with Q/P occupying one excluded slot, we can't accommodate both L and O on the excluded side. This is our answer!

There is no need to confirm that the other answers could be true, but go right ahead for review's sake.

MANHATTAN
LSAT

3. If the doctor sees K third, which of the following must be true?

    (A) She sees N first.

    (B) She sees Q second.

    (C) She sees L last.

    (D) She sees P.

    (E) She sees O.

(A) is correct.

Let's put K third and see what we see. With K third, M must be either fourth or fifth. But as we learned in the last question, we can't have M last (since it would force both L and O out), so M must be fourth, with either L or O last. What else? Since we can put only one of the L/O option last, we know that the other will be out. This means we're left with:

$$\underset{1}{\underline{\quad}} \quad \underset{2}{\underline{\quad}} \quad \underset{3}{\underline{K}} \quad \underset{4}{\underline{M}} \quad \underset{5}{\underline{L/O}} \quad \Bigg| \quad \underline{Q/P} \quad \underline{L/O}$$

At this point we could start looking at the answer choices, but by asking "who's left?" we'll uncover almost everything. We'll have to have Q or P in, as well as N. And we know for sure that N will go first. Now the answers are a breeze, and (A) is obviously correct.

4. Which of the following must be true?

    (A) If the doctor does not see L, she will also not see Q.

    (B) If the doctor does not see N, she will also not see P.

    (C) If the doctor does not see Q, she will also not see P.

    (D) If the doctor does not see Q, she will also not see O.

    (E) If the doctor does not see O, she will also not see Q.

(E) is correct.

Glancing at the answer choices, it seems that this question will take a bit more time than others. In a sense, each choice is a Conditional question. Let's see if we can move fast.

(A) can be eliminated using the work from our last question. We know that L could be out and Q could be in. Eliminate.

Imagining that we didn't think of using previous work, it would be time-consuming to test out (A)'s scenario, so it's best to look over the rules and see that L and Q have no connection to each other and defer judgment.

(B) doesn't raise any alarms since there's no obvious connection between N and P. Defer.

(C) is flat out false! We know we need to see either Q or P. Eliminate!

(D) raises alarms since Q and O are connected in our rules. However, nothing leads from –Q to –O. Eliminate.

(E) is the reverse of (D), and something that must be true. Our rules tell us that if –O, then P, and if P, then –Q.

5. If the doctor sees M fourth, which of the following could be true?

   (A) The doctor sees K first.
   (B) The doctor sees K second.
   (C) The doctor sees P first.
   (D) The doctor sees Q last.
   (E) The doctor sees P last.

(B) is correct.

With M fourth, L or O must go fifth. We saw this situation in the third question, and hopefully we remember that this means that either L or O is out. Who's left? N must be in—and first—and we have K and Q/P left. Here's our diagram:

$$\underset{1}{\text{N}} \quad \overset{\frown}{\underset{2}{\text{Q/P}} \quad \underset{3}{\text{K}}} \quad \underset{4}{\text{M}} \quad \underset{5}{\text{L/O}} \quad \Big| \quad \text{Q/P} \quad \text{L/O}$$

We want something that could be true, so we can predict that the answer will involve Q/P, K, or L/O.

(A) can't be true, but (B) can. Pull the trigger and move on. (Every other answer, of course, can't be true.)

6. Which of the following, if true, would determine which patients the doctor will see and the order in which she will see them?

   (A) The doctor sees N first and P third.
   (B) The doctor sees N first and Q third.
   (C) The doctor sees K first and M second.
   (D) The doctor sees K first and O fourth.
   (E) The doctor sees K second and M fourth.

(B) is correct.

We're looking for something that will establish both the members and order of the number line. There isn't much preparation to do before diving into the answer choices, but it's worth 10 seconds to consider what issues (choices) will have to be resolved by the correct answer. First and foremost, we'll need something that will decide between Q and P as well as between P and O.

We can tackle each answer choice by first considering whether the answer would establish the five selected patients. If it does, *then* we can consider whether the order is established.

(A) looks promising. N first and P third almost fills up the line. K – M makes four, but who will fill the last spot? It'll have to be either L or O. Since there's no reason it would have to be one or the other, we can eliminate this answer without even considering whether the answer would establish order.

(B) is similar to (A), but since Q is part of different rules than P is, it's definitely worth a closer look. With Q in, we'd need P out. And, with P out, we'd need O in. The roster is set: Q, O, K, M, N. And, with slots 1 and 3 filled by N and Q, K – M must go in slots 2 and 4, leaving O to come after M in the final slot.

Take a moment to confirm for yourself why (C) through (E) would not determine the roster and order, and consider how you might have eliminated—or deferred—quickly.

Extra Positions

We've looked pretty closely at the first flavor of Mismatch Ordering games—extra elements—so let's move to the other flavor, extra positions.

As we mentioned in an earlier example, if there were only five films available to be shown at eight different showtimes, the game might require us to repeat some films. We would represent this situation in the roster like so (notice that the question marks represent the elements that will repeat):

F J K L M ? ? ?

___ ___ ___ ___ ___ ___ ___ ___
 1   2   3   4   5   6   7   8

Or perhaps the game might call for some positions to remain empty. Even if we weren't sure which positions were empty, we'd want to add those empty slots to our roster:

F J K L M x x x

___ ___ ___ ___ ___ ___ ___ ___
 1   2   3   4   5   6   7   8

(It may go without saying, but you can use whatever letter or symbol you want to represent the empty slots—for some, an "e" makes more sense.)

In some cases, we'll figure out which slots are empty. We'll note that as follows:

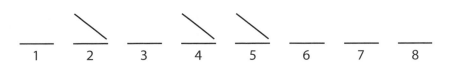

An issue that can come up with extra positions is that empty slots can impact where chunks can go. For example, in the above number line, if K and M had to be consecutive, where could they go? Not too many places!

If you are expected to use elements repeatedly, there often will be special constraints that limit how the elements could fall in the number line, and these rules might be a trigger for framing, or at least for some extra attention. For example, if in the example above we had to use F four times, a typical rule would be, "Two showings of F cannot be consecutive." How many different ways could you arrange those F's? Actually, there are quite a few, but imagine if there were only seven slots….

Regardless of the flavor, and regardless of the specific manner in which you make your notations, it's essential that you notice any mismatches and pay careful attention to the numbers involved. Make sure you're asking yourself the right questions: How many element repeats are needed? Can there be an empty position? How many slots need to double up—or can I have a triple up?

DRILL IT: Mismatch Ordering Setups

Let's quickly practice identifying mismatches and diagramming them correctly. We suggest you check your work after each one.

1. Five political candidates—Hughes, Jones, Kampoyle, Langston, and Nordecki—will appear on a TV talk show during the course of one week, Monday through Sunday. Each candidate will appear exactly once, and no two candidates will appear on the same day. The scheduling of the candidates must adhere to the following conditions:

    Jones must appear after Nordecki and before Kampoyle.

    Either Langston or Hughes must be the last candidate to appear.

    Kampoyle cannot appear on the day immediately following a day on which any other candidate appears.

    Nordecki cannot appear before Tuesday.

2. Exactly four emergency room doctors—Oronsky, Praya, Quayle, and Ralston—must cover all six shifts over the upcoming Wednesday and Thursday. Each day is broken up into three consecutive shifts: morning, afternoon, and evening. Only one doctor will cover each shift, and each doctor must cover at least one shift. The scheduling must adhere to the following rules:

    No doctor can cover consecutive shifts.

    The only shift that Quayle can cover is the afternoon shift on Wednesday.

    Praya will cover the morning shift on Thursday.

    Raltson will cover at least one shift before and one shift after any shift Praya takes.

3. A classical guitarist must perform five different songs from her recent album at an upcoming concert. The album contains a total of eight songs: Revolt, Stampede, Tango, Vein, Waning, Xeric, Yawn, and Zeal. The songs are played one at a time and no other songs are played during the concert. The following rules apply to the order and selection of the songs:

    If S is played, W is not.

    If T is played, it is played third.

    Either X or Y is played, but not both.

    Z is played second.

    V is played.

4. A certain banking website requires a five-digit password that must be composed entirely of the digits 0–6. The following rules apply to any one password:

    No digit may be used twice.

    Either 4 or 5 is the third digit.

    The last digit must be exactly twice the value of the first one.

    Two digits that have consecutive values cannot be used in consecutive positions in a password.

6

Log in to your Student Center for two more (pretty challenging) problems.

SOLUTIONS: Mismatch Ordering Setups

1.

It is easy to assume that L or H must go on Sunday, but there could be an "X" there.

2.

Often you'll figure out the "identity" of one of the mystery repeats as you work through the game's inferences. Above, it became clear we needed at least two R's.

3.

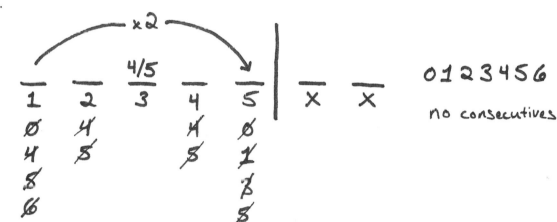

$$\overline{}_{1} \quad \underset{2}{\underline{Z}} \quad \overline{}_{3} \quad \overline{}_{4} \quad \overline{}_{5}$$

S/W	X/Y	
NO	X	

®STVWXYZ

$$S \to -W$$
$$W \to -S$$
$$T \to T_3$$
$$X \longleftrightarrow -Y$$
$$-X \longleftrightarrow Y$$

S

4.

×2

$$\overline{}_{1} \quad \overline{}_{2} \quad \overset{4/5}{\overline{}}_{3} \quad \overline{}_{4} \quad \overline{}_{5} \Big| \quad \overline{X} \quad \overline{X}$$

0123456

no consecutives

1	2		4	5
0̸	4̸		4̸	0̸
4	8̸		8̸	1̸
8				2̸
6̸				8̸

6

Conclusion

Mismatch Ordering games are not very different from the games you've seen so far—except for the mismatch! Mismatches can also show up in other game types, so your ability to handle this twist will be particularly useful.

Key ideas to keep in mind are:

1. Notice the mismatches!

- Don't hesitate to start counting elements and slots. Pay attention to wording about repeats. Don't assume every element is used unless that is stated.

2. Adapt your diagram.

- Draw slots for excluded elements and write multiple copies of elements in your roster if you are sure which elements are repeated. Use place holders—?—if you're not sure.

6

Practice Game 1: PT31, S1, G3

Let's put your brain to work again! Try playing these games back-to-back to work on your endurance. Since we added some extra questions, give yourself a total of 19 minutes for the two games.

During a single week, from Monday through Friday, tours will be conducted of a company's three divisions—Operations, Production, Sales. Exactly five tours will be conducted that week, one each day. The schedule of tours for the week must conform to the following restrictions:

  Each division is toured at least once.
  The Operations division is not toured on Monday.
  The Production division is not toured on Wednesday.
  The Sales division is toured on two consecutive days, and on no other days.
  If the Operations division is toured on Thursday, then the Production division is toured on Friday.

14. Which one of the following CANNOT be true of the week's tour schedule?

  (A) The division that is toured on Monday is also toured on Tuesday.
  (B) The division that is toured on Monday is also toured on Friday.
  (C) The division that is toured on Tuesday is also toured on Thursday.
  (D) The division that is toured on Wednesday is also toured on Friday.
  (E) The division that is toured on Thursday is also toured on Friday.

15. If in addition to the Sales division one other division is toured on two consecutive days, then it could be true of the week's tour schedule both that the

  (A) Production division is toured on Monday and that the Operations division is toured on Thursday
  (B) Production division is toured on Tuesday and that the Sales division is toured on Wednesday
  (C) Operations division is toured on Tuesday and that the Production division is toured on Friday
  (D) Sales division is toured on Monday and that the Operations division is toured on Friday
  (E) Sales division is toured on Wednesday and that the Production division is toured on Friday

16. If in the week's tour schedule the division that is toured on Tuesday is also toured on Friday, then for which one of the following days must a tour of the Production division be scheduled?

  (A) Monday
  (B) Tuesday
  (C) Wednesday
  (D) Thursday
  (E) Friday

17. If in the week's tour schedule the division that is toured on Monday is not the division that is toured on Tuesday, then which one of the following could be true of the week's schedule?

  (A) A tour of the Sales division is scheduled for some day earlier in the week than is any tour of the Production division.
  (B) A tour of the Operations division is scheduled for some day earlier in the week than is any tour of the Production division
  (C) The Sales division is toured on Monday.
  (D) The Production division is toured on Tuesday.
  (E) The Operations division is toured on Wednesday.

18. If in the week's tour schedule the division that is toured on Tuesday is also toured on Wednesday, then which one of the following must be true of the week's tour schedule?

  (A) The Production division is toured on Monday.
  (B) The Operations division is toured on Tuesday.
  (C) The Sales division is toured on Wednesday.
  (D) The Sales division is toured on Thursday.
  (E) The Production division is toured on Friday.

P

Now try a question that we wrote for this game:

19. Which of the following, if substituted for the rule that if the Operations division is toured on Thursday, then the Production division is toured on Friday, would have the same effect in determining when each division is toured?

   (A) If the Production division is toured on Friday, the Operations division is toured on Thursday.

   (B) If the Operations division is not toured on Thursday, the Production division is not toured on Friday.

   (C) The Production and Operations divisions must be toured on consecutive days at least once during the week.

   (D) The Production division cannot be toured on consecutive days.

   (E) If the Operations division is toured on consecutive days, one of those days must be Wednesday.

MANHATTAN
LSAT

Practice Game Solution 1: PT31, S1, G3

Picture the Game

We've got to fill five slots—Monday through Friday—with three different types of tours. Before looking at the rules, we know that some of the divisions will have to be toured multiple times. Glancing at the rules, we can see a conditional rule and some restrictions on elements. Let's bust out our number line and move to the rules.

Notate the Rules and Make Inferences

> Each division is toured at least once.

The first rule is straightforward. If each division is toured at least once, we have only two extra tours to account for.

> The Operations division is not toured on Monday.
> The Production division is not toured on Wednesday.

The second and third rules offer simple restrictions.

> The Sales division is toured on two consecutive days, and on no other days.

The fourth rule gives us two pieces of information. 1) that there are two S's, and 2) that those S's are a consecutive chunk.

> If the Operations division is toured on Thursday, then the Production division is toured on Friday.

The last rule is a simple conditional that should be noted to the side. If we're not disciplined, this is the sort of rule that's easy to forget about once we're knee-deep in the questions. We probably don't need to write out the contrapositive, but it's something to keep an eye on.

Our diagram looks like this so far:

No inferences came to mind as we notated each rule. And still, with a second glance, nothing is coming to mind!

The Big Pause

The only issue that seems worth considering in this game is the SS chunk. How many different places could that go? There are four possibilities. And does each one have significant consequences? With such a limited number of elements, it seems more than likely. Is it worth framing? Sure! (That said, it's 100% possible to solve this game without frames, and, as you'll see in the solutions, the frames don't make the game significantly easier.)

If you didn't frame this game, take a moment to write out the four frames based on the possibilities for placing the SS chunk.

Here's what you should have come up with:

You might have filled in a bit more, though the above is fine as is. For example, in frame #3, you might have written in "O/" and "O/" in the Tuesday and Friday slots (though it'd be important to remember that O could go in both). On the flip side, in frame #2, maybe you didn't realize that you must have an O and P in the last two slots since you can't have two P's in those slots—we need at least one O during the week—and two O's would violate the O on Thursday rule. But you probably would have figured that out when you went to use the third frame

With our without our frames, let's move to the questions.

Attack the Questions

14. Which one of the following CANNOT be true of the week's tour schedule?

    (A) The division that is toured on Monday is also toured on Tuesday.

    (B) The division that is toured on Monday is also toured on Friday.

    (C) The division that is toured on Tuesday is also toured on Thursday.

    (D) The division that is toured on Wednesday is also toured on Friday.

    (E) The division that is toured on Thursday is also toured on Friday.

(C) is correct.

This is not our standard Orientation question; we can't just use each rule and tick off wrong answers. Plus, it's a must be false question! How dare the LSAT make us do some thinking this early on in the game? But even though it's not a standard Orientation question, it is the first question of the game. Thus, if we've done a decent job of picturing the game, diagramming, and making inferences, we should find this question pretty easy. Let's look at how we might approach the question with and without frames.

We're looking for something that must be false.

Without frames

(A) seems to have no problems—couldn't we have SS on Monday and Tuesday?

(B) seems to be OK as well. The right answer to this first question shouldn't require much thought, so we probably should defer on this choice. But with such a small number of elements, it won't be hard to quickly think up the rough outline of a

scenario: P would have to be the tour on Monday and Friday. We can definitely find somewhere to place the SS chunk and the O. Eliminate.

(C) effectively blocks out the SS chunk. With Tuesday and Thursday taken up by a tour other than S (since the SS chunk must be in consecutive slots), where could we place the chunk? Nowhere. This is our answer.

With frames

	M	T	W	Th	F
4	P		O	S	S
3	P		S	S	
2	P	S	S	O P (circled)	
1	S	S	O	P (circled)	

Ø   P

$O_{th} \rightarrow P_f$

(A) is possible in frames 1, 3 and 4. Eliminate.

(B) is possible in frames 2 and 3. Eliminate.

(C) is not possible in any frame. Correct!

(D) is possible in frame 1.

(E) is possible in frames 1 and 4.

15. If in addition to the Sales division one other division is toured on two consecutive days, then it could be true of the week's tour schedule both that the

(A) Production division is toured on Monday and that the Operations division is toured on Thursday

(B) Production division is toured on Tuesday and that the Sales division is toured on Wednesday

(C) Operations division is toured on Tuesday and that the Production division is toured on Friday

(D) Sales division is toured on Monday and that the Operations division is toured on Friday

(E) Sales division is toured on Wednesday and that the Production division is toured on Friday

(B) is correct.

Our first Conditional question is an unusual one! We'll look at this both with and without frames.

Without Frames

Along with SS, we have either an OO or a PP chunk. What does this mean? It's hard to say—it seems that the chunks could go in lots of places. Let's turn to the answer choices.

(A) isn't easy to eliminate without a bit of thought. With P on Monday and O on Thursday, we'll need to put a P on Friday because of the last rule. The only place for our SS chunk is Tuesday and Wednesday. Consider the situation for a moment; we already have five tours, from Monday to Friday: P S S O P. Where's the second chunk? Eliminate.

(B) works out easily. The arrangement could be P P S S O.

With Frames

(A) looks possible in frame #2, but we won't be able to have a second double chunk, since Thursday and Friday cannot be OO. Eliminate.

(B) is possible in frame #3: P P S S O.

Take a moment to confirm for yourself why each of the other answers cannot be true.

16. If in the week's tour schedule the division that is toured on Tuesday is also toured on Friday, then for which one of the following days must a tour of the Production division be scheduled?

(A) Monday
(B) Tuesday
(C) Wednesday
(D) Thursday
(E) Friday

(A) is correct.

Let's consider the impact of the new condition. Who could show up on both Tuesday and Friday? It obviously can't be S. And it can't be P, since with two P's and two S's occupying Tuesday through Friday, we'd be left putting O on Monday, which is illegal.

Thus, we know the arrangement is P O S S O (which, incidentally, means "May I" in Italian).

No need to use frames here! The answer is clearly (A).

17. If in the week's tour schedule the division that is toured on Monday is not the division that is toured on Tuesday, then which one of the following could be true of the week's schedule?

   (A) A tour of the Sales division is scheduled for some day earlier in the week than is any tour of the Production division.
   (B) A tour of the Operations division is scheduled for some day earlier in the week than is any tour of the Production division.
   (C) The Sales division is toured on Monday.
   (D) The Production division is toured on Tuesday.
   (E) The Operations division is toured on Wednesday.

(E) is correct.

Here's another unusual Conditional question. What can we infer if Monday's and Tuesday's tours need to be different? That means S can't be on Monday, and since O can never go on Monday, we know we have P there. Who could be on Tuesday? Either O or S.

$$\frac{P}{M} \quad \frac{O/S}{T} \quad \frac{\quad}{W} \quad \frac{\quad}{Th} \quad \frac{\quad}{F}$$

What else can we infer?

Eek—nothing is coming to mind. The clock is ticking, so we'll dive into the answer choices and eliminate those that can't be true.

(A) can't be true since we know the week starts with a P.

(B) is wrong for the same reason as (A).

(C) is clearly wrong.

(D) is clearly wrong.

(E) is fine; we'd put another O on Tuesday, and the SS chunk on Thursday and Friday.

Here's a great example of a Conditional question in which there's not much to infer from the new condition, but the question writer made the answer choices easy to eliminate regardless. You don't have to panic when a new condition doesn't lead to a cascade of inferences.

18. If in the week's tour schedule the division that is toured on Tuesday is also toured on Wednesday, then which one of the following must be true of the week's tour schedule?

   (A) The Production division is toured on Monday.
   (B) The Operations division is toured on Tuesday.
   (C) The Sales division is toured on Wednesday.
   (D) The Sales division is toured on Thursday.
   (E) The Production division is toured on Friday.

(A) is correct.

At this point, we're used to these sorts of Conditional questions. If Tuesday and Wednesday have the same tour, we're either facing SS or OO on those days, (P can't go on Wednesday). With S unable to go on Monday in either case, we know that P must go there (since O is always restricted from Monday). (A) wins!

19. Which of the following, if substituted for the rule that if the Operations division is toured on Thursday, then the Production division is toured on Friday, would have the same effect in determining when each division is toured?

   (A) If the Production division is toured on Friday, the Operations division is toured on Thursday.
   (B) If the Operations division is not toured on Thursday, the Production division is not toured on Friday.
   (C) The Production and Operations divisions must be toured on consecutive days at least once during the week.
   (D) The Production division cannot be toured on consecutive days.
   (E) If the Operations division is toured on consecutive days, one of those days must be Wednesday.

(E) is correct.

This a tough Equivalent Rule question we wrote! We should start by understanding the impact of the original rule. Frankly, there's not too much impact! But we can consider the few things the rule prevents and allows on Thursday and Friday: PP, PO, and OP are allowed, but OO is not. We haven't figured out much, but it's a simple rule, so let's move to the answer choices:

(A) is tricky, but if we know our conditional logic it's easy to eliminate this reversal of the original rule. $O_{th} \rightarrow P_f$ does not mean $P_f \rightarrow O_{th}$!

(B) is similar to (A). Negating both sides of a conditional statement is not "legal." Eliminate.

(C) is tough to digest quickly, and might deserve an initial deferral of judgement. However, in the end, (C) is more than we need. Can we think of a scenario that was possible under the original rule that isn't under this one? Yes! P P S S O. The correct answer cannot add more restrictions than the original rule provided. Eliminate.

(D) is similar to (C). Why are we restricting P P S S O? Don't be a hater. Eliminate.

(E) is a tough answer to accept if you were looking only for a simple rewording. This answer hinges on the consequences of the original rule: that we can't have OO on Thursday and Friday. The only options under the original rule—and answer (E)—are that if there is an OO chunk, it falls on Tuesday and Wednesday or Wednesday and Thursday. Either way, one O of the OO chunk lands on Wednesday.

Practice Game 2: PT35, S3, G4

Exactly seven professors—Madison, Nilsson, Orozco, Paton, Robinson, Sarkis, and Togo— were hired in the years 1989 through 1995. Each professor has one or more specialities, and any two professors hired in the same year or in consecutive years do not have a specialty in common. The professors were hired according to the following conditions:

> Madison was hired in 1993, Robinson in 1991.
> There is at least one specialty that Madison, Orozco, and Togo have in common.
> Nilsson shares a specialty with Robinson.
> Paton and Sarkis were each hired at least one year before Madison and at least one year after Nilsson.
> Orozco, who shares a specialty with Sarkis, was hired in 1990.

18. Which one of the following is a complete and accurate list of the professors who could have been hired in the years 1989 through 1991?

    (A) Nilsson, Orozco, Robinson
    (B) Orozco, Robinson, Sarkis
    (C) Nilsson, Orozco, Paton, Robinson
    (D) Nilsson, Orozco, Paton, Sarkis
    (E) Orozco, Paton, Robinson, Sarkis

19. If exactly one professor was hired in 1991, then which one of the following could be true?

    (A) Madison and Paton share a specialty.
    (B) Robinson and Sarkis share a specialty.
    (C) Paton was hired exactly one year after Orozco.
    (D) Exactly one professor was hired in 1994.
    (E) Exactly two professors were hired in 1993.

20. Which one of the following must be false?

    (A) Nilsson was hired in 1989.
    (B) Paton was hired in 1990.
    (C) Paton was hired in 1991.
    (D) Sarkis was hired in 1992.
    (E) Togo was hired in 1994.

21. Which one of the following must be true?

    (A) Orozco was hired before Paton.
    (B) Paton was hired before Sarkis.
    (C) Sarkis was hired before Robinson.
    (D) Robinson was hired before Sarkis.
    (E) Madison was hired before Sarkis.

22. If exactly two professors were hired in 1992, then which one of the following could be true?

    (A) Orozco, Paton, and Togo share a specialty.
    (B) Madison, Paton, and Togo share a specialty.
    (C) Exactly two professors were hired in 1991.
    (D) Exactly two professors were hired in 1993.
    (E) Paton was hired in 1991.

23. If Paton and Madison have a specialty in common, then which one of the following must be true?

    (A) Nilsson does not share a specialty with Paton.
    (B) Exactly one professor was hired in 1990.
    (C) Exactly one professor was hired in 1991.
    (D) Exactly two professors were hired in each of two years.
    (E) Paton was hired at least one year before Sarkis.

And try a question that we wrote for this game:

24. Which of the following, if substituted for the rule that there is at least one specialty that Madison, Orozco, and Togo have in common, would have the same consequence in determining when each professor was hired?

(A) Togo was hired at some point after Madison.

(B) A professor was hired in 1995.

(C) Madison and Togo each share a specialty with Orozco.

(D) Paton was hired at least three years before Togo.

(E) Madison was hired in a year immediately before or immediately after a year in which no other professor was hired, but not both.

P

Practice Game Solution 2: PT35, S3, G4

Picture the Game

We have seven professors and… wait, how many years is that? There's no reason to start subtracting—since we'll be writing out those years, we'll simply count 'em! Even though 95 − 89 is 6, there are actually seven years! (If you subtract to find the number of elements in a set, you have to add one element back to the answer—think about it.) Seven professors and seven years doesn't seem like much of a mismatch! However, in the second sentence we see this clue: "…any two professors hired in the same year…." If two professors were hired in the same year, we have extra positions. Since we aren't told the maximum number of professors hired in a year, for now we'll simply start with a number line (instead of stacking multiple rows).

Along with the nearly hidden mismatch issue, another twist to this game is the rule about specialties. At first glance it might seem like we'll need to assign subcategories to the positions, as in a 3D Ordering game; however, the true impact is different. The specialty rule is used to tell us which elements cannot be consecutive. Tricky!

Notate the Rules and Make Inferences

> Madison was hired in 1993, Robinson in 1991.

The first rule gives us two easy-to-add pieces of information. Nothing yet to infer.

> There is at least one specialty that Madison, Orozco, and Togo have in common.

The second rule is much more complex. If M, O, and T all have one specialty in common, we know that none of them can be next to each other. We can notate each restriction separately—~~MT~~, ~~MO~~, and ~~TO~~—but it's probably enough to simply write the rule down as well as make inferences based on the combination of this and the previous rule.

So far we have:

MTO not consec.

$$\frac{}{89} \quad \frac{}{90} \quad \frac{R}{91} \quad \frac{}{92} \quad \frac{M}{93} \quad \frac{}{94} \quad \frac{}{95}$$

MNOPRST

(with T̸/Ø below 92, 93, and 94)

> Nilsson shares a specialty with Robinson.

The third rule should be immediately translated into "N cannot be next to R" and the restrictions around R added to the diagram.

Paton and Sarkis were each hired at least one year before Madison and at least one year after Nilsson.

The fourth rule provides a hefty piece of relative ordering information. Since it's easy to mix up a rule like this, first notate the rule to the side, and then see how it fits into the diagram. With P and S coming before M, they must fall somewhere from '89 to '92. However, since they must come after N, which cannot be in '90, '91, or '92, we know that N is in '89, and P and S are somewhere between '90 and '92.

Orozco, who shares a specialty with Sarkis, was hired in 1990.

The final rule allows us to make our diagram even more defined. If O is in '90, and can't be next to S, S can only come in '92.

With so many rules and relationships, let's definitely take one more tour through the rules to see if there are any more inferences we can glean. One fruitful line of thought here is to consider where T can go. The second rule tells us that it can't be next to M or O, so the only place it can go is '95.

What goes in '94? Apparently nothing, and indeed the scenario never states that a professor is hired in each year. So our final diagram should look something like this:

The Big Pause

What seems to be the issue that this game will hinge on? Since everything other than P's placement is set, we can be sure that a lot of questions will hinge on P! With so little left undetermined, there's no reason not to dive into the questions.

Attack the Questions

18. Which one of the following is a complete and accurate list of the professors who could have been hired in the years 1989 through 1991?

    (A) Nilsson, Orozco, Robinson
    (B) Orozco, Robinson, Sarkis
    (C) Nilsson, Orozco, Paton, Robinson
    (D) Nilsson, Orozco, Paton, Sarkis
    (E) Orozco, Paton, Robinson, Sarkis

(C) is correct.

As in the last game, our first question is not best approached using the standard Orientation approach. Since we've inferred so many placements, let's just compare the answers against our diagram. Eliminate (B), (D), and (E) since they each contain an S, which must come in '92. If you misinterpreted the question, both (A) and (C) might seem correct. (A) is a possible list—one that could work—but it is not a complete list of those who could have been hired in that time frame, since it is missing P.

If you're still confused, compare these two question stems:

Which one of the following is a complete and accurate list of the professors who could have been hired in the years 1989 through 1991?

Which one of the following could be a complete and accurate list of the professors hired in the years 1989 through 1991?

Note the different placements of the word "could."

The actual question—the first one—is asking for *a list of all possibilities*, while the second one is asking for *a possible list*.

19. If exactly one professor was hired in 1991, then which one of the following could be true?

    (A) Madison and Paton share a specialty.
    (B) Robinson and Sarkis share a specialty.
    (C) Paton was hired exactly one year after Orozco.
    (D) Exactly one professor was hired in 1994.
    (E) Exactly two professors were hired in 1993.

(A) is correct.

The new condition in this question tells us that P was hired either in '90 or '92. With that in mind, it's easy to evaluate and choose (A). If P were hired in '90, there'd be no reason P and M couldn't share a specialty.

Notice that three of the four incorrect answer choices are NEVER true, while the remaining choice, (C), cannot be true given this new condition.

20. Which one of the following must be false?

    (A) Nilsson was hired in 1989.
    (B) Paton was hired in 1990.
    (C) Paton was hired in 1991.
    (D) Sarkis was hired in 1992.
    (E) Togo was hired in 1994.

(E) is correct.

We can quickly work from our original diagram. (A) through (D) either are true or could be true; (E) is false.

21. Which one of the following must be true?

    (A) Orozco was hired before Paton.
    (B) Paton was hired before Sarkis.
    (C) Sarkis was hired before Robinson.
    (D) Robinson was hired before Sarkis.
    (E) Madison was hired before Sarkis.

(D) is correct.

With a diagram that's almost fully determined, it's no surprise that we're facing another easy question. What's there to say other than that (D) must be true? (A), (B), (C), and (E) either must be false or could be false.

22. If exactly two professors were hired in 1992, then which one of the following could be true?

    (A) Orozco, Paton, and Togo share a specialty.
    (B) Madison, Paton, and Togo share a specialty.
    (C) Exactly two professors were hired in 1991.
    (D) Exactly two professors were hired in 1993.
    (E) Paton was hired in 1991.

(A) is correct.

If we place P above S in '92, P is at least two slots from both O and T, and there's no problem if they share a specialty. (B) through (E) are all clearly false.

23. If Paton and Madison have a specialty in common, then which one of the following must be true?

    (A) Nilsson does not share a specialty with Paton.
    (B) Exactly one professor was hired in 1990.

    (C) Exactly one professor was hired in 1991.
    (D) Exactly two professors were hired in each of two years.
    (E) Paton was hired at least one year before Sarkis.

(E) is correct.

If P and M cannot be next to each other, P must be in either '90 or '91. Either way, P was hired *at least* one year before S.

(A) could be false if P was hired in '91.

(B) would be false if P was hired in '90.

(C) would be false if P was hired in '91.

(D) is always false. There is always exactly one double year—the year in which Paton is hired.

24. Which of the following, if substituted for the rule that there is at least one specialty that Madison, Orozco, and Togo have in common, would have the same consequence in determining when each professor was hired?

    (A) Togo was hired at some point after Madison.
    (B) A professor was hired in 1995.
    (C) Both Madison and Togo share a specialty with Orozco.
    (D) Paton was hired at least three years before Togo.
    (E) Madison was hired in a year immediately before or immediately after a year in which no other professor was hired, but not both.

(B) is correct.

This is the question we wrote for this game. The original rule required us to keep M, O, and T apart. Since we learn through other rules that M was hired in '93 and O was hired in '90, the only relevant impact of this rule is that T must have been hired in '95. With that in mind, let's look at the answer choices.

(A) is easy to eliminate, since it would allow T to be hired in '94.

(B) seems too "weak" to be the correct answer, but if we must have a professor hired in '95, who could it be? N, P, O, R, S, and M are already locked in before '94, so it must be T.

(C) seems very similar to the original rule, but the slight difference in wording is crucial. The original rule has M, O, and T all sharing at least one specialty. While (C) would also allow that, it also permits a situation in which M and O share one specialty and T and O share a different specialty. In this case, M and T might be hired consecutively, and we'd end up with T in '94.

(D) is tempting, but since P could have been hired in '90 or '91, this rule would allow T to be hired in '93 or '94.

(E) is tricky! It requires that there be an "empty" year either before or after M, and since M was hired in '93 and S in '92, we know that we must leave '94 blank. However, does T have to be hired in '95? No! Under this rule, T could have been hired in '93.

P

Chapter 7
of Logic Games

Timing

In This Chapter...

Timing

At this point, you've learned several different game types and you've played a fair number of games. If you've been following our timing suggestions for practice games, you've probably already experienced some timing struggles. Don't worry; at first almost everybody struggles to finish the games section within 35 minutes. Furthermore, you're already on your way to understanding the primary solution: picturing games, effectively notating the rules, and making inferences before attacking the questions. Later in this book you'll learn how to diagram Grouping games. You will speed up quite a bit once that's all in place. But it's also time to start working on some of the more timing-specific strategies—the icing on the timing cake. Let's start by looking at the games section as a whole.

Section Timing

35 minutes ÷ 4 games = 8:45/game. Right?

That formula would work well if every game were the same difficulty level. But, as you surely already know, there are games and there are GAMES. Fortunately, the test writers balance out the difficulty of the games so that the overall difficulty of games sections is fairly consistent. On test day, most prepared test-takers find one or two games quite easy, one or two average, and one tough.

The difficulty of the games generally increases from the first game to the last. However, this is very much a generality. It's quite possible that you—or even most everyone taking an LSAT—will find the third game to be the hardest of the section. The difficulty of each game falls into a general range:

7

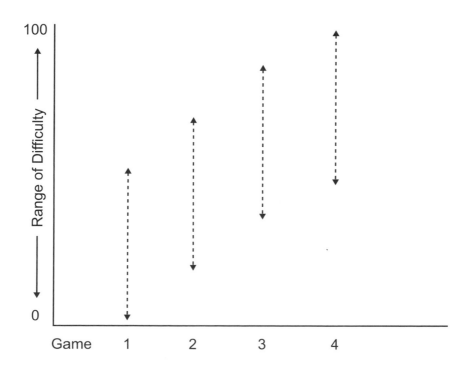

And, while the specific difficulty of each game might vary and fall "out of order," the section's difficulty will average out:

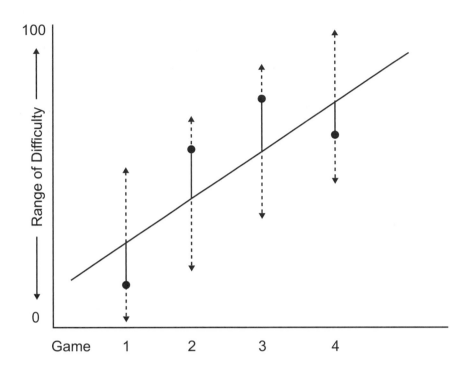

In general, you want to spend less time on the easy games and more time on the tougher ones. Perhaps your timing will be such that you spend 7 minutes on the easiest game, 8 on the next hardest, 9 on the next, and 11 on the hardest one. But it's unrealistic to expect this to happen, or, more importantly, to try to make your game playing fit into that plan. You might face two easy games and two harder ones, requiring a 6, 6, 11, 12 timing. Furthermore, you won't know the difficulty of each game until you are in the midst of it. A rigid timing strategy is counterproductive.

Instead, develop a flexible timing strategy. We suggest that you use what we call the "Time Bank." The idea is to allot each game 8 minutes, leaving 3 minutes in the bank. If the first game takes only 6 minutes—and that's possible—you now have a total 5 minutes in the bank. Then, if the second game ends up taking 9 minutes, you're now down to 4 minutes in the bank. And then if the third game... you get the idea!

Skipping Games vs. Skipping Questions

One obvious way to put more time in the bank is to skip an entire game. This is not a strategy we recommend—and we'll explain why—but let's spend a moment understanding why some might be attracted to this plan. Planning to skip a game automatically gives you an average of 11:40 minutes per game, making it much easier to work through a game and recover from errors. If someone uses a lot of time-consuming trial and error, having 11:40 minutes per game is useful. But the downside is obvious—you can expect to miss almost all the questions on the game you skip! Planning to skip a game is a strategy we would suggest only to students who are a week away from test day, have never been able to finish all four games, and are usually in a mad rush on the last two games. For everyone else, we recommend that you set a goal of finishing all four games. If skipping is required, **skip tough and time-consuming questions**.

To illustrate why this is a better strategy, compare these two performances by the same average (or slightly below average) hypothetical test-taker on the same hypothetical logic games section:

Grant "the Game Skipper"	Quinn "the Question Skipper"
Game 1: 10 minutes. 5/6 correct. One wrong because of a silly mistake.	Game 1: 9 minutes. 5/6 correct. One wrong because of a silly mistake.
Game 2: 13 minutes. 6/6. Perfect performance! That fifth question was a doozy, though!	Game 2: 9 minutes. 5/6 correct. Had to skip and guess (incorrectly) on that fifth question when it was clear that it would be too time-consuming.
Game 3: 1 minute. 1/5 correct. Skipped the game when he realized it was tough, and guessed (D) for every answer.	Game 3: 10 minutes. 3/5 correct. Last two questions skipped (guessed incorrectly) when they quickly proved very difficult.
Game 4: 11 minutes. 4/5 correct. Had to guess (incorrectly) on that last really tough fourth question after spending two and a half minutes on it.	Game 4: 7 minutes. 4/5. Had to skip and guess (incorrectly) on that really tough fourth question when it was clear that time was running out.
Guesses: 6 Score: 16/22	Guesses: 4 Score: 17/22

Clearly, the point of the dramatic game-by-game comparison is that skipping questions is a better strategy than skipping games. But why did it work out better? It wasn't because Grant guessed on significantly more questions—Quinn guessed on four! Quinn did better because she didn't spend a lot of time on the hardest questions of the section. Instead, she invested that time in the easier questions of the game that Grant skipped. In short, she got the easy ones right, and the hard ones wrong. Grant, on the other hand, got many easy ones right and several—in the skipped game—wrong, and he conquered only a couple more of the hard ones than Quinn. Furthermore, if Grant had actually needed three minutes to figure out that the third Game was the one he wanted to skip, he might have found himself performing even worse on the final game of the section.

We've made our point, but the truth is that we've fudged the numbers—it's highly unlikely that anyone who needs to skip an entire game could actually perform as well as Grant. If you are able to correctly answer all or close to all of the questions for three games, you already have significant skills at Logic Games and it's likely that by improving your approach—for instance, by learning to follow the inference chain instead of using trial and error—you can get to all four games.

If you ignore our number-fudging, Quinn did only one point better than Grant. That's not incredibly compelling. But if Quinn sticks with her strategy through months of prep, she'll develop the ability to tell when a question is too tough for her and she'll also be regularly challenging herself to move faster. Grant will focus on becoming better at confirming the answers to his three games, probably using time-consuming trial and error, and he will not expose himself to the hardest games under the pressure of the clock, since he'll be skipping those.

Join Quinn's question-skipping team; commit to trying every game and question. As you develop your abilities, you should soon find yourself skipping only two or three questions per section. And because you'll be comfortable moving on from impossible questions, you will not fall for the most deadly of Logic Game traps: wasting so much time on two tough questions that you have no time for four easy ones.

In summary, **if you're not expecting to get a perfect score on the games section, get the easy and average ones right, and the hardest ones wrong.** Quickly tackling the easy questions and skipping the impossible ones gives you time in the bank to spend on the challenging-but-doable ones.

Developing Your Personal Timing Strategy

The Time Bank is designed to adapt to the reality of whatever game section you're facing. In one sense, it's impossible to plan how it will work out. However, it's useful to set some goals to push yourself to move faster. Each person's timing strategy will be different, and it's up to you to develop your own. Base it on the data you'll gather as you take many practice tests—especially the ones you take after you've learned all the game types. But the truth is that it's too early in your prep for you to decide what overall section timing strategy works best for you. Since you still don't know all the game types, for now, simply note the time each game takes you and start noticing what timing patterns emerge. How fast can you go on those easier games? When you spend 13 minutes on a game, do you get all the questions right, and do you have enough time for the subsequent games? In other words, is it worth it to spend that much time? When you skip time-consuming questions, does it seem to "pay off?" Can you finish the games we assign in this book in our recommended time limits if you let go of one question?

Game-Specific Timing

Hitting your timing goals requires you to manage your timing within each game. Part of this is understanding when to speed up and when to slow down. The Big Pause is a great example of how slowing down can allow you to speed up later. Another piece of the puzzle is being comfortable adapting your game timing to both front-end and back-end games.

As you know, front-end games require more time in their setup phase. There are important inferences to be made before tackling the questions. On the other hand, there are few inferences to be made during the setups for back-end games, but the questions will take longer. Here is a chart showing the tendencies of the games we've looked at so far in terms of where your time will probably be spent:

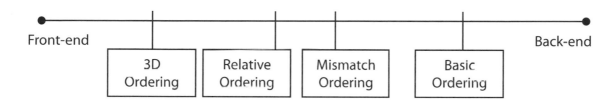

Obviously, these are broad tendencies. Can there be a Basic Ordering game that calls for a complex diagram involving frames? Of course. The idea is not that you see a Basic Ordering game, decide that you should be into the first question after 1:30, and freak out when you're not. You clearly have to adjust to the game in front of you. More important than memorizing which game type falls where on the spectrum is developing a sense of whether a specific game's diagram deserves more time. Erring on either side of that decision—not thinking enough about a front-end game, or spinning your wheels for a long time on a back-end diagram when there is nothing more to discover—will slow you down.

Reordering Questions

Clearly some questions are easier than others. Some students thus reason that if their job is to get the easier ones right and the hardest ones wrong, they should start with the easier questions to make sure they get to them. We do not recommend this strategy, but, as we did with the idea of skipping a game, let's spend a moment examining it.

To some extent, we agree: if you're in a mad dash for time on the last game, go for the easier questions. The first two questions of a game are generally much easier than the rest. Conditional questions can be a bit easier to jump into since they give you something to work with and some Unconditional questions are quite time-consuming—since there's no condition setting off a chain of inferences, each answer choice may require some thinking.

However, there are some problems with turning this under-the-wire strategy into how you approach every game. Many questions do not neatly follow the "law" about difficulty levels—Conditional questions can be much harder than unconditional ones. Furthermore, since the questions in a game are laid out in a generally increasing order of difficulty, moving through the game in the given order means that earlier questions serve as warm-ups for the harder ones. Each question is an opportunity to further "own" the rules and to prepare to apply them on later questions in more complex ways.

Your focus should be on understanding the game and attacking each question correctly. Picking and choosing questions is a distraction, and it takes up precious time. If you're aiming for a 170+ score, few questions, if any, should be out of your reach.

What we *do* recommend is *skipping* questions. As we discussed earlier, know how many questions you can get wrong and still achieve your goal, remember that every question is worth the same number of points, and develop your sense of when enough is enough on a given question. Finally, recognize that some question types are simply designed to take more time (Equivalent Rule questions, unconditional could be questions with dense answer choices, etc.). If you're in a rush, circle the question and guess at the answer. Then, come back later and try it if you have time.

Practice Makes Perfect

You cannot wait until the last few weeks of your prep to improve your timing. You need to start now. That doesn't mean that you can never allow yourself extra time during your practice sessions. It can be useful to take a little more time when first implementing a new diagram, or when replaying a game to see where it went wrong. But in general, set goals for each game and stick to them. It's just as important to practice making the hard choice to skip a question as it is to defeat the insane time-consuming questions. You can always go back after your time is up, reset the timer for 1:30, and give that tough problem another shot. Practice timing as much as you practice everything else.

With that in mind, the next chapter includes a really tough four-game section that we cobbled together with rogue games. It's unlikely that you'll finish within 35 minutes, and it's unlikely that you'll see such a section on a real LSAT. It might seem like an extra-hard section is not the right place to begin working on your timing, but it's actually perfect. You know that the section is "rigged," so give yourself permission to skip questions.

Chapter 8
of Logic Games

Ordering Review

In This Chapter...

What Have We Done?

Are you ready to stop putting things in order? We hope not—look at how often ordering shows up on recent LSATs:

Game Type	Percent of All Games *(PT41–63)*
Basic Ordering	18%
Relative Ordering	13%
3D Ordering	10%
Mismatch Ordering	9%
Ordering Total	**50%**
Open Conditional Grouping	8%
Closed Conditional Grouping	4%
Basic Grouping	9%
Open Grouping	11%
3D Grouping	2%
Grouping Total	**34%**
Hybrid	**14%**
Misc	**2%**

Ordering Family games make up about half of all the games you'll see. As you'll learn in a later chapter, Hybrid games also include ordering, so nearly two out of every three games involve ordering. With so many opportunities to grab points, let's spend a moment reviewing what we've learned and putting it into practice once again.

The Big Ordering Issues

Logic Games are based on either **ordering elements** or **putting elements in groups**, or—as we'll see later—both! The list of twists is limited to the following:

- Elements are further defined by subsets (e.g., "R, S, T, and V are girls, while W, X, and Y are boys").
- Positions are further defined by subsets (e.g., "Three of the interviews will be conducted in person, and four will be conducted on the phone.").
- There can be mismatches (extra elements or extra positions).

With only two major families and just those three twists, it's tempting to say, "That's it!" But we all know that the folks writing the LSAT are devilishly talented at making those twists very twisty! The more important takeaway is that the games and their twists are almost always based on a few "moves" that you can become familiar with. This is NOT to say that you should have a specific plan for every

8

possible game. Inevitably, on your LSAT there will be a twist that seems novel to you, and for which you're going to need to tinker with your usual approach. We're back to MacGyver!

Clearly you're not going to become a MacGyver by simply reading about games and twists. You'll need to do some serious practice, and maybe get a new haircut. To make that practice count, keep two ideas in mind:

1. Quantity

You want to do *a lot* of practice logic games before test day. Unlike the geeks writing this book, most likely you're not playing logic games as part of your job, so you'll need to allocate plenty of time for repeated practice.

While we recommend real LSAT games over "fakes," if you have seen most of the available games, or you'd like to play some particularly challenging ones, look on our site for some games that our teachers have written (http://www.manhattanlsat.com/logic-games-practice.cfm).

2. Quality

Simply playing game after game will not lead you to break through to your highest possible score. You also need to learn from your missteps and use each game to tighten your game playing.

Carefully dissect and replay tougher games immediately after your timed practice sets (and *before* you check your answers). Consider which of the three twists, if any, were used in the game. For an easier game, could you have played it any faster? For any game, could you have arranged your base differently? Could you have framed it in some novel way? What scrappy moves could you have used to speed up? Notice what sort of questions suck you in and leave you doing a lot more work than you need to when really the answer is just waiting for you with a "d'oh!" For the toughest games, rework them until you can solve them quickly and smoothly.

After you've learned what you can—and perhaps read our thoughts by flipping to the back of this book or to our forums (www.manhattanlsat.com/forums)—wait about 10 days and replay the game. This amount of time should help "seal in" what you learned from the game. If needed, rinse and repeat.

8

A Ridiculously Hard Sample Section

Here comes one final practice set before we leave the Ordering Family. While we're tempted to give you an opportunity to revel in how much you've learned by throwing you a standard set for you to knock out of the park, we're instead going to show you some tough love and throw you one of the twistier games sections you'll ever see. We've specifically chosen these four games to give you a chance to stretch your ordering brain. They all have an interesting twist, and some are harder to unlock than others. Don't be surprised when you find yourself struggling far more than you normally do, and don't give up or go over time.

At the end of the section, we'll ask you to reflect on how you did in terms of the four stages (Picture the Game, Notate the Rules and Make Inferences, The Big Pause, and Attack the Questions) and to identify your areas for development.

When you're done with the set, resist the temptation to check your answers immediately. Instead walk through the review process with us.

Enough talk, let's do some games! Give yourself 35 minutes.

8

Practice Game 1: PT36, S4, G2

A radio talk show host airs five telephone calls sequentially. The calls, one from each of Felicia, Gwen, Henry, Isaac, and Mel, are each either live or taped (but not both). Two calls are from Vancouver, two are from Seattle, and one is from Kelowna. The following conditions must apply:

> Isaac's and Mel's calls are the first two calls aired, but not necessarily in that order.
> The third call aired, from Kelowna, is taped.
> Both Seattle calls are live.
> Both Gwen's and Felicia's calls air after Henry's.
> Neither Mel nor Felicia calls from Seattle.

7. Which one of the following could be an accurate list of the calls, listed in the order in which they are aired?

    (A) Isaac's, Henry's, Felicia's, Mel's, Gwen's
    (B) Isaac's, Mel's, Gwen's, Henry's, Felicia's
    (C) Mel's, Gwen's, Henry's, Isaac's, Felicia's
    (D) Mel's, Isaac's, Gwen's, Henry's, Felicia's
    (E) Mel's, Isaac's, Henry's, Felicia's, Gwen's

8. Which one of the following could be true?

    (A) Felicia's call airs fifth.
    (B) Gwen's call airs first.
    (C) Henry's call airs second.
    (D) Isaac's call airs third.
    (E) Mel's call airs fifth.

9. If the first call aired is from Seattle, then which one of the following could be true?

    (A) Felicia's call is the next call aired after Isaac's.
    (B) Henry's call is the next call aired after Felicia's.
    (C) Henry's call is the next call aired after Mel's.
    (D) Henry's call is the next call aired after Isaac's.
    (E) Isaac's call is the next call aired after Mel's.

10. If a taped call airs first, then which one of the following CANNOT be true?

    (A) Felicia's call airs fourth.
    (B) Gwen's call airs fifth.
    (C) A taped call airs second.
    (D) A taped call airs third.
    (E) A taped call airs fourth.

11. Which one of the following must be true?

    (A) Gwen's call is live.
    (B) Henry's call is live.
    (C) Mel's call is live.
    (D) Felicia's call is taped.
    (E) Isaac's call is taped.

12. If no two live calls are aired consecutively and no two taped calls are aired consecutively, then in exactly how many distinct orders could the calls from the five people be aired?

    (A) one
    (B) two
    (C) three
    (D) four
    (E) five

13. If a taped call airs second, then which one of the following CANNOT be true?

    (A) The first call aired is from Seattle.
    (B) The first call aired is from Vancouver.
    (C) The fourth call aired is from Seattle.
    (D) The fifth call aired is from Seattle.
    (E) The fifth call aired is from Vancouver.

Practice Game 2: PT1, S2, G1

Exactly six trade representatives negotiate a treaty: Klosnik, Londi, Manley, Neri, Osata, Poirier. There are exactly six chairs evenly spaced around a circular table. The chairs are numbered 1 through 6, with successively numbered chairs next to each other and chair number 1 next to chair number 6. Each chair is occupied by exactly one of the representatives. The following conditions apply:

> Poirier sits immediately next to Neri.
> Londi sits immediately next to Manley, Neri, or both.
> Klosnik does not sit immediately next to Manley.
> If Osata sits immediately next to Poirier, Osata does not sit immediately next to Manley.

1. Which one of the following seating arrangements of the six representatives in chairs 1 through 6 would NOT violate the stated conditions?

    (A) Klosnik, Poirier, Neri, Manley, Osata, Londi
    (B) Klosnik, Londi, Manley, Poirier, Neri, Osata
    (C) Klosnik, Londi, Manley, Osata, Poirier, Neri
    (D) Klosnik, Osata, Poirier, Neri, Londi, Manley
    (E) Klosnik, Neri, Londi, Osata, Manley, Poirier

2. If Londi sits immediately next to Poirier, which one of the following is a pair of representatives who must sit immediately next to each other?

    (A) Klosnik and Osata
    (B) Londi and Neri
    (C) Londi and Osata
    (D) Manley and Neri
    (E) Manley and Poirier

3. If Klosnik sits directly between Londi and Poirier, then Manley must sit directly between

    (A) Londi and Neri
    (B) Londi and Osata
    (C) Neri and Osata
    (D) Neri and Poirier
    (E) Osata and Poirier

4. If Neri sits immediately next to Manley, then Klosnik can sit directly between

    (A) Londi and Manley
    (B) Londi and Poirier
    (C) Neri and Osata
    (D) Neri and Poirier
    (E) Poirier and Osata

5. If Londi sits immediately next to Manley, then which one of the following is a complete and accurate list of representatives any one of whom could also sit immediately next to Londi?

    (A) Klosnik
    (B) Klosnik, Neri
    (C) Neri, Poirier
    (D) Klosnik, Osata, Poirier
    (E) Klosnik, Neri, Osata, Poirier

6. If Londi sits immediately next to Neri, which one of the following statements must be false?

    (A) Klosnik sits immediately next to Osata.
    (B) Londi sits immediately next to Manley.
    (C) Osata sits immediately next to Poirier.
    (D) Neri sits directly between Londi and Poirier.
    (E) Osata sits directly between Klosnik and Manley.

7. If Klosnik sits immediately next to Osata, then Londi CANNOT sit directly between

    (A) Klosnik and Manley
    (B) Klosnik and Neri
    (C) Manley and Neri
    (D) Manley and Poirier
    (E) Neri and Osata

Practice Game 3: PT30, S1, G2

The six messages on an answering machine were each left by one of Fleure, Greta, Hildy, Liam, Pasquale, or Theodore, consistent with the following:

> At most one person left more than one message.
> No person left more than three messages.
> If the first message is Hildy's, the last is Pasquale's.
> If Greta left any message, Fleure and Pasquale did also.
> If Fleure left any message, Pasquale and Theodore did also, all of Pasquale's preceding any of Theodore's.
> If Pasquale left any message, Hildy and Liam did also, all of Hildy's preceding any of Liam's.

6. Which one of the following could be a complete and accurate list of the messages left on the answering machine, from first to last?

   (A) Fleure's, Pasquale's, Theodore's, Hildy's, Pasquale's, Liam's
   (B) Greta's, Pasquale's, Theodore's, Theodore's, Hildy's, Liam's
   (C) Hildy's, Hildy's, Hildy's, Liam's, Pasquale's, Theodore's
   (D) Pasquale's, Hildy's, Fleure's, Liam's, Theodore's, Theodore's
   (E) Pasquale's, Hildy's, Theodore's, Hildy's, Liam's, Liam's

7. The first and last messages on the answering machine could be the first and second messages left by which one of the following?

   (A) Fleure
   (B) Hildy
   (C) Liam
   (D) Pasquale
   (E) Theodore

8. If Greta left the fifth message, then which one of the following messages CANNOT have been left by Theodore?

   (A) the first message
   (B) the second message
   (C) the third message
   (D) the fourth message
   (E) the sixth message

9. Each of the following must be true EXCEPT:

   (A) Liam left at least one message.
   (B) Theodore left at least one message.
   (C) Hildy left at least one message.
   (D) Exactly one person left at least two messages.
   (E) At least four people left messages.

10. If the only message Pasquale left is the fifth message, then which one of the following could be true?

   (A) Hildy left the first message.
   (B) Theodore left exactly two messages.
   (C) Liam left exactly two messages.
   (D) Liam left the second message.
   (E) Fleure left the third and fourth messages.

Practice Game 4: PT32, S3, G4

On each of exactly seven consecutive days (day 1 though day 7), a pet shop features exactly one of three breeds of kitten—Himalayan, Manx, Siamese—and exactly one of three breeds of puppy—Greyhound, Newfoundland, Rottweiler. The following conditions must apply:

> Greyhounds are featured on day 1.
> No breed is featured on any two consecutive days.
> Any breed featured on day 1 is not featured on day 7.
> Himalayans are featured on exactly three days, but not on day 1.
> Rottweilers are not featured on day 7, nor on any day that features Himalayans.

19. Which one of the following could be the order in which the breeds of kitten are featured in the pet shop, from day 1 though day 7?

    (A) Himalayan, Manx, Siamese, Himalayan, Manx, Himalayan, Siamese

    (B) Manx, Himalayan, Siamese, Himalayan, Manx, Himalayan, Manx

    (C) Manx, Himalayan, Manx, Himalayan, Siamese, Manx, Siamese

    (D) Siamese, Himalayan, Manx, Himalayan, Siamese, Siamese, Himalayan

    (E) Siamese, Himalayan, Siamese, Himalayan, Manx, Siamese, Himalayan

20. If Himalayans are not featured on day 2, which one of the following could be true?

    (A) Manx are featured on day 3.
    (B) Siamese are featured on day 4.
    (C) Rottweilers are featured on day 5.
    (D) Himalayans are featured on day 6.
    (E) Greyhounds are featured on day 7.

21. Which one of the following could be true?

    (A) Greyhounds and Siamese are both featured on day 2.

    (B) Greyhounds and Himalayans are both featured on day 7.

    (C) Rottweilers and Himalayans are both featured on day 4.

    (D) Rottweilers and Manx are both featured on day 5.

    (E) Newfoundlands and Manx are both featured on day 6.

22. If Himalayans are not featured on day 7, then which one of the following pairs of days CANNOT feature both the same breed of kitten and the same breed of puppy?

    (A) day 1 and day 3
    (B) day 2 and day 6
    (C) day 3 and day 5
    (D) day 4 and day 6
    (E) day 5 and day 7

23. Which one of the following could be true?

    (A) There are exactly four breeds that are each featured on three days.

    (B) Greyhounds are featured on every day that Himalayans are.

    (C) Himalayans are featured on every day that Greyhounds are.

    (D) Himalayans are featured on every day that Rottweilers are not.

    (E) Rottweilers are featured on every day that Himalayans are not.

24. If Himalayans are not featured on day 7, which one of the following could be true?

    (A) Greyhounds are featured on days 3 and 5.
    (B) Newfoundlands are featured on day 3.
    (C) Rottweilers are featured on day 6.
    (D) Rottweilers are featured only on day 3.
    (E) Rottweilers are featured on exactly three days.

P

Evaluate Yourself

Before we start looking at some solutions to the games you just played, go ahead and review your process and then your work. Here's a smart way to do it:

1. Look back over your work and give yourself a grade for each part of the game. Use whatever grading system you like, but as much as you can, note specifically where things went wrong.

	Picture the Game *Did you understand the general way the game works before you started diagramming?*	Notate the Rules and Make Inferences *Did you correctly notate each rule? Did you understand each one?* *Did you draw inferences and put them into your diagram?*	The Big Pause *Did you take the Big Pause before moving on to the questions?* *Were you able to predict the key elements of the game?*	Attack the Questions *Did you attack the questions effectively? Did you move on when you needed to? For Conditional questions, did you make inferences before looking at the answer choices?*
Game 1				
Game 2				
Game 3				
Game 4				

2. Next, go back and replay any games for which you didn't give yourself a high grade. Do this before you check your answers. Figure out if you did what you now feel you should have done. Ideally, when you look at the solutions that follow, they will either confirm what you figured out for yourself, or they'll present an interesting alternative to a successful approach that you crafted.

Practice Game 1 Solution: PT36, S4, G2

Picture the Game

It's clear we have five slots to fill with the calls from F, G, H, I, and M, but what is tricky about this game is that we learn *two* different subsets to apply to those slots! Not only do we need to figure out if each slot is live or taped, but we also need to figure out the location. This is a twisted 3D Ordering game!

One interesting thing about this scenario is that while there are no restrictions on the number of live and taped calls, for location we have specific numbers: two V's, two S's, and one K. That's the sort of thing that's easy to overlook!

Here's our basic framework:

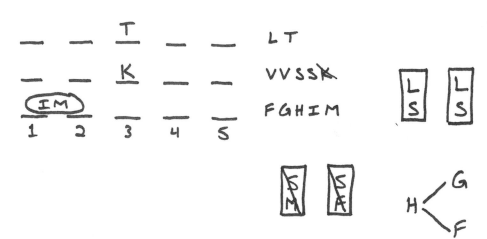

Notate the Rules and Make Inferences

The rules are straightforward—take a look at how each one could be notated:

Hopefully, you're annoyed, saying, "But there's more to figure out!" Indeed, with H before G and F, and slots 1 and 2 occupied by I and M, H must go in slot 3. That leaves G and F to take up slots 4 and 5.

Furthermore, with H in slot 3, we know that all the other callers are in Vancouver or Seattle slots. Since M and F can't be Seattle, they must be Vancouver, leaving G and I for the Seattle slots. But there's more…

Since Seattle calls must be L, we can actually create two chunks: L S I and L S G. However, we don't know where each one is located specifically. Instead, we know that the first chunk is in either slot 1 or 2, and the second chunk is in either slot 4 or 5. It's not straightforward how to represent this, but it's worth devoting some time to laying this out since it captures all the game's possibilities.

Here's one way of representing the situation:

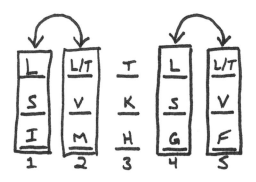

The Big Pause

Let's take a moment…. No! We know we've nailed this diagram! What more could we figure out?

Attack the Questions

7. Which one of the following could be an accurate list of the calls, listed in the order in which they are aired?

    (A) Isaac's, Henry's, Felicia's, Mel's, Gwen's

    (B) Isaac's, Mel's, Gwen's, Henry's, Felicia's

    (C) Mel's, Gwen's, Henry's, Isaac's, Felicia's

    (D) Mel's, Isaac's, Gwen's, Henry's, Felicia's

    (E) Mel's, Isaac's, Henry's, Felicia's, Gwen's

(E) is correct.

Since the answers are only about order and don't reference the subsets, let's use our diagram. It shows us quite a bit about what orders are possible! We see that the order has to be (I M) H (G F).

(A) has H second.

(B) has G third.

(C) has G second.

(D) has G third.

8. Which one of the following could be true?

    (A) Felicia's call airs fifth.
    (B) Gwen's call airs first.
    (C) Henry's call airs second.
    (D) Isaac's call airs third.
    (E) Mel's call airs fifth.

(A) is correct.

With the right diagram, this is a quick slam dunk. Were you disciplined and confident enough to not check all the other answers? It's fine if not, as checking probably took you less than 10 seconds.

9. If the first call aired is from Seattle, then which one of the following could be true?

    (A) Felicia's call is the next call aired after Isaac's.
    (B) Henry's call is the next call aired after Felicia's.
    (C) Henry's call is the next call aired after Mel's.
    (D) Henry's call is the next call aired after Isaac's.
    (E) Isaac's call is the next call aired after Mel's.

(C) is correct.

Let's consider the impact of the new condition. If S is first, we know everything about slots 1–3 except whether slot 2 gets an L or T. You could simply cover up the double-sided arrow over those slots and your diagram would reflect the new condition. Since this is a could be true question and not a must be true, we would typically expect it to be about either that L/T option or something in slot 4 or 5.

(A) is always impossible!

(B) is always impossible!

(C) is definitely true! This is a rare moment when the answer to a could be true question is something that must be true.

Pull the trigger and move on.

10. If a taped call airs first, then which one of the following CANNOT be true?

(A) Felicia's call airs fourth.

(B) Gwen's call airs fifth.

(C) A taped call airs second.

(D) A taped call airs third.

(E) A taped call airs fourth.

(C) is correct.

With this question's condition, we know that the chunks in slots 1 and 2 should be reversed. We're looking for something that must be false. We can expect that most anything about the order of elements in slots 4 or 5 will be incorrect since there's a lot of uncertainty there.

(A) and (B) are clearly possible.

(C) is impossible! Our L S I chunk is in slot 2.

Let's move on!

11. Which one of the following must be true?

(A) Gwen's call is live.

(B) Henry's call is live.

(C) Mel's call is live.

(D) Felicia's call is taped.

(E) Isaac's call is taped.

(A) is correct.

Our diagramming work pays off again!

12. If no two live calls are aired consecutively and no two taped calls are aired consecutively, then in exactly how many distinct orders could the calls from the five people be aired?

(A) one

(B) two

(C) three

(D) four

(E) five

(A) is correct.

Finally, a question with some bite to it! What does this new condition mean? If we can't have LL or TT, then both M and F must get a T. But which chunk goes where? Since we have a T locked into slot 3, we must have L's in slots 2 and 4. Thus, we know we're dealing with this situation:

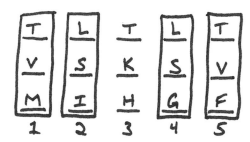

It probably would have been overkill to draw that out, but if you needed to, that's fine. Let's now consider how many options are possible.

One!

13. If a taped call airs second, then which one of the following CANNOT be true?

    (A) The first call aired is from Seattle.
    (B) The first call aired is from Vancouver.
    (C) The fourth call aired is from Seattle.
    (D) The fifth call aired is from Seattle.
    (E) The fifth call aired is from Vancouver.

(B) is correct.

We know what this condition means. Slot 2 is T V M and slot 1 is L S I. We are looking for something that can't be true, so we should expect the right answer to be about the chunks we were able to place definitively.

(A) must be true!

(B) can't be true!

In the final analysis, this was not that hard a game as long as you followed through with making inferences while building the initial diagram. If your diagram was far less developed, practice taking the Big Pause.

Practice Game 2 Solution: PT1, S2, G1

Picture the Game

A circle?! Yes, the LSAT has been known to throw in a circle game every great once in a while. You probably won't see a circle game on your LSAT, but it's great to use such games to improve your flexibility.

In this game, there are six folks sitting around a table that has exactly six seats; we don't have to contend with a mismatch.

When you scanned the rules and the questions, did you notice that there are almost no seat numbers mentioned? Because of this, we don't need to number our positions. This is typical of the few circle games that we've seen, though it's not hard to imagine a circle game in which the positions should be numbered.

Here are two ways you could have successfully represented the game:

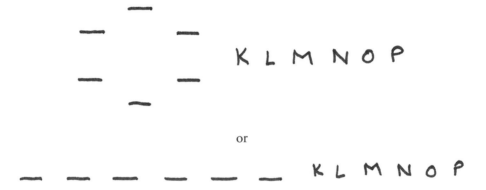

or

K L M N O P

With the linear arrangement, we'll have to remember that the first and last slots are next to each other. You could add a double-sided arrow linking the two if you think you might forget that:

Before reading on, consider replaying the game with the diagram arrangement you didn't use in order to stretch your game brain.

Note that in all but a few places, we'll discuss the game using a circle diagram.

Notate the Rules and Make Inferences

Let's fill in each diagram with our rules to compare how each one would work.

> Poirier sits immediately next to Neri.

Since there are no set positions, we can simply add those elements to our diagrams. We don't have to worry if they're in the "wrong" slots, because it's a circle and, more importantly, because seat numbering is not used in this game:

But what if N is on the other side of P? That might be a valid concern once we have placed other elements. We could draw a cloud around P and N to indicate that they might have switched places.

Let's move to the next rule:

> Londi sits immediately next to Manley, Neri, or both.

This is not an easy rule to represent in a usual manner. Here's one idea:

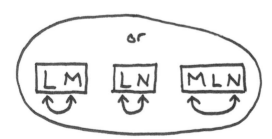

The circle around the whole group is to remind ourselves that these are three options. Note that in the third option, it's only the M and the N that could switch.

We don't know where one of these chunk options will go, nor do we know which chunk option it will be! Onward, with little known so far!

> Klosnik does not sit immediately next to Manley.

Since we have created a way to indicate anti-chunks, this is easy to represent:

And this is another rule that we can't get into the diagram. Let's see what's next…

If Osata sits immediately next to Poirier, Osata does not sit immediately next to Manley.

This is a tricky conditional chunk! But, we can handle this:

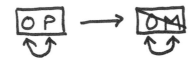

To consider what this really means, see if you can devise a simpler way of notating the rule.

If you can't figure it out, consider what sort of chunk is now impossible. We could never have O next to both P and M:

We have all our rules notated:

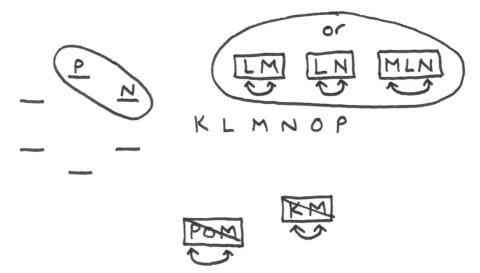

Again, we could have solved this game with a number line—albeit one with no numbers! For some, sticking with a line might be easier. That diagram would look like this:

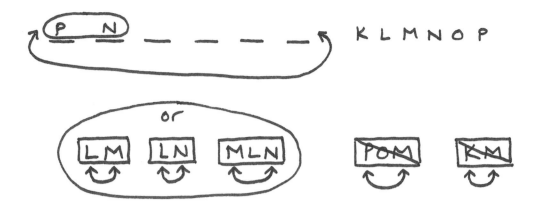

The Big Pause

It looks like there's a lot of uncertainty in this game. We have two elements placed, but we don't know where the LM/N chunk will go, and it's tough to see how the POM and KM restrictions will play out.

Isn't there some big inference we're missing? It definitely feels like that, but there's no evidence that we can find out much more. However, we do see that every element is part of some rule.

It'd be rather remarkable if you framed this game. There are a few cool aha's to be found from framing this game, but if you spent a lot of time on framing this game, you might be looking a bit too hard for framing opportunities. That said, it doesn't hurt to explore the issue for a short while. The most promising division is the LM/N options. If you're feeling particularly geeky, go ahead and play around with it and see what you can come up with.

Attack the Questions

1. Which one of the following seating arrangements of the six representatives in chairs 1 through 6 would NOT violate the stated conditions?

   (A) Klosnik, Poirier, Neri, Manley, Osata, Londi
   (B) Klosnik, Londi, Manley, Poirier, Neri, Osata
   (C) Klosnik, Londi, Manley, Osata, Poirier, Neri
   (D) Klosnik, Osata, Poirier, Neri, Londi, Manley
   (E) Klosnik, Neri, Londi, Osata, Manley, Poirier

(B) is correct.

The first rule eliminates (E).

The second rule eliminates (A).

The third rule eliminates (D).

P

The final rule eliminates (C).

2. If Londi sits immediately next to Poirier, which one of the following is a pair of representatives who must sit immediately next to each other?

    (A) Klosnik and Osata

    (B) Londi and Neri

    (C) Londi and Osata

    (D) Manley and Neri

    (E) Manley and Poirier

(A) is correct.

As is typical of second questions, this question provides a quick confirmation of whether we successfully understood the basics of this game:

With L next to P, we know we have P between L and N. We're still not sure whether it's P N or N P, but since this is a must be true question, whichever way we go, we won't be able to violate the correct answer.

It's hard to know what to do next, so let's ask ourselves, "Who's left?" In this case, it's K, M, and O. We know that K and M cannot sit next to each other (why can't they just get along?), so O must be in the middle. O would then be straight across from P, and K and M could switch between the two seats on either side.

Let's remind ourselves of what we're looking for: a pair that must sit next to each other. Looking at (A), it is clearly correct.

It seems tricky that the LSAT chose a pair that includes K, an element whose position is not fully determined, but try to formulate an answer that doesn't use either K or M. The best one could do is something like "L and P," but that relationship is given to us in the question stem, and such an answer would be silly and un-LSAT like. In this case, there was no option but to use one of the "floaters," but it's actually a common move the LSAT testwriters use even when they don't have to. For example, let's assume that on a Conditional question for some Basic Ordering game we arrive at this question-specific diagram:

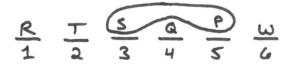

Let's also imagine that the question is: "Which of the following is a pair of bands that must perform consecutively, though not necessarily in the order listed?" There are two very likely answers. See them?

The answer would probably be "Q and S" or "P and Q." Since it can be difficult under pressure to recognize that, for example, Q and S must be consecutive, regardless of which of the two S options is used, this is a tough answer for some to see at first glance.

3. If Klosnik sits directly between Londi and Poirier, then Manley must sit directly between

    (A) Londi and Neri
    (B) Londi and Osata
    (C) Neri and Osata
    (D) Neri and Poirier
    (E) Osata and Poirier

(B) is correct.

This is a question in which we're asked to identify a pair that must straddle M. But what does the new condition mean?

With P and N again locked into place, we'll put K next to P, with L on the other side. What else can we fill in?

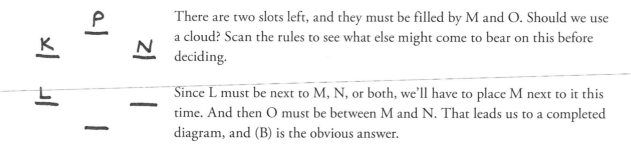

There are two slots left, and they must be filled by M and O. Should we use a cloud? Scan the rules to see what else might come to bear on this before deciding.

Since L must be next to M, N, or both, we'll have to place M next to it this time. And then O must be between M and N. That leads us to a completed diagram, and (B) is the obvious answer.

P

It's time to confess to you that it doesn't matter whether we use N P or P N. If you're not sure why, try that question again, but reverse the positioning of P and N. See if you can figure out why the directional order of the elements doesn't matter. It's not because this is a circle game, as there are other circle games in which this would be an issue.

You should have arrived at the same answer, regardless of the way you arranged P and N, and your diagram should be a mirror image of the one we came up with earlier. The reason that the direction doesn't matter in this game is that neither the rules nor the questions refer to direction—for example, clockwise or counterclockwise—and so it doesn't matter which way the circle goes.

4. If Neri sits immediately next to Manley, then Klosnik can sit directly between

    (A) Londi and Manley

    (B) Londi and Poirier

    (C) Neri and Osata

    (D) Neri and Poirier

    (E) Poirier and Osata

(E) is correct.

What is the impact of the new condition? We'll have a P N M chunk, with L, K, and O left to place. We know that K and M cannot sit next to each other. We also know that we need to place L next to M since LN is no longer an option. Our chunk has grown to P N M L, with K and O left. K is "protected" from M, so nothing to worry about there. Our diagram for this question looks like this:

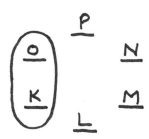

K must fall between O and L or O and P.

5. If Londi sits immediately next to Manley, then which one of the following is a complete and accurate list of representatives any one of whom could also sit immediately next to Londi?

    (A) Klosnik

    (B) Klosnik, Neri

    (C) Neri, Poirier

    (D) Klosnik, Osata, Poirier

    (E) Klosnik, Neri, Osata, Poirier

(E) is correct.

This is a great question for using previous work. Looking back, where do we see L next to M? In #4! We're asked for a list of those that could sit next to L, and thus we know the answer must include both K and O. That allows us to eliminate all but (D) and (E). From there, let's compare what differences those two answers have. The only difference is whether we should include N, so let's test it out.

Let's try placing our LM chunk next to N. We have K and O left (once again), and we can keep K and M separate by putting O in between them. We haven't triggered the P O M restriction, so all is well. N is a possibility, and so (E) is correct.

P

If we had forgotten to use our previous work, the question would still be doable—of course—but testing out scenarios would probably suck up a bit more time. Ideally, we have a firm enough grasp on the rules that we could identify some possibilities by simply thinking it out, and we wouldn't need to write out the scenarios. Try doing it now. It's not easy! This is definitely a question where looking back at earlier work pays dividends.

6. If Londi sits immediately next to Neri, which one of the following statements must be false?

   (A) Klosnik sits immediately next to Osata.
   (B) Londi sits immediately next to Manley.
   (C) Osata sits immediately next to Poirier.
   (D) Neri sits directly between Londi and Poirier.
   (E) Osata sits directly between Klosnik and Manley.

(C) is correct.

It seems like we're playing around with the same issues in many of these questions. If L is next to N, we have a P N L chunk. K, M, and O are left, and O must be in the middle to keep the peace. Working through the answer choices, it's easy to eliminate (A) and (B) and discover the oh-so-tasty correct answer.

7. If Klosnik sits immediately next to Osata, then Londi CANNOT sit directly between

   (A) Klosnik and Manley
   (B) Klosnik and Neri
   (C) Manley and Neri
   (D) Manley and Poirier
   (E) Neri and Osata

(E) is correct.

For a change, the new condition does not immediately link up with P and N. We can draw something vague to help ground our thinking:

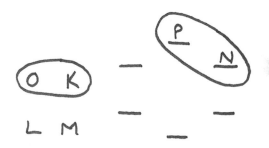

We need to identify a pair that CANNOT straddle L. We could definitely slog our way through the answers by testing them out and deferring judgment. If our control of the game is high—and by the last question, hopefully it is—we should be able to make that strategy work fast enough.

(A) is first up. Can we have L in between K and M? Sure! From the top of the diagram, it's not to hard to imagine, in descending order counterclockwise down the left side: O, K, L, M. No rules violated. Eliminate.

(B) seems fine, too. Starting from P, working clockwise, we'd have P, N, L, K, O, M. We don't violate the K M rule or the P O M one.

(C) is possible as long as we keep K away from M by putting O in between them.

(D) is similar to (C).

(E) can't work. If L is between N and O, we will need to put K and M in the remaining two slots. Those two can't sit together!

That was a rough and tumble way through the answer choices. Can you think of a more nuanced approach to the question? Before reading on, consider what it was about (E) that, perhaps, made it easy to identify as impossible, and thus correct.

What made (E) not work (and be correct) is that it "used up" N, O, and L, and seated them consecutively, leaving K and M to get uncomfortably intimate in the last two slots.

Another approach would have been to sketch out the ways that K and M could have been separated:

With these in hand, the answer choice work should have gone a bit faster. Better yet, you could have eliminated (A) through (D) using previous work (try it now).

That was probably one of the stranger logic games you've seen so far. If you struggled, replay the game before you get up from this prep session. Then play it again in a couple of weeks. What can we learn from this challenge?

1. There wasn't a perfect diagram. Success was not about having the "right" diagram; it was about effectively using whichever one you had. While you probably won't see another circle game in your LSAT career, consider whether you preferred using a circle arrangement or a linear one, and why.

P

2. Flexibility was critical—look at the MacGyver moves we made:

- We turned our number line into a number circle.
- On at least one Conditional question we found ourselves without any major inferences, and so we *set up a framework with which to consider answers*. If you're going to do trial and error, make sure it's well organized.
- We used previous work.

Practice Game 3 Solution: PT30, S1, G2

Picture the Game

This seems like a nice enough game… until you notice the relationships between the last four rules. It's obvious that we should use a circle to represent this game. No, no, just kidding! It's obvious that we should use a standard number line, but we're going to need to pay attention to the relationship between those rules.

Another issue that you need to consider is the odd mismatches that are in effect. There's no requirement that each person leave a message, a fact that becomes more obvious when you read the first two rules.

In short, we have six slots to be filled by up to six people.

Notate the Rules and Make Inferences

The first two rules give us a lot of information about the mismatch nature of the game.

> *At most one person left more than one message.*
> *No person left more than three messages.*

So basically, one person may have left two or three messages. With six slots to fill, we could have six people leave messages, or just five; but we'll definitely need at least four people to leave messages (that would be using the maximum of three messages left by one person, and the remaining three messages left by three others).

It's tough to do anything other than paraphrase these rules to the side.

> "If the first message is Hildy's, the last is Pasquale's."
> "If Greta left any message, Fleure and Pasquale did also."

These rules are simple enough to notate to the side.

> "If Fleure left any message, Pasquale and Theodore did also, all of Pasquale's preceding any of Theodore's."

"If Pasquale left any message, Hildy and Liam did also, all of Hildy's preceding any of Liam's."

These rules, while not particularly difficult to notate, seem oddly connected.

Here's our diagram so far:

O-3 messages each
At most one multiple

$$\underline{\quad}\ \ \underline{\quad}\ \ \underline{\quad}\ \ \underline{\quad}\ \ \underline{\quad}\ \ \underline{\quad}$$
$$1\quad 2\quad 3\quad 4\quad 5\quad 6$$

F G H L P T

$$H_1 \rightarrow P_6$$

$$G \rightarrow F + P$$
$$F \rightarrow P - T \text{ (all)}$$
$$P \rightarrow H - L \text{ (all)}$$

The Big Pause

With so many conditional rules sharing elements, look for links. Indeed, we can combine several of these rules.

One obvious chain is this: $G \rightarrow F \rightarrow P - T$ (all).

Another is this: $G \rightarrow P \rightarrow H - L$ (all).

But wait. Those two chains share elements! Either just notice the connections and remember to keep them in mind, or actually link them up in some strange way like this:

$$G \Big\langle {}^{\nearrow F \longrightarrow P-T\ (all)}_{\searrow P \longrightarrow H-L\ (all)}$$

If you didn't split the G rule (and it's by no mean essential in this game that you do), you might have arrived at a different, strange looking chain:

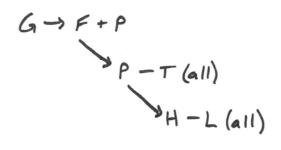

It's worth considering what this cascade of conditionals means for our game. One powerful element is G: if G is in, so is everyone else! F is almost as powerful, forcing everyone but G in. As we work our way down the chain, the elements force fewer and fewer elements in with them.

Considering the mismatch nature of the game, we'll definitely want to keep this in mind. In fact, we can draw an important but subtle inference before even starting. We actually can determine four people who will leave a message in any scenario. Can you figure out who they are before reading on?

If you try to exclude P, T, H, or L, you also have to exclude F, and thus G. Since we have at least four people leaving messages, we know that P, T, H, and L all leave a message. This means that we will always have at least those four people leaving messages.

Attack the Questions

6. Which one of the following could be a complete and accurate list of the messages left on the answering machine, from first to last?

   (A) Fleure's, Pasquale's, Theodore's, Hildy's, Pasquale's, Liam's
   (B) Greta's, Pasquale's, Theodore's, Theodore's, Hildy's, Liam's
   (C) Hildy's, Hildy's, Hildy's, Liam's, Pasquale's, Theodore's
   (D) Pasquale's, Hildy's, Fleure's, Liam's, Theodore's, Theodore's
   (E) Pasquale's, Hildy's, Theodore's, Hildy's, Liam's, Liam's

(D) is correct.

The first rule eliminates (E).

The second rule eliminates nothing! (And with six rules, we should expect that some rules will not be used here.)

The third rule eliminates (C).

The fourth rule eliminates (B).

The fifth rule eliminates (A).

7. The first and last messages on the answering machine could be the first and second messages left by which one of the following?

(A) Fleure

(B) Hildy

(C) Liam

(D) Pasquale

(E) Theodore

(A) is correct.

Resist the temptation to test out the answer choices. Instead, let's think about who would be unable to leave the first and last message. H is a clear no-no, since H first triggers P last. But we still have four answers.

Looking at the remaining answers—F, L, P, and T—all but one of them are involved in conditional/relative ordering rules. Let's consider whether, for example, P's could be the first and last messages. Surprisingly, even though we see "P – T (all)" in our conditional rules, we could have P's fall before and after T as long as there's no F. Without an F, any ordering of P and T is acceptable (likewise, without P, any ordering of H and L works). However, we actually do know that F and P are in. If you're not sure why, reread the question stem and think about why before reading on.

If the first and last messages were the first and second messages left by someone, we know that that person is the only one to leave multiple messages (per the first rule), and since that person's second message is his or her last, that person leaves only two messages. We'll need four more people leaving messages to reach six messages in all. We know we always need to have P, T, H, and L, so who could be the fifth? It must be F! If we were to have G, we'd also be forced to have F, bringing us to six people, with no room for someone to double up.

With F, P, T, H, and L in, we know that we'll trigger P – T (all) and H – L (all), so there's no way that P, T, H, or L could be both first and last. P, for example, could be the first, but since a T must follow all the P's, there's no way that P could be last. Similarly, T couldn't be first. Thus, we can eliminate (C) through (E).

8. If Greta left the fifth message, then which one of the following messages CANNOT have been left by Theodore?

(A) the first message

(B) the second message

(C) the third message

(D) the fourth message

(E) the sixth message

(A) is correct.

With G fifth, what can we infer? G forces every potential element into the number line. We're asked specifically about T, and we know that T must come after P. That means that T can't leave the first message.

9. Each of the following must be true EXCEPT:

    (A) Liam left at least one message.

    (B) Theodore left at least one message.

    (C) Hildy left at least one message.

    (D) Exactly one person left at least two messages.

    (E) At least four people left messages.

(D) is correct.

There's no condition to work from, but scanning the answers, it's clear that this question is about the numbers. As we look for something that could be false, keep in mind that we must have at least four people leave messages.

(A) seems tempting. Can we avoid using L? We know that we must always have P, T, H, and L. (A) must be true! Remember, we're looking for what could be false, so eliminate.

In fact, knowing that P, T, H, and L must always be in allows us to eliminate (B), (C), and (E), as well.

(D) doesn't have to be true. If we use all six elements, there will be no doubling up.

10. If the only message Pasquale left is the fifth message, then which one of the following could be true?

    (A) Hildy left the first message.

    (B) Theodore left exactly two messages.

    (C) Liam left exactly two messages.

    (D) Liam left the second message.

    (E) Fleure left the third and fourth messages.

(C) is correct.

If P leaves the fifth message and no others, we know we have P, T, H – L. We might have three T's, H's or L's, we might have G and F, or we might have F and a doubling up.

That's too many options to explore, so let's look at the answers for one that could be true:

(A) can't be true, since H first means P last.

(B) seems OK until you consider the P – T (all) rule. If we have two T's, we'll need to include F to complete all six messages. That means we'll trigger the P – T (all) rule, and with P in the fifth slot, where would we put two T's?

(C) seems fine. Defer or confirm.

(D) can't be true, since L second means H first, and from our work with (A), we know that can't be true.

(E) is tough to eliminate quickly. With F in the third and fourth slots, we'll have to place P – T and H – L. Since P is fifth, T goes last. That leaves the first two slots for H and L, which brings us back to H in slot 1, which we learned can't be true.

Practice Game 4 Solution: PT32, S3, G4

Picture the Game

From reading the scenario and scanning the rules, we quickly learn that this is not a Basic Ordering game. We have to place *both* a kitten and a puppy each day. It's a 3D Ordering game, with an equal number of options for both rows.

One issue that is hard to pin down is whether each breed must be featured. There's no language to suggest that, so we'll assume not.

Notate the Rules and Make Inferences

Most of the rules should be pretty standard for you to understand at this point in your preparation, but some might have been hard to get into the diagram. Take a look at what we came up with, and at some of the inferences we drew:

We must have an n in puppy slot 7, since the third rule cuts out g and the final rule cuts out r.

One notation that is new here is the use of dots. We'll use this notation more in grouping games, but in short, the way we're using it here is to indicate that if two positions on the same row have a different number of dots, they must have different breeds. It's slightly dicey using this notation here, since the two breeds in position 1 are NOT the same; but since that's a pretty fundamental fact in this game—that puppies and kitties are on different rows—we should be OK.

We're obviously using upper and lower case to differentiate the element subsets. It was a tough decision about whether to make the kittens or puppies upper case. But since cats can be vengeful, we decided to give them top honors.

There's a bit more to infer about this game. For example, you can write "M/S" in kitty slot 1. However, most of these final inferences are pretty obvious and come down more to style. Still, when in doubt, write them in!

The Big Pause

We have a pretty open diagram, and it's definitely worth a moment to consider what's going on. For starters, who is the most important element here?

Definitely H!

Where can those three H's go? There actually aren't that many options, and it wouldn't take long to sketch them out in broad fashion (go ahead and do so now if you didn't earlier).

You could have drawn something like this:

Or you could have gone a bit more into the details:

We could also write out the four possibilities. Though it wouldn't take up much time, it probably isn't worth completely framing this since there aren't significant inferences flowing from each of those frames.

What *is* worth doing is noting that there are not too many ways the three H's can be arranged, and since we can't place an r anywhere we have an H, this is an important issue.

We don't have any rules attached to M or S, nor do we know if we'll actually need to include both of those. Let's move to the questions.

Attack the Questions

19. Which one of the following could be the order in which the breeds of kitten are featured in the pet shop, from day 1 though day 7?

    (A) Himalayan, Manx, Siamese, Himalayan, Manx, Himalayan, Siamese
    (B) Manx, Himalayan, Siamese, Himalayan, Manx, Himalayan, Manx
    (C) Manx, Himalayan, Manx, Himalayan, Siamese, Manx, Siamese
    (D) Siamese, Himalayan, Manx, Himalayan, Siamese, Siamese, Himalayan
    (E) Siamese, Himalayan, Siamese, Himalayan, Manx, Siamese, Himalayan

(E) is correct.

Sorry, puppies; we're focusing only on kitties here.

Let's use our diagram for this one:

> We know that H can't go first, eliminating (A).
> We need three H's, eliminating (C).
> We can't have the first and last be the same, eliminating (B).
> We can't have the same breed shown consecutively, eliminating (D).

20. If Himalayans are not featured on day 2, which one of the following could be true?

    (A) Manx are featured on day 3.
    (B) Siamese are featured on day 4.
    (C) Rottweilers are featured on day 5.
    (D) Himalayans are featured on day 6.
    (E) Greyhounds are featured on day 7.

(B) is correct.

If there's no H in 2, we have to consider where the three H's can go. It must be slots 3, 5, and 7. There are a few inferences we can put into a quick and dirty diagram (notice that we ditched the numbering and are using just one row of lines to speed up our work):

There may be more to infer, but this is the second question, and should be pretty easy. Let's take a look:

(A) is impossible. H is there!

(B) Seems fine. We'd probably confirm it, but we might move quickly through (C) through (E) instead.

(C) is the same as (A)—H is there!

(D) is wrong; there's no H there.

(E) is always impossible!

21. Which one of the following could be true?

    (A) Greyhounds and Siamese are both featured on day 2.

    (B) Greyhounds and Himalayans are both featured on day 7.

    (C) Rottweilers and Himalayans are both featured on day 4.

    (D) Rottweilers and Manx are both featured on day 5.

    (E) Newfoundlands and Manx are both featured on day 6.

(D) is correct.

Nothing to work with on this Unconditional question (other than our impressive brain power and understanding of the game).

(A) is clearly wrong since g can never go in slot 2.

We can add that to our diagram! We'll also note the similar restriction about n in slot 6.

Figuring out more about your diagram mid-game is common; be sure to add in those details to your master diagram.

(B) is a no-no. g can never go in slot 7.

(C) is another silly answer—r and H can never go together.

(D) seems OK. Let's defer, since it'll probably be faster to eliminate (E) than to confirm (D).

(E) is incorrect, since we can't have n in both slots 6 and 7.

And now we have a somewhat better master diagram:

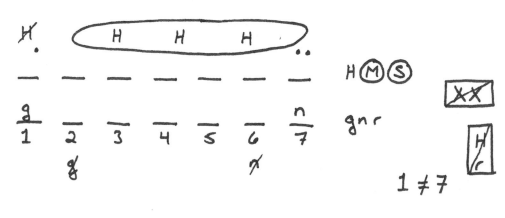

22. If Himalayans are not featured on day 7, then which one of the following pairs of days CANNOT feature both the same breed of kitten and the same breed of puppy?

(A) day 1 and day 3
(B) day 2 and day 6
(C) day 3 and day 5
(D) day 4 and day 6
(E) day 5 and day 7

(B) is correct.

This question stem is tricky, but let's start by making inferences from the new condition. With no H in 7, we must have H's in 2, 4, and 6. We can then draw several inferences about the bottom row based on that and the H and r restriction:

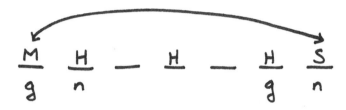

Now it's time to understand the stem. We're asked for two slots that cannot have the same exact pair of breeds. There are a few obvious candidates in our diagram; let's see what the answers give us:

(A) seems OK. Slot 3 is not determined and there's no obvious reason that g and M or S couldn't go in that position.

(B) is our answer! No time to confirm that the rest are wrong, but it's always fine to put a star next to the question, and, if there's time at the end of the section, return to confirm that (C) through (E) are possible, and thus incorrect.

23. Which one of the following could be true?

(A) There are exactly four breeds that are each featured on three days.
(B) Greyhounds are featured on every day that Himalayans are.
(C) Himalayans are featured on every day that Greyhounds are.
(D) Himalayans are featured on every day that Rottweilers are not.
(E) Rottweilers are featured on every day that Himalayans are not.

(A) is correct.

This is definitely a much harder question than the others we've seen in this game. If you struggled a lot, hopefully you moved on and came back to it later; this question could eat up a lot of precious time. Let's look at the answer choices:

(A) is tough to confirm off the bat. It might have felt dangerous to devote the time to testing out whether, for example, we could have 3 H's, 3 M's, 1 S, 3 g's, 3 n's, and 1 r. By the way, best to not use 3 r's in creating a scenario, since that makes trouble for the 3 H's. A smart move with this answer would be to defer judgment.

(B) seems OK as well. Let's defer and try to keep our cool.

(C) is impossible! We have a g in position 1, where H can't go. Eliminate.

(D) is a freebie elimination. Just as with (C), position 1 proves this answer impossible.

(E) takes only a moment to eliminate, using position 1 again. We don't have an H, and we have g rather than r. Bye bye.

We're down to two answers, and now we can simply test out either one. We'll test (B), since there's a bit more to work with. Could we have a G every time we have an H?

Since we couldn't have an H and thus a g in position 2 (there's a g in position 1), we'll start by pushing the three H's down to 3, 5, and 7. Wait, then we'd need a g in slot 7, and we have n there already. Eliminate!

24. If Himalayans are not featured on day 7, which one of the following could be true?

   (A) Greyhounds are featured on days 3 and 5.
   (B) Newfoundlands are featured on day 3.
   (C) Rottweilers are featured on day 6.
   (D) Rottweilers are featured only on day 3.
   (E) Rottweilers are featured on exactly three days.

(D) is correct.

We know the drill on this new condition. With no H in 7, the H's go in slots 2, 4, and 6. We have worked this out already on question #22. We'll look at the work we did there:

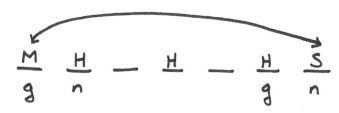

Chapter 8   Ordering Review

Hopefully the answers will be easy:

(A) is impossible, since we have a g in slot 6.

(B) is impossible, since we have an n in slot 2. (Note that we could have written out those restrictions in our diagram, but at this point those are pretty obvious inferences to many of you.)

(C) is impossible. Slot 6 is quite full.

(D) works—there's no problem having an r in slot 3 and then filling up the rest of the diagram with the other elements. Perhaps we'd skip that and simply check that we can eliminate (E).

(E) is indeed incorrect. Where would we fit three r's? We have only three open slots, and they're consecutive. My goodness.

Conclusion

Take another moment to consider how you did on the practice set. If a game was tough, which part did you struggle with? If your struggle was in the setup, do you need to give yourself more time? Did you forget to look at how rules combine? Did you skip the Big Pause?

Remember that we specifically created a set in which each game had a particularly unusual twist or challenge. We wanted to expose your areas for development so that you would know what to work on.

If you were unable to twist right along with each game, don't worry—the night is young! There's plenty more practice with twists coming, and remember that real Logic Game sections are less twisty than this one. Often, the key to conquering a truly nasty game is having moved very quickly on the easier games in order to give yourself enough time. This means that a significant part of improving on the killer games is improving on the easier ones.

At this point, you've finished looking at the Ordering Family and learned how to tackle the vast majority of questions. What you've learned here will be invaluable as you move on to new game types. Most likely, two of the four games on your real LSAT will be in the Ordering family. Give yourself some credit for what you've achieved so far.

Chapter 9

of

Logic Games

Conditional Logic 202

In This Chapter...

Conditional Logic for Conditional Grouping

Alternate Wordings

Compound Conditional Statements

Conditional Logic for Conditional Grouping

We learned the basics of conditional logic in an earlier chapter. Let's now dig a bit deeper in preparation for the next game type, Conditional Grouping. To give you a bit of context for what we're going to learn here, let's quickly introduce this game type.

Conditional Grouping games will involve two types of scenarios:

1. In or Out. In this type of Conditional Grouping scenario, each element is either selected for inclusion as part of a group or not selected for inclusion. Here's an example:

> One or more of exactly seven basketball players—F, G, H, J, K, L, and M—from the
> Riverside High School basketball team will be selected for the league All-Star team.

2. One or the Other. In this type of Conditional Grouping scenario, each element is assigned to exactly one of two groups. Here's an example:

> Seven employees—F, G, H, J, K, L, and M—will each be assigned to exactly one of
> the following two departments: sales, marketing.

Note that these two scenarios are really just variations on the same theme. In each case, your job is to divide up the elements into two groups: in the first case, those who are selected for the team vs. those who are not selected, and in the second case, those who are assigned to sales vs. those who are assigned to marketing.

The rules for these Conditional Grouping scenarios will take the form of conditional statements. Here's how these conditional statements might appear on the LSAT:

> One or more of exactly seven basketball players—F, G, H, J, K, L, and M—from the
> Riverside High School basketball team will be selected for the league All-Star team.
> The following conditions apply:
>
> > If H is selected, then J is also selected.
> > If K is selected, then L and F are not selected.
> > If G is selected, then M is not selected.

Your success on Conditional Grouping games depends on your ability to make valid inferences from these conditional statements. As we'll see shortly, it's not as straightforward as it might seem.

9

Alternate Wordings

We noted earlier that basic conditional statements on Conditional Grouping games are triggered by "If… then" language. However, the LSAT won't always make things so simple for you. In the Modern Era of Logic Games (since the year 2000), the LSAT uses many different wordings in its conditional statements in order to add to the complexity of your task.

The following is a list of rules meant to illustrate the full gamut of advanced conditional statements that have appeared on Conditional Grouping games since the year 2000. Note that it would be highly unlikely for all or even many of these rules to appear in the same game:

1. J and K cannot both be selected.

2. If M is selected, both G and H must be selected.

3. Neither H nor K is selected if L is selected.

4. If J is selected, then G is selected but L is not.

5. F cannot be selected unless H is also selected.

6. L is selected if, and only if, M is also selected.

7. If either Q or R is selected, both must be selected.

8. N and W cannot be on the same team.

If you're not careful, you can get turned around pretty quickly with statements such as these. Ideally, you'll work on them so much that you'll simply have the relevant concepts memorized. For now, however, let's work on a process for deconstructing these difficult statements.

Converting to Simple "If… Then" Form

We know how to use simple "If… then" statements, right? Diagram using an arrow symbol, and reverse and negate to get the contrapositive. You're already a pro at this. It makes sense, then, to tackle these advanced statements by first converting them into simple "If… then" form. Once we convert to simple "If… then" form, we're in the clear. The challenge comes in the conversion.

We'll use a simple box technique to make this conversion. Let's start with the first of our eight examples.

1. J and K cannot both be selected.

This statement is difficult to deal with because it has no "If… then" language. We need to convert it. To do so, let's imagine we have a box that represents selection (a letter placed inside the box has been selected while a letter placed outside the box has not been selected). In this case, we have two letters to the side that are awaiting judgment, so to speak:

9

J
K

The easiest way to derive a simple "If… then" phrase from this difficult statement is to experiment. If we start by putting J in the box, what does that mean for K? Well, since J and K cannot both be selected, putting J in the box means we have to put K outside the box:

Start by putting J inside: J   K

We've just created an "If… then" statement: **IF** J is selected, **THEN** K is not selected. But what if we had started with K? We'll put K in the box to begin with. Since J and K cannot both be selected, we'd have to put J outside the box:

Start by putting K inside: K   J

So we have another simple "If… then": **IF** K is selected, **THEN** J is not selected. Now let's start with J again and see what happens if we put J *outside* the box to begin with. Putting J outside the box doesn't really give us any clues for K. We could put K outside as well, or we could put K inside. Neither of these would break the original rule ("J and K cannot both be selected"):

Start by putting J outside: J K   OR   K   J

So, putting J outside doesn't lead to any reliable "If… then" statement. The same would be true if we started with K outside. In the end, we're left with the two statements we derived above:

  IF J is selected, **THEN** K is not selected.
  IF K is selected, **THEN** J is not selected.

We can express these in symbol form, and then we can take the contrapositives:

IF… THEN FORM	SYMBOL FORM	CONTRAPOSITIVE
IF J is selected, **THEN** K is not selected.	J $\longrightarrow$ -K	K $\longrightarrow$ -J
IF K is selected, **THEN** J is not selected.	K $\longrightarrow$ -J	J $\longrightarrow$ -K

MANHATTAN
LSAT

9

Note that the contrapositives in this case don't give us any new information. So, the original statement "J and K cannot both be selected" leaves us with two pieces of information:

$$J \longrightarrow -K$$

$$K \longrightarrow -J$$

Now that you've got the hang of how to use the box to turn advanced conditional statements into standard "If... then" form, take a look at the remaining seven advanced statements. If you were completely unsure of how to translate them earlier, flip back and give them a second shot now using the box idea.

2. If M is selected, both G and H must be selected.

We can break down this statement into two distinct "If... then" structures: 1) If M is selected, then G is selected, and 2) If M is selected, then H is selected. In general, if you can split up a rule, do so.

IF... THEN FORM	SYMBOL FORM	CONTRAPOSITIVE
IF M is selected, THEN G is selected.	$M \longrightarrow G$	$-G \longrightarrow -M$
IF M is selected, THEN H is selected.	$M \longrightarrow H$	$-H \longrightarrow -M$

In a few pages, we'll talk more about statements with "and" or "or."

3. Neither H nor K is selected if L is selected.

Again, this statement will yield two givens. We can break it down into two distinct "If... then" structures: 1) If L is selected, then H is not selected, and 2) If L is selected, then K is not selected.

IF... THEN FORM	SYMBOL FORM	CONTRAPOSITIVE
IF L is selected, THEN H is not selected.	$L \longrightarrow -H$	$H \longrightarrow -L$
IF L is selected, THEN K is not selected.	$L \longrightarrow -K$	$K \longrightarrow -L$

4. If J is selected, then G is selected but L is not.

This is very similar to the two previous examples. We can break it down into two distinct "If... then" structures: 1) If J is selected, then G is selected, and 2) If J is selected, then L is not selected.

IF... THEN FORM	SYMBOL FORM	CONTRAPOSITIVE
IF J is selected, THEN G is selected.	$J \longrightarrow G$	$-G \longrightarrow -J$
IF J is selected, THEN L is not selected.	$J \longrightarrow -L$	$L \longrightarrow -J$

MANHATTAN
LSAT

5. F cannot be selected unless H is also selected.

This is a tough one. Let's experiment with the box. We know that we can't put F in unless we put H in. So if we start with H in, we can put F in, too. But do we have to? Can we leave F out?

Sure. So we can't build a conditional on selecting H. Similarly, if you can't dance unless there is music, just having music doesn't guarantee dancing.

On the other hand, if we start with F in, what do we know? To put in F, we would need to have H in. After all, we can't select F unless we select H. So we know that if F is in, H must be in.

Start by putting F inside:

IF... THEN FORM	SYMBOL FORM	CONTRAPOSITIVE
IF F is selected, **THEN** H is selected.	F ——→ H	-H ——→ -F

We could also have started by putting H *outside* the box. When H is out, F must be out as well. Notice that this is what our contrapositive tells us.

A quick way to handle "unless" statements is to swap the word "unless" with "if not." For example, using the example above, "F cannot be selected **if** H is **not** also selected." Or, reordered, "If H is not selected, F cannot be selected."

6. L is selected if, and only if, M is also selected.

We've already met this sort of statement, but let's apply our box technique to deepen our understanding, as this may be the most difficult of the advanced statements to decipher.

We'll start by putting M in. L is selected if M is selected, so we must also put L in:

Start by putting M inside:

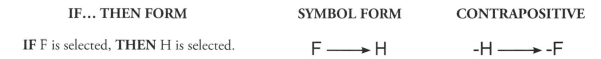

But what if we'd started by putting L inside? What does this mean for M? Well, remember that L is selected ONLY IF M is selected. So if L is in, M must be in as well:

Start by putting L inside:

So, from this original statement, we get two simple "If... then" statements:

IF... THEN FORM	SYMBOL FORM	CONTRAPOSITIVE
IF M is selected, **THEN** L is selected.	$M \longrightarrow L$	$-L \longrightarrow -M$
IF L is selected, **THEN** M is selected.	$L \longrightarrow M$	$-M \longrightarrow -L$

As we learned in Chapter 5, we can also represent these with double-sided arrows:

$$M \longleftrightarrow L$$

$$-L \longleftrightarrow -M$$

7. If either Q or R is selected, both must be selected.

In this case we see two different triggers. Interestingly, including either letter requires us to include the other. Thus, we can derive two statements:

IF... THEN FORM	SYMBOL FORM	CONTRAPOSITIVE
IF Q is selected, **THEN** R is selected.	$Q \longrightarrow R$	$-R \longrightarrow -Q$
IF R is selected, **THEN** Q is selected.	$R \longrightarrow Q$	$-Q \longrightarrow -R$

Note that this statement is different than "Either Q, R, or both is selected." In that case, neither Q nor R is a trigger, but the absence of either one would trigger the inclusion of the other. Again, we could have used double-sided arrows here.

8. N and W cannot be on the same team.

This example is applicable to a Conditional Grouping game in which elements are put on one team or another. It is also another example in which we don't see an "If." However, as in the last example, it turns out that both letters are triggers. If either one is "in," the other must be "out." If we call our teams X and Y, for instance, we know that when N is on Team X, W is on Team Y. And when N is on Team Y? W must be on X.

IF... THEN FORM	SYMBOL FORM	CONTRAPOSITIVE
IF N is selected for team X, **THEN** W is selected for team Y.	$N_X \longrightarrow W_Y$	$W_X \longrightarrow N_Y$
IF N is selected for team Y, **THEN** W is selected for team X.	$N_Y \longrightarrow W_X$	$W_Y \longrightarrow N_X$

Note that we could just as easily have started with the contrapositives of these two statements. Whatever team W is on, N must be on the other. In any case, we have another biconditional on our hands! Our diagram covers all four possible triggers: N_X, N_Y, W_X, and W_Y. To save yourself time and space on the exam, you will probably want to get used to notating with double arrows:

$$N_X \longleftrightarrow W_Y \qquad N_Y \longleftrightarrow W_X$$

Compound Conditional Statements

Compound conditional statements are statements that have a two-part *sufficient* condition (a two-part trigger such as "If X and Y, then… ") and/or a two part *necessary* condition (a two-part outcome such as "…then Y or Z"). Earlier on, we saw a few examples of compound statements. Here's one from before. This particular example has a two-part outcome:

> If M is selected, then both G and H must be selected.

We dealt with this by splitting it into two separate conditionals:

> If M is selected, then G is selected. (M $\longrightarrow$ G)
> If M is selected, then H is selected. (M $\longrightarrow$ H)

While this is the most common type of compound statement that you'll see, it's not the only type. Let's take a moment to define the four types of compound statements that are fair game on the LSAT, starting with the type discussed above.

1. AND in the outcome: If M is selected, then both G and H must be selected.
In this case, M, the sufficient condition, is enough to trigger *both* G and H. In other words, M alone is enough to trigger G, and M alone is enough to trigger H. Thus, we can split the compound statement into two simple statements as we've already learned to do:

> If M is selected, then G is selected. (M $\longrightarrow$ G)
> If M is selected, then H is selected. (M $\longrightarrow$ H)

Of course, from these two simple statements, we can derive two contrapositives:

> If G is not selected, then M is not selected. (–G $\longrightarrow$ –M)
> If H is not selected, then M is not selected. (–H $\longrightarrow$ –M)

It's important to note that type 1 compound statements won't always have the word "and" explicitly written in the statement. For example:

> If M is selected, then G is selected but H is not.

9

This is a type 1 compound statement in disguise! Selecting M triggers two outcomes: G is selected AND H is *not* selected. We could split this up as follows

$$M \longrightarrow G$$
$$M \longrightarrow -H$$

So, it's the same type of statement, just disguised in different phrasing. Be on the lookout!

2. OR in the trigger: If M or G is selected, then H must be selected.
In this case, M on its own is enough to trigger H. We can say the same for G. *Either one* is enough to trigger the outcome, H.

Thus, we can split this compound statement into two simple statements:

If M is selected, then H is selected. (M $\longrightarrow$ H)
If G is selected, then H is selected. (G $\longrightarrow$ H)

Again, we can generate contrapositives:

If H is not selected, then M is not selected. (–H $\longrightarrow$ –M)
If H is not selected, then G is not selected. (–H $\longrightarrow$ –G)

3. AND in the trigger: If M and G are selected, then H is selected.
Here, *both* M and G *together* are enough to trigger H, but neither one *alone* is enough. Thus, we CANNOT split this statement into two parts. We must keep it together:

$$M \text{ and } G \longrightarrow H$$

See if you can figure out the contrapositive of that statement before reading on. Consider what we know if H is not selected.

To find the contrapositive of a statement like this, reverse and negate the elements and SWAP "AND" for "OR" or vice versa (we'll discuss why shortly):

$$-H \longrightarrow -M \text{ or } -G$$

4. OR in the outcome: If M is selected, then G or H is selected.
Notice that M is enough to trigger G or H, but not necessarily both. Thus, we CANNOT split this statement into two parts. We must keep it together:

$$M \longrightarrow G \text{ or } H$$

Again, to find the contrapositive, reverse, negate, and SWAP "AND" for "OR" or vice versa:

$$-G \text{ and } -H \longrightarrow -M$$

By the way, when the LSAT uses "or," unless something like "but not both" is also stated, both is fine. This means that in the above example, if M is selected, G and H might both be selected. This is different from how we often use "or" in everyday life.

Compound statement types #2, #3, and #4 are quite rare on the LSAT, but it's a good idea to be prepared to deal with them when they do crop up. Let's summarize the four types:

Type	Example	Strategy	Notation	Contrapositive	Frequency
AND as an outcome	If J, then K and L.	Split it up	$J \longrightarrow K$ $J \longrightarrow L$	$-K \longrightarrow -J$ $-L \longrightarrow -J$	Common
OR as a trigger	If M or N, then P.	Split it up	$M \longrightarrow P$ $N \longrightarrow P$	$-P \longrightarrow -M$ $-P \longrightarrow -N$	Rare
AND as a trigger	If R and S, then X.	Together	$R \text{ and } S \longrightarrow X$	$-X \longrightarrow -R \text{ or } -S$	Rare
OR as an outcome	If Q, then T or V.	Together	$Q \longrightarrow T \text{ or } V$	$-T \text{ and } -V \longrightarrow -Q$	Rare

To Memorize or to Reason?

For *standard* conditional statements, it's not only unnecessary for us to reason our way to the contrapositive, but it's also dangerous—it creates a potential for error. Reverse and negate and be done with it. If we're told $K \longrightarrow -L$, we know that $L \longrightarrow -K$ and we shouldn't have to think much about why. But a compound conditional statement might require a bit of thought.

While it's easy enough for many people to remember to swap "and" for "or," this is exactly the sort of thing that trips some of us up when we're under the gun. Therefore, it can be helpful to have a process to reason your way to the contrapositive so that your rules make sense. Plus, it's a good brain stretcher even for those who are comfortable with the automation.

To reason your way to a compound contrapositive, start by thinking of the "if" part of the conditional as the "trigger," and the "then" part as the "outcome," as we've suggested previously. Then you can reason your way to the contrapositive as follows:

> "If the outcome isn't true, then the trigger can't be true."

Let's see how this thought process can help us get the contrapositives for four more compound conditionals:

1. If Jean and Fran go, Bill will not.

This can be represented as $J + F \longrightarrow -B$.

We can think of Jean and Fran going as the trigger, and Bill not going as the outcome. Let's apply our reasoning:

> "If the outcome isn't true, then the trigger can't be true."

What would make the outcome not true? *If Bill went.*

What would make the trigger not true? *If either Jean or Fran didn't go.* Be careful if you thought, "If Jean and Fran didn't go"! While both of them not going would mean the trigger didn't occur, it isn't necessary, and thus it's not the logical opposite.

We can represent this contrapositive as follows:

$$B \longrightarrow -J \text{ or } -F$$

2. If neither Ted nor Seth is selected, Raj will be.

This can be represented as $-T$ and $-S \longrightarrow R$.

> "If the outcome isn't true, then the trigger can't be true."

What would make the outcome not true? *If Raj is not selected.*

What would make the trigger not true? *If either Ted or Seth is selected.*

We can represent this contrapositive as follows:

$$-R \longrightarrow T \text{ or } S$$

3. If Carol doesn't go, either Bruce or Erica will go.

This can be represented as $-C \longrightarrow B \text{ or } E$.

> "If the outcome isn't true, then the trigger can't true."

What would make the outcome not true? *If both Bruce and Erica didn't go.*

What would make the trigger not true? *If Carol went.*

We can represent this contrapositive as follows:

$$-B \text{ and } -E \longrightarrow C$$

4. If Matt is on the finance committee, Greg or Jan will not be.

This can be represented $M \longrightarrow -G \text{ or } -J$.

"If the outcome isn't true, then the trigger can't be true."

What would make the outcome not true? *If both Greg and Jan are on the committee.*

What would make the trigger not true? *If Matt is not on the committee.*

We can represent this contrapositive as follows:

$$G + J \longrightarrow -M$$

Let's try one more to discuss what "but not both" might do to the situation:

5. If Sam goes, either Ruth or Tim, but not both, will go.

This one is difficult to represent! We know that if Sam goes, we'll have one of the following situations: Ruth will not go but Tim will, or Tim will not go but Ruth will. We can represent that as the following: $S \longrightarrow (-R + T)$ or $(-T + R)$.

The "but not both" is implied in that representation, since we could never have both $(-R + T)$ and $(-T + R)$. That would require Ruth and Tim to both go and not go at the same time!

"If the outcome isn't true, then the trigger can't be true."

What would make the outcome not true? *In this case, two different situations: both Ruth and Tom don't go, or both Ruth and Tom do go.* Tricky!

What would make the trigger not true? *If Sam doesn't go.*

We can represent this contrapositive as a "compound compound" statement:

$$(R + T) \text{ or } (-R + -T) \longrightarrow -S$$

We can also think of this as two separate triggers that lead to the same outcome:

$$R + T \longrightarrow -S$$
$$-R + -T \longrightarrow -S$$

9

A Geekier Approach

For those who are interested, there is a more formal approach to compound statements. Begin by putting compounds in parentheses to treat them as "blocks." When forming the contrapositive, negate the entire block, as in −(B or T). While the following might give you an unwanted flashback to middle school algebra class, if you want to get fancy, you can "distribute" a negative sign throughout the compound part of a compound rule (i.e., the part you'd put in parentheses). The key is to remember to negate the "and" or the "or," along with each element (again, "and" and "or" are negations of each other). For example, if we wanted to simplify the negative in −(−Q + −T), we would first negate −Q, which gives us Q, then negate the "+" (and), which gives us "or," and then negate the −T. We're left with simply (Q or T).

Here's a chart that shows how we can derive contrapositives from a few compound conditionals using the method discussed above.

Original	Block Negated	Negation Distributed
A + B ⟶ C	−C ⟶ −(A + B)	−C ⟶ −A or −B
−Q + −T ⟶ S	−S ⟶ −(−Q + −T)	−S ⟶ Q or T
P ⟶ −R or Q	−(−R or Q) ⟶ −P	R + −Q ⟶ −P
T ⟶ Y or S	−(Y or S) ⟶ −T	−Y + −S ⟶ −T

Again, we want to stress that for some students, it's far easier to think about conditional logic in a more formal or mathematical fashion, and for others, it's easier to think about these situations by reasoning through them. In fact, we imagine you might know already which process feels more comfortable to you. Learn both, but then use whichever approach feels most comfortable.

We also want to stress that compound conditionals such as the ones above are rare on the exam, and, in our experience, it is not critical that you define and write down the contrapositive during your initial setup. However, it is likely that you will need to think about the contrapositive at some point to answer at least one of the questions.

One important and often confused point to remember is that "or" does not exclude "and." For example, based on the statement "Either Ken or Han is selected," *both* Ken and Han can be selected. This combination is only excluded when it's made explicit that "and" is not okay. It would look like this: "Either Ken or Han is selected, but not both." If this is confusing, or seems completely counterintuitive to you, think of any "or" as "and/or" (unless, again, it's explicitly stated that "and" is not allowed).

Now that you've got a handle on advanced conditional statements, it's time to practice. Then, in the next chapter, you'll learn to apply your understanding of conditional statements and their contrapositives to Conditional Grouping games.

DRILL IT: Drawing Inferences from Advanced Conditional Statements

Convert each of the statements into conditional diagrams, and then derive contrapositive inferences. Keep in mind that some statements may result in "double" diagrams. Be sure to check your responses against the solutions **after each exercise.**

Example: If X is selected, then both Y and Z are selected.

Conversions:	Contrapositives:
X ⟶ Y	–Y ⟶ –X
X ⟶ Z	–Z ⟶ –X

1. Martinez is not chosen unless Jones is chosen.

7. If both P and Q are selected, then R is selected.

2. If H is selected, then J is selected but G is not.

8. L is chosen if, and only if, G is selected.

3. Rolfson and Strapini cannot both be selected.

9. W and X cannot both be chosen.

4. If K is selected, then neither M nor N is selected.

10. If Paulson is selected, then Oster is selected but Vicenza is not.

5. If Fiora is chosen, then both Lane and Newsam are chosen.

11. T is not selected unless R is selected.

6. V is selected if, and only if, P is selected.

12. Neither X nor Y is chosen if Z is chosen.

9

SOLUTIONS: Drawing Inferences from Advanced Conditional Statements

1. Martinez is not chosen unless Jones is chosen.

$$M \rightarrow J \qquad -J \rightarrow -M$$

2. If H is selected, then J is selected but G is not.

$$H \rightarrow J \qquad \cdot J \rightarrow -H$$
$$H \rightarrow -G \qquad G \rightarrow -H$$

3. Rolfson and Strapini cannot both be selected.

$$R \rightarrow -S \qquad S \rightarrow -R$$

4. If K is selected, then neither M nor N is selected.

$$K \rightarrow -M \qquad M \rightarrow -K$$
$$K \rightarrow -N \qquad N \rightarrow -K$$

5. If Fiora is chosen, then both Lane and Newsam are chosen.

$$F \rightarrow L \qquad -L \rightarrow -F$$
$$F \rightarrow N \qquad -N \rightarrow -F$$

6. V is selected if, and only if, P is selected.

$$P \leftrightarrow V \quad OR \quad -V \leftrightarrow -P$$

$$P \rightarrow V \qquad -V \rightarrow -P$$
$$V \rightarrow P \qquad -P \rightarrow -V$$

7. If both P and Q are selected, then R is selected.

$$P \text{ and } Q \rightarrow R \qquad -R \rightarrow -P \text{ or } -Q$$

8. L is chosen if, and only if, G is selected.

$$L \leftrightarrow G \quad OR \quad -G \leftrightarrow -L$$

$$L \rightarrow G \qquad -G \rightarrow -L$$
$$G \rightarrow L \qquad -L \rightarrow -G$$

9. W and X cannot both be chosen.

$$W \rightarrow -X \qquad X \rightarrow -W$$

10. If Paulson is selected, then Oster is selected but Vicenza is not.

$$P \rightarrow O \qquad -O \rightarrow -P$$
$$P \rightarrow -V \qquad V \rightarrow -P$$

11. T is not selected unless R is selected.

$$T \rightarrow R \qquad -R \rightarrow -T$$

12. Neither X nor Y is chosen if Z is chosen.

$$Z \rightarrow -X \qquad X \rightarrow -Z$$
$$Z \rightarrow -Y \qquad Y \rightarrow -Z$$

Chapter 10

of

Logic Games

Conditional Grouping

In This Chapter...

Getting Familiar

Do your best to complete the following game. Use whatever approach you see fit. Give yourself **8:45.**

One or more of six violinists—Greene, Holiday, Liu, Mann, Underwood, and Wilson—will be selected to perform at the year-end concert. No other violinists will be selected. The following conditions apply:

> If Holiday is selected, then Mann is not selected.
> If Liu is selected, then both Mann and Wilson are selected.
> If Underwood is not selected, then Holiday is selected.
> Wilson is not selected unless Greene is selected.

1. Which of the following could be a complete and accurate list of the violinists selected for the concert?

    (A) Holiday, Liu, Wilson, Underwood
    (B) Liu, Mann, Wilson
    (C) Holiday, Liu, Mann
    (D) Liu, Mann, Wilson
    (E) Mann, Underwood

2. Which of the following must be false?

    (A) Liu is selected but Underwood is not.
    (B) Neither Underwood nor Liu is selected.
    (C) Holiday is selected but Liu is not.
    (D) Both Greene and Underwood are selected.
    (E) Holiday is selected but Mann is not.

3. Which of the following could be the only violinist selected for the concert?

    (A) Liu
    (B) Mann
    (C) Greene
    (D) Wilson
    (E) Underwood

4. If Underwood is not selected, then which of the following must be true?

    (A) Wilson is not selected.
    (B) Greene is selected.
    (C) At least two violinists are selected.
    (D) At most three violinists are selected.
    (E) Neither Liu nor Holiday is selected.

5. If Greene is not selected, then each of the following could be true EXCEPT:

    (A) Exactly two violinists are selected.
    (B) Exactly one violinist is selected.
    (C) Mann is selected.
    (D) Holiday is selected.
    (E) Liu is selected.

6. Which of the following CANNOT be a complete and accurate list of the violinists who are selected for the concert?

    (A) Greene, Liu, Mann, Underwood, Wilson
    (B) Greene, Mann, Underwood
    (C) Greene, Mann, Wilson
    (D) Greene, Underwood
    (E) Holiday

7. Which of the following, if substituted for the condition that if Liu is selected then both Mann and Wilson are selected, would have the same effect in determining the violinists who are selected to perform?

    (A) If Liu is selected, then exactly two other violinists are selected.
    (B) If Liu is selected, then both Greene and Underwood are selected but Holiday is not.
    (C) If Mann and Wilson are selected, then Liu is selected.
    (D) If Liu is selected, then Mann is one of exactly five violinists selected.
    (E) If Liu is not selected, then neither Mann nor Wilson is selected.

Recognizing Conditional Grouping Games

About 12% of all games are Conditional Grouping games. Conditional Grouping games tend to be very difficult for those who do not have a repeatable method with which to attack the setup. We'll discuss this method shortly, but first let's take a look at the characteristics that define Conditional Grouping.

Scenario Cues

Remember, there are two main organizational schemes that appear in Logic Games: ordering and grouping. Conditional Grouping scenarios ask you to split the given elements into exactly two groups. In fact, since they're always binary, we considered calling these games "Conditional Binary Grouping Games," but there are only so many words we can fit in without leaving us all tongue-tied. These binary scenarios are presented in one of the following two ways:

1. In or Out. In this type of Conditional Grouping scenario, some elements are selected to be a part of the "in" group, while the remaining elements are left "out":

> One or more of seven actors—Q, R, S, T, V, W, and Y—will be cast in a play at the community theater. No other actors will be cast.

> An investor will purchase shares of at least one of the following six stocks: F, G, H, J, K, and L. The investor will not purchase any other stocks.

> A florist creates a bouquet using one or more of the following flowers: daisies, gladioli, lilacs, roses, snapdragons, and tulips. No other flower types are used.

2. One or the Other. In this type of Conditional Grouping scenario, elements are divided among two distinct groups or categories.

> Each of seven bus drivers—Q, R, S, T V, W, and Y—will be assigned to drive exactly one of two bus routes: the Highland route or the Grasshill route.

> Each of six employees—F, G, H, J, K, and M—will work as part of either the sales team or the marketing team, but not both.

> Six students—S, T, W, X, Y, and Z—enrolled late for the Anthropology Seminar course. Each of these students will be assigned to exactly one of the following course sections: Section I, Section II.

10

Rule Cues

All Conditional Grouping games are characterized by rules that take the form of conditional statements. In the last chapter, we looked at all the different types of conditional statements you are likely to see on the LSAT. When you see a logic game that has all conditional rules, you can bet you're dealing with a Conditional Grouping game. Let's review the common conditional statements we introduced in the last chapter:

1.   J and K cannot both be selected.

2.   If M is selected, both G and H must be selected.

3.   Neither H nor K is selected if L is selected.

4.   If J is selected, then G is selected but L is not.

5.   F cannot be selected unless H is also selected.

6.   L is selected if, and only if, M is also selected.

7.   If either Q or R is selected, both must be selected.

8.   N and W cannot be on the same team.

If you are unsure of what to make of these conditional statements, now would be a good time to review the previous chapter. Your ability to handle Conditional Grouping games depends on your ability to translate conditional statements.

Open vs. Closed Conditional Grouping

Note that each of the scenarios above is "open" with respect to the number of elements that may be assigned to each group. That is, based on the information given, we are not limited in terms of how many people are assigned to one team or another, or how many people take one course or another. On some occasions the LSAT will "close," or define, the number of elements to be assigned to one of the two groups:

> Exactly five people will be selected to serve on the university social committee.
> These five people will be selected from a group of three students—X, Y, and Z; three professors—F, G, and H; and three administrators—O, P, and Q.

In this case, we know that exactly five people must be chosen. The setup for "closed" games is almost identical to that for "open" games (you'll see the differences later in the chapter).

10

Putting It Together

Let's apply these recognition skills to the violinist game introduced earlier in the chapter:

> One or more of six violinists—Greene, Holiday, Liu, Mann, Underwood, and Wilson—will be selected to perform at the year-end concert. No other violinists will be selected. The following conditions apply:
>
> If Holiday is selected, then Mann is not selected.
> If Liu is selected, then both Mann and Wilson are selected.
> If Underwood is not selected, then Holiday is selected.
> Wilson is not selected unless Greene is selected.

In this scenario, violinists are either selected for the concert or they are left out. This is a classic "In or Out" scenario. Notice that there is no limit to the number of violinists that can be selected. Thus, this is an *Open* Conditional Grouping game. Also notice that each of the four rules is written in one of the common conditional forms reviewed above.

Now that we can identify Conditional Grouping games, let's talk about the best way to approach the setup.

Setup: The Logic Chain

The Logic Chain is the best approach for most Conditional Grouping games. The Logic Chain is a diagramming method that may look intimidating at first, but will be easy to use and powerful once you get comfortable with it. Let's set one up:

Step 1: Create Binary Columns

After determining that we are dealing with a Conditional Grouping game, we begin by creating two columns, one that will represent "IN" (selected for the concert) and one that will represent "OUT" (not selected).

IN   OUT

Step 2: Diagram the First Rule

If Holiday is selected, then Mann is not selected.

This first rule contains an H and an M. We want to start our diagram by placing an H and an M in both the "IN" and the "OUT" columns. Note that we place our letters about halfway down the empty space we've left under the column headers. We want to leave room above and below so that we can add in other letters later on.

Now we're ready to draw in our first conditional arrow. The rule tells us: H ⟶ –M. In other words, an H "IN" triggers an M "OUT." We start with the H "IN" trigger (left column) and draw an arrow to M "OUT."

Step 3: Diagram the Contrapositive of the First Rule

The given rule is: H ⟶ –M. So the contrapositive (reverse and negate) is: M ⟶ –H. In other words, M "IN" triggers H "OUT." So, we'll start with the M "IN" trigger and draw an arrow to H "OUT."

Step 4: Move to the Next Rule that Shares a Common Letter

Part of the challenge of the Logic Chain is keeping your diagram neat and tidy so you can read it quickly when you're attacking the questions. In order to facilitate this, we want to place connected letters as close to each other as possible. We currently have H and M on our diagram, so let's find the next rule that contains an H or an M:

✓   If Holiday is selected, then Mann is not selected.
    If Liu is selected, then both Mann and Wilson are selected.
    If Underwood is not selected, then Holiday is selected.
    Wilson is not selected unless Greene is selected.

In this case, the second rule shares an M:

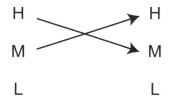

If Liu is selected, then both Mann and Wilson are selected.

Since Liu is directly connected with Mann, we'll put our L's directly below the M's on our diagram, and then we'll place the W's below the L's.

To keep your chain neat, always write the same letters directly across from each other.

Recall from the previous chapter on conditional logic that the second rule actually gives us two distinct relationships: 1) If L is in then M is in, and 2) If L is in then W is in.

MANHATTAN
LSAT   337

To diagram the first part of this, we'll start with the L "IN" trigger and trace an arrow to the M "IN" trigger. Notice that this creates a same-column connection. We want to draw this connection on the outside to keep things neat.

To diagram the second part of this rule, we'll start with the L "IN" trigger and trace an arrow to the W "IN" trigger. Again, this creates a same-column connection.

Step 5: Diagram the contrapositive

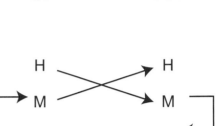

Since we had two statements from this rule, we'll have two contrapositives. If we reverse and negate part 1, we get: If M is out, then L is out. To diagram this, we'll start with the M "OUT" trigger and trace an arrow to L "OUT."

If we reverse and negate part 2, we get: If W is out, then L is out. To diagram this, we'll start with the W "OUT" trigger and trace an arrow to L "OUT."

Now we just need to repeat steps 4 and 5 for the remaining rules. Move to the next rule that shares a common letter with one already on the diagram:

If Underwood is not selected, then Holiday is selected.

Since the U will be connected to the H, we'll draw our U's directly above our H's. Then, we'll start with U "OUT" and trace an arrow to H "IN."

To diagram the contrapositive of this, we'll start with H "OUT" and trace an arrow to U "IN."

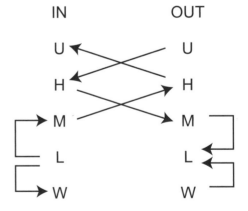

Last rule:

Wilson is not selected unless Greene is selected.

Since the G will be connected to the W, we'll place our G's immediately below the W's in the diagram.

This is an advanced rule that we studied in the previous chapter. If W is selected, we know for sure that G must be selected as well: If W in, then G in. (If you're not quite sure how we came up with the "If... then" statement from this rule, you may want to go back and review Conditional Logic 202.)

The contrapositive is: If G out, then W out.

Let's double-check that we've used all six elements; sometimes there's a floater for which there are no rules.

10

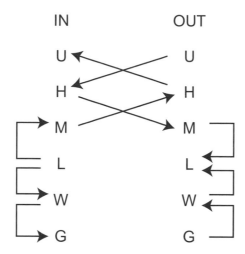

Alternate Approach

Note that some test-takers prefer to start their logic chain by creating two columns listing all of the elements in the alphabetical order in which they are given in the scenario. Though this isn't the method we most recommend, if it feels more comfortable for you, feel free to adapt the chain in this way—it won't prevent you from making any inferences. Do keep in mind that this strategy is very likely to make your diagram look messier, so you will need to take extra care to be neat and organized. The approach of writing down the elements in an order dictated by the rules, which we recommend, may take a bit longer to master, but it will pay off by leading to neater diagrams that are generally easier to use.

Now we have a completed diagram that looks pretty strange! However, we haven't yet seen the real power of the Logic Chain. Let's take a look at how we can use it to our advantage.

Logic Chain Power: Second-Level Inferences

The utility of the Logic Chain tool is that it connects the rules automatically. This will come in handy when we go to answer the questions. Take a look at a few examples that demonstrate the power of the Logic Chain.

What do we know if U is out?

Well, our original rules told us that if U is out, then H is in. However, there's more to be uncovered. Follow the arrows (the logic chain) from U "OUT." If U is out, H is in, which means M is out, which means L is out! We can summarize with a T-chart:

10

in	out
H	U
	M
	L

You MUST remember to read only in the direction of the arrows. A common mistake would be to start with U out, trace it across to H in, then back to M out, then down to L out, *and then down to W out*. L out does NOT lead to W out! Read only in the direction of the arrows to make your inferences.

What do we know if L is in?

Before reading on, create a T-chart and make all the possible inferences from L being in.

L in has two distinct branches coming off it. The bottom one takes us to W in, which leads to G in. The other branch takes us to M in, which leads to H out, which leads to U in. In summary, when L is in we get:

in	out
L	H
W	
G	
M	
U	

In a moment, we'll use our diagram to tackle the questions associated with the violinist game, but first let's practice the mechanics of the Logic Chain setup.

10

DRILL IT: Mini Logic Chain Setups #1

Create a Logic Chain diagram for each of the mini scenarios presented below. Assume that each game is a binary situation. Be sure to check the solutions **after each exercise**. We've started the first one for you.

1. If H is in, then G is in.

in	out
H	H
G	G

4. If V is in, then both P and Q are out.

2. If L is out, then M is in.

5. X plays volleyball only if Y plays squash.

3. R and T cannot both be in.

6. The characters Z and W must be played by actors of different genders.

10

SOLUTIONS: Mini Logic Chain Setups #1

Check your Logic Chains against our solutions. You may have arranged the letters differently, but make sure that all of your connections are the same.

1. If H is in, then G is in.

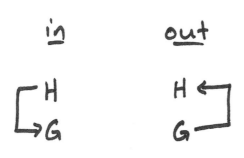

2. If L is out, then M is in.

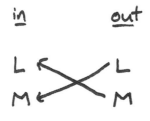

3. R and T cannot both be in.

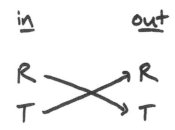

4. If V is in, then both P and Q are out.

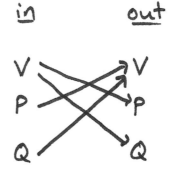

5. X plays volleyball only if Y plays squash.

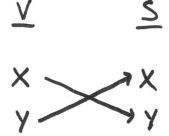

6. The characters Z and W must be played by actors of different genders.

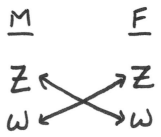

10

Special Situations

The Logic Chain is a powerful diagram for working though Conditional Grouping games; you will feel like a wizard as you follow a string of inferences around the chain. However, as with every game type, there are times when you'll need to adapt the diagram to accommodate some particularly tricky rules. It's worth exploring some of these rules here:

1. Biconditionals. Take a look at this scenario and the accompanying rules:

> Floyd, George and Hank are each being assigned to one of only two camp activities—swimming or tennis. The assignments must adhere to the following conditions:
>
> George and Hank cannot be assigned to the same activity.
> Floyd will be assigned to swimming if, but only if, Hank is.

To start, we can tell this is a Conditional Grouping game because there is a choice between two groups and there are only conditional rules. We'll create the two columns and place the elements that are used in the first rule:

$$\begin{array}{cc} \underline{\text{S}} & \underline{\text{T}} \\ \text{H} & \text{H} \\ \text{G} & \text{G} \end{array}$$

George and Hank cannot be assigned to the same activity.

Now let's think about the implications of this first rule. If G is assigned to swimming, we know that H is assigned to tennis. We also know that if H is assigned to swimming, G is assigned to tennis. So far, we have the chart to the right:

$$\begin{array}{cc} \underline{\text{S}} & \underline{\text{T}} \\ \text{H} & \text{H} \\ \text{G} & \text{G} \end{array}$$

But did you notice another set of relationships? Indeed, if G or H is assigned to tennis, then the other person is assigned to swimming, so we could write this:

$$\begin{array}{cc} \underline{\text{S}} & \underline{\text{T}} \\ \text{H} & \text{H} \\ \text{G} & \text{G} \end{array}$$

But that's a lot of arrows. We can simplify by creating double-sided arrows as in the chart below to the right:

That seems a lot more elegant, but there's one thing to be wary of: at this point you should be well on your way to reading only "down" the arrows. However, with a double-sided arrow you have to read in *both* directions. There's a danger that you might not realize, for example, that H in swimming means G in tennis, since it seems like you're reading illegally "up" that arrow. If you're able to stay aware of the bidirectionality, great. If you think you'll forget, consider using some other symbol at the end of double-sided arrows, like a circle or an "X."

If you use something like what's shown to the right, you'll definitely remember that these arrows are not the usual ones.

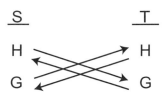

Using the diagram to the right, draw the arrows for the second rule:

Floyd will be assigned to swimming if, but only if, Hank is.

Since "if, but only if" indicates that the relationship is biconditional, you should have drawn something like the following (Of course, you may use double-sided arrows if you prefer):

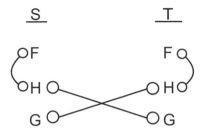

2. Compound conditionals.

Remember from the chapter on conditional logic that we advise you to split all compound statements that can be split, and then take the contrapositives of those individual statements. Also remember that, generally speaking, the compound statements that can be split are those that include an "or" situation in the trigger or an "and" situation in the outcome.

The compound conditionals that cannot be split are, generally speaking, those that include an "and" situation in the trigger or an "or" situation in the outcome. Because they're unsplittable, these statements cannot be drawn easily into your chain, and ought to be written to the side. As we mentioned in the last chapter, these types of statements are relatively rare.

Smart Tip: Find the Contrapositive Rhythm

Have you noticed a rhythm to drawing in contrapositives? In short, it goes like this: "Whatever I end with, I start with its opposite." To demonstrate, consider the rule "If Q is out, R is in." You'd start with Q out and draw an arrow to R in. Now, *start with the opposite* of R in, which is R out, and draw a line to the opposite of Q out. If you find yourself struggling to correctly write contrapositives, use the next drill as an opportunity to practice using the rhythm.

DRILL IT: Mini Logic Chain Setups #2

Create a Logic Chain diagram for each of the mini scenarios presented below. Be sure to check the solutions **after each exercise**.

1. If H is in, then G is in.
    If J is out, then G is out.

2. If K is out, then both L and M are in.
    If L is in, then K is out.

3. S cannot be out unless T is in.
    If R is in, then S is in.

4. If Q is in, then V is in, but P is not.
    If V is in, then P or R is in.

5. Everyone must have exactly one numbered
    locker (1–100).
    X and W cannot both have odd-numbered
    lockers.
    Neither Y nor Z can have odd-numbered
    lockers if W has an odd-numbered locker.

6. If F and N are selected, O will not be.
    If O is selected, P and S will not be.

10

SOLUTIONS: Mini Logic Chain Setups #2

Check your Logic Chains against our solutions. You may have arranged the letters differently, but make sure all of your connections match ours.

1. If H is in, then G is in.
    If J is out, then G is out.

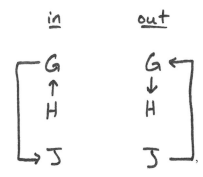

2. If K is out, then both L and M are in.
    If L is in, then K is out.

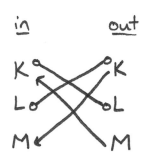

3. S cannot be out unless T is in.
    If R is in, then S is in.

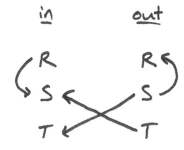

4. If Q is in, then V is in, but P is not.
    If V is in, then P or R is in.

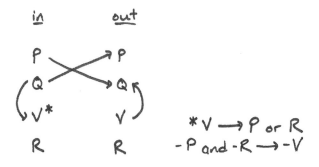

5. Everyone must have exactly one numbered
    locker (1 – 100).
    X and W cannot both have odd-numbered
    lockers.
    Neither Y nor Z can have odd-numbered
    lockers if W has an odd-numbered locker.

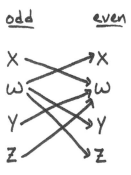

6. If F and N are selected, O will not be.
    If O is selected, P and S will not be.

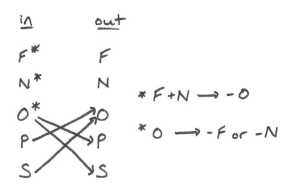

DRILL IT: Mini Logic Chain Setups #3

Another drill already? Yes! Let's move ahead to using our Logic Chains by creating T-charts for Conditional questions. Create a Logic Chain diagram for each of the mini scenarios presented below and then answer the associated questions. Be sure to check the solutions **after each exercise**.

1. Four candidates—P, Q, R, and S—interview for jobs at Microsite, Inc. No other candidates interview for jobs at Microsite, and each candidate who interviews is either hired or not hired. The following conditions apply:

    P cannot be hired unless S is also hired.
    If R is hired, then both Q and P are hired.

(a) What do we know if R is hired? Create a T-chart.

(b) What do we know if R is NOT hired? Create a T-chart.

2. Five commuters—L, M, N, O, and P—each take exactly one of two trains to work: the Highbrook train or the Sullivan train. These commuters take no other train to work, and the following conditions apply:

    If O takes the Sullivan train, then M takes the Highbrook train.
    If P takes the Highbrook train, then L takes the Sullivan train and N takes the Highbrook train.
    M and L cannot take the same train.

(a) What do we know if P takes the Highbrook Train? Create a T-chart.

(b) What do we know if M takes the Sullivan Train? Create a T-chart.

3. Jenny's Juice Store will have a sale on at least one of the following five kinds of juice: grape, mango, orange, pineapple, and tomato. No other juices will be included in the sale. The following rules apply:

> If mango juice is included in the sale, then grape juice is also included but tomato juice is not.
> Pineapple juice is not included in the sale unless orange juice is included.
> If grape juice is included in the sale, then orange juice is also included.

(a) What do we know if mango juice is on sale? Create a T-chart.

(b) What do we know if grape juice is not on sale? Create a T-chart.

(c) What do we know if one and only one of either mango or grape juice is on sale? Create a T-chart.

4. Six kindergarten students—R, S, T, V, X, and Y—will each be assigned to one of two teachers: Mr. Paulson or Mrs. Hanson. None of these six students will be assigned to any other teacher, and the following conditions apply:

> If S is assigned to Mrs. Hanson, then V is assigned to Mr. Paulson.
> If X is assigned to Mr. Paulson, then T is assigned to Mr. Paulson.
> If R is assigned to Mrs. Hanson, then V is also.

(a) What do we know if S is assigned to Mrs. Hanson? Create a T-chart.

(b) What do we know if V is assigned to Mr. Paulson? Create a T-chart.

(c) What do we know if both V and X are assigned to Mr. Paulson? Create a T-chart.

MANHATTAN
LSAT

SOLUTIONS: Mini Logic Chain Setups #3

Check your Logic Chains against our solutions. You may have arranged the letters differently, but make sure all of your connections match ours. If you are missing any connections, or if you misdiagrammed, check the numbered arrows in the diagram against the numbered rules to see where you may have gone wrong. The numbers also represent the order in which we drew the connecting arrows.

1. Four candidates—P, Q, R, and S—interview for jobs at Microsite, Inc. No other candidates interview for jobs at Microsite, and each candidate who interviews is either hired or not hired. The following conditions apply:

   P cannot be hired unless S is also hired.
   If R is hired, then both Q and P are hired.

   (1) P cannot be hired unless S is also hired.
       (P → S)
   (2) CONTRAPOSITIVE (–S → –P)
   (3) If R is hired, then both Q and P are hired. (R → Q, R → P)
   (4) CONTRAPOSITIVES
       (–Q → –R, –P → –R)

(a) What do we know if R is hired? Create a T-chart.

(b) What do we know if R is NOT hired? Create a T-chart.

Be careful! Read only in the direction of the arrows. R not hired tells us nothing about P, Q, or S.

2. Five commuters—L, M, N, O, and P—each take exactly one of two trains to work: the Highbrook train or the Sullivan train. These commuters take no other train to work, and the following conditions apply:

> If O takes the Sullivan train, then M takes the Highbrook train.
> If P takes the Highbrook train, then L takes the Sullivan train and N takes the Highbrook train.
> M and L cannot take the same train.

(1) If O takes the Sullivan train, then M takes the Highbrook train. (Os → Mh)

(2) CONTRAPOSITIVE (Ms → Oh)

(3) The second rule doesn't share any common letters with what we have on the diagram so far (O and M), so we'll skip to the last rule: M and L cannot take the same train.

This one is a bit tricky. If M and L can't take the same train, then M and L are what we would call *mutually exclusive* elements. What happens if M is on a given train? Then L is not. The relationship holds in both directions. If L is on a given train, then M is not. So we have a biconditional!

$$Mh \longleftrightarrow Ls \quad Lh \longleftrightarrow Ms$$

Remember, this bidirectionality is NOT usually valid for normal conditional statements; this is a special case that hinges on the fact that each commuter must take one of the two trains.

On the Logic Chain diagram, we notate these mutually exclusive relationships with special arrosws.

(4) Now we'll double back to the second rule. If P takes the Highbrook train, then L takes the Sullivan train and N takes the Highbrook train. (Ph → Ls, Ph → Nh)

(5) CONTRAPOSITIVES (Lh → Ps, Ns → Ps)

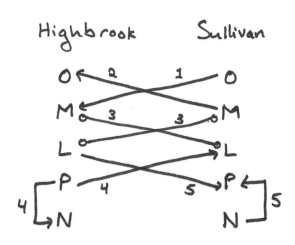

(a) What do we know if P takes the Highbrook train? Create a T-chart.

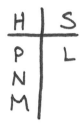

Be careful! It's easy to miss the two-sided arrow coming off L.

(b) What do we know if M takes the Sullivan train? Create a T-chart.

H	S
O	M
L	P

Be careful! Do NOT trace from Ps against the arrow to Ns!

3. Jenny's Juice Store will have a sale on at least one of the following five kinds of juice: grape, mango, orange, pineapple, and tomato. No other juices will be included in the sale. The following rules apply:

    If mango juice is included in the sale, then grape juice is also included but tomato juice is not.
    Pineapple juice is not included in the sale unless orange juice is included.
    If grape juice is included in the sale, then orange juice is also included.

    (1) If mango juice is included in the sale, then grape juice is also included but tomato juice is not. (M → G, M → –T)
    (2) CONTRAPOSITIVES (–G → –M, T → –M)
    (3) The second rule doesn't contain an M, T, or G, so we'll skip down to the third rule. If grape juice is included in the sale, then orange juice is also included. (G → O)
    (4) CONTRAPOSITIVE (–O → –G)
    (5) Now we'll double back to the second rule. Pineapple juice is not included in the sale unless orange juice is included. (P → O)
    (6) CONTRAPOSITIVE (–O → –P)

(a) What do we know if mango juice is on sale? Create a T-chart.

S	NS
M	T
G	
O	

(b) What do we know if grape juice is not on sale? Create a T-chart.

S	NS
	G
	M

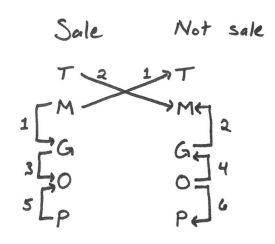

(c) What do we know if one and only one of either mango or grape juice is on sale? Create a T-chart.

S	NS
G	M
O	

We can't have mango on sale, because that would force in grape, too!

4. Six kindergarten students—R, S, T, V, X, and Y—will each be assigned to one of two teachers: Mr. Paulson or Mrs. Hanson. None of these six students will be assigned to any other teacher, and the following conditions apply:

> If S is assigned to Mrs. Hanson, then V is assigned to Mr. Paulson.
> If X is assigned to Mr. Paulson, then T is assigned to Mr. Paulson.
> If R is assigned to Mrs. Hanson, then V is also.

(1) If S is assigned to Mrs. Hanson, then V is assigned to Mr. Paulson. (Sh ➝ Vp)
(2) CONTRAPOSITIVE (Vh ➝ Sp)
(3) The second rule does not contain an S or a V, so we'll move to the third rule. If R is assigned to Mrs. Hanson, then V is also. (Rh ➝ Vh)
(4) CONTRAPOSITIVE (Vp ➝ Rp)
(5) If X is assigned to Mr. Paulson, then T is assigned to Mr. Paulson. (Xp ➝ Tp)
(6) CONTRAPOSITIVE (Th ➝ Xh)
(7) Since there was no rule for Y, we'll simply write it into our chart.

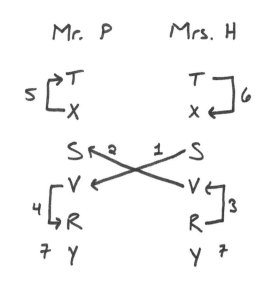

(a) What do we know if S is assigned to Mrs. Hanson? Create a T-chart.

```
 P  |  H
 V  |  S
 R  |
```

(b) What do we know if V is assigned to Mr. Paulson? Create a T-chart.

```
 P  |  H
 V  |
 R  |
```

(c) What do we know if both V and X are assigned to Mr. Paulson? Create a T-chart.

```
 P  |  H
 V  |
 X  |
 R  |
 T  |
```

Try It Again

Now that you've learned how to set up the Logic Chain, it's time to put your skills to good use. Let's revisit our Getting Familiar game. Develop the Logic Chain from scratch, and then use it to tackle the questions. Give yourself **8:45.** We'll work through the solutions together on the pages to come.

One or more of six violinists—Greene, Holiday, Liu, Mann, Underwood, and Wilson—will be selected to perform at the year-end concert. No other violinists will be selected. The following conditions apply:

> If Holiday is selected, then Mann is not selected.
> If Liu is selected, then both Mann and Wilson are selected.
> If Underwood is not selected, then Holiday is selected.
> Wilson is not selected unless Greene is selected.

1. Which of the following could be a complete and accurate list of the violinists selected for the concert?

    (A) Holiday, Liu, Wilson, Underwood
    (B) Liu, Mann, Wilson
    (C) Holiday, Liu, Mann
    (D) Liu, Mann, Wilson
    (E) Mann, Underwood

2. Which of the following must be false?

    (A) Liu is selected but Underwood is not.
    (B) Neither Underwood nor Liu is selected.
    (C) Holiday is selected but Liu is not.
    (D) Both Greene and Underwood are selected.
    (E) Holiday is selected but Mann is not.

3. Which of the following could be the only violinist selected for the concert?

    (A) Liu
    (B) Mann
    (C) Greene
    (D) Wilson
    (E) Underwood

4. If Underwood is not selected, then which of the following must be true?

    (A) Wilson is not selected.
    (B) Greene is selected.
    (C) At least two violinists are selected.
    (D) At most three violinists are selected.
    (E) Neither Liu nor Holiday is selected.

5. If Greene is not selected, then each of the following could be true EXCEPT:

    (A) Exactly two violinists are selected.
    (B) Exactly one violinist is selected.
    (A) Mann is selected.
    (D) Holiday is selected.
    (E) Liu is selected.

6. Which of the following CANNOT be a complete and accurate list of the violinists who are selected for the concert?

    (A) Greene, Liu, Mann, Underwood, Wilson
    (B) Greene, Mann, Underwood
    (C) Greene, Mann, Wilson
    (D) Greene, Underwood
    (E) Holiday

7. Which of the following, if substituted for the condition that if Liu is selected then both Mann and Wilson are selected, would have the same effect in determining the violinists who are selected to perform?

    (A) If Liu is selected, then exactly two other violinists are selected.
    (B) If Liu is selected, then both Greene and Underwood are selected but Holiday is not.
    (C) If Mann and Wilson are selected, then Liu is selected.
    (D) If Liu is selected, then Mann is one of exactly five violinists selected.
    (E) If Liu is not selected, then neither Mann nor Wilson is selected.

10

How Did You Do?

Picture the Game

This game has Conditional Grouping written all over it! Each violinist is either in or out of the concert, and the rules are all conditionals. Other than setting up In and Out columns, there's nothing to do until we start diagramming our first rule in the middle of the chart.

Notate the Rules and Make Inferences

Check your diagram and work against the following explanations. **Read through the ENTIRE explanation for each question, even if you got the question correct.** We've included many general tips and takeaways that you should find useful.

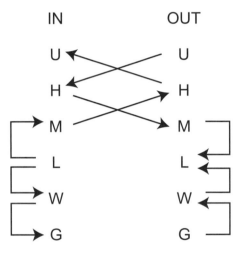

The Big Pause

With Open Conditional Grouping games, there is usually not that much to figure out about the game after you've set up your Logic Chain. That said, it's worth noting whether there are more elements forcing others in than out and whether there are any "big players" that affect a large number of other elements. This will help us particularly on unconditional questions, where we want to be aware of which elements are more likely to create must be true or false situations.

This game seems balanced in terms of how many relationships force elements out and how many force elements in. In terms of "big players," L in is an obvious one to keep an eye on, as is U out.

10

Attack the Questions

1. Which of the following could be a complete and accurate list of the violinists selected for the concert?

    (A) Holiday, Liu, Wilson, Underwood
    (B) Liu, Mann, Wilson
    (C) Holiday, Liu, Mann
    (D) Liu, Mann, Wilson
    (E) Mann, Underwood

(E) is correct.

This is an Orientation question. You can either use the rules in written form, conveniently placed directly above the Orientation question, or you can "read" the rules from the diagram you've created. It's worth trying out this latter approach, as it can force you to engage with your diagram, making it easier to use it for future questions. It's also a good check on your diagram—did you forget to notate a rule? It's imperative that you diagram correctly.

Let's see how this approach of reading the rules from your diagram would play out for Conditional Grouping games. We'll start at the top of our Logic Chain and identify the first rule: U and H cannot both be out. Note that this one statement actually encompasses two rules, one about U out, the other about H out. Scanning the answer choices, this eliminates (B).

Moving down the Logic Chain, the next thing we know is that H and M cannot both be in. This eliminates (C).

The next rule is that L in forces M and W in as well. Eliminate (A). We're left with (D) and (E).

The next rule we can use is that W in requires G to be in. (D) violates this rule, leaving us with (E).

2. Which of the following must be false?

    (A) Liu is selected but Underwood is not.
    (B) Neither Underwood nor Liu is selected.
    (C) Holiday is selected but Liu is not.
    (D) Both Greene and Underwood are selected.
    (E) Holiday is selected but Mann is not.

(A) is correct.

(A) states that L is selected but U is not. What do we know when L is in?

in	out
L	H
M	
U	
W	
G	

Thus, (A) can't be true.

As you become more adept at reading your Logic Chain, you'll probably find that you don't always need to write out scenarios in a T-chart. We suggest that you always use a T-chart for Conditional questions, but for questions such as this one, in which you're looking for a violation, it can be easy to simply trace connections with your finger. Try it out and see if that works for you as you prove to yourself that (B) through (D) could be true (though you wouldn't bother doing so during an LSAT).

3. Which of the following could be the only violinist selected for the concert?

    (A) Liu
    (B) Mann
    (C) Greene
    (D) Wilson
    (E) Underwood

(E) is correct.

Let's start with (A). As we've just seen, L in forces four other violinists in! Eliminate (A).

We can eliminate (B) as well. When M is selected, U must be selected as well.

Answer (C) is more attractive. Selecting G has no further implications. Thus, it seems possible that G is selected alone. However, selecting G alone means NOT selecting the remaining letters. Be sure to consider both columns when evaluating an answer that is supposed to be a *complete and accurate* list of what is in one column. Take H for example. Leaving H out (as we'd need to do if we wanted to select G alone) means putting in U! Also, leaving out U means putting in H. Thus, in every case, we must include either U or H. This means G cannot be selected alone. Eliminate (C).

We can eliminate (D) because putting in W means we need to put G in as well. Plus, we now know either U or H must be in!

At this point we can be fairly confident that (E) is correct. But let's get in a bit more practice by checking. Selecting U does not force the selection of anyone else, so this is good news. But, just as we did for (C), we must check to be sure that NOT selecting the others doesn't lead to some other requirement.

Not selecting H means we must select U (this is okay since U is already selected). We're okay. (E) is the answer.

As you develop mastery of Logic Games you should find yourself increasingly able to predict possible answers. For example, for number three, we know that the answer could not be M, L, or W, since each of those forces another element in. Looking at the answer choices, we only need to consider (C) and (E). And looking at U and H, we can see that at least one of those has to be selected. With a little forethought, we could have predicted that U or H would be the answer, since those are the only elements each of which could be selected on its own.

4. If Underwood is not selected, then which of the following must be true?

   (A) Wilson is not selected.
   (B) Greene is selected.
   (C) At least two violinists are selected.
   (D) At most three violinists are selected.
   (E) Neither Liu nor Holiday is selected.

(D) is correct.

What do we know when U is out?

in	out
H	U
	M
	L

We can eliminate (A) and (B), as we know nothing about W and G when U is out.

We can also eliminate (E), as we know that H must be in.

So it's down to (C) and (D). The only elements we're unsure of are W and G. Notice that if we put W in then G must be in as well. So we *could* have the following:

in	out
H	U
W	M
G	L

10

But notice that we can't have more than three elements in. After all, we know from our T-chart that U, M, and L must be out.

Thus, (D) is the answer.

5. If Greene is not selected, then each of the following could be true EXCEPT:

   (A) Exactly two violinists are selected.

   (B) Exactly one violinist is selected.

   (C) Mann is selected.

   (D) Holiday is selected.

   (E) Liu is selected.

(E) is correct.

What do we know when G is out?

in	out
	G
	W
	L

W and L are out. Thus, it's impossible for L to be selected.

If you found yourself testing out all the answer choices, start working more strategically. On a Conditional question—particularly one that is asking what must be true or false—once you've made some inferences, go look for answer choices that involve those inferences. In this case, you'd want to seek out answers with L or W in them.

6. Which of the following CANNOT be a complete and accurate list of the violinists who are selected for the concert?

   (A) Greene, Liu, Mann, Underwood, Wilson

   (B) Greene, Mann, Underwood

   (C) Greene, Mann, Wilson

   (D) Greene, Underwood

   (E) Holiday

10

(C) is correct.

This is similar to an Orientation question, except that it's asking which CANNOT be a complete and accurate list. Since four answers are possible scenarios, most of the rules will not eliminate any answer choices, and thus we shouldn't use a standard Orientation approach. Instead, we should evaluate answers against our diagram.

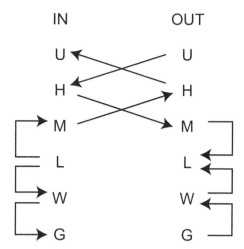

We've seen from our work on #2 that (A) is indeed a possibility. In fact, when L is selected, this is exactly the list we will get. If you somehow overlooked that, a quick review of the implications of G, L, M, U, and W turns up no problems—no violinist on the list is forced out by another, and nobody required is missing. So we'll move on to answer (B).

For (B), if we check the implications of putting in G, M, and U, we don't get any contradictions. It seems like (B) could be true. We could list out the whole scenario to make a definitive elimination, but let's defer. Perhaps we'll find an easier answer later on down the road.

Aha! (C) is our answer. If Mann is selected, Underwood must also be selected. Thus, (C) represents an incomplete list.

No need to evaluate (D) and (E). Who has the time?

7. Which one of the following, if substituted for the condition that if Liu is selected then both Mann and Wilson are selected, would have the same effect in determining the violinists who are selected to perform?

   (A) If Liu is selected, then exactly two other violinists are selected.
   (B) If Liu is selected, then both Greene and Underwood are selected but Holiday is not.
   (C) If Mann and Wilson are selected, then Liu is selected.
   (D) If Liu is selected, then Mann is one of exactly five violinists selected.
   (E) If Liu is not selected, then neither Mann nor Wilson is selected

(D) is correct.

This is an Equivalent Rule question.

The original rule gives us a bunch of arrows on our Logic Chain. It tells us that if L is in then M and W are selected. Using the other rules, we can infer that U and G would also be in, and H would be out. If we remove this rule, we're left with the following:

10

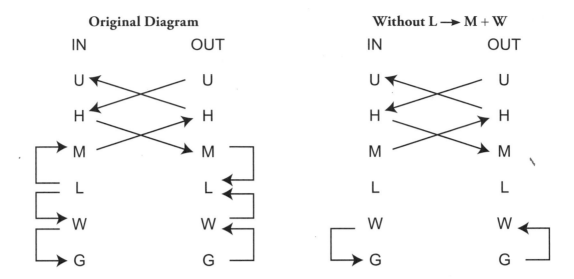

We want to choose an answer that provides the arrows that we're now missing, and that leads us to the same exact result.

Answer (A) doesn't give any indication as to which additional violinists are selected. This is not an equivalent rule to the original. Eliminate (A).

Answer (B) gives us G and U with L and forces out H, but what about M and W? The original rule forces M and W in whenever L is in. (B) does not give us an equivalent result. Eliminate.

Answer (C) gives us reversed logic. If you don't know your Conditional Logic, you might be tempted by this answer, but simply reversing the terms of the rule does NOT give an equivalent rule.

(D) tells us that if L is selected then M is selected as well (this gives us our missing arrow from L in to M in), and five violinists are selected in total. Well, if M is in, we already know that H is out and U is in (follow the arrows from M in). To get to five total, we'd need W and G in as well. This gives us our missing arrow from L in to W in. So, when L is in, this rule forces in M and W. In the end we arrive at the same place we started: L in means M, U, W, and G in, and H out.

Answer (E) is the negation of our original rule. Again, this is a Conditional Logic trap. The negation of a conditional does not provide the same information as the original!

Practice Game 1: PT41, S2, G3

Here's your first chance to put all the pieces together on a new game. Give yourself **8:45** to complete the following game. We'll work through the setup and solutions together on the pages to come.

Each of the seven members of the board of directors—Guzman, Hawking, Lepp, Miyauchi, Upchurch, Wharton, and Zhu—serves on exactly one of two committees—the finance committee or the incentives committee. Only board members serve on these committees. Committee membership is consistent with the following conditions:

> If Guzman serves on the finance committee, then Hawking serves on the incentives committee.
>
> If Lepp serves on the finance committee, then Miyauchi and Upchurch both serve on the incentives committee.
>
> Wharton serves on a different committee from the one on which Zhu serves.
>
> Upchurch serves on a different committee from the one on which Guzman serves.
>
> If Zhu serves on the finance committee, so does Hawking.

13. Which one of the following could be a complete and accurate list of the members of the finance committee?

    (A) Guzman, Hawking, Miyauchi, Wharton
    (B) Guzman, Lepp, Zhu
    (C) Hawking, Miyauchi, Zhu
    (D) Hawking, Upchurch, Wharton, Zhu
    (E) Miyauchi, Upchurch, Wharton

14. Which of the following pairs of board members CANNOT both serve on the incentives committee?

    (A) Guzman and Hawking
    (B) Guzman and Wharton
    (C) Hawking and Wharton
    (D) Miyauchi and Upchurch
    (E) Miyauchi and Wharton

15. What is the maximum number of members on the finance committee?

    (A) two
    (B) three
    (C) four
    (D) five
    (E) six

16. If Miyauchi and Wharton both serve on the finance committee, which one of the following could be true?

    (A) Guzman and Lepp both serve on the finance committee.
    (B) Guzman and Upchurch both serve on the incentives committee.
    (C) Hawking and Zhu both serve on the finance committee.
    (D) Lepp and Upchurch both serve on the incentives committee.
    (E) Zhu and Upchurch both serve on the finance committee.

17. If Guzman serves on the incentives committee, then which one of the following must be true?

    (A) Hawking serves on the finance committee.
    (B) Lepp serves on the incentives committee.
    (C) Miyauchi serves on the finance committee.
    (D) Wharton serves on the incentives committee.
    (E) Zhu serves on the finance committee.

P

Practice Game 1 Solution: PT41, S2, G3

Picture the Game

While this game doesn't present the usual in vs. out situation, this is a binary situation. There are only two committees, and everyone serves on one or the other (as opposed to a situation in which there is a third category, those that don't serve on either). Once we see all the conditional rules, we can quickly conclude that this is a Conditional Grouping game.

We'll carefully note which side of the diagram corresponds to which committee, and dive into our first rule.

Notate the Rules and Make Inferences

This is a tough diagram, so we'll take it step-by-step. However, if you're feeling confident, flip to the completed diagram and see if your confidence is deserved!

The first rule is:

If Guzman serves on the finance committee, then Hawking serves on the incentives committee.
(Gf ➝ Hi, contrapositive Hf ➝ Gi)

We'll start by placing our G's and H's about half-way down, and then we'll draw in the conditional arrows for both the original rule and the contrapositive.

Neither the second nor the third rule contains a G or an H, so we'll skip down to the fourth rule:

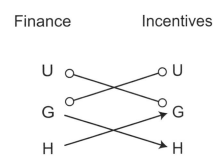

Upchurch serves on a different committee from the one on which Guzman serves.

Since the U will be connected with the G, we'll place our U's directly above our G's in the diagram. Did you notice that this is a bidirectional rule? Since U and G must be on different committees, Uf means Gi (and vice versa), and Gf means Ui (and vice versa). (Uf ⟷ Gi and Gf ⟷ Ui). This is a great time to use the special arrows with circles at each end.

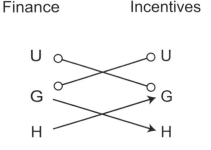

The last rule contains an H, so we can use this one now:

If Zhu serves on the finance committee, so does Hawking. (Zf $\longrightarrow$ Hf, contrapositive Hi $\longrightarrow$ Zi)

Since the Z is connected with the H, we'll place the Z's directly beneath the H's in the diagram.

Finance   Incentives

Now that we have a U on our diagram, we can double back to the second rule:

If Lepp serves on the finance committee, then Miyauchi and Upchurch both serve on the incentives committee.

This gives us two separate relationships: Lf $\longrightarrow$ Mi and Lf $\longrightarrow$ Ui. The contrapositives are: Mf $\longrightarrow$ Li and Uf $\longrightarrow$ Li.

Finance   Incentives

The only rule remaining is the third rule:

Wharton serves on a different committee from the one on which Zhu serves.

This is another bidirectional rule: Wf $\longleftrightarrow$ Zi and Zf $\longleftrightarrow$ Wi.

If you really struggled with this diagram setup, start again from scratch. Do it as many times as required to make the process flawless.

Finance   Incentives

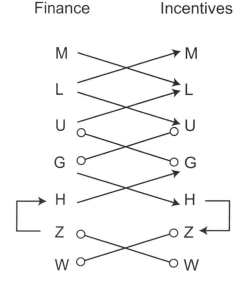

P

The Big Pause

In this game, there are far more elements that force others out (to the incentives committee) than force others in (to the finance one). We should be ready for more situations to be affected by placing elements on the left side, but with two bidirectional arrow pairs, there's a large variety of "moves" happening. In terms of "big players," W out is probably our largest. Take a quick look at how many elements are affected by W out: everyone but M!

Attack the Questions

13. Which one of the following could be a complete and accurate list of the members of the finance committee?

    (A) Guzman, Hawking, Miyauchi, Wharton
    (B) Guzman, Lepp, Zhu
    (C) Hawking, Miyauchi, Zhu
    (D) Hawking, Upchurch, Wharton, Zhu
    (E) Miyauchi, Upchurch, Wharton

(E) is correct.

This is an Orientation question, so we'll use the rules to eliminate. While we could effectively use the rules in their written form, let's "read" the rules from our diagram. We want to keep in mind that the question asks for a complete and accurate list of members for the *finance* committee.

The first rule pair is that M and L cannot be together on finance. No answer choice violates this rule, so we'll look at the next rule pair: L and U cannot be on finance together. Again, no answer violates this rule—let's keep moving along!

The next rule pair we encounter is that U and G cannot be on the same committee; this means we need to see a U or a G, but not both, on finance. We can eliminate (C). Finally something to cross out!

Moving down the Logic Chain, we see that G and H cannot be on finance together—let's cross out (A).

Next, we can apply the rule that Z will serve on finance only if H does. (B) violates this rule.

To choose between (D) and (E), let's use the final rule that Z and W must serve on different committees. We see both Z and W in (D), so we can eliminate it

14. Which of the following pairs of board members CANNOT both serve on the incentives committee?

    (A) Guzman and Hawking
    (B) Guzman and Wharton
    (C) Hawking and Wharton
    (D) Miyauchi and Upchurch
    (E) Miyauchi and Wharton

(C) is correct.

Notice that if H is on incentives, Z must be on incentives. If Z is on incentives, W must be on finance. Watch out for the double arrow! This means H and W cannot both be on incentives.

15. What is the maximum number of members on the finance committee?

    (A) two
    (B) three
    (C) four
    (D) five
    (E) six

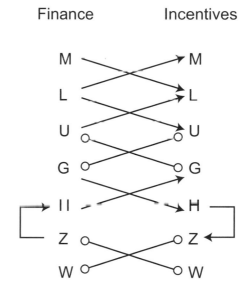

(C) is correct.

This is the toughest of the questions we've seen for this game so far, and the only one that requires a level of logic that goes beyond what is on the Logic Chain diagram itself. You will occasionally run into questions like this one, so it is important to aim to have a couple of extra minutes in the bank.

On these maximum number questions, we always want to start with the biggest answer and work our way down. In this case, let's see if we can put six people on the finance committee without breaking any rules.

We know that either W or Z is on the finance committee, but not both, and we know that either U or G is on the finance committee, but not both (the mutually exclusive double-sided arrows!). Thus, only two of these four people can be on the finance committee, and the other two must be on the incentives committee. If at least two must be on incentives, at most five can be on finance. We can eliminate (E).

P

Can we have five on the finance committee? No. The reasoning here requires us to connect rules. Remember that either U or G serves on the finance committee, but not both. If U serves on the finance committee, L cannot (follow the arrow). If G serves on finance committee, H and Z cannot. Either case would leave at least three people off the finance committee (remember that either W or Z must also be off). The two cases would be:

finance: U
incentives: G, L, and either W or Z

finance: G, W
incentives: U, H, and Z

In each case, we have at least three people on incentives, which means that there couldn't be five on the finance committee. Eliminate (D).

finance	incentives
Z	G
H	L
U	W
M	

Can we have four on the committee? Yes! We can do it with our U example above. We can have U, H, Z, and M on finance, and everyone else on incentives.

16. If Miyauchi and Wharton both serve on the finance committee, which one of the following could be true?

(A) Guzman and Lepp both serve on the finance committee.

(B) Guzman and Upchurch both serve on the incentives committee.

(C) Hawking and Zhu both serve on the finance committee.

(D) Lepp and Upchurch both serve on the incentives committee.

(E) Zhu and Upchurch both serve on the finance committee.

(D) is correct.

What do we know if both M and W are on finance?

finance	incentives
M	L
W	Z

This is all we know for sure. We'll use what we know for sure to hunt down answers that can't be true.

(A) No! L serves on incentives in this case.

(B) No! G and U are always on different committees.

(C) No! Z serves on incentives in this case.

(D) There's no reason to eliminate.

(E) No! Z serves on incentives in this case.

17. If Guzman serves on the incentives committee, then which one of the following must be true?

    (A) Hawking serves on the finance committee.

    (B) Lepp serves on the incentives committee.

    (C) Miyauchi serves on the finance committee.

    (D) Wharton serves on the incentives committee.

    (E) Zhu serves on the finance committee.

(B) is correct.

If you've made your Logic Chain correctly, this is the easiest question in the set to answer. If G is on incentives, U is on finance, and L must be on incentives.

Closed Conditional Grouping Games

The overwhelming majority of Conditional Grouping games are open—the type we've been looking at so far—but occasionally we'll see a Closed Conditional Grouping game. Since this type of game usually hinges on something slightly different, it's worth some time.

The Characteristics of Closed Conditional Grouping Games

In many ways, Closed Conditional Grouping games are very similar to Open Conditional Grouping games: our job is to split the elements into two groups by utilizing a series of conditional rules. However, there are a few characteristics that make closed games slightly different:

1. Defined number of selections. As we discussed previously, *open* games do NOT define the number of selections. In other words, you'll know that some people will be selected for the team, for example, and that others will not, but you won't know *exactly* how many will be selected. The language in *open* games is usually something like "At least one person will be selected for the team…."

By contrast, *closed* games will define the number to be selected: "Exactly five people will be selected for the team." Obviously, this additional rule will have implications for the questions you'll face.

2. Subgroups. In most *open* scenarios, the pool of elements is NOT broken down into subgroups. By contrast, *closed* games will almost always define subgroups, usually three, from the main pool. (In the example to follow, the subgroups are 1960's songs, 1970's songs, and 1980's songs.)

3. Number rules. *Closed* Conditional Grouping games almost always introduce number rules in addition to conditional rules. For example, a rule may limit the number of selections made from one of the three specific subgroups. This information can lead to some very important inferences. Take the following hypothetical example:

> A journalist reads exactly six books out of a pool of nine total books. Of the nine, three are fiction, three are non-fiction, and three are poetry. The journalist reads exactly one poetry book.

Putting together the rule that exactly six books are read and the rule that exactly one of those must be a poetry book, we can draw some very important inferences. We will need either three fiction and two non-fiction, or three non-fiction and two fiction. Regardless, we will need all three of either the fiction or the non-fiction books.

This type of *number* inference is often important on Closed Conditional Grouping games.

4. Fewer Links. The diagrams for Closed Conditional Grouping games usually have fewer arrows (conditional rules) in them than those for their Open counterparts. With so much of the game hinging on subsets and number rules, it would be unfair for the LSAT to also expect us to track a large number of conditional rules.

Setup: The Logic Chain

We use the Logic Chain for both Open and Closed Conditional Grouping games. But now we will need to use the Logic Chain to represent subsets as well as conditional rules. In order to do this, we need to keep the elements segregated by subset. Instead of organizing the elements according to whatever order is convenient because of rule reordering, immediately write out the elements, as given in the scenario, and either leave space between each subset or draw thin lines. You will want to label each subset, and when you are told a rule about the subset that cannot be represented using arrows, write it next to that label.

Before we have you worrying too much about this mysterious game type, let's throw you into one.

P

Practice Game 2

A filmmaker will choose exactly five songs to use in a film project. Of the nine songs that she will choose from, three songs—F, G, and H—were written in the 1960s, three songs—J, K, and M—were written in the 1970s, and three songs—O, P, and Q—were written in the 1980s. The following conditions apply:

    Exactly two songs from the 1980s are selected for the project.
    G and J cannot both be selected.
    H and O cannot both be selected.
    If Q is selected, both G and H are selected.

1. Which one of the following is an acceptable selection of songs for the film project?

    (A) F, G, K, P, Q
    (B) G, J, K, O, P
    (C) G, K, M, O, P
    (D) G, H, K, M, Q
    (E) F, G, H, O, P

2. If Q is selected for the film project, each of the following could be true EXCEPT:

    (A) F is selected for the film project.
    (B) J is selected for the film project.
    (C) G is selected for the film project.
    (D) K is selected for the film project.
    (E) M is selected for the film project.

3. If neither K nor M is selected for the film project, how many of the five song selections are known with certainty?

    (A) one
    (B) two
    (C) three
    (D) four
    (E) five

4. If K is the only song from the 1970s selected for the film project, then which one of the following CANNOT be true?

    (A) O is not selected but F is selected.
    (B) Q is not selected but G is selected.
    (C) F is not selected but P is selected.
    (D) H is not selected but G is selected.
    (E) O is not selected but H is selected.

5. Which one of the following is a song that must be selected for the film project?

    (A) H
    (B) Q
    (C) F
    (D) P
    (E) G

6. If the condition that exactly two songs from the 1980s are selected for the project is replaced with the condition that at least one song from each time period must be selected, and if all other rules remain in effect, each of the following could be true EXCEPT:

    (A) Both O and P are selected.
    (B) Both G and H are selected.
    (C) Both P and Q are selected.
    (D) J, K, and M are selected.
    (E) F, P, and Q are selected.

P

Practice Game 2 Solution

Picture the Game

The game you just finished working on is a Closed Conditional Grouping game. The exact number of selections is defined (exactly five selections are to be made), the pool of songs is broken into three subgroups (1960s, 1970s, and 1980s), and we have a rule that limits the number of selections to be made from the 1980s subgroup (exactly two selections, no more no less).

As we did for the open games discussed earlier in the chapter, we'll use a Logic Chain diagram to notate the conditional rules. As we discussed earlier, the only thing we'll do differently this time is to make certain that we arrange the letters by subgroup. So instead of placing the letters on the diagram according to which rule we're working on, we'll place all the letters on the diagram before we begin to consider the rules. Keeping subgroups together will make it easier for us to keep track of numbers.

Notate the Rules and Make Inferences

Here is a completed diagram for this game:

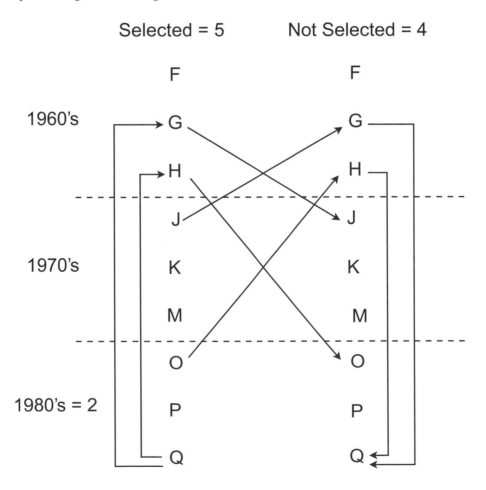

Notice the clear separation of subgroups, and notice the way we've notated the number rules.

The Big Pause

Number Distributions

At this point, we want to pause and consider the possible inferences that might come from this diagram. If exactly two songs from the 80s must be selected, does this tell us anything about the other subgroups?

Take a second and run through a few scenarios in your mind. This quick little exercise will certainly come in handy as you consider the questions, so it's worth sketching out the possibilities on your paper:

$$
\begin{array}{ccc}
60: & \widehat{1} & \widehat{3} \\
70: & \underset{2}{} & \underset{0}{} \\
80: & 2 & 2
\end{array}
$$

We can see that there are four possible distributions. Some game players might want to explore a bit deeper to see if any of those options have specific inferences, but there's not that much to infer here.

Mutually Exclusive Pairs

It can also be very helpful to identify any mutually exclusive pairs that exist in the diagram. We already know that O and H are mutually exclusive (when O is in, H is out, and vice versa), but hidden in this mutually exclusive pair is a second mutually exclusive relationship.

Our diagram tells us that when O is in, H is out, and therefore Q is out. So, when O is in, Q is out. Of course, we also know that when Q is in, H is in, and O is out. So, when Q is in, O is out. O in and Q in are therefore mutually exclusive. Since we must have two songs from the 80s, it turns out that O out and Q out are also mutually exclusive. This has a huge impact on the possible scenarios. Since exactly two 80's songs must be selected, and since O and Q can't be selected together, the two 80's songs must either be OP or QP. Regardless, P must be chosen!

If you didn't see this before starting the questions, it's not the end of the world. We've said before that you won't always get all the important inferences up front. Many people would not spot this inference until a specific question (such as #5) prompted them to consider it. That said, often you'll be able to spot a big inference on a Closed Conditional Grouping game by looking for mutually exclusive pairs, so be on the lookout and give yourself a bit more time up front to poke around.

Finally, any "big players"? Undoubtedly, Q is the song of the hour. Q in affects four different elements.

P

Attack the Questions

Now that we've got the diagram completed and some important inferences made, let's look at the questions. Two new tools you'll want to use on Closed Conditional Grouping games are modified T-charts (to track the subsets) and boxes (to track the numbers). We'll model these both with the second question.

1. Which one of the following is an acceptable selection of songs for the film project?

   (A) F, G, K, P, Q
   (B) G, J, K, O, P
   (C) G, K, M, O, P
   (D) G, H, K, M, Q
   (E) F, G, H, O, P

(C) is correct.

With Orientation questions on Closed Conditional Grouping games—as well as some others—it can be useful to draw lines through the answer choices to show which elements belong to which subgroup. For example, for this question, your lines might look like:

F, G, K, P, Q
G, J, K, O, P
G, K, M, O, P
G, H, K, M, Q
F, G, H, O, P

First rule: Exactly two songs from the 80s are selected. Eliminate (D).

Second rule: G and J cannot both be selected. Eliminate (B).

Third rule: H and O cannot both be selected. Eliminate (E).

Fourth rule: If Q is selected, both G and H are selected. Eliminate (A).

2. If Q is selected for the film project, each of the following could be true EXCEPT:

   (A) F is selected for the film project.
   (B) J is selected for the film project.
   (C) G is selected for the film project.
   (D) K is selected for the film project.
   (E) M is selected for the film project.

(B) is correct.

We'll track our inferences in a modified T-chart. Note that the T-chart below is split into three rows so that we can track the selection of songs from the 60s, 70s, and 80s separately. Also note that we've given two boxes to the 1980s in column and one box to the 1980s out column. These boxes indicate that two songs from the 80s must be chosen and one song must be left out.

in	out
....	....
....	....
□ □	□

The question tells us that Q is selected. If we follow the arrows from Q in, we get G and H in, and J and O out. We'll note these in the proper places in our T-chart:

in	out
G H	
....	....
	J
....	....
Q □	O

The only letter that can fill the remaining 1980s in box is P. Let's add that. (If you inferred that P must be chosen in any scenario, you may have written that before even starting.)

in	out
G H	
....	....
	J
....	....
Q P	O

P

Now that we've followed the chain of inferences as far as we can take it, it's time to answer the question. A quick scan of the answers for what must be false—it's an EXCEPT question!—leads us easily to (B). No need to waste precious time testing out the four could be true answers!

3. If neither K nor M is selected for the film project, how many of the five song selections are known with certainty?

   (A) one
   (B) two
   (C) three
   (D) four
   (E) five

(E) is correct.

Tough question! Again, let's take the additional rule given in the question and see if we can follow the inference chain that it creates. K and M out doesn't really lead to anything further, unfortunately.

In a case like this, when the Logic Chain arrows don't lead to anything concrete, it's best to consider any *number* consequences that the new rule might imply. We already know that exactly two 80's songs must be selected. Thus, we have already placed two of the four out slots, and we know that one 80's song must be out. We can represent this like so:

in = 5	out = 4
	K M
☐ ☐	☐

We still have one more out slot and three in slots to place in the 60s and 70s. Clearly, the out slot will have to go in one or the other, but whichever way we arrange the three in slots, at least two of them will have to be in the 60s (the 70s already have K and M out).

Let's add those two in boxes to the 60s:

in = 5	out = 4
☐ ☐	
	K M
☐ ☐	☐

But we haven't yet filled our in and out quotas. How could the numbers work? Either the 60s will have all three in (and thus the 70s all three out), or the 60s will have one out (and J will be in). Let's think through these scenarios:

Can we place all three 60s in? Yes. And H in would determine which of the 80s songs is out.

It would look like this:

CASE # 1
(no 70's song selected)

in = 5	out = 4
[F] [G] [H]	
	K M [J]
[Q] [P]	[O]

Can we place J in? That would force G and Q out, filling up our out side. We would have this:

in = 5	out = 4
F H	G
J	K M
O P	Q

Is that OK? Check it against the diagram.

O and H can't be in together! Thus, this case is invalid, and we must go with the other case, in which all selections were determined. Thus, we know all five selections: F, G, H, P, Q. (E) is correct.

The key to answering this question was to keep track of the numbers required for each column and to set up a basic framework from which we could consider each possibility.

P

4. If K is the only song from the 1970s selected for the film project, then which one of the following CANNOT be true?

   (A) O is not selected but F is selected.
   (B) Q is not selected but G is selected.
   (C) F is not selected but P is selected.
   (D) H is not selected but G is selected.
   (E) O is not selected but H is selected.

(A) is correct.

If K is the only 70s song selected, J and M are not selected. Since we need exactly two 80s songs, this means we'll have exactly two 60s songs to get to five total songs.

Quickly evaluating answers will work here, but let's see if we can prepare our thinking a bit. We can expect that the correct, and thus impossible, answer choice will trigger a violation of these number rules.

Q in is an obvious suspect, since it forces around so many other elements. However, scanning the answer choices, we don't see one that has Q in, so we should consider what would force Q in. If O is *not* selected, as in (A), then P and Q must be selected. Again, if Q is selected, then G and H are selected, which means F must be left out.

In this case, when O is not selected, F cannot be selected. Answer (A) is impossible.

5. Which one of the following is a song that must be selected for the film project?

   (A) H
   (B) Q
   (C) F
   (D) P
   (E) G

(D) is correct.

This is an inference we made early on! Since O and Q are mutually exclusive, and since we need exactly two songs from the 80s, P must be selected.

6. If the condition that exactly two songs from the 1980s are selected for the project is replaced with the condition that at least one song from each time period must be selected, and if all other rules remain in effect, each of the following could be true EXCEPT:

(A) Both O and P are selected.

(B) Both G and H are selected.

(C) Both P and Q are selected.

(D) J, K, and M are selected.

(E) F, P, and Q are selected.

(E) is correct.

This is a Rule Substitution question. Instead of exactly two songs from the 1980s, we need to include at least one song from each of the three eras. Since this is a "could be true EXCEPT" question, we're looking for the one answer choice that must be false.

We should look for an answer that will force a violation of the new rule—and Q is our heavy hitter when it comes to forcing elements in and out. Let's first evaluate (C) and (E), the answers with Q.

With (C), we can infer that along with P and Q, we'll need G and H, which forces out J and O, but we'll still be able to squeeze in a 70's song. Looks good, so let's move on to (E).

Answer (E) is the correct answer. If F, P, and Q are all selected, then G and H must be selected as well. This brings the total to five, so no other songs are selected, and therefore all of the songs from the 1970s are left out. This violates the new rule, so (E) must be false. While you may have simply started from (A) and worked your way down, notice how strategically choosing which answers to evaluate first can save you a lot of time.

P

Should I *Always* Use the Logic Chain?

The Logic Chain is probably the most exciting diagram you'll learn preparing for the LSAT. (Admit it, you are now such an LSAT geek that a diagram is exciting.) But there are a few folks out there for whom the Logic Chain is not needed. Who are these oddballs? We can call them Logical Freaks of Nature. These people probably don't need to buy a Logic Games book or course because it's pretty clear to them how to solve these games. Go ahead and allow yourself to momentarily marvel at these people and, perhaps, despise them.

Logical Freaks of Nature might feel it's enough to simply write out the rules of a game in standard symbolic form. For example, they might have notated this chapter's Getting Familiar game like so:

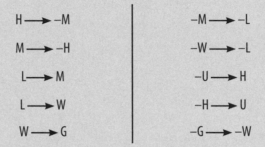

(Separating rules in terms of in or out triggers is smart to do with this approach.)

Can this work? Of course! **Once you've become comfortable with the Logic Chain**, we encourage you to try out the pared-down approach shown above. Try it on the Getting Familiar game and at least one other. If you've done your Logic Chain practice, you'll almost surely find that this approach is not much faster to set up than the Logic Chain. Also, because of the lack of a unified diagram that allows you to quickly see the relationships among all the elements, your work through the questions may be slower. The advantages of this approach are that there is no chance of getting confused by criss-crossing lines, and there is no need to write unsplittable compound conditional statements to the side (though they still can be tough to use if you're not careful).

Despite the few advantages and numerous shortcomings of this method, it's smart to practice at least a couple of games this way, because a couple of games from the last 20 years of LSAT history have so many compound conditional rules that you end up working almost entirely from rules that you write to the side of the chain. Also, the skill of working through a series of conditional statements will help you in some other game types, as well as on some of the Logical Reasoning questions that are heavy in Conditional Logic statements.

The Logic Chain is the most powerful tool available for Conditional Grouping games, but a true LSAT MacGyver has some backup tools available.

Conclusion

1. Practice, practice, practice.

- The Logic Chain takes work. First you need to be very comfortable with your conditional logic basics. If you are still a bit unsure of your ability to read and interpret conditional statements, now's the time to revisit Chapters 5 and 9.

- At this point, you are probably beginning to see the power of the Logic Chain, even if you aren't completely comfortable implementing it. Take the time now to redo the games in this chapter. Do them multiple times. Come back to them in a few days and try them again. The only way you'll get comfortable working with this tool is through repetition.

2. Stay flexible.

- As you encounter Conditional Grouping games in your practice, you'll see some twists. How well will you adapt? Learn and practice the fundamentals of the Logic Chain, and then work to apply it flexibly and with confidence. If a game has too many compound conditionals, put them to the side or, if you feel comfortable, carefully work them into your Logic Chain.

3. Pay attention to double-sided arrows.

- The most common mistake that people make when reading the Logic Chain diagram is failing to see double-sided arrows. Always check the other end of an arrow to see if it's bidirectional. Or replace the arrowheads with a different mark, like an "X" or a small circle, to remind yourself that the arrow is bidirectional. Pay attention to mutually exclusive pairs; they will often help you uncover important inferences during questions.

4. Watch the numbers.

- Your success in Closed Conditional Games will often hinge on identifying possible numerical arrangements. Don't rush into the questions without having considered the possibilities.

P

Chapter 11

Basic Grouping

In This Chapter...

Getting Familiar

Do your best to complete the following game. Use whatever approach you see fit. Give yourself **7:30**.

Six doctors—Haddad, Johnson, Kwong, Lester, Murray, and Nelson—are assigned to the following three training rotations: orthopedics, pediatrics, surgery. Each doctor is assigned to exactly one rotation, and each rotation is assigned exactly two doctors. No other doctors are assigned.

The following conditions must be met:

Kwong is not assigned to the same rotation as Lester.
Murray is not assigned to surgery.
If Lester is assigned to orthopedics, then Haddad is assigned to surgery.
Johnson is assigned to surgery.

1. Which one of the following could be an accurate assignment of doctors to rotations?

    (A) orthopedics: Kwong, Haddad
        pediatrics: Lester, Nelson
        surgery: Johnson, Murray

    (B) orthopedics: Lester, Nelson
        pediatrics: Johnson, Murray
        surgery: Haddad, Kwong

    (C) orthopedics: Kwong, Nelson
        pediatrics: Lester, Murray
        surgery: Haddad, Johnson

    (D) orthopedics: Murray, Nelson
        pediatrics: Kwong, Lester
        surgery: Haddad, Johnson

    (E) orthopedics: Lester, Murray
        pediatrics: Haddad, Kwong
        surgery: Johnson, Nelson

2. If Kwong is assigned to surgery, each of the following could be true EXCEPT:

    (A) Murray is assigned to pediatrics.
    (B) Haddad is assigned to orthopedics.
    (C) Lester is assigned to orthopedics.
    (D) Nelson is assigned to pediatrics.
    (E) Nelson is assigned to orthopedics.

3. It can be determined to which rotation each of the six doctors is assigned if which one of the following statements is true?

    (A) Both Murray and Kwong are assigned to orthopedics.
    (B) Both Kwong and Nelson are assigned to pediatrics.
    (C) Both Haddad and Johnson are assigned to surgery.
    (D) Both Johnson and Lester are assigned to surgery.
    (E) Both Haddad and Nelson are assigned to pediatrics.

4. If Murray and Lester are assigned to the same rotation, for how many of the six doctors is it known to which rotation each is assigned?

    (A) one
    (B) two
    (C) three
    (D) four
    (E) six

5. If Nelson is assigned to surgery, which of the following is a complete and accurate list of doctors who could be assigned to the same rotation as Murray?

    (A) Kwong
    (B) Kwong, Lester
    (C) Haddad, Lester
    (D) Haddad, Kwong, Lester
    (E) Haddad, Johnson, Kwong, Lester

Recognizing Basic Grouping Games

While about half of the games you'll face on the LSAT involve putting elements into groups, in the modern era of Logic Games, only about 9% are Basic Grouping Games. Basic Grouping games are similar to Basic Ordering games in that they are relatively free of complications in comparison to other members of their family. However, while there are no bells and whistles, these games often fall on the more challenging side of the spectrum. The reason? Generally speaking, very few inferences can be made during the setup.

When you're expected to put elements into groups, and you are not facing a Conditional Grouping game (i.e., two groups and all conditional rules), or uncertainty about the number in each group, or a third dimension such as ordering, you're dealing with a Basic Grouping game. Often, you will see references to "assignment" in the scenario, as that is an easy way for the test writers to describe the task of putting elements into groups.

We generally represent ordering horizontally, often with some form of a number line. We will generally represent grouping vertically (which we saw, to some degree, with Conditional Grouping games). We call the diagram for Basic Grouping a "Closed Board" because the number of elements in each group is known. The different groups form the base of the board, with the elements filled into slots above. It's likely that you did this intuitively.

How Did You Do?

The challenge of Basic Grouping is generally not in recognizing what sort of game you're dealing with, nor in flawlessly executing a complex diagram. Instead, the challenge is usually in the questions. There are no fancy diagramming techniques to teach you, so let's just work through the Getting Familiar game and start tackling these challenges.

Six doctors—Haddad, Johnson, Kwong, Lester, Murray, and Nelson—are assigned to the following three training rotations: orthopedics, pediatrics, surgery. Each doctor is assigned to exactly one rotation, and each rotation is assigned exactly two doctors. No other doctors are assigned.

The following conditions must be met:

Kwong is not assigned to the same rotation as Lester.
Murray is not assigned to surgery.
If Lester is assigned to orthopedics, then Haddad is assigned to surgery.
Johnson is assigned to surgery.

11

Picture the Game

This is a classic Basic Grouping situation. We are placing doctors in groups. We could twist this game to say that we're assigning rotations to doctors, using the six doctors as the base of the diagram, but this would make it hard to form groups! We basically would have created a number line with no ordering. We should train ourselves to see that, in a grouping game, we want to arrange a diagram that highlights the groups. With that in mind, we'll place the three rotations as our base, and since each one has two doctors assigned to it, we'll place two lines above each one. Our Closed Board framework looks like this:

$$\frac{\underline{} \quad \underline{} \quad \underline{}}{O \quad P \quad S} \qquad \text{H J K L M N}$$

We can see that we'll use each doctor only once, and there are no mismatch issues to worry about since every slot will be filled.

Notate the Rules and Make Inferences

At this point in your LSAT prep, this is probably a straightforward game to diagram—take a look:

$$\text{H J K L M N} \qquad \frac{\underline{} \quad \underline{} \quad \overset{J}{\underline{}}}{O \quad P \quad S} \qquad \boxed{\frac{K}{L}} \qquad L_O \longrightarrow H_S$$

$$\cancel{M} \qquad -H_S \longrightarrow -L_O$$

Notice that the Closed Board setup process in this case doesn't really lead to any inferences. This is fairly common on Basic Grouping games. The important thing is that we create a visual image of what the grouping structure will be, and that we gather all of the rules, in symbol form, in one place.

The Big Pause

There isn't much to notice, but it's worth noting that there's a lot left undetermined with the five elements left to group. On the other hand, M is limited to two groups, and if the L rule is triggered, we'll have at least half of the elements placed.

From here, we're ready to begin on the questions.

11

Attack the Questions

1. Which one of the following could be an accurate assignment of doctors to rotations?

    (A) orthopedics: Kwong, Haddad
        pediatrics: Lester, Nelson
        surgery: Johnson, Murray

    (B) orthopedics: Lester, Nelson
        pediatrics: Johnson, Murray
        surgery: Haddad, Kwong

    (C) orthopedics: Kwong, Nelson
        pediatrics: Lester, Murray
        surgery: Haddad, Johnson

    (D) orthopedics: Murray, Nelson
        pediatrics: Kwong, Lester
        surgery: Haddad, Johnson

    (E) orthopedics: Lester, Murray
        pediatrics: Haddad, Kwong
        surgery: Johnson, Nelson

(C) is correct.

We know the deal with this question!

The first rule eliminates (D).

The second rule eliminates (A).

We'll skip the third rule, as it's wordy, and use the fourth rule, which eliminates (B).

The third rule eliminates (E).

2. If Kwong is assigned to surgery, each of the following could be true EXCEPT:

    (A) Murray is assigned to pediatrics.
    (B) Haddad is assigned to orthopedics.
    (C) Lester is assigned to orthopedics.
    (D) Nelson is assigned to pediatrics.
    (E) Nelson is assigned to orthopedics.

(C) is correct.

By this point in the book, you should be comfortable rephrasing EXCEPT questions. We can rephrase this question as: "Which one must be false?"

If we're not careful, it's easy to overlook the big inference we can draw from the new condition. If J and K are filling up the S group, we cannot have L in the O group (where would H go?). Thus we know the answer is (C).

3. It can be determined to which rotation each of the six doctors is assigned if which one of the following statements is true?

(A) Both Murray and Kwong are assigned to orthopedics.

(B) Both Kwong and Nelson are assigned to pediatrics.

(C) Both Haddad and Johnson are assigned to surgery.

(D) Both Johnson and Lester are assigned to surgery.

(E) Both Haddad and Nelson are assigned to pediatrics.

(E) is correct.

On a question like this, it can be difficult to know where to start. Do we start with (A) and use trial and error? That's certainly one way to go, but we can be a bit more strategic about our approach. Most likely, this question is going to hinge on one of the major rules. Let's start by looking for answer choices that are directly related to one of those rules. For example, we know that if L is in orthopedics, H must be in surgery. Which answer choices will be directly affected by this?

Answer (C) puts H in surgery, but that doesn't tell us anything about anyone else. Remember, you can't read a conditional rule backwards!

Also, (C) gives us J's placement—something we already know—and so wastes one of the two direct placements that each answer provides. For this reason, we might have suspected in advance that it would be a dud.

We'll jump to (E), because it triggers our contrapositive by placing H in P. We'll assign H and N to pediatrics, thus limiting M to orthopedics:

$$\frac{M}{O} \quad \frac{\frac{H}{N}}{P} \quad \frac{J}{S}$$

Since H is not in S, we know that L is not in O, and thus must go in S. At this point, our diagram is complete.

By starting with answer choices that are directly related to the major rules, we can save ourselves a lot of time.

11

4. If Murray and Lester are assigned to the same rotation, for how many of the six doctors is it known to which rotation each is assigned?

   (A) one

   (B) two

   (C) three

   (D) four

   (E) six

(A) is correct.

Murray and Lester both could be assigned to orthopedics or pediatrics. Since this is a limited game—common for Basic Grouping games—it shouldn't take us long to sketch out each scenario.

We'll start with M and L assigned to O. Remember that if L is assigned to O, then H must be assigned to S. This leaves K and N for P!

So this means we know where each doctor is assigned without a doubt, right? Not quite. Keep in mind that Murray and Lester could also be assigned to pediatrics. From there, none of the unplaced doctors are limited. We could put H in orthopedics, K in orthopedics, and N in surgery, for example.

So if Murray and Lester are assigned to the same rotation, there are at least two viable scenarios:

$$\frac{M}{O} \quad \frac{K}{N} \quad \frac{J}{H} \quad \Bigg| \quad \frac{H}{K} \quad \frac{M}{L} \quad \frac{J}{N}$$
$$\frac{M}{L} \quad \frac{K}{N} \quad \frac{J}{H} \quad \Bigg| \quad \frac{H}{K} \quad \frac{M}{L} \quad \frac{J}{N}$$

The only doctor assigned to the same rotation in each scenario is Johnson. Johnson must be in surgery. Thus, if Murray and Lester are assigned to the same rotation, we can be certain about only one doctor's assignment. (A) is correct.

5. If Nelson is assigned to surgery, which of the following is a complete and accurate list of doctors who could be assigned to the same rotation as Murray?

   (A) Kwong

   (B) Kwong, Lester

   (C) Haddad, Lester

   (D) Haddad, Kwong, Lester

   (E) Haddad, Johnson, Kwong, Lester

(B) is correct.

Since surgery is now filled up, we can't assign L to orthopedics (that would force H into surgery). So, L must be assigned to pediatrics. Since K and L can't be assigned to the same rotation, K must then be assigned to orthopedics. This leaves M for orthopedics and H for pediatrics or vice versa.

$$\begin{array}{ccc} \overline{(H \quad M)} & J \\ \underline{K} & \underline{L} & \underline{N} \\ O & P & S \end{array}$$

Thus, M can be paired with either K or L, but nothing else. (B) is correct.

Once again, the inference chain leads us to a simple answer.

Grouping Variations

While the game we just tackled wasn't super difficult, you'll see that Basic Grouping games can pose serious challenges. The key is to follow inference chains on the questions. Some other game types within the Grouping Family pose different challenges. Here are the major variations:

1. The number of elements in each group may be left uncertain. We call these Open Grouping games, and in these games your focus will be on the number of elements that can be allowed in each group.

2. The groups can be divided into subgroups. For example, imagine that the doctors in the Getting Familiar game were divided into specialists and interns, and each rotation needed one of each. We call these 3D Grouping games.

3. Grouping and Ordering can be combined. This is a heady brew we call Hybrid games. We'll look at all of those twists in future chapters. But here we're focused on Basic Grouping games, which, like Basic Ordering games, are best defined as not having any twists. The one twist we might see within a Basic Grouping game is that elements may repeat (i.e., mismatches). But we're already well-versed in how to deal with these.

Because of the lack of front-end twists, and because of the usually limited number of elements and groups (the Getting Familiar game had a standard number of both), Basic Grouping games are usually back-end games. Thus, it's crucial that you are comfortable with the rules of a Basic Grouping game. Don't rush the diagramming stage just because the diagrams are simple.

It's rare that Basic Grouping games require framing, but, as you surely have learned, even a framing that is not necessary can be a successful way to work through a game.

11

DRILL IT: Rule Juggling

Since the key to many Basic Grouping games is to have a firm grasp on the rules, let's practice quickly handling rules in the questions. Skip the usual steps of the initial diagramming process and instead push yourself to solve these questions as fast as you can, while still maintaining accuracy.

Game 1.

____ ____ ____   L M N O P R

____ ____ ____
 1   2   3

M and P must ride in the same car.
L and O cannot ride in the same car.
R rides in car 1.

1. If O rides in car 3, which of the following must be true?

    (A) M rides in car 1.
    (B) L rides in car 2.
    (C) N rides in a car with R.
    (D) L rides in a car with R.
    (E) N rides in a car with P.

2. Which of the following could be true?

    (A) N rides in a car with R.
    (B) O rides in a car with P.
    (C) O rides in a car with R.
    (D) L rides in car 2 and O rides in car 3.
    (E) N rides in car 2 and L rides in car 3.

Game 2.

____   F G H I J K

____ ____

____ ____ ____
 X   Y   Z

J is kept in Region Y.
K is kept in Region X, if and only if, H is kept in Region Y.
I and G cannot be kept in the same region.
If F is kept in Region Z, then I is kept in Region X.

1. If H is kept in Region Y, which of the following must be false?

    (A) F and I are kept in the same region.
    (B) F and K are kept in the same region.
    (C) F and G are kept in the same region.
    (D) F and K are kept in different regions.
    (E) G and H are kept in different regions.

    ┌─────────────────────────────────┐
    │ ⌨ For more practice, log in to your │
    │   Student Center!   │
    └─────────────────────────────────┘

2. Which of the following could be true?

    (A) K is kept in Region Y and F is kept in Region Z.
    (B) I is kept in Region Y and K is kept in Region X.
    (C) H is kept in Region X and F is kept in Region Z.
    (D) G is kept in Region X and F is kept in Region Z.
    (E) K is kept in Region X and I is kept in Region Z.

SOLUTIONS: Rule Juggling

Note that our solutions to these games skip parts of the setup process. Some of these games can be framed, but to focus the drill on rule juggling, we've skipped that.

Game 1.

1. If O rides in car 3, which of the following must be true?

   (A) M rides in car 1.

   (B) L rides in car 2.

   (C) N rides in a car with R.

   (D) L rides in a car with R.

   (E) N rides in a car with P.

(D) is correct.

If O rides in car 3, the MP chunk must be in 2. This leaves only car 1 for L. Once we place N in the remaining spot in car 3, we have determined all of the placements. Only (D) must be true; the rest must be false.

2. Which of the following could be true?

   (A) N rides in a car with R.

   (B) O rides in a car with P

   (C) O rides in a car with R.

   (D) L rides in car 2 and O rides in car 3.

   (E) N rides in car 2 and L rides in car 3.

(C) is correct.

(A) cannot be true since that would require L and O to form a group. (B) is impossible since M and P are a chunk. (C) is possible! Both (D) and (E) leave no room for the MP chunk.

Game 2.

1. If H is kept in Region Y, which of the following must be false?

   (A) F and I are kept in the same region.

   (B) F and K are kept in the same region.

   (C) F and G are kept in the same region.

   (D) F and K are kept in different regions.

   (E) G and H are kept in different regions.

(D) is correct.

If H is in Region Y, then K must be in X. We're left with F, I, and G to place in the two remaining slots in X and the one slot in Z. Since I and G cannot go together, one must be in Z and the other in X, forcing F to X. Thus, F and K must be in the same region. (B) and (E) must be true and (D) must be false. (A) and (C) could be true, depending on the placement of I and G.

2. Which of the following could be true?

    (A) K is kept in Region Y and F is kept in Region Z.

    (B) I is kept in Region Y and K is kept in Region X.

    (C) H is kept in Region X and F is kept in Region Z.

    (D) G is kept in Region X and F is kept in Region Z.

    (E) K is kept in Region X and I is kept in Region Z.

(E) is correct.

(A)'s two placements force I and G to be together in X. (B) doesn't work because K in X forces H in Y, and there's no room. In (C), our conditional rules force I into X and K *out* of X. Since I is in X, G is also excluded there. With Z full, we now have three elements—J, K, and G—trying to squeeze into the two spots in Y. (D) forces I into X with G. Our work from #1 shows that (E) could be true.

Smart Tip: Turn Your Anti-Chunks Into Groups

Many Basic Grouping games involve chunks and anti-chunks, and it's important to capitalize on them. One way to do so, when the number of elements and groups is quite limited, is to write anti-chunks as two partially filled chunks. For example, if we have six elements—W, Q, R, S, T, and U—that we will place in three groups of two, and we know that T and W must be together but R and Q cannot be, we could draw the chunks and anti-chunks like this:

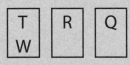

Since we have only S and U left, we could add those in like so:

Try replaying the first game of the drill you just did using that technique.

Conclusion

Before we jump into our practice games, let's review the main points from the chapter:

1. Basic Grouping.

- In Basic Grouping games, the number of positions is equal to the number of elements. Every slot on the Board will be filled, or "closed."

2. Short Setup.

- The Closed Board setup is generally simple and quick, leading to very few extra inferences. The bulk of the work on Basic Grouping games comes during the answering of the questions.

3. Rule Control.

- Basic Grouping games require accurate and quick application of the rules. Slow down initially and make sure that you understand each rule, and that your notations are correct. Consider using your diagram to answer the Orientation question in order to strengthen your grasp on the diagram.

4. Inference Chain.

- On Conditional questions, you will save yourself lots of time if you use the new information given in the question to start an inference chain. Follow this chain to its conclusion before you implement a trial-and-error approach. Often, the inference chain will end with the correct answer.

Practice Game 1: PT52, S2, G2

Here's a chance to apply the approaches we've discussed. Give yourself **16 minutes** to complete the following two games.

On a field trip to the Museum of Natural History, each of six children—Juana, Kyle, Lucita, Salim, Thanh, and Veronica—is accompanied by one of three adults—Ms. Margoles, Mr. O'Connell, and Ms. Podorski. Each adult accompanies exactly two of the children, consistent with the following conditions:

If Ms. Margoles accompanies Juana, then Ms. Podorski accompanies Lucita.

If Kyle is not accompanied by Ms. Margoles, then Veronica is accompanied by Mr. O'Connell.

Either Ms. Margoles or Mr. O'Connell accompanies Thanh.

Juana is not accompanied by the same adult as Kyle; nor is Lucita accompanied by the same adult as Salim; nor is Thanh accompanied by the same adult as Veronica.

8. Which one of the following could be an accurate matching of the adults to the children they accompany?

    (A) Ms. Margoles: Juana, Thanh; Mr. O'Connell: Lucita, Veronica; Ms. Podorski: Kyle, Salim

    (B) Ms. Margoles: Kyle, Thanh; Mr. O'Connell: Juana, Salim; Ms. Podorski: Lucita, Veronica

    (C) Ms. Margoles: Lucita, Thanh; Mr. O'Connell: Juana, Salim; Ms. Podorski: Kyle, Veronica

    (D) Ms. Margoles: Kyle, Veronica; Mr. O'Connell: Juana, Thanh; Ms. Podorski: Lucita, Salim

    (E) Ms. Margoles: Salim, Veronica; Mr. O'Connell: Kyle, Lucita; Ms. Podorski: Juana, Thanh

9. If Ms. Margoles accompanies Lucita and Thanh, then which one of the following must be true?

    (A) Juana is accompanied by the same adult as Veronica.

    (B) Kyle is accompanied by the same adult as Salim.

    (C) Juana is accompanied by Mr. O'Connell.

    (D) Kyle is accompanied by Ms. Podorski.

    (E) Salim is accompanied by Ms. Podorski.

10. If Ms. Podorski accompanies Juana and Veronica, then Ms. Margoles could accompany which one of the following pairs of children?

    (A) Kyle and Salim

    (B) Kyle and Thanh

    (C) Lucita and Salim

    (D) Lucita and Thanh

    (E) Salim and Thanh

11. Ms. Podorski CANNOT accompany which one of the following pairs of children?

    (A) Juana and Lucita

    (B) Juana and Salim

    (C) Kyle and Salim

    (D) Salim and Thanh

    (E) Salim and Veronica

12. Mr. O'Connell CANNOT accompany which one of the following pairs of children?

    (A) Juana and Lucita

    (B) Juana and Veronica

    (C) Kyle and Thanh

    (D) Lucita and Thanh

    (E) Salim and Veronica

P

Practice Game 2: PT16, S1, G1

Eight new students—R, S, T, V, W, X, Y, Z—are being divided among exactly three classes—class 1, class 2, and class 3. Classes 1 and 2 will gain three new students each; class 3 will gain two new students. The following restrictions apply:

> R must be added to class 1.
> S must be added to class 3.
> Neither S nor W can be added to the same class as Y.
> V cannot be added to the same class as Z.
> If T is added to class 1, Z must also be added to class 1.

1. Which one of the following is an acceptable assignment of students to the three classes?

	1	2	3
(A)	R, T, Y	V, W, X	S, Z
(B)	R, T, Z	S, V, Y	W, X
(C)	R, W, X	V, Y, Z	S, T
(D)	R, X, Z	T, V, Y	S, W
(E)	R, X, Z	V, W, Y	S, T

2. Which one of the following is a complete and accurate list of classes any one of which could be the class to which V is added?

(A) class 1
(B) class 3
(C) class 1, class 3
(D) class 2, class 3
(E) class 1, class 2, class 3

3. If X is added to class 1, which one of the following is a student who must be added to class 2?

(A) T
(B) V
(C) W
(D) Y
(E) Z

4. If X is added to class 3, each of the following is a pair of students who can be added to class 1 EXCEPT:

(A) Y and Z
(B) W and Z
(C) V and Y
(D) V and W
(E) T and Z

5. If T is added to class 3, which one of the following is a student who must be added to class 2?

(A) V
(B) W
(C) X
(D) Y
(E) Z

6. Which one of the following must be true?

(A) If T and X are added to class 2, V is added to class 3.
(B) If V and W are added to class 1, T is added to class 3.
(C) If V and W are added to class 1, Z is added to class 3.
(D) If V and X are added to class 1, W is added to class 3.
(E) If Y and Z are added to class 2, X is added to class 2.

P

Practice Game Solution 1: PT52, S2, G2

Picture the Game

We see that we're putting the kids into groups, and there are no fancy bells, whistles, or mismatches; we're facing a Basic Grouping game. We want to start by creating our board, and since we're grouping the children, we'll put the adults along the bottom with two slots above each:

$$J\ K\ L\ S\ T\ V \qquad \underline{\quad}\ \ \underline{\quad}\ \ \underline{\quad}$$
$$\underline{\quad}\ \ \underline{\quad}\ \ \underline{\quad}$$
$$M \qquad O \qquad P$$

Notate the Rules and Make Inferencess

The first two rules are pretty straightforward:

> If Ms. Margoles accompanies Juana, then Ms. Podorski accompanies Lucita.

> If Kyle is not accompanied by Ms. Margoles, then Veronica is accompanied by Mr. O'Connell.

$$J\ K\ L\ S\ T\ V \qquad \underline{\quad}\ \ \underline{\quad}\ \ \underline{\quad} \qquad J_M \rightarrow L_P \qquad -K_M \rightarrow V_O$$
$$\underline{\quad}\ \ \underline{\quad}\ \ \underline{\quad}$$
$$M \qquad O \qquad P \qquad -L_P \rightarrow -J_M \qquad -V_O \rightarrow K_M$$

> Either Ms. Margoles or Mr. O'Connell accompanies Thanh.

> Juana is not accompanied by the same adult as Kyle; nor is Lucita accompanied by the same adult as Salim; nor is Thanh accompanied by the same adult as Veronica.

The first of these two remaining rules tells us that Thanh cannot be assigned to Ms. Podorski, so we'll notate this with a cross-out below the P. The second of the two gives us a bunch of illegal pairings. Because we've set our diagram up with the slots in vertical columns above each adult, we want to represent these illegal pairings as such—illegal *vertical* pairings. This way, we get a visual match with the orientation of the diagram.

As is typical with Basic Grouping games, there aren't any obvious inferences so far.

JKLSTV

$J_M \rightarrow L_P$ $-K_M \rightarrow V_O$

$-L_P \rightarrow -J_M$ $-V_O \rightarrow K_M$

The Big Pause

Once again we see a Basic Grouping game that seems rather back-ended. There are essentially two types of rules to keep in mind. There are rules about who can and can't go with whom (mostly the last rule), and there are conditional rules that are triggered by certain assignments.

We haven't figured out much, so we can expect to do more work during the questions.

Attack the Questions

8. Which one of the following could be an accurate matching of the adults to the children they accompany?

    (A) Ms. Margoles: Juana, Thanh; Mr. O'Connell: Lucita, Veronica; Ms. Podorski: Kyle, Salim

    (B) Ms. Margoles: Kyle, Thanh; Mr. O'Connell: Juana, Salim; Ms. Podorski: Lucita, Veronica

    (C) Ms. Margoles: Lucita, Thanh; Mr. O'Connell: Juana, Salim; Ms. Podorski: Kyle, Veronica

    (D) Ms. Margoles: Kyle, Veronica; Mr. O'Connell: Juana, Thanh; Ms. Podorski: Lucita, Salim

    (E) Ms. Margoles: Salim, Veronica; Mr. O'Connell: Kyle, Lucita; Ms. Podorski: Juana, Thanh

(B) is correct.

At this point, there is no need for us to walk you through Orientation questions.

First rule: (A).

Second rule: (C).

Third rule: (E).

Fourth rule: (D).

P

9. If Ms. Margoles accompanies Lucita and Thanh, then which one of the following must be true?

    (A) Juana is accompanied by the same adult as Veronica.

    (B) Kyle is accompanied by the same adult as Salim.

    (C) Juana is accompanied by Mr. O'Connell.

    (D) Kyle is accompanied by Ms. Podorski.

    (E) Salim is accompanied by Ms. Podorski.

(E) is correct.

Before we start testing the answers, we want to FOLLOW THE INFERENCE CHAIN as far as it will take us.

If L and T occupy Ms. Margoles' column, then K is NOT assigned to M. This triggers one of our conditional statements—V must be assigned to O. So we have J, S, and K remaining. We know that J and K can't be paired together, so J and K must be split between O and P. Thus, S must be assigned to P:

That leads us directly to answer (E). The chain of inferences took us all the way there.

10. If Ms. Podorski accompanies Juana and Veronica, then Ms. Margoles could accompany which one of the following pairs of children?

    (A) Kyle and Salim

    (B) Kyle and Thanh

    (C) Lucita and Salim

    (D) Lucita and Thanh

    (E) Salim and Thanh

(A) is correct.

If J and V occupy P's column, we're left with K, L, S, and T. We know that L and S can't be paired together, so L and S must be split between M and O. We also know that if V is not in O's column, K must be assigned to M. This leaves T for the remaining slot in O's column:

MANHATTAN
LSAT

Thus, Ms. Margoles could be assigned K and L or K and S.

11. Ms. Podorski CANNOT accompany which one of the following pairs of children?

    (A) Juana and Lucita

    (B) Juana and Salim

    (C) Kyle and Salim

    (D) Salim and Thanh

    (E) Salim and Veronica

(D) is correct.

Before you start trying things, check the diagram! We've already made the inference that T can't go in P's column.

12. Mr. O'Connell CANNOT accompany which one of the following pairs of children?

    (A) Juana and Lucita

    (B) Juana and Veronica

    (C) Kyle and Thanh

    (D) Lucita and Thanh

    (E) Salim and Veronica

(C) is correct.

Four of these answers represent pairs that CAN be assigned to O, and one answer represents a pair that CANNOT. Because this question asks us about assignments to O's column, it's very likely that the answer will hinge on our rule that deals with O: $-Vo \rightarrow Km$. So let's look for answer choices that do not contain V, because this will trigger the rule. We'll start with (A). If we put J and L with O, can we place the other letters without any violations? There doesn't seem to be anything stopping us from obeying the conditional and placing K in the M group. J and L are safely paired up, so we just need to separate T and V, and we're in the clear.

(C) also does not contain V, so we'll look at this next. We know that when V is not assigned to O, K must be assigned to M. So if V is not assigned to O, K can't be either. Answer (C) violates this rule. Thus, (C) is the correct answer, as it represents a pair that CANNOT be assigned to O.

P

Practice Game Solution 2: PT16, S1, G1

Picture the Game

We see three groups, with various numbers of elements assigned to each. With three in two of those classes and two in the other, we have a total of eight positions, which exactly matches our eight elements. The rules are about assignment and the relationship between the assignments of elements. This is clearly a Basic Grouping game. Let's set up our framework:

Notate the Rules and Make Inferences

All of the rules are straightforward. Compare your diagram to ours. You might notice one rule "missing" from ours. See if you can figure out why we left it out:

Your diagram probably included a more formal notation noting that Y and S can't be in the same group (similar to the restriction on YW). However, since we already know which group S is in, we need only note that Y can't be in group 3.

There's a lot of uncertainty in the game at this point, as well as a lot of rules. Unfortunately, no inferences are coming to mind.

The Big Pause

In terms of prioritizing the rules, the two anti-chunks—Y W and V Z—seem most relevant since they'll always apply (as opposed to the conditional). It's tough to see exactly how those two pairs will intersect. Y, for example, could be with either V or Z, or with neither. The T Z rule, if triggered, would fill group 1, forcing Y to group 2, W to group 3, and V and X to the remaining spots in group 2. This one rule thus has a large effect, but it is not worth framing per se, since the possibilities when T is not in group 1 are too varied.

Before diving into the questions, circle X, as it has no rules attached to it.

Attack the Questions

1. Which one of the following is an acceptable assignment of students to the three classes?

	1	2	3
(A)	R, T, Y	V, W, X	S, Z
(B)	R, T, Z	S, V, Y	W, X
(C)	R, W, X	V, Y, Z	S, T
(D)	R, X, Z	T, V, Y	S, W
(E)	R, X, Z	V, W, Y	S, T

(D) is correct.

Rule 1 eliminates nothing.

Rule 2 eliminates (B).

Rule 3 eliminates (E).

Rule 4 eliminates (C).

Rule 5 eliminates (A).

2. Which one of the following is a complete and accurate list of classes any one of which could be the class to which V is added?

(A) class 1

(B) class 3

(C) class 1, class 3

(D) class 2, class 3

(E) class 1, class 2, class 3

(E) is correct.

P

Tough question—especially if you didn't use the answer to the Orientation question! We know that answer (D) in the last question works, so we know that V can be part of class 2. That eliminates (A) through (C)! All that's left to do is compare (D) and (E) and test out any difference, which in this case is whether V can be in class 3. Why not just sketch out a possibility? To keep things simple, we'll try to avoid triggering the T Z rule:

It works, and so (E) is correct.

One way to make that sort of work pay off for more than one question is to note which elements can switch places without affecting anything else in the game. In this case, we could have Y and W switch, and we could also have T and V switch. We'll note that, in case we need some scenarios later. Note that this modified diagram does not represent all possible arrangements. For instance, we might swap V and W, or Z and X, but it would be tough to capture all that. We can leverage our existing diagram to prove possibilities, but not to establish what must be true.

3. If X is added to class 1, which one of the following is a student who must be added to class 2?

    (A) T
    (B) V
    (C) W
    (D) Y
    (E) Z

(A) is correct.

What effect does X in class 1 have? It's really not clear at first glance. To help us think this through, let's write out who's left, noting the mutually exclusive pairs:

MANHATTAN
LSAT

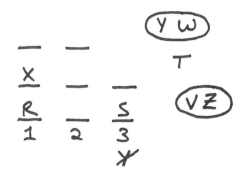

It all seems up in the air, but clearly someone has to be in group 2—look at the question! What about those mutually exclusive pairs? Where could they go? And where can we put T, the one element that isn't in one of those pairs? We know we can't put it in group 1 because of the T Z rule. Let's skip considering group 2 and instead see if it's also restricted from group 3, the other group with only one open slot.

With T in group 3, where would the pairs go? Y and W could span groups 1 and 2, but where would V and Z go? We need to be able to put one of them in group 3, which is filled by T and S in this case. Aha! T must go in group 2. In short, if it's not in group 2, there's no room to spread out those mutually exclusive pairs.

4. If X is added to class 3, each of the following is a pair of students who can be added to class 1 EXCEPT:

   (A) Y and Z
   (B) W and Z
   (C) V and Y
   (D) V and W
   (E) T and Z

(E) is correct.

With X taking up the second and final slot in class 3, we know we'll need to separate our two mutually exclusive pairs between classes 1 and 2. As in the last problem, the only place to put T is in class 2.

Some folks might be able to hold this in their heads, but most of us mortals should write it out:

P

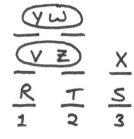

We're looking for a group that can't be in class 1. We know that the LSAT won't give us an answer with S or X in it. That would be too easy and wouldn't be testing whether we drew inferences from the new condition. Thus, we can expect the correct answer to involve T. (E) it is! Note that answers (A)–(D) are simply the four ways we can combine one element each from our two pairs.

5. If T is added to class 3, which one of the following is a student who must be added to class 2?

    (A) V
    (B) W
    (C) X
    (D) Y
    (E) Z

(C) is correct.

This question is similar to the last one, except that all we need to do is switch the positions of T and X. In this case, X must be in class 2.

6. Which one of the following must be true?

    (A) If T and X are added to class 2, V is added to class 3.
    (B) If V and W are added to class 1, T is added to class 3.
    (C) If V and W are added to class 1, Z is added to class 3.
    (D) If V and X are added to class 1, W is added to class 3.
    (E) If Y and Z are added to class 2, X is added to class 2.

(D) is correct.

It's been a while since we've had an Unconditional question in this game! One obvious approach to this question is to simply consider each choice, perhaps testing out some of them, but that is a potential time trap. Let's look at how to work the question with a minimum of writing.

Each answer choice "uses up" two elements in the conditional trigger. Instead of writing them into a diagram, instead cover up those elements in the roster with a finger or two, to help you focus on who is left.

P

For example, with (A), you would cover up T and X in your master diagram:

We see that we have the two mutually exclusive pairs left. There's only one open slot left in class 2, but with two slots left to fill in class 1, and one more in class 3, we should be able to spread out those pairs. And, more importantly, there's no apparent reason we can't fit V into class 1 or 2. Since we were able to "break" (A), we can eliminate it.

Go ahead now and work your way through the other answer choices and see if you can do the maneuvers in your head, with a bit of help from your fingers.

Another approach to this question is to use previous work. Here are two diagrams we developed for this game:

Scenario 1   Scenario 2

Before reading on, see which answers you could eliminate using these two diagrams. Each answer choice begins with a condition, so we want to find the scenario that contains that condition and see if we can "break" the supposed requirement.

We see the first part of (A) in the second scenario. It's tempting to now think this means it must be true, but be careful! We now only can say it *could* be true. Can we "break" this answer? In other words, can we get V out of class 3? Yes! We simply have to switch W and V; no rules are violated, and thus we can eliminate (A).

The sufficient condition of (B), the "if" part, is seen in the first scenario, and T is clearly not in class 3. Eliminate.

The necessary condition of (C) doesn't follow in the first scenario. With a quick check that no rules—like the T Z rule—are triggered, we're done with this answer.

The sufficient condition of (D) is not seen in any scenario, so we'll defer judgment.

The sufficient condition of (E) is possible in the first scenario, where X is in class 3. Eliminate.

No need to confirm (D), but if we have the time, it's easy enough to do.

P

MANHATTAN
LSAT

Chapter 12

of

Logic Games

Open Grouping

In This Chapter...

Getting Familiar

Do your best to complete the following game. Use whatever approach you see fit. Give yourself **8:30**.

The Mizotron Corporation has exactly six managers: Holmes, Jin, Kaufman, Lu, Orr, and Pearson. Each manager has expertise in one or more of the following three areas: finance, marketing, technology. None of the managers has expertise in any other area. The following conditions apply:

> Jin does not share any area of expertise with Orr.
> Holmes has fewer areas of expertise than Lu.
> Jin, Kaufman, and Pearson all have expertise in finance.
> Holmes and Pearson have exactly two areas of expertise in common.
> Orr does not have expertise in marketing.

1. Which one of the following pairs of managers must have at least one area of expertise in common?

    (A) Holmes and Kaufman
    (B) Kaufman and Orr
    (C) Lu and Orr
    (D) Holmes and Jin
    (E) Jin and Orr

2. For how many of the six managers is it possible to determine exactly which of the three areas of expertise they have?

    (A) one
    (B) two
    (C) three
    (D) four
    (E) five

3. Which of the following must be false?

    (A) Exactly four of the six managers have exactly two areas of expertise.
    (B) Exactly one of the six managers has exactly two areas of expertise.
    (C) Exactly one of the six managers has exactly one area of expertise.
    (D) Exactly three of the six managers have exactly one area of expertise.
    (E) Exactly four of the six managers have exactly one area of expertise.

4. Which one of the following is a complete and accurate list of the managers who could have exactly three areas of expertise?

    (A) Holmes, Kaufman, Lu, Pearson
    (B) Kaufman, Lu, Pearson
    (C) Holmes, Lu
    (D) Kaufman, Lu
    (E) Pearson

5. Which of the following must be false?

    (A) Both Jin and Pearson have expertise in marketing.
    (B) Both Lu and Orr have expertise in technology.
    (C) Both Holmes and Lu have expertise in marketing.
    (D) Both Holmes and Orr have expertise in finance.
    (E) Both Kaufman and Pearson have expertise in technology.

6. Exactly how many of the managers could have expertise in both marketing and technology?

    (A) two
    (B) three
    (C) four
    (D) five
    (E) six

Recognizing Open Grouping Games

In recent years, about 9% of all LSAT logic games have been Open Grouping games. Open Grouping games, like Conditional Grouping games, tend to be very difficult for those who do not have a repeatable method with which to attack the setup. We'll discuss this method shortly, but first let's take a look at the characteristics that define Open Grouping.

Putting the "Open" in Open Grouping

Open Grouping games are games in which elements are assigned to groups, and the number of elements that are assigned to each group is unknown or "open."

Compare these two scenarios:

Six students—Harry, Jack, Kylie, Lin, Maxwell, and Nan—will be tutored by exactly three teachers: Mr. Peters, Mrs. Raul, and Mr. Singh. Each teacher will tutor exactly two students, and no student will be tutored by more than one teacher.

Exactly six performers—Q, R, T, V, W, and X—will perform at the county fair. Each performer will perform one or more of the following three acts: juggling, sword swallowing, unicycle riding.

The first example is a familiar Basic Grouping setup. Each of the three teachers will be assigned exactly two students. We can create two slots for each teacher, and every valid arrangement in this game will use all six slots.

$$\begin{array}{ccc} \text{---} & \text{---} & \text{---} \\ \text{---} & \text{---} & \text{---} \\ \text{P} & \text{R} & \text{S} \end{array}$$

Now let's look at the second example. Notice that each performer will be assigned one or more acts, up to a maximum of three. We can think of each performer (group) as having three available slots for acts:

$$\begin{array}{cccccc} \text{---} & \text{---} & \text{---} & \text{---} & \text{---} & \text{---} \\ \text{---} & \text{---} & \text{---} & \text{---} & \text{---} & \text{---} \\ \text{---} & \text{---} & \text{---} & \text{---} & \text{---} & \text{---} \\ \text{Q} & \text{R} & \text{T} & \text{V} & \text{W} & \text{X} \end{array}$$

Note, however, the key phrase "one or more" (sometimes expressed on the LSAT as "at least one"). This means that any particular performer could be assigned one, two, or all three acts. Say, for example, that performer Q performs only as a juggler; two of Q's slots would remain empty. Just because we have three available slots for each performer doesn't mean that all slots will be filled. When the number of slots in each group is not clearly defined up front, and may in fact change from one question to the next, we call this situation Open Grouping.

So, how can we quickly determine whether we're dealing with an Open or Basic (closed) Grouping game? Open situations will usually be cued by one of the following phrases:

1. "One or more":

> Exactly six performers—Q, R, T, V, W, and X—will perform at the county fair. Each performer will perform **one or more** of the following three acts: juggling, sword swallowing, unicycle riding.

2. "At least one":

> At a hospital, each of exactly five doctors—J, K, M, N, and O—will take call on **at least one** of the following three days: Monday, Tuesday, Wednesday.

The Open Board

Let's use our Getting Familiar game to apply and build on the framework we introduced earlier:

> The Mizotron Corporation has exactly six managers: Holmes, Jin, Kaufman, Lu, Orr, and Pearson. Each manager has expertise in one or more of the following three areas: finance, marketing, technology. None osf the managers has expertise in any other area. The following conditions apply:
>
> Jin does not share any area of expertise with Orr.
> Holmes has fewer areas of expertise than Lu.
> Jin, Kaufman, and Pearson all have expertise in
>   finance.
> Holmes and Pearson have exactly two areas of
>   expertise in common.
> Orr does not have expertise in marketing.

This is a classic Grouping situation. In this case we have two sets: managers—H, J, K, L, O, and P—and areas of expertise—F, M, and T. The areas of expertise will be assigned to the managers, thus forming groups.

Is this an Open or Closed situation? Note the key phrase "Each manager has expertise in **one or more** of the following three areas." This phrasing indicates that each of the managers will have three available slots.

However, some of these slots may be left empty. Thus, this is an Open Grouping game.

12

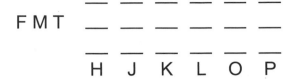

Notice that we have NOT named the rows. For the purposes of the Open Board, there is no finance row, or marketing row, or technology row. You'll see the benefit of this setup momentarily.

Defining the Symbols

The Open Board uses three basic symbols. Let's define them here before we apply them to our game:

____   **The Slot.** An element may or may not be assigned to this position.

◻   **The Box.** An element MUST be assigned to this position.

╱   **The Slash.** An element MUST NOT be assigned to this position.

Setting Up the Board

We'll start by identifying and marking all the slots that we know must be filled. We know from the scenario that each manager has expertise in at least one area. Thus, we know that one slot for each manager must be filled. Which slot? It doesn't really matter. For the purposes of simplicity, we'll put a box in the first slot for each manager:

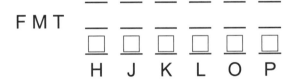

Now it's time for the rules:

> *Jin does not share any area of expertise with Orr.*

In any other system, this rule would be difficult to diagram. After all, we can't really use this to place any letters in the slots, right? But what does this rule tell us about the *number* of slots that will be filled for Jin and Orr? If Jin does not share any area of expertise with Orr, then neither can have expertise in all three areas! We can slash one of Jin's slots and one of Orr's slots:

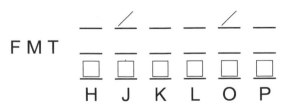

It feels like we should also write out this rule in some more explicit way, but trust us, we'll do that later (if it turns out we need to).

Holmes has fewer areas of expertise than Lu.

Again, we can't use this to place any letters on the board, but we *can* use this to discover more about the *number* of slots that will be filled for Holmes and Lu. If Holmes has fewer areas of expertise than Lu, there are three possibilities: 1) Lu has three areas and Holmes has two, 2) Lu has three areas and Holmes has one, or 3) Lu has two areas and Holmes has one. Regardless, Holmes has at most two areas of expertise and Lu has at least two areas of expertise. Thus, we can slash one of Holmes' slots, and we can add a box to one of Lu's slots:

$$\text{F M T} \quad \begin{array}{cccccc} / & / & \_ & \_ & / & \_ \\ \_ & \_ & \_ & \square & \_ & \_ \\ \square & \square & \square & \square & \square & \square \\ H & J & K & L & O & P \end{array}$$

We can read the Board as follows: Holmes has at least one, and possibly two, areas of expertise. Lu has at least two, and possibly three, areas of expertise.

Jin, Kaufman, and Pearson all have expertise in finance.

This is a rare rule in that it gives us direct information about a particular placement of a letter. We can immediately add F's to Jin's, Kaufman's, and Pearson's columns:

$$\text{F M T} \quad \begin{array}{cccccc} / & / & \_ & \_ & / & \_ \\ \_ & \_ & \_ & \square & \_ & \_ \\ \square & \boxed{F} & \boxed{F} & \square & \square & \boxed{F} \\ H & J & K & L & O & P \end{array}$$

Holmes and Pearson have exactly two areas of expertise in common.

This tells us that Holmes has exactly two areas of expertise (since we know Holmes can't have three), and that Pearson has at least two areas of expertise. We can thus add a box to Holmes' remaining slot, and we can add one more box to Pearson's column:

$$\text{F M T} \quad \begin{array}{cccccc} / & / & \_ & \_ & / & \_ \\ \square & \_ & \_ & \square & \_ & \square \\ \square & \boxed{F} & \boxed{F} & \square & \square & \boxed{F} \\ H & J & K & L & O & P \end{array}$$

12

Orr does not have expertise in marketing.

We can indicate this by putting a cross-out underneath Orr's column:

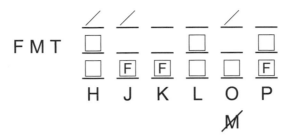

Can we slash a second slot in Orr's column? We slashed the first one because J and O don't share any areas of expertise, but since we don't know which areas J has, we're not sure which element that slash is preventing from landing in Orr's column. We cannot put a second slash at this point.

Cycling Through a Second Time

Now, here's a key step in setting up the Open Board. We need to go back through the rules one more time to see if any further inferences can be made. Sometimes a rule won't give us a whole lot of information the first time, but it becomes more valuable after we've added other information to the diagram. For example, let's look at the first rule again:

Jin does not share any area of expertise with Orr.

If Jin does not share any area of expertise with Orr, then Orr cannot have expertise in finance. After marking this with a cross-out underneath Orr's column, we see that Orr must have just one area of expertise: technology. Thus, Jin cannot have technology.

Remember, we said we'd get to writing out this rule if we needed to? Do we need to?

No! We've been able to write under J and O the actual restrictions that this rule requires. There is no need to write anything else. In some situations, we will still need to notate this sort of rule; later in the chapter, we will discuss how to do this.

Let's look at the second rule one more time:

Holmes has fewer areas of expertise than Lu.

We now know that Holmes has exactly two areas of expertise. Thus, Lu must have expertise in all three areas!

Upon reviewing the remaining rules a second time, we see that no further inferences can be made. This is our final Open Board diagram.

The Key to the Open Board

The biggest mistake that test-takers make on Open Grouping games is misunderstanding the goal of the game. Your job is *not* necessarily to place letters on the diagram. Rather, your job is to track to the best of your ability *how many* assignments each manager, in this case, will get. The slash and box method allows us to track *number* very effectively, while also tracking any assignments that we can make.

DRILL IT: Open Grouping Setups

Work through the Open Board setup for each of the exercises below. Remember that you can often make additional inferences by cycling through the rules a second time. BE SURE TO CHECK YOUR SOLUTION BEFORE MOVING ON TO THE NEXT EXERCISE.

1. YourHome Realty has exactly five condominiums on the market: P, Q, S, T, and V. Each of the condominiums has at least one of the following three features: fireplace, hardwood floors, modern appliances. The condominiums have no other features. The following conditions apply:

   Q has fewer features than S.
   P and T have exactly one feature in common.
   Both Q and V have hardwood floors.
   P has more features than any other condominium.

2. Each of exactly five radio stations—F, J, K, L, and M—plays one or more of the following four types of music: new age, oldies, rock, soul. None of the stations plays any other type of music. The following conditions apply:

   F plays more types of music than any other station.
   K plays new age and oldies, but no other type of music.
   Exactly three of the five stations play rock.
   L does not play new age or rock.
   M plays more types of music than K.

3. The town of Holden has exactly three movie theaters: J, K, and L. Each of the three theaters shows one or more of the following movies: *Rung, Stilted, Trouble*. None of the three theaters shows any other movie. The following rules apply:

   Any theater that shows *Rung* also shows *Trouble*.
   Exactly two of the theaters show *Stilted*.

4. At Riverside High School, six student athletes—Mitembe, Nathan, Paula, Raul, Victoria, and Yolanda—were chosen as Athletes of the Year. Each of the six athletes plays one or more of the following three sports: hockey, soccer, tennis. None of the athletes plays any other sport. The following must be true:

   Nathan plays exactly two of the sports.
   Yolanda plays more of the sports than Victoria.
   Raul and exactly three other student athletes play hockey.
   Victoria plays both soccer and tennis.
   Mitembe does not play any sport that Victoria plays.
   Paula does not play any sport that Mitembe plays.

SOLUTIONS: Open Grouping Setups

1. YourHome Realty has exactly five condominiums on the market: P, Q, S, T, and V. Each of the condominiums has at least one of the following three features: fireplace, hardwood floors, modern appliances. The condominiums have no other features. The following conditions apply:

> Q has fewer features than S.
> P and T have exactly one feature in common.
> Both Q and V have hardwood floors.
> P has more features than any other condominium.

2. Each of exactly five radio stations—F, J, K, L, and M— plays one or more of the following four types of music: new age, oldies, rock, soul. None of the stations plays any other type of music. The following conditions apply:

> F plays more types of music than any other station.
> K plays new age and oldies, but no other type of music.
> Exactly three of the five stations play rock.
> L does not play new age or rock.
> M plays more types of music than K.

12

3. The town of Holden has exactly three movie theaters: J, K, and L. Each of the three theaters shows one or more of the following movies: *Rung, Stilted, Trouble*. None of the three theaters shows any other movie. The following rules apply:

   Any theater that shows *Rung* also shows *Trouble*.
   Exactly two of the theaters show *Stilted*.

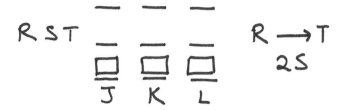

Note: These rules don't give us very much information. All we can do is set up the board and symbolize the rules to the right.

4. At Riverside High School, six student athletes—Mitembe, Nathan, Paula, Raul, Victoria, and Yolanda—were chosen as Athletes of the Year. Each of the six athletes plays one or more of the following three sports: hockey, soccer, tennis. None of the athletes plays any other sport. The following must be true:

   Nathan plays exactly two of the sports.
   Yolanda plays more of the sports than Victoria.
   Raul and exactly three other student athletes play hockey.
   Victoria plays both soccer and tennis.
   Mitembe does not play any sport that Victoria plays.
   Paula does not play any sport that Mitembe plays.

Try It Again

Now that you've learned how to set up the Open Board, it's time to put your skills to good use. Let's revisit the Getting Familiar game. Try developing the Open Board from scratch, and then use it to tackle the questions. Give yourself **8:30**. We'll work through the solutions together on the pages to come:

The Mizotron Corporation has exactly six managers: Holmes, Jin, Kaufman, Lu, Orr, and Pearson. Each manager has expertise in one or more of the following three areas: finance, marketing, technology. None of the managers has expertise in any other area. The following conditions apply:

Jin does not share any area of expertise with Orr.
Holmes has fewer areas of expertise than Lu.
Jin, Kaufman, and Pearson all have expertise in finance.
Holmes and Pearson have exactly two areas of expertise in common.
Orr does not have expertise in marketing.

1. Which one of the following pairs of managers must have at least one area of expertise in common?

   (A) Holmes and Kaufman
   (B) Kaufman and Orr
   (C) Lu and Orr
   (D) Holmes and Jin
   (E) Jin and Orr

2. For how many of the six managers is it possible to determine exactly which of the three areas of expertise they have?

   (A) one
   (B) two
   (C) three
   (D) four
   (E) five

3. Which of the following must be false?

   (A) Exactly four of the six managers have exactly two areas of expertise.
   (B) Exactly one of the six managers has exactly two areas of expertise.
   (C) Exactly one of the six managers has exactly one area of expertise.
   (D) Exactly three of the six managers have exactly one area of expertise.
   (E) Exactly four of the six managers have exactly one area of expertise.

4. Which one of the following is a complete and accurate list of the managers who could have exactly three areas of expertise?

   (A) Holmes, Kaufman, Lu, Pearson
   (B) Kaufman, Lu, Pearson
   (C) Holmes, Lu
   (D) Kaufman, Lu
   (E) Pearson

5. Which of the following must be false?

   (A) Both Jin and Pearson have expertise in marketing.
   (B) Both Lu and Orr have expertise in technology.
   (C) Both Holmes and Lu have expertise in marketing.
   (D) Both Holmes and Orr have expertise in finance.
   (E) Both Kaufman and Pearson have expertise in technology.

6. Exactly how many of the managers could have expertise in both marketing and technology?

   (A) two
   (B) three
   (C) four
   (D) five
   (E) six

12

How Did You Do?

Earlier in the chapter, we discussed how to picture Open Grouping games, and we've already worked through notating the rules and making inferences. Our Open Board is quite filled in so there's no real need for the Big Pause. Let's jump to the questions!

Attack the Questions

1. Which one of the following pairs of managers must have at least one area of expertise in common?

   (A) Holmes and Kaufman

   (B) Kaufman and Orr

   (C) Lu and Orr

   (D) Holmes and Jin

   (E) Jin and Orr

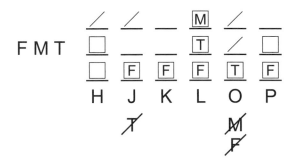

(C) is correct.

K definitely has an F, but all we know about H's assignments is that there are two of them. H could have an M and a T, while K could have nothing more than an F. Eliminate (A).

O has exactly one assignment: T. Again, it's possible that K has nothing more than an F. Eliminate (B).

We can immediately see that L and O both have a T. Thus, L and O must have at least one area of expertise in common. (C) is correct.

Under actual test conditions, we would choose (C) and move on. However, take the time now to disprove (D) and (E).

Before even looking at the answer choices, highly sophisticated game players might notice that L will share an area with every other group, because it has all three. In this case, simply looking for an answer that includes L does the trick!

2. For how many of the six managers is it possible to determine exactly which of the three areas of expertise they have?

   (A) one

   (B) two

   (C) three

   (D) four

   (E) five

(B) is correct.

MANHATTAN
LSAT

While we know that H has exactly two assignments, we don't know which ones. J and K both have an F, but they could potentially have more. L is completely defined. Similarly, we can see that O has one and only one assignment: T. On the other hand, P may have two or three assignments. Thus, only L and O are completely defined.

3. Which of the following must be false?

   (A) Exactly four of the six managers have exactly two areas of expertise.

   (B) Exactly one of the six managers has exactly two areas of expertise.

   (C) Exactly one of the six managers has exactly one area of expertise.

   (D) Exactly three of the six managers have exactly one area of expertise.

   (E) Exactly four of the six managers have exactly
       one area of expertise.

(E) is correct.

It's simple enough to show that (A) through (D) all could be true:

(A) H, J, K, and P could each have exactly two areas of expertise.

(B) H could be the only manager to have exactly two areas of expertise.

(C) O could be the only manager to have just one area of expertise.

(D) J, K, and O could each have exactly one area of expertise.

(E) is impossible since the only managers who could have one area of expertise are J, K, and O.

4. Which one of the following is a complete and accurate list of the managers who could have exactly three areas of expertise?

   (A) Holmes, Kaufman, Lu, Pearson

   (B) Kaufman, Lu, Pearson

   (C) Holmes, Lu

   (D) Kaufman, Lu

   (E) Pearson

(B) is correct.

Our diagram makes it clear that H, J, and O cannot have three assignments. That leaves K, L, and P.

5. Which of the following must be false?

   (A) Both Jin and Pearson have expertise in marketing.
   (B) Both Lu and Orr have expertise in technology.
   (C) Both Holmes and Lu have expertise in marketing.
   (D) Both Holmes and Orr have expertise in finance.
   (E) Both Kaufman and Pearson have expertise in technology.

(D) is correct.

It is certainly possible that both Jin and Pearson have expertise in marketing. Eliminate (A).

We can quickly see that both Lu and Orr indeed do have expertise in technology. Eliminate (B).

Holmes could have expertise in marketing, and Lu definitely has expertise in marketing. Eliminate (C).

While Holmes could have expertise in finance, we can see that Orr has expertise only in technology. (D) is correct.

Take a moment to verify that answer (E) could be true.

6. Exactly how many of the managers could have expertise in both marketing and technology?

   (A) two
   (B) three
   (C) four
   (D) five
   (E) six

(C) is correct.

Four of the six managers—H, K, L, and P—could potentially have expertise in both marketing and technology. J can't have a T, and O is limited to only one element, T.

Choosing Your Base

With most Open Grouping games, it will be quite intuitive which set of elements you should use to form the base of your diagram and which set you should be assigning to those groups. But, consider this scenario:

Four experimental drugs—M, O, P, and R—will be administered to four different patients—W, X, Y, and Z. No other drugs will be administered. Each drug will be used at least once and each patient will receive at least one drug.

This game has all the marking of an Open Grouping scenario. However, notice that both the number of drugs given to patients and the number of patients receiving each drug are "open." We could conceivably create either of these Open Boards:

How will we know which one to use? For some games, one arrangement will be much more advantageous than the other, while for other games, either will be fine. There are two key ideas to consider when choosing your base:

1. Which set of items is listed as being assigned "at least one" or "one or more?" Usually that set should become the base of the board. Think of those letters as "receiving" the other ones.

2. When looking at the rules, which arrangement will allow you to make more numerical inferences (slashes and boxes)?

These two ideas should be enough to help you decide the base for most any Open Grouping game. If you start to diagram and realize you've chosen the wrong base, it's generally best to start over. As you've seen in this chapter, using the Open Board correctly can help uncover many inferences that will make the work of solving the questions much more efficient.

As we mentioned earlier, for most Open Grouping games, the base decision is an easy one. The few fuzzier situations tend to fall into two groups. Either it does not matter which base you use—either one can work fine—or you'll quickly see that you've chosen the wrong base as you start to diagram. As a brain-stretcher, in your review, try replaying Open Grouping games with the "wrong" base. You'll generally see that the diagramming phase quickly fizzles out. However, keep pushing through with the "wrong" diagram—solving games with a suboptimal diagram is a great way to practice your back-end game skills.

12

Back-End vs. Front-End Open Grouping Games

The games you've seen in this chapter have been decidedly front-end. There have been cascades of numerical inferences to uncover. In some cases, it feels as if the test writers decided that typical questions would be too easy to anyone who "cracked the code," and so they had to create questions with especially complex wording just to keep things interesting!

However, in the past few years, we've seen more back-end Open Grouping games than we did in the previous five or so years. Do not be surprised if your diagramming process quickly peters out and the bulk of the work is found in the questions. The skills you developed in Basic Grouping games will prove handy with these games.

Repeat vs. No Repeat

Let's return to the Getting Familiar game. In this scenario, notice that repeats were allowed. What does this mean? Let's look at our Board one more time:

The rules of the game were such that we were allowed to assign more than one F, more than one T, and potentially more than one M. For example, all six managers might have had expertise in technology. This is an example of a "repeat" situation. Now consider the following scenario:

> Exactly five job applicants—J, K, M, N, and O—apply for jobs at exactly three companies—T, U, and V. Each applicant accepts a job with exactly one of the three companies, and each company hires at least one applicant.

In this case, the five job applicants—J, K, M, N, and O—will be assigned to the three companies: T, U, and V. The important thing to notice is that the job applicants CANNOT be repeated. In other words, once J, for example, is assigned to a company, J cannot then be assigned to another company ("Each applicant accepts a job with exactly one of three companies."). So, this is an example of a "no repeat" situation.

This has implications for our setup. First, we want to establish our base. In this case, since the job applicants will be assigned to the companies, we'll put the companies along the bottom:

$$\overline{\underset{\text{T}}{\rule{0pt}{0pt}}} \quad \overline{\underset{\text{U}}{\rule{0pt}{0pt}}} \quad \overline{\underset{\text{V}}{\rule{0pt}{0pt}}}$$

The challenge comes in setting the slots. What is the maximum number of job applicants that any one company could hire? Well, we know that each company must be assigned at least one job applicant. We also know that all five applicants must be assigned. There are two possible scenarios:

SCENARIO 1: One company hires three applicants while the other two companies hire one applicant each (3, 1, 1).

SCENARIO 2: Two companies hire two applicants each while the other company hires one applicant (2, 2, 1).

It is important to note that any one of the three companies could potentially hire three applicants. Therefore, when we set up the slots, we will give each company three slots and we will put a box around one of the slots for each:

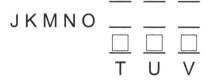

(By the way, it would be worthwhile to note these options on our diagram with a simple "3, 1, 1 or 2, 2, 1.")

So we must always set up our slots based on the maximum possible number of assignments. If at any point during the setup we discovered that one of the companies hired *exactly* two applicants, we would know that we were dealing with a 2, 2, 1 arrangement, and we could slash the third slot for each of the companies.

Also keep in mind that this is still an Open Grouping situation. We have exactly five applicants to be assigned to nine possible slots. We know ahead of time that exactly four slots will be left empty. While this doesn't allow us to add any slashes or boxes, it is a very important numerical restriction to keep in mind.

In "repeat" situations, you might find it hard to conceive of your task in terms of grouping. After all, we typically think of grouping as taking a collection of items and putting each item into one of the available groups. For instance, if you are getting ready for a move, you might sort your possessions into three groups: things to keep, things to give away, and things to throw out. If you are going to keep your old teddy bear, you're not also going to throw it out! However, there are certainly real-world cases of repeat grouping. For instance, one person might be a customer at multiple stores, or a member of multiple organizations. Still, repeat grouping might feel strange to you at first. Make sure you always take note of whether elements can be repeated or not.

12

The Dots

Before we move to a pair of practice games, let's look at one last issue. Go ahead and diagram the game you saw earlier (and be sure to look over the rules to decide which base to use):

> Four experimental drugs—M, O, P, and R—will be
> administered to four different patients—W, X, Y, and Z. No
> other drugs will be administered. Each drug will be used at
> least once and each patient will receive at least one drug. The
> following conditions apply:
>
> Any drug administered to W cannot be administered to Y.
> More drugs are administered to X than to any other patient.
> Fewer drugs are administered to W than to Y.
> M is not administered to X.

This is a particularly front-end game. You can eliminate almost all uncertainty about the number of drugs each patient receives. Check your diagram against ours and replay the setup until you can arrive at ours. Note how we chose to represent the rule about each drug being used at least once.

It's a great-looking diagram, but it's actually incomplete! We drew numerical inferences from the first rule, but our diagram does not tell us that W and Y can't share an element. There are a few ways we can do this:

1. Write out the rule to the side of the diagram. This is simple, but slightly dangerous if you tend to forget to look to the side when solving questions.

2. Draw in some sort of arrow or line notation. Perhaps it would look like this:

MOPR = 1+

This sort of approach is fine as long as it's meaningful to you. It can become a bit messy if you're not careful or if there are several such rules that need to be notated that way.

3. Use dots inside the boxes to show the relationships between the elements. This is our recommended approach. Take a look at what we mean, and see if you can figure out the system before reading on.

MOPR = 1+

Perhaps you've figured it out already: each number of dots represents a different element, though we're not sure which one. However, we do know that mystery element #1 is assigned to W but not to Y, which is assigned two different elements.

To challenge you a bit, how would you add the following rules to the diagram?

> *Exactly two drugs are administered to Z.*
> *No drug is administed to both Y and Z.*

Clearly, you need to add a second box to Z, but since it can't share any elements with Y, which dots should it receive? If you're thinking that it should have four and five dots, you're close! However, there are only four element choices, so five dots—a fifth drug—is not possible. Instead, Z will receive element type #1 and element type #4, so we should put one dot in one box and four dots in another.

12

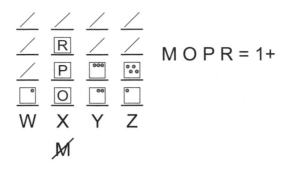

This is a slightly extreme version of the use of dots, but it's also a great example of how using the dots can lead to some otherwise hard to uncover inferences.

Use that diagram to consider this question:

> Which of the following could be true?
>
> (A) R is administered only to X.
> (B) P is administered only to X.
> (C) O is administered only to Y.
> (D) M is administered only to W.
> (E) M is administered only to Z.

Because we see all four elements represented by dots—W has one of the elements, Y has the second and third, and Z has the fourth—we know that between W, Y, and Z, each of the four drugs will be administered once, and one will be administered twice (to W and Z). With that in mind, the answers are easy to evaluate:

> (A) is impossible—R must show up at least once between W, Y, and Z.
> (B) is impossible—P must show up at least once between W, Y, and Z.
> (C) is impossible—O is also administered to X!
> (D) is impossible. Whatever is administered to W is also administered to Z.
> (E) is POSSIBLE—M could be the drug represented by the four dots, which is administered only to Z.

It's worth adding dots to your notation toolkit not only for Open Grouping games, but also for other game types.

To Redraw or Not to Redraw...

Undoubtedly you have made the following decision before: it's the fourth question of a game that has a rather involved diagram. The question is a conditional one, and you don't want to bother writing out the entirety of the diagram; instead you just sketch the important parts, fill in your new condition, and start making inferences.

If that sounds familiar, great. You already figured out that redrawing the entirety of your master diagram is often unnecessary and inefficient. For Open Grouping games, this is a particularly important issue, since the diagrams can be rather involved. By all means, use your discretion on how much to sketch. For example, in some moments, just sketching the bases is enough:

Simply establishing the groups like that is particularly useful with no-repeat games, since there are usually fewer numerical issues in those. Furthermore, when you're several questions into a game, you might feel comfortable with an even sparser diagram: if the group headings are ingrained in your head, you can even skip writing those out.

At other times, particularly when the question is hinging on numerical issues that are hard for you to hold in your head, you may find you want to include the numerical restrictions and possibilities. You can adapt your system on the fly to skip using slashes, only putting slots when an assignment is possible:

Some of our teachers, when quickly sketching out scenarios, will even switch to a horizontal orientation to save space. With all of these diagramming options, what is most important is that you refer to the master diagram when making inferences so that you don't miss anything.

Conclusion

What's the key to Open Grouping games? As much as possible, focus on the numbers! Let's look back at what we've discussed:

1. Thorough set-ups

- When setting up the Open Board, remember to cycle through the rules until there are no more inferences to be made. Many numerical inferences result from the combination of several rules.

2. Variation

- It's becoming increasingly common to see Open Grouping games with fewer numerical inferences. Don't panic if your Open Board is extremely open! Often, we'll see fewer numerical inferences when the game does not include repeats.

3. Choosing your base

- While the base is usually obvious, when it's not, use the rules to determine which arrangement will lead to the most inferences. It's worth spending some time thinking about this, and if you realize that you've chosen the less ideal base, redo the diagram.

Practice Game 1: PT12, S2, G3

Here's your chance to put all the pieces together on some new games. Give yourself **17 minutes** to complete the following two games. We'll work through the setup and solutions together on the pages to come.

Lara, Mendel, and Nastassia each buy at least one kind of food from a street vendor who sells only fruit cups, hot dogs, pretzels, and shish kebabs. They make their selections in accordance with the following restrictions:

   None of the three buys more than one portion of
      each kind of food.
   If any of the three buys a hot dog, that person does
      not also buy a shish kebab.
   At least one of the three buys a hot dog, and at least
      one buys a pretzel.
   Mendel buys a shish kebab.
   Nastassia buys a fruit cup.
   Neither Lara nor Nastassia buys a pretzel.
   Mendel does not buy any kind of food that Nastassia
      buys.

12. Which one of the following statements must be true?

   (A) Lara buys a hot dog.
   (B) Lara buys a shish kebab.
   (C) Mendel buys a hot dog.
   (D) Mendel buys a pretzel.
   (E) Nastassia buys a hot dog.

13. If the vendor charges $1 for each portion of food, what is the minimum amount the three people could spend?

   (A) $3
   (B) $4
   (C) $5
   (D) $6
   (E) $7

14. If the vendor charges $1 for each portion of food, what is the greatest amount the three people could spend?

   (A) $5
   (B) $6
   (C) $7
   (D) $8
   (E) $9

15. If Lara and Mendel buy exactly two kinds of food each, which one of the following statements must be true?

   (A) Lara buys a fruit cup.
   (B) Lara buys a hot dog.
   (C) Mendel buys a fruit cup.
   (D) There is exactly one kind of food that Lara and
         Mendel both buy.
   (E) There is exactly one kind of food that Lara and
         Nastassia both buy.

16. If Lara buys a shish kebab, which one of the following statements must be true?

   (A) Lara buys a fruit cup.
   (B) Mendel buys a fruit cup.
   (C) Nastassia buys a hot dog.
   (D) Nastassia buys exactly one kind of food.
   (E) Exactly one person buys a fruit cup.

17. Assume that the condition is removed that prevents a customer who buys a hot dog from buying a shish kebab but all other conditions remain the same. If the vendor charges $1 for each portion of food, what is the maximum amount the three people could spend?

   (A) $5
   (B) $6
   (C) $7
   (D) $8
   (E) $9

Practice Game 2: PT18, S1, G1

Each of five students—Hubert, Lori, Paul, Regina, and Sharon—will visit exactly one of three cities—Montreal, Toronto, or Vancouver—for the month of March, according to the following conditions:

> Sharon visits a different city than Paul.
> Hubert visits the same city as Regina.
> Lori visits Montreal or else Toronto.
> If Paul visits Vancouver, Hubert visits Vancouver with him.
> Each student visits one of the cities with at least one of the other four students.

1. Which one of the following could be true for March?

   (A) Hubert, Lori, and Paul visit Toronto, and Regina and Sharon visit Vancouver.
   (B) Hubert, Lori, Paul, and Regina visit Montreal, and Sharon visits Vancouver.
   (C) Hubert, Paul, and Regina visit Toronto, and Lori and Sharon visit Montreal.
   (D) Hubert, Regina, and Sharon visit Montreal, and Lori and Paul visit Vancouver.
   (E) Lori, Paul, and Sharon visit Montreal, and Hubert and Regina visit Toronto.

2. If Hubert and Sharon visit a city together, which one of the following could be true in March?

   (A) Hubert visits the same city as Paul.
   (B) Lori visits the same city as Regina.
   (C) Paul visits the same city as Regina.
   (D) Paul visits Toronto.
   (E) Paul visits Vancouver.

3. If Sharon visits Vancouver, which one of the following must be true for March?

   (A) Hubert visits Montreal.
   (B) Lori visits Montreal.
   (C) Paul visits Toronto.
   (D) Lori visits the same city as Paul.
   (E) Lori visits the same city as Regina.

4. Which one of the following could be false in March?

   (A) Sharon must visit Montreal if Paul visits Vancouver.
   (B) Regina must visit Vancouver if Paul visits Vancouver.
   (C) Regina visits a city with exactly two of the other four students.
   (D) Lori visits a city with exactly one of the other four students.
   (E) Lori visits a city with Paul or else with Sharon.

5. If Regina visits Toronto, which one of the following could be true in March?

   (A) Lori visits Toronto.
   (B) Lori visits Vancouver.
   (C) Paul visits Toronto.
   (D) Paul visits Vancouver.
   (E) Sharon visits Vancouver.

6. Which one of the following must be true for March?

   (A) If any of the students visits Montreal, Lori visits Montreal.
   (B) If any of the students visits Montreal, exactly two of them do.
   (C) If any of the students visits Toronto, exactly three of them do.
   (D) If any of the students visits Vancouver, Paul visits Vancouver.
   (E) If any of the students visits Vancouver, exactly three of them do.

Practice Game Solution 1: PT12, S2, G3

Picture the Game

In this case, we have a cross between two sets of elements: people (Lara, Mendel, Nastassia) and food products (fruit cups, hot dogs, pretzels, shish kebabs). We need to assign one set to the other to form groups, but how do we know which set will be assigned and which will be the base?

In order to make this decision, we can start by looking at which set of items is being assigned one or more of the others. In this case, the scenario reads, "Lara, Mendel, and Nastassia each buy at least one kind of food…." It looks like food items are being assigned to people, so we would use the people as the base. Each person can be assigned a maximum of four different kinds of food, and each person buys at least one kind of food. We should notice that repeats are allowed.

In this game, our second tool for deciding on the base—looking at the rules to see which arrangement will garner more numerical inferences—is not very useful. If we were to use the foods as the base, many of the rules would lead to numerical inferences. In fact, it's not that hard to play this game with the food choices as the base. However, since most people probably used the people as the base, and that arrangement is somewhat easier to use, we'll explain the game that way.

If you didn't play the game with the people as the base, go ahead and do so now before reading on. If you did use the people, when you're done reading this solution try playing the game with the food options as the base to stretch the old brain.

Notate the Rules and Make Inferences

> *None of the three buys more than one portion of each kind of food.*

This rule may seem confusing, but it's basically telling us that we can't assign two or more fruit cups, for example, to any one of the people. In other words, each person can be assigned at most one F, one H, one P, and one S. Notice that we have not been told that every food is placed in a group.

> *If any of the three buys a hot dog, that person does not also buy a shish kebab.*

Remember, always think about what the rule tells us about the *number* of elements that can be assigned. Any person assigned an H cannot also be assigned an S. This means that no person can have all four foods! We can slash out one slot for each person.

> *At least one of the three buys a hot dog, and at least one buys a pretzel.*

P

This doesn't give us any further information about the number of filled vs. unfilled slots, but we can keep track of this rule by making a note to the side. So far we have the following:

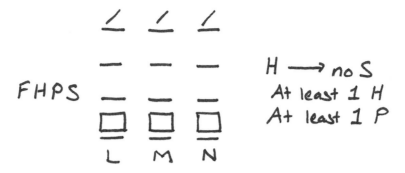

Mendel buys a shish kebab.
Nastassia buys a fruit cup.

These are direct rules. We'll plug this information right into the board. Notice that if Mendel buys a shish kebab, he can't possibly buy a hot dog as well (the contrapositive of "H ⟶ no S" is "S ⟶ no H"). Also, we now know that every food is used in this game.

Neither Lara nor Nastassia buys a pretzel.

We can symbolize this with cross-outs underneath Lara and Nastassia. Also remember that we must have at least one pretzel. If neither Lara nor Nastassia buys a pretzel, Mendel must buy a pretzel.

Mendel does not buy any kind of food that Nastassia buys.

We already know that Mendel has at least two types of food: pretzel and shish kebab. We also know that Mendel can't get a hot dog. Well, if Mendel can't share any food with Nastassia, Mendel can't get a fruit cup either. Thus, Mendel is limited to a pretzel and a shish kebab. Furthermore, if Mendel and Nastassia can't share any food, Nastassia can't get a pretzel or a shish kebab. Thus, the most that Nastassia can get is two foods:

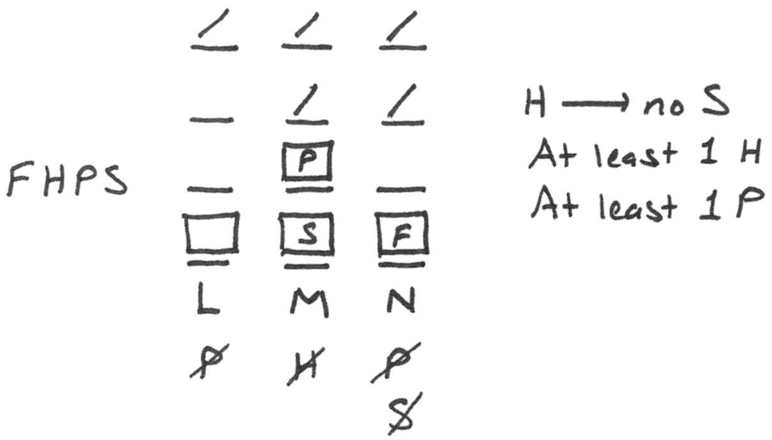

Cycle Through a Second Time

Remember, we must go back through the rules one more time to see if any of them might offer new information after we've filled in our diagram. The second rule proves useful the second time through:

If any of the three buys a hot dog, that person does not also buy a shish kebab.

In the diagram above, Lara is limited to three foods (she can't get a pretzel). However, if she gets the three remaining foods (fruit cup, hot dog, shish kebab), she'll break the H ➞ no S rule. Thus, she can't be assigned all three of the remaining foods. At most she can get two foods:

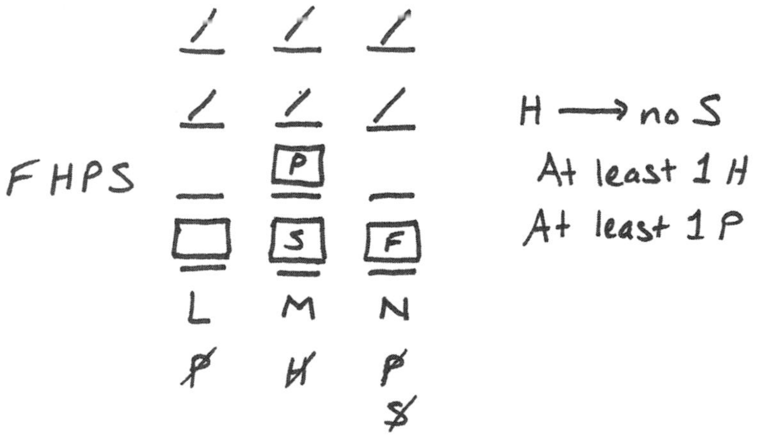

Upon further review, none of the other rules provide any additional information. So this is our completed diagram.

The Big Pause

There's not much uncertainty left in our diagram, but it's still worth a moment to notice which rules are big players. The H ➞ no S rule will clearly come into play, and we'll have to remember to place an H somewhere. In fact, we could write in that H will be assigned to either L or N (or both).

Attack the Questions

Let's use our diagram to tackle the questions:

12. Which one of the following statements must be true?

   (A) Lara buys a hot dog.
   (B) Lara buys a shish kebab.
   (C) Mendel buys a hot dog.
   (D) Mendel buys a pretzel.
   (E) Nastassia buys a hot dog.

(D) is correct.

Easy!

13. If the vendor charges $1 for each portion of food, what is the minimum amount the three people could spend?

   (A) $3
   (B) $4
   (C) $5
   (D) $6
   (E) $7

(B) is correct.

The question is essentially asking about the minimum number of possible assignments. We already have three assignments, and if we place H in L, we don't need to make any other assignments. Thus, at a minimum, we'll have four elements assigned, which translates to $4.

14. If the vendor charges $1 for each portion of food, what is the greatest amount the three people could spend?

   (A) $5
   (B) $6
   (C) $7
   (D) $8
   (E) $9

(B) is correct.

This is essentially the same question, but instead of asking about the minimum number of assignments, it's asking about the maximum number of assignments. Again, we know that Mendel has exactly two.

We also know that both Lara and Nastassia could have at most two assignments. Thus, it seems we have a maximum of six total assignments. A quick check tells us that no rules would be violated, so the answer is $6.

15. If Lara and Mendel buy exactly two kinds of food each, which one of the following statements must be true?

    (A) Lara buys a fruit cup.

    (B) Lara buys a hot dog.

    (C) Mendel buys a fruit cup.

    (D) There is exactly one kind of food that Lara and Mendel both buy.

    (E) There is exactly one kind of food that Lara and Nastassia both buy.

(A) is correct.

If Lara buys exactly two kinds of food, we know for certain that these two foods can't be H and S (remember, H ➞ no S). We also know that Lara can't buy a pretzel. Thus, Lara must buy a fruit cup and either a hot dog or a shish kebab.

16. If Lara buys a shish kebab, which one of the following statements must be true?

    (A) Lara buys a fruit cup.

    (B) Mendel buys a fruit cup.

    (C) Nastassia buys a hot dog.

    (D) Nastassia buys exactly one kind of food.

    (E) Exactly one person buys a fruit cup.

(C) is correct.

If Lara buys a shish kebab, she can't buy a hot dog. So neither Lara nor Mendel buys a hot dog. But remember that we must assign at least one hot dog. This means that Nastassia must buy a hot dog in addition to her fruit cup.

Notice that we DIDN'T examine each answer choice through trial and error. Rather, we started with the new rule given in the question (Lara buys a shish kebab) and we traced this rule through a chain of inferences. "Lara buys a shish kebab" means "Lara does NOT buy a hot dog" which means "Nastassia must buy a hot dog." We arrived a distance of two inferences away from where we started, and this turned out to be one of the answer choices. ALWAYS follow the inference chain as far as you can before implementing a trial and error approach.

P

17. Assume that the condition is removed that prevents a customer who buys a hot dog from buying a shish kebab but all other conditions remain the same. If the vendor charges $1 for each portion of food, what is the maximum amount the three people could spend?

(A) $5

(B) $6

(C) $7

(D) $8

(E) $9

(C) is correct.

This is the toughest question of the bunch, and one that is designed to take up a lot of our time. If we remove the second rule from consideration (H ➔ no S), how does this impact our diagram? The bad news is that we have to start from scratch. The good news—we should be able to draw a new diagram in about 30 seconds or so. If you didn't redraw the diagram to solve this question, do so before reading on.

Here's what we get:

If we count our available slots, it looks like we can have a total of eight assignments. But wait a moment—there's a rule we're overlooking! When we drew our original diagram, we didn't need to notate the rule that Mendel does not buy any kind of food that Nastassia buys. All of the needed inferences from that rule were built into our diagram. However, now that one of the other rules has been removed, and Mendel is free to buy a hot dog, we need to consider this rule again. The fact that M and N can't share any assignments means that at most one of the two could get a hot dog. If we gave the hot dog to Mendel, he would have three assignments and Nastassia would have one. If we gave the hot dog to Nastassia, she would have two assignments and Mendel would have two. Either way, we'd have four total assignments between Mendel and Nastassia. There's nothing stopping Lara from getting everything but the pretzel, so we can add three for Lara to reach a maximum total of seven.

Practice Game Solution 2: PT18, S1, G1

Picture the Game

It's Spring Break! We have five students and three Canadian cities. Each student visits exactly one city (no repeats), but we don't know how many times each city will be visited; thus we should use the cities as the base:

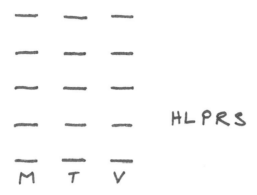

Onc thing to notice is that at this point we have no reason to think that every city will be visited. We should not put boxes in—perhaps one column will remain empty.

Notate the Rules and Make Inferences

> *Sharon visits a different city than Paul.*
> *Hubert visits the same city as Regina.*

The first two rules are easy to notate as a chunk and an anti-chunk. From the first rule, we can also infer that at least two cities will be visited. Since we can't have all five students in one city, we can limit each column to four slots.

> *Lori visits Montreal or else Toronto.*
> *If Paul visits Vancouver, Hubert visits Vancouver with him.*

The next two rules are easy to notate as well. So far there is nothing significant to infer, but we have the following:

P

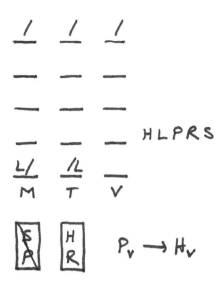

$$P_v \rightarrow H_v$$

Since H is in a chunk, we could also incorporate that chunk into the conditional rule:

$$P_v \rightarrow \boxed{\begin{array}{c} R \\ H \end{array}}_v$$

Each student visits one of the cities with at least one of the other four students.

Our final rule is a bit juicier! Another way of stating this rule is that there cannot be a group with just one student in it. What does this mean in terms of how the game might play out?

With only five elements, there is only one basic arrangement of numbers that works: two will go to one city, and three will go to another (remember, because of the first rule, we can't have all the students go to one city). Thus, one sad city will go visitorless. We should notate this numerical inference somehow!

The first thing we can do is limit the slots in each city to a maximum of three, and then we can write the rest of the inference to the side.

P

HLPRS

3, 2, 0

We now should take another spin through the rules. However, there seems to be nothing more to infer in terms of slashes and boxes. Let's take a moment to gather our thoughts about this game.

The Big Pause

This is a different flavor of Open Grouping game than we've tasted so far. There are far fewer slashing inferences and no boxes! But there is a significant numerical inference nonetheless. We know we'll have two groups, one with three and one with two, and we know that one group has S and one group has P. We could represent this like so:

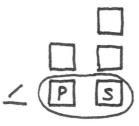

There's more we can infer, though! Where will the H R chunk go? Clearly, it will go in the group of three. That leaves L to fill in the remaining position in the group of two. So far, we have this:

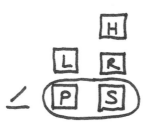

There are two things we have not noted so far: which city goes with which group, and which group will have no elements. We could notate all of these undetermined issues like so:

P

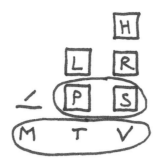

This diagram is far from the standard, but it's pure MacGyver and it represents a lot about this game! Except that we've lost a couple rules. Can you see which ones?

This new diagram no longer notes that L cannot be grouped with V. Nor do we have the Pv → Hv rule. We would need to notate these to the side, or perhaps refer to the original diagram.

We could successfully tackle the game with either of these diagrams:

The fact that we've suggested the "radical" diagram on the left might seem troubling to you if you didn't come up with anything like that. However, instead of troubling you, this should confirm that we don't need to have the "right" diagram to solve a game. Is the diagram on the left a bit more thought-out? Yes. But the truth is that when most of our teachers first solved the game, they used something similar to the one on the right, and they did just fine. In fact, we've intentionally left out some of the cool numerical inferences from the diagram on the right because we don't want to leave you thinking that it's essential to figure out every little nook and cranny of every game.

In terms of rule prioritization, clearly we'll always need to apply the S P and H R rules, but since it is such a contained game (meaning that there are not too many options), we love all these rules equally. Every element is involved in some rule; there's nothing to circle. Enough planning; time to attack!

Attack the Questions

1. Which one of the following could be true for March?

    (A) Hubert, Lori, and Paul visit Toronto, and Regina and Sharon visit Vancouver.

    (B) Hubert, Lori, Paul, and Regina visit Montreal, and Sharon visits Vancouver.

    (C) Hubert, Paul, and Regina visit Toronto, and Lori and Sharon visit Montreal.

    (D) Hubert, Regina, and Sharon visit Montreal, and Lori and Paul visit Vancouver.

    (E) Lori, Paul, and Sharon visit Montreal, and Hubert and Regina visit Toronto.

(C) is correct.

The first rule eliminates (E).

The second rule eliminates (A).

The third rule eliminates (D).

The fourth rule eliminates nothing that is left.

The final rule eliminates (B).

2. If Hubert and Sharon visit a city together, which one of the following could be true in March?

    (A) Hubert visits the same city as Paul.

    (B) Lori visits the same city as Regina.

    (C) Paul visits the same city as Regina.

    (D) Paul visits Toronto.

    (E) Paul visits Vancouver.

(D) is correct.

From the new condition, we can infer that the two groups are S H R and L P. To which cities could these groups be assigned? There are two rules to keep in mind: L can't be assigned to V, and if P is assigned to V, it would need to be with H. Since P and H are separate, we know that P is not assigned to V. Thus, the students must be assigned to either M or T:

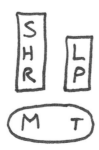

(A) through (C) and (E) clearly can't be true, while (D) can.

3. If Sharon visits Vancouver, which one of the following must be true for March?

    (A) Hubert visits Montreal.
    (B) Lori visits Montreal.
    (C) Paul visits Toronto.
    (D) Lori visits the same city as Paul.
    (E) Lori visits the same city as Regina.

(D) is correct.

What do we know if S is assigned to V? Scanning our diagram, we see that P and L can't go to V. That puts H R in V, too:

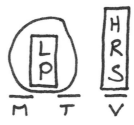

Here's what the answer choice vetting process might look like in real time:

(A) must be false. Eliminate.

(B) could be true, but we could also have L P in T.

(C) is another could be true. Hopefully, there's an easy answer ahead!

(D) D'oh! Of course.

4. Which one of the following could be false in March?

    (A) Sharon must visit Montreal if Paul visits Vancouver.
    (B) Regina must visit Vancouver if Paul visits Vancouver.
    (C) Regina visits a city with exactly two of the other four students.
    (D) Lori visits a city with exactly one of the other four students.
    (E) Lori visits a city with Paul or else with Sharon.

(A) is correct.

No condition to work from. Let's dive in and remember that the wrong answers must be true!

P

(A) looks time-consuming to think about, but, scanning the rest of the answers, they all do! Let's dig in. If P is assigned to V, we know that the H R chunk must follow. Can we place the S L chunk in T, and thereby prove that this answer could be false? Yes we can!

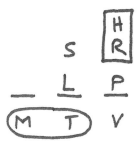

Go ahead and confirm that every other answer must be true. Don't be lazy—do it.

5. If Regina visits Toronto, which one of the following could be true in March?

   (A) Lori visits Toronto.
   (B) Lori visits Vancouver.
   (C) Paul visits Toronto.
   (D) Paul visits Vancouver.
   (E) Sharon visits Vancouver.

(C) is correct.

With R assigned to T, we know H is there as well, along with either P or S. That leaves L for the other group. Since L can't be assigned to V, we know it's assigned to M, along with P or S. If we couldn't hold this in our head—it is a lot—we could write it out like this:

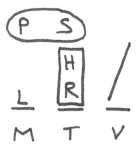

It's easy to eliminate any answer that references a visit to Vancouver, and (C) is clearly the only could be true situation.

P

6. Which one of the following must be true for March?

   (A) If any of the students visits Montreal, Lori visits Montreal.

   (B) If any of the students visits Montreal, exactly two of them do.

   (C) If any of the students visits Toronto, exactly three of them do.

   (D) If any of the students visits Vancouver, Paul visits Vancouver.

   (E) If any of the students visits Vancouver, exactly three of them do.

(E) is correct.

Tough question! For a change, let's begin by discussing the correct answer. Why is (E) correct? To start, who can visit Vancouver of the P S option? It looks like either one. And who could accompany P or S there? We definitely can't have L, so we're stuck placing the H R chunk there, which brings us to three. We don't even need to think about the Pv $\longrightarrow$ Hv rule to confirm (E).

It's clear now that (E) is correct, but how could we have efficiently moved through (A) through (D)? The ideal process would have been to give each of those answers a short consideration and either eliminate it or defer judgment on it. But, at this point in the game, you should be able to quickly work through the wrong answers by using previous work and/or deftly moving elements around the diagram. The process might have looked like this in real time:

We want to "break" answer (A). Can we swing H, R, and S over to M, leaving L and P to T? Sure. Eliminate. We also could have used our diagram from question #2 to do this.

We can eliminate (B) with the scenario that just disproved (A)!

Once again, we can use our (A)-disproving scenario to eliminate (C)! If we weren't so lucky as to have done the above to disprove (A), we could eliminate (C) by quickly thinking out a scenario with two elements assigned to T. That's not too hard to do, especially using the diagram from #2.

Can we have students visit V without P? Sure! H, R, and S visit V, while L and P visit T. Our diagram from #3 could help us think this through. Eliminate (D).

P

Chapter 13

of Logic Games

3D Grouping

In This Chapter...

Getting Familiar

Do your best to complete the following game. Use whatever approach you see fit. Give yourself **8 minutes**.

Eight students—R, S, T, V, W, X, Y, and Z—are paired up into four teams—the Green team, the Indigo team, the Jade team, and the Purple team. Each team will have one leader and one assistant. A student's position is defined by both team and assigned role. The following conditions apply:

  V is assigned to the Jade team, but R is not.
  W and Y are assigned to the same team.
  If S is an assistant, S is teamed with T.
  If S is a leader, S is teamed with X.
  R is not assigned to be a leader.

1. Which of the following could be a list of the leaders for the four teams?

    (A) Green team: W; Indigo team: S;
        Jade team: V; Purple team: R

    (B) Green team: W; Indigo team: S;
        Jade team: V; Purple team: X

    (C) Green team: V; Indigo team: S;
        Jade team: T; Purple team: Z

    (D) Green team: S; Indigo team: T;
        Jade team: V; Purple team: Z

    (E) Green team: W; Indigo team: S;
        Jade team: V; Purple team: T

2. If X is assigned to be an assistant for the Jade team, which one of the following can be determined?

    (A) the students assigned to the Green team
    (B) the students assigned to the Indigo team
    (C) the students assigned to the Purple team
    (D) which student each student is paired with
    (E) the role—either leader or assistant—that each student is assigned to

3. Which of the following must be false?

    (A) W is assigned to be a leader.
    (B) Y is assigned to be a leader.
    (C) X is assigned to be a leader.
    (D) T and Z are teamed together.
    (E) V and Z are teamed together.

4. Which of the following, if true, determines the pairings, though not necessarily the assigned positions, for each team?

    (A) S is teamed with T.
    (B) S is teamed with X.
    (C) V is teamed with Z.
    (D) R is teamed with Z.
    (E) R is teamed with X.

5. If either S or V, but not both, is assigned a leadership role, which of the following must be false?

    (A) Neither W nor Z is assigned a leadership role.
    (B) Neither X nor Y is assigned a leadership role.
    (C) Neither T nor Z is assigned a leadership role
    (D) Neither S nor Z is assigned an assistant role.
    (E) Neither T nor W is assigned an assistant role.

6. If neither T nor X nor Y is assigned to a leadership position, how many different pairs of students can be assigned to the Indigo team?

    (A) 1
    (B) 2
    (C) 3
    (D) 4
    (E) 5

Picturing 3D Grouping Games

Thus far, we've discussed a couple of different grouping game types, with the emphasis on whether the number of elements within a group is defined. In this chapter, we will discuss another type of grouping scenario: grouping games for which the positions within these individual groups are more specifically defined. We call these 3D Grouping games.

There are a variety of twists we might see in 3D Grouping games, and we'll discuss a few different strategies for dealing with the various issues that can arise. While we'll spell out our suggestions, this is a game type in which your flexibility and control of the rules will prove far more important than having the "right" diagram.

The primary diagram that we suggest for 3D Grouping Games is one we call the 3D Board. The 3D Board allows us to use columns to organize information about groups, and rows to organize information about subcategories.

Let's go ahead and use a simple game scenario to discuss how we set up the 3D Board, and how we can use it to effectively deal with a variety of rules:

> Six people—F, G, H, K, L, and N—will ride in three different types of automobiles—a minivan, a roadster, and an SUV—two people per car. In each car there will be one driver and one passenger. The following conditions apply:

Given this scenario, it would be a good idea to set up a board that looks something like this:

$$
\begin{array}{c}
D \underline{} \ \underline{} \ \underline{} \ \ \text{F G H K L N} \\
P \underline{} \ \underline{} \ \underline{} \\
\ \ \text{M} \ \ \text{R} \ \ \text{S}
\end{array}
$$

We are using the vertical orientation to represent groups, and the horizontal orientation to represent subsets. Let's take a look at a variety of rules that we might expect for a game such as this one, and discuss the ways in which we would notate these rules.

Assignment Rules

As with all games, we will get rules that pertain to the assignment of specific elements to specific positions. Here are some examples:

> "K is not the driver of the minivan."

> "N is a passenger in the SUV."

13

If both of these rules appeared in the same game, we could notate them in this way:

$$\begin{array}{c} \overset{\cancel{K}_D}{} \\ \begin{matrix} D \\ P \end{matrix} \; \underline{} \; \underline{} \; \underline{}^{N} \quad \text{F G H K L N} \\ \; M \quad R \quad S \end{array}$$

Note that we've written the "not rule" above the driver line so that we can see the rule a bit more directly as it relates to the position. You might find the subscript to be overkill, and in some instances it can seem unnecessary, but we suggest you use it in order to differentiate slot-specific not rules from group-specific not rules. To see what we mean, think about how you might notate "K is not the passenger in the minivan" and "K is not in the minivan." If you avoid using subscript, those two could end up looking exactly the same.

Grouping Rules

By and large, the manner in which you deal with grouping rules will be largely the same as for other grouping games, but keep in mind that we are now using the rows to differentiate subsets, and this requires us to be a bit more specific in our diagramming.

For example, imagine we were given the rule:

"F and L ride in the same car."

For other grouping games, we would notate like this:

And that representation would be complete and sufficient. However, for a 3D Grouping game, that notation could be confusing.

To see why, think about how you would notate the following rule:

"L is a passenger in the car that F drives."

The very same notation could be an accurate portrayal of this rule, and that's why we run into some trouble here. In order to combat the issue, we have two suggestions:

1. The Double Arrow

The double arrow is something you should be comfortable with by this point, and you can apply it to this situation to mean the same thing it has in other games. The notation would mean that we know F and L ride together, but we don't know which one drives.

13

2. The Vertical Cloud

We already know the cloud well, and we can put it to use here vertically:

Once you've become comfortable with either of the above, be consistent so that you know that such notation means that F and L go in a column together, but that we don't know the exact order.

Subset Rules

The most basic and common subset rules are those that tell us that an element is in a certain subset, or is not in a certain subset.

Imagine we had the following two rules for our hypothetical game:

"N drives one of the cars."
"H is not a passenger in one of the cars."

We could represent these two rules in this way:

$$\begin{array}{cccc} \text{N D} & \underline{} & \underline{} & \underline{} \\ \cancel{\text{H}}\ \text{P} & \underline{} & \underline{} & \underline{} \\ & \text{M} & \text{R} & \text{S} \end{array} \qquad \text{F G H K L N}$$

Keep in mind that we could have just as well notated either of these rules based on the flip side of the information given—that is, for the first rule about N, we could have crossed out N from the passenger row, and for the second rule about H, we could have put H into the driver row. So if you prefer one type of representation, by all means go with that. Of course, if there were three or more subsets, we'd have to be more careful about the "flip side."

More complex subset rules relate elements to one another. Here are some examples:

K drives if and only if N does not drive.
Both G and H drive, or neither of them do.
If K drives one of the cars, G will be a passenger in one of the cars.
If G drives the SUV, F will be a passenger in the minivan.

Let's discuss how we can notate each of these rules:

> *K drives if and only if N does not drive.*

This rule gives us two possibilities—K drives one of the cars and N doesn't, or N drives one of the cars, and K doesn't. Essentially, what that means is that K and N will be in different rows. We can represent it this way:

You may also be tempted to notate it like this:

But keep in mind that we use that notation to mean that elements are in the same column.

> *Both G and H drive, or neither of them do.*

Take a moment to think about how G and H can be placed in the diagram.

This rule essentially means that G and H are in thse same row—either both are in the driver row or both are in the passenger row. We can go ahead and notate this rule as follows:

Again, what the cloud means is that we know G and H go in a row together, but we do not know more about the arrangement.

> *If K drives one of the cars, G will be a passenger in one of the cars.*

$$K_D \rightarrow G_P$$

Note that this is a conditional rule, and like other conditional rules, we want to go ahead and notate it next to our diagram, as opposed to *in* our diagram. Subscript is very effective for rules such as this one. Note that we can't use the cloud here because we don't have a biconditional. If G is a passenger, K might be a passenger also.

> *If G drives the SUV, F will be a passenger in the minivan.*

This is another conditional rule, but this time there's even more to track. You could use a second set of subscript notes here, but keep in mind that when you go to extremes such as a second subscript, don't do so hastily; give yourself ample time to absorb exactly what the rule implies.

13

$$_sG_D \rightarrow {}_MF_P$$

Or you could avoid using subscripts by referencing how the diagram is arranged:

$$\frac{G_D}{S} \rightarrow \frac{F_P}{M}$$

Some people might want to go even further with this idea:

The point is to find a notation style that is meaningful to you under pressure.

Advanced 3D Grouping Considerations

Like other games that throw a variety of rules and information at us, 3D Grouping games have a tendency to be back-end games.

Very commonly, 3D Grouping games will be limited to six elements and six positions. This type of scenario virtually guarantees a back-end game. With the positions so constrained, if there were significant up-front inferences, we would know too much about the game for the questions themselves to pose enough of a challenge.

As with other back-end games, the key to success for these games will be a clear, defined, and usable understanding of the rules. 3D Grouping games are particularly dangerous in that they often have rules that can easily be confused for one another. When you play 3D Grouping games in real time, make sure that you understand your notations completely and correctly before moving on to the questions. Be mindful of ways in which you can misunderstand your own notations; review them, and work to remove ambiguity from your notations.

3D Grouping games rarely require framing. We often don't know even one actual assignment, so we have a board with mostly blank slots (never too inviting). As mentioned before, 3D Grouping games generally are designed so that once a little bit of information is uncovered (say, the positions of three of six elements), the options become very limited and manageable. Therefore, frames can be useful for these games because these games do have a greater amount of uncertainty upfront, but this uncertainty is also why frames are often impossible to use and rarely crucial.

Try It Again

Now that you've learned how to notate the rules you'll meet in 3D Grouping games, let's return to the Getting Familiar game. If you'd like, give it one more shot before we work through it together.

Eight students—R, S, T, V, W, X, Y, and Z—are paired up into four teams—the Green team, the Indigo team, the Jade team, and the Purple team. Each team will have one leader and one assistant. A student's position is defined by both team and assigned role. The following conditions apply:

> V is assigned to the Jade team, but R is not.
> W and Y are assigned to the same team.
> If S is an assistant, S is teamed with T.
> If S is a leader, S is teamed with X.
> R is not assigned to be a leader.

1. Which of the following could be a list of the leaders for the four teams?

    (A) Green team: W; Indigo team: S;
        Jade team: V; Purple team: R
    (B) Green team: W; Indigo team: S;
        Jade team: V; Purple team: X
    (C) Green team: V; Indigo team: S;
        Jade team: T; Purple team: Z
    (D) Green team: S; Indigo team: T;
        Jade team: V; Purple team: Z
    (E) Green team: W; Indigo team: S;
        Jade team: V; Purple team: T

2. If X is assigned to be an assistant for the Jade team, which one of the following can be determined?

    (A) the students assigned to the Green team
    (B) the students assigned to the Indigo team
    (C) the students assigned to the Purple team
    (D) which student each student is paired with
    (E) the role—either leader or assistant—that each student is assigned to

3. Which of the following must be false?

    (A) W is assigned to be a leader.
    (B) Y is assigned to be a leader.
    (C) X is assigned to be a leader.
    (D) T and Z are teamed together.
    (E) V and Z are teamed together.

4. Which of the following, if true, determines the pairings, though not necessarily the assigned positions, for each team?

    (A) S is teamed with T.
    (B) S is teamed with X.
    (C) V is teamed with Z.
    (D) R is teamed with Z.
    (E) R is teamed with X.

5. If either S or V, but not both, is assigned a leadership role, which of the following must be false?

    (A) Neither W nor Z is assigned a leadership role.
    (B) Neither X nor Y is assigned a leadership role.
    (C) Neither T nor Z is assigned a leadership role
    (D) Neither S nor Z is assigned an assistant role.
    (E) Neither T nor W is assigned an assistant role.

6. If neither T nor X nor Y is assigned to a leadership position, how many different pairs of students can be assigned to the Indigo team?

    (A) 1
    (B) 2
    (C) 3
    (D) 4
    (E) 5

How Did You Do?

Picture the Game

The eight students are to be put into four groups, so we'll use the four teams as our base. It's clearly a 3D Grouping game, because the group positions have subsets: leaders and assistants. We have three dimensions to pay attention to: groups, position subsets, and elements.

We'll start by laying out our 3D Board:

Notate the Rules and Make Inferences

The rules for this game are not easy to control. There are a lot of them, and they span all three dimensions of the game. However, each is easy enough to notate if you're careful. Compare your diagram against ours (we haven't put in any inferences yet—and separating notation and making inferences might be helpful with such complex rules):

It's likely that you notated the third and fourth rules like this:

That's perfect, and would be the ideal if there were any possibility of S not being selected. However, since every element in this game is used, the two-chunk notation we showed in the diagram encapsulates the situation a bit more succinctly.

Let's make some inferences!

We'll start with our grouping chunks. Since the J team already has one slot filled, the W Y chunk can't go there.

And while we don't know which of the S chunks is going to be used in any given scenario, we know that neither one could fit on the J team. Be careful not to over apply this inference to T and X! They *can* go in the J group, but just not as part of a chunk with S.

No other obvious inferences come to mind. Here's what we have so far:

```
  /  A   ___   ___   (V)   ___   R S T V W X Y Z
 R/  L   ___   ___   (V)   ___
     G    I     J     P    (W)        S_A →  [ S ]
                R           (Y)              [ T ]
               W
               Y                      S_L →  [ X ]
               S                             [ S ]
```

The Big Pause

It's tough to say which rules will be most important in this game. It seems like all might play a big role in working through the questions. We'll be sure to keep an eye on our chunks, as those will force around the largest number of elements.

There aren't any obvious opportunities to frame this game in a formal sense. However, with so many restrictions on pairings, it's worth outlining the pairs with broad strokes. For starters, we know we have a WY pair. We'll also have S pairing with either X or T. And since neither V nor R will be with S or with each other, they each can start a pair. That leaves T, X, and Z to place. We can represent our thinking as follows:

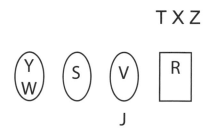

Other than for V, we don't yet know which team each element or group is assigned to, but with this formulation of the game, we've gained a handle on a rather unwieldy game. Similarly, other than for R, we don't know whether each element is assisting or leading.

We can circle Z, as it's the only element that has no rules attached.

Attack the Questions

1. Which of the following could be a list of the leaders for the four teams?

   (A) Green team: W; Indigo team: S; Jade team: V; Purple team: R
   (B) Green team: W; Indigo team: S; Jade team: V; Purple team: X
   (C) Green team: V; Indigo team: S; Jade team: T; Purple team: Z
   (D) Green team: S; Indigo team: T; Jade team: V; Purple team: Z
   (E) Green team: W; Indigo team: S; Jade team: V; Purple team: T

(E) is correct.

The first rule eliminates (C).

The second rule eliminates (D). Since W and Y must be on the same team, one of them must be a leader in any scenario.

The third and the fourth rules work together, and, like the second rule, require a bit of thought to use here. We're either going to have S assisting T or S leading X. That means that if we see S in the list, we can't see X, but if we don't see S, we must see T. This allows us to eliminate (B).

The fifth rule allows us to eliminate (A).

2. If X is assigned to be an assistant for the Jade team, which one of the following can be determined?

   (A) the students assigned to the Green team
   (B) the students assigned to the Indigo team
   (C) the students assigned to the Purple team
   (D) which student each student is paired with
   (E) the role—either leader or assistant—that each student is assigned to

(D) is correct.

Let's work the new condition. If X is the assistant for the Jade team, V must lead. Since S is not with X, S will assist T.

This is where many students will stop making inferences; instead, ask yourself, "who's left?" In this case, we've paired X with V (in J) and S with T. That leaves us R, W, Y, and Z. W and Y must always go together, so that leaves R and Z to be a pair. Finally, R must assist. Let's sketch out the groups:

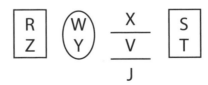

There are no other rules about the teams, so it seems we've hit the end of the inference chain. Let's see if we've done enough to spot the right answer easily.

(A) through (C) all seem highly unlikely. Other than the J team, we have no rules telling us about which team the elements are assigned to.

(D) is clearly what we figured out!

(E) is almost true, except for the W Y group.

3. Which of the following must be false?

    (A) W is assigned to be a leader.
    (B) Y is assigned to be a leader.
    (C) X is assigned to be a leader.
    (D) T and Z are teamed together.
    (E) V and Z are teamed together.

(D) is correct.

This is a tough question! Let's first work through the answer choices as if we had not broadly sketched the pairs during the Big Pause:

(A) can be eliminated based on our answer to the first question.

(B) is the flip side of (A). We don't have any information about who leads the W Y pair.

(C) doesn't appear to trigger any rules. Defer.

(D) seems more promising. There are two elements referenced, so there's more opportunity to violate rules. If T and Z are paired, who's left to pair? W and Y are paired, leaving R, S, V, and X. Since R and S can't be grouped with V, X must be. That leaves S and R, which is not a viable pair according to the two S rules.

It's likely that we would have skipped thinking this deeply about (D) and instead deferred. That would have been a reasonable move. Let's examine (E).

(E) is another answer that's tough to work through quickly, especially if you don't employ the "who's left?" question. If V and Z are together, and so are W and Y, we have R, S, T, and X to pair up. S could go with X, and R could go with T. This could be true, so we can eliminate.

This was undoubtedly a time-consuming question for most people; however, anyone who did the work we did in the Big Pause saw the investment pay dividends here. T, X, and Z can never be grouped together since they were the elements left to fill in the S, V, and R groups!

4. Which of the following, if true, determines the pairings, though not necessarily the assigned positions, for each team?

   (A) S is teamed with T.
   (B) S is teamed with X.
   (C) V is teamed with Z.
   (D) R is teamed with Z.
   (E) R is teamed with X.

(E) is correct.

After our work on the last question, it's somewhat easier to see what this question is asking. What will tell us who the four pairs are? We can dive into the answer choices, but let's take a moment to consider what must be done to find our four pairs.

We'll need to have the S choice settled, which will give us two pairs (since the W and Y pair is established). And then we'll need something that will determine the pairs among the remaining four.

For this question, it might be useful to rewrite the roster next to the question, crossing out or omitting W and Y since they are determined.

(A) seems unlikely. It settles the S issue, but we don't know about the four remaining elements, R, V, X, and Z.

(B) also settles only the S question. What about R, T, V, and Z? V can be paired with either T or Z.

(C) looks promising at first. We have settled V and Z, as well as W and Y, but we don't know whether S will be paired with T or X.

(D) leaves us not knowing about the S pair again.

(E) pairs R with X. We have W and Y already, leaving S, T, V, and Z. Of this group, S can be paired only with T, leaving V and Z to form the final pair.

Notice how (E) works: it settles the "S question" by using one of the possibilities for a different pair. This leaves S with only one pairing option. This is the same little trick that we saw in the second question!

5. If either S or V, but not both, is assigned a leadership role, which of the following must be false?

   (A) Neither W nor Z is assigned a leadership role.
   (B) Neither X nor Y is assigned a leadership role.
   (C) Neither T nor Z is assigned a leadership role
   (D) Neither S nor Z is assigned an assistant role.
   (E) Neither T nor W is assigned an assistant role.

(C) is correct.

We'll sketch out the two possible arrangements. Noting that all the answer choices are about roles, we're not particularly concerned with the teams to which each pair is assigned.

If S leads and V assists, we know that S will be paired with X. We can use the four groups we identified in the Big Pause to help us determine who's left:

Before reading on, quickly sketch out what the other option—V leading but not S—would look like.

If S is assisting, we know it's paired with T. That leaves V leading, and R, X, and Z to place. R must assist, so the other leader will be either X or Z.

With these two frames in place—frames for the condition given in this question—let's dive into the answer choices, remembering that every wrong answer will be something that could be true. Our focus should be on looking for something that must be false; the could be true answers will take up precious time. However, with such involved answer choices, that kind of savvy game playing might be impossible. Thankfully, we have two well-developed frames to rely upon.

Looking at the choices, each one presents a neither/nor situation in which two elements are restricted. Do we need both restrictions to be false for an answer to be false? No. If just one of the restrictions is impossible, the answer is false. Analogously, if someone states that she isn't human and can't be exposed to sunlight, we only have to prove that she can be exposed to sunlight (or that she is indeed human) to prove that her statement is false. Unfortunately, we have more work to do if we want to prove that a choice could be true. In this case, we will need to show that both restrictions could work at the same time.

(A) W can be assigned either role and thus it's possible that W isn't assigned a leadership role. The remaining question is whether Z is prohibited from assisting under the new condition. In the V-leading frame, Z can assist. Thus this is a could be true (or false) answer, not a must be false. Eliminate.

(B) We can ignore Y (like W in the last answer choice), and focus on X. Can X assist? Yes—in either frame.

(C) Can T assist? No. In both frames it must lead. Can Z assist? Yes, but it doesn't matter! We've already proven that this answer must be false. It can't be true that neither T nor Z leads, since T must always lead in this scenario.

Take a moment to work through (D) and (E) to hone your ability to wrestle with these complex answer choices.

6. If neither T nor X nor Y is assigned to a leadership position, how many different pairs of students can be assigned to the Indigo team?

(A) 1
(B) 2
(C) 3
(D) 4
(E) 5

(C) is correct.

This is a big condition! If T, X, and Y are assisting, what do we know? We already know that R must assist, so that leaves S, V, W, and Z to lead. We know W and Y are paired, and if S leads, S and X are grouped together. So we have all the pairs again!

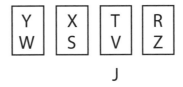

Let's return to the question stem: how many different pairs can be assigned to the Indigo team? The only restriction we have is that V cannot be. At this point, it's just a matter of counting: 1) YW, 2) XS, 3) RZ.

Alternative Methods for Diagramming Grouping with Subsets

The 3D Board is very effective for the majority of grouping games involving subsets, and it's what we recommend you think of first. Having said that, not all 3D Grouping games are created alike, and there are situations for which other notations may be more effective or efficient. Let's further discuss some additional tools that are useful to have in your belt.

Subscript & Cases

Subscript is also an effective way to deal with subsets, and we've been using subscript throughout the book for a variety of issues. For 3D Grouping games, using subscript instead of a 3D Board makes sense when the subsets are more about the elements themselves than about the positions, or when the subsets related to the positions have been left undefined.

Here is an example of a 3D Grouping game that involves subsets but may not require the 3D Board:

> Two Russian novels—G and H—two French novels—J and K— and two Italian novels—M and N—are placed in three different bins, numbered 1, 2, and 3. Two books will be placed in each bin.

Note that in this case the elements to be placed, the novels, have been defined in terms of subsets, but the positions themselves have not been. We could get a rule or two relating subsets to positions (e.g., one French novel is placed in the first bin), but not much more. Therefore, it would be difficult to put together a 3D Board. Instead, it would make sense to use something like this:

$$
\begin{array}{ccc}
\underline{} & \underline{} & \underline{} \\
1 & 2 & 3
\end{array}
\qquad
\begin{array}{cc}
G_R & H_R \\
J_F & K_F \\
M_I & N_I
\end{array}
$$

Here's a different type of 3D Grouping game that also involves subsets, but may not fit into a 3D Board:

> Five veterans—K, L, M, N, and O—and four rookies—S, T, W, and Y—are to be grouped into three teams of three. Each team will have at least one veteran.

Note that in this case we can't use the 3D Board as we have before, because we don't know the exact subset for each of the positions (though we do know the subset for a few of the positions). Therefore, it would be effective to set up our diagram like this:

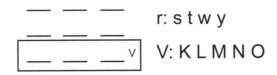

Or, if we'd like to avoid subscripts, we can quickly distinguish our elements by using uppercase for one set and lowercase for the other:

$$\begin{array}{ccc} \underline{} & \underline{} & \underline{} \end{array} \quad \text{r: s t w y}$$

$$\boxed{\begin{array}{ccc} \underline{} & \underline{} & \underline{}_V \end{array}} \quad \text{V: K L M N O}$$

An Additional Layer of Slots

Grouping games can also define entire groups through the use of a subset (instead of defining the members within a group, such as assistant vs. leader). For these situations we can borrow some of the strategies we used for 3D Ordering, and add an additional layer of slots to represent the subset, or characteristic, of the group as a whole.

Consider this example:

> Four different bands—M, P, R, and T—will play on four
> different stages—the North Stage, the South Stage, the West
> Stage, and the East Stage—during a music festival. Each band
> consists of two of the following eight people—F, G, H, I, J, K, L,
> and O—and no person is in two different bands. The following
> conditions apply:
>
> Band R will play on the West Stage.
> F and H are in the same band.
> K plays on the East Stage.

We've included some rules to give a better sense of what this type of game might be about. We have two separate but related mysteries in terms of positioning elements: which band plays on which stage, and which people play on which stage. We can set up a board like this:

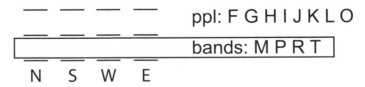

The different "layers" of positions help us to track band information and people information. Notice that we "locked in" the four stage positions. We also could have left the stages subset "floating," on a fourth row, but except in rare situations, it's advantageous to have at least one set of elements in fixed positions to allow easier conceptualization of the game.

DRILL IT: 3D Grouping Setups

Let's get some practice in diagramming 3D Grouping games. More than in any other drill, you'll likely find that your diagram will look different from what we've written. 3D Grouping is one game type for which it's tough to argue that a certain diagram is the ideal. It's most important that you develop your own style and adapt that style to fit the game. That said, you do want to make sure that you haven't made any mistakes, so check every difference between our diagrams to make sure it's simply one of style, and hold yourself to a high standard for correct notation.

1. Four different bomb-detection units must be assembled from five police officers—M, N, Q, R, and S—and five bomb-sniffing dogs—G, H, J, K, and L. No police officer or dog is assigned to more than one unit, and each unit includes exactly one officer and one dog. The assignments must meet the following restrictions:

    Neither N nor M can be assigned to a unit with K.
    Any unit that includes J must also include R.
    L can be assigned only to units with either Q or R.
    S and H form one unit.

2. Four different bomb-detection units—W, X, Y, and Z—must be assembled from six police officers—M, N, Q, R, S, and T—and six bomb-sniffing dogs—F, G, H, J, K, and L. No police officer or dog is assigned to more than one unit, and each unit must have exactly three members. The assignments must adhere to the following conditions:

    Each unit must include at least one officer and at least one dog.
    Q must be in the same unit as K.
    T and M are assigned to Y.
    F must be assigned to Z with one other dog.
    Both G and H must be the only dogs in their respective units.
    Neither R nor S can be in the same unit as F.

3. As part of an unusual three-course meal, a restaurant serves exactly six different dishes—fried banana, green eggs, ham pudding, ice cream, jambalaya, and kiwi soup. Two dishes are served during the appetizer course, two are served during the main course, and two are served during the dessert course. Exactly one dish in each course is considered low-fat. The arrangement of dishes must comply with the following conditions:

> Ham pudding cannot be a low-fat dish.
> Ice cream must be served during the dessert course.
> Green eggs cannot be served with ham pudding or fried banana.
> Kiwi soup can be served as a main course only if fried banana is not.

4. As part of an unusual three-course meal, a restaurant offers six different dishes—fried banana, green eggs, ham pudding, ice cream, jambalaya, and kiwi soup. Two dishes are served during the appetizer course, two are served during the main course, and two are served during the dessert course. Exactly one dish in each course is considered low-fat. Each course is accompanied by exactly one type of wine—Pinot Noir, Riesling, or Shiraz—and each type of wine accompanies only one course. The arrangement of dishes must comply with the following conditions:

> Riesling must accompany green eggs.
> Ham pudding cannot be a low-fat dish.
> Green eggs cannot be served for dessert, but ice cream must be.
> If Shiraz accompanies the appetizer course, it accompanies kiwi soup.
> If Shiraz does not accompany the appetizer course, it accompanies the course in which jambalaya is served.

SOLUTIONS: 3D Grouping Setups

1.

2.

Note that g and h cannot be grouped with the Q k chunk because that chunk already includes a dog, and neither g nor h can be grouped with another dog.

13

3.

H̶ low $\quad \underline{\ }\ \underline{\ }\ \underline{\ }$ FGHI(J)K
$\qquad\qquad \underline{\ }\ \underline{\ }\ \boxed{I}$
$\qquad\qquad\ \ \underline{\ }\ \underline{\ }\ \underline{\ }$
$\qquad\qquad\ \ A\ \ M\ \ D$

$\boxed{\dfrac{H}{G}}\qquad \cancel{\boxed{\dfrac{F}{G}}}$

$K_M \rightarrow \cancel{F}_M$

4.

$\qquad\qquad\qquad\qquad K$

wine $\quad \underline{\ }\ \underline{\ }\ \underline{\ } \quad$ prs

H̶ low $\quad \underline{\ }\ \underline{\ }\ \boxed{I}$ FGHI(J)K
$\qquad\qquad\ \ \underline{\ }\ \underline{\ }\ \underline{\ }$
$\qquad\qquad\ \ A\ \ M\ \ D$
$\qquad\qquad\qquad\quad \cancel{G}$

$\boxed{\dfrac{r}{G}}$

$S_A \rightarrow K_A$

$\cancel{S}_A \rightarrow \boxed{\dfrac{s}{J}} \qquad K_A \rightarrow \cancel{S}_A \rightarrow \boxed{\dfrac{s}{J}}$

Conclusion

At this point in the book, we're looking at variations on standard game types, so you're mostly working with tools you've already developed. However, we've tried to highlight two important skills here:

1. Flexibility

- There are many ways to notate the various rules you'll encounter in 3D Grouping games. By test day, you should have established a standard notation system that encompasses most of the rules you'll encounter, but you should also be comfortable making minor changes if a rule doesn't fit your system.

2. Rule mastery

- Usually, 3D Grouping games are back-end games. This means that your ability to control the rules is crucial. Success is not just about coming up with a great initial diagram; it's about quickly and accurately applying each rule in question after question. If you're stuck on a question, remember to scan your rules.

Practice Game 1: PT7, S2, G2

Give yourself **19 minutes** to complete these two tricky games!

Doctor Yamata works only on Mondays, Tuesdays, Wednesdays, Fridays, and Saturdays. She performs four different activities—lecturing, operating, treating patients, and conducting research. Each working day she performs exactly one activity in the morning and exactly one activity in the afternoon. During each week her work schedule must satisfy the following restrictions:

> She performs operations on exactly three mornings.
> If she operates on Monday, she does not operate on Tuesday.
> She lectures in the afternoon on exactly two consecutive calendar days.
> She treats patients on exactly one morning and exactly three afternoons.
> She conducts research on exactly one morning.
> On Saturday she neither lectures nor performs operations.

8. Which one of the following must be a day on which Doctor Yamata lectures?

    (A) Monday
    (B) Tuesday
    (C) Wednesday
    (D) Friday
    (E) Saturday

9. On Wednesday Doctor Yamata could be scheduled to

    (A) conduct research in the morning and operate in the afternoon
    (B) lecture in the morning and treat patients in the afternoon
    (C) operate in the morning and lecture in the afternoon
    (D) operate in the morning and conduct research in the afternoon
    (E) treat patients in the morning and treat patients in the afternoon

10. Which one of the following statements must be true?

    (A) There is one day on which the doctor treats patients both in the morning and in the afternoon.
    (B) The doctor conducts research on one of the days on which she lectures.
    (C) The doctor conducts research on one of the days on which she treats patients.
    (D) The doctor lectures on one of the days on which she treats patients.
    (E) The doctor lectures on one of the days on which she operates.

11. If Doctor Yamata operates on Tuesday, then her schedule for treating patients could be

    (A) Monday morning, Monday afternoon, Friday morning, Friday afternoon
    (B) Monday morning, Friday afternoon, Saturday morning, Saturday afternoon
    (C) Monday afternoon, Wednesday morning, Wednesday afternoon, Saturday afternoon
    (D) Wednesday morning, Wednesday afternoon, Friday afternoon, Saturday afternoon
    (E) Wednesday afternoon, Friday afternoon, Saturday morning, Saturday afternoon

12. Which one of the following is a pair of days on both of which Doctor Yamata must treat patients?

    (A) Monday and Tuesday
    (B) Monday and Saturday
    (C) Tuesday and Friday
    (D) Tuesday and Saturday
    (E) Friday and Saturday

Practice Game 2: PT36, S4, G3

P

Gutierrez, Hoffman, Imamura, Kelly, Lapas, and Moore ride a bus together. Each sits facing forward in a different one of the six seats on the left side of the bus. The seats are in consecutive rows that are numbered 1, 2, and 3 from front to back. Each row has exactly two seats: a window seat and an aisle seat. The following conditions must apply:

Hoffman occupies the aisle seat immediately behind Gutierrez's aisle seat.

If Moore occupies an aisle seat, Hoffman sits in the same row as Lapas.

If Gutierrez sits in the same row as Kelly, Moore occupies the seat immediately and directly behind Imamura's seat.

If Kelly occupies a window seat, Moore sits in row 3.

If Kelly sits in row 3, Imamura sits in row 1.

14. Which one of the following could be true?

(A) Imamura sits in row 2, whereas Kelly sits in row 3.

(B) Gutierrez sits in the same row as Kelly, immediately and directly behind Moore.

(C) Gutierrez occupies a window seat in the same row as Lapas.

(D) Moore occupies an aisle seat in the same row as Lapas.

(E) Kelly and Moore both sit in row 3.

15. If Lapas and Kelly each occupy a window seat, then which one of the following could be true?

(A) Moore occupies the aisle seat in row 3.

(B) Imamura occupies the window seat in row 3.

(C) Gutierrez sits in the same row as Kelly.

(D) Gutierrez sits in the same row as Moore.

(E) Moore sits in the same row as Lapas.

16. If Moore sits in row 1, then which one of the following must be true?

(A) Hoffman sits in row 2.

(B) Imamura sits in row 2.

(C) Imamura sits in row 3.

(D) Kelly sits in row 1.

(E) Lapas sits in row 3.

17. If Kelly occupies the aisle seat in row 3, then each of the following must be true EXCEPT:

(A) Gutierrez sits in the same row as Imamura.

(B) Hoffman sits in the same row as Lapas.

(C) Lapas occupies a window seat.

(D) Moore occupies a window seat.

(E) Gutierrez sits in row 1.

18. If neither Gutierrez nor Imamura sits in row 1, then which one of the following could be true?

(A) Hoffman sits in row 2.

(B) Kelly sits in row 2.

(C) Moore sits in row 2.

(D) Imamura occupies an aisle seat.

(E) Moore occupies an aisle seat.

P

Practice Game Solution 1: PT7, S2, G2

Picture the Game

At first it seems that this game will involve ordering (which would qualify it as a Hybrid, the subject of the next chapter). In fact, other than one reference to consecutive calendar days, the days are serving as placeholders for the various elements. Thus, this is a 3D Grouping game. The subsets we need to account for are afternoon versus morning positions.

We are not told in the scenario how the mismatch—five days and four activities—will be resolved, except that there will be no empty slots.

We'll begin with our 3D Board and roster:

Notate the Rules and Make Inferences

The basic notations of the rules are straightforward:

But there is a quite a bit to infer from each rule.

To start, notice that we know which five elements will be assigned to the morning slots and which will be assigned to the afternoon ones. The mismatch issue is resolved.

Let's move to our L chunk in the afternoon. Where can that go? Since it must fall on consecutive days, and cannot fall on Saturday, it must occur sometime between Monday and Wednesday. Friday is only consecutive with Saturday, which is off limits. (Tricky game skips Thursday!) Thus, either the chunk will fall on Monday-Tuesday or Tuesday-Wednesday; either way, we know there will be an L on Tuesday. But we can write a bit more than just an L on Tuesday. We know that from Monday–Wednesday there will be the L chunk and a P.

Since we've used our L chunk, the only elements that can go in the afternoon Friday and Saturday slots are P's!

So far we have this:

Moving to our morning, we have a lot of O's to place! With two restrictions on O, the issue is worth some thought.

Since no O can be placed on Saturday, we have four slots in which to place three O's. Furthermore, we can't have O's on both Monday and Tuesday, so between those two, we can place only one O. It turns out that we're not facing much uncertainty about the placement of the O's! One must go on Friday, one on Wednesday, and the final one on either Monday or Tuesday:

There's a bit more we could write in for the morning row. For example, we could note that Saturday must be either P or R. Similarly, the Monday or Tuesday slot that isn't taken by O will have either P or R. However, these are definitely not essential notations.

P

The Big Pause

This game revealed a lot with a bit of focus! This is actually a relatively uncommon situation with 3D Grouping games. With so little uncertainty, there doesn't seem to be much left to consider. Let's move to the questions.

Attack the Questions

8. Which one of the following must be a day on which Doctor Yamata lectures?

    (A) Monday
    (B) Tuesday
    (C) Wednesday
    (D) Friday
    (E) Saturday

(B) is correct.

We figured this out already!

9. On Wednesday Doctor Yamata could be scheduled to

    (A) conduct research in the morning and operate in the afternoon
    (B) lecture in the morning and treat patients in the afternoon
    (C) operate in the morning and lecture in the afternoon
    (D) operate in the morning and conduct research in the afternoon
    (E) treat patients in the morning and treat patients in the afternoon

(C) is correct.

We know there must be an O in the morning. Thus, we can eliminate (A), (B), and (E). (C) has an L in the afternoon, which is permissible, while (D) has an R there, which is impossible.

10. Which one of the following statements must be true?

    (A) There is one day on which the doctor treats patients both in the morning and in the afternoon.
    (B) The doctor conducts research on one of the days on which she lectures.
    (C) The doctor conducts research on one of the days on which she treats patients.
    (D) The doctor lectures on one of the days on which she treats patients.
    (E) The doctor lectures on one of the days on which she operates.

(E) is correct.

P

Slow and steady wins the race on this question:

(A) is breakable. We could put the morning P on Monday, and put an afternoon L there.

(B) is easily broken. Put our R on Monday morning, and push our L's to Tuesday and Wednesday.

(C) also falls when we switch a bit of the last scenario we made, pushing the L's to Monday and Tuesday.

(D) doesn't have to be true either. We can put the one morning P on Saturday.

(E) takes only a moment to confirm. Wherever we put the L chunk, it will fall atop an O.

11. If Doctor Yamata operates on Tuesday, then her schedule for treating patients could be

   (A) Monday morning, Monday afternoon, Friday morning, Friday afternoon
   (B) Monday morning, Friday afternoon, Saturday morning, Saturday afternoon
   (C) Monday afternoon, Wednesday morning, Wednesday afternoon, Saturday afternoon
   (D) Wednesday morning, Wednesday afternoon, Friday afternoon, Saturday afternoon
   (E) Wednesday afternoon, Friday afternoon, Saturday morning, Saturday afternoon

(E) is correct.

There isn't much to infer if O is on Tuesday. There will be either a P or an R on Monday morning. The afternoons of Monday-Wednesday retain their uncertainty. The only inference we can make about P is that it won't fall on Tuesday.

Unfortunately, none of the answers list Tuesday! Fortunately, we already know a lot about P. First, we know that we must have P on Friday and Saturday pm. This eliminates (A) and (C).

What about the morning? We know we have only one P in the am, and in this case it must fall on Monday or Saturday. (B) puts P in two am slots, while (D) puts it on Wednesday, where we already have an O.

Note that (E) also includes the afternoon treatment that must happen at some point from Monday to Wednesday.

12. Which one of the following is a pair of days on both of which Doctor Yamata must treat patients?

   (A) Monday and Tuesday
   (B) Monday and Saturday
   (C) Tuesday and Friday
   (D) Tuesday and Saturday
   (E) Friday and Saturday

(E) is correct.

This is simple with our diagram, especially after the last question.

Practice Game Solution 2: PT36, S4, G3

Picture the Game

This game requires a slow and steady hand to picture correctly.

We have six elements to place in a bus. The seats are arranged in two columns, with three rows. It's difficult to conceive of either the rows or columns as the groups. This is not atypical for 3D Grouping—admittedly, the term "grouping" is getting stretched to its limit in this game! Regardless, we'll need to track both. We also must closely identify which column is the window and which is the aisle.

Let's set up our 3D Board:

$$
\begin{array}{lll}
1 & \_ & \_ \\
2 & \_ & \_ \quad \text{GHIJKLM} \\
3 & \_ & \_ \\
& W & A
\end{array}
$$

Notate the Rules and Make Inferences

Most of the rules are not difficult to notate. The important issue for many of them is to link them to the first rule, which establishes that the GH chunk is in the aisle column. Here's how you could have notated all the rules:

$$
\begin{array}{lll}
1 & \_ & \boxed{\begin{array}{c}G\\H\end{array}} \\
2 & \_ & \_ \quad \text{GHIJKLM} \\
3 & \_ & \_ \\
& W & A
\end{array}
$$

$M_A \rightarrow \boxed{L\,H}$

$\boxed{K\,G} \rightarrow \boxed{\begin{array}{c}I\\M\end{array}}$

$K_W \rightarrow M_3$

$K_3 \rightarrow I_1$

P

We've notated the rules, but what connections between them can we make? Many people would move on to the questions at this point, but taking some time to dig for inferences is what separates the above average test-taker from the pack. Even if there isn't a lot to figure out, considering the game will help you to master the rules rather than to simply notate them.

The last three rules seem connected. They all share K, and I and M both show up twice. If K is in the same row as G, it must be in a window seat, since G is stuck in the aisle in a chunk with H. This triggers our next conditional—if K is in a window seat, then M is in row 3. Since we must have H behind G in the aisle, the only place for our I M chunk is behind K in window seats 2 and 3.

It turns out that *if K and G are in the same row*, we can infer everyone's position!

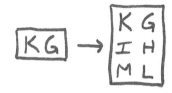

The above inference about the K G rule is probably one most people did not make when they played the game, and for the sake of showing a realistic solution, we'll pretend we did not figure all of that out as we explain the rest of the game. However, we know that you could have figured that out—did you?—if you gave the rules a serious review. To be clear, this chain of inferences doesn't "crack" the game, since it only applies when K is in the same row as G. (If you ever find yourself arriving at a setup that is completely filled in, something has gone wrong! LSAT games are never designed to work that way.)

The Big Pause

There are so many rules in this game! Thankfully, the G H chunk takes up two of the six slots. Other than that chunk, it's difficult to prioritize any of the rules, as each of them is triggered in a very specific situation. It seems the trick to this game will be deft management of the rules.

Attack the Questions

14. Which one of the following could be true?

    (A) Imamura sits in row 2, whereas Kelly sits in row 3.
    (B) Gutierrez sits in the same row as Kelly, immediately and directly behind Moore.
    (C) Gutierrez occupies a window seat in the same row as Lapas.
    (D) Moore occupies an aisle seat in the same row as Lapas.
    (E) Kelly and Moore both sit in row 3.

(E) is correct.

This is a tough first question! It's hard to call this an Orientation question since we have to do some serious work with the rules to eliminate these wordy answer choices. As we've said before, checking each answer is usually the slower route, but it's understandable here.

The fifth rule eliminates (A).

The third rule, with some thinking, eliminates (B). As we figured out above, if G and K are in the same row, we will have M behind I, in rows 2 and 3. Nothing could come behind M in this situation.

The first rule, requiring the G H chunk in the aisle, eliminates (C).

The second rule eliminates (D), since M in the aisle requires that H and L sit in the same row.

How annoying that (E) is the correct answer! It took a while to get here (and perhaps we'd spend a few more seconds proving that (E) is valid to make sure the slog through the other four answer choices didn't mean we missed something about this game). On the bright side, this question—as first questions almost always do—provided a chance to warm up with the rules.

15. If Lapas and Kelly each occupy a window seat, then which one of the following could be true?

   (A) Moore occupies the aisle seat in row 3.
   (B) Imamura occupies the window seat in row 3.
   (C) Gutierrez sits in the same row as Kelly.
   (D) Gutierrez sits in the same row as Moore.
   (E) Moore sits in the same row as Lapas.

(A) is correct.

If L and K are in the window column, what do we know? We know from the fourth rule that M will be in the third row. It's hard to figure out much more, so let's sketch out what we know and who's left:

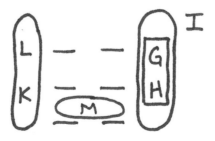

Let's roll into the answer choices:

(A) seems fine (and is). Since this is our first answer, we'd probably choose to confirm it rather than eliminate four other answers. But let's play out how deferring might look.

(B) seems OK. Defer.

P

(C) triggers the K G rule. As we discussed earlier, that requires I M in the window column. This all seems fine if you forget that the question's condition is that K and L are in the window column!

(D) can't be true since M must be in row 3, and G cannot be there.

(E) seems like it would work. We'd need to bring L into the third row with M. Check the rules. Ah! If M is in the aisle, L must be in the same row as H. Eliminate.

We're down to (A) and (B). We can simply try out one to see if it works, since this is a could be true question. (A) indeed works and (B) doesn't.

For review's sake, let's figure out what is wrong with (B). If I is in the window seat of row 3, M is forced into the aisle seat, which requires that L be next to H. That leaves K and G to sit next to each other, which would require the vertical I M chunk. Since M is next to I, that's impossible.

16. If Moore sits in row 1, then which one of the following must be true?

   (A) Hoffman sits in row 2.
   (B) Imamura sits in row 2.
   (C) Imamura sits in row 3.
   (D) Kelly sits in row 1.
   (E) Lapas sits in row 3.

(D) is correct.

With M in row 1, what do we know? This triggers the contrapositives of the K W and K G rules. Thus, we know that K is in the aisle (where it clearly cannot be next to G). So far, we know this:

If we move into the answer choices with just that, we'll find that every answer seems to be a could be true. There's more to figure out! Scan the rules once more, looking for triggers.

We have triggered the contrapositive of the K_3 rule, since I cannot be in the first row. Thus, K must be in front of the G H chunk, which is why (D) is correct.

17. If Kelly occupies the aisle seat in row 3, then each of the following must be true EXCEPT:

    (A) Gutierrez sits in the same row as Imamura.

    (B) Hoffman sits in the same row as Lapas.

    (C) Lapas occupies a window seat.

    (D) Moore occupies a window seat.

    (E) Gutierrez sits in row 1.

(B) is correct.

With K in the aisle seat in row 3, what do we know? We know that the G H chunk is in rows 1 and 2. I, L, and M must go in the window column, and since K is in row 3, I must be in row 1. That leaves L and M's positioning slightly undetermined:

It's tempting to keep pushing this inference chain further. However, notice that this is a must be true EXCEPT question, meaning that the correct answer doesn't have to be true. There must be some uncertainty left in this diagram! Let's leave our diagram as is, and go look for answers that include L or M.

(B) proves to be something that could be true or false.

18. If neither Gutierrez nor Imamura sits in row 1, then which one of the following could be true?

    (A) Hoffman sits in row 2.

    (B) Kelly sits in row 2.

    (C) Moore sits in row 2.

    (D) Imamura occupies an aisle seat.

    (E) Moore occupies an aisle seat.

(C) is correct.

Let's follow the old inference chain one last time! If G isn't in row 1, we know that the G H chunk is in rows 2 and 3. We'll have to place I floating in those rows on the window side. Who's left? K, L, and M. So far we have this:

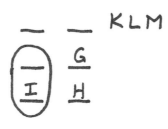

P

Scanning the rules—which we seem to have to do over and over in this game—we can infer that since we can't have I in the first row, we have triggered the contrapositive of the K_3 rule. Thus, K must be in row 1 or 2.

Let's keep thinking. The element that has the most rules attached to it is K. Is K really free to go anywhere other than the third row?

If we put K next to G in the second row, we'd need to have M behind I. But there'd be no room for that, so K cannot go next to G. Thus, K must go in the first row.

We end up with this diagram:

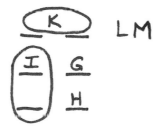

(A) and (B) are clearly impossible.

(C) seems doable, but it'd be smart to defer and see if (D) and (E) can be eliminated as easily as (A) and (B).

(D) is a clear elimination.

(E) seems fine. Let's check! The only available aisle seat is in the first row. That would force K into the window seat, which would require that M be in the last row! So (E) is impossible—M cannot be in an aisle seat with the new condition.

Chapter *of* 14
Logic Games

Hybrid Games

In This Chapter...

Getting Familiar

Give yourself **8 minutes** to complete this game.

A photographer will take three photographs of a high school math team. The seven members of the team—P, R, S, T, V, W, and X—will each appear in exactly one of the photographs. There will be exactly one member in the first photograph, three members in the second photograph, and three members in the third photograph. The following conditions apply:

   P does not appear in a later photo than does T or X.

   R and S will appear in the same photograph together.

   V and X will not be photographed together.

1. Which of the following could be the assignment of members to photographs?

   (A) Photo 1: V
       Photo 2: T, R, S
       Photo 3: P, W, X
   (B) Photo 1: V
       Photo 2: R, S
       Photo 3: P, T, W, X
   (C) Photo 1: V
       Photo 2: P, R, S
       Photo 3: T, W, X
   (D) Photo 1: P
       Photo 2: S, T, X
       Photo 3: R, V, W
   (E) Photo 1: P
       Photo 2: T, V, X
       Photo 3: R, S, W

2. Which of the following must be false?

   (A) W appears in Photo 2.
   (B) T appears in Photo 1.
   (C) P appears in Photo 3.
   (D) V appears after X.
   (E) X appears after V.

3. If P is photographed with S, in how many different ways can all seven members be assigned to photographs?

   (A) 1
   (B) 2
   (C) 3
   (D) 4
   (E) 5

4. If R is in an earlier photograph than X, how many different team members could be in the first photograph?

   (A) 1
   (B) 2
   (C) 3
   (D) 4
   (E) 5

5. Which of the following pairs of assignments would determine the team members for each photograph?

   (A) V is in Photo 1 and R is in Photo 2.
   (B) V is in Photo 1 and R is in Photo 3.
   (C) P is in Photo 1 and R is in Photo 2.
   (D) P is in Photo 1 and V is in Photo 3.
   (E) W is in Photo 1 and R is in Photo 2.

6. If the rule that V and X will not be photographed together is replaced with a rule that V and X must be photographed together, each of the following could be true EXCEPT:

   (A) W appears in Photo 1.
   (B) W appears in Photo 2.
   (C) W appears in Photo 3.
   (D) P appears in Photo 2.
   (E) P appears in Photo 3.

Hybrid Games

We are almost at the end of our journey through LSAT Logic Games, and, if we do say so ourselves, we've reached an impressive depth of understanding.

Let's go back to basics for a minute.

All games involve assigning elements to positions. Games are further defined by having these positions be in **order**, or by having these positions be in **groups** with one another.

Hybrid games are games that involve both ordering and grouping.

About one in every eight games is a Hybrid, and on average Hybrid games tend to fall on the higher end of the difficulty scale.

Why are Hybrid games more difficult? In general, it's not because they require more complicated inferences, or because the problems require more layers of work out of us. It's typically because it's just more difficult for us to work with a variety of information than it is for us to work with a lot of the same type of information. An analogy can be made to juggling (we've moved on from spinning plates). Hybrid games are typically difficult in the same way that juggling tennis balls and bowling balls is more difficult than juggling just one or the other.

If you are nervous about juggling bowling balls and tennis balls, keep in mind that there is also a lot of good news to report about Hybrid games. Hybrid games don't tend to require the long chains of inferences that some other games, such as Relative Ordering or Conditional Grouping games, do. For most problems, if you can simply understand the rules clearly and use them efficiently, you will be fine.

Furthermore, you should feel like you are coming into this with a full head of steam, because you actually already know *everything* you need to know about Hybrid games. You know how to deal with all ordering and grouping issues that may come up. The key to Hybrid games success is going to be how you bring these various skills together.

Let's look at how we'll bring things together in a bit more detail:

Order × Group (+ Assignment)

As mentioned above, the challenge of Hybrid games is that of bringing together, and organizing, a varied set of restrictions. Let's quickly look at the three primary issues for all Hybrid games.

Issue 1: Assignment

Rules of assignment describe a relationship between a specific element and a specific position (e.g., X is assigned to the second group). Every logic game involves assignment at some point.

14

Issue 2: Order

Rules of order relate elements to each other or to positions.

In general, we've been diagramming ordering rules in a horizontal plane, with earlier to the left and later to the right. We want to continue that habit for Hybrid games.

Issue 3: Groups

Grouping rules relate elements to each other in terms of groups (e.g., M and O are in different departments).

We have diagrammed most every grouping rule on a vertical plane, and we want to continue that habit for Hybrid games.

Notating Hybrid Rules (you already know this)

Let's use a very basic Hybrid game scenario to confirm our understanding of how we'd deal with these various types of rules. Imagine we were given the following scenario:

> Eight people—M, N, O, P, Q, R, S, and T—will play in a total of four different tennis matches. The four matches will take place in order, and exactly two players will play in each match.

We have the order of the matches, and we are also grouping elements into pairs that will play together. For this basic scenario, we'd probably want to begin with a diagram that looks something like the frameworks we've used for some other grouping games:

$$\frac{\quad}{\ } \quad \frac{\quad}{\ } \quad \frac{\quad}{\ } \quad \frac{\quad}{\ } \qquad \text{M N O P Q R S T}$$
$$\ \ 1 \qquad 2 \qquad 3 \qquad 4$$

We'll use the horizontal orientation to represent ordering rules and the vertical orientation to represent grouping rules.

Here are some common rules that may appear in a game like this one. These are all rules you've seen before, so you should be able to quickly picture how you would notate each of them. Check the notations on the next page (note that we didn't put any inferences in), marking any rules that might give you some trouble to remind yourself to review them later. Each set is to be diagrammed separately.

Sample Assignment Rules

M plays in the second game.
T does not play in the fourth game.
If P plays in the thir`d game, R will not play
    in the first game.

Sample Ordering Rules

S plays at some point after N plays.
M plays before, but not immediately before,
    R does.
Q does not play before T.
P plays after N but before Q, or before N but
    after Q.

Sample Grouping Rules

O plays against T
P plays neither Q nor R.
If S plays M, N will play R.

Rules That Combine Assignment, Order, and/or Grouping

If N is second, M must play later than N
    does.
If M does not play against T, M must play
    first.
T does not play last, nor does T play against
    P.

Suggested Notations

Assignment Rules

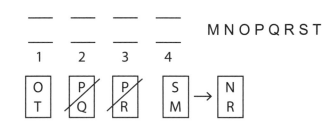

Grouping Rules

Ordering Rules

Combination Rules

Keep in mind that our diagrams above are only suggestions; depending on the game, writing some of those rules differently might be wise. We strongly encourage you to remain flexible. There is a subtle but significant difference between those who try to fit what they see on test day into what they are already comfortable with, and those who are able to adapt their skills to the unique situations the exam provides. You will be in much better shape if you are in the latter category.

Let's look at the scenario for a slightly different Hybrid game:

> A building has three floors, numbered 1 to 3 from bottom to top. Six different companies—F, G, H, J, K, and L—are to occupy the building, and exactly two companies will go on each floor. The following conditions apply:
>
> G must be on a higher floor than K.
> H and F cannot be on the same floor.

Note that in this case it would make a lot more sense to think about the order vertically, and the group horizontally. We would then write out ordering rules in a vertical fashion, and grouping rules in a horizontal fashion. An effective diagram might look something like this:

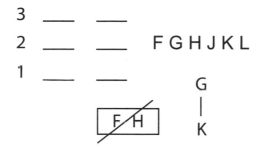

Even though this doesn't match what is typical, hopefully you feel comfortable enough with your skills that you can adapt your systems to match the unique characteristics of any game.

Further Complications

Just like non-Hybrid ordering and grouping games, Hybrid games can be made more complicated through the introduction of other game characteristics. You're already familiar with each of these:

Subsets

Subsets are the most significant and challenging of the possible complications. The manner in which you deal with them is going to be dependent primarily on how much information about them you are given. You want to think about these subsets as presenting two often overlapping but different challenges: are the subsets there to give you additional information to juggle, or are they central to the inferences that you'll be expected to make by bringing rules together?

Whenever possible, you want to represent subsets in Hybrid games by using subscript. That way, the primary forms of organization on your diagram—vertical and horizontal organization—are devoted to the two fundamental issues—ordering and grouping. However, when the subsets themselves are at the heart of the inferences to be made, you may need to add another layer to show them more explicitly in the diagram.

14

To understand the difference between the situations that require these strategies, take a look at these two similar mini-game situations:

Six students—M and N from school X, O and P from school Y, and R and S from school Z—will appear in three dance routines. The routines will take place one at a time and in order. Each routine will involve two students, and each student will dance exactly once. The following conditions apply:

At least one student from school Y dances in the first routine.

No one from school Z performs in the third routine.

Two-person dance teams from three different schools—X, Y, and Z—will perform one at a time and in order during a recital. Six students—M, N, O, P, Q, and R—will perform. The following conditions apply:

The team from Z will not perform after the team from X performs.

O dances in the second performance.

P is from school Y.

Note that both mini-games involve similar situations. We have six students performing in pairs in three different routines. However, in the first game, we know which school each student is from, but the students don't have to perform with their schoolmates. In the second game, the students perform in school teams, but we don't know which students are on which team, and the order of team performance is a primary issue.

For the first game, the subsets are more clearly defined, and though they present challenges, the subsets are not central to the inferences we're expected to make. Therefore, it will most likely be best to handle these subsets using subscript. Here's a sample of how we could have laid out the diagram for the first game:

$$
\begin{array}{ccc}
\underline{\hspace{1.5em}} & \underline{\hspace{1.5em}} & \underline{\hspace{1.5em}} \\
\underline{\quad y \quad} & \underline{\hspace{1.5em}} & \underline{\hspace{1.5em}} \\
1 & 2 & 3
\end{array}
\qquad
\begin{array}{l}
M_X\,N_X \\
O_Y\,P_Y \\
R_Z\,S_Z
\end{array}
$$

$$\cancel{R}$$
$$\cancel{S}$$

We could also have written "O/P" in the bottom slot for group 1, since those are the only two students from school Y.

For the second game, both the order and the assignment of the teams are central to what we are expected to infer about the game. Furthermore, we don't have the benefit of knowing who is from each school ahead of time. Therefore, we want to integrate the subsets into the base of our diagram. We can do this the same way that we did for 3D Ordering games: by adding an additional level to our diagram:

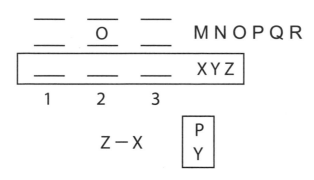

14

Mismatches

Like non-Hybrid games, Hybrid games can have the number of elements not equal the number of positions. All of the strategies you have learned for mismatch issues that appear in Ordering and grouping games will serve you well.

Open Numbering

While many Hybrid games establish how many elements should go in each group, others are open. Apply the techniques and notations you learned with Open Grouping games.

Diagram Ambiguity

Because Hybrid games use ingredients from many other game types, at times your diagram for these games will be quite unusual. Don't be surprised if, for example, a large number of relative ordering rules leads you to a Tree diagram with grouped positions.

Hybrid games are the hardest games to fit into a category. Our teachers often disagree about whether a certain game is best categorized, for example, as a Hybrid game or as a Mismatch Ordering game that requires a lot of "doubling up." Similarly, a 3D Grouping game may add in a small dash of order, making us wonder if it's a Hybrid game, even though the ordering of the elements may be almost irrelevant to how the game is played. This slipperiness is not important, since our goal is to picture the game and create a diagram that is useful; we're not scored on whether we can accurately categorize the game.

It is in these ambiguous moments that you must call upon your inner MacGyver!

How Did You Do?

Picture the Game

We clearly have three groups in which to place seven members. A bit unusually, the groups are not of equal size.

Scanning the scenario and rules, we see references to group—"R and S will appear in the same photograph"—as well as one to order—"P does not appear in a later photo than does T or X."

We'll set up a board with the right number of slots for each group.

Notate the Rules and Make Inferences

The first rule is the most difficult to master. Be careful not to assume that this rule means—as it would in a standard Relative Ordering game—that P comes before T and X. In this game, P, T, and X could all be in the same group!

However, since group 1 has only one slot, T or X in that group would require P to come after. Thus, we can restrict T and X from group 1. Similarly, since R and S must be together, they cannot be in group 1's single slot.

Compare your work to our diagram:

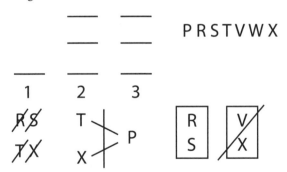

The Big Pause

While we have not inferred a great deal, it's clear that this game will involve a lot of work with all three rules. The relative rule involves almost half of the elements, the chunk fills up most of either group 2 or 3, and any time we place either member of the V X anti-chunk, we'll know the other member is not in that group.

We should remind ourselves of what the relative ordering rule really means. In our own words, the rule means that P can come at the same time as, or earlier than, T and X. It can't come after either of them.

There's no strong reason to consider framing this game. The only candidate for a division is the placement of the R S chunk. However, there are no significant consequences.

Finally, the only element not mentioned in a rule is W—circle it!

Attack the Questions

1. Which of the following could be the assignment of members to photographs?

    (A) Photo 1: V

       Photo 2: T, R, S

       Photo 3: P, W, X

    (B) Photo 1: V

       Photo 2: R, S

       Photo 3: P, T, W, X

    (C) Photo 1: V

       Photo 2: P, R, S

       Photo 3: T, W, X

    (D) Photo 1: P

       Photo 2: S, T, X

       Photo 3: R, V, W

    (E) Photo 1: P

       Photo 2: T, V, X

       Photo 3: R, S, W

(C) is correct.

Rule 1 eliminates (A).

Rule 2 eliminates (D).

Rule 3 eliminates (E)

We're done with rules, but we have two answers left! We could spin through the rules one more time to see if a rule is used twice—sometimes rules are used more than once—but that will lead nowhere in this case, so let's review the scenario to look for rules embedded there. It turns out that (B) violates the numerical arrangement of the groups.

14

2. Which of the following must be false?

    (A) W appears in Photo 2.

    (B) T appears in Photo 1.

    (C) P appears in Photo 3.

    (D) V appears after X.

    (E) X appears after V.

(B) is correct.

Can W appear in group 2? There seems to be plenty of room to place the chunk and the anti-chunk, as well as to make sure that P doesn't fall after either T or X.

Can T appear in group 1? No! We already figured that out. (B) is our answer.

3. If P is photographed with S, in how many different ways can all seven members be assigned to photographs?

    (A) 1

    (B) 2

    (C) 3

    (D) 4

    (E) 5

(A) is correct.

If P is with S, we have a super chunk: P R S! Since P can't come after T and X, the chunk must be placed in group 2 to leave room for T and X in group 3. That means that V must be in group 1 to avoid violating the V X anti-chunk. W clearly goes in the remaining slot in group 3. Every element is placed—how satisfying!—and the answer is (A).

4. If R is in an earlier photograph than X, how many different team members could be in the first photograph?

    (A) 1

    (B) 2

    (C) 3

    (D) 4

    (E) 5

(C) is correct.

If R is earlier than X, we know that the R S chunk must be in group 2 and X must be in group 3. Let's write out the remaining elements to the side: P T V W. We'll use that to organize our thinking.

MANHATTAN
LSAT

Hopefully, our control of the rules is strong enough that we can visualize the rest without using our pencil:

$$
\begin{array}{ccc}
 & \overline{} & \overline{} \\
 & \text{R} & \quad \text{P T V W} \\
\overline{} & \overline{\text{S}} & \overline{\text{X}} \\
1 & 2 & 3
\end{array}
$$

We can eliminate (E) since there are only four elements left to place.

Let's next figure out how many of the four we can place in group 1: Can P go in group 1? Sure! T and X would come after it, and there's room for V in group 2.

Can T? No! We can never place T in 1.

Can V? There's no problem with that. We can fit P into group 2 and T into group 3. The anti-chunk is safe as well.

Can W? Yes! P and T can go in group 3 along with X, leaving the last slot in group 2 for V.

5. Which of the following pairs of assignments would determine the team members for each photograph?

    (A) V is in Photo 1 and R is in Photo 2.
    (B) V is in Photo 1 and R is in Photo 3.
    (C) P is in Photo 1 and R is in Photo 2.
    (D) P is in Photo 1 and V is in Photo 3.
    (E) W is in Photo 1 and R is in Photo 2.

(E) is correct.

It's fine to dive right into the answers on a question like this, but it's also smart to take a moment and consider what will have to be settled by the correct answer. In this case, it will have to place the R S chunk, arrange P, T, and X, and place V somewhere apart from X. That's a lot!

With this sort of question, many people will have to quickly write out the placements in each answer choice in order to think it out. Ideally, your control of the rules should be strong enough that you have to write out only the two placements given in each answer and think about the rest. But it should take only a few more seconds to notate the other elements if needed.

(A) establishes the position for V and the chunk. Since T and X cannot precede P, both must be in 3. However, groups 2 and 3 each have one remaining slot, and W or P could go in either one.

(B) is even less settled. We will have to put P in group 2, but either T, X, or W could go in group 3.

(C) locks in P and the chunk. We need to separate V and X between 2 and 3. This forces T and W into 3, but V and X are interchangeable.

(D) places P, X, and V in groups 1, 2, and 3, respectively, but we don't know where to place the RS chunk.

(E) locks in the chunk, but does not address the anti-chunk. With W taking up group 1, we'll need to spread V and X between groups 2 and 3, and we still have P and T to deal with. It might seem that we have too many options, but since X can't be before P, it can't go in the remaining position in group 2, meaning that V goes there and P, T, and X form group 3. Voila!

6. If the rule that V and X will not be photographed together is replaced with a rule that V and X must be photographed together, each of the following could be true EXCEPT:

(A) W appears in Photo 1.
(B) W appears in Photo 2.
(C) W appears in Photo 3.
(D) P appears in Photo 2.
(E) P appears in Photo 3.

(E) is correct.

If V and X must be photographed together, we have two chunks. Let's sketch out what we have, along with the remaining elements and relationships, remembering that these are not yet in an established order:

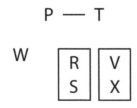

Why have we notated P before T? Well, remember that originally we had to leave open the possibility that P would appear together with both T and X. Now that we have V and X together, this is no longer a possibility. While P and X could be together, P cannot appear together with T, because the chunks leave only one empty spot left for each photo. Thus, P must precede T.

With this sketched out, it's easy to see that (A) through (D) are all possibilities, while (E) is not.

DRILL IT: Hybrid Setups

Diagram each of the following scenarios to stretch your brain, then answer the question that follows. **Be warned, these are extremely difficult.** Check your diagram and answer against the solutions after each one.

1. As part of a simulation, the MLSAT volunteer firefighter battalion is planning its response to a hypo-thetical fire that has spread to all floors of a four-story building, the floors of which are labeled 1–4, from bottom to top. There are exactly eight firefighters in the battalion—Farber, Gilad, Jorgeson, Mary, Nielsen, Palomba, Sherman, and Tyrrell. Each firefighter is assigned to exactly one floor, in accordance with the following requirements:

   Two floors are assigned exactly one firefighter.
   The first floor has more firefighters assigned to it than any other floor.
   Gilad and Mary are assigned to the same floor.
   Tyrrell, who is the sole firefighter assigned to his floor, is assigned to a higher floor than both
       Jorgeson and Palomba.
   At most one firefighter is assigned to a higher floor than Farber.

   If Nielsen is assigned to the same floor as Sherman, and Jorgeson is assigned to the same floor as Mary, which of the following is a complete and accurate list of the floors to which Tyrrell can be assigned?

   (A) 2
   (B) 2, 4
   (C) 3, 4
   (D) 2, 3, 4
   (E) 1, 2, 3, 4

2. Bettelheim Motors swill produce three differently-priced models of a certain car. Each model will come with two of the following options—Q, R, S, T, U, and W—and each model will come in only one of three colors—green, hot red, or indigo. The options and colors of all the cars must adhere to the following rules:

> No color or option is used on more than one car model.
> W and R are used on the same model.
> The green model is more expensive than the hot red one.
> T is not used on the least expensive model.
> The indigo car is more expensive than the car that includes R.

If the car that has S is more expensive than the one that has T, how many different arrangements of colors and options are possible?

(A) 1
(B) 2
(C) 3
(D) 4
(E) 5

3. The Geekettes are planning a series of four consecutive concerts in exactly four states—Maryland, Nebraska, Oregon, and Pennsylvania. One concert will be played in each state. The Geekettes will invite three opening bands—R, S, and T—and three special guests—F, G, and H. There will be an opening band or a special guest at each concert and each opening band and guest will play at exactly one concert. The following rules apply to the concert schedule:

> S will play either in Maryland or Pennsylvania.
> The third concert is in Oregon.
> R will not play at a concert after the one that H plays at.
> No opening act will play between the concerts at which R and T play.
> There will be no opening act at the concert immediately following the concert at which F plays.

If T plays in Pennsylvania at the Geekettes' last concert of the tour, each of the following cannot be true EXCEPT:

(A) G plays at the second concert, held in Maryland, with no opening band.
(B) G plays at the third concert, held in Oregon, with S as the opening band.
(C) G plays at the first concert, held in Maryland, with S as the opening band.
(D) G plays at the second concert, held in Nebraska, with R as the opening band.
(E) G plays at the first concert, held in Oregon, with R as the opening band.

 For more practice, log in to your Student Center!

SOLUTIONS: Hybrid Setups

Note that your diagram might look somewhat different from ours. Keep an eye out for differences that indicate that you made a mistake. If you like how we notated a rule, then steal our style!

1. Diagram:

Question:

(D) is correct.

If M and J are together, we have a G M J chunk, which must go on 1. P must join them because all the other elements—T, F, and the N S chunk—have some restriction that keeps them from going to the first floor. This is the situation:

T can go on 4, with F on 3 and the N S chunk on 2. T can go on 3 with F above on 4 and N S on 2. T can go on 2, with F on 4 and N S on 3.

14

2. Diagram:

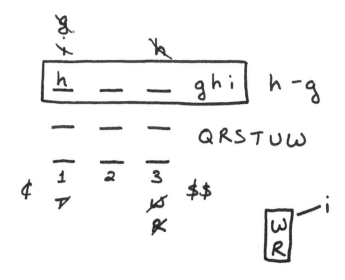

(D) is correct.

If T must come before S, they must go in slots 2 and 3, respectively. The W R chunk must go in slot 1. All that's left are Q and U, which are floating between slots 2 and 3. From the rules, slot 1 will always have to be H, since both I and G have to come after something. So G and I are also floating between slots 2 and 3. Thus, we have this:

There are four ways to arrange what's still undetermined: 1) G I & Q U, 2) I G & Q U, 3) G I & U Q, 4) I G & U Q.

MANHATTAN
LSAT

3. Diagram:

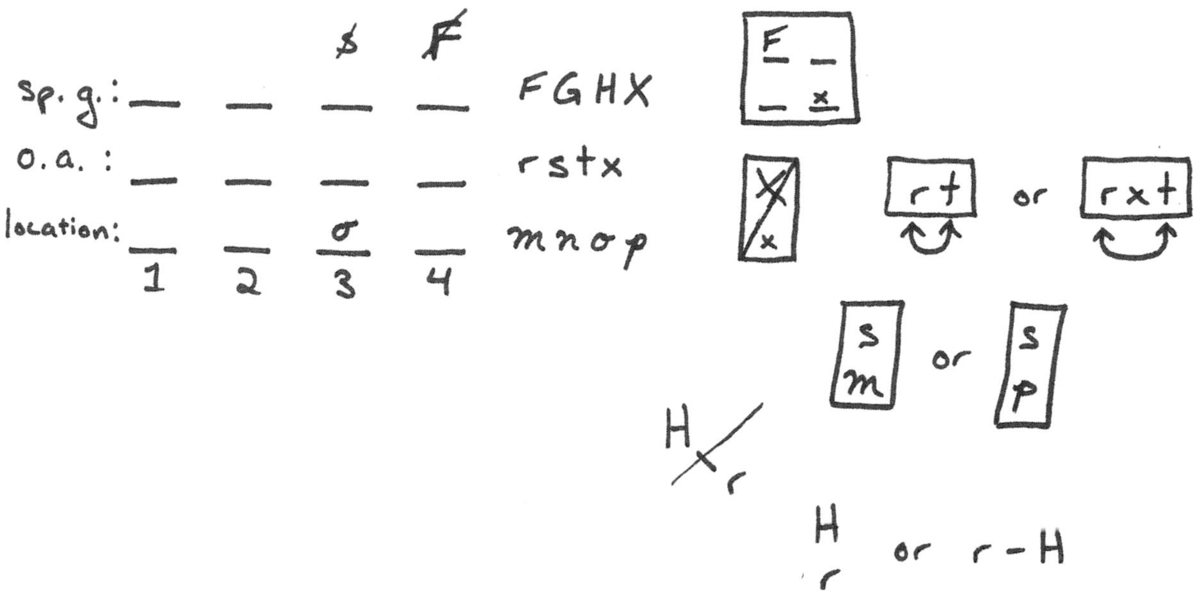

14

(C) is correct.

If T and P go in group 4, there are two options for R. Either we can place it in group 2, with no opening act in 3 (thus, an "X"), or we can place R in group 3. This is a particularly tough question, since it requires some time-consuming framing. If you didn't frame this, try it now before looking at the diagram below.

In the R X T frame, S must go in 1 with M, leaving N for 2. And with no opening act in 3, F must go in 2 as well. We cannot have another X in group 3 and H cannot go in 1 since it would be ahead of R.

In the R T frame, there must be no opening act in group 2 in order to fit in F (into group 1). S is forced into 1, with M. N is left to be the location for 2. We cannot have two X's in group 2, so we need to place G there. (H cannot go in 2, since it would be ahead of R.) This leaves X and H to fill slots 3 and 4 in some order.

The frames look like this:

Armed with those, it's easy to eliminate answers. Tough question!

Conclusion

On Hybrid games, we once again see these two themes:

1. Flexibility

- There are many ways that ordering and grouping rules can be combined. Set up your board, but be ready to adapt.

2. Rule mastery

- If you don't own the rules, they will own you!

MANHATTAN
LSAT

Practice Game 1: PT36, S4, G4

Give yourself **17 minutes** for both of these games (or, if you're feeling confident, just 16).

An airline has four flights from New York to Sarasota—flights 1, 2, 3, and 4. On each flight there is exactly one pilot and exactly one co-pilot. The pilots are Fazio, Germond, Kyle, and Lopez; the co-pilots are Reich, Simon, Taylor, and Umlas. Each pilot and co-pilot is assigned to exactly one flight.

> The flights take off in numerical order.
> Fazio's flight takes off before Germond's, and at least one other flight takes off between their flights.
> Kyle is assigned to flight 2.
> Lopez is assigned to the same flight as Umlas.

19. Which one of the following pilot and co-pilot teams could be assigned to flight 1?

    (A) Fazio and Reich
    (B) Fazio and Umlas
    (C) Germond and Reich
    (D) Germond and Umlas
    (E) Lopez and Taylor

20. If Reich's flight is later than Umlas's, which one of the following statements cannot be true?

    (A) Fazio's flight is earlier than Simon's.
    (B) Kyle's flight is earlier than Reich's.
    (C) Kyle's flight is earlier than Taylor's.
    (D) Simon's flight is earlier than Reich's.
    (E) Taylor's flight is earlier than Kyle's.

21. If Lopez's flight is earlier than Germond's, which one of the following statements could be false?

    (A) Fazio's flight is earlier than Umlas's.
    (B) Germond is assigned to flight 4.
    (C) Either Reich's or Taylor's flight is earlier than Umlas's.
    (D) Simon's flight is earlier than Umlas's.
    (E) Umlas is assigned to flight 3.

22. What is the maximum possible number of different pilot and co-pilot teams, any one of which could be assigned to flight 4?

    (A) 2
    (B) 3
    (C) 4
    (D) 5
    (E) 6

23. If Simon's flight is later than Lopez's, then which one of the following statements could be false?

    (A) Germond's flight is later than Reich's.
    (B) Germond's flight is later than Taylor's.
    (C) Lopez's flight is later than Taylor's.
    (D) Taylor's flight is later than Reich's.
    (E) Umlas's flight is later than Reich's.

Try one more question on the next page…

Here's a devilish one that we've written for this game:

P

24. Each of the following, if substituted for the rule that Fazio's flight takes off before Germond's, and at least one other flight takes off between their flights, would have the same effect on the assignment of pilots and co-pilots EXCEPT:

    (A) Fazio's flight takes off first.

    (B) Fazio's flight takes off before Kyle's.

    (C) Fazio's and Germond's flights do not take off consecutively, but Fazio's and Kyle's do.

    (D) Lopez's flight takes off immediately before or immediately after Germond's.

    (E) Lopez's flight takes off after Fazio's, and at least one other flight takes off between their flights.

Practice Game 2: PT29, S3, G4

Exactly six piano classes are given sequentially on Monday: two with more than one student and four with exactly one student. Exactly four females—Gimena, Holly, Iyanna, and Kate—and five males—Leung, Nate, Oscar, Pedro, and Saul—attend these classes. Each student attends exactly one class. The following must obtain:

Iyanna and Leung together constitute one class.
Pedro and exactly two others together constitute one class.
Kate is the first female, but not the first student, to attend a class.
Gimena's class is at some time after Iyanna's but at sometime before Pedro's.
Oscar's class is at some time after Gimena's.

20. Which one of the following students could attend the first class?

(A) Holly
(B) Leung
(C) Oscar
(D) Pedro
(E) Saul

21. Which one of the following is a complete and accurate list of classes any one of which could be the class Gimena attends?

(A) the fourth, the fifth
(B) the fourth, the sixth
(C) the second, the fourth, the fifth
(D) the third, the fifth, the sixth
(E) the second, the third, the fourth

22. Which one of the following pairs of students could be in the class with Pedro?

(A) Gimena and Holly
(B) Holly and Saul
(C) Kate and Nate
(D) Leung and Oscar
(E) Nate and Saul

23. If Oscar and Pedro do not attend the same class as each other, then which one of the following could be true?

(A) Gimena attends the fifth class.
(B) Holly attends the third class.
(C) Iyanna attends the fourth class.
(D) Nate attends the fifth class.
(E) Saul attends the second class.

24. Suppose the condition that Oscar attends a class after Gimena is replaced with the condition that Oscar attends a class before Gimena and after Kate. If all the other conditions remain the same, then which class must Holly attend?

(A) the second
(B) the third
(C) the fourth
(D) the fifth
(E) the sixth

Practice Game Solution 1: PT36, S4, G4

Picture the Game

We have to place each pilot and co-pilot into one of four ordered groups. Classic Hybrid! To keep the pilots and co-pilots differentiated, we have several options. Perhaps the cleanest is to assign each subset its own row, and, for added clarity, use lower and upper case. However, using subscripts would also work.

Notate the Rules and Make Inferences

Compare your diagram against ours. It is crucial to infer the position of F! Once that's done, we actually don't need to refer to the F G chunk rule.

The Big Pause

The bottom row of this diagram is well-developed, and there's actually only one rule—the U L chunk—that we still can put to use during the questions.

The questions will surely play on the top row and the G L uncertainty.

We could circle all the co-pilots other than u.

Attack the Questions

19. Which one of the following pilot and co-pilot teams could be assigned to flight 1?

    (A) Fazio and Reich

    (B) Fazio and Umlas

    (C) Germond and Reich

    (D) Germond and Umlas

    (E) Lopez and Taylor

P

(A) is correct.

This is not the standard Orientation question, but it's just as easy. We can eliminate all the answers that don't include F, namely (C) through (E). (B) is easily eliminated because of the L u chunk.

20. If Reich's flight is later than Umlas's, which one of the following statements cannot be true?

    (A) Fazio's flight is earlier than Simon's.

    (B) Kyle's flight is earlier than Reich's.

    (C) Kyle's flight is earlier than Taylor's.

    (D) Simon's flight is earlier than Reich's.

    (E) Taylor's flight is earlier than Kyle's.

(C) is correct.

If we have to have R after u, we know that u must be in 3 with L, and r must be in 4 with G. The two remaining co-pilots—s and t—come in some order in the first two groups.

(C) is impossible since K is second, and that is the latest that t could go.

21. If Lopez's flight is earlier than Germond's, which one of the following statements could be false?

    (A) Fazio's flight is earlier than Umlas's.

    (B) Germond is assigned to flight 4.

    (C) Either Reich's or Taylor's flight is earlier than Umlas's.

    (D) Simon's flight is earlier than Umlas's.

    (E) Umlas is assigned to flight 3.

(D) is correct.

L must come third, along with u; G must be in the fourth group. Since we're looking for what could be false, we'll keep our eyes out for answers referring to the elements that are left: r, s, and t.

(A) through (C) must be true. (D) could be false, since s could be in 4.

22. What is the maximum possible number of different pilot and co-pilot teams, any one of which could be assigned to flight 4?

(A) 2
(B) 3
(C) 4
(D) 5
(E) 6

(C) is correct.

It's best just to count them out. L can be last, and only with u. G can be last with any co-pilot but u. Lu, Gr, Gs, and Gt = four groups.

23. If Simon's flight is later than Lopez's, then which one of the following statements could be false?

(A) Germond's flight is later than Reich's.
(B) Germond's flight is later than Taylor's.
(C) Lopez's flight is later than Taylor's.
(D) Taylor's flight is later than Reich's.
(E) Umlas's flight is later than Reich's.

(D) is correct.

This new condition forces L and u into group 3 and s and G into group 4. We're unsure where r and t will go between groups 1 and 2, thus (D) could be false.

And finally, the devilish one that we've written for this game:

24. Each of the following, if substituted for the rule that Fazio's flight takes off before Germond's, and at least one other flight takes off between their flights, would have the same effect on the assignment of pilots and co-pilots EXCEPT:

(A) Fazio's flight takes off first.
(B) Fazio's flight takes off before Kyle's.
(C) Fazio's and Germond's flights do not take off consecutively, but Fazio's and Kyle's do.
(D) Lopez's flight takes off immediately before or immediately after Germond's.
(E) Lopez's flight takes off after Fazio's, and at least one other flight takes off between their flights.

(C) is correct.

There's never been an EXCEPT Equivalent Rule question on the LSAT, but we figured we should keep you on your toes! Remember to start by identifying the effects of the original rule.

F having to come at least two spots before G is what forced F into group 1. With K taking up the pilot slot in group 2, there was no choice but to have F in group 1 and G and L floating between groups 3 and 4.

Keep in mind that the four wrong answers will be valid equivalents:

(A) forces F into slot 1; thus G and L will have to take the last two pilot slots. Eliminate.

(B) accomplishes the same thing as (A).

(C) looks good, but this rule would allow an otherwise prohibited arrangement: G K F L! We have our answer.

For review's sake, let's look at the rest:

(D) requires that the only two consecutive pilot slots—3 and 4—be occupied by G and L, leaving F to take slot 1.

(E) is tricky. Just as the original rule pulled L into either group 3 or 4 even though it wasn't explicitly mentioned, this rule pulls G back there.

Practice Game Solution 2: PT29, S3, G4

Picture the Game

This is not an easy game to picture. We have six groups, four of which are "groups" of one. We can't easily set up a Closed Board, as we don't know which groups have only one member.

When you're unsure of how to arrange a game, be sure you've scanned the rules. The final three rules are all Relative Ordering ones, so we can actually set this game up as a Tree! This is particularly possible because we know one of the two groups that has more than one member, but even if that were not so, we could still work with a Tree arrangement and keep in mind that some elements will be grouped together.

We have six groups and nine elements. Since four groups will have only one member, that leaves five elements to fill the two other groups. There's only one way to break five into two groups that each have at least two members: 2 and 3.

Notate the Rules and Make Inferences

> *Iyanna and Leung together constitute one class.*
> *Pedro and exactly two others together constitute one class.*

The first rule settles who forms one of the two groups. We'll chunk them together. And the second rule gives us the other group! We'll notate these like so:

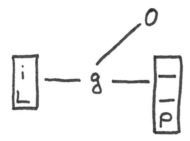

Kate is the first female, but not the first student, to attend a class.

That's a rather complex rule, and it's unclear how it fits into what we have so far. Let's skip it for a moment and see if it's easier to incorporate later. Since we're building a Tree, it makes sense to reorder the rules.

Gimena's class is at some time after Iyanna's but at sometime before Pedro's.

Oscar's class is at some time after Gimena's.

The last two rules fit in nicely with what we've learned so far. It's important not to assume that O is necessarily part of the P group.

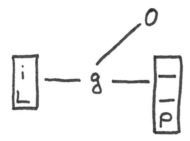

Let's swing back to the third rule about K. She's the first female, but not the first student. This means that she's before the i L chunk, and that a male must come before her. We can notate that like this:

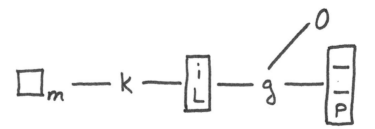

This leaves us with a lot of uncertainty. Let's try to reduce that uncertainty by identifying who's left. We haven't yet placed h, N, or S. We have three open slots, so it seems like a good fit. Right?

Watch out! We don't have to put O in the P group, but we can. Thus, while we'll need to use h, N, or S to complete that group, we may end up using only one of them. With regard to the first empty position, we'll need a male, meaning it's either N or S.

And, since h is a female, we know that she comes at some point after k. Our final diagram should look like this:

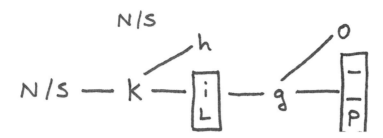

The N/S that is floating above the diagram is to remind us that whichever one of the pair that is not placed first will need to be placed somewhere—possibly in the P group, though not necessarily.

The Big Pause

As is often the case with Tree diagrams, a lot of the game's original uncertainty is settled. We still don't know who will fill the P group, and the positions of N and S are still in the air (although we know that one will be filling the mandatory male slot before k).

It seems that a lot will ride on the P group's membership. Let's keep an eye on that.

Attack the Questions

20. Which one of the following students could attend the first class?

    (A) Holly
    (B) Leung
    (C) Oscar
    (D) Pedro
    (E) Saul

(E) is correct.

Everyone but N or S must come after someone.

21. Which one of the following is a complete and accurate list of classes any one of which could be the class Gimena attends?

    (A) the fourth, the fifth
    (B) the fourth, the sixth
    (C) the second, the fourth, the fifth
    (D) the third, the fifth, the sixth
    (E) the second, the third, the fourth

(A) is correct.

At least three groups (N/S, k, i L) must precede g, so the earliest it could go is fourth. P's class must follow g, so g can't go last.

22. Which one of the following pairs of students could be in the class with Pedro?

  (A) Gimena and Holly
  (B) Holly and Saul
  (C) Kate and Nate
  (D) Leung and Oscar
  (E) Nate and Saul

(B) is correct.

We know that the membership must be drawn from the three strays N/S, O, and H (we can consider N/S one element in this case, since one has to come first). We can thus eliminate any answer that has any element outside those. We're down to (B) and (E). (E) illegally puts both N and S into the P class, leaving no male to come before k.

23. If Oscar and Pedro do not attend the same class as each other, then which one of the following could be true?

  (A) Gimena attends the fifth class.
  (B) Holly attends the third class.
  (C) Iyanna attends the fourth class.
  (D) Nate attends the fifth class.
  (E) Saul attends the second class.

(D) is correct.

The new condition tells us that O is not in the P group, meaning that N/S and h must be. If we need to, we can sketch out the situation:

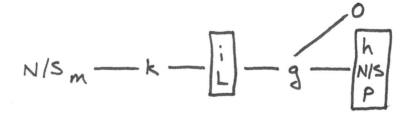

Since this is a could be true question, we can expect that the answer will play on the uncertainty around the order of the final two classes.

(A) through (C) clearly must be false. (D) puts N in the P class, which definitely could come before O's class.

24. Suppose the condition that Oscar attends a class after Gimena is replaced with the condition that Oscar attends a class before Gimena and after Kate. If all the other conditions remain the same, then which class must Holly attend?

P

(A) the second

(B) the third

(C) the fourth

(D) the fifth

(E) the sixth

(E) is correct.

We have to switch the order of O and G. It shouldn't take long to sketch this out:

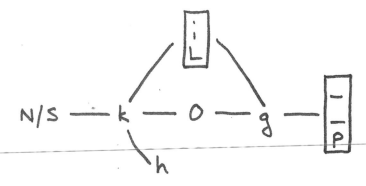

But now we've placed O out of the running for filling P's group. That means that h and the other N/S must go there. It's clear that h must go in the final class.

Chapter 15
of
Logic Games

Conclusion

In This Chapter...

Conclusion

You've made it! You've put in countless hours studying hypothetical scenarios about cat washings and toy trucks, figuring out better ways to notate conditional rules, and generally drawing your way into becoming a better lawyer. So…

What can possibly go wrong?

Professional athletes talk about the importance of a positive mind-set, the importance of being able to "picture" victory or success. That's all well and good, and envisioning success is very helpful, but we at Manhattan LSAT feel some kinship with the Woody Allen camp. We find it more comforting to go into the exam with a positive attitude *and* with eyes wide open to everything that could possibly go wrong. With that said, let's start this chapter by running through a list of…

15

The Five Most Common Pitfalls to Avoid on Test Day

5. You forget that each problem is only worth one point.

For all but a handful of us, missing a few problems will not make or break our games section. However, it's easy to spend three minutes on one problem, miss it (or not), and allow it to distract you from the rest of the section, and thus cause you to score significantly worse than you otherwise would have.

Make sure that you do not overinvest time or energy in any one question. Develop guidelines for when you will force yourself to move on. For many students, a useful gauge is "two attempts." If, after two different approaches, you are still unable to unlock a question, you should take an educated guess and move on. This should work out to you moving on at about 1:20 (none of your approaches should be such that, when they do work, they take any more than a minute). If you're short on time, skip questions that will probably be time-consuming. You know the usual suspects: Equivalent Rule questions, or Unconditional "could be true" questions with dense answer choices.

Overinvesting time on difficult questions is one of the most common mistakes that test-takers make, and nearly everyone who doesn't prepare for this issue will suffer from it at some point during the exam. The bad news is that you can't just tell yourself not to overinvest time and expect that to work. We all have a tendency to get lost in our work, especially when we are engrossed in games, and you only need to get lost once or twice to significantly and negatively impact your overall performance.

The good news is that this is a fairly easy issue to remedy with training and practice. Make sure that you take your practice exams (especially those final ones) as realistically as possible, and that you develop habits for moving on. If you get in the habit of giving yourself extra time in your practice, it increases the likelihood that you will waste time on the real exam. If you can make moving on a habitual decision, rather than a conscious one, your chances of going astray on the real exam will be minimized. If this is a significant issue for you, it may be worth your while to time individual questions with a stopwatch for a while. Monitoring your activity for the final few exams will be helpful in setting your internal clock.

Now, let's move on to the next common issue…

4. You have made a mistake or failed to understand something important about the game.

Oh, each element can be used more than once! Oh, there may be slots that are not used! Oh, I misconstrued that conditional statement! Oh, I misread what my notation was meant to stand for….

The vast majority of test-takers will make mistakes or miss significant characteristics for at least one of the four games that they see. Even though the design of the exam tempts us into thinking that it is the fastest and most clever test-takers who perform the best, in reality we know that those top scorers are also deliberate and accurate. If you can avoid making significant mistakes or omissions on test day, you will have an advantage over other test-takers.

These significant mistakes and omissions commonly occur in the first three minutes of the game. Unfortunately, oftentimes you won't realize you have any issues until you are two or three problems in—until you get an Unconditional "could be true" question, say, and not only can you not figure out what could be true, you have significant trouble seeing that many of the answers must be false. Or, you get a Conditional question, run through your chain of inferences, arrive at an answer, don't see it among the answer choices, and at that point realize you made a mistake in how you read one of the rules.

We've all been there. And we've all made such mistakes. The plan, of course, is to not let them hurt you when it actually counts on test day.

Slipups commonly occur because we are nervous, which makes us rush our work and be overly eager to take control of the situation. Timing restrictions are not meant to gauge how fast you can think. They are gauging your ability to prioritize—to focus on what is most important. Take time to set games up correctly; there is nothing more important than that. If making a quick but flawed diagram takes you one minute and thirty seconds, and doing it accurately takes a minute more, that extra minute is worth it.

In addition, if do you run into the unfortunate situation where you realize you've made a mistake or omission two or three problems in, we recommend that you stop and address the issue completely before moving forward. You may have a desire to quickly semi-correct your mistake and forge forward, but this will often lead to you spinning your wheels and not having much success on subsequent problems.

If two or three problems in you get the sense that something is not right, we recommend the following steps:

1. Stop what you are doing and take a look at your diagram. Look at each notation on it, and say to yourself what it means. Then check each notation against the original rules, to make sure that they either a) match the original rule correctly, or b) can be inferred by bringing rules together.

2. If you find an error, redraw your diagram correctly, and pay extra careful attention to inferences you may have made due to a misunderstanding. Students often feel that they won't have time for this, but drawing a second diagram takes far less time than drawing a first one does, and generally the time invested will be worth it. Practice this, and you won't be as nervous about sometimes having to redraw.

3. After you've checked for errors, give yourself a good five seconds to become comfortable with your diagram—the Big Pause! Again, we know it's going to feel like you don't have enough time to do this, but without a big-picture understanding, the questions will take much longer. Look for connections and prioritize what you know about a game.

If your goal is to get a perfect score, or a near perfect score, on the games section, it is important that you build in extra time so you can recover from a serious diagramming error on test day. If you design a timing strategy that accounts for no errors, you won't be able to recover when issues arise. To complete the games section perfectly, you should feel that, on a really good day, you can get through all four games in 32 or 33 minutes.

3. You haven't correctly prioritized the most important issues.

Issues #4 and #5 are black-and-white concerns that all test-takers, experienced and novice, can understand. Our top three issues become more obviously important once you have a secure footing in games, and especially if you are seeking a top games score.

Prioritizing the most important issues is more of an art than a science, and often you won't know whether you did this correctly until after the fact. If you have a correct sense of priorities, questions will often "flow," because you will be thinking about them in the same ways the test writers did. Even if you have a correct diagram, if you have no sense (or an incorrect sense) of a game's priorities, the questions will feel like a grind. They may seem to require unexpected, or unfair, leaps of thought from you.

Reviewing past work can be a great way to fine-tune your instincts in this area. Go back to games you have solved, set them up again, and decide on the priorities—which rules or inferences are most significant for understanding the game and solving problems. Then go through the problems to see if your understanding of priorities was indeed correct, or if there was something else you should have focused on. You should find that you are able to prioritize just fine in most situations, and you may find commonalities in the situations where you have trouble prioritizing.

Finally, we want to mention that confidence tends to play a significant role in terms of prioritizing correctly. When we are uncertain or nervous, many of us have a natural tendency to prioritize that which is most difficult to understand or handle, assuming that the "secret" must be locked inside. For example, when we read challenging text, we tend to focus most on words that we don't know the meanings of. On games, while we do need to understand each rule, our prioritization of rules should be based on an understanding of which ones have the greatest effect, not on a fixation on those with the trickiest wording. Being confident in your abilities, and being in control of your task, can help you to prioritize with a clearer eye.

2. You can't picture the situation.

As learners, we tend to prioritize the conscious mind, the "front room," and this is with good reason: the front room is the one we understand better, and it's the one we can most directly control. However, the reality is that some of the work you do during a standardized exam takes place in the unconscious mind, the "back room." We're not talking about your deep dark animal instincts or childhood fears; your standardized test prep back room is where you somehow sense which answers are worth examining first, and when a game or question is clicking. The back room is much harder to control and manipulate. However, what this back room thrives on is big-picture understanding. If you are able to visualize the situation, it makes it much easier for your brain to organize and relate the rules. If you can't visualize, you can't conceptualize. And if you can't conceptualize, you're dead in the water.

Burdening yourself with a lack of big-picture understanding is another common consequence of rushing and of lacking confidence. Expect to be able to understand the general parameters of a game, and know not to let yourself go forward into the questions without such an understanding.

The good news when it comes to picturing these games is that they are all variations on a theme. You will not face a situation on the exam that is disconnected from what we've discussed. If you can picture the games you've done for practice, you can picture the games that will appear on your official exam.

A good exercise for preparing for this challenge is to go through all of the games that you have done, hopefully mixed up in some fashion, and try to picture how you would set up each game. Don't solve the entire game—just walk through the setup in your mind. Then you can match up what you envisioned with how you actually solved the game, to reflect on how effectively you imagined the situation. Ideally, you want to get to a point where very few games seem unusual in their basic construction, and where—for the vast majority of games—you can quickly understand how to draw the base, and what the relationship will be between the base and the elements.

And now, what we've all been waiting for. The number one reason games cause trouble during the exam is…

1. You don't have control over the rules.

Control. It's a subjective gauge.

But think back to when you started learning games. Maybe you felt in control of rules from the get-go ("Sure, I know what 'M goes before N' means!"), or maybe you felt in control of the rules once you became comfortable with all the notations, but we hope that as you've studied, the level of control that you *desire* to have, and *expect* to have, has risen correspondingly. You should feel far more in control now than you did before, and you should have a much better understanding of what it *feels* like when you are in control—when the process of solving questions feels like it should.

Control over the rules will play a fundamental role in your success. Control does not mean that you solve a game during the setup, and it certainly doesn't mean that every question can be answered quickly. Control does not mean games are going to be easy. Control *does* mean that you understand exactly what each rule means. We expect that you can translate these rules into notations, and that, by the time you go into the questions, you are very comfortable thinking about how these rules relate to the rest of your diagram, and to one another. Control is not about knowing everything. It's about knowing what you know—and what you *don't* know—in a correct and usable way.

In your final few weeks of review, renew your focus on controlling the rules. Make sure you have confidence in your ability to accurately notate and understand rules, to see how rules relate to a game's big picture, to gauge their importance, to relate them to one another, and finally, to use the rules to perform the various tasks that different questions will present.

For different students, the order of dangers will be different, and we are sure that you know of a couple of elements on the above list that are of particular relevance to you, as well as perhaps a few challenges that are no longer issues for you. We do feel that everyone should agree with the following: if you can avoid these five pitfalls on test day, it is highly likely that you will end up very happy with your games score.

From Now Until Test Day

Let's end this book by discussing what your focus should be for your final few weeks of study. At this point, your goal should not be to gather more information or to learn new strategies. Rather, your priority should be to organize and contextualize what you have learned already, so that you can best apply the skills you have developed when it counts. Here are three general areas for you to address:

1.   Review and organize what you have learned.

2.   Set realistic goals and finalize timing strategies.

3.   Immerse yourself in real games played in real time.

Let's touch on each of these briefly:

1. Review and organize what you have learned.

This is the time to take one final comprehensive look at every rare twist and turn that a game might take. More importantly, this is the time to organize and prioritize what is most important to remember about games, and in what order. You might find that in going back and reviewing, you will feel more comfortable with certain games than you did before, and that's a very common and natural consequence of developing a stronger big-picture understanding. You might also find that you are rusty when it comes to making certain types of inferences for certain types of games. A great way to knock that rust off is to replay games (and then replay them again).

2. Set realistic goals and finalize timing strategies.

At this point, you should have a pretty good sense of how comfortable you feel with logic games. You may be at a point where you are consistently able to get through three games well, but commonly run out of time for the fourth. Maybe you get through all four games, but in order to do so you have to make educated guesses on certain questions. Or maybe you are a point where you are *expecting* to get a perfect score, or something close to that, on the games section.

One thing we strongly recommend is that you try to avoid a Clark Kent/Superman mentality; don't try to perform differently on the real exam than how you perform in your practice. If you consistently miss 5–8 questions in the games section, it's very unlikely that you will score −0 or −1 on test day, and altering your strategies can lead to unpleasant consequences. If you set out to miss your usual 5–8 questions, it's actually more likely that you'll beat your usual performance, as you'll be in a better position to capitalize on your strengths and minimize the amount of time you waste on your weaknesses.

Practice your timing strategies enough that they become internalized and require very little energy on test day.

Back in Chapter 7, we laid out a basic timing strategy based on allocating eight minutes to each game, along with three minutes in a "bank." We also discussed the idea of adapting this strategy to match your own specific strengths, weaknesses, and goals. Use your next two practice tests to get a realistic sense of where you are on a good day, or a bad day. Develop your strategies accordingly. Just as importantly, make these plans with plenty of time to spare, so that you can practice applying them on several more practice tests.

Take a look at a few hypothetical game players and the strategies that would work well for each one. Note that the timing goals are written assuming an ascending order of game difficulty, though in practice, the easiest game might be the second one, and thus it would be treated as game 1 in terms of how much time it "deserves." Don't read these with an eye towards choosing the goal score you'd like; instead, look for ideas that ring true about your own strengths and weaknesses.

15

Jon
Goal: 175–180 overall, –0 or –1 on games.

Characteristics: Generally strong at games, and extremely strong and fast with certain games, but very concerned about running into a game that is unusual, or turns into a slog.

Timing Goals
Game 1: 6
Game 2: 7
Game 3: 9
Game 4: 9
Bank: 4 minutes

Notes: Setting such tight goals for games 1 and 2 should help Jon push the pace, and it's likely that if he does run into an unusual and hard game, it will be game 3 or 4. Having an extra four minutes for that particular game can take a huge load off his shoulders.

Karen
Goal: 172–176, –1 or –2 on games

Characteristics: Feels very comfortable with games, and doesn't worry about running into a game that feels particularly different from others. What she does fear is making some silly mistake somewhere, or getting stuck on one or two particular problems and being forced to move on. She knows her margin of error is small.

Timing Goals
Game 1: 7
Game 2: 8
Game 3: 9
Game 4: 10
Bank: 1 minute

Notes: She doesn't need the tight goals Jon does, because she's less afraid of the rogue game. One minute in the bank is not much, but giving herself more time for each game allows her to be more careful and spend a bit of extra time on any particularly tough questions.

15

Luna

Goal: 168, −3 to −4 on games

Characteristics: Feels comfortable with most games, but is usually stumped by one or two really tough questions, spends too much time on them, and ends up having to rush on the last game.

<u>Timing Goals</u>
Game 1: 7:30
Game 2: 8
Game 3: 8:30
Game 4: 10
Bank: 1 minute

Notes: Luna has to be realistic that she won't have a lot of time to waste. Thus, she must expect to skip a couple of questions during earlier games to give herself time for every game.

Jonah

Goal: 162, −5 to −7 on games

Characteristics: Feels comfortable with simpler games, but has often found himself struggling in a significant way with one game per test.

<u>Timing Goals</u>
Game 1: 7
Game 2: 7
Game 3: 8
Game 4: 10
Bank: 3 minutes

Notes: Jonah needs to focus on hitting his timing goals on the simpler games. To have a good chance of getting most of the questions right on the toughest game, he needs time to "play around," perhaps making a mistake in laying out the framework of the game and then starting again.

3. Play, play, play.

Play games you've already played, and then play them over again. More importantly, practice full sets just as if it were test day. Set goals to get even faster at games you are already good at, and practice "surviving" games that are tough for you. Focus on retaining your mental discipline and not making notation mistakes or reading mistakes. You should play enough to be thoroughly engrossed in games, and you should use these final games to make your processes more automatic, and to explore and shore up the final holes in your understanding.

Final Thoughts

What makes for a great surgeon? We don't mean some surgeon that shows up on a list of "Atlanta's Fifty Best" in some airline magazine—we're talking a surgeon whom you would trust with your life.

Sure, that person has to go to school for a long time, and has to know a lot of stuff, the right sort of stuff, but… is this knowledge what makes for a good surgeon? Is the surgeon who knows the most the one who is best in the operating room?

If so, it's only by coincidence.

Surgery is about **performance**. The knowledge in the surgeon's brain does not have a direct impact on the patient—certainly not as direct an impact as the actions of that surgeon's hand. Surgeons are experts, but expertise is only a necessary condition, rather than a sufficient one, for being a great surgeon.

The good news is that no matter how stressful the LSAT may seem, nobody's life is on the line! The bad news (or the other good news, depending on your perspective), the part that you will likely remember on test day, is that the LSAT does have a hugely significant impact on your law school options.

In the pages of this book, you have been exposed to everything you could possibly need to know to deal with any game that the LSAT will throw in your direction. We're going to be validating this point on the following pages—in our addendum are solutions to all published games from the last nine years, all solved with success and simplicity using just the strategies we've discussed in the previous pages.

So, if you've been paying attention, you've got the knowledge part down. It's all in there somewhere. Your performance is what will dictate your score.

A great surgeon has the talent to be both disciplined and flexible. Something that is meant to be routine will stay routine, and will be handled with absolute precision. At the same time, when challenges arise, as they often do, great surgeons must have the willingness and confidence to make decisions and alter the course.

15

In your final few weeks, we suggest that you do what you can to get into the mind-set of a great surgeon. Don't add another thing to learn on top of the pile. A surgeon does not try to learn new techniques a week before a tough surgery. Use this time to reflect on what you know, to organize what you know, and to figure out how best to utilize it. To mix in another analogy, don't work on your half-court shots; instead, work on making sure that all of your fundamentals are sound. Studying that extremely unusual game from 15 years ago won't help you now. Instead, you might try making sure you know exactly how to recognize when Ordering games have number mismatches, and how to deal with these situations. Focusing on the central issues that will most likely define your performance will be a far better use of your final study hours.

Let's get to work.

Appendix A

of

Logic Games

Coached Replays

Coached Replays

In this section, we've reprinted each of the logic games you've met along your way through this book. Replaying games is an essential part of your LSAT prep. When first learning about each game type and optimal diagram, replaying games is an efficient way to master the basic moves. But now that you know the basics—and more—replaying games is a great way to further develop your more subtle skills, which will also enhance your ability to adapt to twists and turns.

You'll notice that these are not simply reprints of the games you saw throughout the book. We've added suggestions at many points in each game. Think of it as having a coach yelling out pointers as you work through your training exercises. As with a good coach, some of the suggestions are meant to keep you in proper form, while others add an extra challenge because your coach suspects the game might be too easy for you. (We will warn you if we're adding an extra challenge.)

Of course there are many ways to tackle a game, question, or answer choice, and different coaches will naturally offer different suggestions. We don't want you to get the impression that any one approach is the only effective one (indeed, you will find that some of the suggestions that follow differ from what you read earlier).

We have grouped the games into four-game sections for obvious reasons (except for one smaller group, for which we do not have enough games). Since you have seen these games before, you might want to consider giving yourself less than 35 minutes per section. Also, since our suggestions take up a lot of room on the page, you're going to have to work on a separate piece of paper. Giving yourself space to work is all the more relevant since the LSAT has started to spread games over two pages.

For your convenience, you will find an answer key at the back of all the sets. Note that we put an asterisk next to any of the questions that we wrote and added to official games, so you don't call LSAC to complain about how hard a game is.

SET 1

To start, we'll just give you a three-game section. Give yourself **26 minutes** to complete them.

_PT7, S2, G2_

Doctor Yamata works only on Mondays, Tuesdays, Wednesdays, Fridays, and Saturdays. She performs four different activities—lecturing, operating, treating patients, and conducting research. Each working day she pserforms exactly one activity in the morning and exactly one activity in the afternoon. During each week her work schedule must satisfy the following restrictions:

> She performs operastions on exactly three mornings.
> If she operates on Monday, she does not operate on Tuesday.
> She lectures in the afternoon on exactly two consecutive calendar days.
> She treats patients on exactly one morning and exactly three afternoons.
> She conducts research on exactly one morning.
> On Saturday she neither lectures nor performs operations.

Don't forget the Big Pause!

If this is not obvious, it's a sign you need to work on your setup.

8. Which one of the following must be a day on which Doctor Yamata lectures?

   (A) Monday
   (B) Tuesday
   (C) Wednesday
   (D) Friday
   (E) Saturday

Predict the element at play to speed things up even more.

9. On Wednesday Doctor Yamata could be scheduled to

   (A) conduct research in the morning and operate in the afternoon
   (B) lecture in the morning and treat patients in the afternoon
   (C) operate in the morning and lecture in the afternoon
   (D) operate in the morning and conduct research in the afternoons
   (E) treat patients in the morning and treat patients in the afternoon

10. Which one of the following statements must be true?

   (A) There is one day on which the doctor treats patients both in the morning and in the afternoon.
   (B) The doctor conducts research on one osf the days on which she lectures.
   (C) The doctor conducts research on one of the days on which she treats patients.
   (D) The doctor lectures on one of the days on which she treats patients.
   (E) The doctor lectures on one of the days on which she operates.

Look for wrong answers! Figure out when treating patients must occur (this will sound like both "on __" and "on _ or ___") and then eliminate.

11. If Doctor Yamata operates on Tuesday, then her schedule for treating patients could be

   (A) Monday morning, Monday afternoon, Friday morning, Friday afternoon
   (B) Monday morning, Friday afternoon, Saturday morning, Saturday afternoon
   (C) Monday afternoon, Wednesday morning, Wednesday afternoon, Saturday afternoon
   (D) Wednesday morning, Wednesday afternoon, Friday afternoon, Saturday afternoon
   (E) Wednesday afternoon, Friday afternoon, Saturday morning, Saturday afternoon

If it's easy and you know it, clap your hands.

12. Which one of the following is a pair of days on both of which Doctor Yamata must treat patients?

   (A) Monday and Tuesday
   (B) Monday and Saturday
   (C) Tuesday and Friday
   (D) Tuesday and Saturday
   (E) Friday and Saturday

Six doctors—Haddad, Johnson, Kwong, Lester, Murray, and Nelson—are assigned to the following three training rotations: orthopedics, pediatrics, surgery. Each doctor is assigned to exactly one rotation, and each rotation is assigned exactly two doctors. No other doctors are assigned.

The following conditions must be met:

Kwong is not assigned to the same rotation as Lester.
Murray is not assigned to surgery.
If Lester is assigned to orthopedics, then Haddad is assigned to surgery.
Johnson is assigned to surgery.

1. Which one of the following could be an accurate assignment of doctors to rotations?

(A) orthopedics: Kwong, Haddad
    pediatrics: Lester, Nelson
    surgery: Johnson, Murray

(B) orthopedics: Lester, Nelson
    pediatrics: Johnson, Murray
    surgery: Haddad, Kwong

(C) orthopedics: Kwong, Nelson
    pediatrics: Lester, Murray
    surgery: Haddad, Johnson

(D) orthopedics: Murray, Nelson
    pediatrics: Kwong, Lester
    surgery: Haddad, Johnson

(E) orthopedics: Lester, Murray
    pediatrics: Haddad, Kwong
    surgery: Johnson, Nelson

The answer is obvious if you follow the chain!

2. If Kwong is assigned to surgery, each of the following could be true EXCEPT:

(A) Murray is assigned to pediatrics.
(B) Haddad is assigned to orthopedics.
(C) Lester is assigned to orthopedics.
(D) Nelson is assigned to pediatrics.
(E) Nelson is assigned to orthopedics.

Scan the rules before looking at the answer choices to anticipate elements at play.

3. It can be determined to which rotation each of the six doctors is assigned if which one of the following statements is true?

(A) Both Murray and Kwong are assigned to orthopedics.
(B) Both Kwong and Nelson are assigned to pediatrics.
(C) Both Haddad and Johnson are assigned to surgery.
(D) Both Johnson and Lester are assigned to surgery.
(E) Both Haddad and Nelson are assigned to pediatrics.

Write out who's left to make it easier to evaluate the answers.

4. If Murray and Lester are assigned to the same rotation, for how many of the six doctors is it known to which rotation each is assigned?

(A) one
(B) two
(C) three
(D) four
(E) six

You should know the answer before looking at the answer choices.

5. If Nelson is assigned to surgery, which of the following is a complete and accurate list of doctors who could be assigned to the same rotation as Murray?

(A) Kwong
(B) Kwong, Lester
(C) Haddad, Lester
(D) Haddad, Kwong, Lester
(E) Haddad, Johnson, Kwong, Lester

One or more of six violinists—Greene, Holiday, Liu, Mann, Underwood, and Wilson—will be selected to perform at the year-end concert. No other violinists will be selected. The following conditions apply:

Challenge: Try playing this game WITHOUT using the Logic Chain. Instead, just write out the rules. Can you make it work?

> If Holiday is selected, then Mann is not selected.
> If Liu is selected, then both Mann and Wilson are selected.
> If Underwood is not selected, then Holiday is selected.
> Wilson is not selected unless Greene is selected.

Notice the mutually-exclusive pairs.

1. Which of the following could be a complete and accurate list of the violinists selected for the concert?

    (A) Holiday, Liu, Wilson, Underwood
    (B) Liu, Mann, Wilson
    (C) Holiday, Liu, Mann
    (D) Liu, Mann, Wilson
    (E) Mann, Underwood

2. Which of the following must be false?

    (A) Liu is selected but Underwood is not.
    (B) Neither Underwood nor Liu is selected.
    (C) Holiday is selected but Liu is not.
    (D) Both Greene and Underwood are selected.
    (E) Holiday is selected but Mann is not.

Predict the answer: Notice who out forces someone in.

3. Which of the following could be the only violinist selected for the concert?

    (A) Liu
    (B) Mann
    (C) Greene
    (D) Wilson
    (E) Underwood

4. If Underwood is not selected, then which of the following must be true?

    (A) Wilson is not selected.
    (B) Greene is selected.
    (C) At least two violinists are selected.
    (D) At most three violinists are selected.
    (E) Neither Liu nor Holiday is selected.

5. If Greene is not selected, then each of the following could be true EXCEPT:

    (A) Exactly two violinists are selected.
    (B) Exactly one violinist is selected.
    (C) Mann is selected.
    (D) Holiday is selected.
    (E) Liu is selected.

Treat this like an Orientation question, and remember what it means if something is not listed.

6. Which of the following CANNOT be a complete and accurate list of the violinists who are selected for the concert?

    (A) Greene, Liu, Mann, Underwood, Wilson
    (B) Greene, Mann, Underwood
    (C) Greene, Mann, Wilson
    (D) Greene, Underwood
    (E) Holiday

This is designed to take time. First understand the original rule, then work wrong-to-right.

7. Which of the following, if substituted for the condition that if Liu is selected then both Mann and Wilson are selected, would have the same effect in determining the violinists who are selected to perform?

    (A) If Liu is selected, then exactly two other violinists are selected.
    (B) If Liu is selected, then both Greene and Underwood are selected but Holiday is not.
    (C) If Mann and Wilson are selected, then Liu is selected.
    (D) If Liu is selected, then Mann is one of exactly five violinists selected.
    (E) If Liu is not selected, then neither Mann nor Wilson is selected.

STOP

SET 2

Allow yourself only **35 minutes** (or less) for these four games.

_PT1, S2, G1_

Exactly six trade representatives negotiate a treaty: Klosnik, Londi, Manley, Neri, Osata, Poirier. There are exactly six chairs evenly spaced around a circular table. The chairs are numbered 1 through 6, with successively numbered chairs next to each other and chair number 1 next to chair number 6. Each chair is occupied by exactly one of the representatives. The following conditions apply:

> Poirier sits immediately next to Neri.
> Londi sits immediately next to Manley, Neri, or both.
> Klosnik does not sit immediately next to Manley.
> If Osata sits immediately next to Poirier, Osata does not sit immediately next to Manley.

Simplify this to what situation cannot occur.

1. Which one of the following seating arrangements of the six representatives in chairs 1 through 6 would NOT violate the stated conditions?

   (A) Klosnik, Poirier, Neri, Manley, Osata, Londi
   (B) Klosnik, Londi, Manley, Poirier, Neri, Osatas
   (C) Klosnik, Londi, Manley, Osata, Poirier, Neri
   (D) Klosnik, Osata, Poirier, Neri, Londi, Manley
   (E) Klosnik, Neri, Londi, Osata, Manley, Poirier

Follow the chain and identify who's left.

2. If Londi sits immediately next to Poirier, which one of the following is a pair of representatives who must sit immediately next to each other?

   (A) Klosnik and Osata
   (B) Londi and Neri
   (C) Londi and Osata
   (D) Manley and Neri
   (E) Manley and Poirier

You should know the answer before looking at the answer choices.

3. If Klosnik sits directly between Londi and Poirier, then Manley must sit directly between

   (A) Londi and Neri
   (B) Londi and Osata
   (C) Neri and Osata
   (D) Neri and Poirier
   (E) Osata and Poirier

Follow the chain and identify who's left.

4. If Neri sits immediately next to Manley, then Klosnik can sit directly between

   (A) Londi and Manley
   (B) Londi and Poirier
   (C) Neri and Osata
   (D) Neri and Poirier
   (E) Poirier and Osata

Sketch out the condition and who's left to anchor your thinking.

5. If Londi sits immediately next to Manley, then which one of the following is a complete and accurate list of representatives any one of whom could also sit immediately next to Londi?

   (A) Klosnik
   (B) Klosnik, Neri
   (C) Neri, Poirier
   (D) Klosnik, Osata, Poirier
   (E) Klosnik, Neri, Osata, Poirier

With who's left, consider which rules apply.

6. If Londi sits immediately next to Neri, which one of the following statements must be false?

   (A) Klosnik sits immediately next to Osata.
   (B) Londi sits immediately next to Manley.
   (C) Osata sits immediately next to Poirier.
   (D) Neri sits directly between Londi and Poirier.
   (E) Osata sits directly between Klosnik and Manley.

Sketch out all the elements, consider what rule the right answer will predictably violate, and figure out the two possible answers.

7. If Klosnik sits immediately next to Osata, then Londi CANNOT sit directly between

   (A) Klosnik and Manley
   (B) Klosnik and Neri
   (C) Manley and Neri
   (D) Manley and Poirier
   (E) Neri and Osata

PT16, S1, G1

Eight new students—R, S, T, V, W, X, Y, Z—are being divided among exactly three classes—class 1, class 2, and class 3. Classes 1 and 2 will gain three new students each; class 3 will gain two new students. The following restrictions apply:

R must be added to class 1.
S must be added to class 3.
Neither S nor W can be added to the same class as Y.
V cannot be added to the same class as Z.
If T is added to class 1, Z must also be added to class 1.

1. Which one of the following is an acceptable assignment of students to the three classes?

	1	2	3
(A)	R, T, Y	V, W, X	S, Z
(B)	R, T, Z	S, V, Y	W, X
(C)	R, W, X	V, Y, Z	S, T
(D)	R, X, Z	T, V, Y	S, W
(E)	R, X, Z	V, W, Y	S, T

If you're not sure, leave this question for later.

2. Which one of the following is a complete and accurate list of classes any one of which could be the class to which V is added?

    (A) class 1
    (B) class 3
    (C) class 1, class 3
    (D) class 2, class 3
    (E) class 1, class 2, class 3

Keep an eye on those anti-chunks.

3. If X is added to class 1, which one of the following is a student who must be added to class 2?

    (A) T
    (B) V
    (C) W
    (D) Y
    (E) Z

Use what you just figured out.

4. If X is added to class 3, each of the following is a pair of students who can be added to class 1 EXCEPT

    (A) Y and Z
    (B) W and Z
    (C) V and Y
    (D) V and W
    (E) T and Z

You should know the answer before looking at the answer choices.

5. If T is added to class 3, which one of the following is a student who must be added to class 2?

    (A) V
    (B) W
    (C) X
    (D) Y
    (E) Z

For an added challenge, try not drawing out anything. Instead, use your master diagram, cover up the elements you've used with your fingers, and think!

6. Which one of the following must be true?

    (A) If T and X are added to class 2, V is added to class 3.
    (B) If V and W are added to class 1, T is added to class 3.
    (C) If V and W are added to class 1, Z is added to class 3.
    (D) If V and X are added to class 1, W is added to class 3.
    (E) If Y and Z are added to class 2, X is added to class 2.

PT30, S1, G3

Exactly five cars—Frank's, Marquitta's, Orlando's Taishah's, and Vinquetta's—are washed, each exactly once. The cars are washed one at a time, with each receiving exactly one kind of wash: regular, super, or premium. The following conditions must apply:

> The first car washed does not receive a super wash, though at least one car does.
> Exactly one car receives a premium wash.
> The second and third cars washed receive the same kind of wash as each other.
> Neither Orlando's nor Taishah's is washed before Vinquetta's.
> Marquitta's is washed before Frank's, but after Orlando's.
> Marquitta's and the car washed immediately before Marquitta's receive regular washes.

It's definitely possible to frame this game. This time around, try without. Optionally, play the game first without frames, and then with.

11. Which one of the following could be an accurate list of the cars in the order in which they are washed, matched with type of wash received?

   (A) Orlando's: premium; Vinquetta's: regular; Taishah's: regular; Marquitta's: regular; Frank's: super
   (B) Vinquetta's: premium; Orlando's: regular; Taishah's: regular; Marquitta's: regular; Frank's: super
   (C) Vinquetta's: regular; Marquitta's: regular; Taishah's: regular; Orlando's: super; Frank's: premium
   (D) Vinquetta's: super; Orlando's: regular; Marquitta's: regular; Frank's: regular; Taishah's: super
   (E) Vinquetta's: premium; Orlando's: regular; Marquitta's: regular; Frank's: regular; Taishah's: regular

Get scrappy: Make the one must be inference and then scan the answers.

12. If Vinquetta's car does not receive a premium wash, which one of the following must be true?

   (A) Orlando's and Vinquetta's cars receive the same kind of wash as each other.
   (B) Marquitta's and Taishah's cars receive the same kind of wash as each other.
   (C) The fourth car washed receives a premium wash.
   (D) Orlando's car is washed third.
   (E) Marquitta's car is washed fourth.

What kind of wash must the last 2 get? Follow the chain; then predict the elements at play.

13. If the last two cars washed receive the same kind of wash as each other, then which one of the following could be true?

   (A) Orlando's car is washed third.
   (B) Taishah's car is washed fifth.
   (C) Taishah's car is washed before Marquitta's car.
   (D) Vinquetta's car receives a regular wash.
   (E) Exactly one car receives a super wash.

A sound setup pays off here. Defer judgment!

14. Which one of the following must be true?

   (A) Vinquetta's car receives a premium wash
   (B) Exactly two cars receive a super wash.
   (C) The fifth car washed receives a super wash.
   (D) The fourth car washed receives a super wash.
   (E) The second car washed receives a regular wash.

Consider who must have a regular wash; then try using previous work to eliminate the last incorrect choice.

15. Which one of the following is a complete and accurate list of the cars that must receive a regular wash?

   (A) Frank's, Marquitta's
   (B) Marquitta's, Orlando's
   (C) Marquitta's, Orlando's, Taishah's
   (D) Marquitta's, Taishah's
   (E) Marquitta's, Vinquetta's

Two more questions on next page…

It's possible to solve this by adding to your original diagram, but this time around, practice going back to square one and see how quickly you can re-draw.

16. Suppose that in addition to the original five cars Jabrohn's car is also washed. If all the other conditions hold as given, which one of the following CANNOT be true?

   (A) Orlando's car receives a premium wash.

   (B) Vinquetta's car receives a super wash.

   (C) Four cars receive a regular wash.

   (D) Only the second and third cars washed receive a regular wash.

   (E) Jabrohn's car is washed after Frank's car.

Start by considering the implications of the rule in question—BOTH of them!

Try a question that we wrote for this game (assume that the rule change in #16 is not applicable):

17. Which of the following, if substituted for the rule that the first car washed does not receive a super wash, though at least one car does, would have the same effect in determining the order of car washes and the type of each?

   (A) Vinquetta's car can receive only a regular or premium wash.

   (B) No more than three cars receive a regular \wash.

   (C) Frank's car receives a super wash if, and only if, Taishah's car receives a regular or premium wash.

   (D) All cars except Frank's and Taishah's must receive either a regular or premium wash.

   (E) Either Frank's or Taishah's car receives a super wash, and no other car can receive that type of wash.

A filmmaker will choose exactly five songs to use in a film project. Of the nine songs that she will choose from, three songs—F, G, and H—were written in the 1960s, three songs—J, K, and M—were written in the 1970s, and three songs—O, P, and Q—were written in the 1980s. The following conditions apply:

Exactly two songs from the 1980s are selected for the project.
G and J cannot both be selected.
H and O cannot both be selected.
If Q is selected, both G and H are selected.

Identify mutually-exclusive pairs, and don't forget to note both the total number in and out.

Leave the first rule for last.

1. Which one of the following is an acceptable selection of songs for the film project?

    (A) F, G, K, P, Q
    (B) G, J, K, O, P
    (C) G, K, M, O, P
    (D) G, H, K, M, Q
    (E) F, G, H, O, P

Remember to add horizontal lines to your t-charts to help you track the different categories.

2. If Q is selected for the film project, each of the following could be true EXCEPT:

    (A) F is selected for the film project.
    (B) J is selected for the film project.
    (C) G is selected for the film project.
    (D) K is selected for the film project.
    (E) M is selected for the film project.

Don't waste too much time on this question.

3. If neither K nor M is selected for the film project, how many of the five song selections are known with certainty?

    (A) one
    (B) two
    (C) three
    (D) four
    (E) five

Frame this on the O/Q division.

4. If K is the only song from the 1970s selected for the film project, then which one of the following CANNOT be true?

    (A) O is not selected but F is selected.
    (B) Q is not selected but G is selected.
    (C) F is not selected but P is selected.
    (D) H is not selected but G is selected.
    (E) O is not selected but H is selected.

5. Which one of the following is a song that must be selected for the film project?

    (A) H
    (B) Q
    (C) F
    (D) P
    (E) G

Predict how the correct answer will violate the game.

6. If the condition that exactly two songs from the 1980s are selected for the project is replaced with the condition that at least one song from each time period must be selected, and if all other rules remain in effect, each of the following could be true EXCEPT:

    (A) Both O and P are selected.
    (B) Both G and H are selected.
    (C) Both P and Q are selected.
    (D) J, K, and M are selected.
    (E) F, P, and Q are selected.

SET 3

Allow yourself only **35 minutes** (or less) for these four games.

PT18, S1, G1

Each of five students—Hubert, Lori, Paul, Regina, and Sharon—will visit exactly one of three cities—Montreal, Toronto, or Vancouver—for the month of March, according to the following conditions:

> Sharon visits a different city than Paul.
> Hubert visits the same city as Regina.
> Lori visits Montreal or else Toronto.
> If Paul visits Vancouver, Hubert visits Vancouver with him.
> Each student visits one of the cities with at least one of the other four students.

Slow down here; there are not too many elements but there are very restrictive numerical rules.

1. Which one of the following could be true for March?

   (A) Hubert, Lori, and Paul visit Toronto, and Regina and Sharon visit Vancouver.
   (B) Hubert, Lori, Paul, and Regina visit Montreal, and Sharon visits Vancouver.
   (C) Hubert, Paul, and Regina visit Toronto, and Lori and Sharon visit Montreal.
   (D) Hubert, Regina, and Sharon visit Montreal, and Lori and Paul visit Vancouver.
   (E) Lori, Paul, and Sharon visit Montreal, and Hubert and Regina visit Toronto.

Sketch the groups, and since it's a could be question, identify what is still undetermined.

2. If Hubert and Sharon visit a city together, which one of the following could be true in March?

   (A) Hubert visits the same city as Paul.
   (B) Lori visits the same city as Regina.
   (C) Paul visits the same city as Regina.
   (D) Paul visits Toronto.
   (E) Paul visits Vancouver.

Figure out the groups!

3. If Sharon visits Vancouver, which one of the following must be true for March?

   (A) Hubert visits Montreal.
   (B) Lori visits Montreal.
   (C) Paul visits Toronto.
   (D) Lori visits the same city as Paul.
   (E) Lori visits the same city as Regina.

Use previous work as much as possible. Challenge: start at (E).

4. Which one of the following could be false in March?

   (A) Sharon must visit Montreal if Paul visits Vancouver.
   (B) Regina must visit Vancouver if Paul visits Vancouver.
   (C) Regina visits a city with exactly two of the other four students.
   (D) Lori visits a city with exactly one of the other four students.
   (E) Lori visits a city with Paul or else with Sharon.

Follow the chain and note who's left and where they can go.

5. If Regina visits Toronto, which one of the following could be true in March?

   (A) Lori visits Toronto.
   (B) Lori visits Vancouver.
   (C) Paul visits Toronto.
   (D) Paul visits Vancouver.
   (E) Sharon visits Vancouver.

Use previous work!

6. Which one of the following must be true for March?

   (A) If any of the students visits Montreal, Lori visits Montreal.
   (B) If any of the students visits Montreal, exactly two of them do.
   (C) If any of the students visits Toronto, exactly three of them do.
   (D) If any of the students visits Vancouver, Paul visits Vancouver.
   (E) If any of the students visits Vancouver, exactly three of them do.

PT36, S4, G2

A radio talk show host airs five telephone calls sequentially. The calls, one from each of Felicia, Gwen, Henry, Isaac, and Mel, are each either live or taped (but not both). Two calls are from Vancouver, two are from Seattle, and one is from Kelowna. The following conditions must apply:

> Isaac's and Mel's calls are the first two calls aired, but not necessarily in that order.
> The third call aired, from Kelowna, is taped.
> Both Seattle calls are live.
> Both Gwen's and Felicia's calls air after Henry's.
> Neither Mel nor Felicia calls from Seattle.

 Challenge! Is your grasp of this game strong enough that you can solve all the questions without putting pencil to paper?

7. Which one of the following could be an accurate list of the calls, listed in the order in which they are aired?

    (A) Isaac's, Henry's, Felicia's, Mel's, Gwen's
    (B) Isaac's, Mel's, Gwen's, Henry's, Felicia's
    (C) Mel's, Gwen's, Henry's, Isaac's, Felicia's
    (D) Mel's, Isaac's, Gwen's, Henry's, Felicia's
    (E) Mel's, Isaac's, Henry's, Felicia's, Gwen's

8. Which one of the following could be true?

    (A) Felicia's call airs fifth.
    (B) Gwen's call airs first.
    (C) Henry's call airs second.
    (D) Isaac's call airs third.
    (E) Mel's call airs fifth.

9. If the first call aired is from Seattle, then which one of the following could be true?

    (A) Felicia's call is the next call aired after Isaac's.
    (B) Henry's call is the next call aired after Felicia's.
    (C) Henry's call is the next call aired after Mel's.
    (D) Henry's call is the next call aired after Isaac's.
    (E) Isaac's call is the next call aired after Mel's.

10. If a taped call airs first, then which one of the following CANNOT be true?

    (A) Felicia's call airs fourth.
    (B) Gwen's call airs fifth.
    (C) A taped call airs second.
    (D) A taped call airs third.
    (E) A taped call airs fourth.

11. Which one of the following must be true?

    (A) Gwen's call is live.
    (B) Henry's call is live.
    (C) Mel's call is live.
    (D) Felicia's call is taped.
    (E) Isaac's call is taped.

12. If no two live calls are aired consecutively and no two taped calls are aired consecutively, then in exactly how many distinct orders could the calls from the five people be aired?

    (A) one
    (B) two
    (C) three
    (D) four
    (E) five

13. If a taped call airs second, then which one of the following CANNOT be true?

    (A) The first call aired is from Seattle.
    (B) The first call aired is from Vancouver.
    (C) The fourth call aired is from Seattle.
    (D) The fifth call aired is from Seattle.
    (E) The fifth call aired is from Vancouver.

PT32, S3, G3

At a concert, exactly eight compositions—F, H, L, O, P, R, S, and T—are to be performed exactly once each, consecutively and one at a time. The order of their performance must satisfy the following conditions:

> T is performed either immediately before F or immediately after R.
> At least two compositions are performed either after F and before R, or after R and before F.
> O is performed either first or fifth.
> The eighth composition performed is either L or H.
> P is performed at some time before S.
> At least one composition is performed either after O and before S, or after S and before O.

Use the easy rules first.

12. Which one of the following lists the compositions in an order in which they could be performed during the concert, from first through eighth?

    (A) L, P, S, R, O, T, F, H
    (B) O, T, P, F, S, H, R, L
    (C) P, T, F, S, L, R, O, H
    (D) P, T, F, S, O, R, L, H
    (E) T, F, P, R, O, L, S, H

13. P CANNOT be performed

    (A) second
    (B) third
    (C) fourth
    (D) sixth
    (E) seventh

Follow the chain & consider who's left.

14. If T is performed fifth and F is performed sixth, then S must be performed either

    (A) fourth or seventh
    (B) third or sixth
    (C) third or fourth
    (D) second or seventh
    (E) first or fourth

Only follow the chain as long as you have to!

15. If O is performed immediately after T, then F must be performed either

    (A) first or second
    (B) second or third
    (C) fourth or sixth
    (D) fourth or seventh
    (E) sixth or seventh

Eliminate 3 obvious answers, test 1 remainder.

16. Is S is performed fourth, which one of the following could be an accurate list of the compositions performed first, second, and third, respectively?

    (A) F, H, P
    (B) H, P, L
    (C) O, P, R
    (D) O, P, T
    (E) P, R, T

Get Scrappy: Create a hypothetical, eliminate what you can, repeat.

17. If P is performed third and S is performed sixth, the composition performed fifth must be either

    (A) F or H
    (B) F or O
    (C) F or T
    (D) H or L
    (E) O or R

Create a hypothetical to see what must be true.

18. If exactly two compositions are performed after F but before O, then R must be performed

    (A) first
    (B) third
    (C) fourth
    (D) sixth
    (E) seventh

PT52, S2, G2

On a field trip to the Museum of Natural History, each of six children—Juana, Kyle, Lucita, Salim, Thanh, and Veronica —is accompanied by one of three adults—Ms. Margoles, Mr. O'Connell, and Ms. Podorski. Each adult accompanies exactly two of the children, consistent with the following conditions:

> If Ms. Margoles accompanies Juana, then Ms. Podorski accompanies Lucita.
>
> If Kyle is not accompanied by Ms. Margoles, then Veronica is accompanied by Mr. O'Connell.
>
> Either Ms. Margoles or Mr. O'Connell accompanies Thanh.
>
> Juana is not accompanied by the same adult as Kyle; nor is Lucita accompanied by the same adult as Salim; nor is Thanh accompanied by the same adult as Veronica.

8. Which one of the following could be an accurate matching of the adults to the children they accompany?

    (A) Ms. Margoles: Juana, Thanh; Mr. O'Connell: Lucita, Veronica; Ms. Podorski: Kyle, Salim.

    (B) Ms. Margoles: Kyle, Thanh; Mr. O'Connell: Juana, Salim; Ms. Podorski: Lucita, Veronica

    (C) Ms. Margoles: Lucita, Thanh; Mr. O'Connell: Juana, Salim; Ms. Podorski: Kyle, Veronica

    (D) Ms. Margoles: Kyle, Veronica; Mr. O'Connell: Juana, Thanh; Ms. Podorski: Lucita, Salim

    (E) Ms. Margoles: Salim, Veronica; Mr. O'Connell: Kyle, Lucita; Ms. Podorski: Juana, Thanh

Before you decide you have reached the end of the inference chain, scan the rules one last time.

9. If Ms. Margoles accompanies Lucita and Thanh, then which one of the following must be true?

    (A) Juana is accompanied by the same adult as Veronica.

    (B) Kyle is accompanied by the same adult as Salim.

    (C) Juana is accompanied by Mr. O'Connell.

    (D) Kyle is accompanied by Ms. Podorski.

    (E) Salim is accompanied by Ms. Podorski.

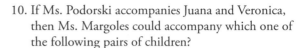

Once again, before you decide you have reached the end of the inference chain, scan the rules one last time.

10. If Ms. Podorski accompanies Juana and Veronica, then Ms. Margoles could accompany which one of the following pairs of children?

    (A) Kyle and Salim
    (B) Kyle and Thanh
    (C) Lucita and Salim
    (D) Lucita and Thanh
    (E) Salim and Thanh

First see if previous work can eliminate some answers. With the ones that remain, track who's left in each situation to help you consider each choice.

11. Ms. Podorski CANNOT accompany which one of the following pairs of children?

    (A) Juana and Lucita
    (B) Juana and Salim
    (C) Kyle and Salim
    (D) Salim and Thanh
    (E) Salim and Veronica

Use previous work to make some initial eliminations.

12. Mr. O'Connell CANNOT accompany which one of the following pairs of children?

    (A) Juana and Lucita
    (B) Juana and Veronica
    (C) Kyle and Thanh
    (D) Lucita and Thanh
    (E) Salim and Veronica

SET 4

Allow yourself only **35 minutes** (or less) for these four games.

PT19, S1, G1

During a period of six consecutive days—day 1 through day 6—each of exactly six factories—F, G, H, J, Q, and R—will be inspected. During this period, each of the factories will be inspected exactly once, one factory per day. The schedule for the inspections must conform to the following conditions:

> F is inspected on either day 1 or day 6.
> J is inspected on an earlier day than Q is inspected.
> Q is inspected on the day immediately before R is inspected.
> If G is inspected on day 3, Q is inspected on day 5.

1. Which one of the following could be a list of the factories in the order of their scheduled inspections, from day 1 through day 6?

    (A) F, Q, R, H, J, G
    (B) G, H, J, Q, R, F
    (C) G, J, Q, H, R, F
    (D) G, J, Q, R, F, H
    (E) J, H, G, Q, R, F

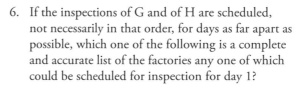

D'oh! (Look for the easy answer.)

2. Which one of the following must be false?

    (A) The inspection of G is scheduled for day 4.
    (B) The inspection of H is scheduled for day 6.
    (C) The inspection of J is scheduled for day 4.
    (D) The inspection of Q is scheduled for day 3.
    (E) The inspection of R is scheduled for day 2.

Don't pick up your pencil! Defer judgment until you find a Must Be False.

3. The inspection of which one of the following CANNOT be scheduled for day 5?

    (A) G
    (B) H
    (C) J
    (D) Q
    (E) R

Work backwards: Choose the two rules most likely to be used and find answers that violate them. You can eliminate four answers like that!

4. The inspections scheduled for day 3 and day 5, respectively, could be those of

    (A) G and H
    (B) G and R
    (C) H and G
    (D) R and J
    (E) R and H

Place the mega-chunk and follow the inference chain. Who's left and what rules apply to them?

5. If the inspection of R is scheduled for the day immediately before the inspection of F, which one of the following must be true about the schedule?

    (A) The inspection of either G or H is scheduled for day 1.
    (B) The inspection of either G or J is scheduled for day 1.
    (C) The inspection of either G or J is scheduled for day 2.
    (D) The inspection of either H or J is scheduled for day 3.
    (E) The inspection of either H or J is scheduled for day 4.

Eliminate two obvious; then start with the greatest distance to determine max distance.

6. If the inspections of G and of H are scheduled, not necessarily in that order, for days as far apart as possible, which one of the following is a complete and accurate list of the factories any one of which could be scheduled for inspection for day 1?

    (A) F, J
    (B) G, H
    (C) G, H, J
    (D) F, G, H
    (E) F, G, H, J

One more question on next page…

Another mega-chunk! Given the elements in the question, anticipate which rule is likely to be triggered.

7. If the inspection of G is scheduled for the day immediately before the inspection of Q, which one of the following could be true?

(A) The inspection of G is scheduled for day 5.

(B) The inspection of H is scheduled for day 6.

(C) The inspection of J is scheduled for day 2.

(D) The inspection of Q is scheduled for day 4.

(E) The inspection of R is scheduled for day 3.

A publishing company published exactly six novels—*Forgiven, Grain, Highwire, June, Lampoon,* and *Melted*—in the years from 1991 to 1996. Exactly one novel was published in each of the six years. Three authors—Robinson, Stewart, and Tamiko—each wrote exactly two of the novels. The following conditions apply:

Exactly one of Robinson's novels was published before the first of Stewart's novels was published.

Be careful with this one…

Neither of Robinson's novels was published in 1991 or 1994.

None of the authors had novels published in consecutive years.

June was published in 1994.

Highwire was published exactly two years after *Melted*.

 Mix it up: Use a combination of the easy rules and your hard-earned inferences.

1. Which of the following could be an accurate representation of the authors and the novels they wrote, listed in order of publication?

   (A) Tamiko: *Lampoon*; Robinson: *Grain*; Tamiko: *Forgiven*; Stewart: *Melted*; Robinson: *June*; Stewart: *Highwire*

   (B) Tamiko: *Lampoon*; Robinson: *Forgiven*; Stewart: *Melted*; Tamiko: *June*; Robinson: *Highwire*; Stewart: *Grain*

   (C) Stewart: *Melted*; Robinson: *Lampoon*; Stewart: *Highwire*; Tamiko: *June*; Robinson: *Forgiven*; Tamiko: *Grain*

   (D) Tamiko: *Melted*; Robinson: *Grain*; Stewart: *Highwire*; Stewart: *June*; Tamiko: *Forgiven*; Robinson: *Lampoon*

   (E) Robinson: *Forgiven*; Tamiko: *Grain*; Stewart: *Melted*; Robinson: *June*; Tamiko: *Highwire*; Stewart: *Lampoon*

2. Which one of the following must be true?

   (A) One of Stewart's novels was published in 1993.

   (B) One of Tamiko's novels was published in 1994.

   (C) One of Robinson's novels was published in 1992.

   (D) One of Robinson's novels was published in 1995.

   (E) One of Stewart's novels was published in 1996.

Follow the inferences, then be lazy…look for the one that must be false.

3. If *Forgiven* was published in 1995, each of the following could be true EXCEPT:

   (A) Stewart wrote *Grain*.

   (B) Tamiko wrote *June*.

   (C) Tamiko wrote *Highwire*.

   (D) Robinson wrote *Lampoon*.

   (E) Robinson wrote *Highwire*.

Mind the chunk!

4. If Tamiko wrote *June*, then which one of the following must be false?

   (A) Tamiko wrote *Melted*.

   (B) Tamiko wrote *Highwire*.

   (C) Stewart wrote *Melted*.

   (D) Stewart wrote *Highwire*.

   (E) Stewart wrote *Forgiven*.

Add to the chunk, further limiting its placement.

5. If *Lampoon* was published in the year immediately preceding the publication of *Melted*, which one of the following must be true?

   (A) Tamiko wrote *Forgiven*.

   (B) Tamiko wrote *Grain*.

   (C) Robinson wrote *Lampoon*.

   (D) Robinson wrote *Highwire*.

   (E) Stewart wrote *Melted*.

6. Each of the following could be true EXCEPT:

   (A) Tamiko wrote a novel that was published in 1995.

   (B) *Melted* was published exactly three years before Grain.

   (C) Stewart wrote *June*.

   (D) *Lampoon* was published before *Highwire* but after *Melted*.

   (E) Both of Tamiko's novels were published before either of Stewart's novels were published.

The correct answer should give us an exact replica of our original diagram.

7. Which of the following, if substituted for the condition that exactly one of Robinson's novels was published before the first of Stewart's novels was published, would have the same effect in determining the years in which the novels were published and the authors who wrote the novels?

(A) Neither of Robinson's novels was published in 1996.

(B) Neither of Stewart's novels was published in 1992.

(C) The earliest that either one of Stewart's novels could have been published is 1993.

(D) The earliest that either one of Robinson's novels could have been published is 1992.

(E) The earliest that either one of Robinson's novels could have been published is 1993.

MANHATTAN
LSAT

PT51, S4, G2

Six hotel suites—F, G, H, J, K, and L—are ranked from most expensive (first) to least expensive (sixth). There are no ties. The ranking must be consistent with the following conditions:

> **It's not necessarily intuitive that most expensive = first and least = sixth. Make sure you follow the game's cue.**

H is more expensive than L.

If G is more expensive than H, then neither K nor L is more expensive than J.

If H is more expensive than G, then neither J nor L is more expensive than K.

F is more expensive than G, or else F is more expensive than H, but not both.

You framed this, right?

With two frames, you have to use the rules.

6. Which one of the following could be the ranking of the suites, from most expensive to least expensive?

   (A) G, F, H, L, J, K
   (B) H, K, F, J, G, L
   (C) J, H, F, K, G, L
   (D) J, K, G, H, L, F
   (E) K, J, L, H, F, G

Establish which frame you're in and eliminate those Must be Falses.

7. If G is the second most expensive suite, then which one of the following could be true?

   (A) H is more expensive than F.
   (B) H is more expensive than G.
   (C) K is more expensive than F.
   (D) K is more expensive than J.
   (E) L is more expensive than F.

Work backwards: Identify all the elements that can be the most expensive.

8. Which one of the following CANNOT be the most expensive suite?

   (A) F
   (B) G
   (C) H
   (D) J
   (E) K

Select your frame and anticipate the element at play.

9. If L is more expensive than F, then which one of the following could be true?

   (A) F is more expensive than H.
   (B) F is more expensive than K.
   (C) G is more expensive than H.
   (D) G is more expensive than J.
   (E) G is more expensive than L.

The wording is a bit tougher here, so take a second to sketch out the conditional first.

10. If H is more expensive than J and less expensive than K, then which one of the following could be true?

   (A) F is more expensive than H.
   (B) G is more expensive than F.
   (C) G is more expensive than H.
   (D) J is more expensive than L.
   (E) L is more expensive than K.

PT32, S3, G4

On each of exactly seven consecutive days (day 1 though day 7), a pet shop features exactly one of three breeds of kitten—Himalayan, Manx, Siamese—and exactly one of three breeds of puppy—Greyhound, Newfoundland, Rottweiler. The following conditions must apply:

> Greyhounds are featured on day 1.
> No breed is featured on any two consecutive days.
> Any breed featured on day 1 is not featured on day 7.
> Himalayans are featured on exactly three days, but not on day 1.
> Rottweilers are not featured on day 7, nor on any day that features Himalayans.

Don't forget the Big Pause!

19. Which one of the following could be the order in which the breeds of kitten are featured in the pet shop, from day 1 though day 7?

    (A) Himalayan, Manx, Siamese, Himalayan, Manx, Himalayan, Siamese
    (B) Manx, Himalayan, Siamese, Himalayan, Manx, Himalayan, Manx
    (C) Manx, Himalayan, Manx, Himalayan, Siamese, Manx, Siamese
    (D) Siamese, Himalayan, Manx, Himalayan, Siamese, Siamese, Himalayan
    (E) Siamese, Himalayan, Siamese, Himalayan, Manx, Siamese, Himalayan

Focus on what must be false.

20. If Himalayans are not featured on day 2, which one of the following could be true?

    (A) Manx are featured on day 3.
    (B) Siamese are featured on day 4.
    (C) Rottweilers are featured on day 5.
    (D) Himalayans are featured on day 6.
    (E) Greyhounds are featured on day 7.

Again, focus on what must be false.

21. Which one of the following could be true?

    (A) Greyhounds and Siamese are both featured on day 2.
    (B) Greyhounds and Himalayans are both featured on day 7.
    (C) Rottweilers and Himalayans are both featured on day 4.
    (D) Rottweilers and Manx are both featured on day 5.
    (E) Newfoundlands and Manx are both featured on day 6.

Follow the chain! Every rule comes into play.

22. If Himalayans are not featured on day 7, then which one of the following pairs of days CANNOT feature both the same breed of kitten and the same breed of puppy?

    (A) day 1 and day 3
    (B) day 2 and day 6
    (C) day 3 and day 5
    (D) day 4 and day 6
    (E) day 5 and day 7

Focus on what must be false. Challenge yourself to work wrong-to-right.

23. Which one of the following could be true?

    (A) There are exactly four breeds that are each featured on three days.
    (B) Greyhounds are featured on every day that Himalayans are.
    (C) Himalayans are featured on every day that Greyhounds are.
    (D) Himalayans are featured on every day that Rottweilers are not.
    (E) Rottweilers are featured on every day that Himalayans are not.

24. If Himalayans are not featured on day 7, which one of the following could be true?

    (A) Greyhounds are featured on days 3 and 5.
    (B) Newfoundlands are featured on day 3.
    (C) Rottweilers are featured on day 6.
    (D) Rottweilers are featured only on day 3.
    (E) Rottweilers are featured on exactly three days.

STOP

SET 5

Allow yourself only **35 minutes** (or less) for these four games.

Exactly seven swimmers—Hewitt, James, Kopov, Luis, Markson, Nu, and Price—will race in the 50-meter freestyle event. Each swimmer will swim in exactly one of seven lanes, numbered 1 through 7. No two swimmers share the same lane. Lane assignments comply with the following conditions:

> James swims in a lower-numbered lane than Kopov.
> Nu swims in either the first lane or the seventh lane.
> Markson swims in a lane numbered two lower than Price's.
> Hewitt swims in lane 4.

Use your diagram.

1. Which of the following could be an accurate list of swimmers, listed in order from lane 1 through lane 7?

    (A) Nu, Luis, James, Kopov, Markson, Hewitt, Price
    (B) James, Luis, Markson, Hewitt, Price, Kopov, Nu
    (C) Nu, Kopov, Markson, Hewitt, Price, James, Luis
    (D) Luis, Markson, James, Hewitt, Price, Kopov, Nu
    (E) Markson, Nu, Price, Hewitt, James, Luis, Kopov

D'oh! (Look for the easy answer.)

2. Which one of the following must be false?

    (A) Price swims in lane 5.
    (B) Price swims in lane 7.
    (C) Markson swims in lane 2.
    (D) Kopov swims in lane 3.
    (E) James swims in lane 6.

Follow the chain & identify who's in "could be" land, and who is not.

3. If James swims in lane 1, then each of the following could be true EXCEPT:

    (A) Kopov swims in a lower-numbered lane than Hewitt.
    (B) Luis swims in a lower-numbered lane than Hewitt.
    (C) Markson swims in a higher-numbered lane than Hewitt.
    (D) Kopov swims in a lower-numbered lane than Price.
    (E) Luis swims in a lowered-numbered lane than Markson.

Follow the chain & identify who's left for could be answers.

4. If Price swims in lane 3, which one of the following could be true?

    (A) Kopov swims in lane 2.
    (B) James swims in lane 6.
    (C) Luis swims in lane 2.
    (D) Nu swims in lane 1.
    (E) Kopov swims in lane 7.

Make it more challenging: start at the bottom.

5. Which of the following could be a partial and accurate list of swimmers matched with the lanes in which they swim?

    (A) lane 1: Nu; lane 2: Markson; lane 6: Luis
    (B) lane 5: James; lane 6: Kopov; lane 7: Luis
    (C) lane 3: Luis; lane 4: Hewitt; lane 5: James
    (D) lane 4: Hewitt; lane 5: Luis; lane 7: Kopov
    (E) lane 2: James; lane 5: Markson; lane 6: Kopov

PT30, S1, G2

The six messages on an answering machine were each left by one of Fleure, Greta, Hildy, Liam, Pasquale, or Theodore, consistent with the following:

> At most one person left more than one message.
> No person left more than three messages.
> If the first message is Hildy's, the last is Pasquale's.
> If Greta left any message, Fleure and Pasquale did also.
> If Fleure left any message, Pasquale and Theodore did also, all of Pasquale's preceding any of Theodore's.
> If Pasquale left any message, Hildy and Liam did also, all of Hildy's preceding any of Liam's.

Big Pause thoughts: What does that long chain mean? Which parts don't have to be triggered?

Use the easiest rules first.

6. Which one of the following could be a complete and accurate list of the messages left on the answering machine, from first to last?

    (A) Fleure's, Pasquale's, Theodore's, Hildy's, Pasquale's, Liam's
    (B) Greta's, Pasquale's, Theodore's, Theodore's, Hildy's, Liam's
    (C) Hildy's, Hildy's, Hildy's, Liam's, Pasquale's, Theodore's
    (D) Pasquale's, Hildy's, Fleure's, Liam's, Theodore's, Theodore's
    (E) Pasquale's, Hildy's, Theodore's, Hildy's, Liam's, Liam's

Don't look at the answer choices until you have figured out the answer by identifying all five elements that cannot be the answer.

7. The first and last messages on the answering machine could be the first and second messages left by which one of the following?

    (A) Fleure
    (B) Hildy
    (C) Liam
    (D) Pasquale
    (E) Theodore

Again, you should know the answer before looking at the answer choices.

8. If Greta left the fifth message, then which one of the following messages CANNOT have been left by Theodore?

    (A) the first message
    (B) the second message
    (C) the third message
    (D) the fourth message
    (E) the sixth message

9. Each of the following must be true EXCEPT:

    (A) Liam left at least one message.
    (B) Theodore left at least one message.
    (C) Hildy left at least one message.
    (D) Exactly one person left at least two messages.
    (E) At least four people left messages.

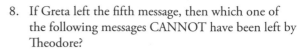

Figure out any restrictions, and who must be in and what rules apply to them.

10. If the only message Pasquale left is the fifth message, then which one of the following could be true?

    (A) Hildy left the first message.
    (B) Theodore left exactly two messages.
    (C) Liam left exactly two messages.
    (D) Liam left the second message.
    (E) Fleure left the third and fourth messages.

PT53, S2, G3

Detectives investigating a citywide increase in burglaries questioned exactly seven suspects—S, T, V, W, X, Y, and Z—each on a different one of seven consecutive days. Each suspect was questioned exactly once. Any suspect who confessed did so while being questioned. The investigation conformed to the following:

T was questioned on day three.
The suspect questioned on day four did not confess.
S was questioned after W was questioned.
Both X and V were questioned after Z was questioned.
No suspects confessed after W was questioned.
Exactly two suspects confessed after T was questioned.

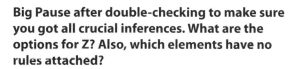

Big Pause after double-checking to make sure you got all crucial inferences. What are the options for Z? Also, which elements have no rules attached?

There's no Orientation question, but the first question should go quickly if your setup is complete. If not, go back!

12. Which one of the following could be true?

(F) X was questioned on day one.
(G) V was questioned on day two.
(H) Z was questioned on day four.
(I) W was questioned on day five.
(J) S was questioned on day six.

Remember that Z's options are limited. "Could be true EXCEPT" translates to…?

13. If Z was the second suspect to confess, then each of the following statements could be true EXCEPT:

(A) T confessed.
(B) T did not confess.
(C) V did not confess.
(D) X confessed.
(E) Y did not confess.

Sketch it out and anticipate the could be elements at play.

14. If Y was questioned after V but before X, then which one of the following could be true?

(A) V did not confess.
(B) Y confessed.
(C) X did not confess.
(D) X was questioned on day four.
(E) Z was questioned on day two.

See your inferences pay off!

15. Which one of the following suspects must have been questioned before T was questioned?

(A) V
(B) W
(C) X
(D) Y
(E) Z

For the next 2 questions, use "who's left?" thinking to get you started.

16. If X and Y both confessed, then each of the following could be true EXCEPT:

(A) V confessed.
(B) X was questioned on day five.
(C) Y was questioned on day one.
(D) Z was questioned on day one.
(E) Z did not confess.

17. If neither X nor V confessed, then which one of the following must be true?

(A) T confessed.
(B) V was questioned on day two.
(C) X was questioned on day four.
(D) Y confessed.
(E) Z did not confess.

One more question on next page…

These questions are meant to be time-consuming, so take your time! Re-do the diagram without this rule; then look for an answer that creates an exact replica of your original diagram.

Try a question that we wrote for this game:

18. Which of the following, if substituted for the rule that exactly two suspects confessed after T was questioned, would have the same effect both in determining the order in which suspects were questioned and in identifying which suspects confessed during questioning?

(A) The final suspect to confess was the sixth suspect questioned.

(B) W and the suspect questioned immediately before W were the last two suspects to confess.

(C) W was the last suspect to confess.

(D) The suspects questioned fifth and sixth both confessed.

(E) S was questioned last and immediately after W.

Eight students—R, S, T, V, W, X, Y and Z—are paired up into four teams—the Green team, the Indigo team, the Jade team, and the Purple team. Each team will have one leader and one assistant. A student's position is defined by both team and assigned role. The following conditions apply:

V is assigned to the Jade team, but R is not.
W and Y are assigned to the same team.
If S is an assistant, S is teamed with T.
If S is a leader, S is teamed with X.
R is not assigned to be a leader.

Big Pause: Forget the teams, think about the four pairings.

Challenge: Try getting to the correct answer using only the first four rules.

1. Which of the following could be a list of the leaders for the four teams?

    (A) Green team: W; Indigo team: S;
         Jade team: V; Purple team: R
    (B) Green team: W; Indigo team: S;
         Jade team: V; Purple team: X
    (C) Green team: V; Indigo team: S;
         Jade team: T; Purple team: Z
    (D) Green team: S; Indigo team: T;
         Jade team: V; Purple team: Z
    (E) Green team: W; Indigo team: S;
         Jade team: V; Purple team: T

2. If X is assigned to be an assistant for the Jade team, which one of the following can be determined?

    (A) the students assigned to the Green team
    (B) the students assigned to the Indigo team
    (C) the students assigned to the Purple team
    (D) which student each student is paired with
    (E) the role—either leader or assistant—that each student is assigned to

Eliminate three using previous work, then either check your pairing diagram or test out one answer.

3. Which of the following must be false?

    (A) W is assigned to be a leader.
    (B) Y is assigned to be a leader.
    (C) X is assigned to be a leader.
    (D) T and Z are teamed together.
    (E) V and Z are teamed together.

Look at your pairing diagram and predict how the correct answer will work.

4. Which of the following, if true, determines the pairings, though not necessarily the assigned positions, for each team?

    (A) S is teamed with T.
    (B) S is teamed with X.
    (C) V is teamed with Z.
    (D) R is teamed with Z.
    (E) R is teamed with X.

Frame it, look for three easy eliminations, and then...

5. If either S or V, but not both, is assigned a leadership role, which of the following must be false?

    (A) Neither W nor Z is assigned a leadership role.
    (B) Neither X nor Y is assigned a leadership role.
    (C) Neither T nor Z is assigned a leadership role
    (D) Neither S nor Z is assigned an assistant role.
    (E) Neither T nor W is assigned an assistant role.

6. If neither T nor X nor Y is assigned to a leadership position, how many different pairs of students can be assigned to the Indigo team?

    (A) 1
    (B) 2
    (C) 3
    (D) 4
    (E) 5

SET 6

Allow yourself only **35 minutes** (or less) for these four games.

Exactly eight rock bands—M, N, O, P, R, S, T, and V—perform consecutively at a showcase on Friday night. No band performs more than once, and no two bands perform simultaneously. The following conditions apply:

> T and P both perform at some time before O.
> S performs at some time before R.
> T performs at some time before N.
> V performs at some time after S.
> M performs at some time before V and at some time after O.

Try using the "String Technique" (your diagram) to eliminate answers.

1. Which of the following could be the order of the performances from first to last?

   (A) P, T, O, M, R, S, V, N
   (B) T, N, M, P, S, O, V, R
   (C) P, T, N, O, M, V, S, R
   (D) T, P, N, O, S, M, V, R
   (E) T, N, O, S, P, R, M, V

Use the first couple of questions to verify the accuracy of your diagram. This should go quickly!

2. Which of the following must be true?

   (A) At least four bands perform at some time after P.
   (B) At least four bands perform at some time after T.
   (C) At least two bands perform at some time after M.
   (D) At least two bands perform at some time before N.
   (E) At least two bands perform at some time before R.

Use the first couple of questions to verify the accuracy of your diagram. This should go quickly!

3. If P performs fifth, then each of the following could be true EXCEPT:

   (A) R is the sixth band to perform.
   (B) N is the fourth band to perform.
   (C) S is the second band to perform.
   (D) T is the third band to perform.
   (E) R performs at some time before N but at some time after T.

Build a new tree and make sure you don't lose any of original rules.

4. If S performs at some time after N, and P performs at some time before T, which of the following could be true?

   (A) N performs earlier than P but later than O.
   (B) R performs earlier than M but later than N.
   (C) O performs earlier than N but later than S.
   (D) R performs later than S but earlier than T.
   (E) P performs earlier than O but later than R.

Beware of zig-zags on this one!

5. Each of the following could be true EXCEPT:

   (A) V performs earlier than N.
   (B) R performs earlier than T.
   (C) N performs earlier than P.
   (D) S performs later than O.
   (E) M performs earlier than P.

Draw all absolute inferences first; then use clouds to help organize the uncertainty.

6. If T performs third and V performs sixth, then exactly how many different orders are there in which the bands can perform?

   (A) 1
   (B) 2
   (C) 3
   (D) 4
   (E) 5

Think about the earliest placement for N and the latest for S to determine max distance.

7. There can be at most how many bands that perform after N but before S?

   (A) 1
   (B) 2
   (C) 3
   (D) 4
   (E) 5

PT31, S1, G3

During a single week, from Monday through Friday, tours will be conducted of a company's three divisions—Operations, Production, Sales. Exactly five tours will be conducted that week, one each day. The schedule of tours for the week must conform to the following restrictions:

> Each division is toured at least once.
> The Operations division is not toured on Monday.
> The Production division is not toured on Wednesday.
> The Sales division is toured on two consecutive days, and on no other days.
> If the Operations division is toured on Thursday, then the Production division is toured on Friday.

Framing is definitely possible, but let's try it this time around without frames.

You know the drill...mind the chunk first!

14. Which one of the following CANNOT be true of the week's tour schedule?

   (A) The division that is toured on Monday is also toured on Tuesday.
   (B) The division that is toured on Monday is also toured on Friday.
   (C) The division that is toured on Tuesday is also toured on Thursday.
   (D) The division that is toured on Wednesday is also toured on Friday.
   (E) The division that is toured on Thursday is also toured on Friday.

Challenge: Try this unusual conditional question without touching your pencil. Remember, options are quite limited!

15. If in addition to the Sales division one other division is toured on two consecutive days, then it could be true of the week's tour schedule both that the

   (A) Production division is toured on Monday and that the Operations division is toured on Thursday
   (B) Production division is toured on Tuesday and that the Sales division is toured on Wednesday
   (C) Operations division is toured on Tuesday and that the Production division is toured on Friday
   (D) Sales division is toured on Monday and that the Operations division is toured on Friday
   (E) Sales division is toured on Wednesday and that the Production division is toured on Friday

Challenge: Try this unusual conditional question without touching your pencil. Remember, options are quite limited!

16. If in the week's tour schedule the division that is toured on Tuesday is also toured on Friday, then for which one of the following days must a tour of the Production division be scheduled?

   (A) Monday
   (B) Tuesday
   (C) Wednesday
   (D) Thursday
   (E) Friday

Don't dawdle before jumping into the answer choices—infer what you can and get going!

17. If in the week's tour schedule the division that is toured on Monday is not the division that is toured on Tuesday, then which one of the following could be true of the week's schedule?

   (A) A tour of the Sales division is scheduled for some day earlier in the week than is any tour of the Production division.
   (B) A tour of the Operations division is scheduled for some day earlier in the week than is any tour of the Production division.
   (C) The Sales division is toured on Monday.
   (D) The Production division is toured on Tuesday.
   (E) The Operations division is toured on Wednesday.

Again, the conditional gives us pretty limited options—sketch them out and keep it scrappy.

18. If in the week's tour schedule the division that is toured on Tuesday is also toured on Wednesday, then which one of the following must be true of the week's tour schedule?

   (A) The Production division is toured on Monday.
   (B) The Operations division is toured on Tuesday.
   (C) The Sales division is toured on Wednesday.
   (D) The Sales division is toured on Thursday.
   (E) The Production division is toured on Friday.

One more question on next page...

Start by asking yourself what scenarios the original rule prevents. Remember, these questions are meant to be time-consuming.

Now try a question that we wrote for this game:

19. Which of the following, if substituted for the rule that if the Operations division is toured on Thursday, then the Production division is toured on Friday, would have the same effect in determining when each division is toured?

    (A) If the Production division is toured on Friday, the Operations division is toured on Thursday.

    (B) If the Operations division is not toured on Thursday, the Production division is not toured on Friday.

    (C) The Production and Operations divisions must be toured on consecutive days at least once during the week.

    (D) The Production division cannot be toured on consecutive days.

    (E) If the Operations division is toured on consecutive days, one of those days must be Wednesday.

MANHATTAN
LSAT

PT35, S3, G4

Exactly seven professors—Madison, Nilsson, Orozco, Paton, Robinson, Sarkis, and Togo—were hired in the years 1989 through 1995. Each professor has one or more specialities, and any two professors hired in the same year or in consecutive years do not have a specialty in common. The professors were hired according to the following conditions:

> Madison was hired in 1993, Robinson in 1991.
> There is at least one specialty that Madison, Orozco, and Togo have in common.
> Nilsson shares a specialty with Robinson.
> Paton and Sarkis were each hired at least one year before Madison and at least one year after Nilsson.
> Orozco, who shares a specialty with Sarkis, was hired in 1990.

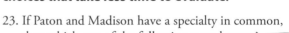

Make sure you're clear on the question task!

18. Which one of the following is a complete and accurate list of the professors who could have been hired in the years 1989 through 1991?

(A) Nilsson, Orozco, Robinson
(B) Orozco, Robinson, Sarkis
(C) Nilsson, Orozco, Paton, Robinson
(D) Nilsson, Orozco, Paton, Sarkis
(E) Orozco, Paton, Robinson, Sarkis

Eliminating the 4 "must be false" is usually the way to go, but when options are limited, it's easy enough to spot the "could be true."

19. If exactly one professor was hired in 1991, then which one of the following could be true?

(A) Madison and Paton share a specialty.
(B) Robinson and Sarkis share a specialty.
(C) Paton was hired exactly one year after Orozco.
(D) Exactly one professor was hired in 1994.
(E) Exactly two professors were hired in 1993.

This is a giveaway with a solid setup.

20. Which one of the following must be false?

(A) Nilsson was hired in 1989.
(B) Paton was hired in 1990.
(C) Paton was hired in 1991.
(D) Sarkis was hired in 1992.
(E) Togo was hired in 1994.

Yet another one—time in the bank!

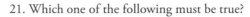

21. Which one of the following must be true?

(A) Orozco was hired before Paton.
(B) Paton was hired before Sarkis.
(C) Sarkis was hired before Robinson.
(D) Robinson was hired before Sarkis.
(E) Madison was hired before Sarkis.

Remind yourself of the impact of the "specialties rule," and save time by starting with the answer choices that take less time to evaluate.

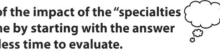

22. If exactly two professors were hired in 1992, then which one of the following could be true?

(A) Orozco, Paton, and Togo share a specialty.
(B) Madison, Paton, and Togo share a specialty.
(C) Exactly two professors were hired in 1991.
(D) Exactly two professors were hired in 1993.
(E) Paton was hired in 1991.

Remind yourself of the impact of the "specialties rule," and save time by starting with the answer choices that take less time to evaluate.

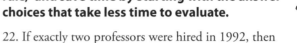

23. If Paton and Madison have a specialty in common, then which one of the following must be true?

(A) Nilsson does not share a specialty with Paton.
(B) Exactly one professor was hired in 1990.
(C) Exactly one professor was hired in 1991.
(D) Exactly two professors were hired in each of two years.
(E) Paton was hired at least one year before Sarkis.

One more question on next page…

Start by considering the impact of the original rule; the correct answer will have the same impact.

And try a question that we wrote for this game:

24. Which of the following, if substituted for the rule that there is at least one specialty that Madison, Orozco, and Togo have in common, would have the same consequence in determining when each professor was hired?

    (A) Togo was hired at some point after Madison.

    (B) A professor was hired in 1995.

    (C) Madison and Togo each share a specialty with Orozco.

    (D) Paton was hired at least three years before Togo.

    (E) Madison was hired in a year immediately before or immediately after a year in which no other professor was hired, but not both.

MANHATTAN
LSAT

PT36, S4, G3

Gutierrez, Hoffman, Imamura, Kelly, Lapas, and Moore ride a bus together. Each sits facing forward in a different one of the six seats on the left side of the bus. The seats are in consecutive rows that are numbered 1, 2, and 3 from front to back. Each row has exactly two seats: a window seat and an aisle seat. The following conditions must apply:

> Hoffman occupies the aisle seat immediately behind Gutierrez's aisle seat.
> If Moore occupies an aisle seat, Hoffman sits in the same row as Lapas.
> If Gutierrez sits in the same row as Kelly, Moore occupies the seat immediately and directly behind Imamura's seat.
> If Kelly occupies a window seat, Moore sits in row 3.
> If Kelly sits in row 3, Imamura sits in row 1.

Be sure you've notated these rules correctly—there are a lot of them!

This is no easy Orientation question. Don't panic; use it as an opportunity to "own" the rules.

14. Which one of the following could be true?

(A) Imamura sits in row 2, whereas Kelly sits in row 3.
(B) Gutierrez sits in the same row as Kelly, immediately and directly behind Moore.
(C) Gutierrez occupies a window seat in the same row as Lapas.
(D) Moore occupies an aisle seat in the same row as Lapas.
(E) Kelly and Moore both sit in row 3.

Tough question. Make it tougher by working from (E) up.

15. If Lapas and Kelly each occupy a window seat, then which one of the following could be true?

(A) Moore occupies the aisle seat in row 3.
(B) Imamura occupies the window seat in row 3.
(C) Gutierrez sits in the same row as Kelly.
(D) Gutierrez sits in the same row as Moore.
(E) Moore sits in the same row as Lapas.

Notice how definitive the answers are. Follow the chain until you reach that level of specificity.

16. If Moore sits in row 1, then which one of the following must be true?

(A) Hoffman sits in row 2.
(B) Imamura sits in row 2.
(C) Imamura sits in row 3.
(D) Kelly sits in row 1.
(E) Lapas sits in row 3.

Since the answer is a could be false, be sure to notate who's left after following the chain.

17. If Kelly occupies the aisle seat in row 3, then each of the following must be true EXCEPT:

(A) Gutierrez sits in the same row as Imamura.
(B) Hoffman sits in the same row as Lapas.
(C) Lapas occupies a window seat.
(D) Moore occupies a window seat.
(E) Gutierrez sits in row 1.

Tough question! Follow the chain; it ends with some limited options.

18. If neither Gutierrez nor Imamura sits in row 1, then which one of the following could be true?

(A) Hoffman sits in row 2.
(B) Kelly sits in row 2.
(C) Moore sits in row 2.
(D) Imamura occupies an aisle seat.
(E) Moore occupies an aisle seat.

STOP

Set 7

Allow yourself a full **35 minutes** for this tough section.

Doctor X will see exactly five of seven patients—K, L, M, N, O, P, and Q—that are all waiting in the lobby. She will see these patients one at a time and in order. The following conditions apply:

> She will see both K and M, and she will see K before M.
> If she does not see O, she will see P.
> She will see Q or P, but not both.
> If she sees either L or O, she will see them after M.
> If she sees N, she must see N first.

1. Which of the following could be the order of patients that Doctor X sees, from first to last?

    (A) N, Q, K, M, P
    (B) N, Q, K, O, M
    (C) N, Q, K, M, L
    (D) N, Q, K, M, O
    (E) N, Q, M, K, O

Use this unconditional question to confirm your setup, and defer judgment.

2. Each of the following could be true EXCEPT:

    (A) The doctor sees Q first.
    (B) The doctor sees M second.
    (C) The doctor sees K fourth.
    (D) The doctor sees P last.
    (E) The doctor sees Q last.

Follow the chain; then scan rules to see which is triggered.

3. If the doctor sees K third, which of the following must be true?

    (A) She sees N first.
    (B) She sees Q second.
    (C) She sees L last.
    (D) She sees P.
    (E) She sees O.

Look for elements that are connected by the rules to speed things up.

4. Which of the following must be true?

    (A) If the doctor does not see L, she will also not see Q.
    (B) If the doctor does not see N, she will also not see P.
    (C) If the doctor does not see Q, she will also not see P.
    (D) If the doctor does not see Q, she will also not see O.
    (E) If the doctor does not see O, she will also not see Q.

Follow the chain and go for easy eliminations.

5. If the doctor sees M fourth, which of the following could be true?

    (A) The doctor sees K first.
    (B) The doctor sees K second.
    (C) The doctor sees P first.
    (D) The doctor sees Q last.
    (E) The doctor sees P last.

Think first about whether each choice will determine the patients seen; THEN think about order.

Alt: Put pencil to paper, but only sketch in the elements in the answer choices and consider who's left mentally.

6. Which of the following, if true, would determine which patients the doctor will see and the order in which she will see them?

    (A) The doctor sees N first and P third.
    (B) The doctor sees N first and Q third.
    (C) The doctor sees K first and M second.
    (D) The doctor sees K first and O fourth.
    (E) The doctor sees K second and M fourth.

PT36, S4, G4

An airline has four flights from New York to Sarasota—flights 1, 2, 3, and 4. On each flight there is exactly one pilot and exactly one co-pilot. The pilots are Fazio, Germond, Kyle, and Lopez; the co-pilots are Reich, Simon, Taylor, and Umlas. Each pilot and co-pilot is assigned to exactly one flight.

> The flights take off in numerical order.
> Fazio's flight takes off before Germond's, and at least one other flight takes off between their flights.
> Kyle is assigned to flight 2.
> Lopez is assigned to the same flight as Umlas.

Not many elements and some restrictive rules: take your time.

As usual, the first two questions are easy IF you have a solid diagram.

19. Which one of the following pilot and co-pilot teams could be assigned to flight 1?

    (A) Fazio and Reich
    (B) Fazio and Umlas
    (C) Germond and Reich
    (D) Germond and Umlas
    (E) Lopez and Taylor

20. If Reich's flight is later than Umlas's, which one of the following statements cannot be true?

    (A) Fazio's flight is earlier than Simon's.
    (B) Kyle's flight is earlier than Reich's.
    (C) Kyle's flight is earlier than Taylor's.
    (D) Simon's flight is earlier than Reich's.
    (E) Taylor's flight is earlier than Kyle's.

21. If Lopez's flight is earlier than Germond's, which one of the following statements could be false?

    (A) Fazio's flight is earlier than Umlas's.
    (B) Germond is assigned to flight 4.
    (C) Either Reich's or Taylor's flight is earlier than Umlas's.
    (D) Simon's flight is earlier than Umlas's.
    (E) Umlas is assigned to flight 3.

Count 'em up!

22. What is the maximum possible number of different pilot and co-pilot teams, any one of which could be assigned to flight 4?

    (A) 2
    (B) 3
    (C) 4
    (D) 5
    (E) 6

Follow the chain and identify who's left.

23. If Simon's flight is later than Lopez's, then which one of the following statements could be false?

    (A) Germond's flight is later than Reich's.
    (B) Germond's flight is later than Taylor's.
    (C) Lopez's flight is later than Taylor's.
    (D) Taylor's flight is later than Reich's.
    (E) Umlas's flight is later than Reich's.

Focus on eliminating answers.

Here's a devilish one that we've written for this game:

24. Each of the following, if substituted for the rule that Fazio's flight takes off before Germond's, and at least one other flight takes off between their flights, would have the same effect on the assignment of pilots and co-pilots EXCEPT:

    (A) Fazio's flight takes off first.
    (B) Fazio's flight takes off before Kyle's.
    (C) Fazio's and Germond's flights do not take off consecutively, but Fazio's and Kyle's do.
    (D) Lopez's flight takes off immediately before or immediately after Germond's.
    (E) Lopez's flight takes off after Fazio's, and at least one other flight takes off between their flights.

PT29, S3, G4

Exactly six piano classes are given sequentially on Monday: two with more than one student and four with exactly one student. Exactly four females—Gimena, Holly, Iyanna, and Kate—and five males—Leung, Nate, Oscar, Pedro, and Saul—attend these classes. Each student attends exactly one class. The following must obtain:

> Iyanna and Leung together constitute one class.
> Pedro and exactly two others together constitute one class.
> Kate is the first female, but not the first student, to attend a class.
> Gimena's class is at some time after Iyanna's but at sometime before Pedro's.
> Oscar's class is at some time after Gimena's.

Make sure your diagram contains all nine people.

This should be easy. If not, go back and work on your diagram.

20. Which one of the following students could attend the first class?

    (A) Holly
    (B) Leung
    (C) Oscar
    (D) Pedro
    (E) Saul

Identify where she can't go and eliminate.

21. Which one of the following is a complete and accurate list of classes any one of which could be the class Gimena attends?

    (A) the fourth, the fifth
    (B) the fourth, the sixth
    (C) the second, the fourth, the fifth
    (D) the third, the fifth, the sixth
    (E) the second, the third, the fourth

Look for easy eliminations.

22. Which one of the following pairs of students could be in the class with Pedro?

    (A) Gimena and Holly
    (B) Holly and Saul
    (C) Kate and Nate
    (D) Leung and Oscar
    (E) Nate and Saul

23. If Oscar and Pedro do not attend the same class as each other, then which one of the following could be true?

    (A) Gimena attends the fifth class.
    (B) Holly attends the third class.
    (C) Iyanna attends the fourth class.
    (D) Nate attends the fifth class.
    (E) Saul attends the second class.

Re-draw your diagram!

24. Suppose the condition that Oscar attends a class after Gimena is replaced with the condition that Oscar attends a class before Gimena and after Kate. If all the other conditions remain the same, then which class must Holly attend?

    (A) the second
    (B) the third
    (C) the fourth
    (D) the fifth
    (E) the sixth

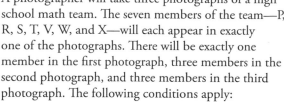

A photographer will take three photographs of a high school math team. The seven members of the team—P, R, S, T, V, W, and X—will each appear in exactly one of the photographs. There will be exactly one member in the first photograph, three members in the second photograph, and three members in the third photograph. The following conditions apply:

P does not appear in a later photo than does T or X.
Be careful!
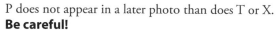
R and S will appear in the same photograph together.
V and X will not be photographed together.

1. Which of the following could be the assignment of members to photographs?

    (A) Photo 1: V
         Photo 2: T, R, S
         Photo 3: P, W, X
    (B) Photo 1: V
         Photo 2: R, S
         Photo 3: P, T, W, X
    (C) Photo 1: V
         Photo 2: P, R, S
         Photo 3: T, W, X
    (D) Photo 1: P
         Photo 2: S, T, X
         Photo 3: R, V, W
    (E) Photo 1: P
         Photo 2: T, V, X
         Photo 3: R, S, W

2. Which of the following must be false?

    (A) W appears in Photo 2.
    (B) T appears in Photo 1.
    (C) P appears in Photo 3.
    (D) V appears after X.
    (E) X appears after V.

3. If P is photographed with S, in how many different ways can all seven members be assigned to photographs?

    (A) 1
    (B) 2
    (C) 3
    (D) 4
    (E) 5

Follow the inference chain and then note who's left.

4. If R is in an earlier photograph than X, how many different team members could be in the first photograph?

    (A) 1
    (B) 2
    (C) 3
    (D) 4
    (E) 5

Tough question! Before diving in, consider what the correct answer will "have to be."

5. Which of the following pairs of assignments would determine the team members for each photograph?

    (A) V is in Photo 1 and R is in Photo 2.
    (B) V is in Photo 1 and R is in Photo 3.
    (C) P is in Photo 1 and R is in Photo 2.
    (D) P is in Photo 1 and V is in Photo 3.
    (E) W is in Photo 1 and R is in Photo 2.

Try framing the two ways you can arrange the chunks.

6. If the rule that V and X will not be photographed together is replaced with a rule that V and X must be photographed together, each of the following could be true EXCEPT:

    (A) W appears in Photo 1.
    (B) W appears in Photo 2.
    (C) W appears in Photo 3.
    (D) P appears in Photo 2.
    (E) P appears in Photo 3.

MANHATTAN   561
LSAT

Set 8

PT38, S2, G1

A car drives into the center ring of a circus and exactly eight clowns—Q, R, S, T, V, W, Y, and Z—get out of the car, one clown at a time. The order in which the clowns get out of the car is consistent with the following conditions:

> V gets out at some time before both Y and Q.
> Q gets out at some time after Z.
> T gets out at some time before V but at some time after R.
> S gets out at some time after V.
> R gets out at some time before W.

Use the string!

1. Which one of the following could be the order, from first to last, in which the clowns get out of the car?

   (A) T, Z, V, R, W, Y, S, Q
   (B) Z, R, W, Q, T, V, Y, S
   (C) R, W, T, V, Q, Z, S, Y
   (D) Z, W, R, T, V, Y, Q, S
   (E) R, W, T, V, Z, S, Y, Q

2. Which one of the following could be true?

   (A) Y is the second clown to get out of the car.
   (B) R is the third clown to get out of the car.
   (C) Q is the fourth clown to get out of the car.
   (D) S is the fifth clown to get out of the car.
   (E) V is the sixth clown to get out of the car.

Follow the chain and identify who's left and who is the most "free" element among them.

3. If Z is the seventh clown to get out of the car, then which one of the following could be true?

   (A) R is the second clown to get out of the car.
   (B) T is the fourth clown to get out of the car.
   (C) W is the fifth clown to get out of the car.
   (D) V is the sixth clown to get out of the car.
   (E) Y is the eighth clown to get out of the car.

Get scrappy: See how few inferences you can make to get to the must be true answer.

4. If T is the fourth clown to get out of the car, then which one of the following must be true?

   (A) R is the first clown to get out of the car.
   (B) Z is the second clown to get out of the car.
   (C) W is the third clown to get out of the car.
   (D) V is the fifth clown to get out of the car.
   (E) Y is the seventh clown to get out of the car.

An EXCEPT question! What characteristic will the correct answer choice have?

5. If Q is the fifth clown to get out of the car, then each of the following could be true EXCEPT:

   (A) Z is the first clown to get out of the car.
   (B) T is the second clown to get out of the car.
   (C) V is the third clown to get out of the car.
   (D) W is the fourth clown to get out of the car.
   (E Y is the sixth clown to get out of the car.

Get scrappy: See how few inferences you can make to get to the must be true answer.

6. If R is the second clown to get out of the car, which one of the following must be true?

   (A) S gets out of the car at some time before T does.
   (B) T gets out of the car at some time before W does.
   (C) W gets out of the car at some time before V does.
   (D) Y gets out of the car at some time before Q does.
   (E) Z gets out of the car at some time before W does.

Challenge yourself to re-draw the diagram as quickly as possible. You're getting faster!

7. If V gets out of the car at some time before Z does, then which one of the following could be true?

   (A) R is the second clown to get out of the car.
   (B) T is the fourth clown to get out of the car.
   (C) Q is the fourth clown to get out of the car.
   (D) V is the fifth clown to get out of the car.
   (E) Z is the sixth clown to get out of the car.

The Mizotron Corporation has exactly six managers: Holmes, Jin, Kaufman, Lu, Orr, and Pearson. Each manager has expertise in one or more of the following three areas: finance, marketing, technology. None of the managers has expertise in any other area. The following conditions apply:

Challenge: We taught you this game using the managers are the base; try it the other way.

Jin does not share any area of expertise with Orr.
Holmes has fewer areas of expertise than Lu.
Jin, Kaufman, and Pearson all have expertise in finance.
Holmes and Pearson have exactly two areas of expertise in common.
Orr does not have expertise in marketing.

1. Which one of the following pairs of managers must have at least one area of expertise in common?

   (A) Holmes and Kaufman
   (B) Kaufman and Orr
   (C) Lu and Orr
   (D) Holmes and Jin
   (E) Jin and Orr

2. For how many of the six managers is it possible to determine exactly which of the three areas of expertise they have?

   (A) one
   (B) two
   (C) three
   (D) four
   (E) five

3. Which of the following must be false?

   (A) Exactly four of the six managers have exactly two areas of expertise.
   (B) Exactly one of the six managers has exactly two areas of expertise.
   (C) Exactly one of the six managers has exactly one area of expertise.
   (D) Exactly three of the six managers have exactly one area of expertise.
   (E) Exactly four of the six managers have exactly one area of expertise.

When you are down to two answers, notice the differences.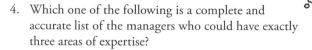

4. Which one of the following is a complete and accurate list of the managers who could have exactly three areas of expertise?

   (A) Holmes, Kaufman, Lu, Pearson
   (B) Kaufman, Lu, Pearson
   (C) Holmes, Lu
   (D) Kaufman, Lu
   (E) Pearson

Defer judgment as you look for the must be false answer.

5. Which of the following must be false?

   (A) Both Jin and Pearson have expertise in marketing.
   (B) Both Lu and Orr have expertise in technology.
   (C) Both Holmes and Lu have expertise in marketing.
   (D) Both Holmes and Orr have expertise in finance.
   (E) Both Kaufman and Pearson have expertise in technology.

Work from largest answer down.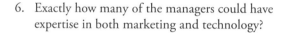

6. Exactly how many of the managers could have expertise in both marketing and technology?

   (A) two
   (B) three
   (C) four
   (D) five
   (E) six

PT12, S2, G3

Lara, Mendel, and Nastassia each buy at least one kind of food from a street vendor who sells only fruit cups, hot dogs, pretzels, and shish kebabs. They make their selections in accordance with the following restrictions:

None of the three buys more than one portion of each kind of food.

If any of the three buys a hot dog, that person does not also buy a shish kebab.

At least one of the three buys a hot dog, and at least one buys a pretzel.

Mendel buys a shish kebab.

Nastassia buys a fruit cup.

Neither Lara nor Nastassia buys a pretzel.

Mendel does not buy any kind of food that Nastassia buys.

If this first question is tough, work on your diagram some more.

12. Which one of the following statements must be true?

(A) Lara buys a hot dog.
(B) Lara buys a shish kebab.
(C) Mendel buys a hot dog.
(D) Mendel buys a pretzel.
(E) Nastassia buys a hot dog.

13. If the vendor charges $1 for each portion of food, what is the minimum amount the three people could spend?

(A) $3
(B) $4
(C) $5
(D) $6
(E) $7

Just add to the diagram you drew for the last question.

14. If the vendor charges $1 for each portion of food, what is the greatest amount the three people could spend?

(A) $5
(B) $6
(C) $7
(D) $8
(E) $9

15. If Lara and Mendel buy exactly two kinds of food each, which one of the following statements must be true?

(A) Lara buys a fruit cup.
(B) Lara buys a hot dog.
(C) Mendel buys a fruit cup.
(D) There is exactly one kind of food that Lara and Mendel both buy.
(E) There is exactly one kind of food that Lara and Nastassia both buy.

16. If Lara buys a shish kebab, which one of the following statements must be true?

(A) Lara buys a fruit cup.
(B) Mendel buys a fruit cup.
(C) Nastassia buys a hot dog.
(D) Nastassia buys exactly one kind of food.
(E) Exactly one person buys a fruit cup.

Re-draw your diagram.

17. Assume that the condition is removed that prevents a customer who buys a hot dog from buying a shish kebab but all other conditions remain the same. If the vendor charges $1 for each portion of food, what is the maximum amount the three people could spend?

(A) $5
(B) $6
(C) $7
(D) $8
(E) $9

MANHATTAN
LSAT

PT41, S2, G3

Each of the seven members of the board of directors—
Guzman, Hawking, Lepp, Miyauchi, Upchurch,
Wharton, and Zhu—serves on exactly one of two
committees—the finance committee or the incentives
committee. Only board members serve on these
committees. Committee membership is consistent with
the following conditions:

Take your time with this diagram.

> If Guzman serves on the finance committee, then
> Hawking serves on the incentives committee.
> If Lepp serves on the finance committee, then
> Miyauchi and Upchurch both serve on the
> incentives committee.
> Wharton serves on a different committee from the
> one on which Zhu serves.
> Upchurch serves on a different committee from the
> one on which Guzman serves.
> If Zhu serves on the finance committee, so does
> Hawking.

**Notice each mutually-exclusive pairs and
consider which side the two cannot be together.**

**Use your diagram. Don't forget that those not
listed are on incentives.**

13. Which one of the following could be a complete
    and accurate list of the members of the finance
    committee?

    (A) Guzman, Hawking, Miyauchi, Wharton
    (B) Guzman, Lepp, Zhu
    (C) Hawking, Miyauchi, Zhu
    (D) Hawking, Upchurch, Wharton, Zhu
    (E) Miyauchi, Upchurch, Wharton

**Challenge: Predict the elements at play by
identifying who on incentives forces other to
finance.**

14. Which of the following pairs of board members
    CANNOT both serve on the incentives committee?

    (A) Guzman and Hawking
    (B) Guzman and Wharton
    (C) Hawking and Wharton
    (D) Miyauchi and Upchurch
    (E) Miyauchi and Wharton

**User your mutually-exclusive pairs to eliminate a
couple of answers; then try a scenario.**

15. What is the maximum number of members on the
    finance committee?

    (A) two
    (B) three
    (C) four
    (D) five
    (E) six

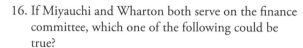

**Draw a t-chart and note who's left below it. Then
work wrong-to-right.**

16. If Miyauchi and Wharton both serve on the finance
    committee, which one of the following could be
    true?

    (A) Guzman and Lepp both serve on the finance
        committee.
    (B) Guzman and Upchurch both serve on the
        incentives committee.
    (C) Hawking and Zhu both serve on the finance
        committee.
    (D) Lepp and Upchurch both serve on the
        incentives committee.
    (E) Zhu and Upchurch both serve on the finance
        committee.

**Follow the chain, then remember it's a must be
true question.**

17. If Guzman serves on the incentives committee, then
    which one of the following must be true?

    (A) Hawking serves on the finance committee.
    (B) Lepp serves on the incentives committee.
    (C) Miyauchi serves on the finance committee.
    (D) Wharton serves on the incentives
        committee.
    (E) Zhu serves on the finance committee.

Coached Replays Answer Key

Set 1

PT7, S2, G2	Manhattan LSAT – Doctor Rotations	Manhattan LSAT – Violin Concert
8. B	1. C	1. E
9. C	2. C	2. A
10. E	3. E	3. E
11. E	4. A	4. D
12. E	5. B	5. E
		6. C
		7. D

Set 2

PT1, S2, G1	PT16, S1, G1	PT30, S1, G3	Manhattan LSAT – Filmmaker's Songs
1. B	1. D	11. B	1. C
2. A	2. E	12. A	2. B
3. B	3. A	13. B	3. E
4. E	4. E	14. E	4. A
5. E	5. C	15. B	5. D
6. C	6. D	16. A	6. E
7. E		*17. E	

Set 3

PT18, S1, G1	PT36, S4, G2	PT32, S3, G3	PT52, S2, G2
1. C	7. E	12. A	8. B
2. D	8. A	13. E	9. E
3. D	9. C	14. A	10. A
4. A	10. C	15. E	11. D
5. C	11. A	16. C	12. C
6. E	12. A	17. C	
	13. B	18. D	

Set 4

PT19, S1, G1	Manhattan LSAT – Publishing Novels	PT51, S4, G2	PT32 S3, G4
1. B	1. B	6. B	19. E
2. E	2. C	7. C	20. B
3. C	3. E	8. A	21. D
4. E	4. B	9. D	22. B
5. D	5. C	10. D	23. A
6. D	6. A		24. D
7. C	7. C		

MANHATTAN
LSAT

Coached Replays Answer Key

Set 5

Manhattan LSAT – Swimming Race	PT30, S1, G2	PT53, S2, G3	Manhattan LSAT – Colored Teams
1. B	6. D	12. B	1. E
2. C	7. A	13. E	2. D
3. C	8. A	14. A	3. D
4. C	9. D	15. E	4. E
5. E	10. C	16. A	5. C
		17. D	6. C
		*18. D	

Set 6

Manhattan LSAT – Rock Band Showcase	PT31, S1, G3	PT35 S3, G4	PT36, S4, G3
1. D	14. C	18. C	14. E
2. B	15. B	19. A	15. A
3. A	16. A	20. E	16. D
4. B	17. E	21. D	17. B
5. E	18. A	22. A	18. C
6. D	*19. E	23. E	
7. C		*24. B	

Set 7

Manhattan LSAT – Doctor X	PT36, S4, G4	PT29, S3, G4	Manhattan LSAT – Math Photos
1. D	19. A	20. E	1. C
2. C	20. C	21. A	2. B
3. A	21. D	22. B	3. A
4. E	22. C	23. D	4. C
5. B	23. D	24. E	5. E
6. B	*24. C		6. E

Set 8

PT38, S2, G1	Manhattan LSAT – Mizotron Corporation	PT12, S2, G3	PT41, S2, G3
1. E	1. C	12. D	13. E
2. D	2. B	13. B	14. C
3. C	3. E	14. B	15. C
4. D	4. B	15. A	16. D
5. D	5. D	16. C	17. B
6. E	6. C	17. C	
7. E			

Appendix B

of

Logic Games

Logic Game Solutions

From PrepTest 40 On...

Logic Game Solutions

On the following pages you will find solutions to all the logic games from PrepTests 40 through 66 (and online you'll find solutions to any LSATs released subsequent to PT66). They are done in a coded short-hand, so be sure to take a moment to learn the code below before reading on. In writing these solutions, we initially hoped to authentically show you the work an expert would do—particularly on paper—to solve these specific games in real time. However, it soon became apparent that such solutions would not be particularly enlightening, since top test-takers may write fewer notations on their paper than others. Thus we have tried to show a sophisticated approach to each game—for those who handled the game alright but want to see if there was a faster way to handle the game—while at the same time explaining the games clearly—for those who are lost about how a game, question, or answer works (or does not). Some solutions lean more one way or the other.

As we've stressed throughout this book, there is rarely (never?) one right way to solve a game. Do not despair if you find that you solved the game in a totally different manner than we show. Furthermore, these solutions were written and edited by a specific pair of teachers. If you were to ask another pair to draw up solutions to these same games, they would invariably approach some of the games quite differently. This variation would probably be most acute in the Big Pause and To Frame or Not to Frame discussions for each game.

If you find that your solution to a game is more elegant than the one written here, go right ahead and post it on our forums—www.manhattanlsat.com/forums. We're interested.

Key to the Code:

Darker shade = information provided explicitly by the game's rules, by a specific question stem, or by the information in a given answer choice

Lighter shade = inferences made on the basis of that provided information

Ⱥ = answer eliminated

Ⓐ = correct answer

"Prev. work" = an answer choice was eliminated/selected based on a consideration of scenarios that were written for previous problems. The problem # used is listed in parentheses.

MANHATTAN
LSAT

A
Ⓑ
C
D
E

When only the correct answer is circled, this means that the test taker actively looked for the correct answer and found it, without pausing to specifically eliminate wrong answers.

If a hypothetical scenario is written out to test an answer choice and the scenario turns out to be invalid, there will be an "X" beside it.

A̶
B̶
C   Ⓒ
D̶
E̶

When the correct answer is written to the side of the answer choices, rather than just being circled, this indicates that the correct answer was chosen because the other four answers were found to be wrong. The correct answer itself was not evaluated.

A̶
B̶
C̲
D̶
E̲

When 2 or 3 answer choices are underlined, this indicates that some eliminations were easy (the crossed-out answers that are not under-lined), while the underlined choices needed careful consideration. Here, it would be an arbitrary choice whether we started by testing (C) or (E).

A̶ 3
B̶ 2
C   Ⓒ
D̶ 1
E̶ 4

On Orientation questions, the number next to the eliminated answer choice indicates which rule the answer choice breaks (some answers break more than one rule, but only one is listed).

"fyi" = the correct answer could have been obtained without evaluating these answer choices, but explanation of why they are wrong is provided.

in   out
Ⓣ/V   V/Ⓣ

The placeholder indicates that early in the deduction process, the test taker split up these two elements. The circled letter shows that ultimately the test taker real-ized that only one of those choices works.

PT40, G1

K — M — T

$M_3 \rightarrow L_6$

$\cancel{L_6} \rightarrow \cancel{M_3}$

$Z_1 \rightarrow L - O \rightarrow M_3$

$O - L \rightarrow \cancel{Z_1}$

```
___ ___ ___ ___ ___ ___   (K,L,M,O,T,Z)
 1   2   3   4   5   6
 T̸                   T̸  M̸
                         K
```

BIG PAUSE

· Basic ordering, but 2 conditional rules to keep an eye on.
· No chunks, no floaters.
· Last 2 rules both deal with T, K. Need to keep an eye on how those rules interact.

To Frame or Not to Frame?

No chunks or important either/or's, so no frames.

① A   rule 3
   B̸   rule 1
   C̸   rule 4
   D   Ⓓ
   E̸   rule 2

② A
   B
   Ⓒ
   D
   E

PT40, G2

F, G, H, I, K, L, M

if both In
```
┌─────────┐
│ H — G   │
│ K — F   │
└─────────┘
```

M → F and H

K̸ or F̸ → M̸

```
F/G  L   ( I )  │  Out
___ ___ (____)  │ ___ ___
(best)  (worst)
```

BIG PAUSE

· Mismatched ordering. 7 things, 5 spots, so add 2 Out spots.
· F is mentioned in three rules, G and H mentioned in two. How do those rules interact?

To Frame or Not to Frame?

Either/or in spot 1 affects other rules.

i. F L (I, H, M/G) │ K G/M

ii. G L (I, K-F) │ H M

⑥ A̸   Rule 1
   B̸   Rule 3
   C̸   Rule 6
   D   Ⓓ
   E̸   Rule 5

⑦ Use frames
   A
   B
   Ⓒ   frame 2
   D
   E

---

③ ___ ___ ___ ___ ___ L
   Z̸
              O-L → Z_1

Ⓐ
B
C
D
E

④ A̸   ___ L M_3 ──────→ L_6
   B̸   ___ ___ ___ M T/k L
                              X
  Ⓒ   ___ O ___ ___ M T/k
   D̸   Z_1 → L - O → L_6
                    K, T?
   E̸   Z M ___ ___ ___ ___
              X

⑤ Z ___ ___(T/k - M - K/T)___
              L-O
              M̸

A
B̸] Z T/k L M O K/T
C̸
Ⓓ   L=4 forces M=3
E̸   Z T/k L O M T/k

---

⑧ F, L, I always in
   Ⓐ
   B̸
   C
   D
   E

⑨   Spot 5
   frame 1: I, H, M, G
   frame 2: I, F

   A
   B
   C
   D
   Ⓔ

⑩ i. F L I (H M/G)
  ii. G L I K F

   A
   Ⓑ
   C
   D
   E

MANHATTAN
LSAT

PT40, G3

H, M, P, T, V

/ / / / —
/ / X / —
— — ☐ — —
—————
H M P T V
⫫ ⫫   ⫫
⫫

H → T   ⫫ → ⫫
(T ≥ H)

$P_T → R_x$ $P_V → R_f$

BIG PAUSE
- Weird game! Using open board helps to record quantity inferences, but each connection will have to be written twice (i.e. if P and T are connected, a 'T' goes in P's column and a 'P' goes in T's column).
- Montreal is most limited, Vancouver is least limited.
- H → T rule could be important.

PT40, G4

in = 6   out = 3

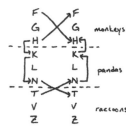

F ⨯ F
G ⨯ G   monkeys
H → H
K   K
L   L   pandas
N ⨯ N
T   T
V   V   raccoons
Z   Z

in	out
—	F/H N/T
	M

BIG PAUSE
- Not too bad. Logic chain has some decent connections.
- OUT column more limited than IN.
- Max 2 monkeys in, but it seems like all 3 P's and all 3 R's could be IN (though not at the same time).

To Frame or Not to Frame?

No chunks or either/or's.

(11) A
⟨B⟩ Rule 1
⟨C⟩ Rule 3
⟨D⟩ Rule 4
⟨E⟩ Rule 2

Ⓐ

(12)
/ / H   / —
— — M — —
P P T/V P V
— — — — —
H M P   T ⫫
⫫   ⫫

A
B   Ⓑ
C
D
E

(13) Ⓐ   if M connects w/H, it must also
B   connect w/ T, but M
C   only has 1 connection
D
E

To Frame or Not to Frame?

Conditional grouping almost never benefits from frames.

(18) A   Rule 2
⟨B⟩ Rule 1
⟨C⟩ Rule 4
D   Ⓓ
⟨E⟩ Rule 3

(19)
H | F
K |
L |
N |
———
   | T

A
B
C Ⓒ
D
E

(20) Use logic chain

A
B
Ⓒ   K → N → ⫫
D
E

---

(14) / / / / —
Ⓐ → V P M V H T   works
     H M P T V H

⟨B⟩
⟨C⟩
⟨D⟩ → Leaves nothing for H to connect with
⟨E⟩ → Someone must connect w/ H,
        + that city will also connect w/ T

(15)   / / T M /
         — — — T —
         V V/T T V H
         H H V P P
         ⫫ ⫫ ⫫
⟨A⟩
⟨B⟩
⟨C⟩
Ⓓ
⟨E⟩

(16) 13 open spots, so max 6 pairs.
But can almost all spots be filled?

A
Ⓑ   / / M / /
C   P P T P T
⟨D⟩   V P H V H   maxed
⟨E⟩   H M P T V   out
                ⫫ ⫫

(17) Only city that can have 4
is Vancouver, so all cities
are connected to V.

A
B
Ⓒ
D
E

F G	H
L	N K
T V	
Z	

(21)
⟨A⟩
⟨B⟩
⟨C⟩   Once HNK are out, that's 3
⟨D⟩   out, so all others must be in.
⟨E⟩

(22) Same diagram as 21!

Ⓐ
⟨B⟩
⟨C⟩
⟨D⟩
⟨E⟩

(23) ⟨A⟩ prev work (21)
Ⓑ   or, from initial inferences, 3 P's
     + 3 R's imposs b/c N + T
     can't both be IN.
⟨C⟩ prev work (21)
⟨D⟩ (19) H L K N V Z | F T G
            m p p p r r   m   m
⟨E⟩ prev work (21)

PT 41, G1

G, L, P, R, S, W

G - P   SL

$\frac{R/}{1}$	$\frac{}{2}$	$\frac{W/S}{3}$	$\frac{}{4}$	$\frac{}{5}$	$\frac{/R}{6}$
R	S				~~W~~
~~L~~					~~S~~

BIG PAUSE

· SL chunk = high priority
· R only has two options
· Spot 3 only has two options
· G - P = last priority (No Floaters)

To Frame or Not To Frame?

SL chunk has 4 options. Probably should just go to questions.

① A
   ~~B~~   3
   ~~C~~   Rule 1
   ~~D~~   4
   ~~E~~   2

② ~~A~~   G = odd / S = odd
   Ⓑ   G can only be 1 or 5.
   C
   D $\frac{G}{R}$ $\frac{}{}$ $\frac{S}{W}$ $\frac{L}{S}$ $\frac{}{L}$ $\frac{R}{G}$ $\frac{}{P}$
   E

③ A   S can only = 4, so W = 3
   B
   C
   D $\frac{}{}$ $\frac{}{}$ $\frac{W}{}$ $\frac{S}{}$ $\frac{L}{}$ $\frac{}{}$
   Ⓔ
   (CBT quest. with a MBT ans.)

④ A
   B
   C $\frac{G}{}$ $\frac{P}{}$ $\frac{}{}$ $\frac{}{}$ $\frac{}{}$ $\frac{R}{}$
   D
   Ⓔ

⑤ A
   Ⓑ   Can't happen when R is 1 or 6
   C
   D   Note: You can elim. the other
   E   four from previous work in #2

⑥ A
   B   Can't happen when R is 1 or 6
   C
   Ⓓ   Note: You can elim.
   E   E from #2, and C from #1

⑦ A $\frac{}{1}$ $\frac{}{2}$ $\frac{S}{3}$ $\frac{W}{4}$ $\frac{}{5}$ $\frac{}{6}$
   B $\frac{S}{}$ $\frac{W}{}$
   C $\frac{}{1}$ $\frac{}{2}$ $\frac{}{3}$ $\frac{}{4}$ $\frac{}{5}$ $\frac{}{6}$
   Ⓓ
   E   SW   G - P

Only 2 options for SW chunk

PT 41, G2

Songs - NQRS

Instrum - f g h k

$\frac{S}{k} \rightarrow \frac{R}{h}$ $\frac{Q}{k} \rightarrow \frac{N}{f}$

R	_	N
	k	

S	_	_	_	_
I				
	1	2	3	4
	~~k~~			

BIG PAUSE

· Rule 4 is a great chunk; it only has two options. Probaby worth framing

To Frame or Not To Frame?

Definitely frame Rule 4's two options:

$\frac{S}{I}$ $\frac{R}{}$ $\frac{\%N}{k}$ $\frac{\%}{}$ $\frac{}{}$ $\frac{S}{I}$ $\frac{\%}{}$ $\frac{R}{}$ $\frac{\%}{k}$ $\frac{N}{}$

Either S or Q will always be with k, so Rule 2 or 3 will always be in effect. 4 frames would cover everything:

①	S	R	Q	N	S
	I	g/h	k	f	h/g

②	S	S	R	Q	N
	I	g h	k	f	

③	S	R	S	N	Q
	I	h	k	g f	

④	S	Q	R	S	N
	I	g	h	k	f

⑧ ~~A~~   3
   B   Ⓑ
   ~~C~~   1
   ~~D~~   3
   ~~E~~   4

⑨ ~~A~~
   ~~B~~
   ~~C~~
   ~~D~~
   Ⓔ   frame 2 + 3

⑩ ~~A~~   frame 3
   ~~B~~   frame 1
   Ⓒ
   D
   E

⑪ ~~A~~
   ~~B~~   Frames 2 and 4
   ~~C~~
   ~~D~~
   E

⑫ Ⓐ
   B   Frame 2
   C
   D
   E

MANHATTAN
LSAT

PT41, G3

Fin   Inc

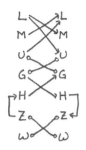

L   L
M   M
U   U
G   G
H   H
Z   Z
W   W

Fin	Inc
Z/W	W/Z
U/G	G/U

BIG PAUSE

· Chain looks pretty readable, just need to be aware of the UG and WZ double-headed arrows.

To Frame or Not to Frame?

Conditional rules (and Conditional Grouping games) almost never lend themselves to frames.

(13) A̶   1
     B̶   5
     C̶   4
     D̶   3
     E   (E)

(14)

Use chain to see if 1ˢᵗ guy in Inc forces 2ⁿᵈ guy to Fin

A
B
(C) $H_I \rightarrow Z_I \rightarrow W_F$
D
E

---

(15)

F	I
U	G
W	Z
M	L
H	

M, H, L left at most 2 can be F

A
(B̶)
C
D
E

(16)

F	I
M	L
W	Z
U	G

A̶
B̶
C̶   (D)
E̶

(17)

F	I
U	G
	L

A
(B̶)
C
D
E

PT41, G4

F, G, H, I, K, Ⓜ, O, Ⓟ

"Across" = 3 in between

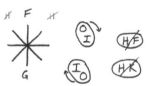

or clockwise →   [O I]

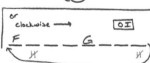

BIG PAUSE

· Yikes! Circular seating is a big curveball. We can use an unconventional circular diagram or use a conventional number line (but remind ourselves that 8 is next to 1).
· [O I] chunk seems most useful and it will be tricky to place.
· M + P are floaters.

To Frame or Not to Frame?

Chunk seems to have 4 options. Normally that's too many to frame, but weirdness of game may incline some to sketch these out just to have a better grasp.

(18) A̶   1
     B̶   1
     C   (C)
     D̶   3
     E̶   2

(19)   [H G O I]

F __ H G O I __ K, M, P
    M/P
    K

A̶
B̶
C̶
(D)   FKPH
E̶

(20)   (G4)

only 2 options for H

A
B
C
D
E

---

(21)   [M O I]

K, H, P

F M O I G H P K
F K P H G M O I

A
B
(C̶)
D
E

(22)   prev work (19), FKPHGOIM was pos.

(A̶)
B
C
D
E

(23)   [O I __ __ __ K] or [K __ __ __ O I]

A
(B)
C̶
D̶
E̶

prev work (21)

(24)

A
B
C
D
E

(O I), M, P

PT42, G1

in				out	
_ _ _ _ _				K/M _ _ _ _	
b c z				c	

F   F
G   G   Bot
H   H
$b \geq 1 \rightarrow z = 1$ K   K
L   L   Chem
$z \geq 1 \rightarrow b = 1$ M   M
P   P
Q   Q   Zoo
R   R

BIG PAUSE

· Got to keep track of conditional rules for both which letters are In/Out and the # of representatives from each category.
· Could be helpful to think through numerical possibilities of subgroups

Bot	Chem	Zoo	(In)
1	1	3	
1	2	2	
2	2	1	
3	1	1	

To Frame or Not to Frame?

Conditional rules/games don't lend themselves to framing.

① start w/ rules 3, 4, 5

A̶   3
B̶   4
C   Ⓒ
D̶   4
E̶   5

②

in				out			
M	P	R	_ Q	L	K	_	_
c	z	z	b z	c	c	b	

must be = b c z
     1 1 3

A
B
C
D
Ⓔ

---

③

in				out			
F	L	Q	R P	G	H	K	M
b	c	z	z	b	b	c	

$z \geq 1 \rightarrow b = 1$

A
B
C
D
Ⓔ

can't put M in b/c that forces P in.

④

in				out			
P	_	_	_	Q	R	M	
z	b	b	c	z	z	c	

Could be: b c z
A   2 2 1
B   (G,H)(K,L)(P)
C   or   b c z
Ⓓ   3 1 1
E   (FGH) (L) (P)

⑤

in				out		
G	H	_	_	_	M	
b	b	z		z	z	c

$b \geq 1 \rightarrow z = 1 \rightarrow M$

A
B   Could be   b=2, c=2, z=1
C   GH, KL, P/Q/R
D   or   b=3, c=1, z=1
E   FGH, L, P/Q/R

PT42, G2

F, G, L, M, P, T

M?
F - [PT] - L - G

F/M					G/M
1	2	3	4	5	6

BIG PAUSE

· Five out of six are in a chain. [PT] chunk is top priority.

· M is a floater.

To Frame or Not to Frame?

Chunk has only 2 options, so frame them if you'd like.

i. F   (PT)   (L - G, M)

ii. (FM)   (PT)   L   G

⑥ A   Ⓐ
B̶   1
C̶   2
D̶   4
E̶   3

⑦ Ⓐ
B
C
D
E

⑧

[M_G] or [G_M]
G can only be 5 or 6, only G/M can be last, so it must be [M—G] / 4 6

A
B
Ⓒ   F (PT) M L G
D
E

---

⑨ From Frames or Tree, L can only be 4 or 5

A
B
C
Ⓓ
E

⑩ A̶   poss in Frame 2
B̶   poss in Frame 1
Ⓒ
D
E

⑪ Gotta be [TPL], so F - [TPL] - G. M?

A
B
Ⓒ
D
E

⑫

F/M	M/F	T	P	L	G

A
B
Ⓒ
D
E

MANHATTAN
LSAT

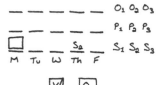

PT 42, G3

BIG PAUSE

- 9 things, 15 potential spots. It never says at least one batch per day, so a day could be empty.
- $O_2 P_1$ chunk is highest priority. Its earliest is Tues (forcing O_1 on Mon), and its latest is Wed (forcing $P_2 + P_3$ on Thu + Fri)

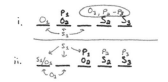

To Frame or Not to Frame?

Frame! Chunk only has 2 options

i. O_1 P_1 $(O_3, P_2 - P_3)$ S_2 S_3 $\overset{S_1}{\to}$

ii. S_1/O_1 $\overset{S_1\downarrow}{\underset{O_2}{P_1}}$ P_2 P_3 S_2 S_3 $\overset{O_1}{\to}$

⑬   A   Ⓐ
    B̶   4
    C̶   2
    D̶   3
    E̶   3

⑭   frame 1: Tues, Thu, Fri could have 3
    frame 2: Wed, Thu, Fri
    Only Mon ≠ 3

Ⓐ
B
C
D
E

⑮   Frame 1
A̶ $O_1 S_1$
B̶ $P_1 S_1$
Ⓒ
D
E

⑯   Frame 1
A
B
C
Ⓓ O_1 P_1 ✗ P_2 P_3 O_2 S_2 S_3
E $\underset{S_1}{\to}$ $\underset{O_3}{\to}$

⑰   Frame 1
Ⓐ O_3
B̶ O_1 P_1 P_3 P_3 S_2 S_3
C $\underset{S_1}{\to}$
D
E

⑱   1 + 3 could only be together on Wed, so Frame 1
A
B
C
D
Ⓔ O_1 P_1 S_1 O_3 $(P_2 - P_3)$ S_2 S_3

PT 42, G4

S, T, U

K < M
L < M
L ≠ J
M ≠ J

Exactly 2 columns match

BIG PAUSE

- O is the "floater" column. We could leave as is, or have 2, or have all 3.
- Interplay between J and M is most important — whichever of S/T/U J has, M will have the other two.

To Frame or Not to Frame?

Diagram is already very limited (and bulky to re-write). There aren't any chunks or crucial either/or's. Don't frame.

⑲   We know K + O can't be in answer choice, since they have T. M can't be because it reviews 2 plays.

Ⓐ
B̶   ∅
C̶   J ≠ L
B̶   K, ∅
E̶   M

⑳   A   J, L = 1
    Ⓑ   M = 2, J = 1
    C
    D
    E

㉑   3 U's → must go to L, M, O.
If J got U, L + M couldn't have U.

$\overset{/}{\underset{S/T}{\underset{J}{—}}}$ $\overset{/}{\underset{T}{\underset{K}{—}}}$ $\overset{/}{\underset{U}{\underset{L}{—}}}$ $\overset{□}{\underset{U}{\underset{M}{—}}}$ $\overset{U}{\underset{T}{\underset{O}{—}}}$

A̶
B
C̶
D̶
Ⓔ

㉒   Everyone who has T must include K and O
A̶   O?
B̶ ⎤ either M or J must have T
C̶ ⎦
Ⓓ
E̶   K?

㉓   Using inference from Q22, either M or J must have T, so if J ≠ T → M = T

A
B
C
Ⓓ
E̶

PT43, G1

F, G, (J), M, P, V

(front)   (back)

1	2	3	4	5	6
M	G̶	M	G̶	P̶	G̶
V̶	M		P̶	P̶	P̶
	V̶				

P ___ ___ +M

F __ V

BIG PAUSE
· Key will be balancing the F__V chunk with the fact that P and M can't get too close.
· G = lower priority
· J = floater

To Frame or not to Frame?

F__V chunk has four options. Probably should just go to questions. If we did frame, we'd get these:

F	P	V	J	G	M
	F		V		
G	P	F	J	V	M
			F	M	V
1	2	3	4	5	6

① A̶   Rule 1
  B̶   1
  C̶   2
  D
  E̶   1

② P — FGV — M, so G = 3

P F G V S/M M/S

A
B
C
D
Ⓔ

---

③ Ⓐ   FPV __ +M
  B
  C   F P V J G M
  D
  E   G/J F P V J/G M

④ A
  B
  C̶
  D̶
  Ⓔ

J=5, so G=1 or 3.
Only 1 option for F__V in each frame

P F G V J M
G F P V J M

⑤ A   prev. work (#4)
  Ⓑ
  C   prev. work (#3)
  D
  E   prev. work (#4)

G J P __ __ M ✗
__ __ G J __ ✗
P __ __ M G J ✗

No place for F__V

PT43, G2

L, M, O, S, V, Z

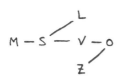

```
      L
M — S — V — O
      Z
```

(front)   (back)
M/Z̶   O/L
| 1 | 2 | 3 | 4 | 5 | 6 |

BIG PAUSE
· Nice tree, what more could we ask for?
· Keep an eye on L & Z, who are strays.

To Frame or Not to Frame?

No need to frame when we have a tree.

⑥ (Not orientation)
  A̶   If L=6, then O would be 5
  B   If S=3, (MZ) would be 1&2
  C
  D̶   If O=5, then L=6
  E̶   If V=3, then M-S would be 1&2

⑦ __ __ __ __ V O
  A
  B
  C
  D
  Ⓔ

⑧ M S L (V Z) O
  A
  B
  C
  D
  Ⓔ

---

⑨ Ⓐ
  B
  C
  D
  E

⑩ Z = Stray
  Can't go last, but that's it.
  A
  B
  C
  Ⓓ
  E

⑪
```
          L
M — S — V — Z — O
```
  Ⓐ
  B
  C
  D
  E

⑫
```
        L
  S — M
      V — O
      Z
```
  A
  B
  Ⓒ   only Z can go before S
  D
  E

PT43, G3

Q, (R), S, T, V, Z

$$
\begin{array}{c}
M \quad \underline{\quad} \; \underline{\overline{(-)}} \; \underline{\quad} \; Z \\
P \quad \underline{\quad} \; \underline{(V)} \; \underline{\quad} \; S \\
 \quad 1 \quad\;\; 2 \quad\;\; 3
\end{array}
$$

S – Z

Q ≠ T

BIG PAUSE

· 6 things, 6 spots. 2nd rule is potentially confusing because Q & T could be in the same period.
· 1st priority (or basis for frames) would be whether V is M2 or P2

To Frame or Not to Frame?

Only 2 options for V, which affects S and Z.

i.
$$
\begin{array}{c}
M \; \underline{\;\varnothing\;} \; \underline{(Z)} \; \underline{\quad} \\
P \; \underline{\;S\;} \; \underline{\;V\;} \; \underline{\quad} \\
 \; 1 \quad 2 \quad 3
\end{array}
$$
ii.
$$
\begin{array}{c}
M \; \underline{\quad} \; \underline{\;V\;} \; \underline{\;Z\;} \\
P \; \underline{\quad} \; \underline{(S)} \; \underline{\;T\;} \\
 \; 1 \quad 2 \quad 3
\end{array}
$$

13. A̶   2
    B   (B)
    C̶   1
    D̶   3
    E̶   1

14.
$$
\begin{array}{c}
M \; \underline{\quad} \; \underline{\;V\;} \; \underline{\;Z\;} \\
P \; \underline{\quad} \; \underline{\;S\;} \; \underline{\quad}
\end{array}
$$
[frame 2]

   A̶
   B   (B)   answers can't
   C̶   have V or Z
   D̶
   E̶

15. A̶] prev $M \; \underline{(Q)} \; \underline{\;V\;} \; \underline{\;Z\;}$ Both Q
    B] work $P \; \underline{\;\;} \; \underline{\;T\;} \; \underline{\;S\;}$ +T are poss.
    C̶   R is also poss. $M \; \underline{\;T\;} \; \underline{\;V\;} \; \underline{\;Z\;}$
    (D) $P \; \underline{(R)} \; \underline{\;S\;} \; \underline{\;Q\;}$
    E̶   Z ≠ 1 or Priv

16.
$$
\begin{array}{c}
M \; \underline{\quad} \; \underline{\;V\;} \; \underline{\;Z\;} \\
P \; \underline{\quad} \; \underline{\;S\;} \; \underline{\;Q\;}
\end{array}
$$
  Frame 2

$\underline{\boxed{\;}\;}_Q$?→ If Q needs something before, it must be P3

   A
   (B)
   C
   D
   E

17. $\boxed{Z \; T}$ → frame 1
$$
\begin{array}{c}
M \; \underline{\;R\;} \; \underline{\;Z\;} \; \underline{\;T\;} \\
P \; \underline{\;S\;} \; \underline{\;V\;} \; \underline{\;Q\;}
\end{array}
$$

   A
   (B)
   C
   D
   E

PT43, G4

X, $\underset{3}{Y}$, Z

I > S   F ≠ P

(T, I have 2 in common)

$$
\begin{array}{cccccc}
\underline{/} & \underline{\;} & \underline{/} & \underline{/} & \underline{/} & \underline{/} \\
\boxed{\;} & \boxed{\;} & \boxed{X} & \boxed{\;} & \boxed{\;} & \boxed{X} \\
\boxed{Y} & \boxed{Y} & \boxed{Z} & \boxed{Y/Z} & \boxed{\;} & \boxed{Z} \\
F & H & I & P & S & T
\end{array}
$$

BIG PAUSE

· F needs one more = X or Z
       (P gets the other)
· H is the "floater" column = leave as is, give it 2, give it 3
· I is okay but could have 3
       (must stay > S)
· P gets one: X or Z
       (determines F + vice versa)
· S could have 1 or 2
       (must stay < I)
· T is done
· Only 1 more Y

To Frame or Not to Frame?

Most of game figured out, no need to frame.

18. A̶ ←
    B   F has Y
    C̶ ←   F = 2
    (D)
    E̶ ←

19. A
    B
    (C)   P gets X or Z, both of which
    D   I already has.
    E

20.   I < H → I = 2 and H = 3
               S = 1

$$
\begin{array}{cccccc}
\underline{/} & \underline{X} & \underline{/} & \underline{/} & \underline{/} & \underline{/} \\
\boxed{\;} & \boxed{Y} & \boxed{X} & \boxed{/} & \boxed{/} & \boxed{X} \\
\boxed{Y} & \boxed{Z} & \boxed{Z} & \boxed{\;} & \boxed{\;} & \boxed{Z} \\
F & H & I & P & S & T
\end{array}
$$

   A
   B
   C
   D
   (E)

21.   Only H and I could have all 3

   (A)
   B
   C
   D
   E

22. A
    B
    (C)   P = 1
    D
    E

PT 44, G1

$F_1, F_2, F_3, M, Ⓡ, S, T$

$\boxed{FF}$

$\boxed{TS}$

1 2 3 4 5 6 7
X̶   X̶
8   D̶

BIG PAUSE
- Key will be balancing the $\boxed{TS}$ chunk with the need to space out the three F's.
- M = low priority.
- R = floater.

To Frame or Not to Frame?

- $\boxed{TS}$ chunk seems to have 6 options
- Spacing out the 3 F's seems to have many options: 1-3-5, 1-3-6, 1-3-7, 1-4-7, 2-4-7, etc. Not worth it.

① A̶   Rule 1
  B̶   2
  C
  D̶   3
  E̶   4

②   F̲ M̲ F̲ T̲ S̲ F̲ R̲
     F̲ T̲ S̲ F̲ M̲ F̲ R̲
  A̶
  B̶
  C̶   The 3 F's must go 1-3-6
 Ⓓ   or 1-4-6 so $\boxed{TS}$ chunk
  E   can fit in.

③   R̲ F̲ M̲ F̲ T̲ S̲ F̲
     R̲ F̲ T̲ S̲ F̲ M̲ F̲
  A
  B   The 3 F's must go 2-4-7
  C   or 2-5-7 so $\boxed{TS}$ can
  D   fit in.
 Ⓔ

④ $\boxed{TSR}$
     F̲ T̲ S̲ R̲ F̲ M̲ F̲
     F̲ M̲ F̲ T̲ S̲ R̲ F̲
  A
  B $\boxed{TSR}$ only has 2 options,
  C   in order for the 3 F's
  D   to fit.
 Ⓔ

⑤   T̲ S̲ F̲ ᴹ/ᴿ F̲ ᴿ/ᴹ F̲
  A̶
  B̶   3 F's must go 3-5-7
  R̶   to fit.
 Ⓓ̶
  E̶

⑥ $\boxed{R\ M}$ $\boxed{T\ S}$

     F̲ _ _ F̲ _ _ F

 Ⓐ
  B   With two chunks, the 3
  C   F's must go 1-4-7.
  D
  E

PT 44, G2

G, H, K, L, P, S

$\boxed{\begin{matrix}L\\P\end{matrix}}$ $\boxed{\begin{matrix}G\\H\end{matrix}}$ $K_M \rightarrow G_T$
                         $S_W \rightarrow H_T$

_ _ _

M   T   W

BIG PAUSE
- Typical rules – a chunk, an anti-chunk, and conditionals.
- 1st priority is placing the chunk, then dividing up G & H into the remaining two groups, then checking to see whether conditionals apply.

To Frame or Not to Frame?

The chunk has three possibilities, but only one seems to cause chain reactions (putting the chunk on Tuesday activates the conditionals). Debateable.

⑦ A̶   1
  B̶   3
  C̶   2
  D̶   4
  E   Ⓔ

⑧ A
 Ⓑ   if K and S were together,
  C   G and H would be together,
  D   since L & P are always
  E   together.

⑨   ᴳ/ᴴ   L̲   ᴴ/ᴳ
     S̲   P̲   K̲
 Ⓐ ↰
  B   from contrapositives
  C   G̶_T → K̶_M
  D   H̶_T → S̶_W
  E

⑩ $\boxed{\begin{matrix}G\\K\end{matrix}}$ ← Can't go on Mon
     + $\boxed{\begin{matrix}L\\P\end{matrix}}$ + $\boxed{\begin{matrix}S\\H\end{matrix}}$ ← Can't go on Wed.

  A
  B
  C
  D
 Ⓔ

⑪   (K̲G̲) L̲ | L̲ (K̲G̲)
     H̲ S̲ P̲ | P̲ H̲ S̲
  A̶
  B̶
  C̶
 Ⓓ̶
  E

⑫   _ L̲ _ | _ L̲ _
     G̲ P̲ H̲ | H̲ G̲ P̲
 Ⓐ
  B
  C
  D
  E

PT44, G3

Archeol – F, G, H

Century – 8, 9, 10

Exactly 1 G, [10/G]

$8^{th} \rightarrow$ [8/O] $\cancel{O} \rightarrow 8^{th}$

BIG PAUSE

· G goes exactly once, and it must be 3rd or 5th, since it must be $\frac{10}{G}$

· F and O have no minimum or maximum, neither do the 8's, 9's, or 10's. It's okay to not use everything

· Even though all 8th's must be O, O is still allowed to be 8/9/10.

To Frame or Not to Frame?

Good deductions so far. Plenty of flexibility remains. Not worth framing.

⑬ [Use rules + diagram for this ordering orientation]

A̶   O ≠ 4, diagram
B̶   G ≠ 1, diagram
C̶   G ≠ 2, diagram
D̶   3
E   Ⓔ

⑭

A
B
Ⓒ
D
E

---

⑮ Ⓐ
   B
   C
   D
   E

⑯ A
   B
   C
   D
   Ⓔ

⑰ Must be exactly 10, but the last could be F.

   A
   B
   C
   Ⓓ
   E

PT44, G4

$X > $Z, so [10/X̶] [15/Z̶]

$W > $F, so W≠10, F≠15   ⑱ [Use inferences on 3D ordering orientation.]

#Z > #X, so

X	Y	Z
1	1	3
1	1	2

⟨ W>F ⟩
    10̶   15̶
10,12,15 __ __ __ 15 __

X,Y,Z __ __ __ __ __
       M   T   W   Th F
                      Z̶

A̶   Ⓐ
B̶   W > F and X > Z
C̶ ⟩ X = 1
D̶ ⟩
E̶   Z ≠ Th

⑲ A
   B
   C
   D
   E

BIG PAUSE

· Need to always figure out how to assign the 10/12/15 to X, Y, and Z.

   15 12 10
   Y x z
   X Y/Z 2/Y

· Mon/Tues have no rules.
· X can only occur once.

---

⑳ $\frac{12}{F}$, so $\frac{15}{X̶}$ $\frac{10}{Y}$

   __ __ 12 **15** 10
           F̶   X   Y

   (only 1 X)

   A
   B
   C
   D
   Ⓔ

㉑ A
   B
   C
   Ⓓ
   E

㉒ [Wed & Thurs ≠ 10]

   X A   only 10 ... 15 **15** 12
   X B   ... 10 15 **15** 12
   Ⓒ
   D̶
   E̶

   You could also make this inference that if Mon alone worked, then Tues alone would also work. Since (A) and (B) can't both be right, they must both be wrong.

PT 45, G1

R, S, T, U, Y, W

S - [Y W] - T

U - R

$$\frac{S/U}{1} \quad \frac{}{2} \quad \frac{}{3} \quad \frac{}{4} \quad \frac{}{5} \quad \frac{T/R}{6}$$

BIG PAUSE

· All six elements accounted for in our two ordering chains.
· Chain of 4 is our top priority.
· Too many restrictions on element positions to notate all.

To Frame or Not To Frame?

[Y W] chunk only has three options, but they don't lead to great chain reactions. Use frames only if you're quick and comfy setting them up.

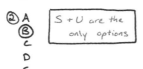

① ~~A~~ Rule 1
   ~~B~~   2
   ~~C~~   3
   ~~D~~   4
   Ⓔ

② A
   Ⓑ | S + U are the only options |
   C
   D
   E

---

③ A
   B
   Ⓒ   prev. work (# 1)
   D
   E | If U=3, there's no place for the WY chunk. |

(Frames could have been useful for this question.)

④ A
   B
   C   [S Y W] - T
   Ⓓ   U - R
   E   (Both W and T must come after Y.)

⑤ A
   Ⓑ   S (Y W) T U R
   C
   D
   E

⑥ ~~A~~ | Similar to orientation question, but no W shown. Use S-Y-T and U-R |
   B
   ~~C~~
   ~~D~~
   Ⓔ

PT 45, G2

L, N, O, P, S, T ≥ 1
    1 1   2

$$\frac{}{1} \quad \frac{}{2} \quad \frac{}{3} \quad \frac{L}{4}$$

       [S O S]

BIG PAUSE

· 6 things, 8 spots.
  4 of them go once, 2 of them go twice (S for sure, and L/P/T seem possible)
· [S O S] chunk is #1 priority.

To Frame or Not to Frame?

[S O S] chunk only has two options. Frame them.

i. (T=2 and/or 4, N,P, duplicate L/P/T)

$$\frac{S}{1} \quad \frac{O}{2} \quad \frac{S}{3} \quad \frac{L}{4}$$

ii.

$$\frac{L}{1} \quad \frac{S}{2} \quad \frac{O}{3} \quad \frac{S}{4}$$
$$\frac{P/N}{} \quad \frac{T}{} \quad \frac{N/P}{} \quad \frac{L}{}$$

⑦ A   Ⓐ
   B   1
   ~~C~~ 4
   ~~D~~ 3
   E   2

⑧   No consecutives poss. in frame 2, so frame 1

   Ⓐ
   ~~B~~   N=1
   ~~C~~   O=1
   ~~D~~   [S O S]
   ~~E~~   T=2 and/or 4

---

⑨   T=4, frame 1

   (N, P, 4P/T) → $\frac{S}{1} \quad \frac{O}{2} \quad \frac{S}{3} \quad \frac{L}{4}$ (T above 4)

   (A)
   ~~B~~
   ~~C~~
   ~~D~~
   ~~E~~

⑩ Ⓐ   frame 2
   B
   C   } Not poss. in either frame
   D
   E

⑪   who CAN play against Tyrone?
    In frame 2 = S
    In frame 1 = O or L

   A
   B
   Ⓒ
   D
   E

⑫   O=3 → frame 2
   A
   B
   C
   D
   Ⓔ

PT45,G3

In   Out

```
 ┌U        U┐
 └→S        S←┐
  └→W    →W←┘
   T ╳ →T
   R╳  ╳R
   Y╳  ╳Y
   Z        Z
```

BIG PAUSE

· Z is a floater.
· Everything else looks pretty
  typical.

To Frame or Not to Frame?

Conditional rules/games almost
never lend themselves to framing.

(13) A̶   4
     B   (B)
     C̶   4
     D̶   1
     E̶   1

(14)   I | O
         ─────────
         TZ | WSU

     A
     B
     C
     D
     (E)

---

(15)   I | O
         ──────────────
         R↗ | YWSU
         TZ is all that's left

     A
     B
     C
     (D)
     E

(16)   I | O
         ──────────────────────
         UZ S̲W̲Y̲ | TR
           3 others

     A
     (B)
     C
     D
     E

(17)   3 in | 4 out
          I | O
         ──────────────────
         S Z W Y | TR
         Too many!

     (A)
     B
     C
     D
     E

PT45,G4

O,R,S,T,W ≥ 1

```
 __  __  __
 __  __  __
  X   Y   Z
      └→≠←┘
```

$\boxed{\dfrac{W}{O}}$ $S_x \longleftrightarrow S_y$

         $R_y \longrightarrow T_x$ and T_z

BIG PAUSE

· 5 things, 6 spots. One thing
  has to go twice. From rules
  2 and 3 it seems like S or
  T will normally be the duplicate.
· Bi-conditional rule: either both
  things happen, or both things
  don't happen (which means
  S would go to Z).

To Frame or Not to Frame?

It might be worth picturing the
two possibilities from Rule 2.

i. __ __ __   ii. __ __ __
    S   S   S
    X   Y   Z   X   Y   Z
        R̶ S̶   T̶   T̶
    forces 2 T's

(18) A   (A)
     B̶   3
     C̶   1
     D̶   4
     E̶   2

(19)   S   S   R
        ─────────────
        T (W O)
        X   Y   Z

     (A)
     B
     C
     D
     E

---

(20)   R̶ R̶ T
        ──────────   (Frame 1)
        S   S   W
        X   Y   Z

     A
     B
     C
     D
     (E)

(21) A
     B
     (C)   Frames
     D
     E

(22) A
     B̶   prev work (20)
     (C)   creates 3 T's
     D
     E
```
```

PT46, G1

F, G, H, L, M, Ⓟ

F – L – M – H

F/P		G/	/G		H/P
1	2	3	4	5	6

BIG PAUSE
- Nice, easy chain of 4.
- G has two options in middle.
- P's freedom creates most of the uncertainty.

To Frame or Not to Frame?

- G only has two options, but neither placement triggers anything definite.

Don't frame.

① A 1
  B̶ 3
  C̶ 3
  D̶ 2

Ⓐ

② Ⓐ ___ ___ ___ F G L–M–H
  B
  C
  D
  E

③ F L M G (HP)
  A
  B
  C
  Ⓓ
  E

④ F L G M (M̄ HP)
  F L M G
  if M ≠ 5, then M = 4 or 3

  Ⓐ
  B
  C
  D
  E

⑤ A
  B
  C
  D
  Ⓔ

⑥ F – [LM] – H
  F L M G (HP)
  (FP) G L M H

  Ⓐ
  B
  C
  D
  E

PT46, G2

J ___ ___ ___ FHJR ×2

F/J				R F
1	2	3	4	
H	X̶			
R				

BIG PAUSE
- Having two of each is weird, but okay.
- The whereabouts of the two F's seem important.
- The two H's appear to be fine anywhere in the six slots of 2/3/4.

To Frame or Not to Frame?

No chunks. Lots of uncertainty. Best to just go to questions.

⑦ A̶ 3
  B̶
  ✗C J=3, R=1
  D̶ 2
  E̶ 4

Ⓑ

⑧ A̶ | J R H F | counterexample
     | J R H F |
  B | J F R H | counterexample
     | F F R H |
  Ⓒ | J R ___ ___ |
     | R̶ |
  D   If you can see this flexibility
  E   mentally, don't write it out

⑨ A̶ forces R F to happen | J ___ ___ F |
                            | J ___ ___ H |
                            | R̶ |
  Ⓑ | J H H R |
     | F F J R |
  C̶ leaves nothing for column 1 }
  D̶ ↳same   } fyi
  E̶ too much jazz   }

⑩ A rule 2
  B rule 3
  Ⓒ | J F H F |
     | J R H R |
  D
  E

⑪ A prev. work (8)
  Ⓑ | J H R ___ | forces R F
     | ___ H R ___ |
  C
  D
  E

Note: Unusual game in that there are no conditional questions. Some people will be able to answer these unconditional questions by just visualizing the scenarios. Others will need to write more out.

PT 46, G3

Towns – J, L, N, O, P

Precip – r, h

	h			r,h	
__	N	P	3/	/J	J,L,N,O,P
1	2	3	4	5	
~~J~~	~~L~~		~~L~~		
	~~O~~		~~N~~		
	~~J~~				

r   r   L > J
[L] [O]   N > J

BIG PAUSE
· J can only be 4 or 5,
and some chain reactions
would result. Might be
worth framing.

To Frame or Not to Frame?

i.   r h __ r r   ii.   r h __ r
   L N P J O   ~~O~~ N P ~~L~~ J

(12) | We know N=2, P=3 |

A   (A)
~~B~~
~~C~~
~~D~~
~~E~~

(13) | O–J, frame 2 |

A
B
(C)
D
E

---

(14) | L — only r, frame 2 |

   r h __ r r
   O N P L J

A
B
C
D
(E)

(15) | J–O, frame 1 |

A
B
C
(D)
E

(16) | O–L, frame 2 |

   r h __ r
   O N P L J

A
(B)
C
D
E

PT 46, G4

F, G, H, I, M, P

6 ppl, 9 spots
3, 2, 1, 1, 1, 1

[F / G] [H / I]

__ = __ = __
__ = __ = __
1   All Three ← Must be M or P
           due to Rules 2+3

BIG PAUSE
· Having only 6 ppl to fill 9 spots
is unusual, but rule 1 clears
up some uncertainty. M/P will go
3 times, and one other person
will go twice.
· 1st order of business with
each question: M or P All Three?

To Frame or Not to Frame?

We could create one frame
with 3 M's, another with 3 P's,
but we wouldn't get any chain
reactions in either.

(17) [F / M] → P is All 3

__ __ __
P P P

A
B
(C)   Everyone is in a committee with P
D
E

(18) F → P   Not sure if this
     G → P   determines All 3

F	G	__	__		F	G	H	}Breaks
P	P	P	P		M	M	M	rule
✓						✗		

~~A~~   forces H / I
~~B~~   no room for M/H and M/I
(C) →   H H M
D   F G I
E   P P P

---

(19) M → I   M can't be All 3

   M __ __   (H, and a
   I F G   copy of
   P P P   someone)

~~A~~
(B)
C
D
E

(20) ~~A~~
~~B~~
~~C~~
(D)   Sure, when P is All 3. prev. work (18)
E

(21) ~~A~~   prev. work (18)
~~B~~   prev. work (19)
~~C~~   prev. work (19)
~~D~~   prev. work (18)
(E)   since one or the other is
     All 3, bound to happen

(22) ~~A~~   prev. work (18)
~~B~~   prev. work (19)
C
(D)   3, 2, 1, 1, 1, 1 every time
E

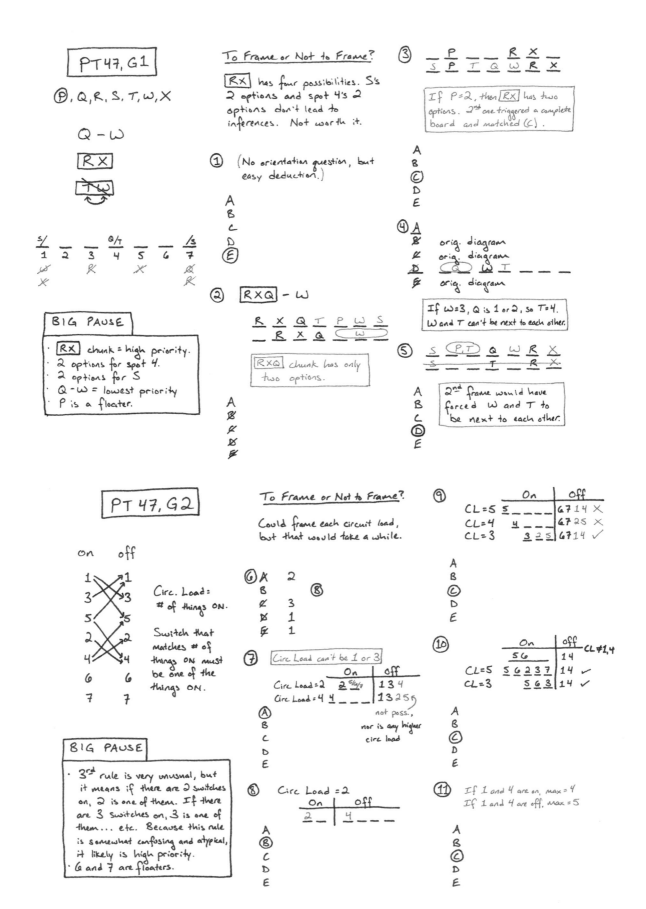

PT 47, G3

f, j, o, r
2

V ≠ Z

			F	
			J	
	O		O	
J	R		R	
S	T	V	X	Z

BIG PAUSE

- T and X are done.
- Only things left to worry about are S, who gets all but one of F, J, O, R, and the relationship between V + Z.
  If V = 2, Z = 1
  If Z = 2, V = 1
  But they could also both have 1.

To Frame or Not to Frame?

With so little left to determine, there's no need for frames.

12. ~~A~~   S = 3
    ~~B~~   T = O + R
    ~~C~~   V ≠ 3
    ~~D~~   X = 4
    (E)

13. ~~A~~   V ≠ Z
    ~~B~~   J = 2
    ~~C~~   S + X are the 2 J's
    (D)
    ~~E~~   X has O

14. f = 1, so X has the only f.
    S = J, O, R
    Z = O/R
    V = R/O

    ~~A~~   V = 1
    (B)
    C
    D   ⎤ fyi, all wrong b/c V = 1
    E   ⎦   + Z = 1

15. A
    B
    (C)   S = 3, Z = 2 or 1
    D
    E

16. r = 3, T, V, and X
    so S = J, O, F
        V = R
        Z = O/F (R) ⎤ could have 1 or 2

    A
    B
    (C)   S = J, O, F + Z = O/F at minimum
    D
    E

17. S = F, J, O/R
    V = F + maybe 1 more
    Z = O/R + maybe 1 more

    ~~A~~
    (B)   could be S = F, J, O + Z = R
    C
    D
    E

PT 47, G4

Sup _ _ _ _ _ (J, N, P)
     M Tu W Th F

[NN]

S ✗ P₁

K → [K/X₂]

BIG PAUSE

- Big mix of things to keep track of. 6 things, 10 spots. Up to 4 people could go twice (we know O and N go at least twice).
- Last 3 rules are all we need to keep track of — 2 of them refer to someone's FIRST day.

To Frame or Not to Frame?

[NN] chunk appears to have four options, too many to frame.

18. ~~A~~   2
    ~~B~~   5
    C   (C)
    ~~D~~   4
    ~~E~~   3

19. _ O O K
                P₁ S
       M Tu W Th F

    A
    B
    C
    D
    (E)

20. A
    (B)   similar inference to 19
    C   If K then S has no
    D   P₁   legal spot.
    E   Fri

21. Monday = earliest slot
    Any rules deal with who can't
        go 1st?

    (A)   S/Mon forces S – P₁
    B
    C
    D
    E

22. ~~A~~   [NN]
    (B)   Tricky, but fine if S/M O/Tu
    ~~C~~   K on Wed breaks, not O's 1st
    ~~D~~   K on Thu breaks, same reason, not
    ~~E~~   No supervisor   N's 1st

PT48, G1

Use   Not

T ⟶ T
H ✕ H
R ⟶ R

V ⟶ T, H, R out

T or H or R ⟶ V out

M   M

(This could go on chain, but would make chain too messy.)

BIG PAUSE
- All the rules force something OUT when another thing is IN. Can't have much IN at the same time.
- V and H are powerful, they each force 3 things OUT.
- M is a floater.

___

To Frame or Not to Frame?

Conditional rules/games don't lend themselves to framing.

① A̶   1
   B̶   2
   C   Ⓒ
   D̶   3
   E̶   3

②
```
            If in. forces 3 out.
                ↓   If in. fires
                ↓      3 out.
 _  _  _ |  M   V   H
```
A
B
C
D
Ⓔ

___

③ A
   B
   C
   D
   Ⓔ   V=in forces 3 out, so max 2=in

④
```
                    V=in forces 3out
                         ↓  (2 max IN)
 M   R   T |  V   H
                         ↑
                    H=in forces 3 out
                        (2 max IN)
```
Ⓐ
B
C
D
E

⑤ Ⓐ   H=in ⟶ R and T = out
   B
   C
   D
   E

⑥ Ⓐ   Prev. work (Q4)
   B   Hard enough to get 3 IN,
   C   4 is imposs.
   D
   E

___

PT48, G2

G, H, J, K, L, M, P, T

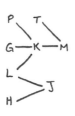

```
 P   T
  \ / \
   G—K—M
  /
 L
  \
   J
  /
 H
```

```
 _  _  _  _  _  _  _  M/J
 1  2  3  4  5  6  7   8
```

BIG PAUSE
- Tree is a little denser than usual, but not too bad.
- 5 options for spot 1, but only 2 options for spot 8.

___

To Frame or Not to Frame?

We have a Tree. No need to frame.

⑦ | Not orientation, but basic Tree inferences |

   A̶
   B̶
   C   Ⓒ
   D̶
   E̶

⑧
```
 _  _  _  _  _  _  M  J
```
A
Ⓑ
C
D
E

⑨ A
   B
   Ⓒ   M has 5 things that must
   D   come before (T,K,P,G,L)
   E

___

⑩
```
 (L-H)  J  _  _  _  _  M
```
A
B
C
D
Ⓔ

⑪

```
    (P )
    (G )—K, T
    (L )            H   (M J)
 _  _  _  _  _  _  _
```
A
B
C
Ⓓ
E

⑫
```
 (P, G, H, T)  L  (K—M, J)
 _  _  _  _  _  _  _
```
A̶
B̶
C̶
D̶
Ⓔ

MANHATTAN
LSAT

PT 48, G3

R, T, V
4

∠	∠	∠	—	∠	V
∠	☐	—	—	V	T
R	R	—	R	T	T
R	R	R	R	T	R
S	U	W	X	Y	Z

BIG PAUSE

· X is "floater" column: leave
  as is, give it 2, give it 3.
· U needs one more T/V.
· W can have 1 or 2, but R.
· S, Y, Z are done.

To Frame or Not to Frame?

Very little uncertainty remains.
No frames.

⑬ S, Y, Z

A
B
C
D
E

⑭ Ⓐ   They both do R, and since
B   S only does 1 thing, it
C   will have to be exactly
D   1 in common.
E

⑮ A
B
C
Ⓓ   U=2 and Y=2
E

⑯ X̶   S=1, U=2
B̶   U has R, Y doesn't
Ⓒ
D
E]   X has R. W+Y can't.

⑰ A
B
Ⓒ   U=R and V/T   Y= V and T
D
E
        either way,
        exactly one match

PT 48, G4

G_f, H_f, L_f, P_r, Q_r, T_r

N   V/   __ __   X
S   X   __ __   /P
    6   8   10 12
    Ø̶   Ɠ̶
    H̶

G_f — H_f | —r | or | —s |
             | — | | — |
             | 10 | | 10 |

Ⓛ/T | —↑ | —↑ |
           | —↓ | —Q |

BIG PAUSE

· Lots of complexity and variety.
· Rules 3+5 may interact, based
  on where folk does/doesn't happen.
· No floaters

To Frame or Not to Frame?

Rule 3 gives an interesting either/or

i. N V/ __ —s X   ii. N V% (L)(Q)r X
    S X   __ —s /P   S X G/H(T) H/V
       6   8 10 12   6   8 10 12
    Ø̶H̶   Ø̶   Ø̶H̶   Ø̶

⑱ A   Ⓐ
  B̶   4
  C̶   2
  D̶   4
  E̶   5

⑲ from frame 2 = Q, T, H, P could
  all be 10 or later

  Ⓐ try counterexample
  B̶ →   P_r T_r G_f X X
  C   X   Q_r L_f H_f /
  D̶   ↳ Breaks Q's rule
  E̶

⑳ from frame 2 = P or G

  Ⓐ verify → G L Q X
  B̶ diagram   X H T P ✓
  C
  D̶ diagram
  E

㉑ Q = 12, frame 1

  P_r (G_f)(H_f) X
  X   T_r L_f   Q

  A
  B
  C
  Ⓓ
  E   (breaks rule 4)

㉒ frame 2

  A
  Ⓑ
  C
  D
  E

PT 49, G1

(F) G (H) I N (T) = 2 of each avail.

I → [IN]

G → [GIN]

I̶   N̶   I̶   N̶   G̶   I̶
      G   G

BIG PAUSE

- Weird mismatch – 12 elements, six spaces. No requirement that each film be used. Possible to just use 3 of them twice.
- Using G or I creates chunks, so they are #1 priority.
- F, H, T are all floaters.

To Frame or Not to Frame?

The chunks don't have to be used, so no frames.

① A̶   2
   B̶   1
   C̶   2
   D̶   2
   E   (E)

② __ I N __ I N

   A
   B
   C
   (D)   Can't use N 3 times
   E

③ 2 × I = 2 × [IN] ←
   __ I N I N _N __ ⎤ Too
   __ I N I N _I _N ⎦ poss.

   (A)
   B
   C
   D
   E

---

④ A   From deductions, I = 2,4,5
   (B)   Also, from prev. work (#3)
   C
   D
   E

⑤ __ __ F __ F
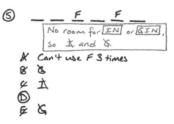
   No room for [IN] or [GIN], so I̶ and G̶

   A̶   Can't use F 3 times
   B̶   G̶
   C̶   I̶
   (D)   I̶
   E̶   G̶

⑥   H, H, N,N,T,T   G̶
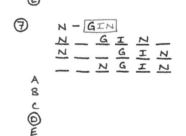
   A   __ H/T __ H/T __ __   I̶
   B   out
   C   if I̶ → G̶
   D
   (E)

⑦   N − [GIN]
   N __ __ G I N
   N __ __ __ G I N
   __ __ N G I N

   A
   B
   C
   (D)
   E

PT 49, G2

F, L, M, P, (S)

$L_R → P_J$

P_G or $P_R → L_J$

F can't be alone

__   __   __
F [P/S]   [ ]   [ ]
  G   J   R
  L̶
  M̶

BIG PAUSE

- 5 things to distribute among 3 groups, could either be 3-1-1 or 2-2-1.
- Not many rules so lots of flexibility. G has fewest options, so start there while keeping tabs on conditional.

To Frame or Not to Frame?

No chunks, lots of flexibility, so no frames.

⑧ A̶   setup (no P)
   B   (B)
   C̶   1
   D̶   2
   E̶   3

⑨ 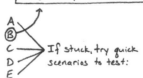 Inf: based on rules 1+2, J must always have L or P.

   A
   (B)
   C   → If stuck, try quick
   D   scenarios to test:
   E

   F   M   F   M
   S P L   S L P
   G J R   G J R
    ✓   ✓

   F   P   F   M
   S M L   P S L
    ✗   ✗

---

⑩ 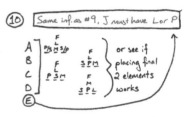 Same inf. as #9, J must have L or P

   A ⎤ F L
       P/S L M S/P   F   or see if
   B   S P M   placing final
   C   P S M   F   2 elements
   D   M   works
   (E) ⎦   S P L

⑪   If Rini has L, triggers rule 2, so start with B + C
   A
   (B)   F M L P S X
   C
   D
   E

⑫ (M) (S)   either J or R

                 F
       M   M
   _S_   P L S
   L̶   L̶
  Forces F to   ✓
  be alone
    ✗

   A̶
   B̶
   C̶
   D̶
   (E)

MANHATTAN
LSAT

PT 49, G3

offered   not

M → L or S (not both)

(L,S) or (L̸,S̸) → M̸

BIG PAUSE
· Need to keep an eye on
  the M/L/S rule, since it
  doesn't work with chain notation.
· Be wary of multiple connections
  from G, S, L.

To Frame or Not to Frame?

Conditional rules/games don't
lend themselves to framing.

⑬ A
   B̸   4
   C̸   1
   D̸   2
   E̸   1

Ⓐ

⑭

Ⓐ̸
B̸
Ⓒ
D
E

⑮

Ⓐ
B̸
C
D
E

⑯

A
B
C
Ⓓ
E

⑰ A
   B̸   prev work (14)
   C̸   prev work (16)
   B   prev work (16)
   Ⓔ   G=in → Z=in → S=out

PT 49, G4

F, G, H, J, K, L, M, O

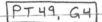

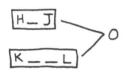

(fastest)   (slowest)

F/G __ __ __ __ __ __ __
    1   2   3   4   5   6   7   8
                              M̸

BIG PAUSE
· Got to always find a way
  to fit both chunks in
  spots 2-7.
· Spot 1 only has two
  options

To Frame or Not To Frame?

K̲ ̲_̲_̲_̲ ̲L̲ chunk has three
options. Frames are debateably
worth it.

F/G K __ H L J Ⓞ
F/G __ K __ __ L Ⓞ
F/G __ H K J __ L O

⑱ Ⓐ̸   Rule 3
   B
   C̸   2 and 4 combined
   D̸   4 and 5 combined
   E̸   Rule 6

Not an orientation quest., but
anticipate it will make simple
use of many rules.

⑲ A   H̲ ̲_̲ ̲J̲ - O
   B
   C   At least three things
   D   must come after H.
   Ⓔ

⑳ A̸   H̲ ̲_̲ ̲J̲ ⟍
   Ⓑ   ⟩ O - F
   C̸   K̲ ̲_̲_̲ ̲L̲ ⟋
   D̸
   E̸   So G is 1ˢᵗ

   G H K J M L O F

㉑ A̸   M - J
   B
   C̸   J's earliest in this game is 4
   Ⓓ   F/G H M J K ⟍ L - O
   E̸
        Doesn't work, try J=5.
        F/G M H K J G/L L O

㉒ A̸   prev. work (20)
   B̸   F/G K M H L J G/F O
   Ⓒ   Earliest spot for K̲ ̲_̲_̲ ̲L̲ is 2-5.
   D̸   prev. work (21)
   E̸   prev. work (20)

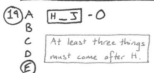
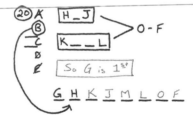
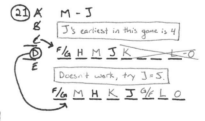

PT50, G1

```
**
L̶N̶
M̶N̶
```

```
         _____ same _____
         |                           |
        _1_ _2_ _3_ _4_  N/O  __   L,M,N,O
                          _5_  _6_
            |_____|
              same
```

BIG PAUSE

· 4 elements, 6 positions. No requirement that we use all 4 elements.

· Spot 5 affects who can go 1–6 and who can go 2–4. That interaction is our #1 priority.

<u>To Frame or Not to Frame?</u>

The either/or in spot 5 might be worth investigating, since it affects 1,2,4,6

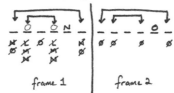

frame 1   frame 2

① A̶   1
   B̶   3
   C̶   4   Ⓓ
   D
   E̶   2

② N=5   frame 1

```
L/M   O     O   N   __
___  ___   ___ ___ ___
```

   A
 Ⓑ
   C
   D
   E

---

③
```
N  M   O  M   O  N | L
_  _   _  _   _  _ | out
ø  ø      ø      ø
```

A
B
Ⓒ
D
E

Have to use N+M in 1+2, but can't have MN

④ From frames, O must either be spot 2 or not used in 1, 2.

A
B
C
D
Ⓔ This forces spot 5 to either match spot 4 or 6.

⑤ O=2 → frame 1

```
__ _O_ __ _O_ _N_ __
                    N̶
                    ø
```

   A
 Ⓑ
   C   O in 6 means O in 1, which
   D̶   makes 1 and 2 the same.
   E̶

PT50, G2

in = 5   out = 5

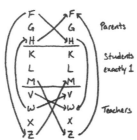

Parents

Students exactly 1

Teachers

```
    in        |  out    M/Z
 _  _  _  _  _ | F/H  U/W
               |  _   _   _
    S          |  P   S   S   T
```

BIG PAUSE

· Max of 3 Teachers selected.
  Max of 2 Parents selected.
  Numerical possibilities:

S	P	T
1	2	2
1	1	3

<u>To Frame or Not to Frame?</u>

Logic Chain should be all we need.

⑥ A̶   1
   B̶   5
   C̶   6
   D̶   4
   E   Ⓔ

⑦
```
H | F
  | M
W | V
Z |
```

   A
   B̶   S = 1
   C̶
 Ⓓ
   E̶

⑧ (Use chain)

   A
 Ⓑ   F → Z → M̶
   C
   D
   E

---

⑨
```
H | F
__|__
W | V
```

Ⓐ   could have just looked at chain instead
B
C
D
E

⑩

A
B
C
D
Ⓔ

⑪
```
        in          |       out
 W̶/U̶ X  G  H  M  | K  L  Z  F  U̶/W̶
  T  T  P  P  S  | S  S  T  P  T
```

   A
 Ⓑ
   C̶
   D̶
   E

PT 50, G3

$R_g, S_g, T_g, \circled{R_c}, S_c, T_c$

$S_c - \overset{S_g}{R_g} - T_g - T_c$

At least
one
grad
___ ___ ___ ___ ___
 1   2   3   4   5

BIG PAUSE
· 6 things, 5 spots. Okay to
  put more than one thing
  per spot. Okay to leave a
  spot blank. Chain of 4
  means at least 4 spots will
  have something.
· R_c is a total floater.

<u>To Frame or Not To Frame?</u>

· Spot 3 is either $\overset{S_g}{R_g}$ or T_g.
  Chain reactions follow. Frame.

i. R_c?   ii. R_c?

$\underline{\circled{S_c} \;\; \overset{S_g}{R_g} \; T_g \; T_c}$ | $\underline{S_c \;\; \overset{S_g}{R_g} \; T_g \; \circled{T_c}}$

⑫ A̶ $R_g \neq 1$
  Ⓑ   frame 2
  C
  D
  E

⑬   Only T_c or R_c can = 5

  A
  Ⓑ
  C
  D
  E

⑭ Ⓐ S_c & R_c, either frame
  B̶ S_c & R_c, frame 1
  Ⓒ   only R_c can go in 3
  D
  E

⑬ Ⓐ
  B
  C
  D
  E

⑯ T_g spot 4 in Frame 1
     R_c spot 3 in Frame 2

  A̶   either frame
  B̶   frame 2
  C̶   frame 2
  D̶   frame 2
  Ⓔ   frame 2

⑰ S_g = 3, Frame 1

  A
  B
  C
  D
  Ⓔ

PT 50, G4

$T, U, W, X, Y, Z = 1$

___ ___ ___
▭   ▭   ▭
1   2   3
Y̶   X̶
U̶   T̶
X

$T - U$ $\boxed{\overset{U}{Y}}$ or $\boxed{\overset{U}{Z}}$
$X \not{-} U$
$W - Y$ $\overset{Y}{\underset{Z}{\cancel{ }}}$

BIG PAUSE
· 6 things will be distributed
  3-2-1 or 2-2-2
· Highest priority might be
  figuring out $\overset{U}{Y}$ vs $\overset{U}{Z}$ each time
· Otherwise, just ordering
  relationships to verify.
· Z can't be with Y, but
  otherwise Z is free.

<u>To Frame or Not to Frame?</u>

Chunk isn't set in stone, but
we might write:

i.   ii.
    ↗X↘   ↗X↘
T —⟨U⟩   T —⟨U⟩
W —⟨Y⟩   ⟨Z⟩
  ↖___Z___↗   W — Y

⑱ A̶   3
  B   Ⓑ
  C̶   3
  D̶   1
  E̶   2

⑲   Y = alone, frame 2
     $\boxed{\overset{U}{Z}}$ = 2 or 3

     X   X
  W U   T U
  $\underline{T \; Z \; Y}$ or $\underline{W \; Y \; Z}$
  1 2 3   1 2 3

  A̶
  B̶
  C̶
  Ⓓ
  E̶

⑳ $Z = 1 \rightarrow$ frame 1

  T
  W U   ⟨$\overset{T}{W}$⟩   X
  Z Y X   or   Z __ U
  1 2 3   1 2 Y
                         3

  A
  B
  C
  D
  Ⓔ

㉑ A̶
  B̶ ⎫ Z was okay alone in #20
  C̶ ⎭
  D   Ⓓ
  E̶   X can never be 1

㉒   Y/Z
               X
  __ T U
  1   2   3

  Ⓐ   we could have had
  B
  C   X
  D   W   U   in #20
  E $\underline{Z \; T \; Y}$

PT S1, G1

1 plaid, 1 solid (share 1 color)
(multi-color) (one-color)

i. Plaid J, Solid O	ii. Solid J, Plaid O

i. Plaid J, Solid O

G
R
V   R/V
J   O

ii. Solid J, Plaid O

R/V   —
J   O
    R,V,Y

BIG PAUSE

· Unusual game. The first 2 rules provided the 2 frames for the game.
· The fact that they must share a color limits what the solid color can be.
· Not much to figure out once we know which frame to use.

To Frame or Not to Frame?

Rules provided 2 frames.

① A̶   2
  B̶   3
  C̶   5
  D   Ⓓ
  E̶   2

② 2 colors = Frame 2

Ⓐ
B
C
D
E

③ J has G = Frame 1

A̶
B̶
C̶
D̶
Ⓔ

④ A̶   frame 1
  B̶   frame 1
  Ⓒ   neither frame
  D
  E

⑤ 3 colors = Frame 1

A
B
C
D
Ⓔ

PT S1, G2

F, G, H, J, K, L

H – L

G – H → J < K/L

H – G → K < J/L

H – F – G or G – F – H

BIG PAUSE

· Looks like Relative Ordering, except rules 2,3, + 4 aren't typical.
· Hard to create a Tree because rules 2,3, + 4 create either/or possibilities.

To Frame or Not to Frame?

Frame! Using last rule, we can create 2 trees.

i.   H – F – G
    L
  K   J

ii.   G – F – H – L
    J
     K

⑥ A̶   2
  B̶   Ⓑ
  C̶   3
  D̶   4
  E̶   1

⑦   J   G   (F – H – L, K)

    (Gotta be frame 2)

A̶
B̶
Ⓒ
D
E

⑧ (Spot 1 in frame 1 = H or K)
   (Spot 1 in frame 2 = G or J)

A   Ⓐ
B̶
C̶
D̶
E̶

⑨ (gotta be frame 1)

    H
  L — F — G
  K   J

A̶
B
C̶
Ⓓ
E

⑩ (Gotta be frame 1)

      F — G
K – H – J
      L

A̶
B̶
C̶
Ⓓ
E̶

PT 51, G3

Songs - S, T, V, W, X, Y, Z

Type - R/N

N __ __ __ N R N R/N
(T-W,Y) S X/V Z V/X STVWXYZ
1 2 3 4 5 6 7

T-W ⟩ S   R → NR
  Y   if N can't go before
                R → R

BIG PAUSE

· With each question, only need to worry about X/V in 5 or 7, Y in 1/2/3, T-W.
· Be careful about adding more R's on top, since each one comes with an N before it.

To Frame or Not to Frame?

Deductions have already gone quite far. No need for frames.

⑪ | We know S=4 and Z=6. We also know 5 and 7 must be X and V. |

A̶
B̶
C̶
D
E̶   Ⓓ

⑫ A̶   V could be 7
   B̶   W could be 2
   C̶
   D̶   T could be 1, Y could be 3
   Ⓔ

⑬ A
   B
   C
   Ⓓ   whether it's 5 or 7, it's N
   E

⑭   W-Y
   N __ __ __ N R N
   T W Y S X/V Z V/X

   A
   B
   C
   Ⓓ
   E

⑮ | Y __ __ V |
   N __ __ __ N R N
   T Y W S V Z X

   A̶
   B̶
   C̶
   D̶
   Ⓔ

PT 51, G4

G, H, J, K, L, M, N, O

   H — L
 N⟍ ⟍
   M — G — O
 J⟋   ⟍ K

__ __ __ __ __ __ __ %/L
1 2 3 4 5 6 7 8

BIG PAUSE

· 4 options for spot 1, only 2 for spot 8.
· L and K are strays.

To Frame or Not to Frame?

We have a tree. No need for frames.

⑯ A̶ 6
   B̶ 5
   C̶ 4
   D   Ⓓ
   E̶ 3

⑰ A
   B
   Ⓒ   L, M, G, O all come after H
   D
   E

⑱ (H, N, J) M (G—O, L)
           K
   __ __ __ __ __ __ __
   A
   B
   C
   Ⓓ
   E

⑲ (N, J, K) H (M-G-O,L)
   Ⓐ
   B
   C
   D
   E

⑳ A̶
   Ⓑ
   C
   D
   E

㉑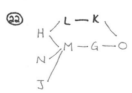
   A
   B
   Ⓒ   L, M, +G would have to fit in spots 5 and 6
   D
   E

㉒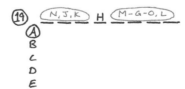
   A
   B
   Ⓒ   5 things must come after H
   D
   E

PT52, G1

G, H, I, K, L, N, O, P

```
        K — I
        P → H — O — L
        N        G
```

```
___ ___ ___ ___ ___ ___ ___ L/I
 1   2   3   4   5   6   7   8
```

BIG PAUSE

· 4 things could go 1st, only 2 can go last.
· I and G are Strays

To Frame or Not to Frame?

We have a Tree. No need to frame.

---

① K̶   5
  B̶   2
  K̶   4
  D̶   3
  Ⓔ

② A
  B
  Ⓒ   K has 4 things (I, H, O, L)
  D   after it.
  E

③   K I (P,N → H-O, G) L
  A
  Ⓑ
  C
  D
  E

To Frame or Not to Frame?

No chunks, no crucial either/or's.
Go to questions.

⑧ A̶   1
  B
  K̶   2   ⑧
  D̶   4
  E̶   3

⑨   L   V   S
    T (J K)
    M   O   P
  A
  B
  C
  D
  Ⓔ

---

④ ___ ___ ___ ___ ___ ___ L I
  A
  Ⓑ
  C
  D
  E

⑤ A
  B
  C
  D
  Ⓔ   If 5 before N, N=6 which
         doesn't leave room for H-O-L

⑥ (P,N,G) K (H-O-L, I)
  A
  Ⓑ
  C
  D
  E

⑦   G K I (P,N → H-O) L
  A
  Ⓑ
  C
  D
  E

⑩   K   T   J
    (L S)   V
    M   O   P
  Ⓐ
  B
  C
  D
  E

⑪ A
  B
  C
  Ⓓ   rule 3
  E

⑫ A   K   J
      T/V   L   V/T   looks fine
       M   O   P
  B̶   prev work (9)
  Ⓒ   ___ K ___   Rule 2 forces
        ___ T ___   V into O
         M   O   P
  D̶   prev work (10)
  E
```

## PT52, G2

J, K, L, S, T, V

```
___ ___ ___
 M   O   P
         T/V
```

```
 J → L        ┌ J ┐
 M    P       │ K │

 K → V        ┌ T ┐
 M    O       │ V │      ┌ L ┐
                         │ S │
```

BIG PAUSE

· 6 things, 6 spots.
· Several anti-chunk rules and 2 conditionals. Hard to prioritize one "key" rule, but start with conditionals.
· T has only 2 options.
· Might want to re-write (re-think) rule 2 as K/S or K/P → V/O.
```

PT 52, G3

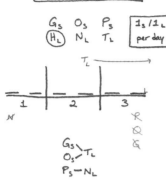

G_S O_S P_S | $1_S / 1_L$ per day |

(H_L) N_L T_L

$T_L \longrightarrow$

```
   |       |
___|_____|____
 1     2     3
```
N

R
Q
G

$G_S \searrow T_L$
$O_S \nearrow$
$P_S - N_L$

| BIG PAUSE |

- 6 things, 6 spots. Just have to use annoying subscripts to keep track of $1_S / 1_L$ per day.
- T_L seems limited; earliest would be spot 2 on day 2. T_L is #1 priority.

To Frame or Not to Frame?

T_L has 3 options + triggers other stuff.

i. | O/G • H | G/O T_L | P | N |

X. | O/G | G/O | T_L | P_S | X   Blows up. So, only two frames.

ii. | $P_S - N_L$, G/O, H | O/G T_L |

iX. | ___ ___ ___ | O/G T_L |
     $\emptyset$

(13) A.   2
    B   (B)
    C.   3
    D.   1
    E.   2

(14)   G = 1, either frame

$$\frac{G}{S} \; \frac{H}{L} \; | \; \_\_ \; \_\_ \; | \; \_\_ \; \_\_$$

   A
   B
   C
   D
   E   (E)

(15)

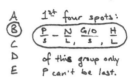

   A
   B
   (C)
   D
   E

(16) Frame 1 only allows T, so we must be dealing with frame 2.

   A
   (B)   1st four spots:
   C $\left(\frac{P}{S} \; \_\_ \; \frac{N}{L}, \; \frac{G/O}{S}, \; \frac{H}{L} \right)$
   D
   E   of this group only P can't be last.

(17)   H = day 2 $\longrightarrow$ frame 2

$$\frac{P}{S} \; \frac{N}{L} \; \left| \; \boxed{\frac{H}{L} \; \frac{G/O}{S}} \; \right| \; \frac{O/G}{S} \; \frac{T}{L}$$

   A
   B
   C
   (D)
   E

PT 52, G4

F, G, H, K, L, M

$F - G - K$
$H \nearrow$

$M \begin{smallmatrix} H \\ < \\ K \end{smallmatrix}$ or $\begin{smallmatrix} H \\ > \\ K \end{smallmatrix} M$

$F - M \rightarrow L - H$

$H - L \rightarrow M - F$

| BIG PAUSE |

- More complicated than most relative ordering. Can't get a complete Tree due to rules 3 and 4.
- Need to create 2 trees based on rule 4, and see if that sheds any light on rule 3.

To Frame or Not to Frame?

Need 2 frames, for each version of rule 4.

i. $F - G - K$
    $H \nearrow$
    $M \nearrow$

Doesn't tell me if F-M or H-L

ii.   L-H
     $F - G - K - M$

In this one, we know F-M so we can add L-H

(18) A.   3
    B.   4
    C   (C)
    D.   1
    E.   2

(19) (M-H, L)   F   G   K
    Must be Frame 1

   (A)
   B
   C
   D
   E

(20)
$$\begin{smallmatrix} F \\ H \end{smallmatrix} - G - K$$

$M \; \frac{F/H}{} \; \frac{H/F}{} \; G \; K$
Must be Frame 1

   A
   B
   C
   D
   (E)

(21) A.   prev work (20)
    B   prev work (20)
    (C)   H-K, true in both frames
    D
    E

(22)   K-L
    | must be frame 1 |

$$\begin{smallmatrix} F \\ > \\ M \end{smallmatrix} \begin{smallmatrix} H \\ \end{smallmatrix} G - K - L$$

   A
   B
   (C)   By Rule 3, H-L,
   D   So M-F
   E

$M \begin{smallmatrix} F \\ < \\ H \end{smallmatrix} G - K - L$

(23) A
    B   prev work (19, 20)
    C   prev work (19)
    D   prev work (19)
    (E)   Impossible in both frames

PTS3, G1

T, W, X, Y, Z

—   —   —

☒   ☐   ☐
F   P   S

Ⱦ
Ⱬ

$\boxed{\begin{array}{c}Z\\Y\end{array}}$ $T_s \rightarrow W_s$

BIG PAUSE

· 5 things in 3 groups could
  either be 3-1-1 or 2-2-1.
· $\boxed{\begin{array}{c}Z\\Y\end{array}}$ chunk is #1 priority,
  followed by conditional.

To Frame or Not to Frame?

Chunk can only go 2 places, so
frames could be nice.

i.

$\boxed{X}$ $\boxed{\begin{array}{c}Z\\Y\end{array}}$ $\boxed{W}$
F   P   S

ii.
— — $\boxed{\begin{array}{c}Z\\Y\end{array}}$
$\boxed{X}$ $\boxed{W/T}$ $\boxed{Y}$
F   P   S̸

1) A̸   4
   B   Ⓑ
   C̸   3
   D̸   1
   E̸   2

2) Ⓐ   frame 1
   B̸
   C̸
   D̸
   E̸

3) A̸   frame 2
   Ⓑ
   C
   D
   E

4) A   either frame
   Ⓑ   frame 1, last loose end
   C
   D
   E

5)   frame 2
   A
   B
   Ⓒ   forces 4 ppl in S.
   D
   E

PTS3, G2

G, J, L, M, P, V

P — M — L

$G\!\!\begin{array}{c}{}^J\\{}_L\end{array}$ or $\begin{array}{c}J\\{}_L\end{array}\!\!G$

$V\!\!\begin{array}{c}{}^G\\{}_P\end{array}$ or $\begin{array}{c}G\\{}_P\end{array}\!\!V$

BIG PAUSE

· Doesn't lend itself to 1 Tree.
· We could use Rule 2 or Rule 3
  to create 2 trees with 5 out of 6.

To Frame or Not to Frame?

To manage the data a little better, we
can use Rule 2 (or 3) to make 2 trees.
Arbitrarily using Rule 2, we get:

i. $\begin{array}{c}P-M-L\\G-J\end{array}$ ii. $\begin{array}{c}J\\ \searrow\\P-M-L-G\end{array}$

For both frames, we still could have
$V\!\!\begin{array}{c}{}^G\\{}_P\end{array}$ or $\begin{array}{c}G\\{}_P\end{array}\!\!V$

6) A̸   2
   B̸   1
   C   Ⓒ
   D̸   3
   E̸   1

7) Ⓐ   P — M — L
   B
   C
   D
   E

8) — — — — — L
   $\boxed{\text{Gotta use Frame 1. What must be true in Frame 1?}}$
   Ⓐ
   B
   C
   D
   E

9) J — M $\boxed{\text{works in both frames}}$
   i. $\begin{array}{c}P-M-L\\G-J\end{array}$ ii. $\begin{array}{c}J\\ \searrow\\P-M-L-G\end{array}$
   A
   B
   C
   Ⓓ
   E

10) A
   B
   Ⓒ   P — M — L
   D
   E

11) A̸   M ≠ 1
   Ⓑ $\underline{V}\ \underline{G}\ \underline{P}\ \underline{J}\ \underline{M}\ \underline{L}$ frame 1
   C
   D
   E

MANHATTAN
LSAT

PT 53, G3

Suspects: S T V W X Y Z

C = confessed, N = not confessed

W — S, W —$\overset{all}{N}$, so $\boxed{\frac{N}{S}}$

$Z \overset{\nearrow X}{\searrow V}$ T — $\overset{exactly\ 2}{C}$

_	_	_	N	C	C	N	C/N
$\frac{Z/Y}{1}$	$\frac{\ }{2}$	$\frac{T}{3}$	$\frac{\ }{4}$	$\frac{\ }{5}$	$\frac{W}{6}$	$\frac{S}{7}$	STVWX(Y)Z

BIG PAUSE

· Robust deductions, so all that's left is whether Z is 1 or 2.
· Y is a floater in 1, 2, 4, 5
· 1st 3 spots don't matter in terms of C/N

To Frame or Not To Frame?

Great deductions. No need to frame.

12 A. ~~A~~
    Ⓑ
    ~~C~~
    ~~D~~
    ~~E~~

13 $\boxed{\frac{C}{Z},\ the\ 2^{nd}\ C}$ so, Z = 2, Y = 1

C	C	_	N	C	C	N
$\frac{\ }{Y}$	$\frac{\ }{Z}$	$\frac{\ }{T}$	$\frac{\ }{X/V}$	$\frac{\ }{V/X}$	$\frac{\ }{W}$	$\frac{\ }{S}$

A
B
C
D
Ⓔ

14 Ⓐ $\boxed{Z - V - Y - X}$
    B
    C | _ | _ | _ | N | C | C | N |
    D $\frac{\ }{Z}$ $\frac{\ }{V}$ $\frac{\ }{T}$ $\frac{\ }{Y}$ $\frac{\ }{X}$ $\frac{\ }{W}$ $\frac{\ }{S}$
    E

---

15 A
   B
   C
   D
   Ⓔ   Z = 1 or 2

16 $\boxed{\frac{C}{X},\ \frac{C}{Y}}$

_	_	_	_	N	C	C	N
			$\frac{\ }{T}$	$\frac{\ }{V}$	$\frac{\ }{X/Y}$	$\frac{\ }{W}$	$\frac{\ }{S}$

Ⓐ
B
C
D
E

17 $\boxed{\frac{N}{X},\ \frac{N}{V}}$

N	_	_	N	C	C	N
$\frac{\ }{Z}$	$\frac{\ }{X/V}$	$\frac{\ }{T}$	$\frac{\ }{V/X}$	$\frac{\ }{Y}$	$\frac{\ }{W}$	$\frac{\ }{S}$

A
B
C
Ⓓ
E

PT 53, G4

~~X~~		~~P~~	
_	I	_	(M, N◎, P, S, T)
(Ⓕ, G, H) $\frac{\ }{1}$	$\frac{\ }{2}$	$\frac{\ }{3}$	
H		~~G~~	

P — N $\frac{S}{G}$ $\boxed{\frac{M}{P}}$ (crossed)

G — H

$\frac{S}{G - H}$

BIG PAUSE

· Hybrid task. Need the order of 3 things (F, G, H) and the groups of 2 that go with each.
· Ordering rules for bottom row and P — N.
· Interplay of $\frac{S}{G}$ and G — H may be important.

To Frame or Not to Frame?

G has 2 options + brings S with it.

i. | _ | _ | _ | ii. | O | S | M |
S	T	_		P	T	N
G	(F H)			F	G	H
1	2	3		1	2	3

18 ~~A~~   2
   ~~B~~   3
   ~~C~~   4
   ~~D~~   1+5
   E   Ⓔ

19 Ⓐ $\frac{P}{H} \longrightarrow$ frame 1
   B
   C | S | T | P-N | | %M | P | N |
   D | G | ~~F~~ | H | or | S | T | M/% |
   E | 1 | 2 | 3 | | G | H | F |
                                | 1 | 2 | 3 |

20 $\frac{O}{2}$ = frame 1
  ~~A~~
  Ⓑ | P | O | N |
  C | S | T | M |
  D | G | (F H) | |
  E | 1 | 2 | 3 |

---

21 $\frac{P}{T} \longrightarrow$ frame 1

A | %M | P | N |
B | S | T | M/% |
Ⓒ | G | (F H) | |
D | 1 | 2 | 3 |
E

22 M — H $\longrightarrow$ frame 1

   | (M, P) | N | | M | P | N |
   | S | T | O | S | T | O |
~~A~~ | G | F | H | or | G | H | F |
~~B~~ | 1 | 2 | 3 | | 1 | 2 | 3 |
~~C~~
~~D~~
Ⓔ

23 already seen S with = O, M, P
            (prev. work)
     and S with T
          (frame 2)

~~A~~
Ⓑ
~~C~~
~~D~~
~~E~~

PT 54, G1

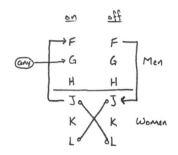

on   off

→ F   F
(any) → G   G   Men
    H   H
    J ⤬ J
    K ⤬ K   Women
    L ⤬ L

on	off
G ³/L	⁴/J

BIG PAUSE

· First 2 rules become bi-
  conditional.
· Since J or L is always ON,
  G must always be ON (no
  need for contrapositive)

To Frame or Not to Frame?

Conditional Rules/Games don't
lend themselves to frames.

① ~~A~~   2
   ~~B~~   4
   C   (C)
   ~~D~~   3
   ~~E~~   1

② A
   B
   C
   Ⓓ   J and L are always split,
   E   1 in, 1 out

---

③   J G F | L   (KH) could be out

A
B
C
~~D~~
Ⓔ

④ | B/c of J/L, can't have all
   3 women, so 2 w, 1 m
   (must be G) ↗ |

A
B
Ⓒ
D
E

⑤ | G, ³/L |

A
~~B~~
Ⓒ
D
E

PT 54, G2

H, I, N, Q, R, Ⓢ = 1

☐ ☐ ☐ ☐
1   2   3   4
∅   ∅   ~~I~~

| N H |

(H/I) or (R/I)   (H/R/)

Q — ¹ₘₐₓ

BIG PAUSE

· 6 things, 8 open spots. 2-2-1-1
  distribution.   (H/R/I)
· Q rule is confusing. Q can
  be 3ʳᵈ if only 1 thing in spot 4.
  Inf.: (H/R/I) ≠ 4
· |N H| seems top priority

To Frame or Not to Frame?

|N H| has 3 options. Debateable,
but here they are:

i.   ↙ I ↘ Q   ii.   ↙ I ↘ ↙ Q
   N H __ __   __ N H __

iii. (R/I/S) ↙ Q ↘
       N H

⑥ A   (A)
   ~~B~~   4
   ~~C~~   3
   ~~D~~   2
   ~~E~~   4

⑦   H/R alone → frame 1
   Ⓐ   S/ ↗ R I/S
   B   N H   R   Q
   C
   D
   E

⑧   (R/S) → (H/I) frame 1 or 2
   A
   B   i. N   H   R   Q
   C   S
   Ⓓ   ii. R   I   H   Q
   E   S   N

---

⑨   N/R/I → frame 1

   N   I
   R   H   (Q S)

~~A~~
~~B~~
~~C~~
~~D~~
Ⓔ

⑩ A
   ~~B~~
   C
   Ⓓ   imposs. in all 3 frames
   E

⑪   R/I → frame 2

      ↙ S ↘
   R   N   H   Q
       I

~~A~~
~~B~~
~~C~~
~~D~~
Ⓔ

⑫   Q, S from prev. work

   A
   Ⓑ   Deduction (H/R/I) ≠ 4
   ~~C~~   (breaks Q's rule)
   D
   ~~E~~

PT 54, G3

L, M, O, R, S, Ⓥ

6 __
5 __
4 __
3 __
2 __
1 __

[R/S chunk box]   [S O I M L column]

BIG PAUSE
- Chain of 4, and the chunk in particular, is #1 priority.
- V is a floater.

To Frame or Not to Frame?

[ML] chunk has three options, but only one of those options seems to have chain reactions. Probably best to skip frames, but this is what we'd get:

```
6  __    __    S
5  __    __    O
4  __    __    M
3  __    M     L
2  M     L     Ⓥ
1  L     V/R   R
```

⑬ A
Ⓑ   Rule 1
Ⓒ   2
Ⓓ   3
Ⓔ   3

⑭ Ⓐ
Ⓑ
C
D
E

[S V I O I M L diagram with R]

The only other element that could be immediately below S is V.

⑮ [box: The other two candidates for top layer are R and V]

A   R   V
B   V   S
C   S   O
D   O   M
Ⓔ   M   L
    L

⑯ Ⓐ   6 S
Ⓡ   5 O
C   4 M
D   3 L
E   2 V
   1 R

⑰ Ⓐ
Ⓑ   prev work (16)
C
D
E

PT 54, G4

H, J, K, R, S, T

$J_4 \rightarrow J <^S_T$ $H<^J_K$

$\cancel{J_4} \rightarrow {}^S_T > J$

```
__  __  __  __  R/S  __
1   2   3   4   5    6
(low)                (high)
     ⌄
   Accepted
   Bid (K/R)
```

BIG PAUSE
- "Accepted Bid" is a curveball. Deal with it when it comes up in the questions.
- The conditional rules have big relative ordering implications. Frames could be nice.

To Frame or Not to Frame?

Frame! Let's see how things look if J is 4 or 4̸.

J=4 $\begin{array}{c}S>J\\T>J\\H<K\end{array}$ J≠4

(H-K, R) J S T __ __ __ __ R/S J

⑱ Ⓐ   2
B
Ⓒ   Rule 1
Ⓓ   3
Ⓔ   4

⑲ Ⓐ
Ⓑ   Frame 1
C
D
E

[box: In Frame 2, H-K, so putting H=4 would leave no room for K.]

⑳ A
Ⓑ   J is 4 or 6
C
D
E

㉑ __ Ⓡ __ __ S __
A
B
C
Ⓓ
E

㉒ Ⓐ   avoidable in Frame 2
Ⓑ   avoidable in Frame 2
Ⓒ   True in both Frames
D
E

㉓ R H K T/S S J/T

Ⓐ
B
C   [box: If R=1, S must be 5 and K must be accepted bid in 2 or 3. H-K forces H=2, K=3.]
D
E

PT55, G1

G, L, M, R, Ⓢ, V

O __ __ __ L
F __ __ __
   1   2   3

ⒼⓂ or ⓋⓂ   G̶/R̶

BIG PAUSE
· 6 things, 6 spots
· Ⓖ or Ⓜ is an either/or chunk, so high priority.
· G and R are in different rows
· S is a floater

To Frame or Not to Frame?

No defined chunks. Everyone seems to have at least 3 possible spaces. No frames. (We also know these types of games are typically back-end).

① A̶   3
   B̶   2
   C̶   1
   D   Ⓓ
   E̶   3

②   could be any of the 3 teams, so think about who are other teams?

L   R
S   V

   A̶
   B̶
   Ⓒ
   D̶
   E̶

③ A   Ⓐ
   B̶   leaves no one for M
   R̶   L̶ never poss.
   D̶   R̶ never poss.
   E̶   M̶ never poss.

④
   R+G diff rows

   A
   Ⓑ
   C
   D
   E

⑤

   A
   B
   C
   D
   Ⓔ

⑥ S   L   G/R   G
   V   R →   , so   M

   A̶
   B̶
   Ⓒ
   D
   E

⑩ L can't be 1ˢᵗ or last

   A
   B
   C
   D
   Ⓔ

⑪ frame 1
   H J L J L H

   A
   B
   C
   Ⓓ
   E

⑫ L₁ ...ᵐᵃˣ... L₂   Both cases,
   frame 1: HJLJLH   only 1 in
   frame 2: JLHLHJ   between L₁+L₂

   A
   Ⓑ
   C
   D
   E

PT55, G2

H, J, L = 1 or 2 each

        1ˢᵗ = Last
H/J __ __ __ .... 4-6 spaces
 &
exactly 1 J

HJ = 1

BIG PAUSE
· Hard to draw number line, since there could be 4, 5, or 6 spaces.
· J is most important, due to HJ chunk, only once in 1ˢᵗ three spots, and could be First/Last.
· Repeating letters can go consecutively.

To Frame or Not to Frame?

2 possibilities for First/Last = H, J

H J L .... H⌉ Picking who's
J .... H J⌋ 1ˢᵗ determines where HJ chunk must be

⑦ A̶   1
   B̶   3
   R̶   2
   D   Ⓓ
   E̶   3

⑧ 2ⁿᵈ frame
   J L L Ⓗ H J

   A
   B
   Ⓒ
   D
   E

⑨ 4 msgs
   Frame 1: H J L H
   Frame 2: J L H J

   Ⓐ
   B
   C
   D
   E

PT55, G3

F, G, H, R, S, T

Nightshift

G, T or S, H

F — G — T
    ╱
R — S — H

(most) F/R __ __ __ __ T/H (least)
   1   2   3   4   5   6

BIG PAUSE

· Looks like easy relative ordering except for "Nightshift" curveball. Only Q17 seems to care about that distinction, so we'll deal with it when we need to.

To Frame or Not to Frame?

We have a Tree, so no frames needed.

⑬ A̶   3
   B̶   4
   C̶   1
   D   Ⓓ
   E̶   5

⑭ R S F (G—T, H)

   A̶
   Ⓑ
   C
   D
   E

⑮ A
   B
   Ⓒ   R — S — H
   D
   E

To Frame or Not to Frame?

No obvious chunks to work with. L being 1 or 2 doesn't seem to have consequences. Don't frame.

⑲ A̶   4
   B̶   1
   C̶   3
   D̶   2
   E   Ⓔ

⑳ __ m̲ __ L̲ __ __ __

Seems like there are still many possibilities

   A
   B
   C
   Ⓓ
   E̶   J ≠ 1

PT55, G4

stops: f l m s

passengers: G J R V

R ≠ M   V — J
J ≠ f ⟷ G ≠ s
J — f ⟷ G — s

J̲   V̶
__ __ __ __ G J R V
            f l m s
 1   2   3   4
         ✗   ✗

BIG PAUSE

· Tough rules! Have to watch out for things being before / not being before other things.
· Last rule is probably most important since it works both directions.
· "L must be 1 or 2" is also very limited.

---

⑯ Want something that forces the two mini-chains (F-G-T & R-S-H) into definite spots.

   A
   B
   Ⓒ   R S H   F G T
   D
   E

⑰   (R-S-H, F) G T
     (F-G-T, R) S H

   A̶
   B̶
   C̶
   D
   E

⑱ From prev work, we know G (13), F (14), H (16), R (17) can be 3ʳᵈ

   From Tree, only T cannot be 3ʳᵈ

   A̶
   B̶
   C̶
   D̶
   Ⓔ

㉑   & R̶
      ‾f̲‾ ‾L̲‾ ‾(m̲ s̲)‾

   J ≠ f, so G ≠ s & R ≠ m (always)

   A̶
   B̶
   C̶
   Ⓓ
   E

㉒   & ̶
      ‾V̲‾ ‾G̲‾
      (L s) (f m)

   A
   B
   Ⓒ
   D
   E

㉓ G — s, so J — f and since V — J, V — J — f

   A
   B
   C
   Ⓓ
   E

PT56, G1

Ⓕ, G, H, J, K, L

J — H

GL — K

J — L

1	2	3	4	5	6
H̶	X̶				X̶
K̶					G̶
					L̶

BIG PAUSE

· J and L each mentioned in a couple rules, which can't be linked because of interchangeable positions.
· Top priority is balancing GL chunk with J—L chunk.
· F is a floater.

To Frame or Not to Frame?

Don't frame. Chunks have multiple possibilities and interchangeable elements.

① A̶   3
   B̶   2
   K̶   4
   D̶   Rule 1
   E

② A   might have JHL
  Ⓑ GL — K
   C
   D
   E

③ A
  B   G L K J H F
  Ⓒ
  D̶ diagram
  E̶ diagram

K=3 was theoretically K's earliest. Completed a scenario to make sure it could work.

---

④ A̶ 4/5 G 3/L H ⟨K,F⟩
  B̶ _ J G? L G?
  Ⓒ _ F G L K J H
  D
  E

⑤ | F ≠ 1 |
Too many other possibilities. Test answers.

Ⓐ G L K/F J F/k H ↰
 B _ J H L G K stop here,
 C _ J H L G K but
 D _ J H/G L G/H/K H/K FYI
 E _ G L K J H

⑥ On 1st pass, nothing sticks out. Test counterexample to each answer

A̶ F J H L G K ✓
B̶ J H L G ⟨K,F⟩ ✓
K̶ prev. work (4)
D̶ scenario for (A) + (B)
E _ _ J G L K (fyi)
    no room for H

PT56, G2

G H J M ≥ 1

_ _ _
R S T

G/S ⟷ H/r   J/T → M/r | G/J |

BIG PAUSE

· Mismatch! 4 things, 6 spots. Since everyone goes at least once, we'll either use one person 3 times (3, 1, 1, 1) or two people twice (2, 2, 1, 1).
· Bi-conditional should be top priority. Either they both happen or they both don't happen.

To Frame or Not to Frame?

The bi-conditional is an either/or, but it's probably not worth framing.

⑦ A   Ⓐ
  B̶ 3
  K̶ 2
  D̶ 1
  E̶ 1

⑧ J _ _   Since
  M _ G   H̶/r̶ → G̶/S̶
  R S T
    &

A
B
C
Ⓓ
E

---

⑨ J/M G M/J
  H H H   H/r → G/S
  R S T

A̶
Ⓑ
C
D
E

⑩ Same 2 in R, T means remaining 2 in S

A̶ rule 3
Ⓑ G H G
   M J M
   R S T
C (breaks rule 2)
D remaining 2 = G, J
E (breaks rule 1)

⑪ _ J _
   M H   G/S → H/r
  R S T
  H̶

A
B̶
K̶
D̶
Ⓔ

MANHATTAN
LSAT

PT56, G3

M, O, S, T } each park has 3 of 4

$\frac{\overline{T}}{\frac{M}{G}}$ $\frac{\overline{T}}{\frac{}{L}}$

$\boxed{\begin{array}{c}M\\S\end{array}} \geq 1$ $O \to T$
($\cancel{T} \to \cancel{O}$)

imposs., so T must be in

BIG PAUSE

· Curious setup. Essentially we're only making 2 decisions: which of the four is NOT in each group.
· Mismatch = check the min/max for the elements. It never said that each variety appears at least once. Hence, the two groups could potentially match.

To Frame or Not to Frame?

$\boxed{\begin{array}{c}M\\S\end{array}}$ chunk has three options: G, L, or both.

i.		ii.		iii.	
T	M/S	M	T	T	T
M	T	T	M	M	M
S	O	O	S	S	S
G	L	G	L	G	L

12 A 3
    B̶ 2
    C̶ 3
    D (D)
    E̶ 4

13 A̶ frame 2 ⎤ counter examples
    B̶ frame 1 ⎦
    (C) T must always be in
    D
    E

PT56, G4

To Frame or Not to Frame?

F only has 2 possible positions.

(Q,R,S,T,V) [☐ ☐ ☐]

(F,H,Ⓜ) $\frac{}{1}$ $\frac{}{2}$ $\frac{}{3}$
         R̶   Ø
         T̶

$Q <^R_T$ $\frac{/}{}$
             $\frac{}{}$
$V \neq S$ ☐ F — H

i.	ii.
/ _ _	_ _ /
☐ ☐ ☐	☐ ☐ ☐
Q/S	M F H
F (H M)	1 2 3
1 2 3	

17 A
    B̶ 4
    C̶ 3   (A)
    D̶ 1
    E̶ 2

18 A̶
    (A) $\frac{R}{T}$ → frame 1
    B $\frac{}{2}$
    C   /
    D   Q T   (V,S)
    E   F (H M)

19 A̶
    B̶ $\boxed{\begin{array}{c}Q\\S\end{array}}$ → frame 2, spot 1
    (C)
    D   _ / _
    E   Q / _   (R,T,V)
          S ☐☐
          M F H

BIG PAUSE

· Have to put F, H, M in order as well as Q, R, S, T, V, who will be in groups of 1-2-2 or 1-1-3.
· Determining F's position and Q's position is top priority.

---

14 Both have S = frames 1 + 3

    (A) ——→ i. T S
    B   M T
    C   S O
    D   iii. T T
    E   M M
                     S S

15 use frames

    A   (Alternatively, we might
    B   have seen from the
    C   outset that O→T
    D   and $\boxed{\begin{array}{c}M\\S\end{array}}$ can't coexist.
    E   Hence, O can't be in both.)

16 use frames

    A̶
    B̶
    C̶
    D̶
    (E) frame 3

20 A̶   Q R
         S V T
         F H M
    B̶   prev work (18)
    C̶   S R $\boxed{\begin{array}{c}Q\\S\\V\end{array}}<^R_T$
         Q T V
         F H M   fyi   H
    (D) ←—   but H can't be 1
    E̶   prev work (18)

21 $\frac{Q}{M}$ → either frame

    A̶   Q   S
    B̶   ☐ V T   Q
    C̶   F M H   V ☐ T
    D   1 2 3   M F H
    (E)   1 2 3

22 A̶   prev work (21) ⎤
    B̶   prev work (20) ⎥ counterexamples
    C
    D̶   frame 2
    (E) frame 1 + frame 2

23 $\frac{S}{F}$ → either frame

    A̶   / /~   / V
    (B) / ↓ T   / R
    C   S Q R   Q S T
    D   F (H M)   M F H
    E   1 2 3   1 2 3

PT57, G1

G, H, J, K, L, M

K - [HG]

[MJ] - L

1	2	3	4	5	6	G/L
~~K~~	~~L~~			K	~~G~~	
~~H~~	~~B~~				~~H~~	
~~G~~					~~M~~	
					~~J~~	

BIG PAUSE
· All six elements are used in our two chains of 3.
· Top priority is finding where the two chunks go.

To Frame or Not to Frame?

Each chunk has 4 options. Too many. Not worth it.

① A   4
  ~~B~~   2
  ~~C~~   3
  D
  ~~E~~   Rule 1

② A
  Ⓑ   ↙K↘ __ H G   no room for [MJ] chunk
  C
  D
  ~~E~~   prev work (1)

③ A
  B
  Ⓒ   ↙Nothing can go 1st.
  D   __ K __ __ __ __
  E

④ A
  ~~B~~   prev work (1)
  C   Nothing can go 6th.
  Ⓓ   __ __ __ __ L ↘
  E

⑤   With rule, L could only
     go 3,4, or 6. [MJ] - L

  A   Different. Previously L could be 3
  ~~B~~   Diff. L always had to be after J
  Ⓒ   Same effect as before: [MJ] - L
  ~~D~~   Diff. L could be last, previously.] fyi
  ~~E~~   Diff. L was always after J.

PT57, G2

G, O, R] 2 each

O₁ - R₁

ⒼⓇ = at least 1

at least 1 in common
↓   ↓
__W̶ __Th __F __Sat
  &̶

1 - 3 ppl/day

BIG PAUSE
· 6 things, 4 spots. Since every day must have something, the 6 things will either be distributed 2-2-1-1 or 3-1-1-1.
· ⒼⓇ chunk and Thu|Sat match seem like highest priorities

To Frame or Not to Frame?

ⒼⓇ can be Th, F, and/or Sat. Might be worth framing.

i.	O/G̶ / W	GR / Th	F	G/R / Sat
ii.	G / W	O / Th	GR / F	OR / Sat
iii.	O/G̶ / W		GR / Th	F	GR / Sat

⑥ A̶   3
   B   Ⓑ
   C̶   1
   D̶   No one on Friday
   E̶   2

⑦   G O R ↙G↘ OR

   A̶
   Ⓑ
   C
   D
   E

⑧ A
   B̶   prev work (7)
   ~~K~~   prev work (7)
   D
   Ⓔ   forces R to go Wed/Thu, & R can't go Wed

⑨
  ✓ A̶   O OG R GR   possible] Do
   B   prev work (6)   this ↓
  ✓ ~~K~~ O GR R OG   poss.   ] or
  ✗ Ⓓ   __ OG OR GR Nothing] this
                         on Wed!
   E̶   prev work (7)

⑩ A̶   R can't be on Wed
  B   No one left to be Thu AND Sat
  Ⓒ   prev work (7)
  D
  E

⑪   GO R O GR
    G   O R GRO

  A
  Ⓑ
  C
  D
  E

PT57, G3

(g, m, r, y)

dinos – I, L, P, S, T, U, V
colors – g   y   r

2 m = IN

V → ꭒ̸   U → ꞙ̸

L and U → m̶m̶ (both)

in		out
_ _ S _ _		ꭒ/v _
m m r		

BIG PAUSE

- Seems like a 3D Closed Conditional Grouping game.
- Gotta keep track of 5 IN, 2 OUT and keep track of colors (some set, some undetermined)
- Out column is very limited
- Last conditional is confusing, need to keep an eye on that one

PT57, G4

M,   T, W, Y
2   1–2

6 max, so only one of T, W, Y can go twice

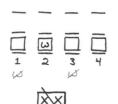

1	2	3	4
w	w	w	w

XX

BIG PAUSE

- Must use 2 M's non-consecutively, top priority
- Other 3 letters can go just once, or one of them can go twice
- Not much space to write scenarios! May need to squeeze in the nooks & crannies.

To Frame or Not to Frame?

No frames, per se, but worth thinking through who could be the 2 m's. Only V, U, L and T can be m. L and U can't both be m. So,

in		out
ꭒ,V,T S _ _		ꭒ/v _
m m r		

(12) A   S
B   LPSTU / yr
C̶   ILPSU / g m y r m   X 6   (B)
D̶   2
E̶   S

(13)
in		out
L ꭒ/v S I P		ꭒ/v T
m m r g y		

A
B
C
(D)
E

(14)   answers all deal with (ꭒ, V, T)
A   (A)
B̶   → ꭒ V / m m can't both be IN
C̶   → V T / m m, U and V can't both be IN
D̶   → L V / m m, U and V can't both be IN
E̶   → m̶ m̶, L and U can't both be m

To Frame or Not to Frame?

2 non-consecutive M's have 3 options

i.   M W M ▢
ii.   M W ▢ M
iii.   ▢y Mw ▢y M

(18) A   4
B̶   5
C   (C)
D̶   3
E̶   2

(19) A̶   frame 1 + 2
B̶   frame 1
C̶   frame 3
(D)   this would create 7 total w/ 2 M's + at least 1 T
E

(20) ▢w → any frame, spot 2 or 4

A   frame 3?
B   frame 3?   looks poss., defer
C   frame 1?
D   frame 1?
E   W ≠ 3 ever, and if ▢Y is 2 or 4, then Y ≠ 3

---

(15)
in		out
L ꭒ/v S T I/P		ꭒ/v P/I
m m r y g/y		

A
B
C
D
(E)

(16)
in		out
_ _ S I U		V
r g		

of what's left, P is most limited. Try in + out

T P S I U	V L
m y r g	

L T S I U	V P
m r g	

(A)
B
C
D
E

(17)   L, T, ꭒ/v
in		out
_ _ S I _		ꭒ/v P
m m r g g		

A̶
(B)   T L V / g m m
C̶
D̶
E̶

---

(21)   2–1 1 1 = 5 spots
M is the only thing going twice
Works in all frames.

A   2 Y's
(B)
C̶   2 W's
D̶   Y / T W _ _ ← No way to legally place 2 M's
E̶   Y T W _ _ ←

(22) A ⎤
B ⎬ if it seems poss., defer
C ⎦
(D) forces 2 M's to be 2 + 3
E

(23) A   where do T's have to go?
B   same as (A), but for Y.
C   M T/Y W ← M↓? which other two?
D   _ _ W _ _
E   M W T/Y W   M, T, Y

PT58, G1

F, G, H, L, M, Ⓢ

G – L – F

M ___ ___ | H ___ ___

(M/G/S) ___ ___ ___ | ___ ___
1   2   3   4   5

BIG PAUSE
- Weirder than normal, but still 6 things / 6 spots.
- 2 out of the 3 (M, G, S) must go first, so if any of them shows up elsewhere, the other two are automatically first.
- S is a floater.

To Frame or Not to Frame?

No chunks, don't frame.

① A̶   4
   B̶   2
   C̶   1
   D̶   3
   E   Ⓔ

② Based on G–L–F, L could be 2ⁿᵈ to last, but that would leave no room for H.

A
B
Ⓒ
D
E

③ A̶ M G L F (S H)
   B
   C
 XD S G M L (H F)
   Ⓔ S M G L F S H

Tested choices that prompted at least some chain reaction

④ Ⓐ   F's earliest is 3, which forces M to be 1 or 2
   B
   C
   D
   E

⑤ A̶ ___ ___ L H F ⌉ Trying to
   B̶ ___ ___ L F ___ | prove L
   C̶ ___ ___ L H F | doesn't have
   D̶ ___ ___ L F ___ | to be 2
   Ⓔ L S (F H) ⌋

⑥ G – L – M F

   S G L M (F H)

   A̶
   B̶
   Ⓒ
   D
   E

PT58, G2

In   Out

L ⟵ L
R ⟵ R
M → M
T ⤬ T
F ⤬ F
V ⤬ V
S ⤬ S

BIG PAUSE
- Looks great!
- L/R/both must be IN
- V/S/both must be IN
- T/FV/all 3 must be OUT

To Frame or Not to Frame?

Conditional rules/games don't lend themselves to framing.

⑦ A̶   4
   B̶   2
   C   Ⓒ
   D̶   1
   E̶   5

⑧   V L | T M R

   A̶
   Ⓑ
   C̶
   D̶
   E̶

⑨   L ⱽ/ₛ | T M R

   A
   B
   Ⓒ
   D
   E

⑩   M T S ⁴/R | F V

   A̶
   B   Ⓑ
   C̶
   D̶
   E̶

⑪   F L | T M R

   Ⓐ
   B
   C
   D
   E

⑫ i.e. Does putting one OUT force the other one IN?

   A
   Ⓑ   L=out → R=in → M=in
   C
   D
   E

PT58, G3

Planes: P_f Q_f R_g S_g T_g

type: D/I

$$\boxed{\frac{I}{P_g}} \quad \boxed{\frac{D}{Q_f}} \quad \boxed{\frac{D}{R_g}}$$

$$\frac{I}{P_g} - \frac{D}{R_g} - \frac{D}{Q_f}$$

All
I's – D's

All
$$\frac{D}{g's} - \frac{D}{f's}$$

$$\underline{I} \; \underline{} \; \underline{} \; \underline{D} \; \underline{D} \quad D, I$$
$$\underline{} \; \underline{} \; \underline{} \; \underline{Q_f} \quad P_f, Q_f, R_g, \textcircled{S_g} \, \textcircled{T_g}$$

BIG PAUSE

· Just have to manage uncertainty
of S_g and T_g. If they're
domestic, then P_g is 1st.
If they're international, they can
go before or after P_g, but
definitely before R_g.

To Frame or Not To Frame?

Good deductions. No chunks.
Don't frame.

13) A ⎤
    B̶ ⎥ We know Q is last
    C̶ ⎦
    D̶   P – R
    E   Ⓔ

14) ┌─────────────────────┐
    │ The only one that can't │
    │ be 2nd is Q_f │
    └─────────────────────┘
    A
    B
    C
    Ⓓ
    E

15) $$\frac{I}{S_g} - \frac{I}{P_g} - \frac{D}{R_g} - \frac{D}{Q_f}$$

    T_g?

    A
    Ⓑ
    C
    D
    E

16) A
    Ⓑ
    C
    D
    E

17) $$\underline{I} \; \underline{} \; \underline{} \; \underline{D} \; \underline{D} \; \underline{D}$$
    with boxes: $\boxed{\frac{I}{P_f}}$ $\boxed{\frac{D}{R_g}}$ $\boxed{\frac{I/D}{T_g}}$? S_g ... g ... Q_f
    1, 2, 4

    A
    B
    Ⓒ
    D
    E

PT58, G11

        3+
    In   Out

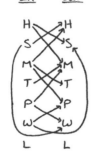

H → H
S   S
M   M
T   T
P   P
W   W
L   L

(3 or 4) in | out
           H/SM M/PT W/PS

BIG PAUSE

· Slightly odd set of rules.
  Conditionals all push things OUT.
· L is a floater. We may need L
  to be In a lot based on rules.
· No rules chain together.
· Smaller possible OUT column is
  3 things: H, M, W.

To Frame or Not to Frame?

Don't frame conditional games.

18) A̶ 1
    B̶ 1
    C   Ⓒ
    D̶ 3
    E̶ 2

19) from placeholders in OUT column,
    min. of 3 OUT, so max 4 IN.
    confirm: _____
             SLTP | HMW works

    A
    B
    C
    Ⓓ
    E

20) in | out
    L _ _ | P W M/T H/S

    A
    Ⓑ verify LST | PWMH
    C
    D̶
    E

21) in | out
    M L S/W | T P H W/S

    A
    B
    C
    D
    Ⓔ

22) A prev work (21)
    B Ⓑ
    C̶ prev work (18)
    D̶ prev work (20)
    E̶ prev work (20)

23) With rule: in | out
                 M | P T
                    | M

    A̶ M → S or W (defer. M didn't
       seem to force something IN)
    Ⓑ M → R and T̶ and H̶ Same as before!
    C̶ This allows M and T to both be IN
    D̶ This allows M and P to both be IN
    E̶ P and T → M̶
       M → R or T̶
       Before, it was P̶ and T̶

PT59, G1

F, H, I, L, P, S, T

T _ _ _ _
M _ _ _ _
B _ _ _ _

PT | H/I | L _

BIG PAUSE

· 7 things, 12 spaces. But since L claims entire floor, there's really 6 things with 8 remaining spaces (3-3 or 4-2)
· F and S are floaters
· Determining L's floor is #1 priority, then place the chunks.

To Frame or Not to Frame?

H/I chunk has only two possibilities.

i.
T | H _ _ _
M | I _ _ _ — PT F,S
B | L

ii.
T | L
M | H _ _ _
B | I _ _ PT F,S

① A̶ 2
   B̶ 1
   C̶   Ⓒ
   D̶ 3
   E̶ 2

②
T | H _ _ _ _ F,S
M | I P I _ _   frame 1
B | L

Ⓐ
B̶
C̶
D̶
E̶

③ A   Top floor, frame 1
   B̶   Mid floor, frame 1
   Ⓒ   Neither frame, leaves no room
   D   for H, I, + L
   E

---

④ FS either frame, but can't share floor w/ PT

H _ FS _ _   L _
I _ PT _ _   H _ FS _ _
L _   I _ PT _ _

A
B
C̶
Ⓓ
E

⑤
T | P I _ ∠ either frame
M |
B |

L _   F S H _
P I H ∠   P I I ∠
F S I _   L _

A
B
Ⓒ
D
E

PT 59, G2

F, G, H, I, K, L, M

H - GK

I L

M = 1, 2 or 3

F/ _ _ _ _ _ _ /F
 1 2 3 4 5 6 7
H̶ ẋ̶   M M M̶ M̶
G̶   M̶ M̶
ẋ̶

BIG PAUSE

· Two chunks to worry about
· F has only 2 options
· M has only 3 options

To Frame or Not To Frame?

The chunks have 6 options. Way too many. Don't frame.

⑥ A̶   Rule 1
   B̶   2
   C
   D̶   3
   E̶   5

⑦   H - L I G K | Chunk has only 2 options |

A̶   M H L I G K F
B̶   F (H,M) L I G K
C̶   H̶
B̶
Ⓔ

⑧ A   (H, M) G K
   B̶   H ← GK →
   C̶   L/M I M/L _ _ _ _
   Ⓓ   L I M H G K F
   E

---

⑨ No inferences from M=2 Test answers

A̶   F M H GK , IL
Ⓑ   _ M _ _ H _ _

C
D
E   Can't fit our 2 chunks.

⑩   Rule forced H - GK
    H ≠ 1, 6, 7

A̶   Diff. Prev work (8). F=7, H=4
B̶   Diff. Prev work (8). L was able to be 1.
C̶   Gives correct possibilities for H, but doesn't force H-GK
D   Confusing, hold off.
E̶   F-H-K is diff. Previously F could be 7th.

fyi   [H₂ → M - H - G
      [H ₘ/ᴳ → H₂

PT 59, G3

```
   4        4
   in      out
```

R   R
J   J
M   M
W   W
S9   S9
P   P
G   G
S3   S3

in	out (w/s9)
_ _ w/6 6/3	3/4 w/6 _ _

BIG PAUSE

· Looks like good ol' Conditional Grouping.
· Be careful with G↔W double-arrow.

To Frame or Not to Frame?

Normally wouldn't frame Conditional game, but we could use GW rule.

i.   _ _ 6/3 G | w 3/4 _ _

ii.   S3 R 3/4 w | G S9 P 3/4

(11) A 4
    B 1
    C 2
    D (D)
    E 5

(12) A (GW)
     B (JM)
     C] fyi (PW)
     D
     (E) frame 2

(13)   R _ _ _ | _ _ _ _

    A
    B] frame 2, not fully determined
    (C) R P S9 G | W _ _ _
    D
    E

---

(14)   w → S9

    A (A)
    B P → S9 ⎤ She can't
    C w → S9 ⎥ take both
    D P → S9 ⎥ stats classes
    E w → S9 ⎦

(15)   (J and M is impossible, so
        must be RM or RJ)
    S3 G 3/4 3/J | S9 w P 3/4

    A
    B
    C
    (D)
    E

(16)   S9 → D2 → G
    P →   or
        S3

    (A) P R S3 w | G S9 J M
    B either R or J must be IN
    C M → R
    D G → D2
    E G → D2

PT 59, G4

L, M, (N), T, V, W

M _ _ T   V _ _ L

T - L   V W

BIG PAUSE

· Tricky! 3 chunks but all with interchangeable positions. VW chunk could be inside V _ _ L or outside. Balancing the 3 chunks in only 6 spaces is top concern.
· N is a floater.

To Frame or Not to Frame?

Each chunk seems to have 3 possibilities, but b/c they have interchangeable parts it would be more like 6 possibilities. Don't frame.

(17) A
    B Rule 1
    C 4
    D 2
    E 3

(18) A
    B
    C → M V W T L N
    D
    E

(19) A M/T V _ T/M L
    B _ _ T _ _ M   V-L 1/4 or 2/5
    C _ _ _ N _ _
    (D) V W T L N M
    E

---

(20) ⎡ Already seen W=2 (19)
      ⎣ and W=3 (18)

    A
    B ⎤
    C ⎥ Try W=1 or W=6
    D ⎥
    (E) ⎦   W V T N L M

(21) A M V W T L N
    B M W V T N L
    C
    D if M=1, V _ _ L
    E   has two options

(22) A diagram
    (B)
    C forces T=6
    D L _ _ V _ _   no room for T
    E diagram

(23) A prev work (21)
    B
    C prev work (21)
    D prev work (21)
    E prev work (21)

PT 60, G1

J, K, N, Q, R, S

am __ __ __ (J, N/s,)

pm __ __ __ (R, K/q,)
     W Th F
          K   ∅
          N̸

[J / K/q] [N/s / R]   Q < K
                                  N

BIG PAUSE
· Not too bad. 6 things, 6 spots.
· 2 partial chunks and Q's
  position are all we need to worry
  about
· If Q went on Th, both
  K+N on Fri

To Frame or Not to Frame?

Q is pretty limited, probably only
has 3 options. Debateable.

i. S J Ⓚ
    R Q N
    W Th F

ii. S/s __ __
    Q __ __
    W Th F

    __ Q Ⓚ   Breaks!
        __ N   No way
    __ __ __   to fit in
    W Th F   J
              K/q

iii. Q J N
     S K R
     W Th F

① A̸   3
  B
  K̸   3   Ⓑ
  D̸   2
  E̸   1

② A
  B
  C
  Ⓓ
  E

③   use frames if poss.
  Ⓐ   never happens!
  B   frame 2 ⎤
  C   frame 3 ⎥ fyi
  D   frame 2 ⎥
  E   frame 1 ⎦

④ Ⓐ   frame 1!   frame 1 or 2
  B   ↓
  C   check answers
  D   against frame 1
  E   to see if we get lucky.

⑤   Q __ __   frame 3
  A   W Th F
  B
  C
  D
  Ⓔ

⑥   frame 1: S
    frame 3: Q
    frame 2: J, (prev work #1)
  A
  B   or think K, N, R ≠ Wed AM
  Ⓒ
  D
  E

PT 60, G2

G, H, J, L, M, P

P
 ⟩ J   M-P → H-G
L
 ⟩ H   G-H → P-M
M

__ __ __ __ __ J/H
 1   2   3   4   5   6
                     G

BIG PAUSE
· 5 of 6 organized in Relative
  Tree.
· Conditional gives G a
  relationship to the tree.

To Frame or Not To Frame?

The conditional and its
contrapositive bring G into the
rest of the tree. Good idea
to frame, however, the trees
are unusually ugly.

if M-P

M-P
    ⟍
    H-G ⟍ J
    ⟋
L

J = last

if G-H
              G
P — M — H
    ⟍
     J
    ⟋
L

H/J = last

⑦ A̸   2
  B̸   3   Ⓔ
  C̸   1
  D̸   4
  E

⑧ A
  B
  Ⓒ L has at least 1 after it (J, H)
  D
  E

⑨ A
  B
  C
  Ⓓ J, H
  E

⑩ A   P — J — M — H
  B̸ ⟍ L
  C̸
  D̸ ⟍
  E̸   ⎡ If we used frames, J-M
         ⎢ tells us we're in the G-H
         ⎢ frame, eliminating C/D/E
         ⎣

⑪   P
  [L G]   ⟋ J   ⎡ and since
  A   ⟍ H   ⎢ G-H, P-M
  B   ⟍ M   ⎣
  Ⓒ L has at least G, J, H after
  D
  E

⑫ A   ⎡ M=1 means M-P frame ⎤
  B
  Ⓒ
  D
  E

PT 60, G3

M, M, M, S, S, S, S

3 cleanings = max

| 1 | 2 | 3 | 4 | M 5 | 6 | 7 |

BIG PAUSE

· What kind of game is this?
Only two different types of
things and two puny rules?
Since so little
time + game seems so unfamiliar,
it might be good to play with
a few scenarios to get
oriented.

To Frame or Not to Frame?

Can all the M's be together?   Yes

S	S	S	S¹	M	M	M
S	S	S¹	M	M	M²	S
S	S¹	M	M	M²	S	S

Can all the M's be apart?   Nope

| M¹ | S² | M³ | S⁴ | M | S | S |

Can 1 M be alone?   Maybe (if M is 1 or 7)

| S¹ | M² | S³ | M | M | ⁴ S | S | X |
| M¹ | S² | M | M³ | S | S | ✓ |

13. A | M¹ | S² | M³ | S⁴ | M | S | S |
B | S¹ | M | M² | S³ | M⁴ | S | S |
C | S¹ | M² | M | S³ | M⁴ | | |
D | S¹ | M | S² | M³ | M⁴ | | |
E   (if you did frames, you could use
them to see this is poss.)

14. A
B   prev. work (last frame)
C   prev work (1ˢᵗ frame, 3ʳᵈ line)
D   All 3 M's apart = Too many
E   cleanings

---

15. | S | S | M | M | M | S | S |

(MSM) would result in too
many cleanings

A
B
C
D
E

16. 2 cleanings = MMM   345 or 456

A
B
C
D
E

17. ~~MMM~~   ~~SSS~~

MM & M = only works when M is
1ˢᵗ or last

		M ↷			
M	S		M	S	S
S	S	M	M	S	M

↖ forces 3 S's

A
B
C
D
E

PT 60, G4

F, G, H, J, K, L

P __ __ (J̄) (H, F/k)
W __ __ __ (K/F)
   R   S   T
      K

SAME row
(G L)
infer: can't be in top row
(H, G, L) in top row forces (J, k, F)
in bottom

P (F/k, H) J
W (F/k, G, L)
  R   S   T
    K

BIG PAUSE

· 6 things, 6 spots. No floaters,
no chunks. No rule seems
especially important. Key will be
systematically going through all
rules to follow inference chain.

To Frame or Not to Frame?

F/k choice doesn't lead to
any inferences. Not worth it.

18. A
B
C   **A** We know it
D   must be H, J, and F/k
E   K ≠ 5

19. A
B | P | F | H | J |
C | W | __ | __ | __ |
D
E | P | K | H | J |
    | W | F | __ | __ |

20. A | H |
B | F | → frame 2
C
D
E | K | H | J |
    | G/L | F | L/G |

---

21. | P | K | H | J | H, J, K
  | W | (G | L | F) | G, L, F

A
B
C
D
E

22. | K | | G |

P | K | H | J | H, J, K
W | G | (L | F) | G, L, F

A
B
C
D
E

23. A   prev. work (22)
B   prev. work (20)
C   H is in J's row + J has Tuscany.
D
E   prev. work (20)

PT 61, G1

F, G, H, J, K, L

DRV 1   2

D [H / F/G]   D [J / F/k]   (G L)

BIG PAUSE

· Flexible quantities, hence use some open board conventions.
· 6 ppl will either be distributed 3 - 3 or 4-2.
· It's poss. that H + J are in the same car, with F driving. If F is a passenger, G + K must drive.

PT 61, G2

F, H, J, N, P, T

```
      N
      J → T
F <
      H
```

P < H N   or   H > N P

BIG PAUSE

· 5 out of 6 in a Tree, but P has two options. We can make 2 trees.

To Frame or Not to Frame?

We should make 2 Trees, one for each version of Rule 3.

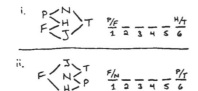

To Frame or Not to Frame?

There is a (G L) chunk, but it doesn't seem like placing it determines anything else.

① A
   ~~B~~ 2
   ~~C~~ 3
   ~~D~~ 1
   ~~E~~ 2   (A)

② A
   B
   C
   D
   (E)   doesn't accomodate F/G

Answer needs to accomodate F/G and F/k.

③

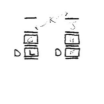

   (A)
   B
   C
   D
   E

⑥ A
   ~~B~~ 2
   ~~C~~ 3
   ~~D~~ 1
   ~~E~~ 2   (A)

⑦   P/F in Frame 1, P/N in Frame 2, so P, F, N

   A
   B
   (C)
   D
   E

⑧ (A)   In Frame 1, (H, J, T) must
   B   come after F. In Frame 2,
   C   (J, T, H, P) must come
   D   after F.
   E

⑨   P N F ___ ___ ___
    [Must be Frame I]

   A
   B
   (C)
   D
   E

④
   D

   A
   B
   (C)
   D
   E

⑤ ~~A~~
   ~~B~~
   ~~C~~
   (D)
   ~~E~~

⑩   P F/N ___ ___ ___ ___
    [Must be Frame I]

   A
   (B)
   C
   D
   E

⑪

i.
```
   P < N
   F > H   T?
       J
```
```
   N
   J ≠ T
```
ii.
```
      J
   F < N   T?
      H - P
      N'
```

~~A~~   T and H had no relationship in either frame before
~~B~~   This rule takes care of N, but does nothing to limit J
~~C~~   This rule allows T < N J to be true. That was not allowed before
(D)   F N J > T so T must be 4, 5, or 6
~~E~~   Does nothing to limit J

MANHATTAN LSAT

PT61, G3

Q, R, S, T, U

Q → QT   Ⴕ ⟷ R/2/R
                U ⟷ S/3/S

—   —   —   — | —
1   2   3   4   out
    S   S

BIG PAUSE

· Not too many ingredients. We have a potential chunk, if Q is in, and then we have the bi-directional U/R rule. Those are top priority.

To Frame or Not to Frame?

The possible chunk has 3 positions. The bi-directional rule has 2 poss.

i. Ⴕ, R/2/R   ii. U, S/3/S
    — R — — | U   — — — S | S
               out   R   out

(12) A   4
      B   2
      C   1
      (D)
      E   3

(13) By 1st rule, T → Q. Since there's only 1 out position, T can't be out.
      A
      B
      C
      (D)
      E

(14) Something that forces Frame 1 would do it.
      A
      (B)   Frame 1
      C
      D
      E

(15) RS can't go 1/2 or 3/4, because S can't go 2 or 4. RS can't go 2/3 because if R=2, we get frame 1.

      A
      B
      C
      D
      E

(16) Frame 2   U   —   S | S
                     R   out

      S is either 3 or OUT
      U T S R | Q
      U Q T R | S

      A
      B
      C
      D
      (E)

(17) from frame 1, S could be 1
      frame 2: Q T S U | R
      A
      (B)
      C
      D
      E

PT61, G4

F, G, H, J, K, L, M

L – F – GK

M – J

H __ __ +M

—   —   —   —   —   —   —
1   2   3   4   5   6   7
    K

BIG PAUSE

· Looks friendly, no floaters. Balance the chain of 4 with H + M's spacing requirement.

To Frame or Not To Frame?

GK chunk seems to have 4 options (really only has 3). Best to just move on.

(18) A   4
      B   5
      C   3
      (D)   D
      E   1

(19) A   M   J   L-F-GK , H
      B   L   M   J   F   GK , H
      (C)   H/M   L   F   M/H   J   G   K
      D   ↑   ↗ ↘
      E   L≠2   only things
                           that can come
                           after are H or GK

(20) See work for 19b
      A   forces L=2
      B   K's earliest = 6
      C   no room for GK
      (D)
      E

(21) L – F – GK – M – J
            ↑
            H
      A
      (B)
      C
      D
      E

(22)   L – F   G K H/J
            L-F, M-J   G K H
            L   F H/M G K J ✗
            ↑
            L≠2
      A
      (B)
      C
      D
      E

(23) (A)   prev. work (22)
      B
      C
      D
      E   L – F – GK
                  L can't be in
                  last 3 spots

PT62, G1

G, L, P, S, T, W

W — L

$P \begin{smallmatrix} G \\ < \\ S \end{smallmatrix}$

$\overline{\text{L/P/W}}$
1 2 3 4 5 6̶

BIG PAUSE

- Basic ordering, although no chunk and rule 3 is unusual.
- Whereabouts of L/P/W in 2 and 3 seem most important since L/P/W affects the 2 ordering rules.

To Frame or Not to Frame?

No chunks, but only 3 poss. pairs for spots 2+3. Debateable.

i.   T   (PW)   (G, S, L)
ii. W   (PL)   (T, S/G)   G/S
iii. P/   W   L   /P   G/S
                          ̶T̶

① A̶   2
   B̶   4
   C̶   1
   D   Ⓓ
   E̶   3

②
              P
              L
              W
   ___ ___ ___ ___ ___ ___
              S̶
              T̶
              G̶

   T   W   L   P   (G S) frame 3
   T (P W) L (G S) frame 1

   A
   B
   C
   D
   E

To Frame or Not to Frame?

No real chunks and TONS of flexibility. Definitely a back-end game.

---

③ A̶   prev work (2)
   B̶   prev work (2)
   C
   D
   E   All three frames

④   Use frames and/or prev work

   A̶   frame 1
   B̶   frame 1
   C̶   prev work (2)
   D̶   frame 2
   E̶   W = 1, 2, or 3

⑤   G ≠ G, S, T, W, P
     T (PW) (G S) L   frame 1

   A
   Ⓑ
   C
   D
   E

⑥   Previously, T could be 1, 4, 5

   Ⓐ
   B̶   frame 1 wouldn't be allowed anymore
   C̶   frame 2 allowed L — T
   D̶   TSG was okay for 4-5-6
   E̶   L was okay at 6

PT62, G2

G, O, P, R, Y ≥ 1
          2

$\begin{smallmatrix} G \\ P \end{smallmatrix}$ = exactly 1

       Y → G̶ and Q̶ → P
   O or G → T̶
       R → O → T̶
       Q̶ → P

inf. = every window has O, P, or both

1   2   3

BIG PAUSE

- Unusual game with lots of uncertainty and chances to re-use elements.
- Conditional rules seem to involve 3 or 4 elements at a time, so probably most important, while keeping track of R=2 and $\begin{smallmatrix} G \\ P \end{smallmatrix}$ = 1

---

⑦ A̶   4
   B
   C̶   1
   D̶   3
   E̶   2

⑧   Inf: you GOTTA have O, P, or both

   A
   B
   Ⓒ   P̶ → O
   D
   E

⑨ A̶   needs O/P
  ✓Ⓑ R P R   seems to work ✓
   C̶   FYI, other
   D̶   needs O/P   group of 2 must
   E̶   contain R, and
                   be O/P, leaving P̶
                   for final group, which
                   leaves no spot for Y.

---

⑩   P ⟨R⟩
   A   R G P
   Ⓑ   O P Y
   C   T̶ Q̶
   D   Q̶
   E

⑪   O > G   G⟨ (2 R's)
     2   1   P P
                    O O Y
   O ≠ 3 b/c we   T̶ T̶ Q̶
   must use Y → Q̶   Q̶
   Ⓐ   poss in 1st column
   B̶
   C̶
   D̶
   E̶

⑫   All 3 ≠ Y, G, O, R
                conditionals only
                exclude others twice
   A
   B
   Ⓒ
   D
   E

⑬   ⟨R⟩ → G Y
   A   P P P/G̶
   B   R R O
   C   T̶ Q̶ T̶
   D   Q̶
   Ⓔ

PT62. G3

Q, R, S, T = 2
        X = 2

— — — — —
F G H I L
Ø R Ø
      R

2 of these 3
Q: G, I, L   (S)(Q)(S)
R: F, I, L   (T)(T₁)(R₁)

BIG PAUSE

· 8 things, 10 spots, so two
  blank (X) spots.
· 2 chunks are highest priority.
  Next would be keeping track
  of Q's and R's limited options.

To Frame or Not to Frame?

Each chunk only has 2 possibilities
(arbitrary choice, so just pick either
one to frame).

i. S _ _ (Q)   ii X Q X S Q
    R₁ _ X (R)   S T₁ T₂ R₁ R₂
    F G H I L   F G H I L

⑭ A   3
   B   2
   C   (C)
   D   4
   E   5

⑮   frame 1
        S Q X _ _
        R T₁ X _ _
               (Q₂, T₂)
   (A)
   B
   C
   D
   E

---

⑯(A)   Test S/R in L
         S Q X Q S
         R T₁ X T R
         F G H I L
   B   R ≠ G
   C] from Frames, we know that
   D] S/R can be in F or I.
   E

⑰   S Q X R X   (frame 1)
      R₁ T₁ (S T) Q
      F G H I L
   A
   B
   C
   (D)
   E

⑱   S Q X X Q   (frame 1)
      R₁ T₁ ³/T R ¹/₃
      F G H I L
   A
   B
   C
   D
   (E)

PT62. G4

M, R, S, T, U, W

[ST] or [SU]

U < R
      W

[TM] or [WM]

— — — — — —
1 2 3 4 5 6
            Ø Ø

BIG PAUSE

· Lots of flexibility. Only 1
  concrete rule. 2 pairs of
  possible chunks.
· 1st priority is figuring out
  which chunk from each pair is
  happening in a given scenario.

To Frame or Not to Frame?

Don't frame. No definite chunks.

⑲ A   2
   B   (B)
   C   3
   D   1
   E   2

⑳   T = 1 → [SU], since [ST]

      T M S U (R W) [TM]
      T S U (R, [WM]) [WM]
   A
   B
   C
   D
   E   (E)

㉑   S = S → [SU], since U ≠ M
       So [ST] → [WM], since [TM]
       U (R,[_+_]) S T
   (A)
   B
   C
   D
   E

㉒(A)   U W M T _ _   No ST or SU
   B
   C   prev work (20)
   D
   E   prev work (20)

㉓ A   S U (R, [TM or WM]) ✓
   B   prev work (20)
   C   prev work (20)
   (D)   U T _ _ _ _   fyi No SU or
   E   prev work (21)   ST poss.

PT63, G1

H, (J), K, L, (M), (O), P

—
—
—
—

(H) P
L	K
A	T

BIG PAUSE

· Incredibly simple game.
There's really only one rule
to keep in mind, the (P) rule.
Once we split them up, we
only have 1 more opening
on Appellate.

To Frame or Not to Frame?

Nothing frame-worthy here.

① A̶   1
   B̶   3
   C̶   2
   D̶   3
   E   (E)

② A
   (B)   only 1 more spot avail in A,
   C   besides L and H/P
   D
   E

③ (A)   same reason as Q28
   B̶
   C
   D
   E

④ | O | J |
           |---|---|
           | H/P | M |
           | | P/H |
           | L | K |

   A
   B̶
   (C)
   D
   E

⑤ A̶   allows H+P to be together in T
   B̶   same ↗
   C̶   J was a floater before
   D̶   allows H+P to be together in T
   (E)   L+K already split up, so
         this prevents H+P from
         being together

PT63, G2

L, O, P, T, W, Z

O-P-L or L-P-O

T-W

L/					/L
1	2	3	4	5	6
				T̶	O̶
					Z̶

BIG PAUSE

· Lots of flexibility.
Biggest priority is whether
L is 1 or 6, hence
L-P-O or O-P-L.

To Frame or Not To Frame?

Definitely not frame-worthy
UNLESS you realize that
only L or O can be last.
This leads to two loose but
useful frames:

(O - P, T- W, Z)	L
L	(T-W, Z, P)	O

⑥ A̶   3
   B   (B)
   C̶   1
   D̶   4
   E̶   2

⑦ A̶   L could be last
   B
   C
   (D)   T-W and W can't be last
   E

⑧ A
   B
   (C)   (T-W, O-P, Z)   L
   D   _ _ _ _ _ _
   E

⑨ A   T-(W Z)
   B   +
   C   O-P-L or L-P-O
   (D)   T W Z P _ _
   E   ↑
               messes up
               O/L-P-L/O

⑩ (A)   (LT) -W
   B   ↘ P-O
   C
   D   L T (P, W, Z) O
   E

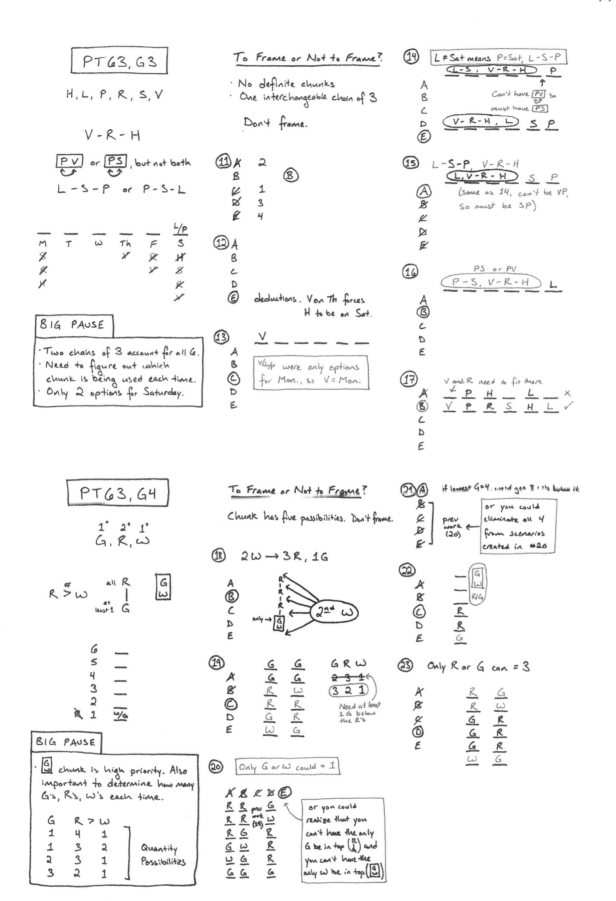

PT64, G1

R S T (V) X Y

T — Y — R (3or4)

S — X

T/S/V		R/	/R		X/N
1	2	3	4	5	6

BIG PAUSE

· Looks like 1:1 ratio basic ordering.
· Spot 6 and R seem most limited, highest priority.
· V is a floater.

To Frame or Not to Frame?

R only has 2 options — might be worth framing.

i. T _ Y _ R _ (S — X, V)

ii. (T — Y) _ R _ (X) _
     S   (before X)
     V anywhere

① A̶   1
  B̶   4
  C̶   2
  D̶   3
  E   (E)

② S — T → frame 2
  S _ T _ Y _ R _ (XV)

  A
  (B)
  C
  D
  E

---

③ answer will have to force floater, V, into a definite position

  A   (XV) in 5+6 (#2)
  B   frame 1 or 2
  (C)   T Y V R S X
  D
  E

④ R = 3or4, Y = 2 or 3
   T = 1or2, X = 5 or 6

  A
  B
  C̶
  (D)
  E

⑤ S — Y → frame 2
   S T _ Y _ R _ (XV)
  (A)
  B̶
  C
  D
  E

⑥ T _ Y _ R _ (S — X, Y)
  A   (frame 1)
  B
  C
  D
  (E)

PT64, G2

   (N/K)   L
   ‾   ‾   ‾ | K/N ‾   (J,K,L,N,O)
   V   Y   Z | out

J → K → N̶

N → K → J̶

O_v → K_y

K_y → O̶_v

BIG PAUSE

· L only has two options, and if L is OUT, J and O are forced IN.
· Figuring out K vs. N in/out seems high priority.

To Frame or Not to Frame?

No chunks, but L's 2 options.

i. _ _ L | K/N _   ii. (J,O,K) | N L
   V Y Z | out   V Y Z | out

⑦ A̶   2
  B   (B)
  C̶   4
  D̶   1
  E̶   3

⑧ (A)
  B̶
  C̶   must include
  D̶   K → J̶   K or N, but
  E̶   not both

⑨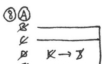
   O _ J _ K | N _ L
   V   Y   Z

   O _ N _ L | K _ J
   V   Y   Z

  A
  B
  C
  D
  (E)

---

⑩ J _ K _ O | N _ L
   V   Y   Z

   O̶ _ K _ L _ N _ O
   J

  (A)
  B̶
  C
  D
  E

⑪ A
  B̶   prev work (9)
  (C)   neither frame
  D̶   prev work (9)
  E̶   prev work (10)

⑫ we had J → K → N̶
       N → J̶ → K

  A̶   Reverse logic
  B
  C
  (D)   J → N̶ → K
  E   N → J̶ → K

PT 64, G3

R S T Y = 1 per day

  | Y S

```
F _ _ R
G _ _
H (T)
J _ _ Y
  1 2
```

BIG PAUSE
- 4 things, 4 spots for each of 2 days.
- Y S chunk seems most important.
- R and Y more limited than S and T.

To Frame or Not to Frame?

Y S chunk only has 2 options.

```
i.  F  Y   S        ii. F  S/T  Y
    G  _   _            G  Y    S
    H   (T)             H  (R,T)
    J  _   _            J   (R)
       1   2               1    2
```

---

⑬ A̶ 1
   B̶ 3
   C   Ⓒ
   D̶ 2
   E̶ 4

⑭ G _ I → frame 1

```
F  Y   S
G  R   T
H  I   Y
J  S   R
```

A̶
B̶
C̶
D̶
Ⓔ

⑮ A̶ prev work (13)
   B̶ prev work (14)
   C
   Ⓓ neither frame
   E

To Frame or Not to Frame?

FM only has 2 options.

```
i.  T □□ ✓ ✓ K̶      ii. 3-3-2
    M I □ _ _           T K O ✓ ✓
    B F □ □ _ Ø/K       M I F M ✓
                        B L G H ✓
```

⑲ Use frames. Nothing matches frame 2, so frame 1.
   FM req'd
   A̶ at least 3
   B   Ⓑ
   C̶ FM
   D̶ Ø
   E̶ FM

⑳ What would force frame 2?
   Ⓐ forces frame 2
   B
   C
   D
   E

---

⑯ A frame 1?
   B frame 2
   Ⓒ neither frame
   D
   E

⑰ either frame seems possible

```
F  Y   S  │  S   Y
G  R/S Y  │  Y   S
H  S/R T  │  R   T
J  T   R  │  T   R
   1   2  │  1   2
```

A̶
Ⓑ
C̶
D̶
E̶

⑱ A̶ prev work (14)   fyi
   B̶ prev work (17)   Y S
   C̶ prev work (17)   S T
   Ⓓ ⟵   T Y
   E̶ frame 2?   R R X
                          confirm
                            T Y
                            Y S
                            R T
                            S R ✓

㉑ Ⓐ true in both frames
   B
   C
   D
   E

㉒ G = top → frame 1

```
T G _ ✓ ✓
M I □ _ ✓
B F M □ M/L
```

A ⎤ if two on Mid,
B ⎦ then four on Btm: FMHL
C̶
Ⓓ
E̶

㉓ O
    I
    L → frame 1
    H

```
T O K/G ✓ ✓
M I L _ _
B F M H _
```

A
B
Ⓒ
D
E

PT 64, G4

F, Ⓖ, Ⓗ, I, K, L, M, O

Top < Btm

```
K   O
|   |
FM  L
```

```
T □ □ _ ✓
M I □ □
B □ □ □ _
```

BIG PAUSE
- 8 things can be split up
      T 2   2
      M 2 or 3
      B 4   3
- Where is FM + which quantity scenario are top priorities.
- G and H are floaters.

PT65, G1

G — [F H]
         ↺
    ↗
K — J

G/K __ __ __ __
 1   2   3   4   5

BIG PAUSE

· Looks very manageable.
· 5 things, 5 spots, 0 floaters.
· [F H]↺ is top priority.

To Frame or Not to Frame?

Toss up: chunk only has 2
options, but game seems easily
manageable w/o frames.

i. (G,K) (F H) J

ii. (G, K—J) (F H)

① A̶   2
   B̶   2
   C̶   3
   D   Ⓓ
   E̶   1

② K — J — G — (F H)↺

   Ⓐ
   B
   C
   D
   E

③ A   frame 1
   B   frame 1 or 2
   Ⓒ   never ← [also clear from our]
   D   [Tree G—(F H)]
   E

④ A̶   G — [F H]
         K — J
   B̶   K — [G F H]
              ↘ J
   C̶   G — [F H J]
         K
   B̶   G — [J H F]
         K
   Ⓔ   G — [K F H] — J

⑤ 4 = F or H

   A
   Ⓑ
   C
   D
   E

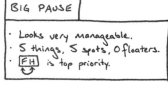

PT65, G2

Y̶   X̶
Ø̶   S̶

__ __ __ __ __ __   [N O P S T W]
                    [J J K K L]

 1 2 3 4 5 6

[K K]

S/K — O/J   T/K — W/L

BIG PAUSE

· 3D ordering, except the 2nd
  layer isn't in doubt. More like
  basic ordering but with 2D pieces.
· 3 K's can't touch. Very limited,
  #1 priority. Could go 1-3-5,
  1-3-6, 1-4-6, or 2-4-6.
  (if K is ever 6, it will have to
  be P/R)

To Frame or Not to Frame?

4 options for the 3 K's. Too
many to frame.

⑥   S—O, T—W, (P S T)

   A̶   1
   B̶   3
   C   Ⓒ
   D̶   2
   E̶   1

⑦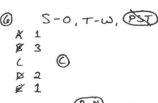
    #1?. where do the other K's go?

   A
   B̶
   C̶
   Ⓓ
   E

⑧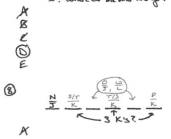
        ← 3 K's? →

   A̶
   B̶
   C̶
   D̶
   Ⓔ

⑨   Hunch: answer will probably
    leave no room for 3 K's

   A   prev work (8)
   Ⓑ   J __ __ J can't fit K's
   C   J K __ K J K
   D   K J J K __ K] fyi
   E̶   prev work (7)

⑩

   A
   Ⓑ
   C
   D
   E

⑪   2 = #7 / #8 / #10   prev work
       N,O S,T   W

   A
   B
   Ⓒ   [Alternatively, K in 2
   D   forces 3 K's = 2-4-6,
   E   and as we inferred,
          if K=6 → P/K]

PT 65, G3

in   out   O = hot food

(F)   (F)   dess.

G   G
(N)   (N)
→O   O   main
oP   P
(T)   (T)
V   V   side
oW   W

(F/N/T)
in | out
_ _ _ | V/N _
d m s

BIG PAUSE
- (PW) both in or out.
- Don't lose track of F/N/T requirement.

To Frame or Not to Frame?

Might be good to see PW in vs. out

i. in | out
    P/O P W | V/N _ _
    d m s

ii. in | out
    G F O T N/I | P W V/N
    d d m s | m s

⑫ (Start from bottom of rules, easier to see)

A̶ 5
B̶   Ⓑ
R̶ 4
D̶ 3
E̶ 2

⑬ i.e. Could you put both OUT? If not, correct.

   out
A F T V/N
B G O V/N
C N T _
Ⓓ O P V/N → forces W in
E   (Also from frames, either P or O is always in)

---

⑭ O = only main → frame 2

in | out
G F O T V | P W N
d d m s |

A
B
C
D
Ⓔ

⑮ F = out → frame 1

in | out
G O N/I P W | V F T/N
d m   m s | d

A̶
B̶
C̶
Ⓓ
E

⑯ T + V = only sides → W = out
                        ↓ frame 2

G F O T V | P W N

Ⓐ
B
C
D
E

PT 65, G4

1 hr.   ½ hr.
G,   R, S, T, W

_   _ | _ _ | _ _
1 1:30 2 2:30 3 3:30

[G<]   [_ I]   R-S

W-T → [WT]

[WT] → T-W

BIG PAUSE
- 5 things, 6 spots. But G is really 2 spots, so things match spots in a slightly weird way.
- G "chunk" only has 3 options, so #1 priority.
- [WT] would have to fall on the hour, so if W is ½ hr. spot → [WT] → T-W.

To Frame or Not to Frame?

G has only 3 options but they don't seem to trigger anything else. Don't frame.

⑰ (Start w/ last 2 rules, easiest to see)

A̶ 2
B̶   Ⓑ
C̶ 1
D̶ 4
E̶ 3

⑱ W T | G | R S
   if W=1 → W-T → [WT]

A
Ⓑ
C
D
E

⑲ ? R | _ _ | _ _
   A̶ (D'oh! 2nd program could be 2:00 if G is 1st)
   B̶
   C̶
   D̶ G | R S/T | W T/W S

A
B
C
Ⓓ
E

---

⑳ X̶ W ≠ T
   R T | S | W | G
   G | R | S | W T

A
B
C
D
Ⓔ

㉑ R/W T | G | _ _ /T

   A → W=1 → T=2
   Ⓑ R ≠ last
   C R T | G | S W
   D
   E

㉒ A̶ prev work (20) if we flip (SW)
   Ⓑ [_ T] - [WR] - S
   C   ↖ nothing could go there
   D
   E

㉓ Previously G had to be 1st, 3rd or 5th

A
B̶ G = 3 was poss before
Ⓒ Looks good!
D
E

PT66, G1

J, K, L, N, O, R

am __ __ __

pm __ __ __ (N)

(K/R) (L/O)

J—O

BIG PAUSE

- 6 things, 6 spots
- (K/R) chunk is top priority, then J—O.

To Frame or Not to Frame?

(K/R) chunk has 3 options. Might be worth framing.

i. [K/R] [J/L] O/N   ii. [J/L] [K/R] O/N
     W Th F   W Th F

iii. [J/L] O [K/R] N
     W Th F

① A̶ 3
   B̶ 4
   C̶ 1
   D̶ 2
   E   (E)

② L ≠ Wed → Frame 1
     Thurs = J, L

   A
   B
   C
   D
   (E)

---

③ [☀ / N̲] = frame 2

   A
   (B)
   C
   D
   E

④ J/L and K/R (and O/N)

   (A)   L = afternoon
   B
   C
   D
   E

⑤ K/R   L/J   O/N   (frame 1)

   A
   B
   (C)   3 others can be
   D   determined = L, O, N
   E

PT66, G2

O, P, R, R, S, T, V

R __ __ + R (T/V) (P%)

P/R __ __ __ __ R/P
 1   2   3   4   5   6   7

BIG PAUSE

- 7 things, 7 spots, although having 2 R's is weird.
- Figuring out 1 and 7 is highest priority, because wherever P goes, % goes next to it (2 or 6). Wherever R goes, there are 2 spots worth of "R" buffer.
- Then, make sure T and V get split up.

To Frame or Not to Frame?

P only has 2 options.

i. P %/v __ __ __ __ R
      ←R→

ii. R __ __ __ __ %/v P
         ←R→

⑥ A̶ 4
   B̶ 2
   C̶ 1
   D̶ 3
   E   (E)

⑦ R S   R,V/o,T   o/v P
     ? ↔ R

   (A)   RSTROVP
   B̶
   C̶
   D̶
   E̶   fyi, V in 4 results in T next to V

⑧ V = 5 → must be (PO)
   P O T R V S R
   R T S R V O P

   A
   B
   (C)
   D
   E

---

⑨ (OS) P (OS) R (TV) R X
        R T (OS) R V P ✓

(only need one working example to get answer — this possibility allows us to eliminate the other four)

   A
   B
   C
   (D)
   E

⑩ __ __ __ S __ __ __

   A̶   prev work (9)
   (B)   P O R S (TV) R X
       R O T S R V P ✓
   C̶
   D̶] prev work (9)   counterexample possible, so (C) doesn't have to be true.
   E̶

⑪ A̶   New rule allows R __ R __ __ __ __
      Old rule didn't
   B̶   Same ↗
   C̶   Same ↗   closest that R = farthest that R
              can get to R   can get from P
   (D)   R __ R __ __ P
     If R=1 and P=7, other R must be = 4,5,6
     If R=7 and P=1, other R must be = 2,3,4
   E̶   New rule forbids (OS)
      Old rule didn't, prev work (#9)

PT66. G3

K, M, P, Q, S, T, U

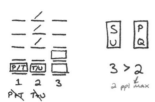

S   P
U   Q

___ / ___
___ / ___
___ / ___
[ ] [ ] [ ]
[P/T] [T/U] [ ]
1   2   3
P/T T/U

3 > 2
2 ppl max

BIG PAUSE
- 7 things, 3 groups, flexible quantities/group.
- 2 chunks and 2 either/or choices are top priority.

To Frame or Not to Frame?

P
Q only has 2 options: 1 or 3

i. P
    Q ___ ___
    1 2 3
    ↗

ii. / □
    S P
  T U
  1 2 3   K, M (either they both go to 3 or one goes to 3, the other to 1)

---

(12) A̶   3
    B   ⑧
    C̶   4
    D̶   1
    E̶   2

(13)   1 > 3 → frame 1

P
Q T
1 2 3

since   1 > 3 > 2,
it must be   4   2   1

A
B
C
D
Ⓔ

(14) Ⓐ → would have to be frame 1

U
K
S
P
Q   T M
     ×
     2 = 3

B̶
C̶   frame 1
D̶
E̶   prev work (13)

S
U
P
Q T M K

---

(15) Ⓐ   prev. (13)
    B
    C
    D
    E

(16)   from 13 we know Q is fine with K, M, S, U, P

A̶
B̶
C̶
D   Ⓓ
E̶

(17)   removed from scoring

(18)   M
     S   → frame 1
     U

          K
          ↓ M
      P   S
      Q   T   U

Ⓐ
B
C
D
E

PT66. G4

M   ___   T   ___   ___   (M, T)
        ↓   ≠
___ ___ ___ ___ ___   (W, Z)
1 2 3 4 5

1 [TT] block

Spot 4 = T or M
         W   Z

at least one
M   ___   any
W   T

BIG PAUSE
- Unusual 3D ordering in that there are only 2 options for 5 spots.
- Either/or in spot 4 and [TT] are biggest priorities.
- 2nd ≠ 5th next concern.

To Frame or Not to Frame?

Spot 4 choice lends itself to frames.

i.   M M   T T   M
    (W) ___ W ___
       ↳ ≠ ↵

ii.   M T T   M
     W ___ ___ Z ___
       ↳ ≠ ↵

(19) A̶   T ≠ 1
     B̶   T̶T̶T̶
     Ⓒ   frame 1
     D
     E

(20)   min = T
             W
frame 1 has at least one.
frame 2, maybe zero?
ii.   M T T M M
      W Z Z Z W

Ⓐ
B
C
D
E

---

(21)   1st = 2nd, either way it's WW
i. M M   T   T M   ii. M T   T   I M
   W W   W Z   W   W Z
                      ↳ ≠ ↵

A
B
Ⓒ
D
E

(22)   5th = T → frame 2
     M   T   T   M   T
     W   Z

A
Ⓑ
C
D
E

(23)   5th = T → frame 2
     M   T   T   M   T
     W   Z   Z   W

A
B
Ⓒ
D
E

ALL TEST PREP IS NOT THE SAME

MANHATTAN
GMAT

MANHATTAN
GRE®

MANHATTAN
LSAT

Elite test preparation from 99th percentile instructors.
Find out how we're different.

www.manhattanprep.com